DEFENDING IRELAND

THE IRISH STATE AND ITS ENEMIES SINCE 1922

EUNAN O'HALPIN

OXFORD

UNIVERSITY PRESS

OXFORD

UNIVERSITY PRESS

Great Clarendon Street, Oxford OX2 6DP

Oxford University Press is a department of the University of Oxford.
It furthers the University's objective of excellence in research, scholarship,
and education by publishing worldwide in

Oxford New York

Athens Auckland Bangkok Bogotá Buenos Aires Calcutta
Cape Town Chennai Dar es Salaam Delhi Florence Hong Kong Istanbul
Karachi Kuala Lumpur Madrid Melbourne Mexico City Mumbai
Nairobi Paris São Paulo Singapore Taipei Tokyo Toronto Warsaw

with associated companies in Berlin Ibadan

Oxford is a registered trade mark of Oxford University Press
in the UK and in certain other countries

Published in the United States
by Oxford University Press Inc., New York

British Library Cataloguing in Publication Data

Data available

Library of Congress Cataloging in Publication Data

Data applied for

ISBN 0–19–924269–0

1 3 5 7 9 10 8 6 4 2

Typeset in Minion
by Jayvee, Trivandrum, India
Printed in Great Britain
on acid-free paper by
Bookcraft Ltd., Midsomer Norton
Nr. Bath, Somerset

For Mary O'Halpin (1926–1994) and her grandsons Patrick and Barry

PREFACE

THIS book explores the pattern of Irish defence and security policy since independence, in terms both of the maintenance of internal security and of the promotion of constructive relations with the outside world. This involves the examination of both declared and submerged values and calculations, and of the secret conduct of business by the state's servants as well as the public articulation of policy by ministers. Other writers have dealt admirably with aspects of these matters, in some cases in more difficult circumstances before the official archives were opened to research, for example Michael Hopkinson and Tom Garvin on the civil war era, Conor Brady on the early years of the Garda Síochána, John Bowman on de Valera and Northern Ireland, Richard English on the republican Left, Joe Carroll, Carolle Carter, Robert Fisk, and more recently Donal O'Drisceoil on aspects of the Emergency, and Patrick Keatinge and Trevor Salmon on the public evolution of Irish security policy. What is attempted here is a gathering together of the various threads of what can broadly be called national security policy and activities in a chronological study.[1]

The book is the outcome of a long-held interest in problems of public order, of security, and of defence policy. Its genesis lies partly in research on aspects of the last decades of British rule in Ireland and of military/police relations which I completed for an MA in UCD in 1978, and partly in a broader interest in the secret world. While working as a research student on the inter-war British Treasury and its mercurial permanent secretary Warren Fisher, I developed my interest in security and intelligence matters, in terms both of British defence and foreign policy in the 1930s and of the evolution of the British intelligence bureaucracy.[2] Thanks largely to Christopher Andrew in Cambridge, I was able to sustain this after returning to Ireland in 1982.

When I began research for this book a decade ago, relevant Irish documents were thin on the ground, and most of the useful material came from British and American records. In the course of the book's gestation, the situation has been transformed through the coming into operation in January 1991 of the National

---

[1] M. Hopkinson, *Green Against Green: The Irish Civil War* (Dublin, 1988); T. Garvin, *1922: The Birth of Irish Democracy* (Dublin, 1996); C. Brady, *Guardians of the Peace* (Dublin, 1974); J. Bowman, *De Valera and the Ulster Question* (Oxford, 1982); R. English, *Radicals and the Republic* (Oxford, 1994); J. Carroll, *Ireland in the War Years* (Newton Abbot, 1975), C. Carter, *The Shamrock and the Swastika: German Espionage in Ireland in World War II* (Palo Alto, 1977), R. Fisk, *In Time of War: Ireland, Ulster and the Price of Neutrality 1939–45* (London, 1983); D. O'Drisceoil, *Censorship in Ireland, 1939–1945: Neutrality, Politics and Society* (Cork, 1996); P. Keatinge, *A Singular Stance: Irish Neutrality in the 1980s* (Dublin, 1984); T. Salmon, *Unneutral Ireland: An Ambivalent and Unique Security Policy* (Oxford, 1989).

[2] E. O'Halpin, *The Decline of the Union: British Government in Ireland, 1892–1920* (Dublin, 1987), and *Head of the Civil Service: A Study of Sir Warren Fisher* (London, 1989).

Archives Act of 1986. There have been parallel though less dramatic developments in the archival policies of both Britain and the United States, particularly in respect of documents dealing with security and code-breaking activities. These have made the task of describing and analysing Irish state security and defence policy and operations at once easier and less manageable: where once it would seem a triumph to track down a single scrap of official paper dealing with Anglo-Irish security relations, since 1991 mounds of documents have been opened touching on even the most secret matters. I have tried, not always successfully, to use the new wealth of detail constructively rather than to wallow in it.

While government records and personal papers are the main sources for this book, I have also been influenced by my own background as the grandson of middle-ranking republicans. My grandfather Hugh Halfpenny (d. 1943) was an IRA commander in East Down in 1921/2 before, like many other Northern IRA men who had served under Eoin O'Duffy, coming south and joining the Garda. My mother's father Jim Moloney, a son of the anti-treaty TD P. J. Moloney, served on Liam Lynch's staff as director of communications during the civil war. One brother, Con, was Lynch's adjutant-general and deputy chief of staff, while another, Paddy, had been killed by British forces in Tipperary in 1921. Jim Moloney, who died in 1981, was a reserved man, and apart from an occasional aside he was not inclined to talk about his 1916–23 experiences to me. His wife Kitby (Kathy) Barry had no such inhibitions. The eldest sister of Kevin Barry, the UCD medical student executed in 1920, she was general secretary of the Irish Republican Prisoners' Dependants' Fund between 1922 and 1924, and was an important link between de Valera and Lynch during the latter stages of the civil war. She also travelled to the United States and to Australia to raise money for the republican cause. She brought up her family in a genteel republican *demi-monde*, denying the legitimacy of the twenty-six-county state but nevertheless accepting its practical existence and on occasion imperiously demanding its assistance. As a schoolboy I was intrigued though slightly scandalized by her anti-Fianna Fáil views and her appetite for the *United Irishman*, but she died in 1969 before I was old enough to ask sensible questions. Partition barely featured in her purist republican litany as I heard it in the 1960s—what mattered was abandonment of the republic in 1921, pure and simple, compounded by de Valera's later apostasy. Kitby Barry's sister Monty was married to Jim O'Donovan, who became the main point of contact between the IRA and Germany in 1938/9, who died in 1979. Unfortunately I never had a serious conversation with him. Another sister, Elgin, who only died in 1997, was a republican activist and hunger striker during the civil war. She later married Mac O'Rahilly, eldest son of the valiant The O'Rahilly, killed during the 1916 rising to which he had been opposed.[3] Mac O'Rahilly encouraged me to look critically

---

[3] M. Mac Ruairi, *In the Heat of the Hurry: A History of Republicanism in County Down* (Castlewellan,

at the received wisdom of the Irish Revolution, and I owe him a particular debt. Although this book is a study of the state rather than of anti-state republicanism there is, consequently, a familial overhang to some of the events and conflicts under discussion. At its simplest, despite early exposure to purist republican historiography and logic I have never been able to fathom how the first generation of anti-treaty republicans could on the one hand deny the legitimacy of the twenty-six-county state, and on the other live quite happily in it while intermittently conspiring against it.

Through my parents I got to know Nora and Charlie Harkin and Frank and Bobbie Edwards, distinguished veterans of the republican Left, who besides showing me great kindness over many years introduced me to the interesting though implausible proposition that revolutionary socialism and Irish republicanism were natural bedfellows. As a student and later a researcher, these family and social links gave me easy access to other people who had been involved on the anti-treaty side in the events surrounding the establishment and consolidation of the state. Amongst these were Maurice Twomey and Peadar O'Donnell, formidable figures whom I interviewed very inefficiently in 1975/6, Bob Bradshaw, and the great C. S. Andrews. On the other side of the treaty divide, in 1983 I met Colonel Dan Bryan, with whom I had many conversations and who gave me transcripts of his memoirs which I have used extensively. He was then 83 years of age, and had brought the absent-mindedness for which he was renowned to a fine pitch. At the same time, he had an extraordinary and subtle memory and a remarkable acuity of observation and perspective. At Bryan's funeral in 1985 Douglas Gageby remarked to me that the elderly man I had known was but a pale shadow of the powerful intellect under whom he had served in army intelligence during the Emergency. If so, the state was indeed fortunate in its unassuming servant.

E.O'H.

April 1998

1997), 71–3, 94; D. Ryan, *Sean Treacy and the Third Tipperary Brigade IRA* (Tralee, 1945), 23, 195, 201; C. S. Andrews, *Dublin made me: An Autobiography* (Dublin, 1979), 281 and 297; D. O'Donovan, *Kevin Barry and his Time* (Dublin, 1989), 199–200.

NOTE TO THE PAPERBACK EDITION

Since this book was completed two years ago, there have been notable developments in Irish security policy. These are briefly dealt with in an addendum on p. 353.

I must also record the sudden death in October 1999 of Commandant Peter Young of the Military Archives. Historians miss him equally for his vast knowledge and sound advice, his enthusiasm and encouragement, and his invariable good humour.

E.O'H.

ACKNOWLEDGEMENTS

In writing this book I have drawn on conversations and correspondence with many people over many years, often initiated for other research projects. In some cases, furthermore, people including serving officials and officers spoke about sensitive and relatively recent events and issues. My acknowledgement of their help has to be anonymous and collective.

I am very grateful to the following people whose comments, recollections, and observations offered to me in conversation or in correspondence over the last twenty-five years I have drawn on in this book: Dr C. S. Andrews, Lord Armstrong, Dr Austin Bourke, Bob Bradshaw, Colonel Tony Brooks, Colonel Dan Bryan, Colonel Sean Clancy, Dr Richard Clutterbuck, Dr Cleveland Cram, Sir James Dunnett, Frank Edwards, Dr Garret FitzGerald, Sir Robert Fraser, Douglas Gageby, Nora Harkin, Professor Sir Harry Hinsley, Group Captain Ron Hockey, Michael Mills, Dr Leon O'Broin, Peadar O'Donnell, Karlo Paice, Sir Edward Playfair, Sir John Stephenson, Maurice Twomey, Group Captain Hugh Verity, and Sir Dick White.

I am also indebted to fellow researchers, friends, and colleagues in Britain and Ireland for advice, assistance, and hospitality over the years, especially Mark Seaman of the Imperial War Museum, Dr Neville Wylie, and Stephen and Pascale Stacey. My particular thanks go to Commandant Peter Young, Commandant Victor Laing, Sergeant John White, and Corporal Brendan Mahony of the Military Archives, Catriona Crowe of the National Archives, and Seamus Helferty of the University College Dublin Archives. I am very grateful to the staff of all the archives and libraries in Ireland, Britain, and the United States who have helped me. I thank the Research Committee and the Business School at Dublin City University for research support for projects partly subsumed in this book, and the Royal Irish Academy and the British Council for grants which enabled me to visit archives in the United Kingdom. I also want to thank DCU colleagues who have given advice or lent a hand in different ways at crucial stages, particularly Helen Fallon, Sheila Boughton, John Horgan, Billy Kelly, Siobhain McGovern, and Gary Murphy. Tony Morris and Ruth Parr have successively been patient editors, Heather Watson imposed order on an unruly typescript, and Helen Litton has produced a reliable index at short notice.

In conclusion, I thank the following institutions and holders of copyright for access to collections of papers: the Director of the National Archives of Ireland; the Controller of Her Majesty's Stationery Office; the Keeper of the Public Record Office of Northern Ireland; the United States National Archives; the Public Archives of Canada; the National Library of Ireland (the Hayes papers);

the Master, Fellows, and Scholars of Churchill College in the University of Cambridge (the Drax, Hankey, and Noel-Baker papers); the Trustees of the Liddell Hart Centre for Military Archives (the Davidson papers); the Bodleian Library (the Curtis papers); the Houghton Library (the Moffat papers); *The Times* (the Dawson papers); the Department of Archives, University College Dublin (the Blythe, Bryan, FitzGerald, Hayes, Kennedy, MacEntee, McGilligan, Ó'Dálaigh, O'Hegarty, and O'Malley papers); the Fianna Fáil party (the Fianna Fáil papers); the Imperial War Museum (the Batstone papers); Professor Risteard Mulcahy (the Mulcahy papers); the Provincial of the Franciscan Order in Ireland (the MacEoin papers); and the Wiltshire Record Office (the Long papers).

CONTENTS

LIST OF TABLES

ABBREVIATIONS AND ACRONYMS

ACA	Army Comrades Association
ARP	Air Raid Precautions
BRO	British Representative's Office, Dublin
CIA	Central Intelligence Agency (American)
CID*	Criminal Investigation Department
CID*	Committee of Imperial Defence (British)
CIO	Command Intelligence Officer
COS	Chiefs of Staff Committee (British)
CPGB	Communist Party of Great Britain
CPI	Communist Party of Ireland
C3	Garda Security Section (1930s–1980s)
DF	Department of Finance
DFA	Department of Foreign Affairs
DJ	Department of Justice
DMP	Dublin Metropolitan Police
DO	Dominions Office
DT	Department of the Taoiseach
FBI	Federal Bureau of Investigation
FCA	Fórsa Cosanta Áitiúil
FO	Foreign Office
GC & CS	Government Code and Cipher School (British, from 1942 styled GCHQ)
GCHQ	Government Communications Headquarters (British)
GOC	General Officer Commanding
G2	Army intelligence directorate (late 1920s–late 1950s)
IDF	Israeli Defence Forces
INLA	Irish National Liberation Army
IO	Intelligence Officer
IRA	Irish Republican Army
IRB	Irish Republican Brotherhood
IRSP	Irish Republican Socialist Party
JIC	Joint Intelligence Committee (British)
KGB	Soviet Union's intelligence service
MA	Military Archives
MI5	Security Service (British)
MI6	Secret Service (British, also known as SIS)
MI9	Evasion and escape organization (British)
MP	Mulcahy Papers
NA	National Archives
NATO	North Atlantic Treaty Organization
OSS	Office of Strategic Services (American)

PAC*	Committee of Public Accounts
PAC*	Public Archives of Canada
PfP	Partnership for Peace
PRO	Public Record Office, London
PRONI	Public Record Office, Northern Ireland
PSOC	Principal Supply Officers' Committee (British)
RAF	Royal Air Force
RIC	Royal Irish Constabulary
RUC	Royal Ulster Constabulary
SIS*	Secret Intelligence Service (British, also known as MI6)
SIS*	Supplementary Intelligence Service (a G2 network)
SOE	Special Operations Executive (British)
TPD	Temporary Plans Division
UCDA	University College Dublin Archives
USNA	United States National Archives

  * In cases where the same acronym was used for two different organizations, the sense should be clear from the text.

1

The State and Civil War, 1921–1923

i. Introduction

The nature and extent of independent Ireland were determined by two funda-mental factors. The first was the settlement negotiated and signed by British and Irish representatives in December 1921. The second was the political and military conflict over acceptance of that settlement which followed in Ireland over the next two years. The divisions marked by treaty and civil war have haunted Irish politics ever since.

The post-treaty conflict had a profound effect on the course of development of the state's public order and defence institutions, and on the system of justice. The nature and powers of the present police force derive from the experience of the first traumatic years of qualified independence. The curious position occu-pied by the Irish defence forces can only be understood by reference to the state's perpetual internal security problem. The paradox of a country which since independence has set its store by the precepts of constitutional democracy, yet routinely puts provisions of its constitution in abeyance, cannot be explained without reference to the state's early experience of disorder, subversion, and civil war.

ii. The Search for Instruments of Order, 1921–1922

The six months following the signing of the treaty saw a struggle for power in Ireland which culminated in civil war. From its establishment on 16 January 1922 the provisional government consolidated its position, taking over from the British what the treaty described as 'the powers and machinery requisite for the discharge of its duties'.[1] However, in the key areas of defence and public order

---

[1] Article 17 of 'Articles of Agreement for a Treaty between Great Britain and Ireland', as published in the second schedule of *Constitution of the Irish Free State* [*English translation*] (Dublin, 1922); on the prelude to and conduct of the civil war see especially Garvin, *1922: The Birth of Irish Democracy*, Hopkinson, *Green against Green*, and J. M. Curran, *The Birth of the Irish Free State, 1921–3* (Alabama, 1980).

the new administration faced enormous difficulties. There, in the nature of events, there was no existing national machinery to be absorbed into the new state.

Where was the provisional government to get its military forces and its police? The IRA had divided on the treaty just as the Dáil had done, and the anti-treaty majority repudiated the authority of the provisional government and of the parliament of southern Ireland (as the Dáil for treaty purposes had become). This placed the new administration in a disastrous position. The anti-treaty IRA presented an enormous threat to government, parliament, and treaty. Until it was either brought under control or destroyed there was no prospect of peace and order in the nascent state. Between January and June 1922 continous efforts were made to produce an acceptable political compromise, but at the same time both the government and the IRA prepared for hostilities.

While they did so disorder and lawlessness flourished. The habit of civic discipline had been eroded in the War of Independence, there were plenty of guns and gunmen and no trained policemen outside Dublin, and there were many grievances to be ventilated. Attacks on British troops and on ex-Royal Irish Constabulary (RIC) men, some simply acts of local vengeance, others calculated to provoke a British military response, caused acute embarrassment to the administration and increased British pressure on it to take firm action against the republicans.[2] Frequent robberies and seizures of property, whether for the cause of the republic or for strictly private gain, emphasized the provisional government's lack of civil authority. Republican attacks on southern Protestants, sometimes in reprisal for those on Catholics in Northern Ireland, sometimes in furtherance of agrarian grievances, sometimes, to use the language of an Irish-American document of April 1923, in pursuit of an exclusively 'Republican, Catholic' and 'Gaelic' Ireland, called into question the new state's ability and will to protect its religious minorities.[3] To anyone not at the bottom of the rural heap, widespread land seizures appeared to threaten the entire social fabric. Labour unrest, including fitful use of the red flag and red rhetoric, seemed deeply menacing despite the enduring modesty of most of the labour movement's demands, methods, and aims.[4]

The provisional government's dilemma in addressing this chaos was acute. While the various strands of disorder were interwoven, their elimination required different approaches. For example, attacks on British troops or ex-police were plainly attributable to the IRA, whether or not the product of local indiscipline or of headquarters' calculation, and were impossible to prevent or

---

[2] Macready (commanding British troops in Ireland) to Collins, 15 Apr. 1922, National Archives, Department of the Taoiseach (NA, DT), S. 2984; Hopkinson, *Green against Green*, 73–4.

[3] 'An appeal to humanity', undated, Apr. 1923, with British consulate general, New York, to Foreign Office, 27 Apr. 1923, DT, S. 1976.

[4] E. O'Connor, *Syndicalism in Ireland, 1917–1923* (Cork, 1988), 140–67.

to punish without a direct confrontation between government and IRA, which both sides wished to avoid. But there was little sympathy for the labour movement within the republican leadership, and the government, accordingly, could contemplate a robust response to labour unrest.[5] The government's injunctions to let southern Protestants alone in the name of tolerance and pluralism, echoed by de Valera, the political leader of the republicans, were not completely consistent with its secret arrangements to wage war in combination with the IRA on the Protestant people of Northern Ireland.[6] Although land agitation was as difficult an issue for the republicans as for the government, the former could afford to ignore it and profit from the government's discomfiture. Republicans had a vested interest in disorder, whether or not they inspired it, because it underlined the provisional government's lack of practical authority in the country.[7] In these circumstances, it is hardly surprising that the government was unable to build a consensus on the restoration of civil order in the months leading up to civil war.

iii. The Policing Problem and the Making of the Garda Síochána, 1922–1923

The need for some form of police force to succeed the RIC had long been recognized, but nothing was done about it until RIC disbandment was almost at hand in January 1922. Local experiments in policing by IRA units and by the 'Republican police' of Dáil Éireann during the War of Independence had been useful mainly for propaganda purposes. After the truce overt political violence waned, yet other public order problems grew considerably in the vacuum left by the collapse of Dublin Castle's police system. In some towns the locals did what they could, organizing groups of men to patrol the streets to discourage crime, but they were no deterrent to any except the most timid and ill-equipped wrongdoer. Tensions within the national leadership, and the rush of other business, meant that the issue of policing was largely ignored.

The government's first response to post-truce policing problems was the establishment in Dublin of an armed plain-clothes force based at Oriel House, and soon to be known as 'Oriel House' or as the 'CID'. Its creation reflected the inevitable confusion surrounding public order policy, as the forces controlled by Dáil Éireann abruptly assumed responsibility for maintaining the peace where before they had operated to disturb it. Oriel House initially combined detective, security, and military and political intelligence functions. In essence, however, it was the creature of Michael Collins, set up by him, answerable to him, and headed by men who had operated under him during the War of Independence on intelligence and assassination work. While intended *inter alia* to

---

[5] Ibid. 158–64.
[6] Hopkinson, *Green against Green*, 83–6.   [7] Garvin, 1922, 101–6.

help to control armed crime in and around Dublin, it lacked the discipline, the organization, or the personnel to serve as a civil police bureau. From early in 1922 Cork had a somewhat similar body, the 'Plain Clothes Squad' or 'City of Cork Police Force', composed of army officers and men, which appears to have been absorbed into a 'Cork Civic Patrol' formed 'by a number of private citizens . . . for the protection of property'. The body's 'duties include escorting postmen, keeping close observation on Banks, Post Offices, Public Institutions etc.', and they enjoyed neither the fame nor the notoriety of Oriel House.[8] Its colourful though brief history is dealt with in a subsequent section of this chapter.

The government's second response was the hasty creation of a police force to replace the RIC. This was the Civic Guard, brought into existence in unpropitious circumstances in February 1922. Its early vicissitudes have been described in detail elsewhere, but they require recapitulation here because they had a profound effect on the eventual development of a disciplined and effective civil police force. The decision to establish one was dictated by the prevailing disorder and by RIC disbandment. What was there to build on? The Dáil 'Minister for Home Affairs' had controlled a police organization of sorts, the 'Republican Police' headed by Simon Donnelly, during the War of Independence. But this was only a simulacrum: the force 'was a small one—probably from 10 to 20', who 'worked in the Minister's offices and were under his control and were paid . . . in the same way as the ordinary' Dáil civil servants.[9] So far from being capable of enforcing the law these men were themselves, like every other activist in the independence movement, continually in danger of arrest by the British authorities. After the truce they were able to operate openly, but they remained a very small, untrained group. Furthermore, they divided on the issue of the treaty. Donnelly and some of his men departed to establish a rival police organization on the republican side. What remained of the force was put under the care of Michael Staines, a pro-treaty TD, and was wound up in January 1922. The Dublin Metropolitan Police (DMP) inherited from the British remained in existence, but it did not seem an inspiring model for a new force. Its political detectives apart, it had survived the War of Independence largely by adopting a position of cowed neutrality.[10] The RIC, by contrast, had fought and lost and was gone. Yet it was the RIC which most influenced the development of the Civic Guard.

Early in February 1922 Collins established a committee under Staines to plan the new force. At the same time the provisional government set up a similar

[8] Brady, *Guardians*, 32; provisional government decision, 4 Sept. 1922, DT, S. 1705; Mortell to director of intelligence, 9 Jan. 1924, University College Dublin Archives, (UCDA), O'Malley papers, P17a/175; army finance office to Ministry of Finance, 25 Sept. 1923, NA, FIN1 747/104.

[9] Justice memorandum, 27 Apr. 1935, DT, S. 2232; *Committee of Public Accounts: Third Report* (Dublin, 1925), 70–1.

[10] O'Halpin, *The Decline of the Union*, 198–9.

group under Richard Mulcahy, the minister for defence. The two groups agreed on the outlines of a scheme, and the Staines group was expanded and asked to work out the details. They quickly produced a set of proposals which the provisional government accepted. The Civic Guard was to be an unarmed body of about 4,500 men, policing by consent rather than by force. With this important exception, apparently predicated on the assumption either that political crime would disappear or that it would be some other organization's business to combat, the proposals largely replicated the disbanded RIC. The Civic Guard would be a non-political force. It would be centrally controlled, and there would be no local input into its operations. Its head would be appointed by and directly answerable to the government.[11]

These proposals made some sense. The RIC had shown itself to be an enormously resilient force, in sharp contrast to the DMP, while in Britain unarmed policing worked very well. But the scheme had many drawbacks. Significantly, it perpetuated a structural weakness in policing in Ireland, the fact that the capital city was the responsibility of a separate force. It also failed to address a serious problem arising from this, which the RIC had recognized but never resolved, the absence of a national detective unit handling political crime throughout Ireland. During the War of Independence this had prompted the British to improvise with a variety of intelligence and security organizations, some civil, some military, some offshoots of British agencies such as MI5 and the Directorate of Intelligence, and others ad hoc local creations.[12] From the British point of view the results had been disappointing. A further weakness of the Civic Guard scheme was that the new force, organized on the same lines, sometimes occupying the same barracks, and administering much the same laws, might be depicted by the republican opposition simply as a new RIC, a creature of central government, insensitive to local needs and conditions, and primarily an instrument of oppression. Such criticisms could perhaps be answered by saying that the new force would be unarmed, and that it would be controlled by an Irish government elected by the Irish people. Thus Collins assured the first recruits that 'you will have one great advantage over any previous regular police force in Ireland and that is that you will start off with the good will of the people, and their moral support in the carrying out of your duties'.[13] In the early months of its existence, however, the reality was that the Civic Guard was not developed along the lines laid down by the Staines committee. What instead transpired was unrest, mutiny, and ultimately the disbandment of the original force. These setbacks were due to a number of factors.

---

[11] Brady, *Guardians*, 43–4.
[12] E. O'Halpin, 'British Intelligence in Ireland, 1914–1921', in C. Andrew and D. Dilks (eds.), *The Missing Dimension: Governments and Intelligence Communities in the Twentieth Century* (Basingstoke, 1984), 55–77.
[13] Notes for speech, n.d., but stamped 26 May 1922, DT, S. 9045.

The first problem was the practical one of finding somewhere for the force to be organized and trained. In this, as in army affairs, the provisional government proved a hopeless quartermaster. Recruits were first housed in the main hall of the Royal Dublin Society and, from April, in part of a military barracks in Kildare which had previously been used for stables. These miserable conditions had their effect on the morale and discipline of the men. The second problem was the government's inability to get the recruits out of training and into police work quickly. The longer this large group of men—1,500 by April 1922—were kept cooped up together, ostensibly to receive training but in fact also because the government feared bringing the new force into operation in the prevailing political climate, the more likely it was that disaffection would spread. The third problem was the conspicuous role allotted to former members of the RIC and DMP. These were mainly men who had covertly worked for Collins's intelligence organization during the War of Independence, and he valued them for that service, for their practical police experience, and—probably—because he could rely on their personal loyalty to him. The difficulty was that the rank and file of the new force, selected by IRA officers acting on Collins's instructions, naturally found it difficult to take orders from men whom they had regarded as the enemy, and whose service to Collins they knew little about and were inclined to discount. The O'Sheil committee of inquiry, established after the May mutiny, commented that, particularly in training, there was 'too extensive use made' of ex-RIC officers 'considering that the main body were ex-IRA men'— of the 160 ex-RIC men who joined in 1922, fourteen were given the rank of superintendent or higher. This was doubly unfortunate because the recruits initially were trained along quasi-military RIC lines, with much emphasis on musketry and drill, which also relates to the fourth problem. This was that, contrary to initial intentions, the Civic Guard was provided with weapons. The O'Sheil report described this as a major mistake: 'arming all the men' encouraged the police to attempt 'to get their alleged grievances settled by threats and force of arms'. It created 'a militaristic instead of a peace outlook in the minds' of the new force, and did nothing 'to assure the public that the militaristic and coercive policeman was at an end in Ireland'.[14] In addition, arming the Civic Guard suggested that the government envisaged them as a gendarmerie to put down political disorder, as the RIC had been used, and the government's republican opponents naturally viewed the force in that light.

The fifth and undoubtedly the greatest problem was politics. Although recruits to the force were screened by men working under Collins's orders, some had anti-treaty sympathies. Furthermore, from March they were commanded

[14] Report by Kevin O'Sheil and Michael MacAuliffe, cited hereafter as 'O'Sheil/MacAuliffe report', 17 Aug. 1922, DT, S. 9045; Brady, *Guardians*, 53; J. Herlihy, *The Royal Irish Constabulary: A Short History and Genealogical Guide* (Dublin, 1997), 109–111 and 153.

by Staines, who was a pro-treaty TD. This was a bad start for a supposedly non-political, impartial police force intended to attract support from all parts of the community. Whatever the exigencies of the time—the provisional government naturally wanted someone on whose loyalty they could rely—Staines's appointment as commissioner made a bad situation worse. Not only was he a TD, but he evidently lacked the ability and the presence to develop the force effectively. The outcome of this succession of mistakes and mishaps was mutiny. On 15 May a self-appointed committee of the men demanded the removal of senior ex-RIC officers, and the next day 'assumed complete control of the [Kildare] camp and took over the armoury'. When Staines sent troops with an armoured car to recover the weapons, as he believed 'they were likely to fall into the wrong hands', the mutineers would not open the camp gates and the soldiers withdrew. After this rather half-hearted attempt to coerce the mutineers the government, already confronted with the IRA's occupation of the Four Courts, and uncertain about the political sympathies and motivations of the mutineers, slowly moved towards conciliating them. Collins made a number of visits to the camp and addressed the men, promising a committee of inquiry into their grievances and stressing the importance of their future role. His proposals were well received, although the mutineers' committee remained in charge in Kildare. When Staines returned to the camp on 9 June, apparently due to a misunderstanding between government and mutineers, he was refused admission. Two other officers who went down separately on his instructions 'seem to have been literally chased out of the Depot and of Kildare. They . . . were pursued by a threatening mob containing many members of the Civic Guard and . . . had to run for their lives and take shelter, after many adventures, in the house of the Parish Priest for the night.' Some days later Rory O'Connor led republicans from the Four Courts garrison into the camp with the connivance of a few sympathizers and cleaned out the armoury. He 'and his friends' also 'did their very best to try and seduce the men . . . to join him', without much success. For that the government were grateful, since it showed that most of the new force remained politically sound. The mutineers were paid for the first time since late May, and the promised inquiry, by Kevin O'Sheil and a Ministry of Labour official, was finally set in train in mid-July. Despite the fiasco of the O'Connor raid, weapons were subsequently provided for detachments assigned to protect roads and installations in various parts of Leinster. Curiously, this further departure from the principle of an unarmed non-combatant force attracted little interest and caused no trouble, perhaps because none of the detachments were involved in any serious engagements with anti-treaty forces.[15]

The report of the O'Sheil inquiry was presented on 7 August. Its findings were a curious combination of practicality and idealism. Its main recommendations

---

[15] O'Sheil/MacAuliffe report; Brady, *Guardians*, 69.

were that the Civic Guard should be disbanded and reconstituted, that no for-mer or serving public representatives should be members of the force, and that ex-RIC and DMP officers should be employed only temporarily. They would be advisers to those holding 'the chief posts', and there should also be at least one experienced ex-policeman in each station in a subordinate position. Senior posts should be reserved for ex-IRA men together with 'one or more highly experienced officers or ex-officers of a foreign police body . . . for preference American, French or German', who would be employed for some years. A 'Gazette or Journal' where 'questions could be discussed . . . and general infor-mation given' should be started. The force would be split up into 'three separate groups or sections': the 'principal body' of unarmed policemen stationed throughout the country; a 'semi-military body, trained to the use of arms . . . a kind of reserve force at Headquarters'; and 'a detective force' which would 'operate in conjunction with if not under the joint control' of the heads of the Civic Guard and of the DMP.

The report also advanced an exalted vision of 'a police body that shall be the servants of the people, and have the confidence of the people; a police body nei-ther militant nor coercive, above party and class, serving the Government of the people, no matter what form of Government the people may elect at any time'. To this end it suggested that, while the force should be centrally controlled, 'it would certainly be a good thing if a local council had the power to hold the local police body directly responsible for certain local duties, contingent on these not infringing on the police duties proper'. It urged the training and use of police-men on 'civilian duties' such as compiling 'statistics of various kinds', 'Ambu-lance and First Aid Work', and 'sanitary Inspection. The latter duty [is] almost entirely carried out by police in some foreign countries.' The effect of all of this would be to promote social harmony, and make people and police inter-dependent.[16]

This curious essay in the philosophy of policing elicited very little immediate response from the government. The civil war had begun, and there was no time for speculation about ideal structures for bringing police and community together, nor for enlisting foreign police advisers. However, the report's crucial recommendation that politicians should be kept out of the police was accepted, and was apparently put to Staines as grounds for his resignation. Furthermore, the force was disbanded and reconstituted, and a new commissioner chosen. The post was first offered to Sean Ó'Muirthuile, a close associate of Collins, but he chose to stay in the new army. The government then offered the job to General Eoin O'Duffy of the army's south-western command, who had also been close to Collins. He accepted, writing to Mulcahy, then both minister for

---

[16] O'Sheil/MacAuliffe report; the recent study by L. McNiffe, *A History of the Garda Síochána: A Social History of the Force, 1922–52, with an Overview of the Years 1952–97* (Dublin, 1997), has little to say either on the development of political policing or on the role of politics within the force.

defence and army chief of staff. O'Duffy recounted the difficulties and achievements of his command—while 'we engage them everywhere . . . other commands are not engaging the Irregulars as they might', denounced the cowardice,
incompetence, and treachery of many of his troops, and pointed out that he had
previously sought 'the position now offered. I would have accepted this position
willingly then, as I had an idea that I could organise a proper Police Force.' Now,
however, due to 'bad handling and weakness', the Civic Guard 'stands very low
in the estimation of the people. It will be difficult to retrieve its position.' Nevertheless, for the good of the nation he was prepared 'to serve in any capacity
that I can be of most value [in]'.[17] This letter was absolutely characteristic of
O'Duffy in its combination of self-glorification, denunciation of others,
reproach, and mock humility, as his eleven years as police commissioner, and
his subsequent drift into authoritarian politics, were to show. What mattered in
1922, however, was that the government had found someone with the energy,
capacity, and personality to rebuild the Civic Guard.

O'Duffy's impact was immediate. Through a combination of melodramatic
exhortation and careful organization he gave the force a sense of purpose and
direction. The principle that the police should be unarmed was finally put into
practice. Despite the general chaos, stations were opened in most parts of the
country by the end of 1922. In many areas there was very little that unarmed
policemen could do to enforce the law, and they were often at the mercy of the
local republicans, but despite their helplessness they appear quickly to have succeeded in their initial aim of winning public support. They also acquired virtual
immunity from assassination by republicans—only one guard was killed in the
course of the civil war, although many were assaulted and their stations ransacked
and burnt out. Republican tolerance of the guards may be evidence of popular
respect for unarmed policing, but it may also reflect an implicit understanding
that the police would not interfere in republican activities. Until 1925 army intelligence officers maintained that the police avoided anything dangerous. One
claimed early in 1924 that 'sergeants in . . . outlying stations in rural districts . . .
close their eyes to a lot of things', and in August 1925 another noted the 'marked
tendency' of the force 'to steer clear of any activity which might be regarded as
bearing on political crime. This was only natural . . . [as] the force was unarmed
and . . . at the mercy of irresponsible gun-men.'[18] This enforced neutrality was an
important factor in enabling the Civic Guard to win public acceptance, which in
turn made feasible its subsequent major involvement in political policing.

In the spring of 1923, as the civil war petered out, the Ministry of Home

[17] Copy of provisional government decision, 18 Aug. 1922, DT, S. 9045; O'Duffy to Mulcahy, 6 Sept.
1922, UCDA, Mulcahy papers (MP), P7/B/1.
[18] Report by Command Intelligence Officer, Waterford, 14 Jan. 1924 and memorandum by director
of intelligence, with director of intelligence to chief of staff, 24 Oct. 1925, Military Archives (MA), file on
'Co-operation with Civic Guards'.

Affairs prepared a Civic Guard bill. Despite the frequently stated hope that the force would be seen as the people's police, not as an occupying body like the RIC, the ministry's draft threatened to turn the Civic Guard into its own private police force, with appointments at all ranks in the hands of the minister for home affairs. The draft did not address the problem of what to do with the DMP, though the attorney-general, Hugh Kennedy, expected the force would be merged with the Civic Guard once legal and financial problems could be overcome. Kennedy accepted that the Civic Guard should be centrally controlled and free from all local influences, but he suggested an important change in the bill. He wrote to the minister, Kevin O'Higgins, pointing out that under the Free State constitution the minister for home affairs was not automatically a member of the executive council, whereas it was necessary that responsibility for the appointment of the commissioner and his chief assistants should lie with the government as a whole: 'it is important to bear in mind that the force is not local, but is an organised national police force . . . No executive government could safely allow such a force to exist outside its immediate authority, or permit the governing heads of such a force to derive authority from any source other than the executive itself . . . I am also of the opinion that all officers [i.e. from the rank of inspector upwards] of the Civic Guard should be appointed by the Executive Council, though of course it would be done on the nomination of the Commissioner.' It appears that these differences about the bill ran deep. When O'Higgins spoke sharply to Kennedy, the attorney-general replied to 'My dear Kevin' in injured tones: he was 'astounded and disturbed' by O'Higgins' complaint about relations between the Ministry for Home Affairs on the one hand and Kennedy and his subordinate, the parliamentary draftsman, on the other. Kennedy had thought himself 'to be on the friendliest terms with Mr O'Freil', the secretary of the ministry: 'Am I then to suppose that honest differences of opinion, different angles of approach to various problems . . . constitute bad relations?' O'Higgins was surprisingly conciliatory: 'It may be that I overstated the case', though 'relations between your office and this Department, and the exact functions of both, simply clamour for definition'.[19] Whatever the root of the quarrel, Kennedy's view prevailed in the final draft.

The civil war was over by the time the bill reached the Dáil in July 1923. The government felt in no position to complete the process of police reform, although they did accept a proposal to rename the force the Garda Síochána. It was only in 1925 that it became a truly national force with its absorption of the DMP, and it was a further year before the new force won undivided responsibility for political policing and domestic intelligence work.[20] Until then, as shall be seen, the government relied extensively on the army in political affairs.

[19] Kennedy's note, 13 May, and draft letter to Kennedy, n.d., UCDA, Kennedy papers, P4/759.
[20] Brady, *Guardians*, 104.

iv. The Problem of Political Policing

Shortly after the truce Michael Collins established the plain-clothes unit which soon became known as Oriel House, and subsequently was officially called the Criminal Investigation Department or CID. Its initial functions were to provide protection for key figures in the independence movement, to monitor the covert intelligence activities of British military and civilian agencies, and to tackle armed crime in Dublin. Its activities subsequently expanded to include intelligence work against opponents of the treaty and, notoriously, the suppression of the anti-treaty IRA in Dublin.

Oriel House was staffed largely by men who had worked in IRA intelligence during the War of Independence, and run by officers personally loyal to Collins. It adopted the form of a civilian detective bureau, rather than a military organization, its staff holding police ranks such as 'detective officer'. Confusingly, however, as an offshoot of the pre-truce IRA intelligence organization, it also had links with the intelligence directorate of the newly formed national army. After the truce military intelligence was dominated by former members of the Active Service Unit (ASU) controlled by Collins as director of intelligence during the War of Independence, when they 'carried out the most objectionable side of the pre-truce operations', the killing of officials, intelligence officers, informers, and collaborators. Experts in clandestine assassination, men of action who had lived on the edge since 1919, they posed a serious problem for Collins once the truce came. An army officer commented in 1924 that 'the very nature of their work' before the truce had 'left them anything but normal . . . if such a disease as shell-shock existed in the IRA . . . the first place to look for it would be amongst these men'.[21] They expected recognition for the risks they had run and the job they had done, and they assumed this would come through senior postings in army intelligence. But as a group they were doers, not organizers or analysers, and they were unsuitable for the bureaucratic environment of a strictly military intelligence headquarters.

This may explain why a number, under the deputy director of intelligence Liam Tobin, were assigned to Oriel House. According to one army officer Tobin, who retained his military intelligence position, was given a vague brief to develop a national detective organization: 'Somebody mentioned Scotland Yard, and at the same time pointed to Oriel House, and beyond that I do not think any further instruction was given' to Tobin. 'A genuine attempt was made to organise a kind of Scotland Yard for Ireland, but there was no time to consider details and consequently interest was lost'.[22] However, David Neligan, a veteran of the DMP, Oriel House, and military intelligence, and subsequently head of

---

[21] Major General Russell's evidence to army inquiry, 10 May 1924, MP, P7/C/29.   [22] Ibid.

the Garda Special Branch from 1925 to 1933, said that the Tobin group formed a 'Military section . . . to do with Military Intelligence', while 'the CID section were to deal with bank robbers, etc. They were armed police and were very necessary because the DMP were unarmed and the Republican Police were inefficient', whereas 'the Military Intelligence men had not much to do in peace time'. When civil war broke out 'all those people' went back to the army.[23] 'Wherever there was anything exciting or dangerous on,' according to another witness, 'these men were to be found in the thick of it.'[24] They remained a hard core of malcontents, convinced once Collins died that neither their past services nor their work was being adequately recognized, and their sense of grievance ultimately led them to mutiny in 1924.

On 8 August 1922 Collins wrote that Oriel House 'is still nominally under' the army's intelligence department, and brusquely ordered the 'immediate removal of the Military Intelligence Officers from it' and its transfer to civil control. This was done on foot of a government decision of 31 July, itself apparently the result of tensions between the military and civil authorities over the division of responsibility for public order.[25] Joseph McGrath TD was later appointed 'Director General, CID', and the Ministry of Home Affairs took overall responsibility for CID affairs. It was funded through a separate vote in the 1922 appropriation act, an important technicality in so far as this meant that the Dáil in principle approved its existence, and that the government had to answer for its activities. However, its status remained unclear. Although it worked amicably with army intelligence during the civil war, it was no longer under military control. While it operated as a civilian agency in Dublin, it stood apart from the DMP, towards whose detectives Oriel House men had 'a feeling amounting to contempt' due both to their role under the British and 'their wretched pandering to the Irregulars'.[26]

When the CID was on the verge of disbandment its commanding officer Captain Pat Moynihan recorded its development and achievements during the civil war. In February 1923 it had over seventy staff 'who were engaged in combating the activities of the armed criminal in Dublin', of whom 'some 30 only could be utilised as Detective Officers. The others were employed on transport, clerical, patrolling and guarding duties'. The CID then absorbed two other plain-clothes groups: the Protective Officers Corps formed in November 1922 to guard ministers, government supporters, public offices, and important commercial buildings, and the Citizens Defence Force, consisting of about one hundred armed 'ex-British soldiers with a sprinkling of Irish Volunteers' organized for patrolling and intelligence-gathering 'on a semi-secret basis', and financed

[23] Colonel Neligan's evidence, ibid.   [24] Russell's evidence.
[25] Collins to director of intelligence, 10 Aug. 1922, MP, P7/B/4; R. Fanning, *Independent Ireland* (Dublin, 1983), 44.
[26] Tom Ennis to Mulcahy, 17 July 1923, MP, P7/B/4.

from the secret service vote. This brought CID total strength up to 'approximately 350 men and women', about 140 of whom were used actively against republicans as detectives, 'street patrols', 'women observers', and 'observers or "Touts" '. In addition, it ran a number of agents 'in Irregular ranks' who sometimes produced 'results that were highly satisfactory'. This extensive surveillance apparatus enabled the capture of over 500 'active Irregulars', weapons, equipment, and documents, and the CID had over two thousand files on suspects. Moynihan was dismissive of the 'lying reports about . . . interrogations' spread by republican propagandists which led 'the average Irregular' to believe 'that the terrors of the Spanish Inquisition were mere lullabys [compared] to the treatment meted out to prisoners'. In fact 'it was never necessary to extract information from a prisoner by other methods than those recognised in other countries. The interrogation of any prisoner was at least as humane as that form at present extensively used in America and known as the Third Degree.' Moynihan noted the paradox that 'propaganda of an unscrupulous type may, while gaining its immediate object with the generally gullible public, have effects which were not foreseen by those utilising it'—many suspects were so afraid of Oriel House that they talked freely rather than experience its methods. Amongst those republicans lucky to survive CID attentions was Tom Derrig, later to serve in de Valera's first governments, who had one eye shot out while in custody.[27] Oriel House succeeded in its task of suppressing small-scale republican activities in the Dublin area, not by the sophistication or the efficiency of its intelligence work—which, like the army's, seems to have been rather poor—but by the more direct method of striking terror into its opponents.

The CID's conduct during the civil war was highly controversial. Allegations soon surfaced not only of widespread ill-treatment of suspects, but of killings—a British army intelligence résumé of 9 September spoke of the 'murder of a number of prominent Republicans . . . Certain of these . . . are laid to the door of Oriel House and most people' believed this.[28] There is little doubt that Oriel House men sometimes killed prisoners in Dublin during the civil war. So too did plain-clothes and uniformed soldiers, and so too did members of the other civilian units eventually amalgamated with Oriel House in February 1923. In some cases there was considerable eyewitness and other evidence. For example, in August 1922 two republicans were bundled out of a car in Drumcondra in broad daylight and shot dead. A British soldier saw 'a Ford car containing 6 men, three in P[rovisional] G[overnment army] uniform and three in trench coats proceeding North from the scene'. In September Patrick Mannion was shot in the head by troops as he lay wounded and defenceless near Mount Street

[27] Report by Moynihan for director-general, 12 Oct. 1923, DT, S. 3331; Ernie O'Malley to Jim O'Donovan, 7 Apr. 1923, in R. English and C. O'Malley (eds.), *Prisoners: The Civil War Letters of Ernie O'Malley* (Dublin, 1991), 35.
[28] Copy of 24th (P) Infantry Brigade weekly intelligence summary, 9 Sept. 1923, in DT, S. 1784.

Bridge. In October Charlie Dalton, one of Liam Tobin's coterie who was then serving in army intelligence, caught three harmless youths in possession of republican posters. The next morning they were found shot dead in a ditch in Clondalkin. Following a CID investigation Dalton was placed under arrest as 'a prima facie case has been established', but he was later allowed to resume his military duties.[29] The IRA man Bobby Bondfield was arrested in St Stephen's Green by some of Cosgrave's bodyguards, and he too was shot dead in Clondalkin.[30] Two months after the collapse of the republican campaign Noel Lemass was grabbed by men in plain clothes who may have been civilians or soldiers; his body was found that autumn in the Dublin mountains.[31] In such a climate, no doubt Oriel House was sometimes blamed for acts done by others. If so, it was a consequence of its own atrocious reputation.

Why did this happen? Part of the explanation lies in the War of Independence. Men who had unhesitatingly killed in cold blood on Collins's orders naturally found it hard after the treaty to play the policeman and to observe the niceties of arrest, charge, and trial or detention of suspects. In addition, sometimes sheer indiscipline or motives of personal revenge were also involved. Furthermore, aspects of the republican approach to civil war, such as attacks on non-combatants, their homes and their families, bespoke a penchant for terror tactics which invited a ferocious response. In this respect it must be asked whether some of these killings were carried out on orders, or at least in pursuit of what was thought to be government policy. On balance this seems unlikely. In relation specifically to Oriel House, there is no evidence that ministers suggested or approved the torture or murder of prisoners by civilian units. The ugly reputation of Oriel House was an acute embarrassment to an administration which so consistently justified its position by reference to law, order, public morality, and democratic values. This probably explains the speed with which the CID was disbanded once the civil war was over. However, there is no doubt that Oriel House's robust approach was an important factor in the campaign against republicans in Dublin. It may have been distasteful, but it seemed to work.

The 'CID' remained a term of obloquy long after the organization was disbanded in the autumn of 1923. It was used in republican circles, including in Fianna Fáil in its early years, to describe the Garda Special Branch. Yet some of those who might fairly be seen as the prime exponents of the methods used by Oriel House and other government forces subsequently rebuilt relations with the republicans whom they had harried so mercilessly—McGrath and Tobin are obvious examples. By contrast, men such as Cosgrave and O'Higgins, who

---

[29] Appendix to 24th (P) Infantry Brigade weekly intelligence summary, 2 Sept. 1922; papers on the Mannion shooting in the FitzGerald papers, P80/285; Supt. Tumbleton to director, CID, 13 Oct. 1922, O'Malley papers, P17a/164; newspaper cuttings on the Clondalkin shootings in DT, S. 1832.
[30] Andrews, *Dublin made me*, 231.   [31] Fanning, *Independent Ireland*, 148.

were undoubtedly uncomfortable at the excesses of the CID and associated units, remained objects of enduring republican contempt.

v. The New Army and National Defence, 1921–1923

The treaty imposed certain restrictions on the nature and size of the Irish defence forces. Article 6 reserved responsibility for 'the defence by sea' of both islands to Britain for an initial period of five years. Ireland was permitted to have seagoing vessels only for revenue and fisheries purposes, while article 7 allowed Britain to retain control of and responsibility for defending specified harbour and other facilities, and guaranteed continued British use and control of transatlantic cables and of war signals stations when needed. Article 8 laid down a rather vague formula restricting the maximum size of the Irish defence forces in relation to the relative populations of Ireland and Great Britain. Implicit in the treaty were two principles fundamental both to Irish defence policy and to Anglo-Irish relations: that Ireland in practice would always rely on Britain to defend the surrounding seas and skies, and that Ireland would never allow her territory to be used by any foreign country to harm Britain's defence interests. Ironically, the latter point had been put altogether more clearly in the ill-fated 'Document Number Two' produced by de Valera as an attempt at compromise between those for and against the treaty. Underpinning this limited recognition of British strategic concerns was a principle on which both pro- and anti-treatyites agreed, that the new Irish state would always stay out of other people's wars.[32]

The immediate concern of the British government after the treaty was not to restrict the size of the provisional government's army but to strengthen it. Unless this was done, the IRA might well defeat the government's forces in an armed confrontation. This overrode other considerations, including the riskiness of nurturing a strong southern army which might ultimately turn its guns on Northern Ireland—as Collins planned in the spring of 1922, and as unionists feared—and a probable reduction in enlistment of Irishmen in the British services.[33] Britain furnished all the weapons and supplies sought by the provisional government for its campaign against the republicans. She also provided twelve armed trawlers for the coastal patrol service set up to prevent gun-running and to provide sea transport for military units, on paper a clear contravention of article 6 of the treaty. The British circumvented this restriction by classifying the trawlers as 'revenue vessels', permitted by the treaty, in return for an

---

[32] 'Document Number Two' as reproduced in Curran, *The Birth of the Irish Free State*, 289–93.
[33] Hopkinson, *Green against Green*, 127; text of ? to secretary, Ministry of Home Affairs, Northern Ireland, 7 July 1922, O'Malley papers, P17a/181. On British considerations see P. Canning, *British Policy Towards Ireland, 1921–1941* (Oxford, 1985), 37–49.

undertaking that 'they should not be used against foreign ships outside British or Irish territorial waters'.[34] The Irish made other minor concessions, for example agreeing that in the event of Britain mobilizing she should have first call on any of her reservists serving in the Free State forces, but beyond what was outlined in the treaty no major pledges on the size and composition of the new state's permanent defence forces were sought or given.[35]

The transformation of pro-treaty elements in the IRA into a formally organized, paid national army under government control was difficult. Problems of equipment, morale, training, and inexperience were compounded by the reality that the army's first opponents would most likely be their former comrades in the IRA. However, the new army had some advantages over the anti-treaty IRA. The first was that the government which controlled it had British backing. The second was that it could look for guidance to Collins, who, in the words of one army officer, 'in pre-Truce days was . . . the Commander in Chief and the man. He was everything . . . Anybody knows that.'[36] The third was that its chief of staff Richard Mulcahy had a clear view of what he wanted to achieve, a permanent defence force controlled from the centre which would take its orders from the elected government. These elementary principles meant that, for all the indecision, ineptitude, lack of will, and want of co-ordination which at times afflicted the provisional government's forces, there existed functioning machinery for prosecuting the war under central control.

On the outbreak of fighting, the contending forces were roughly equal in strength, and the balance of combat experience probably lay with the anti-treatyites. However, unlike the republicans the government had the resources necessary quickly to expand its army, and could obtain equipment from Britain relatively easily. As the conflict progressed the army grew spectacularly, to the point that after peace was secured it itself for a time became the most potent threat to government authority. When the fighting began in June 1922 the government had about 10,000 men under arms. When resistance ceased eleven months later that number had increased fivefold, and the forces included a small air unit and a coastal patrol service.[37]

The expansion of the defence forces was due simply to the imperative of enforcing the government's writ throughout Ireland. There is no evidence that ministers had any further strategic aim in mind, whether the eventual occupation of Northern Ireland or the creation of a peacetime defence establishment along the lines of other British dominions. Such considerations had to wait until the civil war was almost over, when the planning of a peacetime army was begun. Until then, the army expanded piecemeal. It was given many civilian functions by default, and it established units such as the Railways Protection

---

[34] Acting secretary, provisional government, to Colonial Office, 5 Dec. 1922, DT, S. 1980.
[35] Governor-General to Colonial Office, 27 Mar. 1923, DT, S. 3238.
[36] Russell's evidence.   [37] Hopkinson, *Green against Green*, 127 and 265.

and Maintenance Corps, the Military Customs Brigade, and the Special Infantry Corps which had no place in a conventional military defence force. Throughout the civil war the army was dogged by the inadequacies of many of its officers, by the ill-discipline, poor condition, and inexperience of its troops, by ill-feeling and disputes between senior commanders, by the weakness of central control and the disastrous performance of its supplies organization. Military policy, performance, discipline, and commitment were the subject of sometimes hysterical attacks by Kevin O'Higgins and other ministers impatient to see the republicans crushed and order restored. In noting such tensions, it is important to stress that in broad terms the army swiftly achieved its primary military goal: within two months of the outbreak of fighting, serious republican resistance was limited to parts of the south and south-west, and the republican military effort had declined into a series of uncoordinated local guerrilla actions. The considerable military achievements of the early months of the war were, however, largely overlooked in the recriminatory atmosphere which grew up within the Free State leadership as residual republican resistance dragged on, and as the new force's inevitable administrative and other weaknesses became plain to see. It was these failings, rather than its positive achievements in its basic task of subduing the republican military challenge to the new state's existence, which were to shape its destiny in the following years.

vi. Army Intelligence and Internal Security, 1922–1923

Army intelligence is the only facet of military activity which requires detailed consideration here. In intelligence, as in everything else, the organization of an effective service was bedevilled by politics, by inefficiency, and by the unsuitability of some of those involved. It was only after the civil war had ended that an adequate organization controlled from headquarters emerged.

In some repects this was surprising. Because of his success during the War of Independence, Collins placed a premium on good intelligence, and most of his pre-truce workers remained loyal to him. But people who had been successful assassins did not always make good organizers of men or analysers of information. As rapidly became clear in the new army and in Oriel House, his principal pre-truce lieutenants were simply not suitable for the largely administrative work of building up an efficient state intelligence machine, either civil or military. It was only when, in the chaotic first weeks of civil war, that Collins turned his mind to the overall intelligence problem that army intelligence received the direction it needed. We have already seen that, on his terse orders, the officers attached to Oriel House were recalled to the army proper. A circular to all the commands was prepared, complaining that 'INTELLIGENCE has not for some time past been given the attention, thought and energy that is vitally necessary', stressing that 'there was never a time when a thoroughly efficient intelligence Service was more vitally essential', and detailing the duties of each command Intelligence Officer (IO). A week later McGrath, the newly appointed director of intelligence, told Collins that the army's 'Intelligence service is only being reorganised. So far no reports have been received from the commands.' The biggest difficulty was to 'get the Officers to interest themselves in Intelligence', presently 'looked upon with something like contempt. I find that both Officers and men prefer to be more actively engaged than doing Intelligence work.' An efficient service would require 'the willing co-operation of the various staffs at GHQ and the five Commands'. Ironically, the leading republican Ernie O'Malley had almost identical criticisms to make of the IRA's approach to intelligence. It was 'extremely difficult to get a good man in charge' as 'there is too much of the touting idea about intelligence here . . . and higher intelligence has been neglected'.[38]

Despite his other preoccupations as commander-in-chief, Collins continued to press for action to improve intelligence. His conception of how army intelligence should be organized and what it should do owed at least as much to his clandestine experience during the War of Independence as to conventional military thought. His instructions show that, whatever the nominal division of responsibility between Oriel House and the army, the army organization he wanted would be concerned with political as well as with military intelligence, both inside and outside the state, and would also deal with counter-intelligence against British and Northern Irish espionage. It would be highly centralized and secure, with its own 'fully developed' communications system and codes. Crucially, the command IOs would keep in constant independent touch with intelligence headquarters by these means, and would not be simply the creatures of the command GOCs. He told McGrath to establish an 'Intelligence System' in Northern Ireland, 'on the basis of one Command for the entire area' under a single command IO, and he asked him to trace and watch two ex-RIC brothers named Greer thought to be 'connected with the British secret service'. He gave orders to collect information on republicans through well-disposed Irishmen in Britain, and he said that telephone tapping should be organized in conjunction with the Post Office, who would also assist with postal interception: 'We could start off with . . . the prominent politicians, well-known Anti[-treatyite]s, Bolshevics [sic], Fianna, Cumman [sic] Na mBan, I[rish] W[omen] W[orkers] Union], etc.' He complained to McGrath about one command IO: 'Are we receiving definite reports from Commandant Thornton: . . . When he does come to town I am anxious to see him', as it 'appears to me that he is not confining himself to the Intelligence System in the Command . . . He must be

---

[38] Draft circular, 17 July, and McGrath to Collins, 25 July 1922, MP, P7/B/4; O'Malley to Lynch, 16 Aug. 1922, O'Malley papers, P17a/176.

instructed strictly in his own duties'.[39] This comment is particularly interesting: Collins had evidently realized that the penchant for action which Frank Thornton shared with other former members of the 'Squad' was an impediment to effective intelligence work.

Had Collins lived longer, it is likely that many of the army's intelligence difficulties would have been addressed and overcome. His death in August left a void of experience, drive, and authority at the centre which no other senior officer could fill. In October McGrath left army intelligence to become director-general of the CID. He was replaced on a temporary basis by Diarmuid O'Hegarty, the secretary to the provisional government, who carried out a survey of military intelligence activity in the various commands. He found that while some IOs showed skill and initiative, nothing at all was known at headquarters of the activities of others. In Limerick, 'only one report' had been received from the former south-western command, in which it was 'stated that an Intelligence Service was being set up, but so far we do not know of its existence beyond the absolute lack of any form of communication with this Department', while it was 'impossible at the moment to say anything definite as to the Intelligence work' in Cork. A fortnight later he held out hopes of 'better results and finer co-operation' throughout the south, but soon afterwards Mulcahy heard from Collins's brother Johnny that intelligence was going a begging in Cork for the want of 'machinery of any kind of an intelligent type to take it'.[40]

Until the spring of 1923, intelligence remained largely the preserve of the commands, where progress depended on the initiative of individual IOs and the interest of local commanders, and contact with army intelligence at headquarters was a matter of chance. Even in Dublin, where they worked side by side, co-ordination between headquarters and the eastern command IOs was inadequate, and operations were complicated by differing priorities. Dan Bryan, a very successful IO in Dublin, complained many years later that for most of the war intelligence headquarters completely failed in its proper functions of co-ordination, analysis, and distribution. This he attributed to a pervasive raiding mentality, with armed officers hanging around the office hoping the next tip-off would give them premises to search or a suspect to arrest, instead of leaving such action to the CID. Bryan maintained that local successes such as the discovery of the IRA's plan to destroy railway bridges around Dublin were not properly exploited, and that the thousands of IRA documents seized in raids were never adequately appraised. Thus, he believed, the chance was lost of crushing the republicans' military campaign in the autumn of 1922.[41]

[39] Collins to McGrath, 14 July and 1, 3, and 7 Aug., and to Tobin, 19 and 24 July 1922, MP, P7/B/4.
[40] Report by O'Hegarty, 13 Oct. 1922, UCDA, O'Hegarty papers, P8/7; weekly report by O'Hegarty, 28 Oct., and Mulcahy to Dalton, 7 Nov. 1922, O'Malley papers, P17a/164.
[41] Bryan interview, 1983; Andrews, *Dublin made me*, 237. The initial tip-off which led to the thwarting of the bridge-blowing plan and the capture of the IRA's most active Dublin units appears to have come

Contemporary evidence suggests that the indifferent performance of the army's intelligence organization did give cause for concern: in February 1923 the army council called for a 'scheme for Military, Secret Service, Foreign [intelligence], to be submitted at the earliest possible moment', and a week later it directed that all captured documents should be forwarded to headquarters, a significant step in the development of a central intelligence bureau.[42] The council also decided that the 'raiding of houses for persons or materials' was to be left to 'plain clothes police', along with 'all shadowing of persons and places'. The army was also to hand over to the police all 'intelligence information with regard to persons and places to be watched'.[43] These orders presaged a major reorganization at the end of April 1923, just days after the republicans formally abandoned the fight, which is discussed in the following chapter.

vii. The Monitoring of the Republican Movement's External Contacts, 1922–1923

Republican activities abroad were of considerable interest and potential importance to the new Irish government. Information on them came from a surprisingly broad assortment of sources, including army agents in Britain, British police forces, British diplomats and consuls abroad, the British Admiralty, Irish diplomats in the United States and Europe, American police forces, and a New York private detective agency. These were the state's first and largest external intelligence operations.

Britain remained the most important centre of republican activity outside Ireland, just as it had been during the War of Independence. But republican activities were now hampered by the fact that the groups engaged in gun-running, propaganda, and assisting IRA operations were very insecure, because many of their members were known to people loyal to the treaty side. From the early days of the civil war army agents in Glasgow, Liverpool, and other cities in Britain reported on republican activities including the movements of suspects, arms smuggling, and plans to send parties of men across from Liverpool to mount surprise attacks on key points in Dublin. Their reports on their former comrades reflect a combination of familiarity and animosity: in Liverpool Paddy Walsh was 'Chief man for shipping the Goods to Ireland', Mick Joyce was 'helping to get stuff from Antwerp', while Sean Kearns was 'a communist—an awful blackguard'. A draper with an 'organising mind' had 'several bitches of

---

from the wife of the manager of the Maypole Dairy in George's Street, where an assistant had left early as he had to attend an IRA meeting. See C na D [?], IO, 2nd Eastern Division, to director of intelligence, 7 Aug. 1922, MP, P7/B/4.

[42] Army council minutes, 27 Feb., and O'Hegarty to all GOCs, 5 Mar. 1923, MP, P7/B/178 and 83.
[43] Army council minutes, 5 Mar. 1923, P7/B/178.

daughters'—an earlier version of this list had spoken of 'several wrong daughters'—and Tom O'Malley 'raided and created a terrible row in the house of Neill Kerr who was at that time Irish Government Agent in Liverpool'. One propagandist in Glasgow was a 'strong Communist' who 'received £40 [worth] of explosives from me for nothing and sold' them to the Citizen Army for '£30 in 1918. When exposed dropped out of movement.' As British police and security agencies also kept republicans under surveillance, activists were under constant pressure.[44]

The main problem for the Irish government was not to uncover republican activity in Britain but to find a way of dealing with it, since it occurred beyond their jurisdiction. For this they had to rely on the British authorities for help. In some matters, such as the issuing of passports to Irish people wishing to travel outside the British Isles, complete co-operation was automatic—the Irish authorities had the final say in which Irish applicants received passports and which did not.[45] In questions such as the extradition of wanted men and the suppression of republican propaganda, while the British were sympathetic, there were considerable legal obstacles in the path of effective action. Unless republicans in Britain broke British law, they could not be arrested there. Unless the Irish issued warrants for specific offences, they could not be extradited.

In October Mulcahy discussed these problems with A. W. Cope, the British official in charge of liaison with the provisional government. Mulcahy was concerned about arms smuggling, propaganda, and fund-raising by republican groups in Glasgow and elsewhere, about the safety of 'a dozen of our men in Glasgow who are engaged on intelligence work and who run risks at the hands of Irregular agents there', and about allowing these 'secretly and efficiently' to 'pass information' about 'arms traffic to the British Police'. Most importantly, however, he enquired if, 'without having definite charges' against key republicans 'we ask that the British police arrest them, and have them handed over to the Irish Government, will this be done?' In reply Cope undertook to arrange that Irish agents be issued with firearms permits, accepted the need for liaison between these agents and the British police, and said he thought pressure could be brought to bear on the proprietors of halls rented for republican fund-raising functions. He was also optimistic on the crucial question of extradition, agreeing that there would be no difficulty in sending suspects over on charges which would then be dropped, thus enabling the Irish to intern them.[46]

This proposal, on the face of it a flagrant abuse of the British courts, opened a Pandora's box of legal and political complexities which no subsequent British or Irish governments have been able to close. The specific scheme agreed by

[44] O'Hegarty to Sean Golden, one of the army's principal agents in Britain, 16 Dec. 1922, O'Malley papers, P17a/182; lists of suspects, one n.d., one of 12 Jan. 1923, ibid.

[45] Collins to McGrath, 5 Aug. 1922, MP, P7/B/4.

[46] Mulcahy to O'Hegarty, 14 Oct. 1922, O'Malley papers, P17a/197.

Mulcahy and Cope proved unworkable, despite British anxiety not 'to place any difficulties in our way', because it 'was questionable whether there was any statutory authority competent to issue warrants at that time in Ireland'. Only one extradition under warrant was sought, and it fell through for other reasons.[47] Increased liaison between army intelligence and Scotland Yard, and between Irish agents in England and Scotland and the local police and prosecuting authorities, ensured that the pressure on republicans was kept up, but the Irish authorities still wanted to have suspects under lock and key in Ireland. Eventually circumstances changed, following evidence that Liam Lynch had sent Pa Murray to revitalize the IRA organization in Britain and to mount operations there. Diarmuid O'Hegarty visited Scotland Yard in March 1923, and shortly afterwards British police arrested over one hundred suspects and shipped them to Ireland, where they were interned. Although Murray was not picked up then or afterwards, the British action broke the back of the IRA in Britain, as well as disrupting republican activities against the Irish government.[48]

Matters did not go so well in the courts: the House of Lords soon deemed the deportations illegal. The British were then obliged to ask for the return of all the 'internees with the exception of [the] small number . . . against whom criminal proceedings are contemplated'. By then the civil war was effectively over, and the Irish complied with the request. Art O'Brien, one of those released and sent back to Britain, was immediately rearrested there on conspiracy charges prepared with Irish assistance, convicted and jailed for two years.[49] In subsequent years extradition from Ireland to Britain and to Northern Ireland became what it has remained, a process fraught with political and legal difficulties. There is, therefore, considerable irony in the history of the first extradition problems between the two jurisdictions, and in the eventual intervention of the British courts to vindicate the rights of Irishmen improperly handed over to the Irish authorities.

The United States was the next most important centre of republican activities abroad. There the Irish government faced greater difficulties in obtaining information and in thwarting republican schemes. While well disposed towards the new Irish state the federal government had no great interest in the Irish issue. Dublin consequently had to rely mainly on its diplomatic representative Professor T. A. Smiddy. Smiddy, a fussy academic, was in many respects an unlikely choice to defend the interests of the new state in the rough-house of Irish-

---

[47] O'Hegarty to executive council, 7 June 1923, Kennedy papers, P4/659; Home Office memorandum, with Colonial Office to governor-general, 16 Dec. 1922, MP, P7/B/84.

[48] Hopkinson, *Green against Green*, 255; copy of Colonel Carter (Scotland Yard) to O'Hegarty, 17 Apr. 1923, MP, P7/B/83; Canning, *British Policy*, 79–80.

[49] Colonial Office to governor-general, 15 May 1923, O'Malley papers, P17a/195; minute by Cosgrave, n.d., DT, S. 6903.

American politics, where the most important émigré organization, Clan na Gael, had come out against the treaty. But he was at ease in dealing with officials and with national politicians, and in cultivating respectable opinion generally. Surprisingly, when the need arose he also donned cloak and dagger with some zest, warning Dublin that it was 'very inexpedient to mention names in anything connected with intelligence except by code', signing his telegrams 'Sinbad', and asking that any 'confidential letters' for him be addressed to 'Dr Henri Cortial, Cosmos Club, Washinton DC'. There are hints of scepticism in the records about his performance, including the cost to the secret service vote, but he continued to hold a watching brief on republican activities long after the civil war had ended.[50]

Smiddy had two main concerns: to detect and report on republican arms purchasing and smuggling, and to watch the movements and activities of prominent republicans in America. Unsure of whom to trust in Irish émigré circles, he enlisted the help of 'the most efficient Intelligence Detective Agency in the States' to shadow 'a Dublin Jew', Robert Briscoe, whom he believed—probably correctly—to be on a republican arms mission. In addition, he gave the agency a 'general direction to make investigations if there are any guns going to Ireland from the principal ports on the East Coast'—some months later he speculated that 'the activities of our agents' were 'seriously impeding' republican arms smuggling.[51] Smiddy also received reports on republican activities from British consulates throughout America, although until 1924 these were sent via London and Dublin and so could take weeks to reach him.[52] Smiddy was hampered by the fact that the purchase and export of arms was not illegal under American law, and that consequently the federal authorities had no reason to intervene or even to take an interest. The same held good in respect of visiting republicans, whom the authorities were not disposed to harry. One conspicuous exception was the labour leader James Larkin, whom Smiddy initially termed a leading arms smuggler. The Americans first jailed and then deported him, not for gun-running but for his activities as a labour agitator.[53] This illustrates an important point: whatever their indifference to Irish republican activities, in the 1920s many governments, including the British and the American, were acutely conscious of the dangers of communism, kept an international watch on it, and were sometimes willing to share information concerning it with Dublin.

[50] Smiddy to External Affairs, 2 Feb. and 20 Apr. 1923, DT, S. 5785 and 1976; Cosgrave to Smiddy, 8 Apr. 1923, S. 5785; government decision, 3 Apr. 1923, DT, G2/1.

[51] FitzGerald (minister for external affairs) to Mulcahy, 15 Dec. 1922, enclosing report by Smiddy, FitzGerald papers, P80/338; report by 'Sinbad', 20 Apr. 1923, DT, S. 1976.

[52] Governor-General to Colonial Office, 12 Jan. 1923, and Dominions Office to governor-general, 6 Apr. 1924, ibid.

[53] Governor-General to Colonial Office, 22 Feb. 1923, S. 2009; reports by 'Sinbad', 2 Feb. and 20 Apr. 1923, DT, S. 7785.

Links between communism and republicanism formed an important part of the government's investigations of republican activity in Europe. It was natural that left-wing groups should express sympathy for the republican cause—there were cries of 'Long live Ireland' in the Italian parliament during discussion on the arrest of Donal Hales, a republican activist, on the eve of a visit to Rome by members of the British royal family—but there were also more serious problems.[54] The government shared the general European mistrust of the new Soviet regime, both because it preached world revolution and because it provided inspiration for Irish socialists. In January 1923 Michael McDunphy, an official of the government secretariat, visited Irish diplomatic posts in Europe. Alarmed at evidence of meetings between a republican emissary and Soviet representatives, he advised that 'immediate steps' should be taken in France to set 'in motion the machinery of the Secret Police on the track of Irregular and allied Bolshevist activities in Paris', in Switzerland and in 'other countries likely to be affected'. The various police forces could supply reports 'at regular intervals . . . regarding the activities of . . . Irregulars abroad, as well as special reports in cases of urgency'.[55] Another official, Michael MacWhite, sent a more detailed account of republican overtures to the Soviets. In some respects this was reassuring, as it appeared that the woman bearing the 'dispatches from de Valera to Chicherin', the Soviet foreign minister, in Lausanne, was not taken 'seriously' by the Soviets or anyone else. MacWhite had received a somewhat dubious report that the republicans sought a loan of ten thousand pounds as well as an arms shipment 'which could easily be landed . . . in a western Irish port', and he suggested the government give this as much publicity as possible in Ireland and the United States.[56] Cosgrave subsequently spoke in public about this alleged intrigue, prompting a Soviet denial which was almost certainly true given their lack of interest in Ireland.[57] This episode was important not because it bespoke any sudden upsurge in republican/Soviet links, but because it suggested that the republican party and the IRA which controlled it were willing to seek an accommodation with the country then most feared by Britain. This propensity to seek help from Britain's enemies—first the Soviets, then the Germans—and thereby implicitly to undertake to help them against Britain—had ramifications for Anglo-Irish relations out of proportion to the generally feeble efforts of the republican movement to make such concordats effective.

The documents suggest that during the civil war the government had three main classes of information on republican activities in Europe and America.

[54] Copy of British ambassador in Rome to foreign secretary, 30 May 1923, S. 3114.

[55] McDunphy to FitzGerald, 26 Jan. 1923, FitzGerald papers, P80/752.

[56] MacWhite to FitzGerald, 13 Jan. 1923, and attached undated report, possibly a translation of a document originally prepared in French, DT, S. 3147.

[57] Text of Monsieur Klishko to foreign secretary, 21 Feb. 1923, S. 2108; S. White, 'Ireland, Russia, Communism, Post-Communism', *Irish Studies in International Affairs*, 8 (1997), 156–8.

The first was the intelligence obtained by its own forces in Ireland through interrogation of prisoners, interception of correspondence, and analysis of captured documents. The second was that which came directly from the handful of Irish officials abroad. The third was that provided by the British government, which came from British intelligence agencies, from British diplomats and consuls, and from material passed to the British by friendly governments. The British were to continue to be Dublin's principal external source of intelligence on republicanism abroad, although as the new state consolidated its standing internationally a certain amount of information came directly from foreign governments and police and security agencies.

viii. The Course of the War, 1922–1923

The civil war was, as recent research has admirably demonstrated, a miserable and confused business.[58] The kindest thing that could be said for the government's military performance was that it was less bad than the opposition's. Its forces were poorly organized, weakly led, and initially small in number. However, from the first the government controlled the levers of power, it had the assurance of British support, it had considerable legitimacy as a result of the June 'Pact' election which had returned a clear majority of pro-treaty TDs, and it had a clear political aim, to retain power and to vindicate the treaty. Collins put it thus on 14 July:

What the Army is fighting at present is largely mere brigandage, and when not this it is opposition to the People's will. What they are fighting for is the revival of the Nation . . . this revival and restoration of order cannot in any way be regarded as a step backwards, nor a repressive, nor a re-actionary step, but a clear step forward.[59]

The theme of defending the popular will again occurs in a sombre note written in August by W. T. Cosgrave, evidently for publication in the event of his death, after learning that 'members of the Government are on the list to be shot'. This plan he termed, rather charitably, 'misguided patriotism . . . The people who so act are irresponsible and must not be allowed to cow or awe the people of Ireland.' Even if the entire government 'are shot and die others will be found to take their places. None of us could be indispensable . . . My place will be easily filled.' The 'people of Ireland . . . must prevail against any minority seeking to order their will or their life save under the laws which the people's representatives pass'. Cosgrave forgave whoever might kill him, and asked 'those who are in arms against the Government to consider if it be not possible to come to an

---

[58] Hopkinson, *Green against Green* is best on the civil war. For political developments see J. Lee, *Ireland 1912–1985: Politics and Society* (Cambridge, 1989), 56–69.

[59] Collins to Griffith, enclosing draft statement, 14 July 1922, DT, S. 1318.

agreement with the nation. No member of the Government wishes to continue any war on any section.'[60] This note of melancholy determination was perhaps peculiar to Cosgrave, but his government colleagues were equally fixed in their will to see off the republicans once the fighting had started.

Underlying the civil war split was the re-emergent divide between two streams in separatist thought which had come together after the 1916 rebellion. In essence the anti-treatyites, while quibbling about the mechanics of the June 1922 election, were dismissive of electoral opinion as the deciding factor in national affairs. Until the republic, pristine and complete, was achieved, the popular will did not matter because the people were not in a position to make the right choice.[61] This left electorally minded republicans, and in particular Eamon de Valera, in a deeply ambiguous position: as he wrote in September, resistance to 'the decision of the majority of the people' implied 'the repudiation' of what republicans 'recognise to be the basis of all order in government and the keystone of democracy—majority rule'. The anomalies in de Valera's stance, having attempted to forge a compromise on the treaty and having subsequently seen only 21 per cent of votes go to anti-treaty candidates, were obvious enough: as one northern republican who had come south in order to avoid internment put it to a former comrade,

I am as I have always been in my national outlook, but I certainly must vehemently protest against the methods some people are using to further their ideas of principle. The Irregulars have (a great many of them) no principles other than that of opposition, destructive opposition to the Free State. They are not even against the connection with England, as witness de Valera's pronouncement on Document No 2. You will remember my attitude when the Treaty terms were first published . . . I ran amok, but since I came to the Free State I have been compelled by my reason and logicality and against my conscience to look facts in the face . . . I disagree altogether with armed opposition without reason.[62]

The republican opposition were unprepared for the conflict which they had precipitated, and were divided about how to proceed. The aim of the militarist group which had occupied the Four Courts since April had been to destroy the authority of the provisional government and to provoke the British army into a fight, and thereby to reunite the independence movement. Once this failed with the provisional government's attack on their positions in June, no coherent

---

[60] Note by Cosgrave, 12 Aug. 1922, DT, S. 2817.

[61] This argument is admirably advanced in Garvin, *1922*, 27–62. For a contrasting, republican legitimist view see B. Murphy, *Patrick Pearse and the Lost Republican Ideal* (Dublin, 1990), 139–44, 181–2.

[62] R. Sinnott, *Irish Voters Decide: Voting Behaviour in Elections and Referendums since 1918* (Manchester, 1995), 96–7; extract from de Valera to McGarrity, 10 Sept. 1922, quoted in S. Cronin (ed.), *The McGarrity Papers: Relations of the Irish Revolutionary Movement in Ireland and America, 1900–1940* (Tralee, 1972), 124; extract from Hugh Halfpenny (my grandfather) to Thomas Branagan, n.d. [1922], Public Record Office Northern Ireland (PRONI), HA/5/1921. See Mac Ruari, *In the Heat of the Hurry*, 71–2, 94.

military or political strategy emerged to replace it. In Dublin, as their occupation both of the Four Courts and of buildings in O'Connell Street showed, republicans were beset by their elevation of symbolism above military practicality; elsewhere, while some units performed competently, the lack of a functioning national command meant that their efforts had only a local and temporary impact.[63] The government's decisive success in quickly evicting republican forces from the main cities and towns put paid to the IRA's initial strategy of inflicting military defeat on the national army. Without political leadership once the fighting broke out as de Valera floundered in the background—in October 1922 he allowed himself to be appointed head of a republican government subordinate to the army council of the IRA, a make-believe arrangement which was to be a political millstone around his neck until he finally cast it off in 1925—the IRA havered between quasi-conventional warfare and the guerrilla tactics of the War of Independence. By contrast, and for all its deficiencies of organization, of training, of equipment, of leadership, and of morale, the army operated as a national military force under the control of a civilian government. Its operational performance during the first phase of the conflict could, furthermore, scarcely be faulted. It quickly established physical control of most of the country other than the south-west, reducing republicans to fragmented hit-and-run tactics. Ships were successfully used to transport troops around the coast, resulting in the almost bloodless reoccupation in July of Waterford and Westport, and in August of Cork and of other key towns still behind republican lines. After 11 August, when republicans under Liam Lynch abandoned the barracks at Fermoy, the anti-treaty forces held not a single military installation in the state.[64]

The republican campaign developed through a succession of hasty improvisations. After the abandonment of attempts to hold fixed positions in key towns, it grew to include not only action against military and police targets, and widespread destruction of roads, bridges, and railway lines, but also attacks on civilians believed to be government supporters, as well as incidental raids for money or supplies. In response to the Public Safety Act which gave military courts the power to deal with a wide range of capital offences, Liam Lynch declared open season on the persons and property of all pro-government TDs, all senators, and all prominent supporters of the government. For a combination of reasons from distaste to inefficiency, this policy of reprisal assassinations was only haphazardly applied. Nevertheless it represented both a further

---

[63] Hopkinson, *Green against Green*, passim; C. S. Andrews interview, 8 June 1982. Dr Andrews's memoir *Dublin made me* is a valuable republican account.

[64] The (IRA) army executive resolution appointing the republican government was moved by Con Moloney, my grandfather's brother. F. O'Donoghue, *No Other Law: The Story of Liam Lynch and the Irish Republican Army, 1916–1923* (Dublin, 1954), 276–7 and 342–3; on Lynch's strategy see ibid. 266–7; N. Harrington, *Kerry Landing August 1922: An Episode of the Civil War* (Dublin, 1992), 81–120.

upping of the stakes, and a reversion to War of Independence tactics.[65] Republicans showed a greater appetite for the less vicious tactic of arson, sometimes with fatal consequences. The government TD James McGarry lost his son when his house was set ablaze, and the father of Kevin O'Higgins was shot dead during an attempt to burn his home in Laois. O'Higgins, not surprisingly, treated with contumely a 'message . . . of maudlin regret for the murder . . . and an assurance that it was quite "unofficial"' from Lar Brady, a leading Laois republican. The 'only assurance that the Minister could give him [Brady] was that *his* home and *his* family would be secure and that he need be in no anxiety about a reply in kind'.[66] Agrarian and sectarian as well as political motives clearly played a part in the arson campaign. A weekly situation report of 21 April 1923 is a typical catalogue: in Cavan 'house of Mr Moore' and in Longford 'Mrs Richardson's house' were burned; in Westmeath there were 'house burnings [in] Aughavass & Rhode', and in Meath 'house burning—Major Bomford'; in Offaly, 'Colonel Biddulph's house', in Carlow, 'house of Robert Power', and in Cork 'Frank Pitt's house' were all attacked. Other actions were harder to fathom: what on earth possessed the armed group in Ballina who 'demolished the park enclosure and released the hares', causing the abandonment of a coursing meeting?[67] Such venting of local spleen was no substitute for concerted military action. The leaders of the IRA proved hopeless generals, unwilling to adopt and to follow a coherent national strategy. Instead they stayed in their own bailiwicks, waiting for the enemy to come to them and to pick them off piecemeal.

Despite the shambolic campaign over which he nominally presided, to the day of his death in April 1923 Liam Lynch clung to the illusion that he could transform the military situation once enough weapons were secured. A captured letter to Sean Moylan in New York in February 1923 illustrates this:

Further re Jetter [Captain J. T. Ryan, a Berlin-based Clan na Gael leader who had fled the United States in 1917 fearing arrest for involvement in German/Irish intrigues]: money for a few pieces of artillery should only be spent, as all finance possible is required here. I understood guns and submarine were on hands with our friends there, then why not push them here at once? Would that submarine have a few guns to hit up a few British ships? Nothing but artillery will clear up this war quickly. We have hopes also in another direction.

That Lynch was not simply fantasizing is indicated by another captured document, a letter sent by Moylan to a London cover address:

[65] Lynch to Michael Hayes (ceann comhairle of Dáil Éireann and speaker of the Southern Parliament), 28 Oct. 1922, UCDA, Hayes papers, P53/47; Hopkinson, *Green against Green*, 190.
[66] TJ Coyne (private secretary to O'Higgins) to adjutant-general, 23 Feb. 1923, O'Malley papers, P17a/188.
[67] Army situation report, 23 Apr. 1923, MP, P7/B/138, and daily calendar of incidents, 3 Jan. 1923, O'Malley papers, P17a/173.

We can get you any ammunition you want in any quantity. I have written 'the Boss' about a scheme we had for getting stuff in direct . . . We have one hundred silencers . . . Your news about the 'Artillery' is good. We have a man in Germany negotiating the same stunt and expect to pull off a big thing.

The 'big thing' was the purchase of four batteries of mountain artillery, four heavier guns, the appropriate shells, and millions of rounds of .303 ammunition. These were to be smuggled to Ireland by Ryan, accompanied by one hundred English-speaking military instructors. Lynch's hope that the submarine would be able to 'hit up a few British ships', presumably to draw Britain back into the fight, reflects a preoccupation with the symbolic which dominated the IRA's thinking and which was completely inappropriate to a military campaign intended to win physical control of the country.[68] This partly explains the IRA's failure in the early weeks of the civil war. Then, while at least as strong in numbers and morale, and collectively more experienced in fighting, than the fledgling government forces, it proved completely unable to devise and adopt a concerted military strategy. Instead the government was given time to consolidate its grip, first in Dublin and then in the key cities of Limerick and Cork. Thereafter the course of the war dictated that small-scale guerrilla tactics were the only ones viable against an enemy who controlled all the centres of population, the transport and communications systems, the bureaucracy and the national treasury and which, as the June election had indicated, enjoyed majority support. While sabotage, arson, and assassination made the country hard to govern, they failed to win political power for the republican movement, and they begot savage retribution. This we must now consider.

ix. Government Policy on Subduing Unrest, 1922–1923

From the outbreak of the civil war the government's policy was clear and inflexible. It would not tolerate armed resistance to its rule. It would introduce and operate draconian laws against those who challenged its authority. It would restore social order, discipline, and respect for the law. Above all, it would fight fire with fire, even beyond what emergency legislation permitted or envisaged. In all of this, it believed, it had the support of a large majority of the people. There were bitter differences on aspects of the campaign, particularly those between O'Higgins and Mulcahy on the army's alleged military and other failings, but to the world the government presented a united and uncompromising

---

[68] Lynch to Moylan, undated [early 1923?], and ? [probably Moylan], New York, to 'Mr Brooks', London, 27 Feb. 1923, UCDA, FitzGerald papers, P80/791. It is likely that this letter was intercepted or seized by the British and passed on to Dublin. Cronin, *The McGarrity Papers*, 69, 99, 105, and 134–5; Andrews, *Dublin made me*, 271–2; Hopkinson, *Green against Green*, 237.

face. Despite the sudden deaths in quick succession in August first of Arthur Griffith and then of Michael Collins, it pursued its aims with unwavering and ruthless will.

There were three strands to this ruthlessness. The first was the government's willingness to use harsh laws, most notoriously making the mere possession of arms a capital offence. Some ministers urged the use of these measures not merely to defeat the IRA but to crush social disorder, which they saw as a poisonous by-product of republican defiance. The second was its unwillingness or inability to curb the excesses of its own forces, most importantly the murder of prisoners. The third was its willingness to go beyond its legal powers in the widespread detention of republicans by the army and, more dramatically, in the summary execution of four unconvicted republican leaders in December 1922.

There was nothing new about the use of emergency legislation to quell disorder in Ireland, nor about allowing military courts to dispense justice for capital crimes. The provisional government simply took up where the British left off. Conditions were abnormal, the ordinary system of justice could not function, and harsh measures were therefore required as a temporary measure to help restore order. What distinguished the Cosgrave government's approach was its single-minded and calculated use of the death penalty under the Public Safety Act of October 1922. Under this legislation emergency judicial and punitive powers were granted to the army. Following a brief amnesty for anyone prepared to surrender his weapons and to stand aside from the conflict, these powers came into operation. Between November 1922 and May 1923 military courts dispensed justice in a cursory fashion: in the words of one officer, 'proceedings ... showing where the Court was convened, the evidence heard and the prisoner sentenced to death' were sometimes recorded 'on one sheet of foolscap'. Seventy-three republicans were executed after trial, and many more were sentenced to death but remained prisoners around the country, their survival often conditional on the activities of their fellows still at large in the locality. The first men to die were deliberately chosen because they were small fry, as O'Higgins made clear in a notorious Dáil speech. The most senior figure to be shot for possession of a firearm was the propagandist and constitutional thinker Erskine Childers. Apart from Charlie Daly, shot in Donegal in March 1923 in dubious circumstances, and Erskine Childers, an implausible candidate for the role of gun-toting desperado who inspired unusual hatred because of his influence on de Valera, most of those actually executed were foot soldiers of the republic, not, as might have been anticipated in a civil war, the top men.[69]

From November 1922 until the war's end executions and the threat of execu-

---

[69] McAllister to director of intelligence, 28 Oct. 1929, MA, file on 'Intelligence Branch—Co-operation with Civic Guards'; Nora Harkin interview. She met Daly and three other armed IRA men near Stranolar shortly before they were captured. Daly's death caused great bitterness, as he was thought not to have carried out the killing he was accused of.

tions were used as an instrument of policy. By way of illustration, the army council minutes of 12 February 1923 deal with 'Executions. All bad cases taken during the current week are to be ready and dealt with in case . . . executions are necessary next week.' From then on, 'it must be anticipated that no clemency will be shown in any case . . . In every case of outrage in any Battalion area, 3 men will be executed. Men will be immediately concentrated at the Command Centre for this purpose.'[70] In fact executions continued to be at the discretion of the local commanders, who had a variety of factors to bear in mind. These included the state of local feeling, the level and nature of republican activity in the area, and, perhaps, the possibility of drastic reprisals against government supporters. Overall, the policy of selective executions after courts martial was very successful in restricting republican activity in many areas, in lowering republican morale, and in avoiding the national and international opprobrium which a more thoroughgoing approach might have provoked.[71]

During the war, however, the apparent reluctance of many local commanders to execute convicted men was particularly attacked by O'Higgins and his close associate Patrick Hogan, the minister for agriculture. In the social disorder and indiscipline accompanying the war these two men saw the imminent collapse of Irish civilization. The army, they maintained, did not understand that the spirit of anarchy had been loosed upon the nation: it would have incalculable effects if it were not ruthlessly extirpated. They put their views in two remarkable and much-quoted memoranda in January 1923. In an intemperate essay on the failure of security policy, Hogan warned that 'the land war will begin in earnest within a few weeks'. The people behind it were from

the worst elements in the country districts with a pretty liberal sprinkling of wasters from the towns. They are practically all landless. The great majority have no genuine claim to land and would not make a success of farming . . . Their present methods are murder and arson.

Hogan also claimed that 'the time has definitely come when strikes and other disputes are being settled by shooting and arson. In Athy recently a dispute involving some farmers and three to four hundred labourers led to the haggards of seven of the farmers being burned, and one steward being shot through the hand.' He linked such unrest to a general fracturing of the republican campaign, which had become 'a war by different sections, different interests, and different individuals, with no common bond except this—that all have a vested interest in chaos, in bringing about a state of affairs where force is substituted for law.' All this could be easily remedied, if 'we only go about it properly. The people are thirsty for peace, and thirsty for strong ruthless measures.' These should be provided by 'an unusually steady, disciplined army acting with the utmost

[70] Army council minutes, 12 Feb. 1923, MP, P7/B/178.
[71] Hopkinson, *Green against Green*, 288; Andrews, *Dublin made me*, 251–4.

efficiency and ruthlessness', specifically by a new 'highly disciplined efficient reserve, not affected in any way by the provincialism' of the existing army, which would tackle disorder. He also asked for military 'inspectors who would be absolutely independent of the local commands', to overcome local reluctance to carry out executions for possession of weapons or for arson: 'I know that executions are only a second best, and that they cannot be continued indefinitely', but for the moment 'they ought to be going with machine-like regularity'. Hogan concluded by pointing out somewhat cryptically that action was also needed on '(a) Prisons and prisoners; (b) Women; (c) Payment of Army Accounts, and (d) The Drink Question.'[72]

O'Higgins argued on the same lines: 'We are not engaged in a war properly so called, we are combating organised sabotage and a kind of disintegration of the social fabric', so the military should 'perform many duties which, strictly and technically, might be said to be those of armed peace rather than of military'. His concern was not with organized republican resistance, but with the unleashing of 'greed and envy and lust and drunkenness and irresponsiblity' in the countryside. As 'the first sign of a crumbling civilisation' he adduced, bizarrely, the fact that 'the bailiff as a factor in the situation, has failed'. Thus the army should form special units to clear land, enforce court orders, and to assist in 'tracking and stamping out poteen traffic'. In addition, 'there should be executions in every county. The psychological effect of an execution in Dublin is very slight in Wexford, Galway or Waterford . . . I believe that local executions would tend considerably to shorten the struggle.'[73]

Underlying these apocalyptical warnings was a straightforward point: in its prosecution of the war, the army had been unable to compensate for the lack of civil authority in many areas. Disorder flourished in its absence. That point was accepted by the government, and the army agreed to do more in consultation with the civil authorities in the disturbed areas. This initially cheered O'Higgins up remarkably: he told Cosgrave that once the 'little committee of order', as he incongruously termed it, 'starts holding its occasional meetings, the idea will rapidly shape itself . . . Business men will take heart and realise that the courts are no longer an empty shamble, and that credit can be given with reasonable certainty of recovery.'[74] The succeeding fortnight saw no less than twenty-nine of the seventy-three legal executions carried out during the civil war, but with that grisly exception the army dragged its feet on the specific changes O'Higgins had sought: the military detachments he demanded only materialized as the Special Infantry Corps in the spring as a by-product of wider army reorganization. In April O'Higgins told Cosgrave that with the prevailing 'revolt against all

---

[72] Memorandum by Hogan, 11 Jan. 1923, MP, P7/b/96.
[73] Memorandum by O'Higgins, n.d., ibid.
[74] O'Higgins to Cosgrave, 12 Jan. 1923, ibid.

idea of morality, law and social order', 'no greater disaster could happen to the country than that "peace" should overtake it, leaving conditions such as these to be dealt with by a new and unarmed Police Force and by legal processes'.[75] With the war effectively over, he won his point about the deployment of the military. Units of the Special Infantry Corps, sometimes acting in conjunction with unofficial groups organized by farmers, made vigorous and partisan interventions in agrarian and industrial disputes. The labour historian Emmet O'Connor has pointed out that while 'the cabinet was anxious to maintain the values of liberal democracy', to the extent that this was achieved in the new state 'it was realized through the paradox of withholding the conventions of liberalism until after the crisis phase'. Government forces 'did not act within the law, were indisciplined, and often openly partisan' in their interventions throughout 1923.[76]

Hogan and O'Higgins wildly exaggerated both the extent and the depth of social disorder in January 1923, as well as its links with republicanism. The evidence cited by Hogan—a man wounded in the hand, and a few barns destroyed in Kildare—scarcely bespoke impending doom. His ideal remedy appeared to be the apprehension of the perpetrators and their trial and execution just as if they were active republicans caught in arms. Failing this, in his view, the least the army could do would be to shoot a few of its republican prisoners in areas disturbed by land or labour troubles, since this might give the agitators food for thought. Hogan's views though extreme were essentially pragmatic: as minister for agriculture he naturally defended the interests of substantial farmers threatened by strikes, while every politician was well aware that the land issue was a powder keg. He dealt with it, as the British had learned to do before him, not simply by coercion but by reform, putting through the 1923 Land Act which substantially disposed of most of the grievances underlying land agitation. O'Higgins's concerns were altogether more spiritual. He took the view that defeating the republicans militarily was not enough: the land grabber, the debtor, and the drunk were enemies just as menacing. Victory would be achieved only with the return of the bailiff, the restoration of the local credit system, and the extirpation of illicit distilling. Only then would the country rediscover its social discipline and its moral sense. This was a messianic agenda which put local social unrest, agitation, and indiscipline on a par with widespread armed resistance to the government. No other minister attained remotely the heights of verbal morality routinely scaled by O'Higgins, a man who, judging by what he said and what he wrote, saw everyone and everything—the war, land agitation, the army, industrial unrest, intemperance, republicans, even his colleagues—in terms of starkest black and white. Yet persistent shrillness should not be confused with consistency: we shall see that,

---

[75] O'Higgins to Cosgrave, 5 Apr. 1923, DT, S. 582.
[76] O'Connor, *Syndicalism in Ireland*, 163.

whatever his tirades and declamations, O'Higgins was as capable of equivocation in words and in policy as any of the fellow politicians whose prevarications and evasions he habitually denounced.

From the outbreak of hostilities the government was willing to go beyond its legal powers. Its justification was firstly that, unlike its opponents, it enjoyed majority support and was fighting to vindicate democracy, and secondly that, unless it gave an unequivocal display of its resolution, it might lose the civil war. Early on in the conflict, for example, Collins gave characteristically robust orders that in Wexford 'any man caught looting or destroying property should be shot at sight'.[77] The army also detained many people in advance of legal power to do so. In the context of civil war, minor breaches of the law in furtherance of public order and safety were an unimportant technicality. Summary executions, however, were another matter. On 8 December 1922 four prominent republicans, one from each province, Dick Barrett, Liam Mellows, Rory O'Connor, and Joe McKelvey, in prison since the capture of the Four Courts, were taken out and shot on government orders. This was a calculated act, done without any pretence of legality. The executions followed the killing by republican gunmen of a government TD, Sean Hales, and the wounding of another, the deputy speaker of the Dáil. That attack came on foot of an order from Liam Lynch directing the IRA to kill, amongst others, all deputies and senators who had voted for the Public Safety Act. In the IRA's view this enormous extension of the concept of collective responsibility from members of the government, already scheduled for assassination, to virtually anyone who publicly supported government policy, was morally superior to the only alternative it saw, that of shooting prisoners. It is an interesting illustration of a peculiarly militarist philosophy—those soldiers beaten in battle could be spared, those civilians victorious in politics should die. In fact Sean Hales had not voted for the offending act, being absent when it was passed, he had distinguished himself against the British and was still highly respected by republicans, one brother Tom was a leading IRA man in Cork, and another, Donal, was the republican representative in Italy. The republican historian Dorothy Macardle found some solace in the specious technicality that Hales was also an army officer, but the murder was a characteristically inept piece of work by the IRA.[78]

The declared policy of shooting public representatives invited a drastic response from a government which drew its legitimacy from the Dáil. The outcome was an act of state terror, of a kind never seen again in Ireland, as the government turned Liam Lynch's expansive logic of collective responsibility back

[77] Collins to director of intelligence, 10 Aug. 1922, MP, P7/B/4.

[78] Andrews, *Dublin made me*, 251; D. Macardle, *The Irish Republic* (1st edn., London, 1937; Corgi edn., London, 1968), 750. Despite his republican activities, Hales's Italian-based brother Donal reportedly commissioned a commemorative statue in Genoa in 1928, to be erected in Bandon. Appeal for subscriptions, n.d. (Oct./Nov. 1928), UCDA, MacEoin papers, QMG 344H.

onto the republican elite. The IRA got the message: no more TDs or senators were killed in the civil war, although the homes of a number were burned down. Whether this justified the government's action is a moot point. It already had ferocious legal powers with which to crush its enemies, and it was already militarily and politically in command of most of the country. The men it shot had been in custody for months, had not been convicted of anything, and had nothing to do with Lynch's order. This ferocious premeditated act also made it difficult for the government, if indeed it had the will, to control unofficial reprisals and murders by its own forces. Finally, the executions undermined one central tenet of its case, that the rule of law must always prevail. However, the absence of significant protests at the time from non-republican sources, and the results of subsequent elections, suggest that the general public acquiesced in drastic measures. This was an important practical lesson, which later governments took to heart. Whatever the theoretical objections to exceptional laws and actions against political crime, harsh measures never did serious political damage to an incumbent administration provided the response was seen to be proportionate to the immediate challenge posed by militant republicanism.

The four men shot on 8 December 1922 were not the only men to be killed outside the law. During the civil war and its aftermath a large number of republicans, perhaps as many as one hundred and fifty, were murdered while in custody or while supposedly evading capture. These killings can be divided roughly into two categories: those perpetrated by soldiers, and those by members of civilian or at any rate plain-clothes bodies such as the CID. The practice was first seen in Dublin, and as the fighting spread throughout the south and west so too did the murders, most notoriously in Kerry. Most army atrocities were committed either in hot blood in the immediate aftermath of engagements, or as calculated reprisals for republican attacks. For example, in September 1922 a number of soldiers were blown up by a mine near Macroom. An armed republican who then attempted to surrender was killed. Mulcahy defended this action in the Dáil, saying it was understandable that the surviving men should want to avenge their comrades. In fact, however, Emmet Dalton, the GOC in Cork, complained to Mulcahy that local troops were appalled at the man's death: while 'I personally approve of the action . . . the men . . . are of such a temperament that they can look at seven of their companions being blown to atoms by a murderous trick without feeling annoyed—but when an enemy is found . . . they will mutiny if he be shot'. The killing was 'the work of the Squad', the Dublin assassination unit set up by Collins during the War of Independence, and Dalton asked that they be withdrawn.[79] The atrocities in Kerry in March 1923 were also the work of hard men sent down from Dublin, in this case the Dublin Guards under P. T. Daly, as reprisals for the deaths of five soldiers killed

---

[79] Dalton to Mulcahy, 19 Sept. 1922, MP, P7/B/82.

by a republican mine. In one bloody week three groups of captured republicans were taken from prison and tied to mines which were then detonated. Eighteen prisoners were killed. These gratuitously savage acts—after all, the army had plenty of convicted prisoners which it could have executed quite legally—naturally caused an outcry. The government was acutely embarrassed, but it was unable or unwilling to investigate the deaths thoroughly lest it upset the army, and all ministers seem to have concurred uneasily in this. By contrast, when in June Daly and two other officers were accused of manhandling two daughters of a Kenmare doctor, on the face of it a rather less sinister offence than blowing prisoners to pieces, ministers were outraged at such lewd behaviour: O'Higgins, who, characteristically, threatened resignation over the army's unwillingness to punish those involved, and then changed his mind when the military refused to act, said the incident 'is in a class to itself . . . It is going to ring the death-knell of either discipline or banditry.' It was also another stick with which he could beat Mulcahy in their developing dispute over the army's performance and future.[80]

Unauthorized killings and other crimes perpetrated by civilian agencies did not excite the same criticism within the government. We have seen that Oriel House—the CID and satellite plain-clothes units—were responsible for a number of murders during and immediately after the civil war, as well as for widespread maltreatment of prisoners. Because such units operated in plain clothes, it was seldom possible to identify the people and units involved in individual cases. The motives for many killings were also obscure: it is said that personal vendettas were behind some of the most notorious murders. There is no evidence that any ministers were implicated, either directly or indirectly, in directing this terror: they can, however, fairly be criticized for the public equanimity with which they greeted unequivocal and repeated evidence of murder by government agencies.

Republicans, politically and militarily on the defensive from the outset, were appalled at the government's ruthless prosecution of the war. Their leaders took refuge on the moral high ground, contrasting the government's behaviour in introducing the death penalty for possession of arms with their own observance of 'the recognised rules of warfare'.[81] No matter that republicans were highly eclectic in their interpretation of such rules. For example, in Wexford the IRA warned that anyone giving information to government forces 'will be considered as military combatants and are liable to be shot by all the rules of warfare'.[82] Which such rule permitted the killing of defenceless relations of ministers? What legitimate war objective was met by the burning down of the homes of

---

[80] Quoted in Hopkinson, *Green against Green*, 264; T. de Vere White, *Kevin O'Higgins* (London, 1948; Tralee, 1996), 159. See Harrington, *Kerry Landing*, for a healing account of the Kerry campaign.

[81] Lynch to Hayes, 28 Oct. 1922, as in n. 65 above.

[82] IRA notice, with Brennan-Whitmore to director of intelligence, 12 Aug. 1922, O'Malley papers, P17a/176.

the Anglo-Irish, or the shooting of prominent government supporters? What honourable military purpose was served by the slaughter of Protestants in rural Cork?[83] Republican complaints about the government's attitude are revealing of an enduring strain in republican thought, whereby an extraordinarily strict litmus test of legality, of due process, and of general fairness is applied to actions of everyone save those in the movement itself. The role of state law in republican thought is paradoxical, since the movement on the one hand routinely denies the legitimacy of laws it happens not to like yet consistently complains that they are not fairly and correctly administered. This emphasis on unfairness is deeply rooted in republican critiques of the state, and goes well beyond the necessary sophistries of defence counsel. It remains a central though puzzling part of republican doctrine and propaganda.

x. Conclusion

There is no doubt that the government's political and military resolve came as a profound shock to republican opponents, who saw themselves as the military and political elite of the independence struggle. With Griffiths and Collins dead, the government appeared a ragbag of obscure lightweights, a group of opportunists who had come to prominence only when the British were leaving and it was safe to do so. To be outmanoeuvred politically by such tyros was bad enough, although, to the despair of the redundant de Valera, the IRA leadership had already abandoned any attachment to conventional concepts of democratic politics; to be outfaced in terror and to be defeated in guerrilla war was an even greater blow to republican pride, because it showed that even in the sphere of pure militarism into which the IRA had retreated they could be bested by a collection of untried nonentities.[84] The government might well have won without recourse to all the measures used, and without the various atrocities for which its forces were responsible. But at some point or other the government had to meet force with greater force, and IRA terror with state terror. It was death sentences and executions, not murders, that broke the IRA's morale. The introduction and use of such draconian laws did not provoke a crisis of legitimacy for the Cosgrave government: on the contrary, the evidence suggests that the majority of the people accepted these laws as necessary for the suppression of disorder. The complaints of republicans against both the savagery of the laws and the way in which they were applied were vitiated by the lawless ambience and undisciplined ruthlessness of the IRA's own campaign.

---

[83] P. Hart, 'The Protestant Experience of Revolution in Southern Ireland', in R. English and G. Walker (eds.), *Unionism in Modern Ireland: New Perspectives on Politics and Culture* (Basingstoke, 1996), 81–98.

[84] Andrews, *Dublin made me*, 251–2; Andrews interview.

The course of the civil war saw the definitive military defeat of the anti-treaty forces. Thereafter republicans working against the state had either to channel their activities into politics, or to work covertly as members of the underground IRA. Vindicated by the result of the civil war, the government's prosecution of it nevertheless raised awkward questions. Making hostages of condemned men, tolerating murder by state forces, shooting unconvicted republican leaders as a deterrent, using civil war legislation and the army to quell social and industrial unrest—all this set a grim precedent which some future government confronted with disorder might follow.

2

The Civilianization of Internal Security, 1923–1932

i. Introduction

The four years between April 1923 and August 1927 saw the steady consolidation of the new state, beginning with republican collapse in the civil war and culminating in de Valera's grudging entry to the Dáil. In retrospect the victory of constitutional politics has the appearance of inevitability. At the time, however, matters did not seem so simple: the violent deaths of key political figures mark key points in the period. The republican irreconcilable Liam Lynch was killed in action in April 1923, and Kevin O'Higgins, the passionate advocate of the rule of law, was assassinated while walking to mass in July 1927. As he lay dying O'Higgins forgave his killers but warned his friends to beware of de Valera. He was right: his death forced Fianna Fáil into parliamentary politics. In so doing it wrought not only the marginalization of militant republicanism which O'Higgins had hoped for, but also the electoral triumph in 1932 of the man whom he and his colleagues loathed the most.

The problems facing the government in April 1923 were enormous. Roads, bridges, and railways had suffered great damage, threatening the country's economic life. In many areas the local taxation system had almost collapsed, jeopardizing the provision of essential services. Land agitation in the west and south, fanned by the civil war but largely independent of it, seemed to challenge the established social order. Labour unrest added to the sense of menace. The explosive issue of the boundaries of Northern Ireland remained on the agenda. Despite military defeat, republicanism was still a potent political force. The state was almost bankrupt, faced with enormous reconstruction costs but saddled with large, expensive, and truculent security forces. Yet economic recovery required not only the restoration of order but a reduction in the level of state taxation and spending, and hence radical cuts in the security machine on which the state depended for survival. What was to be done?

There were five strands to the government's response to these issues. These were a gradual switch to civilian policing, ameliorative land legislation, the establishment of a coherent civil court system, a careful relaxation of emergency powers of detention and imprisonment, and drastic cuts in security and defence spending. Within a few years an apparently stable, peaceful, democratic, and conservative polity had emerged. This remarkable transformation has, somewhat ironically, led some commentators to deprecate as paranoia the continuing unease of the Cosgrave administration about political and social unrest once the civil war had been won.[1] But they were ex-revolutionaries themselves, whose fear of subversion derived from their own success in destroying Britain's authority in Ireland, and who appreciated the political potential of apparently random and unpopular acts of violence. As they considered the implications of O'Higgins's murder in 1927, they could not know that it was an isolated act and not the calculated prelude to a renewed campaign of violence against the state. As they observed de Valera's contortions during the mid-1920s, and his sustained efforts to remain on good terms with armed republicanism even after he split with Sinn Féin and with the mythic Irish republic and headed grudgingly but purposefully towards participation in the Free State's imperfect Dáil, they had every right to be sceptical of his intentions and fearful of his ability to harness the gunmen for another push against the treaty settlement.

ii. The Restoration of Order, 1923–1924

The collapse of organized republican resistance in the spring of 1923 left the government with enormous public order problems. Land and labour agitation, army demobilization, and the absence of civil authority in many parts of the country provided conditions in which lawlessness flourished. The courts system was in chaos. Many armed republicans remained at large. The Garda Síochána was still in an early stage of development. By now an unarmed force, it was neither organized nor trained to deal with widespread armed crime. The army was in the throes of demobilization, an exercise which unquestionably would increase the pool of potential criminals. How were public order problems to be solved?

O'Higgins had no doubts. Although a virulent critic of the army on grounds both of inefficiency and ill-discipline, he told Cosgrave in April 1923 that it was up to the military to restore order. Two months later he stressed that 'the maintenance of order and public peace and the enforcement of law are primarily the responsibility of the police and other civil authorities'. The army, nevertheless, 'may have to be used when armed opposition to the law is anticipated or in cases of riot or organised violence beyond the powers of unarmed police', although 'only . . . when requested by the civil authorities', to address instances of land occupation, cattle driving, attacks on rates collectors, strikes, and other forms

---

[1] Brady, *Guardians*, 100.

of disorder.[2] He had his way: until the country fell quiet and the police were firmly established, the army had to cope.

The decision to use the army as a surrogate police force was understandable and inevitable. How else could public order be restored and protected, given the government's lack of practical authority in many parts of the country? This presented the military, already wrestling with the nightmarish task of peacefully reducing its size by two-thirds, with considerable difficulties. It also cut across Mulcahy's professed aim of turning the army into a compact, apolitical, and highly trained defence force, one 'that would be absolutely responsible to even a de Valera Government'. Instead, the army remained the government's Jack of all security and allied trades, to the unease of its senior officers. The Special Infantry Corps intervened in agrarian disputes, formally to enforce court orders and in practice to subdue agitation. The Military Customs Brigade operated in border areas in lieu of a civilian customs and excise service. Army intelligence became the government's chief source of information and analysis on the range of domestic threats to public order, but also assumed what were essentially detective duties combating armed crime. Most strikingly, however, thousands of troops were deployed on what were properly civilian police duties.[3]

For the army the implications were grim. Instead of concentrating units for reorganization and training along conventional military lines, it had to provide many small detachments to act in lieu of civilian police throughout the country. This unwelcome duty was complicated by two predictable factors: as O'Higgins later acknowledged, soldiers 'make bad policemen. There is a fundamental difference of outlook.' Furthermore, the army was the source of much of the crime it was supposed to suppress: in January 1924 the director of intelligence reported that, while republicans and freelance criminals were very active in the south and west, and while 'agrarian and labour disputes have led to a good deal of crime' in some areas, 'a high percentage of the crimes committed during the second half of 1923 have been definitely traced to members or ex-members of the Army'. This view was echoed in an RUC report obtained by army intelligence which spoke of 'armed outrages' by 'roving bands . . . of discontented ex-soldiers', while discharged members of the CID and other semi-civilian units were also frequently implicated.[4] The saga of Commandant Joe Owens illustrates the near anarchy which prevailed in the months following the republican defeat.

During the civil war Owens had commanded Cosgrave's bodyguard, but in the spring of 1923 he was dismissed and placed under close arrest. He was 'an

---

[2] O'Higgins to Cosgrave, 5 Apr. 1923, and attached memorandum, n.d., DT, S. 582 and S. 3306.

[3] Note of talk between Cosgrave, Mulcahy, and McGrath, 26 Jan. 1924, MP, P7/B/105; army council minutes, 13 May and 15 June 1923, P7/B/178; 'Summary of intelligence', undated [1984], UCDA, Bryan papers, P71/171(3).

[4] Report by director of intelligence, 8 Jan. 1924, and text of Royal Ulster Constabulary (RUC) monthly intelligence summary for Jan. 1924, MP, P7/B/140.

erratic type of gentleman, as I have known him to do holds up [*sic*] for the purpose of stealing Motor Cars, drink etc., even whilst he was serving in the Army'.
On his release in June 1923 Owens and two CID men embarked on a series of
armed robberies in Dublin. He was captured and released by troops at least once
before finally being arrested by the army in the course of a robbery in Westmeath. When brought to Dublin, his two companions were 'recognised as CID
men' and immediately released, but Owens was sent for trial. He was promptly
acquitted because of 'his past record in the Volunteer Movement', and he
returned to crime. Owens was eventually interned in November 1923 under the
Public Safety Act, on the face of it a clear misuse of an emergency measure aimed
at suppressing political violence. Despite Cosgrave's reservations, he was freed
in June 1924. He was then awarded an ex gratia grant of £50 as he was 'more or
less down and out and unless he has some means of sustenance . . . is apt to
again resort to violence . . . bad as he has been in the National Army some of the
others were not angels either'.[5]

In retrospect, what is striking about the first year after the civil war is not the
extent but the transience of disorder, violence, and public indiscipline in the
country. There was no shortage of weapons in unauthorized hands. Demobilization returned thousands of men to civilian life with few prospects of
employment. Starting in the autumn of 1923, twelve thousand republicans were
gradually freed; the Northern Ireland authorities also released and expelled
most of their internees, swelling the pool of potential malcontents. Agrarian
and labour tensions, largely dormant during the civil war, flared up once the
fighting had ceased. Guns were used not only for robberies but to settle political
and personal scores. In the most drastic though not the last anti-Semitic crime
that independent Ireland was to see, someone took advantage of the general
atmosphere of lawlessness to murder in succession two inoffensive Dublin
Jews.[6] The Garda and the DMP were too weak to cope with such disorder, while
the army proved an inadequate and undisciplined surrogate police force. The
system of justice was in chaos, with two distinct but overlapping court systems
in operation. Yet the country gradually calmed down. There were three key reasons: government policy towards republicans; a combination of repressive and
ameliorative measures to deal with labour troubles and with agrarian disputes;
and the rapid development of good relations between the police and the community in most parts of the state.

When the civil war ended the government's twelve thousand prisoners posed
an awkward problem. If released precipitately, they might resume their former
ways—they had only 'dumped arms', not admitted defeat, and many anticipated a return to combat when the time was right. If held indefinitely, however,

---

[5] Unsigned reports, 3 and 27 July 1923 and 14 Jan. 1924, MA, file marked 'Intelligence' and 'Owens,
Joseph'; private secretary, president, to Military Pensions Board, 20 Oct. 1924, DT, S. 2209.
[6] DT, S. 4073; Bryan interview, 1983.

they would attract increasing public sympathy. In July a further Public Safety Act was introduced, which closed a legal loophole by permitting the continued detention in peacetime of unconvicted civil war prisoners. Government policy was to let the republican rank and file go free in dribs and drabs once they had given written undertakings not to resume subversive activities. This approach has been criticized as narrow-minded and ungenerous. However, all the evidence suggests that most republicans viewed their continued detention simply as one further act of Free State spite, although there is no doubt that some prisoners owed their continued incarceration to 'a state of confusion' and a lack of proper records. Cosgrave, who initially was 'in favour of an amnesty', came to the conclusion that such a gesture would fly in the face of 'the intense feeling there is against release of these prisoners' amongst government supporters. It is also difficult to see how an immediate amnesty would have won republican hearts and minds.[7] Furthermore, the government's policy was calculated to demoralize the republican movement while diluting public sympathy for it, and in this it plainly succeeded. In reaction to continued internment, and to harsh conditions in Mountjoy jail, the IRA made a major mistake. Buoyed up by the republicans' unexpectedly good showing in the August general election, when the abstentionist Sinn Féin party won 44 of the 153 Dáil seats against an expected 30, in October the IRA leadership sanctioned a mass hunger strike of prisoners. The deaths of Thomas Ashe in 1917 and Terence MacSwiney in 1920, and the release of prisoners from Mountjoy jail in 1920 had demonstrated the political capital that could be made from such strikes against a regime bereft of popular support. But the October 1923 strike was unplanned and uncoordinated, and it proved a disaster. Within a week it had begun to crumble, provoking discord and despair amongst the men in the various prisons and camps. A handful held out for almost six weeks, until the strike was called off following the deaths of two prisoners. The government took advantage of the collapse in republican morale to resume what Cosgrave termed the 'dribble out of prisoners', eventually dispensing with the pledge of future good behaviour, and by the spring of 1924 all but a handful had been freed.[8]

There were important practical lessons for both sides in the conflict. Cosgrave and his ministers handled the crisis with considerable skill, allowing the republicans to make all the moves and all the mistakes. For the republican movement, the outcome demonstrated a curious inverse relationship between the number of hunger strikers and the level of public sympathy generated. Both government and IRA were to revisit these issues in later decades. It has been argued that, by not releasing all the prisoners once the strike had collapsed in

---

[7] Brady, *Guardians*, 98; Andrews, *Dublin made me*, 293; Cosgrave's MS notes, 3 Jan. 1924, DT, S. 581; unsigned memorandum [by Dan Bryan], 13 Aug. 1925, MA, file marked 'Co-operation with Civic Guards'.

[8] Cosgrave's comments, 3 Jan. 1924, DT, S. 581.

November 1923, the government dissipated the advantage it had gained and afforded republicans the time to heal 'the schisms of the strike'. But this point, typical of republican complaints about repressive policies, only holds water if there is evidence that softer treatment would have diluted the militancy of those still detained. While republicans spoke and wrote bitterly of their detention, no one who afterwards remained true to the IRA's vision of the republic attributed their continuing militancy to the harsh policies of the Cosgrave administration. On the contrary, it seems more likely that for most prisoners the strike was the last straw: it underlined the government's power and practical authority, the futility of resuming armed resistance, and the continuing political ineptitude of the IRA.[9] The men who remained active adherents of armed struggle after 1923 were a small minority of those who began the strike, and the movement they led for a generation shrank progressively in size and power. The vast majority of released prisoners, however embittered by their prison experiences, subsequently took their lead from de Valera, already embarked on his tortuous journey towards strictly constitutional politics. Overall, the government's policy towards republican prisoners after the civil war while ungenerous was amply justified both by circumstances and by events.

Government policy towards labour and land agitation involved a combination of coercion and amelioration. Ministers were unwilling to see the benefits of their civil war victory lost through what they regarded largely as civic indiscipline and hooliganism. There was pressure from business and farming interests to contain a recrudescence of the labour militancy seen in 1921–2: in Cork in October 1923 a merchant 'inquired why the Civic Guard did not prevent "peaceful picketing" (it is anything but peaceful) and lamented the absence of the RIC'. Who was to deal with 'the Red Flag men, many of whom are armed'?[10] In rural districts, unrest amongst farm labourers damaged the interests of the large farmers seen as the backbone of the agricultural industry, while land agitation threatened the social fabric of rural Ireland.

The government's response to this unrest was robust. Coercion was applied, largely through the army's Special Infantry Corps, which intervened in a wave of farm strikes in south Leinster and north Munster over the summer and autumn of 1923. This was bad for the army but it worked well enough and it saved the Garda from 'the odium' associated with strike breaking. Land seizures, which were widespread in many counties, presented more complex problems of social control. Soldiers could not be dispatched to clear every contested acre, and the mass of disputes about occupancy and ownership were best addressed through the slow but inexorable processes of the ordinary law.

---

[9] J. Bowyer Bell, *The Secret Army: A History of the IRA 1916–1970* (London, 1970), 44–5; P. O'Donnell, *The Gates Flew Open* (Dublin, 1932; Mercier Press edn., Cork, 1965), 86–100, 102–4; Andrews, *Dublin made me*, 301–2.

[10] Army intelligence report, 4 Oct. 1923, MP, P7/B/140.

However, exemplary action was taken along lines suggested by Patrick Hogan, who also pressed the need for accompanying steps 'to tackle the question of land purchase'. This was successfully done through the 1923 Land Act, a substantive attempt to redress the legitimate grievances of landless men. Despite the best local efforts in subsequent years of gifted agitators such as Peadar O'Donnell, once the 1923 act came into operation the issue of land reform faded from national politics.[11]

iii. The Army and the State, 1923–1925

As the country gradually calmed down, so the Garda consolidated its position. In January 1924 the army director of intelligence reported that the new force was 'slowly but surely asserting its authority', and a month later emphasized that 'there is no doubt that the Gardai have earned both the confidence and respect of the people whose attitude to the military is frankly hostile'. In the turbulent conditions of the time this was a remarkable achievement. It was partly the product of the policy decision to disarm the force after the 1922 mutiny; however, two other important factors were also involved. Until 1925, the Garda did not operate in Dublin, the cockpit of political intrigue and the area most affected by armed crime. Secondly, until its amalgamation with the DMP in 1925 the force had no formal responsibility for dealing with political crime or with subversion and did not generally attempt to do so: army intelligence officers were frequently critical of what one described as the propensity of policemen to 'close their eyes to a lot of things when they could pass a lot of important information on to us', while in some areas they were hesitant to call on the military for any assistance, for fear of arousing local hostility.[12] In its crucial first years the force prudently stuck to enforcing the ordinary law, and left it to other agencies to tackle armed crime, to harry the republican movement, and to monitor political and labour conditions.

For all the unrest and disorder in the months following the civil war, the greatest threat faced by the government came not from the republican movement but from its own side. Within the army unrest, already obvious during the war, grew further under the peacetime pressures of demobilization and reorganization, and culminated in mutiny in March 1924. The genesis of the mutiny lay in the circumstances of the army's creation and hasty expansion in 1922. As already discussed, a significant group of officers, led by Collins's one-time

---

[11] O'Connor, *Syndicalism in Ireland*, 163; unsigned memorandum [by Hogan], 22 Dec. 1922, DT, S. 1943.

[12] Director of intelligence's monthly reports, 9 Jan. and 5 Feb. 1924, MP, P7/B/138; report from Waterford CIO, 14 Jan. 1924, with other CIO reports in similar vein, MA, file on 'Intelligence Branch—Co-operation with Civic Guards'; notes from GOC's meeting, 15 Dec. 1923, MP, P7/B/179.

assistant General Liam Tobin, had grown restive at their treatment during the civil war, when they were gradually excluded from key positions in the interests of discipline and efficiency. In January 1923 they had agreed to 'build an organisation', the Irish Republican Army Organization or 'Old IRA', which 'when strong would demand a strong voice in Army Policy', and would 'make every effort to get control of the vital sections of the Army', weed out 'those undesirable persons who were and are holding these positions', and force a reappraisal of what they thought was the government's unduly pro-British policy.[13] Once the war petered out they were threatened with further indignity through the government's plans for rapid demobilization of at least thirty-five thousand of its fifty-five thousand soldiers. Who was to go, who was to stay, and who was to get the best jobs?

The government's handling of the army was complicated by increasingly strained relations within the executive council between Mulcahy and most of his colleagues. Mulcahy had borne the brunt of criticism of the army during the civil war, and this continued after the republican collapse. In particular, O'Higgins spoke of the army's discipline and performance with a combination of hysteria and withering contempt; Cosgrave and other ministers did little to offset these outbursts, whether because they broadly agreed with them or because they were simply in awe of O'Higgins's powers of invective. By the spring of 1923 Mulcahy was isolated within the government, and his arguments consequently carried little weight. This in turn weakened his authority within the army, where the malcontents were encouraged in their activities by the minister for industry and commerce Joseph McGrath, who was on close terms with Tobin and other leading dissidents whom he had known since the War of Independence and with whom he had worked in Oriel House during the civil war.

In the summer of 1923 the leading Tobinites, accompanied by McGrath, met Cosgrave and Mulcahy to outline their grievances. These talks were sanctioned by the executive council in the hope of avoiding a split in the army in the run-up to the August general election. While they may have bought time, the meetings were something of a humiliation for Mulcahy and Cosgrave: the Tobinites were aggressive and discourteous, and their demands extravagant. They, who had prosecuted the war against the republican movement with particular ferocity, now complained of the government's abandonment of the republican ideal of national independence and unity. More pertinently, they argued that the army council was giving preferment to ex-British officers and to others 'never known to be anywhere' or to have 'cleared out of this country when there was danger', while there 'are easily IRA men who could hold these positions and use their brains'. They warned that the army was now riddled with incompetents and

---

[13]   OIRA questionnaire on 'Intelligence', with chief of staff to minister for defence, 24 Nov. 1923, MP, P7/B/195.

British spies, complained about attempts by Mulcahy and the army council to use the Irish Republican Brotherhood (IRB) within the army as a focus of loyalty to the government, and demanded 'a Committee to be set up at once to enquire into the position of the Army. "They" [were] to have 50% representation on that Committee.' The Tobinites did not get the inquiry they sought, and in succeeding months, encouraged in their truculence by McGrath, they continued to organize. They were particularly strong inside intelligence, a factor which hindered effective monitoring of their activities. Mulcahy hoped that the IRB would rally support within the officer corps for the government, but such reliance on an oath-bound secret society blurred the basic issue of loyalty to the existing state. It also lent some credence to the conspiracy theories of the Tobinites, who claimed the IRB was being reorganized 'only with the intent of undermining the old Republican position'—there is little doubt that one of the reasons for IRB reorganization was to stop it falling into republican, anti-treaty hands. The atmosphere of intrigue was further thickened by the establishment of an informal caucus of ex-British officers to protect their interests, and by associated rumours of Masonic influence: for example, in November 1923 an agent in the Curragh reported that 'our friends of the square and compass are nicely enough set here. I believe there is a house where they meet Friday nights in the Camp and I will keep my eyes skinned this week for it.'[14]

The crisis deepened during the remaining months of 1923 as army numbers were slashed. The Tobinites grew increasingly restive, convinced that they were being excluded from favour by an IRB clique. Their attitude to the treaty derived from personal loyalty to Collins, not to his government colleagues and successors. They were quite prepared to play the green card: an Old IRA document circulated in the autumn claimed the organization had been formed 'with a view to securing complete INDEPENDENCE when a suitable occasion arose', and complained that the 'Army is not a National Army. It is composed of 40% IRA, 50% ex-Britishers and 10% ex-Civilians. The majority of the Civilians were, and are, hostile to the National ideals.' In November, following a protest at the Curragh against the demobilization of some officers with good War of Independence records, a three-man executive council committee, including McGrath but not Mulcahy, was set up to review the army council's decisions on the demobilization of officers. This committee endorsed each action taken, provoking McGrath to resign from it; its mere establishment nevertheless further undermined the authority of Mulcahy and the army council, and it bolstered the belief of army dissidents that the government would eventually cave in on demobilization if only sufficient pressure was applied.[15] Thereafter some moves were

[14] Notes of meetings, 25 June and 7 July 1923; OIRA questionnaire as above; director of intelligence's report, 6 Nov. 1923, P7/B/140.
[15] M. Valiulis, *Portrait of a Revolutionary: General Richard Mulcahy and the Founding of the Irish Free State* (Dublin, 1992), 204–7; OIRA questionnaire, as above.

made to placate the Tobinites by 'handling discharges in a tactful manner, so as not to outrage the feelings of our Old IRA supporters', and Cosgrave urged generous demobilization terms for officers, but the crux of the issue was not addressed. Mulcahy sought support for his high-minded view that 'the essential was an Army that would be absolutely responsible to even a de Valera Government, if such a Government were returned'. While he accepted the

necessity and the possibility of utilizing the older roots of the Army it is no part of my conception of my policy to keep in the Army men who are unfitted for it, who, when they had the opportunity of doing any work, did not do it, or did it badly, and who have not got the proper attitude with regard to discipline. My general attitude too is that these men must be weaned away from the idea and the use of arms, and that in the new situation in which a war in our new circumstances would find us here, they would be of little use, that the State must look to an efficient Army machinery of its present best officers as a clear definite headline of military discipline.[16]

Cosgrave and most of his colleagues agreed with the aim of a disciplined, apolitical professional army. However, they were fearful of the Old IRA and were unwilling to support Mulcahy wholeheartedly. Furthermore, McGrath, the Old IRA's executive council patron, was accorded at least as much attention as Mulcahy and rather more respect. McGrath depicted the Old IRA as an essentially loyal organization, driven to protest only by Mulcahy's intransigence and his reliance on an IRB clique. Despite the implications for military discipline, this was a relatively reassuring analysis: for all their rumblings about the treaty settlement the Old IRA had no wider political agenda than the redress of legitimate grievances about due recognition of past services. At its most basic, the Old IRA could be bought off, if Mulcahy would only allow this.

The government's obvious unwillingness to support Mulcahy or to curb McGrath's activities evidently emboldened the Old IRA. However, in the absence of any government decision formally to alter stated policy the process of demobilization and reorganization continued along the lines set out by Mulcahy and the army council. Matters came to a head on 6 March 1924, when the Old IRA issued a written ultimatum to the government. This demanded the removal of the army council and the suspension of demobilization and reorganization, complained that the government had betrayed the ideal of eventual unity, and warned that unless its demands were met the Old IRA would 'take such action that [sic] will make clear to the Irish people that we are not renegades or traitors to the ideals that induced them to accept the Treaty ... we can no longer be party to the treachery that threatens to destroy the aspirations of the nation'. About fifty officers then tendered their resignations, and some

---

[16] Director of intelligence to IO, Athlone, 1 Oct. 1923, MA, file marked 'Demobilisation of national forces'; note of talk between Cosgrave, McGrath, and Mulcahy, 26 Jan.; Mulcahy's notes of 11 Jan. 1924, as shown to Cosgrave, MP, P7/B/195.

absconded with weapons. The 'army crisis' had begun, as it was to end, in confusion. What was the Old IRA really more concerned with, jobs for the boys or the ending of partition? Why had some of its supporters resigned their commissions, and others not? Why had some taken weapons, and others not? Were any or all of the Old IRA leadership in league with the republican movement?[17]

Mulcahy and the army council had no doubt that they were facing mutiny. They sought and got authority from the government to arrest the signatories of the ultimatum, Liam Tobin and Charles Dalton, and to refuse negotiations on the Old IRA's demands. McGrath resigned in protest. Hesitation then began to creep in. Cosgrave, who besides Mulcahy was the minister best versed in the travails of the army over the past year, suddenly took ill. As vice-president of the executive council O'Higgins took over in his absence. O'Higgins's distrust of Mulcahy and his army adherents had deepened, not lessened, since the end of the civil war. He was covertly in touch with a disaffected officer, Colonel Jephson O'Connell, who presented an alarming picture of Mulcahy-sponsored IRB intrigue within the officer corps. Other ministers also began to shift their ground, distancing the government from Mulcahy and his generals. In the Dáil and at a number of meetings of the Cumann na nGaedheal parliamentary party McGrath defended the patriotism and loyalty of the mutineers, placing the blame for the crisis squarely on Mulcahy's shoulders for treating old comrades unfairly and for promoting the IRB within the army. On 10 March the executive council appointed the Garda commissioner General Eoin O'Duffy to the new post of general officer commanding and inspector-general of the defence forces, without however defining what his standing would be in relation to the minister and to his chief of staff. This was effectively an endorsement of the mutineers' complaints about the army's high command. Two days later, after McGrath had acted as a go-between, the government announced further significant concessions: army searches for the leading mutineers would cease, an amnesty was introduced for the return of stolen weapons, and an inquiry into army administration was promised. In return the mutineers pledged their loyalty to the government, their republican grievances about the 'aspirations of the nation' mysteriously disposed of. In Cosgrave's absence on 12 March it fell to O'Higgins, the high priest of civil supremacy, since 1922 the scourge of military indiscipline, to pass off the mutiny to an incredulous Dáil as really nothing more than a series of innocent misunderstandings amongst patriotic men which had arisen from the insensitive handling of the delicate issue of demobilization. Any embarrassment at having to present so far-fetched an

---

[17] Quoted in de Vere White, *O'Higgins*, 160. For a succinct account of the politics of the mutiny, see Lee, *Ireland*, 95–105. The two officers interviewed who served during the crisis, Dan Bryan (in 1983–5) and Lt.-Col. Sean Clancy (in 1997), maintained that the mutiny was the product of disappointment and indiscipline rather than of any grander conspiracy.

interpretation of events was more than offset by his victory over his old enemy Mulcahy, humiliated and abandoned by the executive council.[18]

Events did not, however, rest there. Tobin and his followers evidently took the government's emollient approach as a sign of weakness. So far from being content with the concessions they had won, they began to plan further action. Inadequately shrouded 'in a haze of whiskey', rumours about their deliberations soon reached official ears: there were stories of an impending *coup d'état*, of a McGrath-led junta, of a wave of assassinations of key ministers and officers, even of an alliance with republicans. Some of this was unfounded, some based on hard information. On the evening of 18 March army intelligence, through the simple expedient of telephone tapping, learned of a meeting of leading mutineers in Devlin's hotel in Parnell Street. Mulcahy and the adjutant-general Gearoid O'Sullivan sent troops to arrest those present. They did not consult O'Duffy, who as it happened was still arguing with the government about the terms of his army appointment, or the executive council. When the troops arrived at Devlin's those inside, some of them armed, barred the door and refused to surrender. McGrath turned up and attempted to have the raid called off: he 'was very disagreeable to the Officer i/c Troops and would have been detained himself, were it not for the fact of his position in Government and also that he was under the influence of drink'. After some hours the mutineers surrendered. There were no casualties apart from one officer who was slightly injured while attempting to escape from the lorry bringing him to Portobello barracks.[19]

The raid on Devlin's was amply justified by the information available to those who ordered it, by what it uncovered, and by its outcome. Contrary to their pledges, the mutineers had, however ineptly, continued and intensfied their plotting against both the army authorities and the government. The raid and arrests stopped them in their tracks. The executive council, however, was not satisfied. On the grounds that the raid was in defiance of settled policy—a nonsense since the decision to cease raids had been part of the 12 March understanding with the Old IRA, who had spectacularly broken their side of the bargain by continuing to conspire and to breach military regulations—ministers demanded the resignations of the army council, and advised the still absent Cosgrave to dismiss Mulcahy as minister. O'Higgins telephoned Mulcahy to tell him of the decision on the army council, whereupon Mulcahy resigned in protest not knowing that his colleagues had already demanded his head. The

[18] Valiulis, *Portrait*, 210–14.

[19] Bryan interview; report by GOC, Dublin command, to Mulcahy, 19 Mar. 1924, MP, P7/B/196; note by Maurice Moynihan, secretary to the government, of talk with General M. J. Costello, director of intelligence at the time of the mutiny, 12 Dec. 1948, DT, S. 5478B.

    During his last illness in 1948, a number of the leading mutineers visited Gearoid O'Sullivan to make their peace with him.

adjutant-general and the quartermaster-general also resigned their posts and commissions. The chief of staff, Sean MacMahon, instead asked the government to give their grounds for demanding his resignation. He was peremptorily dismissed. When Cosgrave expressed his disquiet that he had not been consulted about this decision and the concomitant appointment of O'Duffy's nominees to the three vacated posts, he received a terse and barely civil explanation from O'Higgins: the matter was so urgent that the executive council had not had time to consult anyone. By accepting this arbitrary and patently unjust treatment at the hands of the executive council the three sacked officers, who with Mulcahy had consistently espoused the doctrine of civilian control of the armed forces, vindicated that principle. (Unlike his two colleagues, and perhaps with Cosgrave's support, MacMahon was recommissioned as a major-general three months later.) The contrary argument recently advanced that the generals 'could have stood up for themselves by refusing to resign ... This ... would have enabled the army to have been more vigorous in defending its own power within the Department of Defence', is implausible in the circumstances of 1924. The civilians, who had temporized, vacillated, dissimulated, and reneged as only politicians can, unblushingly accepted the resignations as proof that a purge had indeed been necessary to rid the army of those sympathetic to secret societies and to turn it into an obedient instrument of democratic government: once the dust had settled O'Higgins even restored the title of 'mutiny' to what he had previously assured the Dáil was merely the understandable search for justice of patriotic men. No matter that the new head of the army was himself a senior IRB man, or that putting police and soldiers under a single commander was scarcely good constitutional practice.[20] For O'Higgins the arrangement made sense: as Garda commissioner O'Duffy was his man.

The collapse of the mutiny was followed two days later by a serious IRA attack on British troops at Cobh. A group of men, some wearing Free State army uniform, machine-gunned British soldiers standing on a quayside, killing one and wounding many others. This act appeared calculated to provoke the British, and thus to lead to an IRA/army rapprochement in the face of the old enemy. The British, however, were not to be drawn into confrontation. The government's immediate offer of generous compensation was accepted, and it closed the matter. There was even some British sympathy for Cosgrave's difficulties. Lionel Curtis, the intellectual mainspring of the British commonwealth ideal, told Churchill in August:

True he [Cosgrave] has failed to apprehend the assassins, but when were we more successful? Nor have the Government of Northern Ireland been more successful over the McMahon murders. The fact we are too apt to forget is that the Free State Government

---

[20] Valiulis, *Portrait*, 215–19; Theo Farrell, 'The "Model Army": Military Imitation and the Enfeeblement of the Army in Post-Revolutionary Ireland, 1922–42', *Irish Studies in International Affairs*, 8 (1997), 116.

not only risked their own lives but imprisoned many thousands, and executed over 80 of their former associates in order to sustain the treaty.[21]

In May 1924 the government set up the promised inquiry into army administration and indiscipline. Its terms of reference, its limited powers, and its membership all suggested a determination to air the case against Mulcahy and his generals rather than to examine all the events and factors leading up to the mutiny, including the shifts in policy of both the government and of individual ministers. Its proceedings were held in private, and its records were not published. This gave O'Higgins a further opportunity to vent his spleen against Mulcahy as a disloyal colleague, an anti-democratic militarist, and a sower of IRB pestilence, but the committee was none the less constrained by the sheer weight of evidence ultimately to exonerate Mulcahy and the army council from the main assertions made against them. By the time its report was published, however, the heat had gone out of the issue and the government suffered no embarrassment.[22]

The collapse of the mutiny did not put an end to unrest. A new section established within army intelligence in July 1924 to watch the Old IRA 'for a considerable period . . . had a very difficult time in dealing with the activities of these people' within the army, partly because of secrecy and also because 'persons of considerable political and other influences were to a greater or lesser extent in sympathy with and supporting its activities'. Old IRA influence was also apparent within 'the numerous . . . ex-Army Mens' organisations, which were being organised weekly'. As most of the Tobinite leadership had 'considerable experience of the Army and Governmental machine, and in particular of intelligence methods . . . the position at times practically resolved itself into a battle between their Intelligence service and ours'. The 'turning point' for the army came in December 1924, when the government demobilized 'certain officers, NCOs and men'.[23] Old IRA activities amongst ex-army men remained a problem, and towards the end of 1925 there were firm reports of negotiations between Tobinites and 'prominent Irregulars': 'It is believed that they have agreed to act together to overthrow the Government . . . The "Mutineers"['s] . . . attitude is now much more friendly towards the Irregulars and more hostile towards the Government.' These talks produced nothing concrete, although they aided the growing rapprochement between Tobinites and republicans. That rapprochement came to full fruition once Fianna Fáil took office.[24] While politicians such

---

[21] Curtis to Churchill, 19 Aug. 1924, Bodleian Library, MS Curtis 89. T. P. Coogan, *Michael Collins* (London, 1990), 352, deals with the notorious McMahon family murders in Belfast in 1922.

[22] Valiulis, *Portrait*, 221–3. Transcripts of evidence from the inquiry are in MP at various numbers in the files series P7/b and P7/C.

[23] 'Report of workings of Intelligence Department for period 1st October 1924/31st December 1925', undated, MA, file marked 'Annual Report, 21/1/26–27'.

[24] Chief of staff to minister for defence, 30 Oct. 1925, and extracts from report by Captain Feeney, 7 Jan. 1926, FitzGerald papers, P80/847.

as O'Higgins and Cosgrave were still regarded with hatred by many republicans because of their policies while in office, those responsible for some of the worst excesses of the civil war came into Fianna Fáil favour: Joseph McGrath and Liam Tobin, both closely linked with Oriel House, are examples. McGrath developed excellent personal relations with leading Fianna Fáil politicians including Sean Lemass, whose brother Noel had been murdered by plain-clothes men. Tobin, who had led the mutiny against a democratically elected government in 1924, was made superintendent of the Oireachtas in 1940, responsible for the security of the national parliament.[25]

iv. The Struggle for Control of Domestic Intelligence, 1923–1926

Between April 1923 and February 1926 the government made a number of crucial choices affecting the organization of policing and security work. The key figure in these decisions was undoubtedly Kevin O'Higgins. He had a vision of an ordered, tranquil society, protected by an unarmed police force reliant on public support and firmly under the thumb of central government. Achievement of those aims, however, required ruthlessness and guile, qualities with which he was well endowed. That was just as well, because there were other strong views in the government, in the army, and in the police and other civilian agencies about who should be responsible for internal security, for domestic and external intelligence, for countering British and Northern Irish machinations, for monitoring republican and labour subversion, and for combating armed crime.

The first bid for position came from Joseph McGrath, who although minister for industry and commerce was the political head of the CID or Oriel House. Despite its deplorable reputation, McGrath argued for its peacetime retention. On 9 May he circulated a 'rough outline of S[ecret] S[ervice] scheme'. This ambitious document argued for a new 'Secret Service Department'. Its first task would be to gather together and collate the 'mass of detailed information relative to the activities of the enemies of the State ... scattered over the whole country' in the records of various military and civilian agencies. This body 'to be properly run, to get the maximum of information and to maintain secrecy, should be attached to a CID Department' which 'should be on "Scotland Yard" lines in so far as it would have jurisdiction in all parts of An Saorstát'. Its 'functions should be very widespread in so far as that it should have a detailed record of all sections in An Saorstát such as Republican Clubs (if started), A[ncient] O[rder of] H[ibernians], Orange Lodges, Freemasons, Land & Labour, Communists, etc.' It might also subsume the army's foreign intelligence activities, as well as those in 'the Six-County area'.

---

[25] DT, S. 12134A.

McGrath's scheme extended beyond the efficient collation of information. The department would also employ undercover agents throughout the country 'in a position to gain all kinds of information about local clubs, meetings, etc. and generally to report on feelings and views of different classes'. In each area 'he or she would need to be a person who would be loyal to whatever Government would be in power—in other words, he or she would almost need to have no Political views'. Possible agents might include 'a good type of Hotel-keeper or Shop-keeper' or, more fantastically, 'intelligent partly disabled soldiers'.[26]

The immediate motive for these proposals was, transparently, to safeguard Oriel House, an organization sorely in need of defenders. In his plan McGrath was unwittingly echoing a very similar scheme put forward in 1918 by Sir Basil Thomson of Scotland Yard for the post-war organization of domestic British intelligence under his control.[27] The scheme was dismissed at cabinet level, yet the manner in which McGrath made his case illustrates the range of threats which the government believed the new state faced. Some of these now appear bizarre: how could anyone have regarded Irish freemasons as potentially subversive? It is, however, pointless to use the values of late twentieth-century Ireland, and our knowledge of the state's political development, to judge assessments made seventy years ago by men who owed their political careers to their own subversive activities. At the time there was agreement on the multiplicity of threats to be faced. The issue was how to deal with them within the conventional confines of a democratic state.

McGrath's proposals failed for a number of reasons. One was probably the sheer scale, cost, and pervasiveness of the proposed organization, with its elaborate records and its licence to pry. In the aftermath of their civil war victory Cosgrave and most of his colleagues viewed widespread subversion as a transient threat, to be dealt with by exceptional measures rather than by permanent ones. Their policy was directed towards attaining a state of normality in which an unarmed police force and the ordinary law would be sufficient to maintain tranquillity. To this end they did maintain harsh policies, but as temporary expedients. There was no place in their thinking for a permanent and secret political police organization, as this went against the conventional democratic precepts to which most of them subscribed. A second reason for the failure of the McGrath scheme was more immediate: Oriel House had few admirers, and to its appalling civil war reputation had since been added clear evidence of the involvement of some of its men in armed robbery, protection rackets, and other criminal activities, as well as of some collusion with republicans. Furthermore, its continued existence outside police or army structures threatened confusion all round. The Oriel House proposal also cut across the interests of the police forces and of the army, represented in cabinet respectively by O'Higgins and

---

[26] Memorandum by McGrath, 9 May 1923, DT, S. 583.
[27] C. Andrew, *Secret Service: The Making of the British Intelligence Community* (London, 1985), 231–2.

Mulcahy. Mulcahy and his generals had their own plans to improve and expand army intelligence. O'Higgins, for his part, was determined that the conventional police forces should eventually assume responsibility for all crime and security work. All were implacably hostile to the perpetuation of Oriel House as an autonomous organization. Despite protests against the dismissal of 'men who are second to none in the services they have rendered to their country, and who have in such a short time and with no training made a record in police work which it would be very hard to beat', Oriel House's separate existence came to an end in November 1923. A minority of its officers was absorbed into the detective division of the DMP, where under David Neligan they formed the backbone of what later became the Special Branch; some more were employed as bodyguards for ministers; the majority, however, were deemed unsuitable for police work of any kind and were paid off.[28]

Rejection of McGrath's scheme, and the subsequent disbandment of Oriel House, left open the difficult question of who was to deal with the range of security and intelligence tasks still necessary. While O'Duffy for some time remained an advocate of a 'State Intelligence Department' separate from both the army and the police, collating all information on subversion and controlling its own 'Secret Service Agents', in practice all such work eventually fell to the Garda detective division. But this took time: although Neligan was no tyro in intelligence matters—as a DMP man he had been one of Collins's most valuable agents, and at the time of his transfer to the detective division he was acting head of army intelligence—until 1925 he had his hands full with armed crime, he had very few men to spare for political intelligence work, and he had no formal organization outside Dublin. In the interim, the army retained responsibility 'for dealing with any matters having a political or Irregular complexion'. Its activities in these fields were considerable.[29]

Army intelligence emerged from the civil war in rather better shape than it had begun it. The principle had been established that the director of intelligence had direct access both to the chief of staff and to the minister for defence. Intelligence at headquarters had been developed considerably in the last months of the war, being reorganized into six branches: the 'Director's Office', the 'Command Branch', the 'Secret Service Branch', the 'Finance Branch', the 'Cyphers Branch', and the 'Records Branch'. In the autumn of 1923 army intelligence acquired 'the bulk of the files created' in Oriel House, together with the adjutant-general's files on internees. This placed intelligence in control of most of the government's records on political unrest. Furthermore, despite Cosgrave's

---

[28] Ennis to Mulcahy, 17 July 1923, MP, P7/B/195; report by director of intelligence, 29 Nov. 1923, P7/B/140; report by Captain O'Muireadhaigh, 11 Nov. 1923, FitzGerald papers, P80/1047; Brady, *Guardians*, 32–3 and 128–9.

[29] 'Report of workings of Intelligence Department for period 1st October 1924/31st December 1925'; 'Explanatory notes on army organisation', n.d. [May 1924], pp. 3–5, DT, S. 3442B.

'statement' to the army in June 1923 'that Agents in Britain and in [the] Six Counties (if any) should be withdrawn', intelligence retained responsibility for the networks of agents built up in Britain to spy on republican organizations there, and in December 1923 'took control of the remnants of the Intelligence Service' in Northern Ireland. Nevertheless, the effectiveness of intelligence activity until the spring of 1924 was hampered by three factors. The first was the sheer burden of work thrust upon intelligence in the aftermath of the civil war. It was the first port of call for sundry 'Departments and Ministries' requiring 'a vast amount of investigations . . . relating to all kinds of claims and other matters', from prisoners' petitions for release to compensation claims and to passport applications, 'arising from the Anglo-Irish war . . . [the] post-Truce period and period of hostility with the Irregulars'. As a result it became, as one disgruntled Tobinite put it in July 1923, largely 'a machine for putting together a number of files regarding a number of names'. The second factor was demobilization, under which intelligence in the various commands was 'for all practical purposes wiped out', in Dan Bryan's phrase, by 'someone who was looking at British Peace Tables of Organisation and not conditions in Ireland'. The third factor was the growing split within the army, which particularly affected intelligence. The army crisis has been discussed in detail above: here it need only be noted that, as the director of intelligence later reported, 'a very considerable amount of work' was done against the conspirators by officers loyal to the government, and that this had an important bearing on the eventual failure of the mutiny in March 1924.[30]

The growth of the army's intelligence activities up to the spring of 1926 are best described under two broad headings: military and political. The first embraces what one director of intelligence approvingly termed 'real' intelligence: staff work concerning foreign armies; developments abroad in warfare and weapons and their implications for Ireland; and the planning of appropriate security measures to reinforce Irish neutrality in any future war involving Britain. However over-ambitious, such activities reflected and strengthened the process of military professionalization. Some also eventually bore considerable fruit. A start was made on a 'Topographical and Statistical Survey' of each county, as 'militarily speaking, we have no knowledge of Ireland tabulated at present'. The scheme languished for want both of money and of co-operation: one officer described the attitude of the Ordnance Survey 'as "snotty" . . .'.[31] In response to agent reports that the Northern security forces were making considerable efforts to intercept and decrypt wireless communications, problems both of increasing signals security and of reading Northern government traffic

[30] Army council minutes, 15 June 1923, MP, P7/B/178; notes of meeting with disaffected officers, 7 July 1923, P7/B/195'; 'Summary of intelligence'.
[31] Brennan-Whitmore to Costello, 3 June 1925, MA, file on '2nd Bureau Topographical Survey 1924–1925'.

were examined. Experimental work on breaking codes and ciphers, on signals interception, and on detecting secret ink, while of immediate practical use only against the republican movement, at least established the precedent that this was an army intelligence function: when such work was restarted for security purposes in 1938, it was done under army auspices. Similarly, a plan prepared in 1925 for a 'censorship bureau' correctly anticipated both the extent of communications censorship problems, and the fact of army intelligence pre-eminence in censorship policy, after 1939: the proposal stated that Ireland needed 'a comprehensive and all-embracing system of Censorship for the protection of the country and its military forces in war, and . . . the maintenance of neutrality in certain circumstances'. The 'original conception of Censorship which was to protect purely military secrets has now developed into a system designed to cover the whole life of the nation against leakage of information'. In Ireland, such a machine would be an essential prerequisite to neutrality if Britain were at war. It would control all press, broadcasting, postal, and telephone censorship, as well as covert postal and telephone interception and wireless detection. In the domestic and international conditions of 1925, such a proposal seemed both far-fetched and impolitic, and it was evidently suppressed. But the file was dusted off as European war loomed in 1938, and the censorship policy adopted largely followed from the 1925 analysis. (By a curious irony, however, the author of the 1925 proposals, Commandant Brennan-Whitmore, was himself then subjected to covert postal interception because of his pro-German sympathies.)[32]

Intelligence, renamed the 'Second Bureau' at some point in 1924, stepped up its political intelligence work. Operating both from headquarters, and through command and battalion IOs throughout the country, including the Military Customs Brigade, its methods ranged from postal and telephone interception to the penetration of suspect organizations. Outside the state it maintained an extensive network of agents working against the republican movement—over eight thousand pounds was set aside to pay those in Britain in 1925/6—and it also had agents in Northern Ireland supplying information and documents on the security forces, on republican, nationalist, and unionist organizations, and on economic affairs. Amongst its customers was the North-Eastern Boundary Bureau, set up to prepare the state's case for a redrawing of the border. Much of the material supplied was accurate, some highly dubious: in 1924, for example, agent 'No. 76' regularly furnished the text of the RUC's monthly intelligence summaries; on the other hand, it was also reported that the Klu Klux Klan 'is firmly established in the Six Counties. The Northern Government are not taking any precautionary measures . . . considering that they have nothing to fear

---

[32] Papers on signals interception from Jan. 1924 are in the O'Malley papers, P17a/179; files marked 'Papers on liaison, censorship & intelligence organisation', 1925, and 'Censorship regulations and reports', MA, G2/X/0042.

from it.'[33] Within the state the Second Bureau's principal targets were republicans, but it also watched ex-servicemen's groups, suspected agents of the British and Northern Irish authorities, Boy Scout organizations, Orange lodges, trade unionists, communists, and other bodies and individuals thought to pose a potential threat, however slight—at one point its director complained that the police were withholding 'reports made on the Organisations in the Industrial and Communistic circles' whose activities might well some day 'call for intervention by the military . . . the Army is thrown back on its own resources to obtain its knowledge of these bodies'. But the main reason, and the only real justification, for the army's political intelligence work was the threat posed by republicans, and the absence of an effective civilian detective unit to investigate it. Early in 1924 Cosgrave himself asked whether 'there is any hope of getting information' on IRA 'policy' in the wake of the release of most detainees. In fact the army did obtain some intelligence on IRA plans and activities. More significantly, however, it managed to secure good information from within the political side of the republican movement.[34]

Archival evidence shows that intelligence used a range of techniques to monitor political developments within the state. For example, agent '101A' reported in malicious detail on the political and financial travails of the Communist Party of Ireland (CPI), while examples of telephone and postal interception, and of the bugging of prisoners' cells, can be found in the Mulcahy papers.[35] More dramatically, in November 1923 the director of intelligence produced a 'copy of a trial despatch on a line which I have opened to de Valera', imprisoned since August in Arbour Hill gaol. Through this the government was able to read de Valera's forlorn and faintly petulant correspondence with his colleagues in his notional republican government. Although he was 'afraid of double-crossing and suspect[ed] the channels', had trouble with 'this [secret] ink business', and found it tedious to have to memorize code words, de Valera persevered. The intercepted correspondence revealed a profoundly depressed man: 'No mouse was ever watched by a cat as I am.' His main concerns were that his colleagues should not share his fate, and that they should build up the political strength of the movement. He also attempted to organize his escape: 'The elements of the plan are that I should dope the Officer on guard over me', slip across the prison

---

[33] 'Estimate of expenditure for the financial year 1925–26', undated, Bryan papers, P71/3; [RUC], 'Monthly Intelligence Summary for period ending January 31st, 1924', and report circulated by director of intelligence, 1 Feb. 1924, MP, P7/B/140; various reports by 'No. 76' enclosing texts of RUC intelligence summaries are in the FitzGerald papers, P80/939; note by Costello, and Costello to O'Sheil, 20 and 28 Nov. 1923, O'Malley papers, P17a/177.

[34] Memorandum by director of intelligence, 14 Sept. 1925, MA, file on 'Co-operation with the Civic Guards'; undated minute by Cosgrave, 1924, DT, S. 8047.

[35] Reports by '101A', 9 and 30 Jan. 1924; telephone intercept, 7 Nov. 1923, and intercepted letter of 27 Nov. 1923 from Kathleen Barry (my grandmother), general secretary of the Republican Prisoners' Dependants Fund, to Archbishop Mannix; 'Copy of document intercepted in the mails', 1 Dec. 1923, and précis of 'De Valera–Finnerty interview, Saturday' of 5 Jan. 1924, all in MP, P7/B/138 and 140.

yard, and climb over the wall by ladder. It would 'take a month or two to work up . . . My cell is on the corridor with the motto: "Sin no more lest a worse thing befall thee".[36] This useful insight into de Valera's thinking was lost with his release in July 1924, but intelligence had by then secured a wide range of informants in touch with republican affairs. Many of their reports have survived. Some, such as those of 'MM' in Dundalk, of '140 Sligo', and of 'LP[Liverpool]11', deal with purely local matters. Others, from Northern Ireland and from Dublin, cast considerable light on the struggle over policy between the political and military wings of the republican movement, and on the developing split within Sinn Féin on the issue of abstention from the Dáil.[37]

Although the government was the main beneficiary of the Second Bureau's absorption in political affairs, such covert activities were scarcely consonant with the declared policy of moulding a disciplined, apolitical army concerned primarily with external defence, not with internal repression. Once the police found their feet under the charismatic leadership of Eoin O'Duffy, a jurisdictional dispute was inevitable. O'Duffy himself evidently had doubts about the desirability of assuming responsibility for dealing with political crime and subversion. His minister O'Higgins, not a man to shrink from conflict with anyone who stood in his way, had none: in October 1924 he wrote that 'good order can best be preserved' and the 'best arrangements made for the observation, prevention and detection of major crime' by the amalgamation of the Garda and the DMP, 'with an armed Detective Branch operating from Dublin Headquarters all over the country under the aegis of the amalgamated force'. The alternative of improving co-operation between the two existing forces would encounter what he gnomically described as 'grave intangible human difficulties', while he dismissed the concept of 'a special detective department, distinct from two co-existing police forces . . . obviously a utopian idea if it has any merit at all'. With a 'centralised police system . . . it is a confusion of thought to divorce from the police what is undoubtedly real police work, the observation and detection of crime'. Despite the reservations both of O'Duffy and of the chief commissioner of the DMP, O'Higgins had his way in the summer of 1925, shortly after O'Duffy had relinquished the post of army commander given to him during the mutiny. Two crucial pieces of legislation were passed: the Treasonable Offences Act or 'Treason Act', a permanent anti-republican measure, replaced the emergency legislation introduced after the civil war, and the Police Forces Amalgamation Act abolished the DMP, created a unitary national police force under tight central control, and provided an effective framework for civilian policing throughout the country. Despite opposition criticism O'Higgins

---

[36] Costello to director of intelligence, 26 Nov. 1923; texts of de Valera to Kathleen O'Connell and to P. J. Ruttledge (acting president of the Irish republic), and two messages to 'Stormy Petrel', all undated, P7/B/140.

[37] Copies of many such reports are in the FitzGerald papers, P80/847 and 849.

made no apology for these measures: he told the Dáil that violent crime necessitated strong police powers, and he maintained that direct government control of the Garda was the best guarantee of effective policing. Under the new arrangements, the related problems of armed and political crime were to be tackled by an expanded detective division under David Neligan, soon divided into two sections, one dealing with 'crime ordinary' and the other, quickly to become known as the 'Special Branch', with 'crime special', that is crime having a political dimension.[38] This indicated that in future it would be the Special Branch's job to monitor and counter political subversion.

The Second Bureau was aware of the threat to its activities which the police posed. Successive directors of intelligence had been raising the problem of co-operation with the Garda since the autumn of 1923, with the aim of ensuring an adequate interchange on actual crime—which they saw as the main concern of the police—and on the military and political policies of the republican movement, which they viewed as the army's business. Some progress was evidently made: in November 1924 the director had amicable discussions with O'Duffy, then in command both of the army and the police, aimed both at enhancing 'the ordinary inter-departmental co-operation' and at 'the fitting in of the activities of Army Intelligence and the Intelligence duties of the Police forces, so that they become . . . complementary portions of a complete organisation for the surveillance of persons and things likely to call for the actions of the Defence Forces'. Once O'Duffy relinquished his army posts in February 1925, however, goodwill quickly evaporated. The Second Bureau afterwards found that the police, while eager to get information, were most unwilling to give any. Officers complained that, when detectives acting on army intelligence seized republican documents, they refused to furnish details to the Second Bureau. Similarly, while the detective unit was most anxious to learn more about the army's agent networks, it would not pass on relevant material which police agents supplied: 'I think the C[ivic] Guards have definite orders not to help our people in . . . giving such co-operation . . . they are not even as useful as a friendly civilian'. Furthermore, Second Bureau officers, having lamented police inaction for two years, became very critical of the Garda onslaught on republicans following the passing of the Treason Act and the expansion of the detective division throughout the country. In August 1925 Dan Bryan complained that, while the army approach 'has been to collect all possible data with regard to their policy, activities, and organisation, but not to interfere with them except when action would result in the capture of arms or quantities of documents of importance', the

Detective Division are hitting out blindly against any Irregular activities that come under their notice, just as they would do in ordinary criminal cases, and apparently not dealing with the Irregulars as an extensive military organisation with ramifications not

[38] Memorandum by O'Higgins for Executive Council, 3 Oct. 1924, S. 4185; Brady, *Guardians*, 121–2.

alone in An Saorstát, but in the Six Counties, Great Britain, United States and to a limited, though very important degree, on the Continent.

Besides disrupting the systematic study of the republican movement, the 'present policy of raids and prosecutions' might strengthen the 'Military section' within republicanism against those political figures 'not in favour of an aggressive policy' of armed action against the state. This point was echoed by the chief of staff, who told his minister that 'no useful purpose will be served by imprisoning every nonentity who happens to have a seditious document in his possession'. In addition, the Second Bureau argued that 'if the Police took over Intelligence, they would merely be concerned with the getting of guns, dumps, etc. & not . . . with the obtaining of information on the Policy of anti-State organisations'. They had neither the 'disposition nor the records and data' for sustained surveillance of subversive bodies, let alone for the patient monitoring of the possible agents of foreign powers who might operate against Britain through Ireland. Furthermore, 'apart from defending the country from external aggression, the Army must be in a position when called upon to control and suppress the disorderly and violent elements within our borders', from militant republicans to 'communist agitators . . . busy fomenting trouble', and this required accurate political intelligence.[39]

These criticisms illustrate a fundamental difference between policing and security, the one concerned with law enforcement, the other with the long-term study of direct and indirect threats to the state. The solution proposed by the army required a firm delineation between the two activities, clear rules on the exchange of relevant intelligence between the Second Bureau and the detective division, and a commitment from both organizations to co-operate in future. But the contesting forces in this debate were unevenly matched. The police had the backing of the government, determined to get the army entirely out of politics, and the ferocious support of their minister O'Higgins, still distrustful of the army in general and of intelligence in particular. Against him the army had only the political lightweight Peter Hughes, appointed minister for defence as a stopgap measure after the mutiny. He accepted the police case, and in the last months of 1925 gave 'verbal instructions' to begin the process of transferring all the Second Bureau files on individuals, and to relinquish control of all agents and informers in the state, to the police. The system of paid 'touts and agents' in each command was 'almost completely discontinued on instructions towards the end' of the year. In keeping with the doctrine of civil supremacy elaborated

---

[39] Costello to chief of staff, 17 Oct. 1923; director of intelligence to Garda commissioner, 19 Nov. 1924; note by Brennan-Whitmore, 11 Oct. [1924]; unsigned memorandum [by Dan Bryan], 13 Aug. 1925; memorandum by Captain Feeney, same date, all in MA, file marked 'Co-operation with Civic Guards'; note of GOC's meeting, 15 Dec. 1923, MP, P7/B/179; chief of staff to minister for defence, 27 July 1925, Fitz-Gerald papers, P80/849; undated memorandum on 'The Army and the Civil Power. Mutual Obligations and Relations', MA, file on 'Co-operation with Civic Guards'.

by O'Higgins since 1922, the army would pull in its horns and leave all political intelligence and security work entirely to the Garda.[40]

For some months nothing was done to carry out this instruction, probably in the hope that satisfactory arrangements would first be made for the regular provision by the police of adequate intelligence summaries, and that a residual domestic security role would be accorded to army intelligence. The police would agree to no such thing. The transfer of 'between 23000 and 24000 personal files' began accordingly in February 1926. The card index to these records was later sought and reluctantly given, along with 'files for "notorieties". De Valera, etc. etc.' The army's networks of agents and informers in the Free State, Northern Ireland, and Britain were transferred to Garda control or were quickly run down: by 1 April only four 'paid agents' remained, and by December there were only two, one of whom was in Northern Ireland. This transition was reflected in the Second Bureau's budget: in 1925/6 it spent almost eleven thousand pounds, four-fifths of which came from the secret service vote and was used mainly to pay agents and informers; in 1926/7 it spent three thousand pounds, only a quarter of which came from the secret service vote. (By 1928/9 the army's share of this vote came to just £12.) Some months after the transfer Bryan wrote that 'on the 1st April, the surveillance of enemies of the State was handed over to the Civil Powers . . . A year ago our work was almost entirely political, whereas nowadays we know nothing more than the ordinary man about political matters.'[41]

Bryan's comment was disingenuous in his own case, because he took care to remain discreetly in touch with some of his republican and labour contacts, but it was broadly true for the Second Bureau, which turned its attentions to 'actual training and . . . the development of purely Military Intelligence'. In the week following the formal transfer of responsibility for intelligence on political subversion to the police, all battalion IOs attended a Second Bureau course at the Curragh. Designed to give them an understanding of 'the various headings which comprise the very elastic expression, "Army Intelligence" ', the emphasis throughout was on intelligence as an adjunct to conventional military operations—where there were complaints that the Second Bureau had always been weak—although Bryan did give one lecture on 'Special Intelligence Agents'.[42]

---

[40] Chief of staff to minister for defence, 8 Dec. 1925, ibid.; Eastern command intelligence report for 1926 [by Dan Bryan], 31 Jan. 1927; 'Report on workings of Intelligence Department for period 1st October 1924/31st December 1925'; Dan Bryan transcripts, p. 44 (in my possession).

[41] E. O'Halpin, 'Army, Politics and Society in Independent Ireland, 1923–1945', in T. G. Fraser and K. Jeffery (eds.), *Men, Women and War: Historical Studies*, xvii (Dublin, 1993), 167 and n. 62; Eastern command intelligence report.

[42] Ibid.; Commandant McManus to chief staff officer re 'Organisation of the General Staff', 28 Apr. 1925, MA, no file or refence number; document headed 'Course of lectures for junior officers. Syllabus', MA, file on 'Battalion Intelligence Officers' Course held at the Army School [of] Inst[ruction], Curragh XXX 1926'; Clancy interview (Colonel Clancy attended the course).

The transfer of responsibility for the surveillance of subversive organizations and individuals from the army to the police was the logical culmination of the policy of the civilianization of law enforcement on which O'Higgins had embarked in 1922. Just six weeks before national politics was transformed through the establishment by de Valera of the Fianna Fáil party, the army was finally taken out of political affairs. It was thereby spared the embarrassment of continuing to spy on what soon became the state's largest party. However, the change was not entirely for the good, because the Special Branch defined their task almost exclusively in terms of protecting the state against the IRA. While they investigated and harried republicans with some enthusiasm, they evinced no interest in continuing the political intelligence activities of the Second Bureau. Furthermore, Northern Ireland formed no part of the Special Branch's brief, and the army was disbarred from collecting information on affairs there—in any case, as the director of intelligence complained in October 1927, 'it would be very hard to get going again' without the relevant subject files which had been transferred. Active collection abroad of intelligence on the republican movement ceased, and the problem of foreign espionage in Ireland, comprehensible in military terms because of Ireland's defence relationship with Britain, was forgotten. Bryan later complained of this oversight: in practice it served the army well, because when serious security questions were raised by the British in 1938 military intelligence was asked to handle them on the grounds that such matters were dealt with by defence ministries 'in almost all other States', and that the Garda was doing nothing about them.[43] But that lay in the future: for the Second Bureau, in common with the rest of the army in 1926, prospects were grim.

v. The Garda and Political Crime, 1923–1931

The Garda's first unhappy years as an unarmed force in the midst of armed disorder delayed but did not prevent its eventual assumption of primacy in the maintenance of internal security. By the summer of 1924 the disorder which followed the civil war had virtually disappeared: armed robberies, rather than assaults on the state, now appeared the main problem. The IRA had assumed the shape it was to retain for the rest of the decade, a collection of small groups of activists scattered around the country, enjoying more sympathy than active support. The spectres which had haunted O'Higgins—looting, land seizures, unpaid taxes, and repudiation of debts—had largely faded away. What was left was the residue of the civil war, and some associated armed crime. The strategy

---

[43] Director of intelligence to chief of staff, 18 Oct. 1927, MA, file on 'Co-operation with Civic Guards'; Bryan interview; memorandum on 'Defence Security Intelligence', with Bryan to minister for defence, 21 June 1945, NA, Department of Foreign Affairs (DFA), A8/1.

of unarmed policing pursued by O'Duffy and O'Higgins had already begun to
pay off in terms of public acceptance of the Garda even in strongly republican
areas, although not without some cost: in December 1923 a sergeant was killed
during a raid on a Kerry station, and in May 1924 two Gardai were shot dead in
Tipperary while attempting to arrest one 'Sonny Dwyer, Irregular'. Another
Garda was killed during a robbery by ex-army men in Baltinglass in January
1924. Some coherent method of combating armed crime nationally was clearly
necessary.[44]

As has been seen, O'Higgins's solution was a unitary police force with an
armed detective division. This he achieved with the passage of the Police Forces
Amalgamation Act of 1925, in the process disposing of the organizational fault
which had bedevilled policing in Ireland for a century. It also broke the remaining link between policing and local government: with the passing of the DMP
went the Dublin city police rate. Under the new act the provision and funding
of policing became the responsibility solely of central government. This, and
the tight ministerial control exercised from the outset over the Garda, was the
subject of some Dáil criticism. Opposition TDs argued the need for some local
input into policing to enhance both the accountability and the responsiveness
of the new force, suggestions which O'Higgins treated with characteristic contempt. The government's approach to police reorganization has been described
as 'profoundly illiberal', but what else was to be expected in the circumstances of
1925? Its aim was to achieve a system of policing which would be effective, politically reliable, and communally acceptable.[45]

Whatever the defects of the 1925 arrangements, they succeeded in producing
what the government sought and what the public evidently respected. For all
O'Duffy's posturing—he wallowed in the opportunity to present himself as the
personification of a new breed of police chief, honest, disciplined, fearless, and
unarmed, and he overspent wildly while promoting his image at international
police conferences in Europe and the United States—and despite the authoritarian manner in which he ran his force, when it came to the crunch he complied with government instructions. Thus, after two Gardai had been killed
during a co-ordinated series of IRA raids on some twenty police barracks in
November 1926, he submitted a bombastic and near hysterical memorandum
on the moral infirmities of the Irish people. He dismissed the idea of combating
armed crime through strengthening the detective units, and instead pressed for
arming the entire force: 'civics is not taught in the school, citizenship is rarely, if
ever preached in the Church'. His men 'are . . . placed in an impossible position
in being required to enforce the principles of citizenship amongst a population,
the vast majority of whom know or care little about such principles'. Arming the

[44] Brady, *Guardians*, 114 and 131; Garda summary of republican outrages, 1923–1931, DT, S. 5084A.
[45] O'Higgins to executive council, 3 Oct. 1924, DT, S. 4185; Brady, *Guardians*, 132–5.

Garda 'with revolvers will not take away from their character as Police—quite the contrary—nor will it put a military cloak on them . . . The defenders of the lives and property of the people' should be 'clothed in the livery and armed with the weapons of the state', not 'armed plain clothes policemen . . . we should get away from the idea of the plain clothes gun-man. It is not detective work.' By contrast O'Higgins argued that to arm the Garda would turn the force into 'a symbol of oppression', would not deter republican attacks, would risk the loss of the 'moral support received from most sections of the community', would convey an inappropriate sense of panic, and if unrest developed again within the force might lead to a repeat of the 1922 Kildare mutiny. The executive council supported O'Higgins. His apocalyptical warnings notwithstanding, O'Duffy meekly complied with their decision.[46]

The government's view was that armed crime was an aberration attributable to the residue of the civil war, best dealt with in isolation from ordinary policing. Under the 1925 act the DMP detective branch, bolstered through the assimilation of some former CID men, became the nucleus of the Garda detective bureau under David Neligan. Its men were permitted to carry arms where necessary, leaving the uniformed force unarmed. The subdivision of the bureau into non-political and political branches further emphasized the continuing distinction between political policing and ordinary police work, and the unavoidable odium which attached to the Special Branch did not spill over into mistrust of the uniformed force. This was despite the robust approach adopted by Special Branch officers after the passage of the Treasonable Offences Act of 1925. They harried republican activists unmercifully, and they supplemented their legal powers with very rough methods of search, arrest, and interrogation. This engendered intense resentment among republicans, who saw and who portrayed the Special Branch simply as the continuation of the 'CID' of Oriel House days: Todd Andrews wrote that 'we Republicans were completely at the mercy of the police', and he complained bitterly of the treatment meted out by the 'CID'.[47] In contrast to attitudes towards uniformed policemen, who continued to enjoy widespread public support, it is clear that unease about Special Branch methods was not confined to republican sympathizers—the army thought that the Special Branch's indiscriminate approach might stiffen rather than break republican resolve, while some TDs expressed alarm at the nature and scale of repression. The public reaction to police excesses after the murder of a Garda in Waterford in 1926 provoked a crisis in relations between O'Duffy and O'Higgins: the commissioner pleaded provocation in mitigation of his men's actions—'sober, zealous and efficient officers' who, knowing their

---

[46] O'Duffy to O'Higgins, 6 Dec. 1926, and O'Higgins to executive council, 3 Jan. 1927, DT, S. 5260.

[47] C. S. Andrews, *Man of no property: An Autobiography Volume Two* (Dublin, 1982), 23 and 31; Brady, *Guardians*, 145–8.

prisoners to be guilty, 'were not gentle in their handling of them'—where O'Higgins sought their immediate dismissal, and at one point O'Duffy tendered his resignation. But the dispute was eventually overcome with honour satisfied on both sides, and O'Duffy remained. The issue of police brutality remained a sensitive one: once Fianna Fáil took their seats in the Dáil they raised it at every opportunity, and at the turn of the decade the government was to be particularly embarrassed by events in County Clare, where relations between the IRA and the Garda became particularly bitter after one detective was lured to his death.[48]

But, notwithstanding some celebrated instances of brutal treatment of suspects by the police, their excesses did not extend to murder. This was a marked and creditable change from the civil war era. Furthermore, republican complaints about the activities of the Special Branch have to be taken with a grain of salt, because it was a natural propaganda tactic and because the IRA showed no inclination to forswear political violence. On the contrary, it continued to conspire and to mount operations where it could, including occasional attacks on the Garda and on the army and the killing of suspected informers. It also sought to defy the law in more trivial ways, such as illegal drilling, the production of seditious material including the celebrated 'Ghosts' pamphlets of 1928, and involvement in various forms of social and economic protest from land agitation to strikes. Some of these developments presaged the split within militant republicanism which was to emerge in the 1930s between traditional nationalists and those increasingly attracted to the broader agenda of international socialism. At the time, they gave the government legitimate cause for concern that the IRA might become social as well as political revolutionaries, and they led to the red scare of 1931–2.

Amongst IRA operations mounted was the successful Mountjoy prison escape of November 1925, when nineteen prisoners were freed. The following year a series of armed raids on moneylenders was staged in Dublin and elsewhere to demonstrate the IRA's solidarity with the poor. There was also a succession of actions against symbols of British imperialism, from threats against cinemas showing pro-British war films to the burning of the Union Jack and even the disruption of Boy Scout camps. More seriously from the government's point of view, the IRA adopted a policy of making threats and attacks against witnesses and jurors involved in court proceedings against republicans. Most notoriously, one witness, Albert Armstrong, was murdered, and a juror was seriously wounded in 1929. Such assaults were not widespread, but then they did not have to be to make convictions in jury trials a practical impossibility, and they demonstrated the organization's continuing ruthlessness. So too did

---

[48] O'Duffy to Justice, 8 Apr. 1929, FitzGerald papers, P80/851; Justice memorandum, 28 Sept. 1932, DT, S. 2206.

its treatment of suspected informers, although its most celebrated effort to eliminate one was a fiasco—in an episode more appropriate to the streets of Chicago than to the leafy roads of Dartry, the police undercover agent Sean Harling shot and killed one of two gunmen who attacked him outside his home in 1928. Harling, a republican who had been a part-time driver for Countess Markievicz, had been down on his luck and in need of cash when he was suborned by the police. The man he killed, Timothy Coughlan, was both a well-known IRA man and a card-carrying member of Fianna Fáil, an illustration of the continuing links between militant and slightly constitutional republicanism. (Harling was given a grant to flee the country with his family, but he returned against police advice two years later. He made his peace with the IRA, as usual more willing to forgive a fighter than a politician, and obtained work as a messenger in the civil service. When he died in 1974 he was described not as a one-time Free State spy and agent provocateur but as a holder of the altogether more dignified position of aide-de-camp to de Valera from 1919 to 1921—he had been a courier for the first Dáil government.)[49]

Many republican activities in the middle and late 1920s were freelance affairs, either local initiatives or opportunistic actions by individual republicans or by splinter groups. In the latter category can be placed the violence in Clare in 1929, 1930, and 1931, and most of the armed robberies and general banditry seen from time to time. The most significant such act, however, was the murder of Kevin O'Higgins, gunned down while on his way to mass on 10 July 1927. Although threats to his life had been reported in 1924 and 1925, he and his colleagues no longer worried much about security, in itself a reflection of how much the country had calmed down. He was unarmed, and his bodyguard had remained outside his house. O'Higgins was particularly loathed by republicans for his political resolve and for the bitterness of his invective, but other groups including ex-army mutineers and disgruntled CID men also appeared plausible perpetrators. In fact his killers, amongst them Timothy Coughlan, himself to die at Harling's hands a year later, were experienced republican gunmen acting on their own initiative. Over half a century later Todd Andrews, who always adhered to the unforgiving view of O'Higgins as a craw-thumping moralizer who wallowed in republican blood, described the assassination as 'worse than a crime, it was a mistake'. Although the killing was promptly disowned by the IRA, it nevertheless brought upon the movement an avalanche of repression, including a public safety law more draconian than anything seen since 1923. This was hardly surprising: the government were not to know that the murder was an isolated and unplanned act of terror. What they did know was that

---

[49] There are papers on this in UCDA, MacEntee papers, P67/775; DT, S. 5598; Garda commissioner's confidential report, with O'Duffy to minister for justice, 24 June 1931, FitzGerald papers, P80/856. Attacks on Boy Scout camps are discussed in NA, Department of Justice (DJ), H280.

militant republicans remained dedicated to the overthrow of the state, that there were plenty of weapons in the wrong hands, and that democratic politics could be thrown into turmoil by one well-placed shot. The wave of political assassinations which ministers feared in 1927 did not materialize, but some attacks did take place: in two incidents in November 1930 shots were fired at Cosgrave's car in Terenure, and an army sergeant on guard outside the house of Michael Hayes TD, the speaker of the Dáil, was wounded by two gunmen. Had either of these attacks resulted in the deaths of their presumed targets, or had an alleged plot to kidnap Cosgrave's two young sons in 1931 succeeded, Irish politics would once more have been convulsed.[50]

The electoral legislation passed in the wake of O'Higgins's murder forced de Valera finally to accept the practical legitimacy of the Free State and its institutions by casting off the millstone of abstentionism or, as the Fianna Fáil party minutes more cumbersomely put it, 'deviating from our former line of action and the strict letter of our pledges with respect to non-subscription to the Free State formula [oath of allegiance] for entry', and leading the party into Dáil Éireann.[51] Although he thereby finally crossed the constitutional Rubicon, he and his party retained amicable links with many of those former comrades who remained on the other bank, adherents to the notional republican government and Dáil which not even de Valera's flair for metaphysical exposition had been able to keep in being in the face of the achievements of the Cosgrave regime. These links were to serve the party well until 1933, but they underlined the conditional nature of Fianna Fáil's conversion to conventional parliamentary politics. It was a point of which the Cosgrave government and its advisers were well aware.

Although the murder of O'Higgins and its legislative aftermath transformed the face of Irish politics, its direct impact on militant republicanism was less severe. The new Public Safety Act, like the old, depended on the operation of trial by jury in the ordinary courts. In retrospect this was a serious flaw: first, juries were not always to be relied on in political cases, particularly where the alleged offence was minor and symbolic; secondly, juries were open to intimidation. In practice, the legislation allowed republicans to present themselves as persecuted idealists while generally enabling them to escape conviction (in fact, between 1929 and 1931, when the law was changed to strengthen Garda powers of arrest, a succession of republicans won damages in actions for false arrest and assault against detectives).[52] They received enthusiastic support from Fianna Fáil spokesmen in the Dáil, who declaimed against repressive legislation and police excesses. The gun still had its uses in Irish politics.

---

[50] Andrews, *Man of no property*, 83; reports on the shootings, both dated 26 Nov. 1930, FitzGerald papers, P80/851(a).

[51] Minutes of fifth meeting of Fianna Fáil TDs, 5 Aug. 1927, Fianna Fáil archives, FF/437.

[52] Brady, *Guardians*, 157; papers on these actions are in NA, DJ, S. 66/29.

vi. External Aspects of Internal Security, 1923–1932

Two important aspects of internal security under the Cosgrave governments remain to be explored: the influence of external powers and political ideologies on political events within Ireland, and the implications for Anglo-Irish security relations of potential foreign involvement in Irish affairs. Neither of these elements has received much consideration hitherto, being treated simply as by-products of the struggle between republicans and the new state after 1922. But they were of some significance in the 1920s, and they acquired considerable importance during the Second World War.

There were three potential sources of external influence on domestic politics in the decade up to 1932. These were firstly Britain, and the competing ideologies respectively of Soviet-inspired communism and of European fascism. Some ministers had considerable intellectual sympathies with elements of fascist ideology such as its emphasis on corporatist governance and on national discipline, and there was also widespread admiration for Benito Mussolini, seen as the strong man who had rescued Catholic Italy from chaos and the scourge of communism. The Italian fascist experiment appeared one from which Ireland could learn without abandoning her newly established democratic structures. Consequently, the first tentative flowerings of organized fascism in Ireland caused little alarm. In commenting on developments in January 1928 the army journal *An t-Óglách* heartily endorsed the concept of a movement charged with 'proselytising the spirit of nationality' to young people, though it objected to the establishment of an 'Irish Command of the British Fascisti . . . Ireland seems to be fast becoming a happy hunting-ground for all sorts of non-Irish juvenile organisations'. It 'should not be outside the range of practicability' to establish an indigenous movement to promote national allegiance and discipline. The British fascist organization in Ireland also caused some irritation because of its links with British ex-servicemen's groups.[53] Events after 1932 were to show that fascism, so far from inculcating discipline, loyalty, and good citizenship, was a force for political chaos: under Eoin O'Duffy the crypto-fascist Blueshirts emerged as a major threat to the state in 1933, while ultramontane fascist groups became a security embarrassment in the late 1930s because of their links with Italy.

For the state in the 1920s, however, other threats were more apparent. Amongst these, at least for a time, was possible British interference in Irish affairs. We have already seen that the Second Bureau took a keen interest in supposed British and Ulster unionist machinations in relation both to the border and to Irish domestic politics. There is evidence that the Northern authorities

---

[53] *An t-Óglách*, 1/2: 2; papers on this are in DJ, S. 89/28.

did collect some information covertly on political conditions along the border, just as the Free State did on Northern Ireland, and that they kept an eye on the army.[54] Once the existing border was confirmed in the autumn of 1925 as a consequence of the boundary commission fiasco, however, there was little incentive for either state to spy directly on the other. At local level along the border the respective police forces, customs services, and other authorities had more to gain from co-operation in the administration of the ordinary laws in relation to petty crime, to smuggling, and to agricultural regulations than from a continuation of the sporadic intrigues of the 1922–5 period. While some in the Free State, not all of them republicans, believed that Britain continued to exercise an unseen influence on politics through the masonic order, the *Irish Times*, the Boy Scout movement, and the Church of Ireland, there is no evidence whatsoever that Britain had either the intention or the capacity to influence Irish affairs by covert means. After 1925 this was the conclusion generally reached in government circles in Dublin. The reality was that the British political and administrative establishment collectively washed their hands of Irish affairs in 1922, and when occasionally called upon subsequently to deal with Irish issues displayed a combination of reluctance, amnesia, and ignorance remarkable in a power which had so recently relinquished control (although they could probably decode Irish diplomatic cables, as they did messages to and from foreign diplomatic missions in Dublin). The only remotely clandestine activity of which evidence has emerged reflects this: in 1926, apparently without consulting either the British government or the other service departments, the Royal Navy adopted the practice of using Irish residents whom they considered reliable to report on the political bona fides of southern Irish applicants. This ludicrous arrangement exposed the navy's Irish friends—ex-officers and their families, and Irish loyalists—to the charge that they were at best recruiting agents for the crown, at worst British spies. In 1936 it was to cost the elderly Admiral Somerville his life. It was also pointless: under an informal arrangement between the British and Irish governments, whenever the War Office wanted to check on the background of an Irish recruit they simply sent a telegram or wrote in 'plain envelopes' to the local Garda station, a system which worked perfectly well.[55]

If the malign hand of British intrigue was conspicuous by its absence, the new state had somewhat more grounds for its sharper and more enduring concerns about communist activities. The Second Bureau and after 1926 the Special

    [54] Examples of RUC intelligence from 1924 can be seen in PRONI, CAB 9G/63 and G/67, and HA/32/1/441.
    [55] For code-breaking examples, see decrypts of Stimson (Washington) to Sterling (Dublin), and reply, 14 and 21 Oct. 1930, on Irish accession to the London naval treaty, PRO, HW 12/136; Allen (War Office) to Congdon (Admiralty), 16 May 1936, PRO, ADM 178/144; executive council decision, 17 Nov. 1931, DT, S. 6091A.

Branch took an active interest in left-wing political and labour organizations as well as in the mainstream republican movement. By 1931, when the government sought to play the red card, evidence of communist sympathies within a segment of the republican movement was available in abundance; evidence of practical subversive achievement was not.

The revolutionary Left had a thin time in the 1920s. Despite the political upheaval of the civil war, despite local unrest over land, despite the frequently miserable conditions of the urban poor, despite the legacy of Connolly and the return of the firebrand labour leader James Larkin in 1924 after his release from prison in the United States, the body politic proved incorrigibly conservative. In the first years of the state overt communist activity languished—at one point early in 1924 the CPI was dissolved amidst an unseemly squabble about misappropriated funds and unpaid bills—as most people hostile to the Free State grouped themselves around de Valera, Sinn Féin, or the IRA. The Communist International or Comintern, the natural vehicle for the dissemination of communist ideology, made some rhetorical efforts from 1924 onwards to fan the flames of revolution, but it was hamstrung by three factors. The first was simply that Ireland was far down the Soviets' agenda, of significance only if the country could be used in some way against Britain. The second factor inhibiting the Comintern was its approach to the task of spreading the word in Ireland, relying on the Communist Party of Great Britain to supply the necessary drive and organization. To place Irish communists in a subordinate position to their British comrades was a highly insensitive act, and it did not bode well for the spread of communist ideas amongst a predominantly rural population. The third factor hampering Comintern activities was the personality of their first chosen instrument: the Soviets found James Larkin, the leading Irish delegate to the Comintern, just as untameable as had everyone else who ever attempted to work with him. So far from assisting CPGB organizers in establishing a robust Workers Party in Ireland, in the autumn of 1925 Larkin was alleged to be obstructing them. He also demanded direct links between Dublin and Moscow, and he sought money from Moscow to set up his own Workers Union of Ireland (he was always a hopeless manager of money). In 1926 a Garda report, prepared at the request of External Affairs for transmission to the American government, noted with some satisfaction that 'Larkin is in serious trouble with his friends in Moscow' and his 'influence in Irish labour circles is practically nil'. In forwarding this, an American diplomat assured Washington that 'Irish labor as a whole is weak . . . neither the whole nor any part of it is probably capable of any serious disturbing action'. That remained the case for decades.[56]

---

[56] Justice to commissioner, 3 May 1926, DJ, S. 47/23; Hathaway to State Department, 13 May 1926, quoting a Garda report, United States National Archives (USNA), State Department records, 841/d.oo/849; M. Milotte, *Communism in Modern Ireland* (Dublin, 1984), 73–95.

Nevertheless, the Left did get its chance after the establishment of Fianna Fáil in 1926. This led in time to a haemorrhage of political talent from militant republicanism, and left an intellectual gap in the extremist movement which a coterie of left-wingers moved to fill. The last years of the decade saw a spectacular flowering of activities and organizations devoted to workers, peasants, friendship with the Soviet Union, and other pet Comintern causes. Groups of well-wishers made trips to the Soviet Union under the aegis of the Ireland Russia Friendship Society; a handful of men were dispatched to study propaganda techniques in Moscow in 1928 and 1929; and the Soviet-controlled Russian Oil Products opened a Dublin office. Most of these developments were promoted and supported by the same small pot-pourri of committed communists, maverick republicans, and assorted eccentrics: surveying the field in 1930, the Department of Justice observed that 'much the same people appear to be behind several organisations'. These groups provided an ideological bridge between communism and militant republicanism, and although revolutionary politics achieved nothing in practice, they came to provide alternative inspiration for a minority of activists. The vast majority of republicans, however, remained true to the visceral, atavistic, insular Catholic nationalism on which they had been weaned.[57]

The Comintern was the most public but not the only vehicle for communication between the Soviet Union and Ireland. Until 1926 the most significant contacts were made not through recognized class warriors such as Larkin and Jack Kearney, who as delegates to the Comintern held forth about the revolutionary potential of the Irish peasantry and of the working class, but through mainstream republican emissaries seeking practical help in the struggle against the Free State. We have already seen that during the civil war the republican side had, for purely opportunistic reasons, sought Soviet assistance. Further efforts were made in the aftermath of military defeat: in June 1925 Sean Russell, a prominent IRA man utterly devoid of left-wing sympathies, and Gerry Boland, one of de Valera's closest political associates, travelled to Moscow to ask for weapons. They did this in the name not simply of the IRA but of de Valera's notional republican government. No arms materialized, but Russell did make detailed arrangements for espionage against Britain. He 'was instructed on my return from Moscow . . . to call on Mr X in Berlin and arrange a line between Berlin and London'. Sean Lemass, then minister for defence in the make-believe government, 'instructed me to meet Mr X' in London 'and introduce him to OC Britain as the link between Dublin and Berlin. I had an earnest conversation with Mr X and OC Britain', Pa Murray, 'when future meeting places, postal and hand communications were fixed up for both sides'. Mr X provided a detailed

---

[57] On the travails of the republican left, see especially English, *Radicals and the Republic*; Justice memorandum on revolutionary organizations, 4 Apr. 1930, DT, S. 5074B.

list of information required, including 'drawings from Patent Office of the new optical instrument for directing aeroplanes', 'sample of new gas mask', and other military items. Murray was reportedly successful 'in supplying all his requirements' within weeks, but Russell became worried lest Mr X might be using Murray 'as one of his agents "just [as] an individual" . . . although he is willing to pay us for our services it may not come under the notice of the people in Moscow that we as an organisation are rendering any assistance . . . if we continue to assist these people it should be made clear that our assistance is coming to them officially'. Lemass agreed: Murray 'must be on terms of absolute equality with Mr X's Government or there can be no liaison as far as we are concerned'.[58] The relationship evidently fizzled out, although the IRA continued to seek Soviet money, weapons, and help for its activities, and in 1927 formally adopted a resolution proposed by left-wingers committing the organization to side with Russia in any future Anglo-Soviet war. That decision receives only passing mention in the standard histories of the IRA, while the earlier espionage link is not mentioned at all.[59] In republican terms IRA overtures to the Soviet Union were explicable simply in terms of the enduring imperative to make friends with Britain's enemies: just as in 1796 revolutionary France and in 1914 imperial Germany had been courted, so in the mid-1920s it was natural that Godless Russia should become a focus of separatist diplomacy.

The Cosgrave administration shared the antipathy of most governments towards communism in all its forms, seeing it as the greatest threat to world order throughout the 1920s. Consequently there were few inhibitions about exchanging information on communist activity with other countries, both within the framework of dominions co-operation and with foreign powers including the United States and Germany. Despite predictable squabbles about the cost, the fostering of links with other police forces was encouraged both to keep in touch with 'developments, experiments and research' in the 'scientific investigation of crime', and to 'get first hand information' on 'the spread of Communism in European countries'.[60] While Ireland received far more information than she provided on communist activity, this was a consequence of geography rather than of reticence. Not surprisingly, Britain was the main source of intelligence: she had most to fear from communist intrigue in Ireland, and she was also best placed to observe communications between the Comintern and its Irish acolytes in so far as these were maintained via the CPGB, itself naturally the target of intense surveillance. Liaison between Dublin and London on communist activity was run through the respective police forces, albeit on an evidently fitful and cautious basis. This is reflected in Neligan's

---

[58] T. P. Coogan, *The IRA* (London, 1970; Fontana edn., 1971), 125–7; report by IRA quartermaster-general, n.d., and Lemass to chief of staff, 3 Oct. 1925, FitzGerald papers, P80/869.

[59] Bell, *The Secret Army*, 65.

[60] O'Duffy to Justice, 6 Dec. 1929 and 8 Sept. 1931, DJ 4/114.

deadpan report on his visit to London in December 1924 to seek information about Larkin's activities abroad:

I saw Colonel Carter [of the Special Branch] . . . I informed him of my mission and he replied that Larkin 'cut no ice' now, and that he was not taken seriously in Russia, that Carter never bothered about getting reports on him, and that the English Communists with whom Larkin was dealing were quite harmless. He then turned the conversation onto other topics and questioned me on the following:

What were the Irregulars doing? De Valera, Stack and Dan Breen. I replied things were quiet . . . at present, and that the Irregulars were going in for constitutional methods. He next asked how was the National Army: what were Mulcahy and Tobin doing? Had they joined hands?

I told him the Army was well disciplined and that the persons mentioned were not under notice as doing anything remarkable.

To questions as to their political behaviour I answered that I was only a minor official and that I had no information as to recent developments except what I read in the Press. The same answer I gave to his query as to 'what do your people propose doing on the Boundary business?'

He next questioned me as to whether I did political work, and what were my relations with the Director of Army Intelligence? I replied that I did police work and that the Director of Intelligence did army work.

The next question was 'How was Mr Cosgrave?' I replied that I had no information . . .

He asked what would happen if the Irregulars won at the General Election: and I said I did not think they would. He stated he heard the Government election machinery was very ineffective. He informed me that the British people would not stand for a Republic, and that we were to be allowed to work out our own salvation, as the British had no Agents in Ireland. He asked me for a report on the Egyptian Students in Trinity College, and another on St Nihan Singh, whom he alleged was a revolutionary emissary. He also asked that I should let him know of anything of interest re plots against the British etc., and that he would do everything he could for the Free State.

When I was leaving he gave me a history of Larkin, which I attach. It contains nothing of any importance.[61]

This report scarcely bespeaks close co-operation on a range of matters of mutual interest. Neligan evidently wanted to confine exchanges strictly to material about communist and associated activities, while Carter was openly fishing for material on Irish political conditions. Scotland Yard's Special Branch was and remained the operational handmaiden of the security service MI5, which at that time viewed subversion and espionage primarily from an imperial defence perspective; by contrast, what became the Garda Special Branch was emphatically a domestic police organization. This probably explains the apparent equanimity with which the Special Branch received the evidence of the IRA's efforts at espionage in Britain on behalf of the Soviet Union. They took it as just

61   Neligan to commissioner, 18 Dec. 1924, DJ, S. 47/23.

another piece of republican mischief-making rather than as a potentially grave threat to British security and consequently to Anglo-Irish relations (the British do not seem to have found out about it). When the Second Bureau belatedly saw the IRA documents, officers analysed them in terms of Britain's defence security concerns and were consequently alarmed at the ramifications for Anglo-Irish relations. Until the late 1930s, however, no one else shared this view.

Contrasting British and Irish perspectives on security questions were also reflected in the crucial matter of passport control. The First World War had demonstrated the enormous security advantage which the United Kingdom enjoyed as a pair of islands with a limited number of points of entry and exit and a relatively homogeneous English-speaking population amongst whom continental Europeans and other foreigners stood out a mile. This had proved an enormous security asset, and it was one of which British security organizations remained acutely conscious. After 1918 Bolshevism replaced Germany as the *raison d'être* for the passport control system which, in the words of Sir Basil Thomson in 1921, 'serves a double purpose . . . it is a fine-meshed sieve through which the stream of alien visitors to this country is filtered', and it 'provides an all important intelligence service on the movements of international revolutionaries'.[62] The common travel area maintained under the treaty, and the creation of a highly permeable land border between the Free State and Northern Ireland, consequently had considerable implications for British security: it meant that anyone landing in Ireland from a foreign country could make their way unsupervised into the United Kingdom. A firm Anglo-Irish understanding on passport control was therefore vital to prevent undesirable foreigners from slipping undetected into Britain through the Irish back door, while the police, the Inland Revenue, and other domestic departments were anxious that no one should be able to evade British justice by slipping away through Ireland.

In practice, passport control did not become an issue in Anglo-Irish relations until the spring of 1924, because until then ambitions to issue Free State passports were thwarted by a dispute with Britain about the precise wording to be used, and any Irish person seeking travel documents had to make do with British ones. Domestic political pressures eventually led the Cosgrave government to proceed with their plans, notwithstanding British objections, from 3 April 1924. This development has already been examined in terms of the lofty issues of Irish sovereignty and of relations between Britain and her dominions; its practical consequences have not been discussed.[63] The Irish decision to begin issuing passports, and to open a passport office in New York which could also provide visas to foreigners wishing to visit Ireland, caused consternation in the shadier recesses of Whitehall, where defence, security, and intelligence officials

---

[62] Memorandum by Sir Basil Thomson, 29 Apr. 1921, PRO, T161 501/S. 9242/1.
[63] J. P. O'Grady, 'The Irish Free State Passport and the Question of Citizenship, 1921–4', *Irish Historical Studies*, 26/104 (Nov. 1989), 396–405.

contemplated the circumvention of their 'fine-meshed sieve' by swarms of undesirable aliens let into or of domestic criminals let out of the United Kingdom by the feckless Irish. An interdepartmental conference involving the Foreign Office, the Home Office, the India Office, MI5, MI6, and its offshoot the Passport Control Office was convened to discuss the problem. The conclusion was reluctant but emphatic: the only way to preserve the passport control shield around the British Isles was to persuade the Irish that it was in their interests to help to maintain it. To that end it was agreed to ask them to operate the British passport watch list. This extraordinary document listed both persons whom the British wished either to exclude or to monitor should they attempt to enter the United Kingdom, and people who might seek to leave the jurisdiction unnoticed. As well as suspected spies and subversives, the list included such exotica as 'suspected white slave traffickers', 'proprietors of fraudulent theatrical enterprises', 'cases of anticipated wife desertion', and tax defaulters. Apart from suspect 'British Indians', whose names were removed at the behest of the India Office, the Irish were given the full list for passport control purposes.[64] In practice what this meant was that when someone on the list presented himself at an Irish port, or sought a visa from an Irish diplomatic mission abroad, the Irish authorities would notify their British counterparts.

Whatever reservations there may have been in Whitehall about Irish reliability in matters of passport control were soon swept away by experience. The Irish had little insight into Britain's strategic security concerns, but for reasons of practicality it was in Ireland's interests to co-operate with her neighbour: the Irishwoman assigned to deal with passport questions in New York actually received a fortnight's training from her British counterparts before opening an 'Irish Free State Passport Control Office', and for the first couple of weeks of business she was assisted by a British official. Furthermore, the Cosgrave government and its successors loathed Bolsheviks and communists just as much as the British did, they shared British suspicion of Europeans in general, they had no sympathy at all for the native peoples of the British empire, they regarded it as axiomatic that to admit foreigners was to give away Irish jobs, and they thought it essential to social harmony to preserve the homogeneity of the populace by keeping strangers out. Even those few foreigners who managed to establish themselves in Ireland remained objects of official interest. Reviewing the system in the 1950s Justice exulted in the results of the arrangements, which it believed had worked disproportionately in Ireland's favour: in return for meeting Britain's security concerns through co-operating on passport control, the British did Ireland the inestimable favour of operating the most rigid immigration controls on her behalf, helping to preserve the ethnic and religious

---

[64] Note of a meeting, 11 Feb. 1924, and attached memorandum, PRO, FO 372/2091, and Adams (Foreign Office) to Treasury, 5 July 1924, FO 372/2649.

purity of the Irish people. This is how, during the tidal waves of European refugees before and after the Second World War, Ireland managed to exclude all but a handful of aliens without incurring the public odium of being seen to turn back refugees: the job was done on the state's behalf by British officials at the English Channel ports or in consular offices on the continent. In return Britain received the wholehearted though scarcely foolproof assistance of Irish immigration officials in screening arrivals to and departures from the British Isles.[65]

One final external aspect of internal security merits consideration: the border and relations with Northern Ireland. Uncertainty about the border disappeared with the boundary commission report in 1925; thereafter, the issue is conspicuous by its absence from the records. It appears that, while the two governments steered clear of close contacts, the various elements within their respective bureaucracies whose operations were most affected by the border quickly achieved a modus vivendi. Reciprocal local permission for the RUC and Garda to cross the border as a matter of convenience has already been noted, while mundane problems such as smuggling, animal disease control, and the administration of the law could only be dealt with on a co-operative basis, however informal or—in the case of the criminal law—illegal the methods used. Extradition from the Free State to Northern Ireland was banned by a High Court judgement in 1929, and in consequence the Northern authorities declined to act on Free State warrants. These problems were accentuated in 1930 by a British refusal of requests from both the Northern authorities and the Free State to include offences punishable by less than one year's imprisonment in legislation on extradition—the Home Office wanted to prevent the extradition of people sought for illegal fishing. The Garda and the RUC got around the petty offenders' problem by a simple expedient: as a senior Justice man cheerfully explained to a Home Office official in 1938, 'it sometimes happened' that a person wanted in one or other jurisdiction would 'find himself' on the wrong side of the border, where the local police would be waiting to pick him up. This procedure had been severely criticized in the 1929 High Court proceedings, and its perpetuation underlined the propensity to maintain cross-border co-operation at local level, away from the glare of politics and publicity, however frosty formal relations were.[66]

vii. Public Order and Politics, 1931–1932

The flowering of left-wing political organizations and thought within the republican movement in the late 1920s ensured that within the IRA men with

[65] C. R. Bannesman to R. D. Sharp (State Department), 3 Nov. 1924, USNA, 841D.111; Justice memorandum, 15 Feb. 1952, DT, S. 15273A.
[66] G. Hogan and C. Walker, *Political Violence and the Law in Ireland* (Manchester, 1989), 281; note of a talk with Mr Duff, 3 Mar. 1938, PRO, HO45/14513.

a radical social and economic as well as nationalist agenda such as Peadar O'Donnell, George Gilmore, and Michael Fitzpatrick grew in influence. This apparent radicalization caused the government some alarm. In addition, by 1929 the IRA was visibly growing in strength and confidence, it had regained its appetite for action, and it continued to work for the overthrow of the state. Despite the various public order laws passed since 1923, the police found increasing difficulty in dealing with political crime. Trial by jury became a pointless exercise once the IRA's policy of threatening jurors took root, and the courts had become very critical of Garda harrying of republican suspects. Furthermore, despite de Valera's conditional conversion to constitutional politics Fianna Fáil remained avowedly sympathetic to the IRA and hostile to state action against the republican movement, and there was every prospect that the party's strength would grow rather than diminish at the next general election.

The growing political turmoil was exacerbated in the autumn and winter of 1930 and in the early months of 1931 by an increase in IRA activity. In addition to the abortive attacks on Cosgrave and on Michael Hayes already discussed, there were a number of significant killings. In January 1931 Patrick Carroll, an IRA battalion OC who had become an informer three years earlier, was shot dead in Dublin. In March came the shooting of Superintendent Curtin in Tipperary. Curtin had made energetic efforts to prosecute IRA men for illegal drilling. Although unable to secure convictions, he had antagonized the local IRA to such an extent that they sought GHQ's permission to kill him. He was duly murdered outside his house. Three months later, a local man who had given evidence for Curtin was abducted and killed, again with GHQ sanction. The Curtin assassination was a monumental miscalculation by GHQ: while in fact a one-off episode, it appeared to mark a new IRA policy of assassination of senior police officers, a very serious escalation of activity which was asking for trouble from an already nervous government. As usual, the IRA was to be taken aback by the cumulative consequences of its own operations when the government finally acted.[67]

The state's response to the upsurge in violence and to the IRA's flirtation with revolutionary socialism was governed by two factors. The first was its practical experience of political subversion—the Cosgrave administration has become so caricatured as a collection of pious, penny-pinching, wing-collared conservatives that their previous history as successful revolutionaries has been forgotten. The second was its perception that it faced not one but three related enemies: the IRA, communism, and Fianna Fáil. These foes were attacked by a combination of legal, moral, and political measures. The legal response, the most drastic since the end of the civil war, was directed against the IRA: in

---

[67] Bell, *The Secret Army*, 82–6.

October 1931 a further Public Safety Act was passed in the form of an amendment to the constitution, article 2A, to enable the introduction of military courts to try political offences. This departure from the conventional democratic norms by which the Cosgrave government set such store had three results. First, it disposed of the problem of jury intimidation, and provided a draconian alternative: the virtual immunity conferred on those engaged in acts of defiance against the state by the failure of the jury system was now gone. Secondly, the reintroduction of military courts upped the stakes for all the government's republican opponents: they did not have to cast their minds back very far to recall the dispatch with which the army had performed similar functions during the civil war. It also left open the possibility that internment might be reintroduced. Thirdly, the emergency measures succeeded in their immediate aim of curbing political violence, providing a relatively peaceful climate in the months leading up to the momentous general election of February 1932.

As a prelude to the Public Safety Act the government launched a vigorous attack against communist influence within the republican movement, including Fianna Fáil. This 'Red Scare' was not simply the product of ministers' overheated and partisan imaginations, in that there was some evidence of communist intrigue. In October the Catholic hierarchy was supplied with lengthy Justice memoranda detailing the illegalities of both republicans and communists since 1923, and pointing to links between the two. The bishops duly issued a pastoral letter denouncing communist activity and influence. The memoranda given to them were accurate: the IRA had become more active and more brazen, as the murder of Superintendent Curtin demonstrated; within the IRA, left-wingers had come to prominence; there had been a proliferation of communist inspired or controlled political and labour organizations; under the aegis of the CPGB Irish communists were working to the Comintern's rhetorical agenda; a handful of Irishmen had received political training in Russia; the IRA and the phantom republican government had on various occasions solicited help from and expressed sympathy with the Soviet Union; and the new IRA offshoot Saor Éire was, in the words of an American military observer, 'frankly communist in its outlook'. But the alarmist construction which the government put on these piecemeal developments begs the question of whether ministers genuinely thought that communism posed a serious threat to the state, or whether they simply calculated that they could damage both the IRA and Fianna Fáil by tainting them with the communist brush. In the months leading up to the election, government supporters sought to build on public loathing of communism by casting de Valera in the improbable role of a Bolshevik stooge. This was accompanied by the rather more plausible accusation that Fianna Fáil was in cahoots with the IRA, for which plenty of evidence was to emerge during and after the election campaign. Unfortunately for the government, such charges did not deter the electorate from voting de Valera into power.[68]

The final weeks of the Cosgrave government saw a decidedly more serious threat to the stability of the state than that offered by the machinations of enthusiastic but inept communists. It came from the man charged with leading the fight against subversion, the Garda commissioner Eoin O'Duffy. After his early successes both as commissioner and as army commander in 1924/5, he had gradually fallen out of favour with the government, mistrustful of his idiosyncratic leadership of the police and irritated by his bombastic manner. The sense of the dramatic which O'Duffy brought to his commissionership extended to his analysis of trends in the political sphere, and his progressive estrangement from ministers cannot have improved his judgement. The Fianna Fáil victory in the February 1932 election was, therefore, the last straw rather than the original cause of his disenchantment with the conventional political system. O'Duffy viewed Fianna Fáil as an IRA auxiliary, and he feared that de Valera's victory would see the destruction of the institutions of state so laboriously consolidated since 1922. More prosaically, he realized that his job was in jeopardy. In the autumn of 1931 he had begun taking soundings amongst his former army subordinates on the possibility of a coup should Fianna Fáil come to power. The people would be saved from the evil of a de Valera-led administration by a military government headed by himself. Whatever their fears and reservations about a Fianna Fáil government, the prospect of forcibly putting O'Duffy in charge of the nation's destinies cannot have been very attractive for anyone with previous experience of his distinctive and capricious style of command. In the weeks between the declaration of the poll and the convening of the Dáil to elect a new president and executive council, O'Duffy decided to act. However, he did not get the support he expected either from the army or from his own Garda subordinates. Michael Brennan, the chief of staff, quietly removed suspect officers from positions in which they could assist a coup and made it clear that it was the army's duty to accept whatever government emerged. Cosgrave got to hear something and warned O'Duffy off, and the plot fizzled out. Rumours of a coup prompted some Fianna Fáil TDs to bring weapons to the first meeting of the new Dáil, but proceedings passed off without incident. After Cosgrave had been proposed and rejected for the post of president of the executive council, a majority of TDs voted de Valera into office. Constitutionality had finally triumphed over conspiracy in mainstream Irish nationalist politics.[69]

[68] D. Keogh, 'De Valera, the Catholic Church, and the "Red Scare", 1931–1932', in J. A. Murphy and J. P. O'Carroll (eds.), *De Valera and his Times* (Cork, 1983), 131–59; Milotte, *Communism in Modern Ireland*, 107–11; military attaché's report, 9 Oct., with Atherton (London embassy) to State Department, 12 Oct. 1931, USNA, 841.00B/3.

[69] Brady, *Guardians*, 167–9; J. P. Duggan, *A History of the Irish Army* (Dublin, 1991), 157–8; Bryan and Clancy interviews. Each maintained that the coup talk had been so much hot air.

viii. Conclusion

The first decade of independence saw the consolidation of the institutions of the new state and the development of a law-bound, democratic polity. A largely unarmed police force won widespread public acceptance and esteem, an initially truculent army was cajoled and humiliated into submission, an independent judiciary flourished under the umbrella of a liberal democratic constitution. The impressive culmination of that process was the peaceful transfer of power, at the behest of the electorate, from the victors in the civil war to the losers.

However, in marking this achievement we should not lose sight of other aspects of the state's development. Its first decade saw the repeated and unashamed bypassing of constitutional safeguards in the name of public security. Expedients such as internment without trial, intrusive domestic political surveillance, and the use of the army to dispense justice, were adopted to meet the continuing challenge from militant republicanism and the associated evil of communism. It also saw the discreet adoption of the outlook and assumptions of the British state in relation to the outside world, including the enthusiastic and unquestioned operation of passport and immigration controls. Finally, while the decade saw the absorption of mainstream republicanism into constitutional politics, to many observers the conversion of de Valera and his followers to strictly democratic methods appeared entirely opportunistic.

3

Ireland's Defence Dilemma, 1923–1932

i. The Provisions of the 1921 Treaty

Resolution of the problem of the army's domestic intelligence activities was only one in a number of dramatic changes of status, scale, organization, purpose, and prospects endured by the army between 1923 and 1932. Much of this was, at least in principle, as welcome to the military as it was vital for the government. In practice, the changes represented the progressive marginalization of the army in Irish political life. In April 1923 the government was utterly dependent on the military; by 1932 the army was cowed, emaciated, and resigned to further decline. This transformation in military fortunes was wrought by a government which, in common with most of its successors, steadfastly refused either to articulate or to make provision for a coherent national defence policy.

The problem had been obvious since the end of the civil war. The government's internal security needs could be met by a small number of lightly armed units along the lines of a gendarmerie distributed throughout the country. It had no military designs on Northern Ireland, and it had made its peace with Britain. Attack from outside the island was the only plausible military threat, and in such circumstances the government anticipated that Britain would intervene vigorously to protect her own strategic interests. Soviet-inspired communism or Bolshevism was regarded as a real ideological danger to Ireland, but it was one which manifested itself and had to be confronted as a political rather than a military threat. So why have defence forces at all?

There were a number of reasons why the state needed an army. First, as a matter of national pride and a symbol of virile independence. Ireland had gained freedom partly through force of arms, and the maintenance of an army was one of the litmus tests of sovereignty: almost every other independent state had one. Secondly, the state needed an army to lay claim to the mantle of the Irish Volunteers, who had begun the fight for freedom in 1916, lest this be appropriated by the republican IRA. Thirdly, the state needed to provide an effective counterweight to violent republicanism, as the police were generally unarmed. Fourthly, in times of crisis the existence of the army gave the government ready access to a supplementary and draconian system of justice based not on the delicate checks and balances of the civil constitution, but on the robust imperatives of national defence. Those republicans who defied or obstructed the ordinary law and courts ran the risk of provoking the use of the military to dispense justice. Finally, the state needed an army for purposes of external defence. It is evident that the Cosgrave government had a firm grasp of the first four considerations: where they and their successors had trouble was in the fifth, on which the first four depended. On the one hand, in a conventional democratic polity the *raison d'être* of a national army had to be external defence. On the other hand, ministers, preoccupied with internal security, found it hard to imagine what external defence might mean. This last point merits more detailed examination here.

The 1921 treaty dealt with defence issues primarily from the British perspective. Her strategic needs were identified and accepted in article 7 and in the annexe to the treaty. Britain was permitted to retain naval installations on the northern and southern coasts, in Lough Swilly, Queenstown, and Berehaven, including 'facilities in the neighbourhood of the . . . Ports for coastal defence by air'; to place her 'war signals stations' in 'the charge of care and maintenance parties'; to retain control of existing wireless stations and submarine cables, to land new cables or establish new stations as she wished, and to exercise a veto on anyone else doing so; and in times of crisis to demand the use of other facilities needed for the defence of the ports. These provisions were made against a background of considerable confusion about who Britain's next enemy would be. Germany, demilitarized, bankrupt, and under partial Allied occupation, was far down the list of possibilities. The British armed services looked instead at the powers which had emerged victorious from the First World War. In 1919 the Admiralty had pointed towards the United States as a potential danger, and in the early 1920s both the Royal Air Force (RAF) and the navy regarded a future war with France as a distinct possibility. It is important to appreciate that, despite the chastening experience of 1917 when U-boats almost severed Britain's Atlantic supply lines while the Grand Fleet wallowed impotently at its moorings, the navy still saw the battleship as the ultimate expression of maritime power and the weapon which would win future wars for Britain. The Admiralty put a low priority on anti-submarine operations based on Irish ports: rather, the navy envisaged Berehaven 'occupying the same position in a war against France as had Scapa Flow [the Grand Fleet anchorage in the Orkneys] in the war against Germany'.[1]

---

[1] 'Articles of agreement for a treaty between Great Britain and Ireland', reproduced in L. Kohn, *The Constitution of the Irish Free State* (London, 1932), 413–18; O'Halpin, *Head of the Civil Service*, 12; G. Sloan, *The Geopolitics of Anglo-Irish Relations in the Twentieth Century* (London, 1997), 180–4; Canning, *British Policy*, 176. At 179–97 he deals concisely with the various strands of British military and naval opinion on the treaty ports up to 1938.

The treaty was also vague on Ireland's defence rights and obligations. Article 6 stated that any Irish 'military defence force' should be proportionately no larger than were British home-based forces to the population of Great Britain, and that 'the defence by sea of Great Britain and Ireland' would remain the sole responsibility of the British for five years, after which the two governments would hold discussions 'with a view to the undertaking by Ireland of a share in her own coastal defence'. In the interim, Ireland could deploy craft only on revenue (i.e. customs) and fisheries protection duties. These measures to restrict Irish defence activity were partly explained by the strongly held British view that, because of her strategic position, 'Ireland was not . . . a Dominion when it came to defence'. Curiously, it is clear that most Irish politicians were reasonably happy with these terms in 1921: indeed, de Valera, who opposed the treaty root and branch on other grounds, addressed Britain's strategic concerns at far greater length in his controversial 'Document Number Two' during the treaty debates. He envisaged a transitional period of five years during which the British would be entirely responsible for coastal defence, after which a conference would be convened to 'hand over . . . coastal defence' to Ireland 'unless some other arrangement for naval defence be agreed . . . in the common interest of Ireland, Great Britain, and the other associated states', an unequivocal recognition of Ireland's responsibilities as a member of the British commonwealth. The document also included an explicit promise that after the five-year transitional period,

so far as her resources permit, Ireland shall provide for her own defence by sea, land and air, and shall repel by force any attempt by a foreign Power to violate the integrity of her soil and territorial waters, or to use them for any purpose hostile to Great Britain and the other associated states.

He offered a further undertaking that Ireland would not build submarines without the consent of Britain and the other dominions. Document Number Two failed for other reasons, though de Valera remained attached to the underlying principle that it was simply not possible for independent Ireland to ignore Britain's strategic concerns. In that, ironically, he was if anything more prescient than his pro-treaty opponents.[2]

ii. Defence Policy and Practice, 1923–1932

Even before the civil war had ended, it was clear that the country could not indefinitely sustain fifty-five thousand men under arms. Considerations of cost, of political stability, and of Anglo-Irish relations all dictated a rapid reduction

---

[2] 'Document Number Two', reprinted in Curran, *The Birth of the Irish Free State*, 289–93. See the collection of statements on defence in DT, S. 10701A; Canning, *British Policy*, 176.

in the army and the uses to which it would be put. Mulcahy and his military advisers were well aware that the army required drastic pruning, on grounds of efficiency as well as of economy. Their aim was a compact, highly trained infantry force divided into nine commands, supported by various specialist corps, and capable of rapid expansion in times of crisis. A small air service and a coastal defence unit were included in their plans. Their initial proposals envisaged a peacetime establishment of about twenty-eight thousand men, together with proper reserves. This would, they reasoned, allow the development of an efficient military force while enabling the army to continue to discharge the unwelcome public order duties thrust upon it by the government.[3] Issues of organization and development were left vague: while British influence was unavoidable, the intention was not to produce a British army in miniature but a distinctive national force.

Between 1923 and 1932 the army produced a succession of such organization schemes, encompassing desiderata such as a staff college and a proper system of reserves. While these schemes varied in details, they all rested on the premises that the army had external defence as well as internal security functions, that its peacetime organization should be such as to facilitate rapid expansion in times of crisis, and that high levels of training and mobility were prerequisites to military efficiency. From the surviving documents it is obvious that these schemes, whatever their military merits, were hopelessly ambitious in scale, thrust, and cost: the pace and direction of demobilization and reorganization reflected instead the emphatic victory of civilian over military priorities. Even O'Duffy, in a strong position to influence the government because of the circumstances of his appointment, could do little to defend the army's long-term interests. He described the reorganization plan he submitted in the aftermath of the mutiny in 1924 as 'really the fifth scheme . . . that has been under consideration during the past year and I trust that the Army will not have to stand the shock of another one'. Understandably from a police commander, it was predicated on the assumption that 'internal disorder is more imminent and more to be apprehensive of [*sic*] . . . our experience has shown that the highly trained and mobile Infantry man was the most effective weapon used against the Irregulars'. O'Duffy proposed an army of some twenty-eight thousand men, with three geographic commands, a number of specialist corps, and the Curragh training establishment—'the most valuable asset in the possession of the Army'. While he maintained that 'money spent on bands is money well spent', he showed none of the conventional military nostalgia for cavalry: 'no conceivable use could be found for it against irregular warfare' in 'this close and well fenced country'. More questionably, he was dismissive of the case for developing

---

[3] 'Memorandum on demobilisation and reorganisation of the army', July 1923, MA, file marked 'Demobilisation of national forces'.

military aviation, arguing that its 'practical utility' during the civil war had been negligible. All O'Duffy wanted was one mixed squadron of one hundred and fifty-five men, 'the smallest Aerial Unit which would be sufficient to keep progressive thought stimulated ... to give our troops a knowledge of the value of aerial co-operation, train a small number of Infantry as Pilots', and keep an eye on developments elsewhere.[4]

O'Duffy's scheme was accepted by the government without much difficulty. In reality there was not the remotest prospect of its being made to work as planned. Critics maintained that the reorganization 'weakens the authority of GHQ and increases the authority of the Command GOCs', and also that it left the chief of staff only *primus inter pares* with the adjutant-general and the quartermaster-general at army headquarters. O'Duffy dismissed these arguments: he could afford to, because of the unique control which he enjoyed as general officer commanding and inspector-general and because he also had his Garda job to occupy him. Two years after his departure from the army, however, the system of geographic commands was abandoned and replaced by seven brigades directly under the chief of staff, assisted by a strengthened inspectorate. The change was made on grounds of efficiency and practicality: so far from attaining the twenty-eight-thousand strength required by O'Duffy's plan, by then the army had shrunk to under twelve thousand men and more cuts were in prospect. Curiously, however, the system of commands was subsequently reinstated in 1935, when numbers had almost halved again.[5]

The position of the chief of staff was further circumscribed under section 8 of the Ministers and Secretaries Act of November 1924. Under it military members of the council of defence could not serve continuously for more than three years, thereby limiting the term of office of the chief of staff to that length of time. The intention was presumably to restrict the authority and control of any one senior officer, and thereby to render the army more amenable to government direction, whatever the cost in terms of military efficiency. Despite emasculation the post of chief of staff, like that of Garda commissioner, remained a hazardous one: of the six incumbents between 1923 and 1940 only two, Peadar MacMahon (1924–7) and Michael Brennan (1931–4, 1934–7, and 1937–40), served for a full three-year term. Four others, Sean MacMahon (1922–4), Dan Hogan (1927–9), Sean MacEoin (1929), and Joseph Sweeney (1929–31) resigned or were forced out early. Brennan bucked the trend by being reappointed twice, but even his departure in 1940 was an unwilling one. This turnover is all the more striking when it is remembered that the officers in question were products of the War of Independence and were very young men on appointment: even

---

[4] Military secretary to assistant secretary, executive council, 1 July 1924, and attached memorandum by O'Duffy, 2 May 1924, DT, S. 3442B.
[5] Memorandum by O'Duffy, 2 May 1924, pp. 27, 36, 44, and 55, as in n. 4 above; memorandum by chief of staff, and council of defence minutes, 1 and 6 Apr. 1927, MA.

Brennan, who had served for over eight years, was able to point to his growing family as grounds for claiming employment from the government in addition to his pension in 1940.[6]

The discussions on the appropriate size and organization of the army which took place after the civil war were in reality purely academic. Retrenchment saw to that: in 1923–4 eleven million pounds went on defence, almost a third of total government spending in that year. Within a year of accepting O'Duffy's plan for a twenty-eight-thousand-strong army, the executive council set a limit of ten thousand men. In 1926–7 just two million pounds was spent on defence (including pensions), about one-twentieth of overall spending. All the government was prepared to fund was a small, docile infantry army, just sufficient in size to cowe the republican movement. Demobilization progressed on that basis: by the time of the mutiny numbers stood at sixteen thousand, and they were reduced progressively thereafter. By 1927 there were less than twelve thousand men in the regular forces, and by 1930 these had contracted to under seven thousand. The public rationale for this approach was financial: money could not be spared for a large military establishment. However, the process of retrenchment was underpinned by assumptions and calculations about the role of the army in the political system, about future defence policy, and about Anglo-Irish relations. These we must now examine.

Evaluation of the government's underlying attitude towards defence policy in its first years is hampered by the absence of documentary evidence. Once the civil war was over, the only military issues that appear to have attracted significant government attention until the summer of 1925 were the role and performance of the army as a surrogate police force, demobilization, and the associated problems within the officer corps which culminated in the mutiny. One reason for this was undoubtedly the growing supremacy of the civilian side of Defence over the military. After the vast expense, waste, profiteering, and financial chaos in procurement and administration seen during the war, the department, at the insistence of Finance and of the Dáil, imposed an enormously rigid set of bureaucratic controls.[7] As the size of the army shrank, so the number of forms deemed necessary to run it multiplied. This had a paralysing effect on army administration, absorbing the energies of officers in elaborate bookkeeping and compliance rituals which were then replicated by civilian staff in Defence. An obsession with financial minutiae has bedevilled the army ever since: in 1990 the authoritative Gleeson report observed that

the centralised bureaucracy and the slow processing of decisions through extended chains of command create a sense of powerlessness and disillusion among military

---

[6] Papers on the early chiefs of staff are in DT, S. 3721. Papers on Brennan's retirement are in S. 11607.

[7] Committee of Public Accounts, *Third Report* (1925), xxxix–xlix; L. O'Broin, *No Man's Man: A Biographical Memoir of Joseph Brennan—Civil Servant & First Governor of the Central Bank* (Dublin, 1982), 120–1.

personnel, resulting in lower morale and widespread feelings of frustration. Discontent and frustration in the face of what is perceived as an insurmountable bureaucracy were frequently cited as causes of complaints.[8]

This system also gave the civilian side of Defence an undue pre-eminence over the army in matters of policy, facilitating the suppression of unwelcome and potentially costly professional military assessments of affairs and statements of requirements. Civilian hegemony was attained primarily through financial controls, assisted by continuity: in the first thirty-five years of the state's existence there were a dozen chiefs of staff, but just two secretaries of Defence. The first, Cornelius O'Connor, a highly decorated ex-British army officer and one-time junior official, did not enjoy good relations with the army, and in 1927 retired early. His successor was Lieutenant-General Peadar MacMahon, who moved over from being chief of staff. MacMahon proved an extreme example of a poacher turned gamekeeper. As secretary he was the main conduit of advice to the various ministers whom he served, and as an ex-chief of staff he could second-guess the army even on purely military matters. Furthermore, he remained secretary for the inordinately long period of thirty-one years.[9]

There were no compensating factors for the army in the massive reductions it endured in these years. In 1926 an 'Army Reorganisation Board' argued the need to convert the force 'from its present semi-immobile basis, designed to deal with internal disorder solely' to a 'mobile basis' to counter the threat of invasion. It could not even obtain adequate maps, a problem which remained a perennial source of friction with the Ordnance Survey, and it had neither the vehicles nor the equipment to train for field operations in strength: for example, 'improvised mobile wireless sections' could only be furnished for manoeuvres in 1925 through 'almost superhuman efforts, and by reducing routine [signals corps] operations to a minimum'. The handful of sections thus formed 'had to be transferred from Command to Command' as there were not enough to go round, and the exercise demonstrated that 'immediately the troops take the field on a war footing, the whole [communications] machine breaks down . . . at the moment we have no means of maintaining communications in the field'. The work of the artillery corps of three batteries of field guns was 'greatly handicapped through lack of ammunition', the 'allowance being 400 rounds for the entire corps each year'. The army was an early victim of the chronic failings of the British motor industry: the Vickers tank bought for training purposes in 1928 proved one of those nightmarish one-off purchases with which the defence forces were already very familiar, as its engine had been 'improperly assembled at the firm's works', while mechanical problems also plagued the heavy

---

[8] *Report of the Public Services Organisation Review Group* [the Devlin report] (Dublin, 1969), 247–8; *Report of the Commission on Remuneration and Conditions of Service in the Defence Forces* [the Gleeson report] (Dublin, 1990), 21.

[9] DT, S. 3109; Bryan interview.

transport fleet after it was decided, for reasons of ease of supply, to replace excellent Benz lorries with Leyland vehicles.[10]

The executive council was impervious to such difficulties. The stream of plans, recommendations, pleas, and warnings which emanated from the army were ignored by the government, which instead insisted on reductions in costs and numbers far beyond what the professionals advised, and which discouraged almost to extinction serious consideration of what the long-term role of the defence forces was to be. This had particularly damaging effects for aerial and maritime defence. The government took the view that future defence needs could be met simply by the retention of a small land force: air and naval defence was entirely discounted. Thus the coastal patrol service improvised at considerable expense during the civil war for 'controlling the coast' against arms smuggling and for 'despatching troops by water', which might have served as the nucleus of a fisheries protection and coastguard force, if not of a permanent naval arm, was hastily scrapped just after taking possession of a dozen armed trawlers: the minister commented that it was 'more satisfactory, and more administratively healthy to get rid of all those vessels, even if we had to start in two or three years' time to rebuild the service'.[11] The diminutive air arm fared little better: optimistic suggestions from its officers that it should become the nucleus of a national civil aviation service, and that it should be deployed not only in support of the army but also on other functions such as fisheries protection, won no political backers. Its unpopularity may have owed something to the fact that of necessity it remained heavily dependent on ex-British pilots and technical officers. However, the service at least survived on the organization charts, and it received a considerable boost in 1928 through the participation of Colonel James Fitzmaurice in the first successful east/west transatlantic flight. It also discharged some of the state's responsibilities as a signatory of international conventions on air travel in relation to the reporting of weather conditions and of aircraft movements.[12]

The minimalist views on the proper role of the defence forces advanced by O'Duffy were not shared by all his army subordinates. This became obvious once he relinquished his army posts in 1925: within a few months an 'army reorganisation board' was appointed by the chief of staff, while a remarkable plea for a more positive definition of defence policy was sent by the council of defence to

---

[10] Undated memorandum, with council of defence minutes of 26 July 1929, MA; 'Report of the army reorganisation board 1925–1926', MA, box marked '2/1926 Org'; G-2 report by Lieutenant John G. MacArthur, assistant military attaché, London, 28 Apr. 1928, cited hereafter as 'US report, 1928', USNA, 841d.20/1; 'Army half-yearly report to March 1930', UCDA, Blythe papers, P24/224.

[11] Memorandum by minister for defence, received 25 Sept. 1923, DT, S. 1980; minute, 7 Oct. 1931, PRO, DO 35/402/10.

[12] 'Report of the army reorganisation board', 24–6; council of defence minutes, 3 Feb. 1926, MA; memorandum by O'Duffy, 2 May 1924, DT, S. 3442B, and 1927 file on reporting of aircraft movements, S. 5303.

the executive council in July. This memorandum pressed 'the necessity for placing us in possession of at least the outlines of the Defence Policy of the Government', as without it 'it is impossible to organize and equip the Forces to any very useful purpose'. Policy 'since the formation of the army has been the establishment of forces for the suppression of the Irregulars and the education of our regular officers and men in the ABC of their profession', but a longer view was now needed. While the country's internal security difficulties were familiar to everyone, external defence problems required close consideration because 'Ireland by reason of her geographical position may be said to be the aerial and submarine key to England . . . as likely to become a cockpit for the belligerents in a war . . . as Belgium was before the Great War'. The army could not as it stood take 'any really effective part in the defence of the country against a modern army, navy or air force'. Unless it were made capable of sustained independent defence, Britain would 'assume control of the country', with or without Irish acquiescence, to prevent it falling into enemy hands. The memorandum defined three policy options: the development of defence forces capable of mounting a serious campaign against any attacker; development of an army 'which would be an integral part of the British Imperial forces and would, in the event of war, be controlled by the Imperial General Staff'; and 'the abandonment to England of responsibility for defence against exernal enemies, and the formation of a force to deal with internal disorders'. It discussed the three options in some detail, while clearly inclining towards the first, independent defence: 'Without being aggressive we can be sufficient of a hornet's nest to any outsider to make him keep his hands off in his own interests'. On this its recommendations were wildly ambitious, requiring the peacetime organization for defence purposes of almost every area of economic life, from food production to scientific research. Air strength could be built up by rapid expansion of civil aviation to provide 'a maximum number of Airmen and machines' for mobilization in wartime; food and weapons production should be promoted to ensure self-sufficiency; a coastal defence service should be formed through 'the development of our fishing industry and . . . Mercantile Marine' and, although the 'construction of submarines is not feasible in the immediate future . . . there is no reason why we should not keep the matter in mind'; the Irish diaspora which existed 'in almost every country' could be organized to carry out sabotage 'by way of reprisal or otherwise'; the state should develop 'friendly and intimate relations with USA, France and Germany, all of whose interests would be served by an independent Ireland'; and a 'Chemical Warfare Service . . . could be organised and developed in conjunction with medical, industrial and agricultural research'.[13]

From his annotations it is clear that Cosgrave disagreed with the Anglophobe thrust of the document, writing 'Do not visualise anything but alliance with GB'

---

[13] Memorandum by the council of defence, 22 July 1925, S. 5451.

alongside the suggestion that Ireland court the USA and European powers. The government was itself determined that the Free State should not be seen as a client state of Britain in international affairs: in December 1923 Ireland had incurred British displeasure by joining the League of Nations, which was viewed as the best guarantor of the rights of small nations, and throughout the 1920s Dublin quietly pursued an independent line in commonwealth affairs.[14] But the suggestion that the state could enhance its security by courting Britain's most likely enemies was palpable folly given economic ties, as well as the fact that Britain retained the treaty ports. In any event, the defence memorandum laid the seeds of its own destruction with its outlandish recommendations. However, its analysis of Ireland's defence dilemma, and its emphasis on British concerns, did pose serious questions. After the options had been 'discussed at length', the government gave its response. The army

must be an independent national Force capable of assuming responsibility for the defence of the territory of Saorstát Éireann against invasion, or internal disruptive agencies; but it must also be so organised, trained and equipped as to render it capable . . . of full and complete co-ordination with the forces of the British government in the defence of Saorstát territory whether against actual hostilities or against violation of neutrality on the part of a common enemy.

Ministers believed that 'the present international situation does not . . . justify the hope that recourse to arms will in future be rendered impossible'. While it was their 'earnest desire . . . to avoid participation in any international struggle', if 'some foreign power' attempted to 'utilise our geographical position either as a base for an offensive against Great Britain or against seaborne traffic' between Irish ports and 'other countries, we would be forced into taking action'. The government concluded that a 'standing Army 10,000 to 12,000 strong should suffice both as a deterrent against internal disorder and as the nucleus of a defensive force against external attack'. It should be 'capable of rapid and effective expansion', and all personnel should be trained 'in duties of a more advanced nature than those normally associated with each rank'. Its 'equipment and training' should involve 'specialised preparations of plans to resist invasion from any quarter', including the 'study of likely landing places'. The problem of aerial defence was not mentioned, while it would 'not be practicable to take any special steps' in coastal defence until discussions were held with Britain under article 6 of the treaty. The wilder proposals for the fostering of strategic industries were simply not mentioned, although the army, inspired partly by British thinking on the need for imperial self-sufficiency, continued to hanker after such an approach: four years later the minister assured his generals that 'the requirements of national defence will be held in view in connection with industrial development'.[15]

---

[14] On this see especially M. Kennedy, *Ireland and the League of Nations, 1923–1946* (Dublin, 1996).
[15] Undated annotations by Cosgrave on council of defence memorandum of 22 July 1925, S. 5451; council of defence minutes, 17 July 1929, MA.

Despite the inadequacy of the executive council's conclusions, they at least laid down clear, if militarily unattainable, lines of defence policy. The country would not go to war unless neutrality were violated—membership of the League of Nations was evidently not then envisaged as implying any positive military obligations. The army should plan for independent land defence, but also anticipate close co-operation with British forces. Air defence would, by inference, be left entirely to Britain, while the issue of coastal defence would be dealt with under the five-year review of arrangements provided for in the treaty. The problems of the supply of defence equipment to Ireland, and the protection of sea traffic to and from Ireland, would presumably also be addressed through a future understanding with Britain. That, however, was a distant prospect: while Britain was the country's most logical defence partner, she was also Ireland's most recent enemy. Whatever the exigencies of the treaty and of Anglo-Irish relations, an officer corps composed largely of men who had fought against Britain was unlikely rapidly to embrace overt co-operation with her.

Despite its statement of policy, the government was unwilling to allow the army to proceed on the basis indicated. So far from retaining the strength prescribed by the executive council, the army was progressively weakened. One reason was undoubtedly money. The decline in military spending was precipitous, from over eleven million pounds in 1923–4 to less than two million in 1928–9. In 1929 the minister for finance Ernest Blythe, when also acting minister for defence, assured the council of defence that, as military spending had now been 'brought down to a normal figure, he considered that such very detailed scrutiny of proposals will no longer be necessary', and that in future 'due weight' would be given 'to the views of the responsible military chiefs'. This message seems not to have reached his Finance subordinates, whose cheese-paring intensified in subsequent years. A second reason, presumably, was a fear that too large an army might again get out of hand. A third was the fact that, in contrast with most state services, there was no parliamentary pressure to increase defence spending: on the contrary, even before Fianna Fáil entered the Dáil, opposition TDs criticized the government for squandering money on the army, not for starving it of funds and purpose. Fianna Fáil politicians regarded the army as the incarnation of Free State repression; they saw no likely external enemy except Britain; they were emotionally predisposed towards irregular warfare, drawing inspiration from the War of Independence and discounting the chastening experience of republican forces during the civil war; many of them retained very close links with the IRA, which still styled itself the true national army; and they feared that the military might block the path to power if they looked like winning an election. In November 1927 the parliamentary party agreed that 'our policy should be to re-organise the army on a volunteer, territorial basis, with a small permanent training and maintenance staff'. A fourth reason for the neglect of defence questions was probably a misplaced faith in the capacity of the international community to protect small nations: in 1929 a Defence document observed that 'we . . . suffer from the disadvantage that compared with other countries, a large proportion of our diplomatic activities centre on the League of Nations, with the result that undue importance is attached . . . to the activities of disarmament conferences, and other such bodies, which have in fact achieved no tangible results'.[16]

iii. Anglo-Irish Defence Discussions, 1923–1932

So loath were both Britain and Ireland to settle the defence problems left hanging in the treaty that the five-year review stipulated in article 6 never took place, much to Irish relief. Awkward questions did, nevertheless, arise. In December 1923 the Admiralty furnished a lengthy list of points for discussion. As well as detailed arrangements for the working of the defence provisions of the treaty in peace and in war, the Admiralty insouciantly suggested the establishment of an Irish coastwatching service, and asked if Irish 'revenue vessels' could be 'turned over to Imperial Navy in time of war'. These indelicate proposals naturally caused some alarm: Cosgrave noted that while such requests might be 'reasonable' in terms of the treaty, 'they may nevertheless be negotiable on the grounds of safety'. The necessary arrangements were discreetly made and honoured with the Admiralty and the War Office for the maintenance of the treaty ports, defences and installations, including measures which ranged from the passage of British army convoys through Free State territory to provision for the exemption from Irish motor tax of the private cars of British officers stationed in Ireland. The Irish authorities also checked out the family and political backgrounds of Irish volunteers to the British army. For their part the British made some co-operative gestures: Irish troops in uniform were even allowed to pass through Northern Ireland while on pilgrimage to Lough Derg, on condition that they did not disembark from their trains while in transit.[17] The bigger questions posed by the Admiralty were, however, left severely alone. In the prevailing political conditions the government was wary of the perils of stumbling into an overt defence alliance with Britain. The paradox in this was that it almost certainly strengthened Britain's hand, because the Irish army was given no opportunity to define, negotiate, and plan for a credible role for itself in any future crisis in which Britain would be involved.

Despite the 1925 ruling that the army should be capable of close co-operation

---

[16] Council of defence minutes, 7 and 8 Nov. 1929, MA; Fianna Fáil parliamentary party minutes, 15 Nov. 1927, Fianna Fáil archives, FF/438; TS 'notes on attached memo', n.d. [1929], DT, S. 4541.

[17] 'Agenda for next Monday's conference at the Admiralty', with Loughnane to Mulcahy, 4 Dec., and Cosgrave to Kennedy, 6 Dec. 1923, Kennedy papers, P4/493. Examples of such arrangements can be seen in DT, S. 4779 and S. 1978.

with Britain in the event of attack or invasion, no discussions were held to plan for this eventuality. Indeed, there were virtually no Anglo-Irish military contacts at all, other than on officer training and on the purchase of equipment and supplies, and even these were inadequate. Both government and army were wary of any substantive Anglo-Irish exchanges on defence issues, an attitude reciprocated in Whitehall, where the Free State was still regarded with suspicion. Paul Canning has written that Committee of Imperial Defence papers 'routinely circulated to the other Dominions were withheld from it as a matter of course', while it was not 'invited to send representatives to attend [CID and its subcommittees] meetings as were the other Dominions'. However, one significant exception to this practice should be noted: the adjutant-general and a staff officer attended a meeting between the Principal Supply Officers Committee of the CID and representatives of the dominions arranged during the London imperial conference in November 1926 to discuss the 'supply of war materials and other essential requirements' in time of war. That meeting produced three recommendations: that each dominion should set up its own supply committee analogous to the PSOC; that such committees should keep in touch with the PSOC; and that they should 'exchange annual reports'. Notwithstanding the possible implications for foreign policy, the chief of staff endorsed these recommendations because the issue of 'supply in war', and related problems such as the safety of shipping to and from Ireland 'must become the subject of an understanding between the Saorstát and Great Britain'—Ireland would need British weapons, and Britain would need Irish food.[18] While conscious of the danger of 'committing ourselves to British military policy' implicit in appointing a military attaché to London, as the other dominions had done, for some years the army sought to persuade the government to put 'our relations with the British on a more satisfactory working basis', and to sanction 'informal consultation between our General Staff and the British General Staff' on questions of 'training and equipment'. No such high-level contacts were permitted, although for a time an officer was deputed to liaise with the War Office.[19]

The Irish did take one significant initiative in 1927, during the limited and informal 'technical discussions on coastal defence' held in lieu of the review prescribed by the treaty. Possibly in order to divert attention from other issues, the Irish side asked the British to cede the peacetime defence of the treaty ports. In Britain, official opinion was divided on the merits of retaining full control of the ports: while the Admiralty insisted on this, the War Office, which had to provide troops to guard them, and the Dominions Office, which aimed to improve relations with Dublin, were disposed towards conciliating the Irish.

---

[18] Council of defence minutes, 15 June 1927, and associated documentation, MA.

[19] Undated memorandum with council of defence minutes, 26 Aug. 1930, and memorandum by Captain Rooney, seen by assistant chief of staff on 2 Nov. 1927, MA, no file or box number; Canning, *British Policy*, 182.

However, the matter was decisively settled in the Admiralty's favour at cabinet level before the 'technical discussions' took place. Instead, when British and Irish officials met the British again pressed issues which the Admiralty had touched on in December 1923: Ireland should 'take over certain aspects of its local defence, such as minesweeping, coastal patrol and at least certain aspects of naval intelligence or coast watching'. The British 'refused to discuss the handing-over' of the defences of the treaty ports, on the grounds that they were 'integral to Imperial defence . . . The British must have been well aware that we were technically ill-equipped to man those defences, and that the Saorstát proposal . . . was based on questions of general prestige, and not defence considerations'.[20]

The fact that neither country sought to fulfil the treaty requirement for a review of defence provisions is clear evidence that each was satisfied to leave matters as they were. For Britain, the main consequence was that the War Office had grudgingly to continue to secure the fortifications around the treaty ports; maintenance of the status quo also lessened the danger, however slight, of any upsurge of revanchist sentiment in Ireland being translated into aggression against Northern Ireland. For Ireland, the impact was more profound, because it meant that the government could postpone indefinitely further consideration of problems of external defence. Had ministers been concerned primarily with increasing Ireland's defensive preparedness, then they could have acted on other aspects of coastal defence as the British had suggested. These would be essential anyway, should the port defences eventually be handed over, or should Britain go to war again. Instead, while the minister did tell the council of defence in 1929 that 'it could be assumed that Government policy may include a share in the Coastal Defence and that staff should include provision accordingly', no money was made available and nothing at all was done. The government view appeared to be that if the British insisted on defending the ports themselves, then it was entirely up to them to do so effectively.[21]

Between 1927 and 1932 there was little dialogue with Britain on defence questions. The army from 1928 became preoccupied with American approaches to questions of military organization and operations. This diluted the influence of the British model, and perhaps distracted attention from the strategic desirability of developing a clear defence understanding with Britain. The shift in outlook can be explained partly by politics, but also by developments in officer training and education from the mid-1920s on. These must now be discussed.

[20] Canning, *British Policy*, 180–1; 'Fundamental Factors affecting Irish defence policy', marked 'G2/057, dated May 1936', with private secretary, minister for defence, to private secretary, minister for finance, 23 May 1936, UCDA, MacEntee papers, P67/91, p. 54, cited hereafter as 'Fundamental Factors'. This document was 'at least 90%' written by Bryan, who had been involved in the 1927 discussions. Bryan transcripts, p. 2.

[21] Council of defence minutes, 17 July 1929, MA.

iv. The Professionalization of Military Service, 1923–1932

Despite the chaos, parsimony, and incoherence of the government's approach to defence questions, despite the debilitating rundown of numbers, despite the unrest which remained after the mutiny, despite poor prospects for advancement and uncertainty about pensions, despite shortages of basic equipment, of weapons, and of men, despite the continual demands to carry out security and other tasks which should by rights have been the responsibility of the civil authorities, the army underwent a transformation in the mid-1920s. The Defence Forces Act of November 1924 put the army on a stable footing, and disposed of problems of allegiance by forbidding membership of oath-bound societies and of political organizations. Those officers who survived demobilization consciously turned away from politics, espousing the conventional doctrine of military subservience to elected government and immersing themselves in the assumptions, forms, and trappings of military professionalism. It is no coincidence that, in an era of savage retrenchment, the army school of music flourished, under the direction of a former German officer, Colonel Fritz Brase. This can easily be dismissed as a frivolous preference for ceremony over military effectiveness, for brass over steel. O'Duffy, admittedly a man temperamentally disposed towards public display, disagreed: bands were good value, producing 'that most essential quality . . . Esprit de Corps'. Military tattoos featuring 'massed bands, massed P[hysical] T[raining] displays, massed drill displays and historical pageants' were staged in Dublin in 1927 and in 1929 to stimulate public interest. A visit by a British army boxing team in 1926 proved an enormous success: 3,500 people were said to have attended their first contest against an army team at Portobello barracks. The travels and achievements of the army's show-jumping team after 1926, again under the direction of a foreign officer, Colonel Rodzanko, were also a source of considerable pride and of public enthusiasm. Not everyone was impressed: in 1930 an pseudonymous officer wrote that 'an army cannot be justified by incidentals. Horse-jumping is not its prime function, nor the production of bands, nor gymnastic displays for public entertainment.' The army should be judged on how it fulfilled its primary function of national defence: 'let it not be justified by trivialities if it deserves to be damned for its military futility'. On the other hand, an American officer who visited Ireland in 1928 'was told that the authorities feel that a good band and snappy turnout is a good political argument for maintaining the Army'. As it shrank in size, the army also became more pronouncedly Catholic in ethos: mass parades, pilgrimages, and other semi-public devotional acts became an integral part of its activities, although even such displays of piety were insufficient to satisfy some purists. The perils to morality inherent in military service were as obvious in the Free State army as they had been under British rule: in

1924 the military hospital at Haulbowline alone contained over one hundred and forty men afflicted with venereal disease, and the soldiery always remained under suspicion of licentiousness. More surprisingly, however, in 1929 the *Catholic Pictorial* roundly accused the army of 'encouraging Stopery [contraception]' amongst its men by only providing allowances and accommodation for a maximum of four children of each married soldier.[22]

Training became very important. Each year a handful of officers travelled abroad, mostly to Britain, to attend specialized courses in artillery, chemical warfare, aircraft maintenance, and the like. More significantly, however, early in 1925 it was suggested that Ireland should either send 'a few officers to a military academy' in America or arrange for 'USA Army officers to come here' as instructors in the military college envisaged under O'Duffy's reorganization scheme, and O'Duffy himself was asked to take soundings while in the United States to attend an international police convention. In December the government approved the 'Military Mission', the dispatch of a number of officers for training in the United States. It was to have a profound impact on the army's development, and it represents the one positive initiative taken by a government otherwise concerned only to run down the army as quickly and as much as possible.[23]

The decision to dispatch officers to the United States was a conscious effort to broaden the horizons of the new army and to lessen dependence on British approaches to military organization, although British blessing for the mission was obtained. It sat somewhat oddly with the executive council's July 1925 decision that the army should be so trained and organized as to be capable of operations in tandem with British forces. The choice of the United States was evidently dictated more by linguistic and political considerations than by any assumptions about American military science: an Anglophone country was required, and it would have been impolitic to turn for help to fellow dominions such as Canada, Australia, or South Africa, although their defence arrangements like Ireland's were complicated by membership of the commonwealth. By contrast, no nationalist could complain about taking advice from the American army, however inapplicable its experience and approach to training might be for a small semi-island Atlantic state like Ireland. Six officers, led by the assistant chief of staff Major-General Hugo MacNeill and Colonel M. J. Costello, spent just over a year in various military establishments in the United States: two officers at the command and staff school at Leavenworth, three at the infantry

---

[22] Memorandum by O'Duffy, 2 May 1924 as in n. 4 above; D. Fitzpatrick, ' "Unofficial emissaries": British Army Boxers in the Irish Free State, 1919–31', *Irish Historical Studies*, 30/118 (Nov. 1996), 227; 'US report, 1928'; M. Hogan, 'International Military Show-Jumping', and 'Irish Army International Show-Jumping', *An t-Óglách*, 2/2 (Aug. 1929), 27–9 and 3/1 (Jan. 1930), 82–6; P. Young, 'Pageantry and the Defence Forces', *An Cosantóir*, 45/9 (Sept. 1985), 296; 'XYZ', 'Why should we apologize?' and 'NCOs and men', *An t-Óglách*, 3/1 (Jan. 1930), 8 and 18, quoting the *Catholic Pictorial*.

[23] Council of defence minutes, 21 Apr. 1925, MA; executive council decision, 12 Dec. 1925, DT, S. 4559.

school in Fort Benning, and one at the artillery school at Fort Sill. The aims of the mission were, in MacNeill's words, to produce recommendations 'for the application to Irish needs' of the American military system or 'particular features of it', and to prepare the ground for the establishment of a military college.[24]

On his return MacNeill cautioned against unthinking imitation of the American model of military organization—the 'wide difference in the character of the problem which faces the two countries requires very different treatment in each case . . . the answer to the Irish problem must be found in the study of the Irish needs and situation'. The immediate outcome of the mission was the establishment at his behest of a 'Temporary Plans Division' (TPD) in January 1928 to develop 'a suitable Theory of War on which the defence of An Saorstát should be based'; to formulate 'tactical doctrines covering the employment of all arms and branches'; to suggest any 'necessary addition or amendments to existing schemes of organization . . . for peace and war'; to draw up 'tables of equipment and supply'; to produce 'recommendations re Command, Staff, Administration and Supply'; and to draft mobilization schemes and plans for 'Military Education for the Forces'. The TPD was set up in the Hibernian Schools in Dublin, and fifteen officers were assigned to it full time including MacNeill as its director, Costello as the officer in charge of 'Command' studies, Dan Bryan in charge of 'Intelligence', and two officers who had attended staff college in Britain. There was also provision for the part-time participation of other officers, and about one hundred took part as students.[25]

While the TPD experiment was in operation, principles were agreed and tactical doctrines developed for dissemination amongst the officer corps. Problems were set and discussion papers written on the various aspects of organization and operations outlined by MacNeill. A visiting American officer was impressed: he thought the 'business-like way in which General MacNeill and his assistants seem to be going about their work . . . particularly noteworthy'. Most of those attending 'seem to be interested', though 'some of them perhaps have scarcely the educational background to attack problems in major tactics'. Some doubted 'the value in considering divisions and corps when in the nature of the case they would be limited to operations with small units', and others with 'first-hand knowledge of the subject' from the civil war were 'heard to comment rather unfavourably on a lecture on street-fighting'. The almost exclusive reliance on 'Leavenworth and Gettysburgh maps . . . for map problems' also raised eyebrows (though the reason may have had as much to do with the army's continuing difficulties with the Ordnance Survey as with slavish reliance on

---

[24] 'General recommendations re establishment of Defence Plans Division . . .', n.d. [1928], cited hereafter as 'Military mission report', MA, box 2/TPD & 24 Org.

[25] Ibid.; chief of staff circular letter to officer commanding signals corps, 18 Jan. 1928, MA, box 2/TPD & 24 Org.

what MacNeill and Costello had been taught in America). The attaché also observed that with the development of a staff college for 'advanced studies' a number of officers 'may not find themselves qualified to continue' in the army, a conclusion also reached by some British military sources.[26]

MacNeill intended the TPD not as the vehicle for a one-off reassessment of military doctrine but as the precursor of both a proper staff college and a 'Defence Plans Division' with 'a permanent place in our Military Organization . . . under the direct control of the Chief of Staff'. The first two aims were realized; the third was not. The TPD's analysis of military doctrine was accepted, and schemes of organization and tables of strength were revised accordingly. The military college was finally established at the Curragh under MacNeill in 1930 to teach the theory of war and the tactical doctrines which the TPD had developed. Despite the intention to eschew the British approach to military education, the teaching materials used included British as well as American studies and handbooks. This was inevitable, given continued dependence on Britain for equipment and for specialist training. As the American attaché had anticipated, some of the less sophisticated of those officers who had survived earlier purges were weeded out by the notorious 'Hunt board' in 1928–9, as the army sought to retain a cadre of officers showing future promise in the midst of yet more cuts. Legend has it that, in addition to the novelties of military science, officers were schooled to act like gentlemen, to extinguish the mess lights by use of the switch instead of revolver fire, and even to drink crème de menthe in place of pints of stout.[27] But no permanent planning section was created along the lines MacNeill had recommended, and no systematic action was taken to address such vital issues as the training of proper reserve and volunteer forces, and the securing of an appropriate and timely supply of weapons, munitions, and vehicles, which were central to the operation of any defence plan in time of crisis.

The concern of some officers to come to grips with long-term defence problems is reflected in the surviving documents on organization, training, and planning. Earnest memoranda were produced urging the application of the lessons of military science: compared with most 'modern armies . . . we deviate from the accepted principles in a good number of ways'. The need for a military topographical service was pressed, for example, and, as has already been noted, the establishment of a skeletal military censorship office capable of taking over all communications censorship in times of crisis was suggested. Another document urged systematic experimentation in the production of weapons and equipment, as

---

[26] 'Military mission report'; 'US report, 1928'; Fitzpatrick, 'Unofficial emissaries', 221.

[27] 'Military mission report'; memorandum on 'Courses at Foreign Military Schools', undated, with council of defence minutes, 26 Aug. 1930, MA; there is a miscellany of instructional material in MA, boxes MM & TPD and MM; information from Fr. Mícheál McGreil, SJ, 1993.

we cannot, because our military policy and organisation is different, take over such weapons as England provides for her army, and purchase from other countries is not a sound proposition . . . It is therefore necessary that we explore every possible source of supply in An Saorstát and that we consider the capabilities of those Foundries and Workshops which exist and have already turned out war material for both the British and ourselves . . . our needs can only be satisfactorily met by production here.[28]

Officers found a more public outlet for their opinions in the journal *An t-Óglách*, which had come under army auspices in 1922. After O'Duffy's departure, its recasting as an 'Army Journal . . . worthy of its mission' was described by the adjutant-general as promising 'more than anything hitherto to assist the army to maintain its rightful position in the national life of the country'. It was eventually reorganized in 1927, and in 1928 Costello became its editor. In its new form historical and descriptive articles were joined by surprisingly forthright editorials, vigorous discussions on contemporary defence issues, analysis of the declared policies of the major political parties, foreign press surveys prepared by intelligence, and arguments for the adoption of this or that innovation in military organization.[29]

Most such proposals, however, remained just that, purely theoretical pieces written more in hope than in expectation. There was no political interest in or money available to spend on such arcane activities as defence preparations. The government was willing to announce important initiatives such as the development of reserve and volunteer forces, all necessary if the regular army was to fulfil the brief assigned to it of becoming the highly trained nucleus of a larger military organization capable of mobilization at short notice, but not to take the steps necessary to bring these into effective existence. The regular army was markedly reluctant to become embroiled in the training of any part-time soldiers until the requisite equipment had been provided and proper programmes of instruction prepared—both of which developments were dependent on significant extra spending which Finance was simply not going to provide—while ministers, for all their policy statements, were probably wary of remilitarizing the country: rifle clubs and even Boy Scout organizations were regarded as potentially subversive. Furthermore, politicians remained fearful that the army itself might once more get ideas above its station, and that the old problem of the ultimate allegiance of its officers might arise again. They sought to contain the army by denying it money and by exercising extremely tight control on every aspect of its activities. The post-mutiny 'army leaders' have recently been criticized for accepting such control and for not defending 'their own interests more vigorously', but it is hard to see how they could have resisted retrenchment

---

[28] Defence memorandum, 3 Feb. 1926, MA, file marked 'Experimental works: Research etc. in Defence Forces Saorstát Éireann'.

[29] Army memorandum, 8 July, and adjutant-general to chief of staff, 16 July 1925, MA, file on '*An t-Óglách*—publicity'; unsigned MS note, 15 Apr. 1930, FitzGerald papers, P80/1043.

without appearing dangerously insubordinate. The financial climate may explain the abrupt resignation of Daniel Hogan as chief of staff in 1929 after less than two years in the post, just as other aspects of ministerial intervention contributed to the departure of his successor Sean MacEoin after just three months.[30]

The government's wariness about army affairs is also illustrated in its treatment of two offshoots of the TPD fervour, the National Defence Association and the revived *An t-Óglách* which acted as its journal. The association had been formed in the autumn of 1929 following the return of the military mission, to stimulate informed discussion of military affairs and to contribute to the education of the public on questions of defence 'from a professional and national standpoint, and standing clear of political differences'. Its founders had hoped to elect MacEoin, the recently departed chief of staff, as its first chairman, but he declined. Hugo MacNeill, the high priest of the new cult of military professionalism, thought this 'a great mistake . . . your prestige both inside and outside the Service would have been a great acquisition to us'. Despite his passion for military science, however, MacNeill was and remained throughout his career hopelessly insensitive to political affairs. Thus, although 'I believe it is a false step' for a serving officer, he agreed to become chairman himself. The association was initially a spectacular success: by November 1929 three-quarters of all regular officers, and two-thirds of all officers of the reserve, had enrolled. However, it was disastrously compromised from the outset by the remit which it set itself. Its main declared aim of educating the public in strategic realities was likely to cause friction with the government, since it threatened the prospect of soldiers publicly airing the case over the heads of ministers for an adequately financed and coherent defence policy. Its subsidiary aims were even more impolitic for an officer corps still tainted by the 1924 mutiny: while MacNeill stressed that it must not 'embark on anything of a trade union nature; such a step would be fatal both to the Service and to the Association', he saw no harm in enunciating 'grievances affecting the efficiency and the interests of the Service, as a whole' such as the 'long overdue Army Pensions legislation'.[31]

The government baulked at this latent threat to discipline. In January 1930 the acting minister Ernest Blythe complained forthrightly about 'the type of matters which were being raised by the Association, and . . . the fact that they were being put forward' by MacNeill, 'a serving officer, from his official residence'. He also attacked 'certain matters published' in *An t-Óglách*: 'the substance . . . was not at all what he would expect to find', and 'the wording . . . was unsuitable and the general tone objectionable'. He 'directed that Colonel

---

[30] Farrell, 'The "Model Army"', 118. Hogan's departure remains something of a mystery. He was shot dead in the United States in the early 1940s; Clancy interview.

[31] MacNeill to MacEoin, 6 Oct. 1929, UCDA, MacEoin papers, CR71/308; minutes of first annual general meeting of National Defence Association, 8 Nov. 1929, in *An t-Óglách*, 3/1 (Jan. 1930), 111 and 113.

Costello should cease to be editor'. In October he 'intimated that he intended to dissolve' the association and gave instructions accordingly.[32]

The army's new-found enthusiasm for military science and for the discussion of strategic issues was not entirely wasted. It imparted a sense of purpose which transcended the prosaic demands of maintaining internal security, and so contributed to the development of a professional military ethos. It also influenced the thinking of career officers who, as European war loomed in the late 1930s, suddenly found themselves being taken seriously by the government. In the 1920s, however, the cuts just went on and on, and the army's development continued to suffer from a chronic shortage of money. Even where recruitment was sanctioned, it was very difficult to attract and to retain skilled men for the various technical corps. This was true throughout the army, though the air service was particularly affected: there the expedient of training ground staff from scratch was adopted, but this was hampered by a shortage of instructors and by the ready availability of better paid work in Britain for apprentices once they had completed their courses. The provision of detachments to guard key buildings and installations throughout the state made great demands on manpower, inhibiting training activities and causing considerable dissatisfaction amongst the men because of the long hours of duty involved. Orders to provide drivers and armed guards for key political figures after the O'Higgins murder also took their toll: in 1930 the chief of staff reported 'a large number of discharges and transfers to the Reserve' of men employed in the 'special Protective Unit', where 'guard duty has been very heavy generally'. There was also a steady trickle out of experienced men drawn by the wider vistas for professional soldiering offered by the British army. Although one officer drew comfort from this, it was and remained a debilitating feature of army life: 'The type of man we have in . . . is much superior to the type of recruit got in England or Scotland. Our soldiers are anxious to improve their position, and they look to the future. So far the British Army offers greater facilities than we do to help the soldier to do this.'[33]

In 1928 the minister had commented that 'his idea is the biggest army possible for the least money'.[34] What policy in practice produced between 1923 and 1932 was an army militarily incapable of anything more than static garrison duty, operating in a strategic policy vacuum. The delicacy of Anglo-Irish relations meant that ministers shied away from the private discussion, let alone the public airing, of elementary facts of strategic life inherent in the Free State's location, her economic links with Britain, and Britain's defence rights under the treaty. By 1932 the Free State had neither the resources, the framework, nor the

---

[32] Council of defence minutes, 4 Jan. and 16 Oct. 1930, MA.

[33] Army half-yearly reports to Mar. 1929 and Mar. 1930, Blythe papers, P24/223 and 224; memorandum by Major Liston, 15 Jan. 1927, following council of defence minutes, 22 Oct. 1926 to 26 Nov. 1927, MA.

[34] 'US report, 1928'.

doctrine to mount any serious defence of her territory, her seas and skies. The army was militarily incapable of anything more than keeping the IRA quiet. There was only the frailest simulacrum of an air service and, despite Ireland's position in the Atlantic, no maritime capability of any kind—not even to police the country's coastal fishing grounds, or to report on traffic in Irish waters, neither of which services would have met with British objections. On the credit side, however, the army had developed an increasingly educated officer corps. In Irish circumstances the litmus test of their professionalism, identified by Mulcahy in 1923, and reiterated endlessly after 1924 by the army itself, was neither operational competence nor strategic insight, but a more basic democratic requirement: willingness to serve whatever government the people chose. That willingness was put to the test when Fianna Fáil won office in February 1932.

v. The Army and the Transfer of Power, 1931–1932

The political prelude to the election has already been discussed: here we need only consider its implications for the army. The Public Safety Act of September 1931, established in response to the growth in political disorder, set up military tribunals to dispense justice in cases of political crime. This measure was portrayed not only by the IRA, against whom it was directed, but by Fianna Fáil, as a blatantly unjustifed and partisan ploy by an insecure government to stifle legitimate opposition and to distract attention from its own failings. With a general election due within a year, which Fianna Fáil might very well win, it was not a propititious development for an army anxious to distance itself from political controversy.

The prospect of a de Valera government was viewed with dismay by most officers. They had good reason: in addition to an understandable fear of republican revenge, which could well result in wholesale dismissals to make way for republican placemen, any officer interested in problems of external defence could only have been alarmed at the disdain of Fianna Fáil politicians for conventional military organization, their fixation with Britain as the source of all of Ireland's woes, and their rhetorical preference for irregular warfare: shortly after entering the Dáil in 1927, de Valera had argued that 'we should . . . reduce' the army 'to a small standing force and a volunteer territorial army instead of the present one'. It is against that backdrop that the O'Duffy coup proposal should be considered here: its appeal lay not simply in the understandable reluctance of those who had won the civil war to see their enemies taking control of the state, but in the argument that some pre-emptive action was necessary actually to safeguard the newly professionalized army from the depredations of an irresponsible, demagogic republican regime bent on destroying the positive achievements of Cosgrave's decade of power. Such logic has, precisely by catering to the conventional professional military disdain for civil politics, facilitated military seizures of power in newly independent states the world over. That it did not do so in Ireland in 1932 is to the credit both of Cosgrave and of the most senior officers, who knocked talk of a coup on the head. In the aftermath of that momentous election the army stayed in its barracks. Apart from the discreet destruction of many sensitive civil war records, no special steps were taken in anticipation of the new regime.[35] The army awaited its fate under its former foes nervously but quietly.

[35] *Dáil Debates*, vol. 24, col. 1450, 16 Nov. 1927; Bryan interview.

4

Internal Security and External Defence, 1932–1939

i. Fianna Fáil's First Year, 1932–1933

De Valera's peaceful installation as president of the executive council on 9 March 1932 was a watershed in Irish politics. He was elected as head of a minority government supported by the Labour party, a constraint for which he may on reflection have been grateful. The transfer of power took place through the relatively dignified medium of a vote in Dáil Éireann. The process was the antithesis of what many on both sides of the civil war divide had anticipated: there was no shooting, no rioting, and surprisingly little overt rancour or triumphalism. Despite its sympathy with the militant republican movement, Fianna Fáil had become an essentially constitutional party. Despite the bitterness of its defeat and its fears for the future, Cumann na nGaedheal remained one.

The following weeks vindicated the peaceful transfer of power. Whether through magnanimity or through statecraft, the victors did not claim all the spoils. There was no serious bureaucratic bloodletting, no sidetracking of judges, and no clear-out of soldiers or policemen who had incurred republican enmity since 1921. Indeed, so few changes were made that de Valera was rebuked at the next Fianna Fáil ard fheis for 'forgiving his enemies and forgetting his friends'.[1] De Valera set out to control the machinery of government, not to purge it. This attitude had a considerable bearing on policy in the succeeding years. It meant that, apart from the sensitive matter of how to deal with militant republicanism, most security and defence issues continued to be handled much as before by much the same people in the civil service, the police, and the army.

The most striking examples of this unexpected continuity were to be found at the top. Peadar MacMahon, the secretary of Defence since 1927, held on to his post—to the army's regret, he remained there for a further twenty-six years.

[1] Andrews, *Man of no property*, 120. The speaker was Dr Con Murphy, who had lost his public service position in the 1920s through refusing to swear allegiance to the Free State. Earl of Longford and T. P. O'Neill, *Eamon de Valera* (London, 1970), 275–6.

The chief of staff Michael Brennan, who had been appointed in 1931, was left undisturbed, as were his senior officers. Brennan had an outstanding War of Independence record, and he was not personally associated with civil war atrocities. His retention was nevertheless a striking indication of de Valera's political sophistication. This was also demonstrated in the choice of Frank Aiken as minister for defence. On the one hand, Aiken had impeccable republican credentials, and as a South Armagh man he could not easily be outflanked on the issue of partition. On the other hand, he had made strenuous efforts to prevent the civil war, though he became one of the very few anti-treaty leaders to emerge from it with his military reputation intact. This counted for something with the army: he was the first minister since Mulcahy with significant fighting experience. Equable and reserved, one associate later described him as 'indifferent to the opinions of either his political friends or opponents, or indeed of anyone except de Valera'. From the outset he made it clear to the army that there would be no witch-hunts—though after the declaration of the poll there had been a bonfire, as sensitive intelligence records were burnt—that he took its loyalty for granted, and that business would proceed as usual. Aiken proved a straightforward and honourable minister, though like most politicians of his generation he was oblivious to the military differences between the insurgencies in which he had fought and serious national defence. But he was a man in whom the army could have confidence, and in 1932 that was what mattered most.[2] The new government's actions in relation to the Garda were equally circumspect. On the face of it the force had much to fear. Since 1925 it had been the government's main weapon against the republican movement, and its detectives, agents, and informers had unearthed and chronicled the close links between Fianna Fáil, the IRA, and other subversive organizations. This had earned them the enmity of their new masters: as one Cumann na nGaedheal critic put it many years later, between 1927 and 1932 Fianna Fáil's 'remedy' for republican violence had been to urge the disbandment of the Special Branch. If that were done, 'the decent young Republicans would cease their activities'.[3] Republican support in the election campaign had been useful, and some reciprocal gesture from Fianna Fáil was now expected. Yet de Valera proceeded very cautiously. Changes in policy there would be; changes in personnel would depend on how serving officers accommodated themselves to the new regime. As his minister for justice de Valera nominated not some republican firebrand but James Geoghegan, a one-time member of Cumann na nGaedheal. More remarkable still, despite his reputation and his anti-Fianna Fáil activities, O'Duffy was left undisturbed as Garda commissioner. To some Fianna Fáil supporters, and to all other republicans, this appeared to be carrying moderation to extremes. O'Duffy's theatri-

[2] Bryan transcripts, p. 1.
[3] Michael Hayes to Gerry Boland, 26 Apr. 1966, UCDA, Hayes papers, P53/276.

cality and his Catholicism combined effectively in the arrangements for the Eucharistic Congress in June, a long-scheduled jamboree which bestowed a fortuitous benediction on the new regime, enabling de Valera to confound accusations of communist sympathies in an orgy of public piety.

The experiment in cohabitation was otherwise not a success, and its failure presaged alarming developments in extra-parliamentary politics.[4] But it was a risk worth taking for de Valera: it demonstrated his willingness to work with even the most enthusiastic servants of the Cosgrave regime so long as they were prepared to work with him, and it probably bolstered police morale. De Valera's policy towards his former comrades in the republican movement was, predictably, radically different to that of his predecessors in government. His intention was to woo as many as possible into constitutional politics, to consolidate his grip on popular republican sentiment, and to marginalize those activists who would not come into the Fianna Fáil fold. He anticipated not a Pauline conversion of his former comrades but a gradual drift into conventional politics as the wisdom of Fianna Fáil's approach became clear. His policy had five strands: first, the undermining or removal of symbols of imperial subordination in the constitution such as the oath of allegiance and the governor-generalship; secondly, the adoption of modestly progressive social policies, most notably in housing; thirdly, the retention of the land purchase annuities due to Britain under the treaty, a decision which sparked a trade war particularly damaging to the larger farmers who formed the backbone of Cumann na nGaedheal's rural support; fourthly, the systematic adoption of tariffs to foster indigenous industrial development; and fifthly, a conciliatory approach towards the IRA and its offshoots.

Cumulatively, de Valera's policy decisions in 1932 appeared to his Cumann na nGaedheal opponents to represent not only the undoing of the 1921 settlement, but the destruction of the ordered polity which they had created. His depredations in constitutional and economic affairs were compounded by his handling of the IRA and its left-wing satellites. This was no policy of covert appeasement: instead, the operation of the Public Safety Act and its attendant military courts was suspended, almost one hundred republican prisoners were released, and an indulgent attitude adopted towards republican activities generally. Special Branch harassment of republicans virtually ceased, the practice of searching for arms and documents was abandoned, and uniformed Gardai shied away from confrontation. The opposition claimed that de Valera had given his republican allies carte blanche, while a British MP who took soundings in September reported to the prime minister that the IRA 'have the Fianna Fáil government entirely in their power, and it is believed that President de Valera can neither move forward nor back and that he is under continued threats by the extremist

[4] Brady, *Guardians*, 178.

wing of the IRA'.[5] The IRA found itself in a situation akin to the months after the truce in 1921: its units could now recruit, drill, parade, and demonstrate to their hearts' content, safe from prosecution as long as they did not bear arms in public or attempt to import weapons, and within a year numbers had risen to about thirty thousand men.[6] But, as the mainstream IRA leadership understood rather better than de Valera's other Irish and British critics, and as Fianna Fáil made clear to them in private and in public, the honeymoon would last only so long as republicans did nothing seriously to discomfort the new government. If the IRA chose to rely on de Valera to undo the 1921 settlement, they would have a long wait. If they resumed their campaign against the institutions of the Free State, the common bond with Fianna Fáil would be sundered. This set the IRA an awkward dilemma, though it had the incidental benefit of enabling the traditionalists to push the leftists to one side: the veteran republican turned communist George Gilmore recalled that ' "Don't embarrass Fianna Fáil" became a defence' against calls for the revival of Saor Éire.[7] Despite the IRA's greater ostentation, serious political crime virtually disappeared for the remainder of 1932 as the republican movement and the government sought to maintain their understanding.

IRA forbearance did not, however, extend to toleration of Fianna Fáil's political opponents. Republicans turned their energies to the disruption of Cumann na nGaedheal meetings and to the intimidation of that party's supporters. The police were loath to intervene. Rioters might be beaten with batons, but they were seldom charged with any offence. When action was unavoidable, the mildest possible charges were pressed: thus an IRA man shot and captured during an armed raid on a private house was charged only with illegal possession of a firearm.[8] In reaction to official unwillingness to curb the IRA, Cumann na nGaedheal politicians increasingly looked to muscular elements amongst their own supporters for protection. Violent—though unarmed—clashes became common.

The new government's indulgence towards the IRA was part and parcel of a broader political programme aimed at removing the most objectionable features of the treaty. That programme had the inevitable and probably welcome result of producing a marked deterioration in Anglo-Irish relations. Fianna

---

[5] Quoted in D. McMahon, ' "A transient apparition": British policy towards the de Valera Government, 1932–5', *Irish Historical Studies*, 22/88 (Sept. 1981), 336.

[6] Draft reply to Dáil question by McGilligan, 6 June 1932, DT, S. 4107. According to Bell, *The Secret Army*, 101, the IRA imported arms from the United States. On 24 August 1932 Lord Sankey, a member of the British cabinet's Irish situation committee, noted that the shipment of arms from the continent 'has been going on more or less the whole year and we informed the Irish Free State Gov[ernmen]t of the fact', Bodleian Library, Sankey diary, MS Eng. hist. c. 286.

[7] Justice memorandum, 29 June 1932, DT, S. 2206; G. Gilmore, *The Republican Congress 1934* (Dublin, n.d.), 24; Twomey interview, 1975; Bowman, *De Valera and the Ulster Question*, 123–6.

[8] Brady, *Guardians*, 186; Patrick McGilligan instanced this and other cases during an adjournment debate on 1 Aug. 1933, *Dáil Debates*, vol. 49, cols. 1047–8.

Fáil's approach appeared to bear out many of the fears both of its domestic opponents and of the British government. The British, comically ill-informed about Irish politics, discomfited by the election of someone they saw as a dangerous fanatic, and alarmed by the implications for dominions relations of the constitutional experiments upon which de Valera was pledged to embark, unwisely took counsel with Cumann na nGaedheal emissaries, one of them a serving public official, sent by Cosgrave to London: de Valera was an incorrigible gambler, a cat's-paw of the IRA, an impetuous, unscrupulous, irresponsible demagogue who would do anything to court popularity. Britain should make no concessions, and should instead let him be wrecked by his own extremism. His government was a minority one, dependent on Labour support to stay in office, and its days were clearly limited. This was an important exchange: that so self-righteously constitutional a party as Cumann na nGaedheal would proffer secret advice to the British on how best to see off de Valera, and with him a set of national aspirations which had plainly been endorsed by the electorate, demonstrates the depths of despair to which Cosgrave and his followers had plunged. The makers of a democratic Ireland were in danger of repudiating the very principle on which they had based their case for ten years: that the people must decide. For some months British policy was based on the Micawberish assumption that the Irish electorate would soon come to their senses, evict de Valera, and restore Cumann na nGaedheal to power. In March the British began decoding Irish diplomatic cables, and in August the British army agreed to investigate the possibility 'of obtaining information as to activities in the Irish Free State, both from the point of view of military intelligence and also of political intelligence', but London's analysis of Irish politics remained hopelessly naive. In September a cabinet committee rejected a possible compromise on financial issues in telling terms: 'it would be unthinkable in Mr Cosgrave's interests, as well as in our own'. Time was to bring out further ironies: de Valera used the fact of such covert contacts between the opposition and the British to argue the case for IRA restraint, while it was thanks largely to the Cosgrave government's own achievements in dominions diplomacy since 1922 that de Valera was able to accomplish his heinous anti-imperial aims entirely through 'constitutional devices, which almost fortuitously lay ready to hand'.[9]

The despair felt within Cumann na nGaedheal at de Valera's depredations in constitutional and economic affairs was amplified by the problems of public order which stemmed from his treatment of the IRA. The election had been characterized by the frequent disruption of Cumann na nGaedheal public

[9] Bowman, *De Valera and the Ulster Question*, 110–12; extracts from minutes of Irish situation committee, 5 Aug. 1932, PRO, ADM 178/91; minutes of same committee, 27 Sept. 1932, quoted in McMahon, 'A transient apparition', 344; Sankey to prime minister, 10 Aug. 1932, PRO, PRO 30/69/701; de Valera to McGarrity, n.d., Sept. 1933, quoted in Cronin, *The McGarrity Papers*, 156; N. Mansergh, *The Unresolved Question: The Anglo-Irish Settlement and its Undoing, 1912–1972* (London, 1991), 289.

meetings by republicans of all hues bent on revenge for the decade of harassment which they had endured. In the course of the campaign, the Army Comrades Association (ACA) came quietly into existence. Although initially
regarded and presented as an apolitical, non-party benevolent organization for
ex-soldiers, in the months after the election the ACA came under the effective
control of Colonel T. F. O'Higgins, who in August became its president.
O'Higgins's affiliations were crystal clear: he was a Cumann nGaedheal TD, and
his father and his brother Kevin had both been murdered by republicans. It was,
therefore, not surprising that under his leadership the ACA moved closer to
Cumann na nGaedheal. While pledged to support the 'lawfully constituted government of the state', the ACA also committed itself to opposing the spread of
communism in all its guises, and to the protection of free speech. In furtherance
of this, the ACA announced the formation of a volunteer wing.[10] Cumann na
nGaedheal would now have its own protectors.

Recourse to the ACA was a reflection of the desperation felt by men who
feared that the achievements of a decade were on the point of destruction.
When in office Cosgrave had been at pains to take the army out of politics, and
he knew from bitter experience how unmanageable and how dangerous ex-
servicemen's organizations could be. But the pressure to do something to counter
republican disruption became intense in the venomous months after the election, as republicans continued their 'no free speech for traitors' campaign
unabated. As one Cumann na nGaedheal supporter put it decades later, Fianna
Fáil had exploited republican muscle, so why should Cumann na nGaedheal
not arrange to safeguard 'the right of free speech' in the face of 'organised
obstruction of meetings by supporters of the Gov[ernmen]t'?[11] The problem
was that Cumann na nGaedheal's recourse to an extra-parliamentary force was
bound to deepen, not to lessen, the public order crisis, and it inevitably led to
violent clashes between rival political gangs. The ACA had other unfortunate
attributes. First, it raised the spectre of the renewed politicization of the army.
As has already been seen, the government had watched ex-servicemen's groups
very closely since 1923, because these were well placed to foment and to manipulate discontent within the army, and because they were composed of men with
military training who in certain circumstances might be persuaded to use it
against the state. Secondly, although it had no visible links with British fascist
organizations in Dublin, there were arguable parallels between the newly
politicized ACA and the populist, militarized movements of the European
Right which preached the virtues of nation, race, faith, discipline, and anti-

---

[10] M. Manning, *The Blueshirts* (Dublin, 1974), 26–39. Detailed studies of the movement are beginning
to appear. See in particular M. Cronin, 'The Socio-Economic Background and Membership of the
Blueshirt Movement, 1932–5', *Irish Historical Studies*, 29/114 (Nov. 1994), 234–49. Despite this, however,
the nature of the Blueshirts remains as much a matter for polemics as for dispassionate analysis.

[11] Notes by Cecil Lavery sent to Michael Hayes, 21 Nov. 1965, Hayes papers, P53/325(2). Cecil Lavery
was a distinguished lawyer who rose to become a judge of the Supreme Court.

communism and downplayed the importance of democratic institutions and processes. The comparison was made by IRA left-wingers, who labelled the ACA fascist as soon as its Cumann na nGaedheal affiliations and its anti-communist mission were publicly declared.[12] Cosgrave, a thoroughly constitutional politician, had no intention of importing fascism to Ireland, any more than de Valera's careful appeasement of the IRA demonstrated that he was under communist influence, as his wilder critics charged. What Cosgrave and the majority of his colleagues saw in the ACA was an effective counter to republican harassment, which would enable their party to mobilize public opinion against the government and to fight the next election free from disruption and intimidation. What they got was an organization which, while it served the immediate purpose of providing some security for public meetings, rapidly acquired a character and a direction of its own: in the autumn the government received advice that the wilder elements within the ACA had access to caches of stolen weapons missing since the 1924 mutiny, and that they might well prove willing to use them against the state. By a fine irony, this warning emanated from the Garda commissioner Eoin O'Duffy, himself soon to become indelibly associated with the ACA.[13]

By the end of 1932, de Valera had achieved a good deal, but his freedom of manoeuvre was hampered by his dependence on Labour party support in the Dáil. In January 1933 he called a snap election. It was bitterly fought, and was characterized by disturbances much greater than those of the previous campaign. De Valera told O'Duffy to ensure complete Garda impartiality, though there were many instances where the police were too few in number to prevent or to contain intimidation, disruption, or rioting. While Cumann na nGaedheal again maintained that they were placed at a disadvantage by republican harassment, the ACA proved a robust defender of the party's interests.[14] The result of the election was a devastating shock both to that party and to those in Britain who looked to Cosgrave to bring Ireland back to its senses: in an unusually high poll Fianna Fáil won an overall majority, and the editor of *The Times* heard 'groans' in London 'on de Valera's now assured victory'.[15] De Valera now had unequivocal popular endorsement for what he had done and for what he proposed to do in economic, political, and constitutional affairs. In the jaundiced words of one opponent, he could also begin to 'take his political cloak off' those republicans whom he 'found . . . he could not carry with him'.[16] The next two years were to see a loosening of the ties that had bound Fianna Fáil and the IRA. They were also to see what was potentially the greatest threat posed to civilian government since the army mutiny, one which emanated not from the IRA

---

[12] Gilmore, *Republican Congress*, 7; Manning, *The Blueshirts*, 31.   [13] Ibid. 83.
[14] Brady, *Guardians*, 178–9; Lee, *Ireland*, 178; Manning, *The Blueshirts*, 16–17.
[15] Geoffrey Dawson's diary, 27 Jan. 1933, Bodleian Library, Oxford, MS Dawson 37.
[16] Michael Hayes to Gerry Boland, 26 Apr. 1966, UCDA, Hayes papers, P53/276.

or its left-wing offshoots but from the right of the political spectrum, the profoundly anti-Fianna Fáil and anti-communist ACA.[17]

ii. Public Order and Internal Security, 1933–1937: The Blueshirts

In the wake of his second victory, de Valera took the action in relation to the
Garda which his supporters had demanded a year earlier. As minister for justice
he appointed P. J. Ruttledge, a resolute Mayo solicitor who had served in the
phantom republican government in the mid-1920s. On 22 February 1933
O'Duffy was dismissed as Garda commissioner, after refusing an alternative
appointment at the same salary as controller of prices in the Department of
Industry and Commerce. The second Garda commissioner to serve the state
thus became the second, though not the last, to be fired by a government of the
day. Special legislation was passed to allow the granting of a pension, a sop
which did nothing to assuage O'Duffy. His removal, coming so soon after a
rowdy election in which the police had obeyed government instructions and
had performed with commendable impartiality, caused a sensation: why sack
him when he had demonstrated his reliability? The answer perhaps lies in a
crisis within the Special Branch described below, but if so this was probably the
occasion rather than the cause of the government's action. Whatever the reason
behind the sacking, the tempestuous general was now free to launch himself on
a dramatic though short-lived political career.

O'Duffy's dismissal was a transparently political act. Cumann na nGaedheal,
drawing a veil over their own difficulties with him when in government,
denounced it as naked appeasement of the IRA. More dispassionately, it has
been argued that O'Duffy had continued to be a highly efficient police chief
under Fianna Fáil, while there was also an obvious case for keeping so turbulent
a personality inside the tent. Against this must be put the grounds for getting rid
of him. These included most obviously his would-be coup in 1931/2, and the
doubts which that naturally accentuated about his reliability. There were also
other factors. He had been in charge for a decade, and he had set a highly personal stamp on the force. There was a case for change simply on those grounds.
In addition, his qualities of drive and leadership were matched by his itch for
excitement. His assessment of political developments of any sort had always
been melodramatic, in contrast to the deadpan reporting of the Special Branch,
and he had developed an unprofessional obsession with the communist menace. Finally, despite Fianna Fáil's pursuit of reconciliation with the republican
movement there had been continuing problems within the Special Branch. In
August 1932 two prominent IRA men, George Gilmore and T. J. Ryan, had been

---

[17] M. Manning, *Irish Political Parties: An Introduction* (Dublin, 1972), 15.

badly roughed up by two detectives during a labour dispute in Clare, where relations between police and republicans had been particularly bitter for years. A sworn inquiry found that the detectives had assaulted the men, offences which the inquiry chairman attributed 'largely to lack of proper instructions and proper supervision'.[18] Many Fianna Fáilers fastened on this episode as further proof that the Special Branch should be disbanded, but despite pre-election promises the government proceeded cautiously. A cabinet committee was set up to examine the future of the Special Branch, while the two detectives were dismissed and their victims were compensated. Five months later the head of the Special Branch, David Neligan, was suspended after organizing a collection for the dismissed men. Neligan had proved himself a calm and competent policeman since the Special Branch had assumed responsibility for political policing in 1925, but he had an exceptionally ugly reputation because of his alleged conduct during the civil war. The calculated act of defiance which led to his removal spoke a good deal for his courage, but the outcome was inevitable. He was ultimately given a sinecure at the same salary in the Land Commission.[19] In February 1933, his acting replacement Inspector E. M. O'Connell was arrested and charged with a breach of the Official Secrets Act, along with Colonel Michael Hogan of army headquarters. A few days later O'Duffy was dismissed. There followed a somewhat farcical trial, in which it transpired that O'Connell had simply continued Neligan's practice of passing examples of left-wing publications to Colonel Hogan, whose brother Professor James Hogan was engaged in alarmist research on Irish communism. Both Hogan and O'Connell were acquitted. It has been argued that the help given to Professor Hogan was innocuous, scarcely grounds for disciplinary action let alone for a criminal trial.[20] But James and Michael Hogan were brothers of the combative former Cumann na nGaedheal minister Patrick Hogan, and Cumann na nGaedheal had become increasingly reckless players of the red card in their attacks on Fianna Fáil. It was at the least remarkably imprudent for Neligan and O'Connell to continue to use official records to assist research plainly intended *inter alia* to discredit the party now in government—when it appeared later that year, the work proved both alarmist and frankly partisan.[21]

The turmoil within the Garda reflected the government's desire to tighten its grip on the machinery of justice. There were two important changes within Justice itself. First, the head of the prisons division was sent to join David Neligan in bureaucratic exile in the Land Commission, a clear indication of government disfavour. Secondly, Henry O'Freil, the secretary of the department,

---

[18] Cosgrave to Hayes, 8 May 1933, Hayes papers, P53/81; Justice memorandum, 28 Sept. 1932, quoting a letter from Patrick Lynch KC, the inquiry chairman, DT, S. 2206.

[19] Brady, *Guardians*, 173–6; Bryan and Andrews interviews.

[20] Brady, *Guardians*, 176–7. Hogan had served as army director of intelligence in 1923.

[21] DT, S. 2396; J. Hogan, *Could Ireland become Communist?* (Dublin, 1933).

who 'had not in fact had much to do with the office since November 1930, being full occupied with the Tariff Commission', saw his secondment made permanent, much to his displeasure. He was succeeded not by a career official but by D. J. Browne, a solicitor from Tralee alleged to have Fianna Fáil connections. Whatever his political credentials, in less than a year Browne too was rusticated, being sent to the Revenue Commissioners. His replacement S. A. Roche proved more durable, and remained calmly in place until his sudden death in 1947.[22] In public eyes, however, the most conspicuous appointment was that of a successor to O'Duffy as commissioner. The government's choice fell on Colonel Ned Broy, then a relatively obscure chief superintendent, over the heads of a number of more senior but politically suspect officers. Broy was an ex-RIC sergeant who, like Neligan, had become an important IRA informant. After the treaty he had joined the army, before reverting to a police job in 1925. His was an unexpected and, as it transpired, a somewhat unfortunate selection for the post of commissioner. He was not well known inside or outside the force, and his appointment branded him as a Fianna Fáil hack despite his pro-treaty background. Although he had one trait which his flamboyant predecessor conspicuously lacked—caution—he was not a sufficiently strong character to resist political pressure, and during his time in charge he seems to have been largely at the mercy of Justice. But, whatever the force's private opinion of him, his orders were obeyed.

Political conditions worsened following O'Duffy's dismissal. Under Cosgrave, policy had been geared towards defending the more productive farmers, because agricultural goods were by far the country's biggest export; under de Valera, their interests were discounted, for both economic and social reasons, with long-term results which remain debatable.[23] The impact of the economic war on the rural economy was so great that, even without the rifts left by the civil war, some protest movement involving the strong farmers who were heavily dependent on the export trade would have been inevitable. Agitation, intimidation, and violence had never been the sole preserve of the dispossessed in rural Ireland, as events under the Cosgrave government had shown: tillage farmers had organized unofficial militias to fight labour unrest during and immediately after the civil war, for example, while disputes in the nascent sugar beet industry had been characterized by xenophobia and threats if farmers did not receive what they considered a fair price for their produce.[24] What the ACA provided was an organizational and political focus for unrest which had to find some outlet.

---

[22] Justice confidential print on the IRA, 1935–40, p. xiii, MacEntee papers, P67/526; Lee, *Ireland*, 176.

[23] For a recent economic assessment see J. P. Neary and C. O'Grada, 'Protection, Economic War and Structural Change: The 1930s in Ireland', *Irish Historical Studies*, 27/107 (May 1991), 250–66.

[24] J. Cullen, 'Patrick J. Hogan TD, Minister for Agriculture, 1922–1932' (unpublished Ph.D. diss. Dublin City University, 1993), 170–1.

In March 1933 the burgeoning ACA adopted a blue shirt with shoulder straps and black beret as a uniform, and a straight-arm salute later became standard practice. All this was unarguably in imitation of parties of the radical Right in Europe, and it bolstered the case of those who argued that the organization was fascist both in inspiration and in aspiration.[25] The uniform gave a further fillip to the ACA, increasing its visibility and attracting new recruits throughout the country. The promotion of a vigorous 'sporting and social life' for young Blueshirts and Blueblouses, again an echo of European radical movements, greatly enhanced the ACA's appeal to young people in rural Ireland starved of other outlets for recreation and entertainment.[26] The Cumann na nGaedheal leadership, shell-shocked at the outcome of the election, half-demented with fear of the communist menace, and mindful of the Catholic Church's benevolent attitude towards European fascist parties, saw the ACA as the best means of securing both national salvation and political retribution. The government, composed of men with extensive experience both of revolution and of subversion, was alarmed: here was a body which in the space of a year had moved from being a non-party organization concerned with the interests of ex-soldiers to one which was openly hostile to the government's economic and political policies, whose leaders lauded the virtues of physical force as an antidote to republican disruption of political debate, and which had adopted an overtly militarized form. The government's unease deepened in July when O'Duffy yielded to the blandishments of Cumann na nGaedheal emissaries and accepted the leadership of the ACA, which he promptly renamed the National Guard.[27] The organization adopted a new constitution which was a synthesis of Catholicism, anti-communism, nationalism, and economic and social corporatism. Within a couple of months O'Duffy, who in de Valera's words until recently 'had it as his first duty to see that the law was obeyed and that the Constitution was obeyed', began to denounce the inadequacies of parliamentary democracy in general and the Free State constitution in particular, though he explicitly repudiated the suggestion that the Blueshirts were fascist. In July he announced plans for the revival, under Blueshirt auspices, of the annual commemoration for Griffith, Collins, and O'Higgins, hitherto a damp squib of an event held outside Leinster House each August between 1927 and 1931. Arrangements were made to bring Blueshirts from all parts of the country for the occasion. Despite O'Duffy's protestations that the Blueshirts were a strictly law-abiding organization, the parallel with Mussolini's march on Rome was obvious to anyone who followed public affairs (he made the comparison himself in conversation with an Italian official a year later). What would the government's response be?[28]

[25] Manning, *The Blueshirts*, 55–7; Gilmore, *Republican Congress*, 8.
[26] M. Cronin, 'Blueshirts, Sports and Socials', *History Ireland* (Autumn 1994), 43.
[27] Manning, *The Blueshirts*, 69–73.
[28] *Dáil Debates*, vol. 49, col. 1060, 1 Aug. 1932; D. Keogh, *Ireland and Europe, 1919–1948* (Dublin, 1988), 44.

O'Duffy's announcement presented de Valera with both a challenge and an opportunity. There was information—some of it provided by O'Duffy when still commissioner—that elements in the Blueshirts had access to weapons. A parade so close to government buildings and to Leinster House posed obvious dangers, if not of a *coup d'état* then of a loss of government control and authority. Even if the intentions of the organizers were entirely peaceful, and all the Blueshirts unarmed, their appearance en masse would undoubtedly provoke a major counter-demonstration and street violence from republicans. The likelihood of such clashes, and the more tenuous possibility of a Blueshirt plot against the state, prompted three exceptional steps.

First, the Garda visited holders of licensed firearms throughout the country to demand that they surrender their weapons. Amongst those affected were former ministers of the Cosgrave government, some of whom were most reluctant to relinquish the only protection which they felt they had left against republican assaults. They pointed out that de Valera had made no concomitant moves to impound the far more sinister collection of weapons in IRA hands. O'Duffy himself had to hand over two revolvers, which led to Cumann na nGaedheal accusations that the government was deliberately exposing him to assassination; this claim was refuted quite effectively by Ruttledge, who told the Dáil that O'Duffy had demanded that his police bodyguard be withdrawn, and that when 'offered the guard back again to protect him . . . said he was only a tout and would not have him'. The impounding of legally held weapons was clearly calculated to show Cumann na nGaedheal and the Blueshirts that the state would not allow them to become an armed counterweight to the IRA. It had the additional benefit, however, of preparing the ground for the eventual seizure of IRA arms. De Valera's strategy of gently weaning republicans away from violence required action to prevent the IRA's bitterest enemies from arming themselves: how else could he persuade the IRA that their own guns were now entirely redundant and must be put aside?[29]

The furore over legally held arms somewhat overshadowed a more significant innovation in public order policy, the rapid recruitment and deployment of a new intake of armed police initially charged with protective duties. In some respects a throwback to the CID and Citizens Defence Corps of the civil war era, the 'Broy Harriers' differed in that on this occasion the raw recruits given guns, police powers, and a ten-minute lecture on the law were of unimpeachable republican pedigree, men whose only previous experience of the law had been in breaking it. It was widely alleged that they were hand-picked by the Fianna Fáil TD Oscar Traynor, who had commanded the IRA's Dublin brigade at the outbreak of the civil war and who retained close links with his former comrades. Although the government maintained that the new men were simply an over-

---

[29] *Dáil Debates*, vol. 49, cols. 1028–72, 1 Aug. 1932.

due influx needed to bring the Garda back up to its established strength, in effect they constituted a separate unit on whom ministers, somewhat nervous about police and army loyalty, could rely to act vigorously in any confrontation with the Blueshirts. The new intake siphoned off fighting talent from the IRA, but their gradual absorption into the mainstream force was to have serious consequences. While some became useful officers, many remained inefficient and unruly, impervious to discipline because they had Traynor's ear. As both Blueshirts and IRA were to discover, they were prone to rough measures and they were very quick to use their guns. There was considerable friction and mistrust between Harriers and experienced Special Branch officers, who resented having to work alongside, and sometimes under the supervision of, hardened republican political appointees. These tensions probably played their part in the effective demotion of a number of detectives in 1934, action subsequently reversed through a court decision to the great benefit of political policing. Most seriously of all, however, some of the new men never lost their republican roots: in 1939 army intelligence concluded that no less than five Harriers serving in the Special Branch were 'wrong'uns' actively helping the IRA, an indelicate assessment borne out by events in 1940 and 1941.[30]

The third step taken to counteract the Blueshirt threat was to invoke the special powers provided under article 2A of the constitution, a decision later defended in terms virtually indistinguishable from those used by the Cosgrave regime in 1931: the government so acted 'only because there was no other means at its disposal of carrying out its supreme obligation to maintain peace and preserve the democratic institutions entrusted to its care'. The military tribunal was reconvened to try cases brought under 2A, and the Blueshirt parade planned for 13 August was banned. Protesting that his intentions had been entirely legal and pacific, O'Duffy reluctantly complied with this decision. Just over a week later his 'National Guard' was proclaimed an illegal organization. The weapons which Cumann na nGaedheal had deployed when in government to curb the IRA were now being turned against their putative saviour, while the IRA itself remained a legal organization on civil though increasingly strained terms with Fianna Fáil.[31]

The opposition's response to the government's move against O'Duffy's organization was emphatic: within weeks Cumann na nGaedheal and the small Centre Party united with the Blueshirts to form a new political party, Fine Gael, under O'Duffy's leadership, and its TDs took to wearing the blue shirt in Dáil Éireann. The Fine Gael manifesto, while frankly corporatist in its thinking, emphasized its strictly democratic aims and methods, but from the outset there was an ambiguity about its ultimate direction and purpose. What O'Duffy and

[30] Bell, *The Secret Army*, 107; Brady, *Guardians*, 197–200; Bryan interview.
[31] Sean Moynihan to Norman Thomas, 5 June 1935, DT, S. 2266.

Cosgrave had in common was a fear of communism, a loathing of Fianna Fáil, and a detestation of the IRA. But Cosgrave and the majority of his parliamentary colleagues were concerned primarily to win back political power through the ballot box: they thought that the consequences for farmers of the economic war would turn rural Ireland against Fianna Fáil, and they looked to the Blueshirts to mobilize public support and to provide protection against republican assaults and disruption of their political activities. De Valera's invocation of article 2A, less than two years after he had trenchantly denounced it as an instrument of tyranny, they saw as unwarranted and vindictive, a partisan abuse of the constitution to retard the opposition's political recovery as the impact of the trade dispute with Britain deepened. The Blueshirts played a cat and mouse game with the law, changing the organization's formal title three times to evade proscription, while the anti-Fianna Fáil majority in the Senate blocked a potentially effective uniforms bill intended to make the wearing of the blue shirt illegal. All this was arguably within the spirit of the constitution by which Cosgrave and his colleagues set such store. However, O'Duffy's ambitions were less clear: while his political ideas were and remained eclectic and confused, he revelled in the drama and mob violence which enveloped party politics as the Blueshirts, the Garda, and republicans slugged it out in towns and cities throughout the state.

Analysis of O'Duffy's political intentions and of the Blueshirt movement generally is complicated by a number of factors. The first is O'Duffy's authoritarian and bombastic personality: he saw himself as a man of destiny, but so long as he was in unchallenged command he was relatively indifferent to the direction pursued. Secondly, beyond his anti-communism and his hostility towards Fianna Fáil because they had fired him he had no coherent political agenda at all: some of the more cerebral Cumann na nGaedheal politicians may have grasped the intricacies of corporatist ideology, but O'Duffy was not one of them. He imitated and he borrowed from right-wing exemplars in Europe without any attempt to accommodate their doctrines to Irish social and economic conditions.[32] The third factor complicating analysis of O'Duffy's political intentions is that he and the Blueshirt movement were nurtured by some of those who considered themselves the makers of Irish democracy. Thus, when in August 1933 de Valera had bracketed the Blueshirts with the IRA as 'two forces which will ultimately mean civil war in this country', Patrick Hogan replied that de Valera 'is never more insincere and never more a pettifogger than when he thumps the desk . . . I think there is more real nationality and democracy in General O'Duffy's little finger than in his whole body'. In Cumann na nGaedheal eyes, the Blueshirts offered no threat to anyone or anything operating within

---

[32] E. Broderick, 'The Corporate Labour Policy of Fine Gael, 1934', *Irish Historical Studies*, 29/113 (May 1994), 88–99.

the law and the constitution: they were an unarmed and disciplined movement which stood up for the rights of those hardest hit by the economic war and confronted only those republican and communist forces of disorder which the government would not curb.[33] This vision of O'Duffy as saviour and servant of the treaty settlement, vanquisher of communism and charismatic counterweight to de Valera's populism led Cumann na nGaedheal and the small Centre Party into their short-lived merger with the Blueshirts. That alliance fell apart within a year, as O'Duffy and his acolytes moved from condoning to encouraging outright illegality, including street violence against republicans and on occasion against the Garda, non-payment of land annuities, the withholding of local authority rates, organized disruption of communications, and resistance to sequestration of the property of rates defaulters. This changed the nature of Blueshirt activities from being anti-republican to being directly anti-state. The systematic non-payment of legal debts and the 'disappearance of the bailiff' was, as has been seen, a spectre which had haunted the imagination of Kevin O'Higgins, the high priest of the rule of civil law, in the early 1920s. Furthermore, the political reputations of Cosgrave and his colleagues as consolidators of the state rested partly on the resolution with which they had tamed recalcitrant local authorities unwilling to collect local taxes.[34] O'Duffy's incitements to illegality were undermining the very principles of law-bound, upright civic society which Cosgrave held most dear. Furthermore, as the *Catholic Bulletin* observed, the 1934 local elections 'sounded the Last Post for Fascism in Ireland', painfully demonstrating majority support for Fianna Fáil despite a burgeoning of Blueshirt membership, and the hardships brought about by the economic war.[35]

This new reverse threw Fine Gael into turmoil. Not only did the Blueshirt leadership's penchant for street violence go against the grain for men who had spent a decade in office attempting to corral political dispute within the confines of the Oireachtas, but it did not produce electoral benefits. Underpinning these disappointments was the sense that O'Duffy was too volatile and egocentric a leader for a constitutional political party. His policy pronouncements were frequently contradictory, he maintained a bellicose line on partition quite alien to Fine Gael's Cumann na nGaedheal heritage, and if not a fully fledged fascist himself he was in amicable contact with fascist politicians in other countries. In September 1934, under pressure from Cosgrave and other leading party figures, he resigned the leadership. A power struggle then ensued within the

---

[33] *Dáil Debates*, vol. 49, col. 1071, 1 Aug. 1933. This comment may have owed more to Hogan's remarkable talent for political invective than to conviction, because he entertained private doubts about O'Duffy. Manning, *The Blueshirts*, 101. For Hogan's political career see Cullen, 'Hogan'.
[34] E. O'Halpin, 'The Origins of City and County Management', in *City and County Management: A Retrospective* (Institute of Public Administration, Dublin, 1991), 4–12.
[35] 'Romanus', 'The Truth about Irish Fascism', *Catholic Bulletin*, 24/9 (Sept. 1934), 740.

Blueshirts, as rival factions emerged for and against the turbulent general. Here we need only note that O'Duffy's departure from Fine Gael deprived the Blueshirts of the electoral legitimacy which had, however scantily, cloaked the movement's activities.[36] While they remained organizationally formidable for a further year, they had been politically marginalized.

It is unarguable that between 1933 and 1935 the Blueshirts posed a significant direct threat to public order, both by their own activities and by the temptation which they offered to their republican enemies. Despite the occasional shot fired at or by Blueshirts in affrays with republicans and the police, however, they never either planned or threatened organized armed action against the state. Furthermore, contrary to Fianna Fáil fears neither the army nor the Garda wavered in their loyalty to the state, despite some overtures by O'Duffy.[37] The Broy Harriers and uniformed Gardai, sometimes fearsomely equipped with borrowed army weapons and vehicles, were the government's main instrument against them. Troops were used only sparingly, and in a supporting role, to help control potential disturbances. G2—army intelligence—was precluded from any investigation of either Blueshirt or republican activities other than where the army's own internal security was involved: there was an obvious danger of penetration by the Blueshirts, and because both Blueshirt and republican prisoners were held in army custody problems of prison security also arose.[38] The military tribunal, initially convened in October 1931 to jail republicans and communists, became an efficient if somewhat cursory instrument of justice against men from the opposing poles of Irish politics. By 1935, having provided Fianna Fáil with the incidental benefit of proving the reliability of police and army, the public order crisis posed by the Blueshirts had blown itself out.

The sundering of his conventional party political links saw O'Duffy move further down the path of extra-parliamentary action. As he did so the dwindling residue of his movement drifted further from the mainstream of politics, and by 1936 it was no longer regarded as a significant force for good or ill in national affairs. Freed of his penchant for ostentatious street politics, Fine Gael immediately reverted to Cumann an nGaedheal type, respectable, pious, and churlish within the Oireachtas, and virtually invisible outside it. The Blueshirts were not to make domestic mischief again, though the outbreak of the Spanish civil war in the summer of 1936 offered some of the more zealous of the remaining members the opportunity to fight communism and anticlericalism head on. The government made half-hearted attempts to prevent Irishmen travelling to

---

[36] Keogh, *Ireland and Europe*, 47–50.

[37] Bryan interview; Keogh, *Ireland and Europe*, 44–5.

[38] Papers on the loan of military vehicles and equipment to the Garda are in DT, S. 2205; Bryan transcripts, pp. 1–2; Bryan interview. For example, Bryan investigated the smuggling out of messages from both Blueshirt and IRA prisoners. Decades later, at a meeting of the Irish Historical Society, he mentioned this to Maurice Twomey, who said: 'Oh, I had a good book code. You'd be wasting your time trying to solve that problem.'

join the war, but about seven hundred men led by O'Duffy circumvented this embargo and departed on a short-lived 'Crusade in Spain' which began in chaos and continued in farce: their first fatalities were inflicted by fire from their own side, they saw little serious fighting, and after six months almost all voted to return home to Ireland. Their inglorious fate proved a boon to the government, relieved to see such troublemakers depart Irish shores and delighted at the humiliation which they encountered in Spain; what was dangerous, however, was the strengthening of the international fascist credentials of O'Duffy and one or two of his officers. Links between former Blueshirts and kindred spirits in Italy, Spain, and Germany were to cause the security authorities some headaches in succeeding years.[39]

iii. Public Order and Internal Security, 1933–1937: The Republican Movement

In parallel with the growth and decline of the Blueshirts, and for much the same reasons, the mid-1930s saw a sea change in militant republican strategy and ideology. The optimism which had infected republicans in the months following de Valera's advent to power gradually faded. They were particularly stung by what they regarded as unfair police tactics during and after the January 1933 election, by the use of the military tribunal against republicans as well as Blueshirts, by the evident popularity of de Valera's step by step approach to the dismantling of the treaty settlement, and by his repeated public and private appeals to the IRA to lay down their weapons and embrace constitutional politics. Despite the ousters of O'Duffy and Neligan, they saw the Garda and the army as Free State partisans bent on protecting the Blueshirts.[40] They drew little comfort from the creation of the Broy Harriers, rightly seeing this as a device designed partly to wean republican activists away from the IRA. They were also disheartened by the establishment of a new army reserve, the Volunteer Force, which they noted appeared 'the greatest menace which we have at present' because 'the officers . . . are of good records' and because it promised to draw off yet more talent. Compensation for ex-public servants victimized under the Cosgrave regime, and the provision of pensions for republican veterans of the War of Independence, implicitly contingent on good behaviour, cooled the residual ardour of many activists.[41] A concerted response to these developments

---

[39] Manning, *The Blueshirts*, 146–63, 201–7. See E. O'Duffy, *Crusade in Spain* (Dublin, 1938) for his account of this episode.

[40] Gilmore, *Republican Congress*, 8–14; Cronin, *The McGarrity Papers*, 155–8.

[41] Comments attributed to Tom Barry in notebook containing an MS record of the IRA convention of March 1934, MacEntee papers, P67/525. Papers on the review of cases of Gardai dismissed for political reasons are in DT, S. 6442. Bowman, *De Valera and the Ulster Question*, 125.

was, however, difficult to achieve, because the IRA itself was still riven by disputes about its future purpose and direction.

The IRA's difficulties were not all of de Valera's making. The inroads made by the Left into senior positions since the mid-1920s, culminating in the creation of Saor Éire in 1931, had provoked increasing scepticism amongst traditionalists. While all could agree on the desirability of taking on the Blueshirts, many senior figures doubted the wisdom of espousing a doctrine of social revolution which appeared remote from Irish conditions, inimical to public opinion, a great embarrassment because it raised 'the Communistic Bogey', and a monumental distraction from the fundamental task of undoing the treaty. The Left argued that the IRA should not ignore 'the ideal of James Connolly', but they found few takers.[42] The issue came to a head in March 1934 at an IRA convention which considered a series of leftist resolutions by George Gilmore, Peadar O'Donnell, and Mick Price. Their proposals drew an exasperated response from Tom Barry, the IRA's most experienced leader:

I maintain that we are too apt to rely on resolutions. We should apply ourselves to what we can do—not to what we say . . . There has been far too much stress put upon the social side. There is not a word mentioned about the destroyers at present in our harbours, the military in the north & south.[43]

The convention took its lead from Barry, and voted against the Left's attempts to radicalize the IRA's agenda. O'Donnell, Gilmore, and a number of other prominent figures then quit the IRA, and through a flurry of resolutions at a meeting in Athlone established the 'Republican Congress', a new 'revolutionary organisation' to 'give expression to the aims and activities of those desirous of achieving an Irish Workers' Republic' through struggle against both British imperialism and indigenous capitalism. In terms of practical revolutionary politics, this soon proved an ill-judged act: it consigned radical analysis of and protest about economic and political conditions to the verbose backwater of ultramontane communism. Although it continued to attract the dutiful attention of the Special Branch, the revolutionary Left caused the state no further embarrassment or trouble for years. Many of its most active proponents went to fight for the Spanish republic when, in contrast to the inconsequential and dispiriting experience of O'Duffy's volunteers, they saw serious and sustained action and fought with bravery and distinction.[44] This in turn won some belated

---

[42] Criticisms of the IRA for ignoring 'working class politics' by Peter O'Connor, a veteran of the Abraham Lincoln battalion of the International Brigade during the Spanish civil war, in *The Irish Times*, 7 Oct. 1994.

[43] Notes of IRA convention, MacEntee papers, P67/525; Gilmore, *Republican Congress*, 28–30; Twomey interview. He was dismissive of the revolutionary aspirations of O'Donnell and his associates, saying that the Left achieved a short-lived prominence out of all proportion to their influence and position within the republican movement.

[44] Police reports on communist activity in the 1930s and early 1940s can be seen in the MacEntee papers, P67/522 and 526; Bryan interview. The Irish contribution to the defence of the Spanish republic

plaudits for the Irish Left. Partly in consequence, O'Donnell and Gilmore, the men chiefly responsible for the establishment of Republican Congress, in later decades became respected figures well beyond the surreal world of Irish Stalinism. But their departure from the IRA, and the rapid evaporation of their new movement, saw their permanent exclusion from militant republican though not from communist affairs.[45] The IRA, rid at last of class warriors, was left free to pursue its own more narrowly nationalist agenda.

In the course of the year in which it lanced its socialist boil, the IRA finally abandoned the hope that if it displayed what it regarded as restraint its former comrades in Fianna Fáil would come around to its way of thinking. Police action against republican rioters, and the use of emergency powers to jail republicans as well as Blueshirts, was accompanied by a constant stream of public warnings from de Valera that the IRA must either embrace constitutional politics or face inevitable repression: public order ranked above fraternity in Fianna Fáil's priorities, while only the state could be allowed to use armed force. The movement also saw the gradual erosion of its strength as republican-minded men were drawn into the paid ranks of the Broy Harriers and, from early in 1934, of the army's new Volunteer Force. Some senior figures and many ordinary members made their peace with de Valera and joined Fianna Fáil, others simply became inactive. The schism which produced the Republican Congress also weakened the IRA, taking away some of its brightest if most turbulent spirits. Cumulatively the movement was losing talent at every level. The precipitous decline of the Blueshirts after the split in Fine Gael compounded rather than eased the IRA's problems: it was running out of enemies other than the Fianna Fáil-controlled state itself to mobilize against, and that state now had the support of many ex-IRA converts. Units were still allowed to drill unimpeded, but they were now under watchful police eyes: a volunteer later commented that the IRA 'never seemed to realise' the intelligence advantage which they accorded the police by flaunting themselves so openly when it was obvious that a crackdown was likely. Once the government had the problem of Blueshirt agitation firmly under control, some action against what remained of the active IRA was only a matter of time.[46]

---

is covered in various works including S. Cronin, *Frank Ryan: The Search for the Republic* (Dublin, 1980). The late Frank Edwards frequently spoke to this writer of his time in Spain.

[45] Gilmore, *Republican Congress, passim*; W. K. Anderson, *James Connolly and the Irish Left (Dublin,* 1994), 132–5; Bell, *The Secret Army,* 110–15; Twomey interview, 1975; R. English, 'Socialism and Republican Schism in Ireland: The Emergence of the Republican Congress in 1934', *Irish Historical Studies,* 27/105 (May 1990), 64–5. Broadcast interview with Nora Harkin in *Would you believe?,* RTE 1, 13 Jan. 1994.

Despite frequent tensions, the Irish communist movement remained under the nominal control of the CPGB until 1943. On this see B. McLoughlin and E. O'Connor, 'Sources on Ireland and the Communist International, 1920–1943', *Saothar,* 21 (1996), 103–5.

[46] Tape-recorded interview by my late father with Bob Bradshaw, undated, mid-1970s, in my possession, cited hereafter as 'Bradshaw tape'. On Bradshaw see U. Mac Eoin, *The IRA in the Twilight Years, 1923–1948* (Dublin, 1997), 421–8.

Luck played a part in what happened. In February 1935 a Longford IRA unit raided the house of a land agent involved in a dispute with tenant farmers. The agent was injured and his son, Richard More O'Ferrall, was mortally wounded. This inept murder—the intention had been to intimidate the agent, not to shoot anyone—further hardened official attitudes. It was followed a few weeks later by violence during a protracted public transport strike in Dublin, when the IRA declared its 'willingness to assist the workers in their struggle'. A number of Gardai, some armed and some unarmed, were shot and wounded, and army lorries providing an emergency bus service were fired on, actions which suggested that the movement still had a social conscience despite its split with the Left. The government's response to these provocations was to step up pressure on the IRA in Dublin through raids, detentions, and the censorship and subsequent suppression of the republican newspaper *An Phoblacht*, while holding back from proscribing the organization itself.[47] De Valera's strategy of gradual assimilation had already reduced the IRA to a small rump, and proscription now might stir up public support. In addition, the outbreak of serious sectarian violence in Belfast in 1935 underlined the very difficult circumstances in which some northern nationalist communities lived. That in turn probably affected official attitudes towards the IRA: banning the organization might smack almost of collusion with the Stormont regime. It is clear that, while de Valera was fearful of the inflammatory potential of IRA action within Northern Ireland, his government was markedly more sympathetic to the organization's existence there—even as he moved decisively against the IRA within the jurisdiction, the legal fees of a northern republican on trial in Belfast were paid by External Affairs from the secret service vote. Despite Fianna Fáil's increasing severity towards the IRA, furthermore, we should note that thirty-five Blueshirt and republican prisoners, amongst them Con Lehane, a senior and unrepentant figure in the IRA, were freed from prison at Christmas 1935 as an act of clemency. Such early releases were to remain a feature of government policy for decades. They underline one of the enduring paradoxes of Irish politics, that the state's initially ferocious response to serious subversion can be succeeded almost immediately by extraordinary leniency.[48]

The government's patience with the IRA finally snapped in the spring of 1936 after two particularly callous killings, ones which by chance came soon after the Fianna Fáil national executive had urged party organizers of local parades marking the twentieth anniversary of the Easter rising to ensure that they would

---

[47] DT, S. 7494 and 5 contain papers and newspaper cuttings on IRA activity in 1935; Brady, *Guardians*, 227–9; English, 'Socialism and Republican Schism', 54. Maurice Twomey spoke warmly of the IRA's involvement in social action, such as raids on moneylenders, but was at pains to distinguish this from the conventional class war urged by the Left.

[48] Bowman, *De Valera and the Ulster Question*, 135; J. Connolly to J. A. Walshe, 21 May 1936, NA, DFA, P67; executive council decision of 17 Dec. 1935, contained in DT, S. 8395.

do nothing which would discourage committed republican veterans from taking part. In April the retired Vice Admiral Boyle Somerville, 'an old man of over seventy years' who since 1926 had provided references for locals wishing to join the Royal Navy, was shot dead in County Cork. A month later John Egan, a youth who had quit the IRA after being arrested for illegal drilling, was killed 'under the eyes of his mother' in Dungarvan. Each of these operations had the sanction of IRA GHQ, though there is some doubt whether the plan was to warn off Somerville rather than to shoot him, and in each case the logic was clear in traditional republican terms: the admiral was an agent of the enemy, suborning young men from their proper loyalty, while Egan was a deserter and possible informer.[49] Even within the notional framework of military law in which the IRA customarily couched its decisions, however, the killings were a plainly disproportionate response. Large numbers of IRA men, including senior officers, had left the organization unmolested since Fianna Fáil had taken office. Similarly, the IRA's grievance against Somerville was, in the words of one policeman, 'trivial in the extreme'. In providing character references for applicants he had done no more for the navy than the Garda did for the British army. (His death did have a short-term impact on recruiting but the Admiralty soon adopted the War Office procedure of relying on the Garda to screen applicants, as the navy's need for manpower grew.)[50] If it was time for the IRA to provoke a fight with the government, more prominent and deserving targets could surely have been found than a defenceless old man and an obscure youth whose killings inspired widespread revulsion and ecclesiastical condemnation. The action underscored the incoherence of the IRA's response to the political successes of constitutional republicanism.

The IRA paid a high price for its killings. In June 1936 it was finally declared an illegal organization, an indignity deeply resented by republicans despite their professed disdain for the Free State and its laws. The widely respected chief of staff Maurice Twomey, 'a very bright man', was jailed for three years by the military tribunal. Another prominent IRA man, Michael Conway, was convicted of the Egan murder and sentenced to death, although he later said he 'always knew' that he would be reprieved. In 1931 de Valera had spoken for republicans, denouncing the draconian emergency powers brought in by the Cosgrave government to curb the IRA; now he was using precisely the same measures to subdue his former comrades. Republicans protested, just as they had under the British and under Cosgrave, at the injustice of proscription, the iniquity of non-jury trials, the harshness of prison conditions, the futility of tyranny in the face

---

[49] Fianna Fáil national executive minutes, 1 Feb. 1936, Fianna Fáil archives, FF/342; S. Moynihan to N. Thomas, 6 Aug. 1936, DT, S. 2266; Bell, *The Secret Army*, 126–7; Coogan, *The IRA*, 120–4.

[50] Superintendent Croke to chief superintendent, Bandon, 5 Dec. 1958, NA, DFA, P351A; papers on navy recruiting can be found in PRO, ADM 178/91; minute by director of naval intelligence, 30 Apr. and 25 June 1936 and 5 Feb. 1937, ibid.

of the inalienable right of the Irish people to establish the pure republic. Mary MacSwiney, the purist of the pure doctrinaires, lambasted 'poor, poor foolish Dev. How are the mighty fallen!'[51] But it was not the mighty who had fallen, but three insignificant and defenceless men capriciously assassinated by an organization now hopelessly out of touch with popular politics.

The crackdown on the IRA provoked no serious public reaction. The republican movement had lost almost all its popular support, and the remaining ties of affiliation and respect which had bound it and Fianna Fáil together were almost sundered. While this at least removed any residual ambiguities about relations with de Valera, it also demonstrated the movement's utter political failure in the face of his triumphant apostasy. Vigorous Garda action underlined the fact that the government was bent on the thoroughgoing suppression of what remained of militant republicanism. The IRA could plan for the future in the knowledge that the Fianna Fáil state was now one of its principal enemies.

Twomey was succeeded as IRA chief of staff by Sean MacBride, a man of an altogether different stamp. While his pedigree and his personal courage were unimpeachable, by personality and by his legal training he revelled in starting arguments and in winning them, traits inimical to the effective leadership of a disparate movement under growing pressure. He was also one of a group which had urged the development of a new abstentionist republican political party, Cumann Poblachta na h-Éireann, which many of his comrades thought a dangerous distraction and which proved an utter failure.[52] Shortly after becoming chief of staff, he court-martialled his quartermaster-general Sean Russell, an out-and-out militarist who had travelled to America to promote the case for a campaign of attacks in Britain.[53] Russell was convicted of various technical misdemeanours and removed from his post, but the dispute deepened IRA divides between those who looked to and those who forswore any form of electoral politics, and between proponents of varying military strategies. MacBride was replaced in the autumn of 1936 by Tom Barry, and became director of intelligence: ironically in view of his eventual metamorphosis into a patron saint of Irish radicalism and of the international struggle for human rights, he then reportedly made 'the first contact' with agents of Hitler's Germany. In 1938 he withdrew from the IRA, and he gradually shifted his full attentions to his legal practice. He was to do the republican movement much greater service as a skilled courtroom defender in the years ahead than he had done as its military

---

[51] Bryan transcripts, p. 45; R. English, '"Paying no heed to public clamour": Irish Republican Solipsism in the 1930s', *Irish Historical Studies*, 28/112 (Nov. 1993), 428; private information; Bowman, *De Valera and the Ulster Question*, 125. Conway was released within two years.

[52] English, 'Paying no heed to public clamour', 426–31; Bell, *The Secret Army*, 130–1; Andrews interview.

[53] American diplomats in Ireland, chronically ill-informed about Irish politics, described Russell as having 'very pronounced communist views'. Owsley (Dublin) to State Department, 20 Oct. 1936, USNA, RG59, 841D.00/1110.

chief.[54] For the next three years it would be the man whom he had temporarily ousted from GHQ, Sean Russell, who would dominate IRA thinking and policy on armed action to achieve a republic.

Clarification of who its enemies were left the IRA with the problem of choosing what to do and where to act to advance the interests of the republic. Resolution of these dilemmas was complicated by factional disputes within the leadership, differences which have left their mark in contradictory and confused accounts of the evolution of republican policy between 1936 and 1938. A number of points are, however, clear. First, in the wake of the rupture with Fianna Fáil, the IRA felt that future action must appeal to rather than further alienate public opinion within the state. Secondly, by 1937 the IRA in Northern Ireland, emaciated and desperate, and under intense pressure following its killing of two supposed informers, wanted some show of support from their southern comrades. Tom Barry favoured concerted action, beginning with an attack on a military depot in Armagh, followed by the destruction of railway lines, and flying column operations. Implementation of the first phase of these plans was ignominiously aborted because of breaches of security, though Barry remained wedded to the principle that the IRA's first duty was to fight the occupier on Irish soil. There were some disturbances along the border, notably the burning of 'more than twenty Customs Houses' on the occasion of King George VI's coronation visit to Belfast in July 1937, but the bold campaign Barry pressed for never materialized.[55] His policy proposals came into conflict with another strand in republican thinking, that the fight should be taken directly to Britain. For some years Joe McGarrity, the most powerful figure in Irish republican politics in the United States, had urged this course. He won the agreement of Russell, who continued to work towards this end in Ireland and America even after his court martial in 1936. The issue was not resolved decisively until April 1938, when a majority of the army council backed Russell, causing Barry and his supporters to quit the IRA. This led in turn to the calamitous IRA bombing campaign of 1939–40, which is discussed below. Here we need simply to probe the thinking of those who made the case for that campaign, Russell and McGarrity.

Sean Russell was a professional revolutionary of an intensity, commitment, and endurance unusual even within the republican movement. A pure physical force man, he possessed what Richard English has termed 'an anti-political quality of mind'. In Russell's view the only way to advance the cause of the republic was by force. He was not prepared to compromise or to temporize: it

---

[54] Bell, *The Secret Army*, 130–2; G2 report on 'German IRA and related contacts', undated [1940?], MA, G2/X/0093; Andrews interview.

[55] G2 note on 'German, IRA and related contacts', and O'Donoghue note of his June 1940 conversation with Tom Barry, 23 Nov. 1943, G2/X/0093; Bell, *The Secret Army*, 134–5; Home Office memorandum, 30 July 1937, PRO, HO 45/20567.

was every republican's duty to fight Britain until she let go of Ireland. The timing of action would be determined not by political considerations but simply by resources: when enough men, guns, and explosives were in place, the campaign would start. If prosecuted with sufficient vigour, Britain would realize that the partition game was not worth the candle and would make peace on republican terms. Russell's most important supporter was McGarrity, himself the prisoner of a War of Independence mentality which left him disappointed and baffled by the course of republican politics since 1922, who could never fathom how de Valera could be so harsh towards his former comrades and so accommodating towards Britain. McGarrity controlled Clan na Gael, and he was an experienced and accomplished fund-raiser and gun-runner. He used these skills to assist Russell. McGarrity had been involved in the negotiations with German diplomats in the United States which had led to the 1916 rebellion, and he undoubtedly approved of the revival of links which Russell, who had participated in the IRA's abortive liaison with the Soviet Union in the mid-1920s, undertook in approaching the German embassy in Washington in 1936. Tom Barry later claimed that in supporting Russell's plans for a campaign in Britain 'Clan na Gael . . . were acting on behalf of German Agents there and that the source of financial aid was from that quarter also'. There is other evidence to suggest that from as early as 1936, in anticipation of war with Britain, Germany made various efforts through 'a number of different people' to 'get in touch with the IRA and different personalities in it'. Barry himself visited Germany late in 1937, though the American FBI later reported that 'such contact was casual' up to 1939.[56] There was nothing new in republican links with Britain's enemies: such understandings had been a mainstay of Irish separatist conspiracies since the 1790s. The renewal of ties between the IRA and Germany showed both the persistence of the old separatist assumption that England's enemies were automatically Ireland's friends, and the movement's enduring myopia about the political and strategic implications for Ireland and for Anglo-Irish relations of such alliances. De Valera was to show himself considerably more prescient about the dangers to Irish interests posed by any concordat between domestic subversives and foreign powers.

The debate within republican circles about the direction to take after June 1936 was no great secret. Fianna Fáil ministers well understood the minds of their former comrades—de Valera had meetings with both Russell and McGarrity in the year preceding official proscription of the IRA—and it is clear

---

[56] English, 'Paying no heed to public clamour', 436; conversation with Bob Bradshaw, 1976. Cronin, *The McGarrity Papers, passim*; Bowman, *De Valera and the Ulster Question*, 104–5, 125–6, and 193; O'Donoghue note of his June 1940 talk with Tom Barry; F. H. Hinsley and C. A. G. Simkins, *British Intelligence in the Second World War*, iv: *Security and Counter-Intelligence* (London, 1990), 16–17; G2 note on 'German, IRA and related contacts'; memorandum on Irish Republican Army, with J. Edgar Hoover to Adolph A. Berle, State Department, received 30 Sept. 1943, USNA, 841D.00/1421, cited hereafter as 'FBI 1943 report'; Bryan to Walshe, 4 Apr. 1946, DFA, A20/4.

that the police knew in general terms the positions taken by the various factions. But neither ministers nor the Garda appear to have anticipated that the IRA might once more seek outside help for its struggle. Consequently, the government only became aware of the fact of German interest in Russell's proposed campaign long after it had begun. Nor did the Garda seek or find traces of the covert activities of any foreign interests in Ireland—the hapless communist movement apart—until tipped off by the British in the spring of 1938. These were to prove significant intelligence failures.

iv. Anglo-Irish Relations, 1932–1938

The advent to power of Fianna Fáil in 1932, and its emphatic retention of office in the succeeding election a year later, wrought a transformation in Anglo-Irish relations. In retrospect the change appears one more of pace than of direction. For all its supposed deference to Britain, the Cosgrave government had played a forceful part in the redefinition of commonwealth relations on a basis of equality between former ruler and former colonies, and that process would assuredly have continued had Cumann na nGaedheal remained in office. So far from enhancing Ireland's practical independence of Britain through unilateral repudiation of the detested 1921 settlement, furthermore, de Valera pursued his aims through judicious exploitation of the provisions of the treaty, the conventions of commonwealth relations, and the protectionist convulsions of the international economy. The crown jewels of empire—the oath of allegiance, appeal to the Privy Council, the office of governor-general, and ultimately the position of the British monarch in Irish affairs—were prised out of the 1921 settlement through dexterous use of the instrument manufactured to enshrine them, the Free State constitution. Ultimately, and quite legally, that very constitution was replaced in 1937 by one which more accurately reflected Fianna Fáil thinking on social affairs, on the role of organized religion within the state, and on the still-burning issue of partition.[57]

The gradual realization that in pursuing his goals de Valera was playing the game within the written rules, in combination with the hard fact that his policies had proved electorally popular, wrought a gradual change in Anglo-Irish relations after 1933. The fixation with facing down de Valera until such time as Cosgrave would be returned to office, which had characterized the British government's initial discomfited reaction to Fianna Fáil's success, faded away as Whitehall came to terms with the new facts of Irish political life. If the angular, ascetic, enigmatic de Valera still conjured up images of Beelzebub in British minds, he was a devil whom they were gradually coming to know if not to

[57] *Bunreacht na hÉireann* (*Constitution of Ireland*) (Dublin, n.d.); Bowman, *De Valera and the Ulster Question*, 147–60.

understand. Furthermore, familiarity brought on a degree of boredom: between 1933 and the end of 1935 no one in London lost much sleep over Irish affairs, which were allowed to tick over at official level. By 1936, matters had so much quietened down that the War Office judged it safe to allow the dispatch of an army team to the Dublin horse show, something it had blocked since 1932 on the threadbare excuse that one could not be assembled (the Dominions Office was afterwards heartened by reports that the team had received a much warmer reception from the spectators than had de Valera). It is even arguable that the economic war, so far from threatening the fabric of Anglo-Irish relations, helped rather than hindered the maturation of relations between new state and former ruler. It allowed Fianna Fáil to take on Britain in a non-violent arena which fulfilled an atavistic yearning for a further swipe at the old oppressor; it disposed of the vexatious and emotive though highly technical issue of repayments to Britain for land purchase; and, fortuitously or not, it produced at least a rough equality of economic hardship in trade terms, while also serving Fianna Fáil's domestic industrial and employment objectives. From the British point of view, once the Irish had had their tilt against the realities of economic interdependence the visible cost of the war to Irish agriculture brought home to Fianna Fáil the desirability of a predictable and stable trade regime: the Irish-initiated coal/cattle pact of January 1935 marked the first step in that process. For both sides in the economic war honour was satisfied, some political capital accumulated, and no blood spilt. It also had the advantage of providing a suitable starting point for the intricate trade, fiscal, and defence negotiations of 1937/8 which culminated in the Anglo-Irish agreement of April 1938.[58]

In terms of Anglo-Irish relations, the most significant elements of the 1937 constitution were the exclusion of any reference to the British crown or commonwealth, and the irredentist articles 2 and 3. Article 2 defined the national territory of Ireland as the entire island and its surrounding seas, while article 3 deferred the exercise of Irish sovereignty over the six counties 'pending the reintegration of the national territory'. These articles were something of a fudge by de Valera, designed to steer a middle course between the thoroughgoing assertion of national territorial integrity urged by republicans within his party, and recognition of the political reality of a resilient Northern state supported by the majority of its population and forming part of the United Kingdom. Ironically, the claim was regarded by the British government and by unionists as so outrageous as to be completely fatuous, with the result that it had no serious impact on Anglo-Irish relations at all in the years immediately following its enunciation.[59]

[58] Minutes by Antrobus and by Ridgeway, 7 July 1932 and 18 Aug. 1936, PRO, DO 35/355/3. For somewhat contrasting assessments of the economic war see Neary and O'Grada, 'Protection, Economic War and Structural Change: The 1930s in Ireland', 262–3, and Lee, *Ireland*, 190–201; Bowman, *De Valera and the Ulster Question*, 116–21.

[59] Ibid. 146–60.

Trade, constitution, and partition apart, Anglo-Irish relations were characterized by pragmatism after 1932. Three pertinent areas require consideration: exchanges of security information and criminal intelligence, extradition, and immigration and passport control. Contacts on security issues such as communist activity seem to have lessened markedly after 1932, perhaps as much a function of the waning of red scares as of a frostier intergovernmental climate, while discussions with foreign police forces on conventional crime were hampered by a sceptical Finance, which found Broy an altogether less formidable adversary than O'Duffy. Despite the commissioner's claims that forgery, smuggling, passport offences, and the 'traffic in women' were intrinsically international crimes requiring close co-operation—'we have already had cases of international criminals operating here'—Finance dismissed his request to attend a police conference in Copenhagen with hauteur: 'the Minister would point out that the activities of international criminals are really not of much concern to the Saorstát'. More significantly, exchanges on republican activities abroad seem to have ceased for some years after Neligan's ouster from the Special Branch, although as already mentioned the Garda continued to carry out routine security checks on aspiring British army recruits. The absence of dialogue with the British police and security authorities may have contributed to the government's surprising ignorance of IRA/German contacts later in the decade.[60] The second area, the thorny problem of extradition, remained just that. Even when political offences were excluded from the equation, Justice was unable to find a statutory formula which would provide certainty in procedures between Britain and Ireland. In addition, after 1929 extradition simply did not operate between the two Irish states, although the RUC and the Garda notoriously worked out their own unofficial solution of dumping wanted men across the border.[61]

The third significant aspect of Anglo-Irish relations to be considered is that of passport and immigration control. Here, British security interests continued to be taken into account, just as British assistance was implicitly relied on, in the management of visa and immigration procedures. The British continued routinely to provide an updated blacklist, and the Irish authorities did their best to co-operate. Any misunderstandings seem to have been cleared up amicably with the minimum of fuss: for example, when in April 1932 'the "On Wah" . . . troupe of Chinese acrobats', booked to appear in Dublin's Capitol Theatre, were refused visas in Paris by a British official to travel via Britain, the matter was sorted out within days.[62] British concern that Ireland under Fianna Fáil might

---

[60] Memorandum by Broy, 19 Oct. 1934, and Finance to Justice, 16 May 1935, NA, DJ 4/114.

[61] Note of informal discussion with Mr Duff, 3 Mar. 1938, PRO, HO 45/14513; M. Farrell, *Sheltering the Fugitive? The Extradition of Irish Political Defenders* (Dublin, 1985), 31–3.

[62] Walshe (External Affairs) to Dixon (Home Office), 20 May 1932, PRO, HO 45/14631. By chance Collinson, the British official who initially refused the Chinese their visas, was posted to Dublin as passport control officer and MI6 operative in 1940.

become an entrepôt to the United Kingdom for mainland Europeans or other foreigners was misplaced, because the new government's attitude to immigrants was at least as robust as the Cosgrave administration's had been; indeed, in the autumn of 1932 it was claimed that the authorities had embarked on the systematic expulsion of all aliens who could not prove ten years' continuous residence in the state.[63] For all their rhetorical fellow feeling for oppressed peoples everywhere, Fianna Fáil adhered to the Justice view that Ireland was not a suitable location for hordes of importunate foreigners displaced from their own countries by war, by oppression, or by economic misfortune. Justice officials appeared to think that many of those fleeing from religious or racial persecution in Europe from the mid-1930s had done much to bring the catastrophe upon themselves, and would have to cope with the consequences accordingly. This was reflected in the drafting and passage of the 1935 Aliens Act, a measure emphatically intended to tighten immigration controls. While there would always be limited room for people bringing in specialist skills, or large amounts of money for investment, the act augmented the state's formidable battery of defences against inundation by refugees. The government saw Ireland as a small, poor, homogeneous, predominantly Catholic, and commercially innocent country, unfamiliar with the ways of foreigners, ill-equipped to accommodate them, and in perpetual danger of seeing precious national assets fall into the oily palms of devious Europeans abusing the innate hospitality of the Irish people. It was far better to keep them out than to have to ask them to leave, an attitude heartily endorsed by the British government, which had its own security reasons for wishing Ireland to remain free of foreigners. By and large, with exceptions such as some Austrian seminarians accorded asylum after the *Anschluss* on grounds of religious compatibility—and, perhaps, because in those more chaste times it was judged unlikely that they would corrupt Irish women, breed, take over Irish firms, or lend anyone money at usurious rates— the policy of exclusion enshrined in the 1935 act served its purpose. Notwithstanding the explicit recognition of the Jewish religion courageously included in article 44 of the 1937 constitution, only a lucky handful of European Jews fleeing from Hitler were to find refuge in Ireland in the late 1930s. When the government did agree to a minor relaxation in immigration rules, it was decided to concentrate on 'Christians with Jewish blood', and 'approximately 150 "non-Aryan" refugees from Germany were admitted for temporary refuge'.[64] In the state's view, there had to be limits even to Irish generosity and compassion.

---

[63] This claim was vigorously refuted by Duff in a letter to the Home Office of 18 Oct. 1932, PRO, HO 45/15630.

[64] Memoranda by Duff and by Costigan (Justice), 16 Nov. 1938 and 24 Sept. 1945, DT, S. 11007A.

v. Defence Policy and Practice, 1932–1938

The dexterity with which Frank Aiken handled the army as the first Fianna Fáil minister for defence has already been noted. The transition was probably helped by the fact that in the first months of Fianna Fáil rule, the army's energies were fully absorbed in logistical and ceremonial preparations for the Eucharistic Congress. Morale—and public esteem—were probably boosted by the army's important public role: a special mounted unit, the Blue Hussars, was established for ceremonial duties, while a miscellany of Air Corps aircraft flew over Dublin in cruciform formation. The national imperative that arrangements for the Congress run smoothly provided an excellent reason for postponing any tinkering with army structures and personnel, and allowed the military to demonstrate their usefulness to government in an altogether benign, apolitical sphere. Minor changes in security arrangements were made by Fianna Fáil, though the army may have welcomed these as they lessened their involvement in protective duty. A committee was also set up to examine, amongst other security matters, 'the question of establishing a special protective corps for coastal defence and other purposes'. Such a body did not materialize, though the inquiry may have contributed to the eventual establishment of the Volunteer Force in 1934. Only one policy departure threatened serious difficulties: Aiken ended the preferential treatment accorded to ex-soldiers in filling public sector jobs and awarding public contracts, an action which while understandable in the circumstances caused much resentment amongst former soldiers and helped to fuel the growth of the ACA.[65]

Most of the distinctive policy ideas which Fianna Fáil had put forward when in opposition were quietly set aside. Despite its adoption of a thoroughgoing protectionist policy to foster industrial development, the party in office evidently thought better of its earlier proposals for a national munitions industry. In 1932 regular army strength was about six thousand, supported by largely notional reserve forces. In its first year in office the party did reduce defence spending somewhat—in 1932/3 expenditure fell to less than £1.7 million, the lowest annual amount ever reached—but the wholesale retrenchment which had been predicted and promised never took place. Some IRA men were given commissions, but fears that that organization would be absorbed wholesale into the regular army proved unfounded. Contrary to predictions, Fianna Fáil did not jettison the conventional defence policy and establishment which it inherited in favour of the less orthodox organization and approach developed during the War of Independence.

---

[65] Council of defence minutes, 30 Apr. 1932; Hayes to Captain Kelly, July [1932], Hayes papers, P53/289(25); minute by Moynihan, 17 Aug., conveying government decision of 16 Aug. 1932, DT, S. 2206; Manning, *The Blueshirts*, 26.

In many respects it was business as usual for the army. The need for worth-while training had constantly to be balanced against the necessity of providing sufficient troops to occupy the many barracks and installations still in use. The government continued to use the army as a convenient reservoir of disciplined manpower in all manner of civil emergencies: we have already seen that the military were given the invidious duty of providing both courts and prisons for political offenders under article 2A, and that army lorries were pressed into service during the 1935 Dublin transport strike. More positively, in the autumn of 1933 substantial exercises were held for the first time in six years, and the chief of staff led a sizeable contingent of troops on a pilgrimage to Lourdes (his decision to lay a wreath at a war memorial caused some distress to Finance, which argued that he should pay for it himself). The army equestrian team competed in various international events, acting *faute de mieux* as an ancillary intelligence service on military developments abroad.[66] Army records for the period are scant, but the surviving files confirm that the familiar problems of organization, equipment, and finance remained much the same: expenditure continued to be over-whelmingly on pay and allowances; G2's long-running feud with the Ordnance Survey about the provision of adequate maps dragged on; the minister offered to do what he could about unjustified 'delays on the part of some Government Departments, particularly . . . Finance . . . arising out of the proposed purchases of Warlike Stores', but the Finance leopard did not change its spots; and specialist technical posts proved almost impossible to fill because of better opportunities in Britain. Defence policy evidently remained a matter too important for the military to be encouraged to consider: the council of defence met infrequently, and usually dealt with only the most mundane details. For example, its first meeting following the crucial establishment of the Volunteer Force discussed only the 'use of wheatmeal flour at Curragh Bakery', deciding that 33 per cent of bread supplied should be brown, while the subsequent meeting was entirely devoted to 'Curragh Camp Lettings, Sandes' Soldiers Home'.[67]

One major change in defence arrangements was, however, signalled in the immediate aftermath of the 1932 election, when a Fianna Fáil intermediary promised republican leaders that the government would create a 'Volunteer Force', a new army reserve which IRA men could join without compromising their principles. Whether by accident or design, this force did not materialize for two years. Then, it was established in very different political circumstances: it served not to incorporate the IRA into the state's army but to woo men away from the paramilitary world, offering them a small allowance, some elementary

---

[66] Longford and O'Neill, *De Valera*, 335; papers on the Lourdes expedition are in NA, DF, S004/0143/33; information from Colonel Donal O'Carroll, 1990.

[67] 'Transfer of topographical section to Ordnance Survey', and council of defence minutes, 30 Aug. 1933 and 28 Sept. 1934, both MA; the saga of the recruitment of a civilian aeronautical engineer is contained in NA, DFA, S. 44.

training, and the chance to serve under the national flag within the law. Although it had long been policy to regard the regular army as 'essentially a skeleton of highly trained personnel which includes the administrative and technical overhead capable of rapid expansion in time of war', the new force was the first substantial attempt since the foundation of the state to augment the front-line army with a coherent system of reserves relying not on superannuated men who had served their time in the forces but on young volunteers. Short of conscription, a step no government could contemplate, it was arguably the most effective means of providing the male population with some element of formal military training, of building up a system of reserves, and of asserting the state's primacy as the defender of the nation. Within a year the functioning volunteer reserve stood at about eleven thousand men. Despite a predictable equipment, transport, and weapons famine, and a hopelessly underfunded training regime, it was to be the mainstay of the army's dramatic expansion in 1939–40. The relative success of the new reserve force lent a little credibility to the army's proposed war plans, predicated on the assumption of a British invasion from Northern Ireland, which in 1934 envisaged four (later six) well-equipped first-line brigades. These would be used to hinder the advance of British forces, rather than to attempt to hold a static line, while the reserves were called to arms. Once conventional resistance became impossible, the army would revert to the guerrilla tactics of the War of Independence.[68]

From the time that he took office de Valera repeatedly made his foreign policy crystal clear, both in the Dáil and at the League of Nations. First, the state would remain strictly neutral in any war unless directly attacked or unless called upon to act in concert with other members of the League. Secondly, the state looked to the League for protection from aggression, and in return was willing to take an active part in the League's affairs. This was publicly demonstrated in its endorsement, despite a certain amount of bluster from the opposition and from the Catholic Church, of sanctions against Italy for her invasion of Abyssinia in 1935. Recent research has also shown that de Valera was even prepared to offer a contingent of up to 400 men (about 7 per cent of army strength) to join the international military force established to keep the peace during the Saar plebiscite in 1934–5, an offer apparently made without consulting the army as there is no trace of it in Defence records.[69] Thirdly, despite the continuing injustice of partition, the state would never allow itself to become a base for attacks against Britain. The problem with these principles, from the army's point of view, was that they cast no light on what arrangements the government

---

[68] Duggan, *A History of the Irish Army*, 159–62; memorandum by chief of staff, n.d. [1935], with council of defence minutes, 23 Sept. 1935; P. Young, 'Defence and the New Irish State, 1919–39', *Irish Sword*, 19/75–76 (1993–4), 6; Farrell, 'The "Model Army"', 119–20.

[69] M. Kennedy, 'Prologue to Peacekeeping: Ireland and the Saar, 1934–5', *Irish Historical Studies*, 30/119 (May 1997), 423–8.

envisaged to ensure that the country was adequately defended, and did not address the problem of how Ireland could stay out of a conflict involving Britain when Britain had such strong defence rights under the treaty. Furthermore, de Valera's declared policy was based largely on the premise that the League of Nations could protect small states threatened with aggression. As the decade progressed the international climate deteriorated, the League's moral and practical authority was eroded by events in Manchuria and in East Africa, and Ireland's naive reliance on it appeared a less and less judicious option. In February 1936 the director of intelligence commented to the chief of staff that the international 'situation gives cause for great unease. I fear that this unease is not felt outside this Department.' In fact, however, there were already considerable differences within the army on the course which national defence policy should take.[70] Discussion about an appropriate defence policy was complicated by the emergence of a sharp divide on the issue of partition. Fired up by the rhetoric of the economic war, and resentful of partition, a group of officers began 'talking extensively about a military war against the British and the successful manner in which such a war could be waged'. The moving spirit in this extraordinary speculation was Hugo MacNeill, who had the reputation of being a strategic thinker, and who had become the first commandant of the military college. MacNeill was a northerner, and this may have predisposed him to thoughts of a military solution to partition which other officers less engaged by that issue shied away from. Dan Bryan, then second in command of G2, thought the idea 'utter insanity', and he decided to write 'a document which would display the irresponsibility of this attitude effectively'. The outcome was 'Fundamental Factors affecting Irish defence policy', not 'so much a statement of defence policy as a statement of our inadequacies particularly in arms'.[71]

Bryan argued that 'the Saorstát with its own resources could not as an organised state wage war with any reasonably strong state except for a very short period. Munitions, and other technical supplies and financial resources, would become exhausted.' The importation of supplies, and the ordinary trade upon which the Irish economy depended, could only take place with 'the acquiescence of the naval power controlling adjoining waters'. He bemoaned

the general lack of information or non-recognition of [the] existence of such a problem . . . This is due to the fact that the external defence of the Saorstát has been in the practically unchallenged control of Great Britain for a long period . . . the Saorstát may be said to be not relatively but absolutely disarmed . . . [the public] do not realise that in the usual European sense the Saorstát can hardly be said to have a Defence Force at all. This

---

[70] Archer to Brennan, 2 Feb. 1936, with Brennan to minister for defence, 22 Sept. 1936, MacEntee papers, P67/191(3).

[71] Bryan transcripts, p. 2; 'Fundamental Factors'; J. P. Duggan, *Neutral Ireland and the Third Reich* (Dublin, 1985), 181, states that Bryan initially wrote 'Fundamental Factors' as a paper for a command and staff course at the military college.

condition is possible because the Saorstát lies within the sphere of British defence influence and in practice, the British forces intervene between it and all other possible external enemies.

The paper dealt at length with the ramifications of Ireland's strategic position in the Atlantic, the implications in a future war of Britain's retention of the treaty ports, and the fact that Northern Ireland would unavoidably be involved if Britain went to war. It pointed out that, the 1921 treaty restrictions on Irish naval development notwithstanding, Britain had since pressed the Free State to develop a coastal defence and maritime patrol system. Bryan analysed Britain's vital Atlantic naval operations based on Ireland during the First World War, and argued that submarine warfare had increased rather than lessened Ireland's strategic importance. He pointed out that Britain's enemies for centuries had routinely tried to harm her by fomenting rebellion in Ireland, that Germany had achieved an unqualified diversionary success by encouraging the 1916 rising, and that Ireland would 'always' have 'an active if small minority that can be exploited' by a foreign power to make trouble for Britain. Bryan also argued that, should Britain go to war again, she would make extensive demands of Ireland in addition to her use of the treaty ports. These would include not only the extra air and communications facilities also provided for in the treaty, but 'extensive co-operation' on matters including press and communications censorship and other aspects of the 'larger question of Internal Security (protection against espionage, hostile propaganda, sabotage and various other undesirable activities)'. Furthermore, 'it is not generally recognised that effective neutrality imposes definite very onerous military and international obligations as well as giving specific rights to the neutral state'. Failure to meet these obligations would provide Britain with 'adequate excuse for undertaking measures for local defence in addition to seizing the facilities they regard as necessary', which would be 'disastrous' for 'our national prestige and our political problems'.[72]

'Fundamental Factors' was an impolitic though formidable statement of strategic realities, dismissed as 'pro-British' by the clique of officers whose ideas it assailed. This may explain why 'it was never submitted by the chief of staff as an official submission on defence'. Over forty years later Bryan, while he knew that it had been widely read within the army, remained uncertain of its broader distribution and its policy impact. In fact, the archives reveal that it was circulated in its entirety to key ministers, and that it served as the only considered overview of defence issues emanating from the army in the years leading up to 1939. Nothing better illustrates the habitual timidity of the general staff and civilian officials in Parkgate Street than the fact that it was offered to ministers without gloss, explanation, reservation, or endorsement.[73]

---

[72] 'Fundamental Factors', *passim*.   [73] Bryan transcripts, p. 3.

Bryan's document came at a crucial time, because there were already some stirrings of unease in Merrion Street about trends in international politics. Some months previously a cabinet committee on wartime censorship, moribund for years, had been revived. Significantly, both Bryan and the director of intelligence Liam Archer were members, giving defence a crucial toehold in the formation of security policy. Drawing heavily on Britain's First World War experience, it began to lay the groundwork for the press and communications censorship machinery which came into operation in 1939. At the political level, the problems of reconciling neutrality with British security interests had been aired in the Dáil, while the issue of Britain's defence rights under the 1921 treaty also caused concern. In September 1936 a ministerial committee on national defence, consisting of the ministers for defence, for justice, and for local government, and chaired by de Valera, was established. Its brief was to ensure 'the co-ordination of all Governmental activities having a bearing on national defence' while a new Defence Forces bill was being drafted. Defence policy was, quite suddenly, now a matter of considerable political interest.[74]

It was in this climate of dawning ministerial realization of the country's defence inadequacies, of Ireland's strategic importance to Britain, and of the implications of Britain's defence rights under the treaty, that a coherent programme was put forward in September 1936 to 'complete the existing units of the Defence Forces in the shortest possible period'. The chief of staff prefaced the plans with a remarkable admission: in the past, 'as the Defence Forces had no "long term" policy and it was obvious our supplies were infinitesimal there was a tendency to try and obtain additions by any means'. On this occasion, however,

I wish it to be definitely understood that this programme has not been prepared in a bargaining sense or in the hope that if very large demands are made some of them will be granted . . . This programme . . . must be regarded as a basis for a 'long term' policy.

The main thrust of the programme was not a dramatic expansion in the size of the army but in its equipment: 'with the exception of Bulgaria we were spending less on such material', about 5 per cent of recurrent expenditure, than any other European state. The programme envisaged providing the requisite weapons, equipment, transport, and support services to enable the notional wartime establishment of six brigades to operate effectively. The programme also provided for the development of air defences, envisaging nine squadrons of new fighters and light bombers, and twenty-four anti-aircraft guns to protect Dublin city and the Shannon hydro-electric scheme. The estimated capital cost of these developments would be in the region of £2,100,000, and the increased recurrent annual costs would be something under half a million; at the time

[74] Moynihan to private secretary, minister for finance, 12 Jan. 1937, MacEntee papers, P67/190.

total defence spending stood at under two million pounds, the air corps had no modern fighter or bomber aircraft at all, and the army possessed just four anti-aircraft guns. The chief of staff buttressed his plans with copies of 'Fundamental Factors' and of a strongly worded memorandum by Archer. This warned of complacency about the international situation, public ignorance about the army's operational capacity, and a total lack of information from the Department of External Affairs about the trend of affairs in Europe. It also included the prescient comment that 'the earliest year' likely for 'war between Germany and France' would be '1938/39'.[75]

The government's first response was ominous if predictable: in January 1937 Sean MacEntee, the minister for finance, was added to the committee on national defence. Despite his formidable republican record, in style and manner he was cast in a different mould to most of his colleagues. A published poet and something of an intellectual, an insatiable reader of memoranda and a 'woefully long-winded' speaker, he could argue a point indefinitely. As finance minister his spiritual home was the Gladstonian Treasury. Relishing a debate on so obviously economically unproductive an investment as defence spending, he took issue with almost every assumption underlying the army's case.[76] Such action would, Finance argued, be pointless either because there would not be a war, in which case it would prove a complete waste of money, or because there would be, in which case the army would rapidly be overwhelmed by superior force if it attempted to defend Irish territory against a major belligerent. An adequate air defence system was, in Finance's view, similarly impracticable. Despite Europe's increasing drift towards war, no significant increase in defence spending was sanctioned for 1937 on foot of the army's representations. Furthermore, beyond the imperative of staying out of other peoples' wars there was no consensus on what defence policy should consist of. Should the army be confined to a static defensive role or should it be organized and equipped to move quickly in strength against invading forces, should it even attempt to provide air defences, should it police coastal waters? Even within the army these were matters still in dispute. The absence of a unitary military view on defence probably weakened the army in discussions with ministers and with Finance, though it is arguable that the outcome would have been the same no matter how coherent the military case made. The reality was that the government viewed problems of national defence entirely in terms of Anglo-Irish relations. Developments in that sphere finally cleared the way for serious political consideration of defence issues when de Valera, once he had won popular endorsement for his new constitution in a referendum in July 1937, began the exploratory talks with Britain

[75] Chief of staff to minister for defence, 22 Sept., and Archer to chief of staff, 20 Feb. 1936, MacEntee papers, P67/191(3).

[76] O'Broin, *Just like Yesterday . . . an Autobiography*, 100–1. Dr O'Broin was private secretary to MacEntee in Finance in the 1930s.

on trade and other issues which were to culminate in the Anglo-Irish agreement of April 1938. That agreement both brought an end to the 'economic war' and resulted in British abandonment of the rights to ports and other defence and communications facilities guaranteed under the 1921 treaty.

De Valera had far wider political aims in pursuing a rapprochement with Britain once he had his constitution in place, but defence was a central issue in the discussions between the two governments. Invoking the unhappy fate of John Redmond, de Valera initially stressed that while partition remained it would be impossible for any Irish government to lend Britain positive support in a European war, no matter how strong the private sympathies of ministers. His implicit offer of a defensive alliance in return for British abandonment of Northern Ireland was, predictably, rebuffed. Nevertheless, his attempt to link defence and partition allowed him to placate his republican wing, while it also served calmly to remind the British of the likely value of Irish goodwill in a future war. It invited the British government, advised by their service chiefs, to make the calculation which they eventually did: that Britain's strategic interests would be better served by benign Irish neutrality than by the retention against Irish wishes of outmoded and ill-defended facilities which would anyway be of doubtful utility in the kind of conflict which planners anticipated, and which would be impossible to operate in wartime without Irish co-operation. This conclusion was reached in the awareness that de Valera had explicitly refused to give any undertaking to allow Britain to use the ports in time of war.[77] The eventual outcome of the negotiations was a satisfactory settlement all round: the British prime minister Neville Chamberlain tartly informed the Northern Irish prime minister Lord Craigavon that it would 'help our trade and what is more important' increase 'our security' and that of Northern Ireland in the event of war. The trade dispute was finally laid to rest, Northern Ireland was left untouched, and Britain relinquished her defence rights under the 1921 treaty. De Valera told the Dáil that 'the Irish Government . . . and that has been our policy and will remain our policy—is not going to permit its territory to be used as a base of attack against Britain', and that Ireland would resist any 'foreign power' which might 'possibly covet our territory or our possessions' for military purposes.[78] The Anglo-Irish agreement transformed the prospects for a genuinely independent Irish defence policy, and it lent some political urgency to what had previously been mainly military concerns about some aspects of national defence.

The first military fruits of the Anglo-Irish negotiations proved somewhat unpalatable to the army: in February 1938 the British CID, evidently acting on

[77] Canning, *British Policy*, 188.

[78] Ibid. 176–97; Bowman, *De Valera and the Ulster Question*, 160–81; Chamberlain to Craigavon, 12 Mar. 1938, PRO, PREM 1/274; extract from de Valera's comments in the Dáil of 27 Apr. 1938, DT, S. 10701A.

an Irish request for advice, concluded that Ireland needed only an additional £1.4 million in capital spending, and an extra two million pounds recurrently, to build up adequate air and land defences. These relatively modest figures, predicated on co-operation between British and Irish forces, caused the army some alarm. Its own estimate of what was needed, based on the assumption that it must be made capable of the significant independent defence of the national territory, amounted to £10 million of capital spending, and about £3 million recurrently. It seems remarkable that British advice should ever have formally been entertained on what an appropriate Irish defence policy should be, particularly as political sensitivities ensured that all military dialogue arising from the transfer of the ports had been deliberately confined to entirely technical issues: 'there was an [Irish] emphasis on the fact that general staff personnel were not involved' in any discussions, a decision which further obscured the crucial issue of securing a guaranteed supply of the equipment necessary to defend Irish neutrality.[79] Although ministers could hardly endorse the CID's assumption that Britain would be the guardian angel, not the violator, of Irish territorial integrity in a European war, its figures were evidently circulated in order to weaken the army's case for a dramatic increase in defence spending. For the time being national defence preparations were to remain a symbolic rather than a practical exercise.[80]

The Anglo-Irish agreement had a second, largely unremarked impact on the army. This was in the area of security. The British government had been concerned for some years about the political activities of both German and Italian diplomats amongst émigré communities in various countries, including the United Kingdom itself. While the Germans and Italians represented such work as entirely innocent and proper, the imposition of political discipline upon émigrés increased the likelihood of their employment for espionage or sabotage activities in time of war.[81] The British also had some evidence of a growing German intelligence effort against British targets. Shortly after the conclusion of the Anglo-Irish agreement, a warning was passed to the Irish high commissioner in London that the 'espionage activities of Germany extended to Ireland and that these . . . affected British, United States and French defence interests', and that Germany was planning 'to use Irish nationals for espionage against Great Britain'. This information caused alarm in Dublin. The need for a counter-espionage service had been one of the unsuccessful cards played by intelligence during its struggle to retain its domestic intelligence role in 1925/6;

---

[79] Bryan transcripts, p. 3; minutes of meetings of 25, 27, and 28 May 1938 at office of the Irish high commissioner, DFA, S. 77.

[80] CID estimate of Irish defence requirements, Feb. 1938, MacEntee papers, P67/192; unsigned critique of CID estimate, 2 Mar. 1938, ibid., P67/193.

[81] Hinsley and Simkins, *British Intelligence*, 14–17; memorandum by Mallet (British embassy, Washington), 5 Oct. 1937, with memorandum by Dunn, State Department, 13 Dec. 1937, USNA, RG95, 811.OO Nazi/334.

officers had predicted, accurately as it transpired, that the police would take not the remotest interest in so arcane an aspect of security work. We have already seen that the IRA's and the Blueshirts' foreign links had indeed been viewed entirely through the prism of domestic politics, rather than of the state's external security and its relations with its neighbour. The covert political work of German and Italian nationals had received little attention, although the government had expressed its disquiet to the German legation about some of the activities of Helmut Clissman, the Dublin representative of the German academic exchange organization and later to be a key link between the IRA and the Abwehr (the military-controlled German foreign intelligence service). Evidence subsequently emerged that Jupp Hoven had separately established an intelligence organization 'which was quite independent of the IRA and used to send . . . communications . . . through German boats calling at Cobh', which again went unnoticed by the authorities.[82] There are also indications that the French did some intelligence-gathering without attracting official attention, and they also decrypted Irish diplomatic cables. Furthermore, the police were unaware of the haphazard contacts which had already taken place in the United States and on the continent between Clan na Gael, the IRA, and an assortment of German officials and agents. In the light of the British warning, the government concluded that because 'similar' counter-espionage and security problems intelligence problems in 'almost all other States' were dealt with by defence ministries, a new 'defence security intelligence section' should be established within G2. It was a timely decision: the War of Independence had shown that successful security work depended not on weight of arms, but on local knowledge, expertise, and good organization. These were almost the only assets freely available to the army in 1938.[83]

vi. Ireland Prepares to Defend Neutrality, 1938–1939

The return of the ports brought no immediate benefits for the army. Despite the extra direct and indirect costs involved in taking over the port defences, on the face of it an obvious bargaining card for Defence to play, Finance ensured that there was no great increase in spending, apart from unavoidable payments to Britain for the fixed coastal and harbour defences now under Irish control. When the army, eager to exploit increased ministerial awareness of defence issues, sought the enormous extra sum of ten million pounds for war material

[82] Duggan, *Neutral Ireland*, 62. One army file contains information on Clissman dating from October 1938, MA, G2/X/2; note on 'German, IRA and related contacts', n.d., with Bryan to O'Donoghue, 24 Nov. 1942, MA, G2/X/0093.

[83] Information from Dr Peter Jackson of the University of Wales at Aberystwyth; memorandum on 'Defence Security Intelligence', with Bryan to minister for defence, 21 June 1945, NA, DFA, A8/1; Bryan transcripts, p. 4; information from Commandant Peter Young; Duggan, *Neutral Ireland*, 62.

to bring it up to its established strength and capacity, it was given sanction to spend just six hundred thousand pounds, and even this was subject to the usual dilatory purchasing procedures, frequently so slow as to prevent actual spending within the financial year. The chief of staff's call for a 'long term plan of purchases' and 'comprehensive arrangements with the higher supply authorities in London', an argument made on and off since the early 1920s, had no impact.[84] At the height of the Munich crisis in September the general staff informed the government that 'the actual strength and organization of the . . . forces' rendered them useful solely for internal security purposes. In normal times, such an assessment would have caused ministers little concern, but in the fraught international climate it apparently had some effect. Some weeks later de Valera, then also acting minister for defence, chaired an unusually lengthy council of defence meeting on 'Defence Policy'. A scheme of re-equipment, reorganization, and expansion along lines put forward by the army was subsequently agreed.[85] While a less than ideal solution to the country's defence problems, this exchange represented a major improvement. Finance continued to argue against the military's case: British self-interest, and command of the seas, would ensure that no foreign power could mount a successful invasion of Ireland, so there was no point in having a continental-style land army in miniature. All that was needed was adequate 'defence against attack from the air'. However the government, less sanguine about British intentions, now inclined towards the army's view of the problem. A handful of aircraft were ordered for the air corps, together with one motor torpedo boat for the planned naval service.[86] Early in 1939 officers were dispatched to the War Office with lists of material required. As the army had long predicted, the British, with a far-flung empire to arm and to defend, while politely sympathetic were unable to promise rapid deliveries of anything. The supply situation was particularly grim for fighter aircraft and anti-aircraft artillery, ironically the commodities which even Finance accepted were required in numbers. This setback, hardly surprising in view of Britain's own armaments needs, provoked a long overdue reappraisal of purchasing policy. Accompanied by a Finance chaperone, Colonel Costello was sent to the United States, where a handful of one-off ordnance purchases had already been made.[87] His mission was to see whether weapons and equipment requirements could be met more or less off the shelf there. If so, then orders already placed through the War Office would be cancelled. The American government made it clear that any sales would be subject to the approval of the British. In fact, the prices and the delivery times quoted by American manufacturers for most of the army's

---

[84]   Chief of staff to minister for defence, 21 May 1938, MacEntee papers, P67/193.
[85]   Young, 'Defence and the New Irish State', 7; council of defence minutes, 19 Oct. 1938, MA.
[86]   D. Brunicardi, 'The Marine Service', *Irish Sword*, 19/75–6 (1993–4), 78–9.
[87]   The Canadian customs authorities noted the passage of ammunition for a 37 mm. anti-aircraft gun for onward shipping to 'C/O, Ordance Depot, Islandbridge Barracks, Dublin, Ireland', Public Archives of Canada (PAC), RG25, vol. 1894, file 1939–109, part O.

needs proved unsatisfactory, although twenty thousand elderly Springfield rifles were eventually supplied in 1940 after much pressure from Irish and British diplomats. Costello did find an unexpected willingness to provide aircraft, but to his frustration the Air Corps clung to the naive policy of reliance on British manufacturers. That decision was to blight the Air Corps for the next six years: as one veteran pilot observed many years later, 'anything would surely have been better than nothing'.[88] These procurement disasters ensured that, despite the fact that it was at last receiving government support for its efforts to plan seriously for an impending European war, when that war came the army remained hopelessly unprepared and ill-equipped for the defensive role it was expected to fill.

The shock of the Munich crisis provided the impetus for other action in anticipation of war. The outlines of a communications censorship scheme, heavily influenced by British experience and by the army's own 1925 proposals and under discussion since the end of 1935, were quickly and amicably agreed between the military, Defence, and Justice. An emergency powers bill, again drawing heavily on British precedents and on studies prepared in the 1920s, was drafted 'as a matter of extreme urgency' following a government decision of 20 September and approved by the cabinet just a week later.[89] Good staff work could not conjure up troops, weapons, and equipment from thin air, but it proved enormously valuable in 1938/9 in laying down the foundations for the safeguarding of national security once Britain and Germany went to war and Ireland found herself an isolated neutral. Nowhere was this more apparent than in the area of counter-espionage.

Following discussions between Archer and MI5 officers in London, G2 began to make the arrangements which were to carry it through the next seven years. There was no repeat of the squabbles which had preceded the army's removal from domestic security work in 1925/6. The Garda and Justice evidently accepted G2's new role with good grace, perhaps because the full implications only became clear after the European war broke out, but also because the decision was taken at the highest political level: de Valera himself agreed arrangements for Justice to issue postal interception warrants to G2, and he sanctioned visits to Britain by the head of the Post Office's postal investigation section to study methods of interception and censorship, and subsequently to buy modern equipment for both postal and telephone supervision. This official and

---

[88] Young, 'Defence and the New Irish state', 5–6; Finance memorandum, 16 Jan. 1939, MacEntee papers, P67/193; J. Carroll, 'US–Irish Relations, 1939–45', *Irish Sword*, 19/75–6 (1993–4), 101–2; A. Quigley, 'Air Aspects of the Emergency', ibid. 87.

G. C. Peden, *British Rearmament and the Treasury, 1932–1939* (Edinburgh, 1979) is a valuable introduction to the complexities of British armaments planning in the years leading up to war.

[89] Papers on censorship planning and organization in 1925 and in 1938/9 are in MA, P/21560 and G2/X/0042 and in NA, DT, S. 11306 and 10829; council of defence minutes, 23 Sept. 1938, Moynihan (secretary to the government) to O'Donoghue (attorney-general's office), 21 Sept. 1938, DT, S. 10834A.

his deputy 'became very interested in the work, and gave the fullest cooperation' to G2, at whose directions postal interception was initiated in May 1939. MI5 had suggested that G2 recruit someone of the 'rank and capacity of a police inspector' to make inquiries, but Archer, 'a cautious man' mindful of institutional sensitivities, thought it wiser to ask the Garda to carry out all investigations. There already existed a Garda Aliens Office, concerned solely with aspects of the Aliens Act. A small inquiries section was set up within it under Sergeant Michael Wymes, in Dan Bryan's words 'an energetic and active officer' who was ultimately to become Garda commissioner. Although there were some teething problems, these arrangements stood the test of time.[90]

Investigations were soon begun into the activities of foreign visitors and of resident aliens. As the German and Italian communities in Ireland, refugees apart, were under the indirect political control of their home governments, they were obvious subjects for surveillance. Movements to and from the continent were routinely noted by both the Irish and the British passport authorities and were supplied on request to G2. Using postal interception and other methods— the G2 file on Dr Eduardo Tomacelli of Trinity College, since the mid-1930s 'head' of the Italian fascist organization in Ireland, includes a torn-up letter which he evidently drafted before discarding in a hotel waste-paper basket in October 1938, as well as fascist correspondence from Britain and from Rome—G2 gradually built up a mass of knowledge on the lives, allegiances, and activities of foreigners in Ireland. Inquiries about other Italian and German nationals indicated the strength of their political links with their homeland, although it was only after the war began that positive information on the clandestine work of suspect individuals such as Clissman and Hoven came to light. The position of the director of the National Museum, Adolf Mahr, gave particular concern because he was the leader of the Nazi Party organization in Ireland; there were also indications that he had provided topographical information to the German government.[91]

G2's early encounters with foreign espionage led both Defence and External Affairs to recommend in April 1939 that the emergency powers bill then in contemplation should be altered to include 'provisions for dealing with espionage conducted within the state of one foreign power against the interests of another foreign power'. Similar laws already existed in other European neutrals such as Switzerland. Unless this was done, it was argued, a foreign agent in Ireland could quite legally accumulate intelligence inimical to the interests of Britain and her friends, and the authorities would be powerless to act. The attorney-general, however, advised against such a measure. As the case of the German

[90] Memorandum on Defence Security Intelligence; Bryan transcripts, pp. 4–6.

[91] Papers on Tomacelli are in MA, G2/0222 and G2/0222F; memorandum on 'German IRA and related contacts', with Bryan to O'Donoghue, 24 Nov. 1942, MA, G2/X/0093; Hinsley and Simkins, *British Intelligence*, 17; D. O'Donoghue, *Hitler's Irish Voices: The Story of German Radio's Wartime Irish Service* (Belfast, 1998), 22–6.

agent Ernest Weber Drohl was to show early in 1940, the absence of any prohibition on third-party espionage might have caused serious problems to the
authorities after war began, had the state's general powers of arrest and detention not been so extensive under the Emergency Powers Act. In practice, it
did not become a serious issue until the lapsing of most of the provisions of
that act in 1945. Then the government evinced no interest in G2's arguments
on the need to provide a proper legal basis for peacetime counter-espionage
activities.[92]

   G2 was not supposed to concern itself with indigenous subversion or with
domestic political organizations, but some overlap was unavoidable. Take the
issue of anti-Semitic activity, in which G2 began to take an interest for the first
time since the murders of two Dublin Jews in 1923.[93] It might be thought that as
an overwhelmingly Catholic and predominantly rural society Ireland needed
no encouragement to treat its Jewish community as foreign and essentially
undesirable. Despite an abundance of private prejudice, however, the Jewish
religion was explicitly recognized in the 1937 constitution, and the state limited
itself to the relatively obscure act of discouraging Jewish immigration. Some
anti-Semites looked to mainland Europe, and particularly to Germany, for
ideas on how to operate. In May 1939 the Special Branch informed G2 that a
spate of anti-Jewish propaganda in Dublin earlier that year was attributable to a
George Griffin, 'not a very intelligent person and . . . inclined to be slightly
abnormal. He is easily led and is suffering from anti-Jewish mania.' Griffin was
reported to be the tool of 'an organisation known as "The International Fascist
Movement" emanating from the Italian Legation and sponsored by Captain
Liam D. Walsh', a former Blueshirt associate of O'Duffy, 'who is employed there'.
A police agent also reported that two prominent politicians turned business-
men, Patrick Belton TD and J. J. Walsh, were involved in efforts to combat Jew-
ish moneylenders in Dublin through the promotion of the St Stephen's Green
Loan Fund Society. This extraordinary tale of the intermingling of racial preju-
dice, commercial self-interest, and foreign influence may seem far-fetched. But
Liam D. Walsh was soon to act as an intermediary between the Abwehr and the
IRA, and over the next few years was to prove himself a committed fascist.
Belton had since 1935 shown himself a devout Catholic and an admirer of
Italian fascism who saw the mark of Jewish usury in every development he
happened to disapprove of, from industrial development to communism and to
political chaos in Ethiopia. J. J. Walsh was a rabid protectionist—he had quit his
job as minister for post and telegraphs in the Cosgrave government in 1927 on
the issue—a xenophobic businessman obsessed with aliens whom he alleged
were bleeding the country dry. He was, nevertheless, simultaneously an outspoken admirer of Hitler and all things German, and in 1940 was linked in

---

[92] Attorney-General to Moynihan, 8 Apr. 1939, DT, S. 10834C.   [93] DT, S. 4073.

other agent reports with plans to establish a Quisling government should Germany invade.[94]

The interaction of foreign subversion with domestic politics was illustrated in the first big espionage case which came G2's way, the visit of the German agent Oskar Pfaus to Ireland in February 1939. Pfaus, who travelled in the guise of an author, aroused the suspicions of British immigration officials, and when he reached Ireland he was put under Garda surveillance. His itinerary suggests that he was not well briefed on the intricacies of Irish politics: while he told one republican contact that his mission 'was to arrange to have a force of Irishmen organised here to assist Germany on the outbreak of war', in other words to court the IRA, he first sought the assistance of that organization's bitter enemy Eoin O'Duffy. O'Duffy declined to help, saying that 'the time was not yet ripe', but he did not denounce Pfaus to the Garda. O'Duffy's former assistant, Liam D. Walsh, was more helpful, and put Pfaus in touch with the IRA. By this time Pfaus had realized he was under surveillance. He managed to shake off his police shadowers for a time, and then departed rather hurriedly. In succeeding months a stream of German propaganda material was observed in the post from Germany addressed to people whom Pfaus had met and identified as sympathetic. G2, the Garda, and, apparently, MI5 were pleased with this first significant essay in countering foreign intrigue. What was not then realized was that Pfaus had succeeded in arranging for the IRA to send a representative to Germany. The outcome was a series of visits by the IRA's director of chemical warfare Jim O'Donovan between February and August, during which plans were laid for concerted IRA assistance to the German war effort through sabotage and espionage in Britain and Northern Ireland, for radio communications between the IRA and Germany, and for the supply of weapons and money. A radio link was established, and the contacts were to bear fruit of a sort after war was declared.[95] Shortly before the war broke out another G2/Garda investigation, again prompted by an MI5 tip-off, yielded the discovery that a traitor in the French navy was sending reports to his controllers via a German woman resident in Dublin, coincidentally living very close to army headquarters in Parkgate Street. She left 'almost as soon as attention was directed to the matter'.[96] These two cases showed that British concerns about espionage in Ireland were by no means fanciful, and they also gave the agencies involved valuable operational experience. It is worth noting, however, that the formal division of responsibility for counter-espionage and for domestic subversion between G2 and the Special Branch seems to have resulted in a significant intelligence failure: neither

---

[94] Carroll to Archer, 28 May 1939, MA, G2/X/40.

[95] Report on Pfaus, with de Buitléar to Walshe, 22 Apr. 1944, DFA, A7/1; Bryan transcripts, pp. 4–5; Cronin, *The McGarrity Papers*, 170–3.

[96] Bryan transcripts, p. 5; Hinsley and Simkins, *British Intelligence*, 12 indicates that MI5 had by then discovered that the use of third-country 'post boxes' was a frequent Abwehr technique.

organization learned of the success of Pfaus's mission, or of O'Donovan's subsequent trips to Germany, until years later. This is why the concrete evidence of German/IRA co-operation discovered after the arrest of Stephen Carroll Held in May 1940 was to come as such a shock.

A final aspect of subversive activity in the months leading up to war must be considered. This was the IRA's British bombing campaign, agreed on at the IRA convention of April 1938, which began in January 1939. Its timing is explained partly by the fact that, after almost a year of frenzied preparation, Sean Russell, who had 'obtained considerable financial aid from the Germans . . . handled entirely by Joe McGarrity' in the United States, decided that the organization was sufficiently equipped and trained to do the job effectively.[97] The inception of the campaign also owes something to the arcane theology of the republican constitution: in December 1938 Russell persuaded the exhausted remnants of the irredentist Second Dáil to transfer their notional authority as the legitimate government of the Irish republic to the army council of the IRA in perpetuity. This enabled the army council to issue the British government with an ultimatum as one government to another: withdraw from all of Ireland immediately or face war with the mythical Irish Republic. This strategy had little to commend it, and its execution as the 'S-plan' over the next year was inept. The places bombed—cinemas, railway stations, a shopping street in Coventry—meant that every one of the seven people killed and the dozens seriously injured were civilians, something hardly calculated to excite much sympathy in Ireland. It was scarcely to be expected that Britain would meekly surrender to the IRA's demands. It was also likely that de Valera would eventually be forced to take vigorous action against republicans involved in the campaign, despite his fear that the government would be accused of 'acting as a policeman for England'.[98] While the Germans undoubtedly hoped to use the IRA for espionage and subversion in the United Kingdom once war came, the inept timing of the S-plan vitiated its diversionary potential. It also provoked vigorous police and MI5 investigation of republican networks in Britain, enabling these to be largely neutralized before the war began by a combination of arrests and deportation.[99] In Ireland, the campaign increased state pressure on republicans; it is also arguable that the outrageous nature of the bombings placed the IRA in a very poor light, lessening residual public sympathy and legitimizing the very severe action taken against the organization once war broke out. The only benefit for the republican movement was the creation of two martyrs, the hapless Barnes and McCormack, both convicted and executed for involvement in the bungled

---

[97] Bryan to Walshe, 4 Apr. 1946, DFA, A20/4.

[98] Cudahy (American minister in Dublin) to State Department, 13 Feb. 1939, quoted in Bowman, *De Valera and the Ulster Question*, 198–9.

[99] In requests for increases in Special Branch strength between 1934 and 1937, the IRA is not even mentioned as a threat. PRO, HO 45/25479.

Coventry bombing of August 1939. Jim O'Donovan, the author of the S-plan, is said to have had 'a far broader vision of both military and political realities in Europe than did any of the men surrounding Russell', but the campaign scarcely serves as a monument either to his intellect or his perspicacity.[100]

vii. Conclusion

The seven years between de Valera's accession to power and the outbreak of the Second World War saw a transformation in Ireland's domestic politics and in her international relations. In 1932 militant republicanism had been a vibrant and significant force in national politics, on close terms with Fianna Fáil and confident of the future. On the other side of the political and ideological divide, the extra-parliamentary Right had begun to flex its muscles. In the following years de Valera confronted each of them in turn, consigning each of them to the margins of the political stage and consolidating electoral politics and the rule of law: a Fianna Fáil notice urging support for the draft constitution in 1937 triumphantly proclaimed that a 'no' vote was appropriate 'if you are a Communist, or a Fascist, or a Nazi'.[101] On the Right, the Blueshirt movement evaporated after 1935, leaving its effervescent inspiration O'Duffy high and dry. What remained of the IRA reverted to the simple apolitical physical force tradition, an approach doomed to failure because it took no account whatsoever of the impact of electoral democracy on mainstream public opinion, while the republican Left disappeared from political life for two decades.

The marginalization of these forces did not render them harmless. On the contrary, it increased their propensity to seek friends and assistance where they could. Irish fascism was all but dead by 1939, and so had little to offer the Germans and Italians when war came. The IRA, however, retained some organization, some volunteers, and some spirit. It was an obvious ally for Germany in her struggle with Britain, and that alliance was to cause the state intense difficulty.

De Valera's success against domestic subversion owed much to the care with which the coercive institutions of the state were handled in the years immediately after his party came to power. Neither the police nor the army was purged, and both forces proved loyal to the new regime despite the temptations posed by O'Duffy, and the adulteration of the Special Branch by known republicans. The army suffered under Fianna Fáil just as it had done under Cosgrave, deprived of men, equipment, and weapons, its only obvious practical role an internal security one, its warnings about the need for both the policy and the means to defend the state unheeded. Despite these dispiriting circumstances, its officers

---

[100] Hinsley and Simkins, *British Intelligence*, 16–17; Bell, *The Secret Army*, 146–63; Andrews interview.
[101] *The Irish Times*, 1 July 1937.

kept out of politics, did what the government told them to, and stuck to their planning tasks. Vindication of their efforts was to come with the outbreak of European war, when the army, from being treated as little more than a supplier of public order and a provider of public pageantry, became the mainstay of national survival.

There were important developments in foreign policy in the seven years between 1932 and 1939. De Valera continued the policy of reliance on the League of Nations bequeathed to him by the Cosgrave administration. By 1935, however, it was clear firstly that the League was incapable of curbing the expansionist urges of powerful states, and secondly that a general European war was becoming a likelihood. This prompted the injection of some realism into the discussion of how Ireland could protect herself if war came. That in turn led ultimately to what was perhaps de Valera's greatest single achievement, Britain's relinquishing of her defence rights under the 1921 treaty. This was what made Irish neutrality feasible and, arguably, preserved Ireland from the horrors of a further civil war. Neutrality was, however, not easily maintained. The actions and policies adopted in order to keep Ireland out of the war, and the pressures exerted by foreign powers and by domestic subversives to embroil the state in it, must now be considered.

5

External Defence and Security, 1939–1945

i. Neutrality and Public Opinion

De Valera had three principal assets in the autumn of 1939. The first was his firm policy of staying out of a European war, and his concomitant public pledge not to allow Britain's interests to be harmed from Irish territory. This formulation gave him the flexibility which he needed to steer his way through the hazards which confronted him. It not only underlined neutrality, but placed it in a context where British strategic concerns were nevertheless openly acknowledged, and to some extent discreetly addressed from the beginning of the war. This was aided by the timely solution of the question of British diplomatic representation in Dublin through the appointment of Sir John Maffey and the establishment of the British Representative's Office in the first week of the war, an arrangement which proved invaluable to both governments.[1] De Valera stuck to the letter of the deal hammered out in 1938. The British, who were to find themselves faced with circumstances unimagined when they had relinquished their rights to the treaty ports, came very close to breaking their part of that bargain.

De Valera's second asset was national sentiment: from the outset there was virtual unanimity on government policy, what he termed 'a passionate desire in the Irish heart to be neutral'.[2] World affairs were viewed almost exclusively through the narrow prism of Anglo-Irish relations, and many Irish people regarded Britain not as a bastion of democracy in need of reinforcement against tyranny but as the country which had unleashed the Black and Tans and murdered innocents on Irish streets less than twenty years before, and which continued to sponsor the repression of nationalists in Northern Ireland.[3] Dan Breen, perhaps the most celebrated gunman of the Anglo-Irish war, put it thus to a fellow Fianna Fáil TD, the Jewish

---

[1] Mansergh, *The Unresolved Question*, 309.

[2] Memorandum on visit to Ireland by R. G. Menzies, prime minister of Australia, undated [between 5 and 10 Apr. 1941], in W. J. Hudson and H. J. W. Stokes (eds.), *Documents on Australian Foreign Policy 1937–49*, iv: *July 1940–June 1941* (Canberra, 1980), 552, cited hereafter as 'Menzies report'.

[3] Bowman, *De Valera and the Ulster Question*, 207–8; see also G. FitzGerald, *All in a Life: An Autobiography* (Dublin, 1991), 24–5.

immigrant Bob Briscoe, who had reproached him for calling a visiting Jewish journalist a British agent:

If you wish it, I'll state in public that Ziff is an agent. I don't give one damn what views Ziff or yourself hold, that is your own personal affair. I hold the old Irish view and that one is very plain and simple and it has not changed with time . . . the words are 'you can't serve Ireland well without a hatred for England'. This is old, but it is as true today as when it was first spoken. You mention that Mr de Valera has accepted Ziff—what has that got to do with me. Mr de Valera and myself don't always see eye to eye. Yes, I visit both the German & Italian legations. Why not—the Germans and the Italians are not the people that murdered and robbed my people for 700 years. It took your good English friends to do that and they continue to do it . . . today. Finally you state that it is presumptuous on my part to keep an eye upon you. Well Bob if it is presumptuous for me to keep an eye on what my people for generations gave their lives and blood to save then you are right and I'll continue to be so. I consider it a big duty on me to be what you term presumptuous—[I] would be false to my own & my comrades & friends that are gone if I acted otherwise.[4]

To such an atavistic nationalist, Germany's foreign policy accomplishments and declared aims in the years leading up to the war—the reoccupation of the Rhineland in 1935, the *Anschluss* in 1938, even the absorption of the German-dominated Sudetenland after the Munich crisis—could all be interpreted from a safe distance primarily in terms of the legitimate redressing of wrongs inflicted on the German people by the capricious, unfair, and unworkable boundaries set at Versailles by Britain and her allies. While the take-over of what remained of the Czechoslovak state in March 1939 could hardly be placed in that category, in theory the dispute with Poland which was the immediate cause of the war focused on German demands for what was ethnically and culturally a German city, Danzig. Hitler was not universally regarded in Ireland as a madman bent on world domination and on the annihilation of whole peoples. Many saw him rather as a remarkably successful reviser of unfair boundaries and rescuer of Germanic peoples, and above all as imperial Britain's Nemesis—Breen regarded Hitler as the greatest man whom Europe had seen for generations, and cried all day when he learned of the Fuhrer's death.[5] Many people of a nationalist outlook hoped that Germany would win, and thereby bring about the destruction of the British empire. Some thought this would be the prelude to Irish unity. At the outset they saw the war not as a clash between democracy and dictatorship, between darkness and light, between civilization and barbarism, but simply as a rerun of the old imperial conflict of 1914 to 1918 which Britain had, regrettably, won. They recalled the distortions of British propaganda in the early months of the First World War, and were determined not to be misled by atrocity stories again. They were, in any case, predisposed to disbelieve anything

<hr>

[4] Breen to Briscoe, 18 Apr. 1941, DFA, P40.   [5] Private information.

emanating from the British government which, less than two decades before, had lied through its teeth about its own policies and actions in Ireland. Even the country's few communists for once found their views flowing with the main-stream of Irish politics, after Stalin's remarkable pact with Germany in August 1939 and his subsequent invasion of eastern Poland. Those Irish who hoped for a British victory—and these probably included most of the active political elite—felt that Ireland should stay out. There was a real danger of civil war if the state did become involved. It was also clear that the other small countries of Europe were not queuing up to fight, but were instead keeping their heads down and their voices soft—even Germany's staunchest ally, Italy, had belatedly come to the conclusion that it was safer to watch from the sidelines. No polit-ician of national standing argued for Irish participation: initially it was left to the maverick senator Frank MacDermott, someone of whom few Irish people would even have heard, to make a political case for joining the war on Britain's side.[6]

De Valera's third key asset was his own talent for statecraft, for the seamless if to his critics Jesuitical interweaving of the principled and the contingent. In a world conflict which in retrospect was cast as a crusade against Hitler's barbarism, de Valera presented neutrality as a high, unalterable moral prin-ciple. From being the product of sheer pragmatism, national self-interest, and the enduring nationalist grievance over partition, maintained by all manner of sub rosa co-operation with Britain and her allies, it became the proof and the justification of Ireland's title to independent statehood. In the process, it nurtured foreign policy delusions which have afflicted Irish politics ever since.

If foreign policy was crystal clear in 1939, defence policy was not. The state was extraordinarily ill-prepared to defend itself. The army had just six thousand ill-equipped and poorly trained regular soldiers scattered throughout the coun-try, together with a ragbag reserve of uneven quality. For most practical pur-poses the Air Corps did not exist, while the state possessed not even the simulacrum of a naval service. Defence policy during the Emergency—as the war years later became known although the declaration of a state of emergency came only in June 1940—was constructed almost entirely in terms of land operations to defend the national territory from violation or invasion by one or another of the belligerent powers. As a matter of convenience, however, the two subordinate arms of the defence forces, and related issues of air and sea defence, will be discussed first .

---

[6] Bowman, *De Valera and the Ulster Question*, 212. On European diplomacy in the year leading up to war, see especially D. C. Watt, *How War Came: The Immediate Origins of the Second World War, 1938–1939* (London, 1989).

ii. Air Defence during the Emergency

Air defence during the Emergency was conspicuous by its absence. The uncertainty about its purpose which had dogged the Air Corps since its creation intensified rather than abated in the face of the threat of war. In 1939 the notional war establishment was a coastal patrol squadron, a reconnaissance squadron, a bomber squadron, and a fighter squadron, all to be equipped with aircraft of British manufacture. This hopelessly ambitious plan took no account of the likely availability of aircraft in the event of a European war, encouraged the retention of a pot-pourri of aircraft types, spare parts, and maintenance equipment, and left the corps 'woefully ill-equipped' to operate effectively. It imposed high training costs for aircrew and for maintenance staff, and it ensured that, with the arguable exception of land reconnaissance, the Air Corps was of almost no operational use: the chief of staff commented in 1941 that there was 'practically no Air Force', a phrase echoed by de Valera in conversation with the Australian prime minister Robert Menzies. One can sympathize with the crew of an elderly Walrus amphibious biplane who on 9 January 1942 flew to Cornwall in an attempt to enlist in the RAF. They were ignominiously returned to Ireland under arrest, though after dismissal from the service and six months in prison for desertion the pilot concerned finally slaked his thirst for action by enlisting in the RAF.[7]

After two years of inertia, efforts were made to improve matters. A committee was established in reaction to unrest amongst Air Corps officers. Early in 1942 it reported that the only militarily useful machines in service were three obsolete Gloucester Gladiator fighter biplanes, too slow to intercept the modern aircraft of the belligerents which repeatedly violated Irish air space, and six squat and ponderous Lysanders designed for close co-operation with ground forces. Starting in mid-1942, a handful of modern Hurricane fighters were painstakingly acquired, at first through the opportunistic salvage and purchase of crashed RAF aircraft, and later by the more orthodox process of orders placed through the British Air Ministry. The RAF also supplied a pilot instructor, who trained a cadre of thirteen officers on Hurricanes.[8] These developments prompted the abandonment of the grandiose plans for separate bomber and reconnaissance units, and the belated concentration on the development of a credible fighter squadron: in 1943 the chief of staff wrote that 'experience in the present war' had shown the vulnerability of specialist reconnaissance aircraft,

---

[7] 'General report on the Army for the year 1st April 1940 to 31st March 1941', MA. Reports in this series of annual reports will be cited hereafter as 'Annual Report', followed by the appropriate year. 'Menzies report', 550; Quigley, 'Air Aspects', 86.

[8] When the RAF initially said it could supply six Hurricanes if the Irish also accepted a British instructor, the proposal was blocked on political grounds. Minutes of 229th meeting of chiefs of staff sub-committee (COS), 22 July 1940, PRO, CAB 79/5.

while bombers were of 'limited usefulness in a defensive situation'. But the Air Corps never acquired sufficient stocks of fuel or ammunition to operate its fighters in combat conditions. This was despite the development of an extensive bartering system with RAF and American units in Northern Ireland: Allied aircraft which crashed or landed in the state were routinely recovered and brought to the border, where they were exchanged for aviation fuel and other supplies.[9]

The Air Corps's main value lay not in its minimal operational capacity, but in the provision of essentially technical services. The most important of these was the operation of an aircraft identification and plotting system, based on reports from observers throughout the country, which was established in the autumn of 1939 and which operated until 1945. This system allowed the army partially to monitor and record violations of Irish air space, and in so doing protected Ireland from British accusations of negligence. Air Corps officers liaised closely with British and American air units stationed in Northern Ireland on the many practical issues which arose in the course of the war. These included overflights, forced landings, aircraft and aircrew recovery, and the provision of navigational aids along the coastline. The Air Corps also provided control officers for the state's civil air stations, and advised on various aspects of civil air policy. All these were useful roles. Equally, all could have been discharged by appropriately qualified civilians. The wartime experience of the Air Corps raised more questions than it answered about the practical value to the defence forces of having an air arm at all.[10]

The operational inadequacies of the Air Corps were replicated in the state's other air defence arrangements. On the outbreak of war the army possessed the grand total of four medium anti-aircraft (AA) guns with which to defend the principle centres of population, and obvious targets such as airfields, ports, and military installations, from air attack. It had almost no worthwhile detection and fire control equipment, and just four searchlights against a paper requirement of seventy-two. The acquisition of four Bofors light AA guns and a few additional searchlights shortly after European war was declared did little to improve matters. In July 1940 Sir John Maffey persuaded the British military authorities of the desirability of enabling the Irish to strengthen their AA defences, but the newly appointed prime minister Winston Churchill would have none of it. Towards the end of 1941 the British chiefs of staff again recommended the supply of a number of 3.7 inch AA guns to Ireland, this time specifically for airfield defence, but this gesture was also blocked on policy grounds. In the course of the next two years a few AA guns did materialize, as part of the

---

[9] Annual Report, 1942–3; Quigley, 'Air Aspects', 89.

[10] The Air Corps GOC Colonel Delamere was one of three Irish officers whom the Pentagon recommended for the award of the American Legion of Merit after the war. The idea was dropped out of deference to Irish sensibilities about neutrality. Fanning, *Independent Ireland*, 124.

British policy of supplying the Irish with a token allotment of weapons in order to stiffen their resolve to resist German aggression. The guns and lights in position around Dublin went into action on a number of occasions in the early years of the Emergency, but there is no evidence to suggest that they served as an effective deterrent: indeed, it may be that opening fire at night on German aircraft in Irish airspace conveyed the impression to the aircrew that they were over enemy territory and consequently could drop their bombs.[11] The reality was that for the duration of the war Ireland's ground defences against air attack were on a par with her aerial warfare capacity. The state possessed only the vocabulary of an air defence system, and remained entirely reliant on the sometimes leaky British air defence umbrella.

The final aspect of aerial warfare which requires consideration is that of civil defence. The government subscribed to the conventional wisdom of the 1930s, reinforced by the Luftwaffe's spectacular assaults against undefended towns during the Spanish civil war, that aerial bombing of civilian targets would be an inevitable and rapidly decisive tactic in any future European war. As in so many other aspects of emergency planning, the government had looked to Britain for advice and example on how to prepare for such an eventuality. As a result of these inquiries, an air raid precautions act had been passed towards the end of July 1939. This provided for a civil defence framework based on local authorities, but almost nothing was done before war was declared to prepare the public for possible aerial attack, to design and build bomb shelters, to strengthen the fire and ambulance services or to train their personnel, to formulate plans for the evacuation and accommodation of civilians dislocated by bombing, or to secure communications from bomb damage. All of this was left on one of the state's many long fingers until events overtook complacency. ARP experience in the United Kingdom during the war suggests that the measures which the government did belatedly put in place, however enthusiastically operated by the various organizations involved, would have been ineffective in the face of substantial bombing on the scale experienced by many cities, including Belfast in April and May 1941. This, however, was scarcely an excuse for the state's inaction in the years leading up to war.[12]

The prospect of invasion naturally quickened the pace of preparations. On 10 July Sean Lemass, now in charge of the newly created Department of Supply, announced the introduction of extraordinary measures to provide for the continuance of government and the maintenance of public order in the

---

[11] COS (40) 229, 22 July 1940, and COS (41) 333 and 342, 25 Sept. and 3 Oct. 1941, PRO, CAB 79/5 and 14; R. Hawkins, ' "Bending the beam": Myth and Reality in the Bombing of Coventry, Belfast and Dublin', *Irish Sword*, 19/75–6 (1993–4), 142; Duggan, *A History of the Irish Army*, 189–92, 208.

[12] J. Dukes, 'The Emergency Services', *Irish Sword*, 19/75–6 (1993–4), 69–70. The scarcity of suitable materials for civil defence works was a subset of the wider problem of Ireland's pre-war dependence on British suppliers. Despite Fianna Fáil's protectionist instincts, nothing had been done to lessen this dependence before war broke out. Andrews, *Man of no property*, 170–1.

event of a heavy aerial assault or an invasion in which parts of the country might be cut off from Dublin. Perhaps not surprisingly, these improvised measures were virtually a carbon copy of those in place in Britain, where eight regional civil defence commissioners had been appointed under legislation drafted before the war.[13] Lemass informed the public that the government had selected eight experienced civil servants to act as regional commissioners. These would 'be fully authorised, empowered and instructed' to exercise the full powers of government, with the exception of military command, in their designated areas should these be 'wholly cut off . . . from contact with the central government' as a consequence of 'active hostilities proceeding on our territory'. Their 'decrees must be loyally obeyed . . . and disobedience to their orders will be disloyalty to the nation. They will be the last bulwark against anarchy.' Amongst the commissioners accorded these proconsular powers was Leon O'Broin, later a distinguished historian. Because the country did not have to endure sustained attack, the regional commissioners were confined to a useful co-ordinating role between the various local services involved in civil defence, the control of food supplies, and the myriad of other administrative tasks created by the national crisis.[14] In the event, the country's civil defence arrangements were seriously tested on only a few occasions during the war. Nineteen civilians were killed when a beached mine exploded in 1943, a disaster which one veteran unkindly attributes to 'the truculence and stupidity' of some migrant workers, home on leave from Scapa Flow.[15] The only fatalities from aerial attack were three people killed in Co. Carlow, two in Co. Wexford, and twenty-nine in Dublin, all as a result of German bombs. Such isolated episodes fuelled the imagination of conspiracy theorists—the far-fetched claim that the South Circular Road area was singled out for bombing in 1940 because it was Dublin's Jewish quarter still has its adherents. Such myths presupposed a degree of navigational precision under operational conditions in hostile skies which neither set of belligerents possessed until much later in the war. Although some British officials were inclined to the view that Germany deliberately bombed Dublin in 1941 'to give [the] Irish [taste] of horrors of war and keep them neutral', the attacks appear to have been accidents of war, the products of faulty navigation, of sheer confusion, or of the desire of individual bomber crews to dispose of their heavy loads and get back to base quickly.[16]

---

[13] T. H. O'Brien, *Civil Defence: History of the Second World War* (London, 1955), 116–17; O'Broin, *Just like Yesterday*, 137.

[14] Text of Lemass broadcast, 19 July 1940, reproduced in *City and County Management: A Retrospective* (Dublin, 1991), 186–8.

[15] O. Quinn, 'The Coastwatching Service', *Irish Sword*, 19/75–6 (1993–4), 92.

[16] Hawkins, 'Bending the beam', 132–5; note by J. H. Godfrey, director of naval intelligence, on his visit to Ireland, 16 Aug. 1941, JIC (41) 335, circulated to COS (41) 291, PRO, CAB 79/13, cited hereafter as 'Godfrey report'; interview with Group Captain Ron Hockey, 1991.

iii. Maritime Defence and Coastal Surveillance, 1939–1945

Maritime defence presented the government with even graver problems than did the prospect of air attack. With the exception of the somewhat decrepit and poorly sited fortifications at the treaty ports taken over in 1938, Ireland had no coastal artillery or other fixed defences against a seaborne assault on her ports. The British naturally laid extensive minefields in the seas beyond Irish territorial waters, both to hamper German submarine operations and to deter a possible invasion fleet, while some rather primitive domestically manufactured mines were eventually laid by the Irish Marine Service in the approaches to various ports including Cork, Waterford, and Sligo. From 1942 onwards a few guns also materialized from Britain for port defence. By that time, however, their military usefulness had long passed, although the chief of staff still spoke of the 'constant danger' of 'an attack . . . by the Axis powers'.[17] As a 'neutral state', furthermore, Ireland was obliged to ensure that its ports were not used by the navies of the belligerent powers or by transport ships carrying war matériel for any of the combatants. This required the establishment of port controls for the inspection of shipping. The state also had to 'undertake the surveillance of our territorial waters', to provide some protection for its own shipping, and to succour casualties of war.[18] For years the government had, as much on grounds of economy as of high policy, resisted repeated British suggestions of a coastal patrol and minesweeping force. The result was that in September 1939 Ireland had no naval capacity at all with which to carry out any maritime functions. A Marine Service had to be improvised 'which at least wouldn't be seasick, while defending Kathleen ni Houlihain's virginity with five rounds in the magazine'. There was a considerable amount of confusion and delay in getting the service into operation: even the elementary matter of establishing a port control in Dublin was only tackled towards the end of May 1940 after the chief of staff 'in a very forcible manner' demanded action without delay. Initially, the duty was discharged by motor launches of queasy troops 'in tin hats, green uniforms and red ammunition boots . . . with orders to refuse entry to any craft of a warlike nature. Their weapons were 1914 Lee-Enfield rifles.'[19]

When war broke out in September 1939 one motor torpedo boat (MTB) was already on order from Britain—a year earlier the army general staff, who were

---

[17] COS (41) 271, 1 Aug. 1941, CAB 79/13; D. O'Carroll, 'The Emergency Army', *Irish Sword*, 19/75–6 (1993–4), 24 and 37; Duggan, *A History of the Irish Army*, 189–92; Annual Report, 1942–3; Brunicardi, 'The Marine Service', 80–1.

[18] Defence memorandum, received 3 Oct. 1940, DT, S. 11101.

[19] P. Campbell, 'Sean Tar joins up', in *Come here till I tell you* (London, 1960), 220, 226–9. See also his 'Cuckoo in the nest' and 'By the right—Go Mear Mearseail', in *The P-P-Penguin Patrick Campbell* (London, 1965), 110–15 and 119–31, for hilarious accounts of his career in the service from 1940 to 1944. Bryan transcripts, p. 11.

quite unversed in naval matters, had concluded that MTBs would play an important striking role against an invasion fleet. An order was hurriedly placed for six
more, together with some armed trawlers. The latter would undoubtedly have
been useful. Unfortunately they never materialized, apparently because the
British Admiralty blocked the sale. The only vessels immediately to hand were
two craft employed by Agriculture and Fisheries on somewhat desultory fisheries protection patrols inside the state's territorial waters. These were the elderly
Muirchú ('hound of the sea'), which had been the butt of Dublin satirists for
years, and the deep-sea trawler *Fort Rannoch*.[20] These two unlikely men-of-war
were transferred to Defence and fitted out with 12-pounder guns and light armaments. Their crews were impressed en masse into the new service, initially without uniforms or service rank, and were sent to sea to protect Ireland's maritime
interests. Despite their naval limitations, these craft were capable of sedate
patrolling in the rough waters around Ireland. They also acted, *faute de mieux*,
as minesweepers, their crewmen destroying hundreds of drifting mines with
rifle fire. By contrast, the handful of obsolescent MTBs which were slowly
acquired were of little operational value. They were unsuitable for heavy seas and
were prone to mechanical problems, and conditions on them were miserable.
The service also had 'an old steam drifter' incongruously named *Shark*, which
was used as a minelayer, and a miscellany of smaller craft employed on port control work. Amongst these was the *Noray*, a small grease-encrusted tug stationed
in Dublin Bay under the uncertain command of the humorist Patrick Campbell:
'now that she'd joined the navy she was at least painted battleship grey, though
remaining unarmed. Eighteen men, in three watches of twenty four hours, lived
in this iron box continually for four years', boarding foreign vessels 'mainly . . . I
have to admit, in search of tea' to augment their meagre rations.[21]

It is difficult to provide a balanced account of the Marine Service. It did maintain a presence of sorts in territorial waters, and its crews displayed great perse-
verance, often in wretched conditions at sea and on shore. However, it acquired
a reputation for almost comical inefficiency. To a greater degree even than the
Air Corps, it was hamstrung by the fact that it was established under army control. Its regulations, procedures, terms of service, dispositions, and operational
tasks were ultimately determined for it by army officers who had little knowledge of naval matters. The chief of staff's observations revealed exasperation
with the service. In 1944 he observed that while 'it is too small to develop as a
separate service apart from the army . . . most of its problems are purely naval
ones. The lack of suitable officers is another serious handicap.' A year later,
writing at a time when congratulations rather than condemnation were to be
expected, and when he was anxious above all to underline the national

[20] See *Fifteen Years of Dublin Opinion* (Dublin, n.d.), 97, 185, 202, 215, and 245.
[21] Brunicardi, 'The Marine Service', 77–82; Defence memorandum, 10 Sept. 1940, DT, S. 11101; Campbell, 'Sean Tar joins up', 220.

imperative to 'achieve a proper state of preparedness for defence' in the future, he could find few words of praise for the service, which

is not in a satisfactory condition. It has failed to develop properly either along military or naval lines. A general looseness of control and lack of responsibility among the officers, and particularly among the senior officers, has resulted in the whole service being unreliable . . . Probably the underlying cause of all the trouble is that we were unable to pick officers of the best type.

If the service was to be retained in peacetime, 'it will be necessary to make some very drastic changes in personnel. I certainly could not recommend that it continue as at present.'[22]

One crucial aspect of coastal defence was, however, reasonably well organized from the start. In the months before the war plans had been laid and locations identified for a coastwatching service, and these were put into operation relatively smoothly. A total of eighty-eight observation posts were established around the coast, frequently on remote and inhospitable headlands. Local men were employed as observers to report on 'everything that moved on or above the sea'. The service had its teething problems: initially not all posts were equipped with telephones, and there was no machinery for the proper collation and analysis of reports in army headquarters, but within a year the system was providing a reasonably complete and reliable picture—in 1943, an American security officer wrote of its 'great efficiency'.[23] Its effectiveness was increased with the supply of radio transmitters to regional reporting centres, an innovation facilitated by the British since it enabled them to intercept the reports as they were broadcast *en clair* from these centres to headquarters in Dublin, and from Dublin and Cobh to Air Corps aircraft on patrol.[24] The importance of the service did not lie simply in its supply of information to the military authorities. Its rapid establishment undoubtedly served to demonstrate to the British navy that the government had no intention of turning a blind eye to belligerent activity along Ireland's coastline. It also lent credibility to Irish refutations of 'unfounded rumours about the adventures of German submarines in Irish bays and harbours', one of the recurring and damaging themes in British and American press coverage of Irish affairs—one of the first British officers caught making covert inquiries in Ireland, the inept Lieutenant Mason, was arrested after quizzing members of an observation post.[25]

[22] Annual report, 1943–4 and 1944–5. Brunicardi, 'The Marine Service', 77–85, and A. McIvor, *A History of the Irish Naval Service* (Dublin, 1994), 41–96, provide more sympathetic assessments.

[23] Quinn, 'The Coastwatching Service', 91–2; Annual Report, 1941–2; Bryan interview; Bryan transcripts, pp. 14–16; unsigned OSS memorandum [by Marlin], 27 Jan. 1943, USNA, RG226, entry 106, box 0039, file 347.

[24] Guilfoyle (G2) to Walshe, 20 Feb. 1943, enclosing report promised by Bryan on the coastwatching service, DFA, P94; Greig (naval attaché) to Slade, 15 Nov. and 27 Dec., and to Maffey, 15 Nov., and Slade to Greig, 15 Nov. and 26 Dec. 1939, PRO, DO 130/7.

[25] Aide-mémoire by J. A. Hearne, Irish minister in Ottawa, 22 Dec. 1939, PAC, RG25, D1, vol. 781, file 398; Bryan transcripts, pp. 15 and 17.

iv. The Development of the Army during the Emergency: Men, Matériel, and Organization

On 1 September 1939 the government ordered full mobilization of the defence forces, including all reserves. By the end of that month some nineteen thousand men were under arms, the bulk of them partially trained members of the Volunteer Force, although some in reserved occupations were soon discharged. This was about half of the agreed war establishment strength of thirty-seven thousand, and it proved impossible to bring the two brigade structure on which the war establishment was predicated into being. Even this limited expansion proved too much for Finance. Basing its case on the relative calm of the first two months of war, in November it forced the army to begin to contract in size in the interests of economy. On 7 December a cabinet committee chaired by de Valera ordained that the army's war establishment should be cut to twenty-nine thousand. Furthermore, the 'emergency establishment' should be 'based on the smallest number of troops necessary to garrison fixed positions, together with the cadre of two mobile brigades and the number of troops in training', and should be 'substantially below the figure 15350'. In essence this was a restatement, albeit in entirely different conditions, of the Cosgrave government's policy decision of 1925. It had the desired financial effect: by January 1940 army numbers had fallen to sixteen and a half thousand, and by May to thirteen and a half thousand men.[26]

The consequences of this mobilization fiasco were predictable. The opportunity to make the two brigade structure effective was lost. Much of the regular army's energies in the first months of the crisis went not into intensive training and serious defensive preparations, but into the absorption and then into the discharging of those reserves initially called up. Some of the more adventurous of the discarded men were lost to the army for good, because they travelled to the United Kingdom either to enlist in the British services or to take up civilian employment. Military morale was undoubtedly affected by the government's precipitate reversion to naive peacetime priorities and policy. The army was to suffer two further shocks in December 1939.

The first of these was what Dan Bryan later described as 'our Pearl Harbor', the IRA's Magazine Fort raid. The second, which the public understandably took to be a consequence of that coup, was the removal immediately afterwards of the chief of staff, General Michael Brennan. In fact, however, Brennan had been informed days before the raid that he would shortly be replaced, and had been offered a subordinate command. He and Frank Aiken later disagreed on the exact circumstances: Aiken said that during the preparations of the Defence

---

[26] D. Parsons, 'Mobilisation and Expansion, 1939–40', *Irish Sword*, 19/75–6 (1993–4), 11–18; cabinet committee minutes, 7 Dec. 1939, DT, S. 11101.

Forces Act of 1937 he had as minister informed Brennan, who had been chief of staff since 1931, that he would serve for a maximum of three years more. Brennan denied that he had been told any such thing.[27] In any case, the decision evidently reflected government dissatisfaction with the condition of the army. Before news of Brennan's replacement became public, the IRA launched its raid on the Magazine Fort in the Phoenix Park and succeeded in stealing almost all the army's reserves of small arms ammunition. The product of almost unbelievable military slackness and of the treachery of a Defence official, this humiliation made the army a laughing stock inside and outside Ireland, although most of the ammunition was recovered very rapidly. It underlined the internal security menace posed by the IRA, and the organization's potential as a 'fifth column' in the event of an external attack. As news of Brennan's ouster only leaked out after the raid, a London newspaper ill-advisedly linked the two events, a mistake which cost it £500 in libel damages.[28]

The selection of Brennan's successor caused intense surprise: instead of choosing one of the obvious candidates with general staff and command experience such as MacNeill or Costello, the government went far down the list of eligible candidates and appointed the deputy quartermaster-general, Colonel Dan McKenna. Why they did so remains unclear: perhaps Fianna Fáil considered some of the army's more senior officers tainted by their civil war service—McKenna was from County Derry, and had a clean fighting record—or suspected them of pro-German sympathies; perhaps it was simply, as de Valera's official biographers suggest, that McKenna had impressed the taoiseach with his drive and initiative some years earlier. Whatever the reason, it proved an inspired choice.[29]

McKenna later wrote that, when he took over in January 1940,

because of the general weakness of the Army, there were no striking forces available capable of offering prolonged and organised resistance. Furthermore the necessity for disposing our small force throughout the state for reasons of internal security and of providing some elements for coast defence resulted in our being weak everywhere.

Few units were equipped or trained to operate at more than company strength, and there was 'almost a complete absence of the most important weapons, namely, anti-tank weapons, anti-aircraft weapons and automatic weapons', and 'a very considerable deficiency of artillery and mortars'. Radio 'equipment is also seriously deficient'.[30]

The army's equipment problems were along the lines predicted in staff studies dating back to the mid-1920s. The state's engineering industry was very

[27] Memorandum by Brennan, 15 Jan. 1940, DT, S. 11607; Bryan transcripts, p. 26.

[28] Bryan transcripts, pp. 18 and 26; cuttings about the action against the *Daily Telegraph* are in S. 11607.

[29] Longford and O'Neill, *De Valera*, 335; Bryan and Clancy interviews.

[30] Annual Report, 1940–1.

limited in capacity and in sophistication, although a 1938 study privately commissioned by Hankey, the *éminence grise* of inter-war British defence policy, had suggested that Irish firms could produce over two million pounds worth of 'armaments and machined parts per year from the many small concerns in Ireland' if properly organized.[31] But that secret estimate was predicated on British goodwill, because most of the raw materials, the machinery, the designs, and the expertise required for arms manufacture would have to be imported. During the war Irish engineering firms and the army's own workshops did manage to produce some munitions and equipment, but nothing on the scale anticipated in the Hankey study: rough casings for sea and land mines and for grenades, and a variety of makeshift armoured cars built on the chassis of commercial vehicles. Even these were dependent on imports of explosives and of parts from Britain.[32] While testament to a commendable spirit of improvisation, furthermore, they were of doubtful military value. Ireland could only have equipped herself for defence if the British so allowed. In fact, supplies of all kinds were a political issue—we have seen that, even when the chiefs of staff suggested the provision of weapons and aircraft in 1940 and 1941, the British government at first refused permission. There is, in any case, little evidence to suggest that Ireland would have been willing to spend money on the scale required to make the army a credible land force, even had the British been willing to supply every requirement. In practice the bills were never too big, because Britain deliberately provided only an occasional 'token allotment of equipment', usually 'with the object of maintaining our present good relations. The advantages . . . appeared mainly political', as the 'small quantities' handed over were militarily insignificant.[33]

It is in this context that the visit of Frank Aiken to the United States in the spring of 1941 should be seen. Aiken, now minister for the co-ordination of defensive measures, was publicly dispatched by de Valera to seek American food, weapons, and shipping. This mission was announced after the British government abrogated shipping arrangements in place since the outbreak of war, an obvious attempt to use economic blockade to extract Irish concessions on the key issue of the treaty ports. The choice of Aiken as emissary puzzled American officials, since he was considered the most Anglophobe member of de Valera's government and was believed to expect and to favour a German victory. Aiken did press for weapons in an acrimonious meeting which President Roosevelt terminated by throwing his lunch time crockery onto the floor, but his conduct during the trip suggests that its main intention was to acquire

---

[31] Bridges (cabinet secretary) to Hankey, 7 Aug. 1938, returning undated letter addressed to Hankey from Handcock & Metz of Fleet Street, Dublin, Churchill College Cambridge, Hankey papers, HNKY 4/30. [32] O'Carroll, 'The Emergency Army', 39–40.
[33] COS (41) 286, 308, 333, 342, and 401, 15 Aug., 5 and 25 Sept., 3 Oct., and 28 Nov. 1941, PRO, CAB 79/13, 14, and 16.

shipping for food and to cultivate Irish-American support for Irish neutrality. Although the United States government eventually provided two ships, the visit was a diplomatic disaster. Besides excluding the United States as a source of military aid for the rest of the Emergency, it bolstered Roosevelt's hostility towards Ireland. The army remained dependent on whatever inadequate scraps the British chose to provide at their leisure (de Valera prudently declined a German offer of captured British equipment after Dunkirk).[34]

Despite crippling shortages of equipment and weapons, the army underwent remarkable development in the first two years of the Emergency. In May 1940 there were about thirteen thousand men under arms, the level which Finance thought sustainable. The invasion of the Low Countries and the subsequent collapse of France, however, upset all calculations about Ireland's prospects. With Germany now in possession of the Atlantic coastline from Norway to the south of France, Ireland was an obvious candidate for invasion: by Germany, to seize ports and airfields with which to assist the invasion of the British mainland and to threaten Britain's Atlantic lifeline; and by Britain, to gain control of the treaty ports or to pre-empt or repel a German attack. Realization of this wrought a revolution in the government's attitude to defence. The political and financial constraints which had dominated defence policy—it was, after all, only seven months since Finance had forced the army to reduce numbers drastically—suddenly evaporated. On 2 June de Valera, accompanied by the other party leaders, issued a call to arms. It produced an extraordinary voluntary response, evidence both of the popularity of neutrality and of a national resolve to defend it: within five weeks almost twenty-five thousand men had volunteered. De Valera also established a 'defence conference' as a mechanism through which opposition party leaders could be briefed confidentially on defence and security policy and developments. The minutes of the conference suggest that it was a master stroke: it bound Fianna Fáil's parliamentary opponents even more tightly into support for the government's approach while denying them any real say in the management of foreign and defence affairs. Senior opposition figures including Cosgrave and Mulcahy were bitterly critical of the conference, somewhat indiscreetly complaining to Sir John Maffey that they were told virtually nothing.[35]

By March 1941 the army was over forty-one thousand strong. This influx placed intense pressure on the regular army, which had to assimilate, train, accommodate, and deploy the new recruits at the very time when the prospect

---

[34] Andrews, *Man of no property*, 124. For contrasting analyses of the Aiken mission, see J. Rosenberg, 'The 1941 Mission of Frank Aiken to the United States: An American Perspective', *Irish Historical Studies*, 22/86 (Sept. 1980), 162–77, and Longford and O'Neill, *De Valera*, 279–83. Duggan, *Neutral Ireland*, 119; N. Nicolson (ed.), *Harold Nicolson: Diaries & Letters 1939–45* (1st edn., London, 1967; Fontana, 1970), 217.

[35] The defence conference minutes are in DT, S. 11896; Maffey to Machtig, 13 July 1940, PRO, DO 130/12.

of invasion seemed greatest and the need for active defensive preparations most acute. McKenna reported that not all the regulars were up to it: 'a number of the older officers . . . may be said to have largely outlived their usefulness, inasmuch as they are not sufficiently active, and do not possess the necessary physical energy and keenness. The weeding out of such officers will have to be seriously considered.' The problem was compounded by the reluctance of Finance to sanction the commissioning of experienced NCOs, and by the difficulty of recruiting good officer material.[36]

In addition to army expansion, a part-time Local Security Force (LSF), initially established under Garda control primarily as a police auxiliary in each Garda divisional area, attracted many thousands of recruits unsuitable for or unwilling to enlist for full-time military service: by October its strength stood at about one hundred and eighty thousand men. The LSF was divided into two groups. The A group was designated as a combat section intended for protective duties in the event of hostilities, while the unarmed B group was intended for local patrolling, aerial, coastal, and port observation, and routine security tasks. It was an obvious anomaly that the unarmed police should control an armed militia, although the Garda initially appeared enthusiastic at the prospect of organizing resistance to an invader. In January 1941 the A group was reconstituted as the Local Defence Force (LDF) and placed under army command. By March 1941 it had about eighty-eight thousand men, most of them with little or no military training. As in the full-time army, there were problems finding suitable officers: 'The older men have been responsible for the building up of the organisation . . . the general interest demands that in a large number of cases they should be replaced by younger elements. This problem is not easily solved because of the influence and standing of these leaders.'[37] As a new part-time body, the LDF was last in the queue for what weapons and equipment the army possessed: initially many units had to make do with wooden rifles, which goes some way to explain the enthusiasm with which one Louth platoon welcomed the gift of 'sixty Brown Bess flintlock muskets, two brass flintlock blunderbusses and one nine-foot blunderbuss' early in 1941. In 1942 McKenna wrote that the LDF 'is now an integral part of the defence forces, and the responsibilities now entrusted to it have far out-reached those originally envisaged'. However, although some LDF units were later grouped into rifle battalions to carry out garrison duties, the force as a whole never received the training or equipment necessary to make it of much military value: an American military attaché's description of it in 1942 as 'very raw' and very 'poorly equipped' rings true.[38]

[36] Annual Report, 1940–1. Complaints about Finance obstruction of NCO promotions were repeated in 1941–2.

[37] Annual Report, 1940–1.

[38] Annual Report, 1941–2; Dukes, 'The Emergency Services', 68–9 and 71; report on 'The German threat to Ireland and the strength necessary to meet it' by Lt.-Col. Reynolds, 9 Mar. 1942, USNA, 841D.20/40, cited hereafter as 'Reynolds report'.

The regular army was somewhat bemused by the rush to the colours in the summer of 1940. One of the striking features of this voluntary enlistment in the defence forces was not merely the scale but the breadth of the public response to the call for full-time and part-time volunteers for the army, the Marine Service, and the LSF/LDF. This confronted the military with problems of political, religious, and cultural diversity which had not previously troubled them in screening recruits.[39] The assimilation of pro-treaty with anti-treaty men which followed Fianna Fáil's advent to government in 1932 had been a delicate matter, but even that had not prepared the army authorities for the situation which they now faced.

The most obvious danger came from IRA infiltration. The winnowing out of known republican activists from the throng of those wishing to volunteer was a relatively simple exercise. However, many men with republican associations were admitted on trust, although officers were expected to keep an eye on such recruits. The fact that many men with such backgrounds did enlist explains British fears that 'great efforts have been made to seduce the soldiers from their allegiance', and the later warning by the Admiralty's John Godfrey that it would 'be unwise wholly to discount . . . reports which indicate that the IRA have infiltrated considerably into the LDF'—he was not to know that the vast majority had forsworn subversion at least for the duration of their service, although G2 reported that pro-German propaganda directed at the defence forces had had some impact.[40] In the Munster area, hardened republicans who would not dream of taking a Free State oath or of wearing a Free State uniform were secretly recruited to a clandestine intelligence-gathering, security, and 'stay-behind' organization, the Supplementary Intelligence Service (SIS). Established by Major Florence O'Donoghue of G2, one of the few War of Independence veterans who could bridge the political and personal treaty divide, it was organized on the same battalion areas as the pre-1922 IRA in anticipation of an invasion of the south coast by either set of belligerents. In the event, its main function turned out to be that of gathering intelligence on clandestine activities. Its greatest service was the detection of the escape plans of the German agent Herman Goertz and the Special Branch renegade Jim Crofton in Kerry in 1941. The SIS was notionally a secret unit of the LDF, but its members were 'never formally attested' and their names did not appear on any army roll. They were, consequently, legally not eligible for the 1940–1945 Emergency service medal later awarded to members of the defence forces. Special cabinet sanction had to be obtained in 1951 for the secret issue of medals to SIS members, who as committed republicans were still shy of admitting their Emergency activities.[41]

[39] For illustrations of the pre-Emergency screening of recruits, see 'Serving soldiers and recruits accepted, 1927', MA.

[40] Bryan interview; 'Godfrey report'; Parkinson (Dominions Office) to Maffey, 15 Apr. 1940, PRO, DO 130/12.

[41] Defence memorandum to government, undated, Feb. 1951, MA, G2/X/0363. There is no relevant material in O'Donoghue's papers in the National Library of Ireland.

Republicans were at least a familiar breed to the military authorities. Other kinds of recruits posed new challenges. Irishmen, it transpired, came not only in all shapes and sizes, but with an alarming and puzzling variety of religious and cultural allegiances and experience. University graduates, not only from the National University of Ireland but from Trinity College, made their appearance in uniform. Men considered incurably pro-British by breeding, class, education, and religion came forward to defend Irish neutrality. To an extent all were welcome, and yet at first all were slightly suspect. Patrick Campbell recalled that the Dublin Port Control Service consisted of

a hard core of part-time dockers and longshoremen from the North Wall, with a sprinkling of cynical youths ... who'd joined in the belief that even this lash-up couldn't be as bad as the Army. There was also myself, the only Protestant among the whole *elite* corps—an unavoidable disability that caused me for four years to be regarded, philosophically, by my shipmates, as an enemy agent.[42]

The new men who caused the army most concern ranged from 'west British' Catholics—who, however suspect politically, at least were of the right religion— to Protestants of various ilks, and even to Jews. While all such volunteers had a clear reason to fight if Germany invaded, G2 was concerned about their attitude should Britain attack first (the presence of Protestants in the army, LDF, and LSF was a source of some comfort to the British precisely because it was felt that they would not bear arms against British forces).[43] Jewish recruits to the army and ancillary bodies caused particular anxiety: 'it is earnestly pointed out that a concerted movement on the part of any section of the population is bound to have a deleterious effect on the recruitment of other circles, less organised, apart from the present wide-spread objection in the civil population to the Jewish community, recently much swollen in numbers. (The same objection as to the Jews applies also to the Ailesbury Road or Killiney type of outlook.)'[44] A number of Jewish officers were in fact attached to G2 at one time or another during the Emergency, but the presence of Jews in the defence forces remained a highly sensitive issue because of the 'fundamental characteristic of the Jewish people ... that they have no national allegiance and are described by those who have studied the Jewish problem as being supernational or international in character', and the fear that the primary motivation of such recruits might be to obtain military training to be subsequently put to use in an international Jewish army.[45]

[42] Campbell, 'Sean Tar joins up', 223–4. Interview with a former G2 officer (who described himself as 'west British'), 1992. Dan Bryan took particular pride in the religious heterogeneity of G2, which at its largest had about thirty-five officers. This was partly a function of the need for linguists, and partly of the army's propensity to consign people with untypical backgrounds to staff work.

[43] General report on Ireland, July 1940, quoted in Canning, *British Policy*, 287–8.

[44] G2 memorandum, 19 June 1940, MA, G2/X/40. Ailesbury Road and Killiney were considered unreconstructed bastions of pro-British sentiment and Protestant affluence.

[45] G2 memorandum on 'Jewish church parade', undated but post-1941, MA, G2/X/40.

Public enthusiasm for volunteering soon waned as fears of imminent invasion receded. The supply of recruits dried up, and the army never reached its established wartime strength. There were a number of reasons for this. Pay was very poor—in the autumn of 1942 the wage of private soldiers was increased by 50 per cent in belated acknowledgement of what the army had long argued— and conditions of service were sometimes harsh. In addition, men could satisfy their impulse to serve without sacrificing their normal occupations by joining the LDF or the LSF. Furthermore, the government soon reverted to the habit of using the army as a source of cheap manpower for various disagreeable unmilitary tasks: thousands of men were detached in 1941 and in each subsequent summer to work on the cutting and stacking of turf, and in 1941 soldiers were used extensively to bury the carcasses of cattle infected with foot and mouth disease. Such activities were enough to dampen anyone's martial ardour. The problem of recruitment became so serious that by 1944 McKenna was suggesting that the government consider 'some sort of compulsory military service'. This politically explosive proposal got nowhere: the conscription crisis of 1918 had destroyed the moral authority of the British government in Ireland, and whatever the possibility of introducing compulsory service at the time of greatest national peril in 1940, there was no chance at all that any Irish government would risk such a measure once the immediate likelihood of invasion had passed.[46]

One of the principal reasons why recruitment proved so difficult was the simple fact, pointed out by McKenna in 1943, that 'those who have a natural taste for military life are more inclined to join the British Services, where a more exciting career is expected'.[47] There was also plenty of well-paid civilian work available in Britain. Desertion, whether to join the British services or to find other work in Britain, became a serious problem. The highest incidence, perhaps not surprisingly, occurred in units stationed near the border. It has been argued that desertion was a function not of low morale but, as in the case of recruitment, of the fact that there was more money and excitement to be had in Britain, whether as a serviceman or as a civilian worker.[48]

The recruitment of Irish men—and women—to the British armed services was a complicated issue. As late as 1936 the cabinet had sanctioned the continuance of the arrangement under which the Garda carried out security checks for the British authorities on Irishmen enlisting in the British services. While this facility was probably discontinued in 1939, the authorities had neither the will nor the capacity to restrict the movement of Irish people from the state into the United Kingdom. While some controls could be imposed on travel by ship or air between Ireland and Britain, furthermore, neither government could seal the

---

[46] Annual Report, 1943–4; O'Halpin, *Decline of the Union*, 154–5.
[47] Annual Report, 1942–3.   [48] O'Carroll, 'The Emergency Army', 41; Clancy interview.

land border with Northern Ireland effectively: after a visit to Belfast in April 1941 Robert Menzies thought 'the fact must be recorded that recruiting in Ulster is indifferent and . . . some comment is beginning to arise' because 'the existing recruiting is greatly stimulated by a stream [of men] which flows from Eire into Ulster'.[49] In 1940 the Special Branch was directed to launch an investigation into the British Legion, an obvious source of advice and encouragement for anyone thinking of enlisting, which was widely believed to be operating as an unofficial British recruiting agency.[50] Despite the use of agents provocateurs the results were both inconsequential and irrelevant: even if the Legion's officers could be deterred from encouraging or facilitating recruiting, the most that anyone from the south had to do was to take the boat to Liverpool or the train to Belfast and sign up there. Aiken, not noted for his Anglophile tendencies, admitted in 1940 that it would be 'very difficult to intervene' to prevent such enlistment.[51] G2 later attempted to measure the phenomenon through the postal censorship, but this was useful only where people corresponded with recruiting offices in Northern Ireland or in Britain prior to joining up. It disclosed nothing of the intentions of the Irish people who travelled to the United Kingdom each year.[52] It is abundantly clear that the many thousands of Irishmen, and some Irish women, who went to or who already lived in the United Kingdom and voluntarily enlisted in the British armed services during the war did so for a variety of reasons including family tradition, force of circumstances, a desire for excitement, and a wish to aid in the defeat of Germany and her allies. It also seems clear that such enlistment was no indicator of their personal opinions on the rights and wrongs of Anglo-Irish relations.[53]

Despite its manifold difficulties with recruits, transport, weapons, and all manner of supplies, the army developed very considerably in a short space of time under McKenna's direction. It did so in the worst of circumstances: the need for sustained training had to be balanced against the imperative of having as many men as possible under arms and ready to mount organized resistance to any invader, while the government's persistent recourse to the army for non-military tasks also impeded concentration on increasing military effectiveness.

The main organizational innovation was the adoption of a full two-division structure, one to concentrate on border defence, the other on the defence of the southern ports and coastline. This approach had not been envisaged in pre-war studies, and it apparently emerged in discussions between McKenna and de Valera, Aiken, and Oscar Traynor (the minister for defence) in December 1940.

---

[49] 'Menzies report'.
[50] Comments of William Norton TD, Labour party leader, defence conference minutes, 10 Mar. 1941, DT, S. 11896.
[51] Defence conference minutes, 3 July 1940.   [52] Bryan to Walshe, 16 Oct. 1943, DFA, P81.
[53] Bowman, *De Valera and the Ulster Question*, 208; interview with Mrs Ann Brophy, an Irish nurse working in Britain who joined Queen Alexandra's Nursing Auxiliary in 1944.

It is unclear whether or not the chief of staff initially favoured or opposed such a development: the new structure lessened the powers of the GOCs of the various geographic commands, but it did nothing directly to strengthen his hand. The obvious element missing from this new structure was a GOC in overall command of the defence forces. Two decades after the army's foundation, this remained a highly sensitive issue because of the concentration of power in the hands of a single officer which it suggested. Whether through modesty or prudence, McKenna was unwilling to press the government directly on the point, although he proceeded on the assumption that in the event of hostilities he would be appointed GOC. The fact that he was denied that status throughout the Emergency makes his handling of the two strong characters appointed as GOCs of the 1st and 2nd divisions, Generals MacNeill and Costello, all the more admirable.[54]

What distinguished the 1940/1 reorganization from the large number which the army had endured in its first years of existence was the fact that it was put into operation more or less as envisaged. It required a degree of operational sophistication well beyond the army's previous experience. By the spring of 1941, when the two divisions were in process of formation, McKenna reported that 'combat efficiency has progressed . . . from weak scattered defence by mobile units of company and, in a few cases, battalion strength to defence by formations of all arms [brigades] capable of serious fighting independently or in co-operation'. There were three such brigades to cover the border, and a further three to protect the southern coastline. Training was stepped up at the military college, while some 'specially selected officers were sent on British army courses in Northern Ireland' where 'invaluable experience and knowledge were . . . acquired'. Intensive staff work culminated in the exercises of August and September 1942, which were concentrated along the valley of the River Blackwater. Most field elements of the army were involved in these prolonged exercises which, while they threw up many defects in the training and procedures of the new divisions and supporting forces, were judged a major success overall. In his annual report McKenna wrote that 'the training carried out . . . has been much more arduous, more extensive and more progressive than anything attempted since the foundation of the army'. While weaknesses had been revealed, the exercises also demonstrated 'conclusively that the troops have passed from the stage of barrack square training and that the army is now an effective and mobile field force, whose further training must be of an advanced and intensely practical nature'.[55]

This robust assessment of the army's strength was, however, qualified by other considerations. As McKenna's reports made clear, the army still lacked the armour, the aircraft, the anti-tank weapons, and the AA guns necessary for

---

[54] O'Carroll, 'The Emergency Army', 21–2.   [55] Annual Report, 1941–2 and 1942–3.

independent defence. It could only fight effectively if someone else provided those elements of defence which it still so conspicuously lacked. While training continued for the remainder of the Emergency, and while additional equipment trickled in from Britain, the army's underlying weaknesses remained. However enthusiastically led and however well drilled, it was a field force without much of the equipment necessary for sustained combat. An American military attaché described it in 1942 as 'destitute of all equipment necessary to a modern fighting force' although 'I formed a very favorable impression of the character and ability of the officers and the excellent discipline and quality of the troops'. Capable at most of a 'spirited but brief resistance to a German invasion', he argued that it 'seemed best to disregard it' entirely in making plans for an Allied response.[56]

v. British Policy, German Intentions, and Irish Defence Planning, 1939–1945

From the first days of the war British military planners raised the possibility of action to recover control of the facilities relinquished to Ireland under the 1938 agreement. On 4 September 1939 the chiefs of staff heard of 'the importance, from the naval point of view, of being able to use ports in Southern Eire', although the Admiralty acknowledged that 'the political repercussions of such a proposal were not clear'. Churchill had been almost alone in opposing the return of the treaty ports in 1938, being 'listened to with a patient air of scepticism. There was even a kind of sympathetic wonder that anyone of my standing should attempt to plead so hopeless a case.' Now, restored to government at the Admiralty, he 'made no effort to conceal his distaste' for his colleagues' unwillingness to force the issue with the Irish in the changed circumstances of war. Throughout the autumn he continued to argue that the ports must be recovered. In assessing his views and his influence on policy, it must be remembered, in Paul Canning's phrase, that to his colleagues he 'was not yet the hero of the Battle of Britain', but rather the old impetuous Winston whose passion for action had led to the Dardanelles disaster in the First World War.[57] Although his pressure did influence the cabinet's decision to intensify efforts to resolve the impasse through negotiation with de Valera, he remained isolated in his view that if diplomacy failed then *force majeure* should quickly prevail. The majority of the cabinet felt that as matters stood it served British interests better to have Ireland as a friendly neutral than as a sullen and mutinous conscript to the war

[56] 'Reynolds report'.
[57] COS (39) 3, 4 Sept. 1939, PRO, CAB 79/1; W. Churchill, *The Second World War*, i: *The Gathering Storm* (London, new edn., 1949), 248–9; Canning, *British Policy*, 271. This section draws heavily on Canning's incisive account.

effort. Besides, any act of force against Ireland would do great harm in the United States and in the commonwealth, whereas patient negotiation had the benefit of exposing the unreasonableness of de Valera's refusal to help. There were other considerations: Ireland was a fertile recruiting ground for the British armed services; Irish exports and Irish civilian workers were sorely needed in Britain; and if relations deteriorated sharply, Ireland as a major creditor was in a position to do great damage 'by calling us to repay at a most inconvenient time'. (A Treasury official later recalled Finance as 'more Papist than the Pope' in its adherence to British wartime currency regulations.)[58]

Under Churchill's leadership, however, the Admiralty persisted. In the spring of 1940 a new argument was adduced in favour of intervention: the first sea lord bluntly remarked that 'as we were now contemplating action which would infringe the neutrality of both Norway and Sweden, consideration might be given at the same time to the question of occupying Berehaven', which would be 'of the greatest value . . . particularly . . . for anti-submarine forces'. Although pre-war planners had calculated that such a seizure would require a full division, the army view now was that a smaller force could do the job even in the face 'of Irish opposition'. A paper was produced and discussed, but the proposal was set aside as inopportune.[59]

Up to that point, the question of the forcible occupation of Irish ports and facilities was viewed entirely in terms of strengthening naval operations in the Atlantic. No one anticipated serious German action against Ireland.[60] Germany's military conquests in the spring and early summer, first of Norway and Denmark, then of Holland, Belgium, and Luxembourg, and finally of France, changed the picture completely. The original issue of the ports was now bound up with the wider possibility of a German move on Ireland, either as a diversionary attack 'in order to draw our fleet away from the main seaborne expedition' during an invasion of Britain, or to gain ports and airfields from which to attack Britain and to menace her Atlantic shipping. The ease with which Germany had subdued other European neutrals—Copenhagen was taken unopposed by a ship-borne battalion of German troops while German aircraft circled overhead to overawe the Danish population, and Norway and the Netherlands fell within days of being attacked—suggested that she could anticipate gaining a toehold in Ireland at virtually no cost, if she could get a force there in the first place.[61]

As the military situation in France deteriorated, British fears of German action grew. On 15 May the JIC discussed 'information . . . pointing to the

---

[58] Memorandum by Hauser (Treasury), 30 Oct. 1939, quoted in Canning, *British Policy*, 255; Sir Edward Playfair (a wartime Treasury official) to the author, undated, 1980.

[59] Canning, *British Policy*, 271; COS (40) 59 and 75, 26 Mar. and 12 Apr. 1940, PRO, CAB 79/3.

[60] There is no mention of any threat to Ireland in the JIC paper on 'Possible German actions in the spring of 1940', 18 Dec. 1939, PRO, CAB 81/95.

[61] JIC minutes, JIC (40) 79 and 101, 24 May and 6 June 1940, PRO, CAB 81/96.

likelihood of an imminent air-borne attack on Great Britain via the West Coast and Eire', and the next day recommended that the Irish government should be warned of 'probable German attempt to land parachute troops in Ireland'. A few days later the first sea lord asked that 'immediate study . . . be given to the possibility of the Germans making use of bases of various kinds in Eire, so that appropriate action could be taken in good time'. The conclusions of the planners made grim reading: Ireland was virtually defenceless, and could mount little resistance to a German attacking force. The IRA would act as a fifth column in support of the invader.[62]

British thinking on these problems was framed by three considerations. The first was that which motivated the navy, the desirability of acquiring Irish ports and facilities for operational purposes: in June Vice Admiral Tom Phillips, later to die on board the *Prince of Wales* off Malaya, reiterated that German possession of French Atlantic bases made action essential to 'secure occupation of ports in Eire'. The second major consideration was essentially military and defensive: the need to prevent Germany gaining a foothold in Ireland. British planning proceeded on two contrasting assumptions: that of Irish co-operation, and that of Irish hostility. If Britain intervened in support of Irish resistance against a German attack, her forces would generally be welcomed; if she moved into Irish territory in anticipation of a German attack, or simply to seize ports and other facilities, she would incur Irish hostility.[63] If the Germans chose instead to land in Northern Ireland, perhaps posing as liberators of nationalist areas, the best the British could hope for would be Irish inaction. That was a scenario which appealed to some republicans, and which 'particularly terrified' de Valera. At a meeting in August of the grandly titled 'Irish National Unity Council' in Dublin, attended by an assortment of northern nationalists, the German minister Edouard Hempel, and at least one Garda informant, it was decided to 'place the Catholic minority in Northern Ireland under the protection of the Axis Powers'.[64] The third consideration was entirely political and it grew in importance after the resignation of Neville Chamberlain as British prime minister on 10 May. His successor, Winston Churchill, was a man of an entirely different stamp.

There is no doubt that Churchill regarded Irish neutrality almost as a personal affront. He had enormous experience of Irish affairs, not least through his direct involvement in the Anglo-Irish settlement of 1921, but he could never accept that independent Ireland had flown the imperial nest. This was compounded by his extraordinary interest in—though not always mastery of—grand strategy, and by his intense devotion to the navy.[65] He exercised a

[62] JIC memorandum, 16 May, PRO, CAB 81/87; COS (40) 141 and 147, 20 and 24 May, PRO, CAB 79/4; 179 and 181, 13 and 14 June 1940, PRO, CAB 79/5.
[63] COS (40) 186, 19 June 1940, PRO, CAB 79/5.
[64] Bowman, *De Valera and the Ulster Question*, 211; Special Branch report, 9 Nov. 1941, DFA, A23.
[65] Interview with Sir Robert Fraser, who worked in the Treasury from 1914 to 1937, and who bemoaned Churchill's reverence for the navy while chancellor from 1924 to 1929, 1983.

consistently baleful influence on policy towards Ireland in the latter half of 1940 and in 1941, producing a succession of decisions calculated to underline Britain's displeasure at Irish policy. Yet, as his officials sometimes suggested, those measures individually and cumulatively had the effect of reinforcing Irish suspicions about Britain's intentions, and of strengthening rather than of weakening Irish resolve to stay out of the war. The refusal of arms, the imposition of restrictions on supplies, the constant complaints about security, were all legitimate weapons of Anglo-Irish conflict, but they were ones which required calculated deployment to produce desired results. When Ireland more or less ran out of tea as a result of British restrictions, the public did not blame the government for antagonizing the British; rather, they cursed the British for attempting to ration Ireland into war.[66] Where Churchill may have erred was in his miscalculation of the motivations and character of the Irish leadership, and in his naive assumptions about the effect of economic sanctions on Irish public opinion: in December 1940 he reportedly thought that 'refusal to buy her food, to lend her our shipping or to pay her our present subsidies seem calculated to bring de Valera to his knees in a very short time'.[67] But it is difficult to starve a self-sufficient agricultural economy into submission. On the other hand, putting the squeeze on Ireland was politically popular in Britain, where there was 'intense feeling against the neutrality policy', and may even have served to propitiate public outrage.[68]

The increased likelihood of German action against Ireland led to secret exchanges in London on 23 May, with Joseph Walshe of External Affairs and Liam Archer of G2 agreeing principles of military co-operation with British officials. These talks were followed by further clandestine discussions in Dublin about military co-operation in the event of an attack. While at pains to emphasize the army's material weaknesses, McKenna insisted that any British movement into Irish territory could come only after the Irish had first engaged the invader. He was advised not to concede the principle of 'command of the combined military forces . . . being placed under a British General'. Quite apart from the 'insurmountable . . . political and national difficulties', the ill-fated Norwegian campaign had shown that 'our staff are in general definitely more efficient' than their British army equivalents, although the RAF and navy were 'perfectly competent'. The army's hastily produced 'general defence plan no. 1', was geared primarily towards the containment of an 'internal uprising by the IRA' timed to coincide with a German attack: the British warned that 'an invasion is not only seriously planned and prepared with the help of the IRA, *but is imminent*'.[69] The

[66] Andrews, *Man of no property*, 170.

[67] J. Colville, *The Fringes of Power: Downing Street Diaries,* i: *1939–1941* (London, 1985), 363, 3 Dec. 1940.

[68] Menzies to A. W. Fadden, acting prime minister of Australia, 4 Mar. 1941, in Hudson and Stokes, *Documents on Australian Foreign Policy*, iv, 549–50.

[69] C. Mangan, 'Plans and Operations', *Irish Sword*, 19/75–6 (1993–4), 48–9; undated note by Col. J. J. O'Connell, MA, EDP 1/4; Antrobus (BRO) to Boland, 1 June 1940, DFA, A3.

obvious implication of the Irish army's plan was that the British would rapidly intervene, and the British themselves made clear their intention of sending a mobile column from Northern Ireland immediately upon news of a German attack. Speed of response would be crucial, as the success or failure of a German parachute assault might be settled in the first hours, because if paratroops could seize airfields, they could quickly be reinforced by troops and equipment flown in by transport aircraft.[70] The British later revised their counter-invasion plans. A royal marine brigade was moved to Milford Haven ready 'to sail at the shortest possible notice', although within weeks it was once more decided that troops based in Northern Ireland would be responsible for combating any German attack on Ireland.[71]

The discussions between McKenna and the British resulted in detailed preparations for combined action in the event of a German attack. A small British signals detachment was attached to army headquarters in Dublin in order to provide direct communications with British army headquarters in Northern Ireland, and an RAF radio station was also established in Maffey's office.[72] However, the succeeding months saw a heightening of mutual suspicions. On 24 June the British chiefs of staff advised against the supply of any further equipment unless the Irish agreed to co-operate by allowing the use of the ports, although they still 'saw no reason . . . from the military point of view' to depart from the principle of not invading Ireland unless the Germans did so first.[73] Two days later the British government suddenly presented de Valera with the prospect of post-war Irish unity, subject only to Northern Ireland's consent, in return for the provision of naval and air facilities to Britain and for Irish participation in the war. This desperate offer, remarkable though it was, did not contain any guarantee of unionist compliance. Even if it had done, for de Valera to plunge Ireland into war on Britain's side would have been an extraordinary act of faith, when most neutrals and many pro-British observers were expecting a rapid German victory. As John Bowman has observed, in the circumstances of June 1940 'the conclusion seems inescapable that no British offer, other than the establishment of a guaranteed, united, neutral Ireland would have had any serious appeal to the Fianna Fáil cabinet'. Since the British initiative was dictated precisely by strategic considerations, such a proposal was not an option—de Valera himself soon afterwards 'reluctantly acknowledged its impracticability' while Britain remained at war, and Northern nationalists also cautioned him to remember the fate of John Redmond, who had supported Britain's call to arms in 1914 on the assumption that home rule would eventually be granted.[74] His

---

[70] Canning, *British Policy*, 269.   [71] COS 188 and 203, 20 June and 1 July 1940, PRO, CAB 79/5.
[72] Memoranda by Pryce (BRO), 1 and 9 Oct. 1941, PRO, DO 130/16.
[73] COS (40) 192, 24 June 1940, PRO, CAB 79/5.
[74] Bowman, *De Valera and the Ulster Question*, 237; 'Menzies report'; T. Hennessey, *A History of Northern Ireland, 1920–1996* (Basingstoke, 1997), 84–5.

reaction to the British overtures created doubts as to his 'real attitude ... we cannot allow Eire to be handed over to the enemy'.[75] On the Irish side, the arrest in mid-July near Mullingar of a British officer engaged on a covert reconnaissance of routes south caused intense alarm, coming so soon after the army had disclosed its defence plans to the British. What, Walshe asked Maffey, were the Irish supposed to read into this?[76]

The British army in Northern Ireland was slowly strengthened in the autumn in anticipation of a possible 'decisive move on a broad front, should this at any time become necessary': Churchill thought that 'the effect' of this build-up 'in itself might produce the result desired' of intimidating de Valera into co-operation.[77] Britain also embarked on what amounted to a partial economic blockade of Ireland, albeit one heavily qualified by her continued need for Irish supplies and labour: in April 1941 de Valera told Robert Menzies that 'Eire could supply more foodstuffs to Great Britain, but ... Great Britain is prepared to go a little hungry in order to injure Eire'. More importantly in strategic terms, in March 1941 the British began a massive expansion of air and naval facilities in Northern Ireland. These became decisive assets in the Atlantic U-boat war, and they diluted the strategic case for southern Irish bases.[78]

British fear of an immediate German move into Ireland gradually faded in parallel with the prospect of a rapid invasion of the British mainland. On 10 July Churchill observed that he now thought a sudden invasion unlikely given the strength of the Royal Navy. While 'a small raid might be made upon Ireland from Brest ... this also would be dangerous to the raiders while at sea'. By October, the JIC still considered a German invasion of Ireland 'probable' but did not expect it for some months. By January 1941, the estimate was of a seaborne invasion of the southern coast by perhaps as many as five German divisions, intended as a diversionary measure during an assault on mainland Britain.[79] The first hard indications that Hitler had abandoned any intention of committing troops to an invasion of the British Isles did not become available through decrypted signals until mid-January 1941, and these did not have an immediate impact on British assessments of German intentions: in fact John Godfrey commented on a 'recrudesence' of the 'invasion scare' in the following month, despite signals intelligence and other reports indicating the contrary.[80] British

---

[75] COS (40) 204, 2 July 1940, PRO, CAB 79/5.

[76] Maffey to secretary of state, 16 July 1940, PRO, DO 130/12.

[77] Churchill to Eden (secretary of state for war), 12 Nov. 1940, PRO, CAB 120/582.

[78] 'Menzies report'; Sloan, *Geopolitics*, 211–19.

[79] Churchill to Ismay, 10 July 1940, PRO, ADM 223/484; JIC (40) 64, 31 Oct. 1940, PRO, CAB 81/87; JIC (41) 35, 31 Jan. 1941, PRO, CAB 81/88.

[80] M. Gilbert, *Churchill: A Life* (London, 1991), 681–2, 688; Godfrey to Board of Admiralty, 8 Apr., enclosing agent report dated 15 Feb. 1941, PRO, ADM 223/484. The continuing fear of invasion and the chronic lack of intelligence on German intentions are reflected in the diary of Major General F. H. N. Davidson, director of military intelligence from 1940 to 1944, 28 Dec. 1940, 28 and 29 Jan. and 14 Mar. 1941, Liddell Hart Centre for Military Archives, Kings College London, Davidson papers.

forces in Northern Ireland continued to plan for armed intervention across the border, and to study the military and political conditions which they might find. The development of liaison with the Irish army after June 1940, British provision of training for some Irish officers, and the free hand accorded to the British service attachés based in Dublin all served to increase the information available: in April 1941 the director of military intelligence noted that 'we also now covered Eire well'. Despite these improvements, British officers in Northern Ireland were reportedly adamant in 1942 that they were 'in insufficient force and that they lacked the necessary planes, armoured vehicles, and motor transport to knock out a powerful invasion force before it gathers momentum'.[81]

Politically, the most disturbing invasion scenario of all from an Irish point of view was what Bowman has termed 'de Valera's worst fear', a German raid in force on Northern Ireland. What would happen if, say, five thousand airborne troops were sent to seize key points, and the German government were to proclaim that this was the first step in the ending of British rule? Such an eventuality would undoubtedly inspire republican action in Northern Ireland; it would also pose acute difficulties for the Irish state. In such circumstances, would Irish forces (*a*) join the British in repelling the German attackers; (*b*) join the Germans in a campaign against British forces in Northern Ireland; or (*c*) do nothing, and await the military outcome? It was by no means clear that revanchist sentiment within both the general public and the army—some of whose most senior officers had fantasized in the mid-1930s about a successful war to repossess Northern Ireland—would be outweighed by sober calculations of where the state's long-term interests lay.[82]

For over a year after June 1940 Irish military planning proceeded on the basis of the equal likelihood of invasion by Germany or by Britain. In the event of a German attack, the army took British intervention as given, and arrangements were put in place to facilitate it. In December 1941, however, the army concluded that a German invasion of Ireland was 'unlikely' until Hitler had defeated Russia.[83] The more pressing danger came from Britain, most likely through attempts to seize Irish ports and airfields for Atlantic operations. Such action would depend on the complete subjugation of the Irish army which might otherwise harass the occupying forces and hamper sea and air operations. In December 1940 de Valera warned the army that relations with Britain 'had worsened and that there was a danger that the British might attempt a rapid and surprise occupation', and gave directions to intensify planning accordingly. While 'we must not be put into the position of making an aggressive move

---

[81] Davidson diary, 14 Mar. 1941; 'Reynolds report'.
[82] Bowman, *De Valera and the Ulster Question*, 242.
[83] General plan no. 2, quoted in Mangan, 'Plans and Operations', 52.

first . . . the situation might be such that we could assume the offensive particularly in the 6 County areas where the population was friendly'.[84]

Germany's Irish policy after the fall of France was calculated to serve a
number of purposes. The first was to stiffen Irish resolve not to grant facilities
to Britain and to stay neutral. The second was to impress on the Irish the
inevitability of German victory, and the potential which that offered for resolution of the problem of partition. The third was to lure Ireland into the German
sphere of influence, by the offer of military discussions and by the covert provision of captured British weapons. Acting under orders, Hempel made repeated
overtures about military co-operation in the latter half of 1940. He reported that
these were received politely but non-committally, although another legation
official made more headway in December 1940 in secret exchanges with an officer referred to only as 'L'. This was evidently the assistant chief of staff Hugo
MacNeill, who shortly afterwards became involved in discussions on the modal-
ities of an official approach by the chief of staff Dan McKenna to discuss the possibility of German assistance should Britain attack.[85] In such an eventuality the
Irish hoped that the Germans could supply 'British-type' weapons of all kinds,
could provide some air support within two days of the outbreak of hostilities,
could fly troops in to Irish airfields, and could quickly base naval units in the
port of Killybegs in south-west Donegal. In retrospect, these assumptions about
German capacity to overcome British air and sea interdiction en route to Ireland may appear naive. However, they were made in the aftermath of Hitler's
remarkable military successes in Europe, victories which had been characterized by unpredicted breakthroughs, and were partly based on the earlier
British estimates of Germany's ability quickly to dispatch significant forces to
Ireland.[86]

Although some officers probably hankered after an active alliance with Germany to drive the British out of Northern Ireland, the government's apparent
contemplation of a secret understanding with Germany was the product primarily of desperation. There may also have been an element of deception
intended. It was known that amongst the German agents already sent to Ireland
was one, Herman Goertz, who styled himself an emissary rather than a spy and
whose primary aim was to promote a rebellion in Northern Ireland and an
Irish/German understanding if Germany won the war. The government may
have hoped to scotch Goertz's intrigues by appearing better disposed towards
German offers of assistance than they in fact were.[87]

Whatever the reasons for it, the decision officially to anticipate German help

[84] Minutes of meeting to discuss general plan no. 2, 15 Dec. 1940, MA, EDP1/2.
[85] Duggan, *Neutral Ireland*, 119–37, 186; MacNeill to McKenna, 13 Dec. 1940, MA, EDP1/2.
[86] Undated memorandum by Colonel O'Connell, given to chief of staff on 13 Dec. 1940, EDP1/2;
Mangan, 'Plans and Operations', 51–2.
[87] The Goertz case is discussed in the following chapter.

in the event of a British incursion was a dangerous one. If it became known that the government had even considered approaching German diplomats not only for support in the event of a British invasion, but for captured British weapons with which to resist one, it would have provided the British with very good grounds for pre-emptive intervention. Furthermore, it was wildly impractical to suppose that the details of military collaboration could be settled by a few muffled exchanges in the German legation with diplomats unversed in military affairs, while it was difficult to see how Germany could have placed captured British arms in Irish hands without the British getting to hear of it immediately. From the German point of view this might not matter, but it would greatly undermine the case for Irish neutrality, particularly in the United States where the Roosevelt administration's hostility towards Ireland was somewhat constrained by Irish-American sentiment.

Fears of a British invasion gradually faded in the course of 1941, although in April Robert Menzies concluded that it remained de Valera's 'principal obsession' (as an invasion of Britain did the then chief of the imperial general staff Sir John Dill, who a month afterwards was still 'evidently very anxious about invasion and seemed to fear that Winston would insist on denuding this country of essential defensive forces').[88] German overtures to enter into a definite understanding about arms and support, never pressed with any great force by Hempel, ceased entirely as attention switched towards the planned war against Russia. The main thrust of Berlin's diplomatic policy towards Ireland thenceforth was straightforward: to encourage neutrality, and to dissuade de Valera from granting facilities to the Allies. In practice this was somewhat compromised by the continued efforts of the Abwehr to use Ireland as a base for espionage against the United Kingdom, but the broad lines of policy remained unchanged from 1941 to 1945.

British defence policy towards Ireland shifted as her fears of a German invasion of any part of the British Isles receded. The question of the ports and associated facilities gradually reverted to what it had been before the fall of France: a diplomatic issue, which would be dealt with by diplomatic means, not by force. The relatively straightforward issue of access to the treaty ports was gradually redefined: in March 1941 Menzies cabled his Australian colleagues that he had learned from 'intimate discussions with Churchill and others' that the 'real problem . . . is not so much the use of Irish ports as the use of land bases from which to employ fighter aircraft' to provide air cover for Atlantic convoys facing constant U-boat and long-range bomber attack. In August Godfrey, relying on a source 'graded A1'—undoubtedly decrypted Italian diplomatic traffic from Dublin to Rome—wrote that External Affairs had been at pains 'to persuade' the Italian minister in Dublin 'that there was no prospect of joint British-American

---

[88] Menzies report; Hankey diary, 13 May 1941, Hankey papers, HNKY 1/7.

action to obtain Eire bases'. He went on to describe a visit to Dublin, where he had useful discussions with the British and American representatives and with Joseph Walshe, the secretary of External Affairs. He found Walshe 'very interested in the bases question, but ... ignorant of the strategical as distinct from the political aspect' and disposed to think that British 'need of bases was lessened by recent events and developments'. Godfrey also 'attended a private dinner party at which (as always in Ireland) there was a good deal of political talk. The party might be described as a fairly representative and intelligent Dublin gathering', including three TDs and one of McKenna's officers. 'After a long and somewhat exhausting evening', Godfrey came away with a number of striking impressions. The Irish were obsessed with partition. They 'cling passionately to their neutrality', largely in Godfrey's view because of their 'fear of air attacks, which the Germans cleverly keep alive by their occasional raids'. They were 'genuinely puzzled by our refusal to give them arms. They think that we are inconsistent in urging them to stand up against the aggressor and giving them nothing to do it with', the 'usual complaint of the small neutral and never an easy one to answer'. Godfrey found 'their conceit impenetrable and they cannot bear to be ignored', but as a navy man his greatest complaint was about facilities:

The Irish cannot or will not understand the geographical factors which make the need of bases imperative. They cannot see that they and ourselves are like two houses on the edge of a cliff, which will both fall into the sea unless something is done to stop coast erosion. This argument is too realistic for them, and they invariably slide off into politics.[89]

The concerted action to secure facilities which Godfrey still hoped for never materialized. Instead, despite continuing anger at the Irish position, the British government became grudgingly reconciled to the fact that in no circumstances short of a German invasion would de Valera grant access to ports and airfields.

For his part, de Valera was willing to give the British and later also the Americans every possible help short of openly letting them use Irish territory for belligerent purposes: the only real constraint on co-operation was the desirability of keeping it as secret as possible. Britain had to make do with this, extracting concessions resulting in increasingly detailed and complex collaboration on a range of matters with some military bearing. Some of these, such as intelligence, security, and communications control, are dealt with elsewhere; here, however, we may note Irish acceptance of the stationing of British 'shipping advisers' in the principal ports, a necessary quid pro quo for the continuance of shipping to and from the state. As well as 'routeing ships', these men acted as conduits to the naval attaché for all manner of maritime information.[90] The same co-operative approach was adopted from the outset on weather information. The collection

---

[89] 'Godfrey report'.
[90] Boland's note of a meeting with Antrobus (BRO) and two shipping advisers, 20 Nov. 1940, NA, DFA, A10.

of Irish weather data and the preparation of forecasts had been a British responsibility, until 1936 when an Irish meteorological service had finally been established under British tutelage. Staffed by an assortment of British and European
meteorologists—its first Irish recruit did not join until 1939—it naturally
retained close links with its British midwife as well as developing contacts with
the Canadian and United States weather services. These links were allowed to
remain in place after September 1939, despite the obvious military value of
Atlantic weather reporting and the consequent argument that collaboration
was in breach of neutrality. In addition to the practical and political arguments
in favour of continuing collaboration—the Irish service received useful data
from the British, and Irish seaborne trade was entirely dependent on British
tolerance and protection—even in the dark days of June 1940 Industry and
Commerce had their eyes on a long-term economic benefit: an official wrote
that 'it has been our definite policy . . . to avoid giving the British any excuse for
taking up trans-Atlantic forecasting', lest British development of 'meteorological facilities comparable with those' at Shannon would 'adversely affect our
chances of making' Shannon 'a *permanent* port of call for trans-Atlantic aircraft'. Throughout the war, accordingly, the nascent meteorological service sent
encoded reports to Britain hourly using a standard code, from August 1941
encrypted through one-time pads supplied by the Dominions Office; the selection of data which it received in return generally proved sufficient for Irish forecasting purposes.[91] Much secrecy surrounded the dispatch and receipt of these
messages, but the weathermen involved were under no particular security
injunction beyond the standard civil service warnings not to disclose details
of their work. Indeed, one of them became quite friendly with an interned
Luftwaffe meteorologist.[92]

Germany's declaration of war against the United States on 10 December 1941
brought a new complication. Irish hopes that America would act as a guarantor
of neutrality had already been shaken by Roosevelt's undisguised hostility; now
the United States was in the war, and so had an even more direct interest than
hitherto in securing Britain's Atlantic supply routes. America's entry was the
occasion of Churchill's enigmatic telegram to de Valera 'Now is your chance.
Now or never. A nation once again.' The evidence suggests that the prime
minister intended not to guarantee the ending of partition, but rather to urge
unionists to consider this if the south proved its bona fides by helping to beat
Hitler. De Valera, however, took the telegram to be an offer of a British guarantee of eventual unity in return for Irish participation in the war. But even this

---

[91] Fergusson (Industry and Commerce) to Walshe, 6 June 1940, and high commissioner, London, to
Walshe, 20 Aug. 1941, DFA, A14; interview with Dr Austin Bourke, the first Irish graduate to join the
service in 1939, 1994.

[92] Bourke interview; Nagle (director of the meteorological service) to Fergusson, 22 July 1942, DFA,
A41.

was not something which he could agree to, because he did not believe that the Irish public would support such an arrangement at a time when the country was virtually defenceless against air attack, and when Germany was still thought likely to defeat Britain.[93] In fact American entry into the war against Germany, and the much trumpeted arrival of American servicemen in Northern Ireland shortly afterwards, created new difficulties in and added to Anglo-Irish and to Irish–American tensions for the following two years. An outright demand for naval and air facilities under pain of force, a course repeatedly pressed by David Gray, the American minister in Dublin, remained a possibility until the invasion of France in June 1944. But the likelihood was never very great, for a combination of political and military factors, and de Valera knew it. The gradual improvement in the army's effectiveness, while it was never a decisive deterrent factor, had the effect of increasing the size of the military investment which would be required to seize key installations, render them secure for operational use, and subdue Irish resistance. The strengthening of Irish defences also had political implications: while an unopposed occupation could cause little fuss anywhere save amongst the Axis powers, the use of force on the scale necessary to subdue concerted military resistance would be very difficult for the Allies to justify. The principal military and political arguments against allied violation of Irish neutrality were, however, pragmatic.[94] The acquisition and rapid development by the United States of bases from 1941 onwards in Iceland, Greenland, and the Azores, the introduction of effective long-range anti-submarine aircraft, technical improvements in submarine detection, the commissioning of escort carriers for convoy protection, and the prodigious expansion of the Londonderry base, all progressively diluted the strategic case for taking southern Irish facilities by force, although the Allied military staffs saw clear advantages in terms of supporting the invasion of Europe. Furthermore, although the battle of the Atlantic remained undecided until the summer of 1943—when British code-breakers regained their mastery of German U-boat communications after five frantic months during which losses of shipping had soared— once America entered the war British strategic preoccupations shifted from securing national survival to planning for an eventual invasion of the continent.[95] Ireland's position in Allied strategic calculations altered accordingly: what mattered most after December 1941 was not Irish bases, or Irish vulnerability to German assault, but Irish security, defined by the Allies as the prevention of espionage or sabotage activities directed against the United Kingdom, and of the innocent leakage of information from the United Kingdom through Ireland to Germany. These were matters which an autonomous Irish government was far better placed to handle than any occupying force could be if

---

[93] Bowman, *De Valera and the Ulster Question*, 246–8.

[94] J. G. Winant, *A Letter from Grosvenor Square: An Account of a Stewardship* (London, 1947), 186–8.

[95] Sloan, *Geopolitics*, 222–3; Gilbert, *Churchill*, 719–24.

confronted with an antagonistic population. From 1942 on, Irish security policy proved to be the cornerstone of military neutrality.

vi. Signals Intelligence and Diplomatic Communications

In 1939 the state was almost completely incapable of protecting its interests in respect of encoded cable and radio traffic into and out of Ireland, but the years to 1945 were to see a surprising accumulation of expertise in certain aspects of decryption. The main issues can be grouped under two broad headings: the security of the state's own communications, and communications to and from the Dublin diplomatic missions of the belligerent powers. The clandestine communications of foreign agents operating in Ireland are discussed together with their other activities in the next chapter.

In September 1939 the security of the state's own external communications was very limited. The one exception to this was probably meteorological reports. Contact with diplomatic missions abroad was maintained variously by telephone (only to London), by correspondence, and by cabled messages. The perils of the telephone as a medium for confidential discussions were appreciated by all, although the high commissioner in London was sometimes indiscreet just as American and British officials in Dublin on occasion were.[96] The alternatives of the ordinary post, or even of a diplomatic bag, were slow and were always liable to covert interception. By contrast, cable communication was relatively swift and if material was encoded, potentially highly secure. However, the External Affairs codes were evidently vulnerable to foreign code-breakers. A fortnight before the outbreak of war a list of twenty-four code words was sent to missions in Europe to cover various eventualities, but this precaution apart no special steps were taken to improve the security of Irish traffic.[97] Once war came it proved impractical to supply significant revisions or updates to the prewar code system, while the physical security of code documents in missions abroad can never have been high. Consequently it was probable that interested powers would be able to read Irish diplomatic cables at will. These points were as obvious to External Affairs and to its more reflective officials abroad as they are in retrospect: in 1943 Michael MacWhite, unaware that some of his cables had already reached Winston Churchill's desk, wrote from Rome to point out that 'the system we employ is an old one and is not over difficult to break'.[98]

It is certain that from mid-1941 cryptanalysts of the code-breaking agency GC&CS (from 1942 GCHQ) at Bletchley were able to break Irish diplomatic

---

[96] Stephenson interview. In 1941 restrictions on External Affairs/London calls were eased, apparently in return for additional teleprinter facilities for the BRO. DFA, P42.

[97] Walshe to missions in Europe, 24 Aug. 1939, DFA, S75.

[98] MacWhite to External Affairs, 4 May 1943, DFA, P8.

cable traffic from missions in Europe and the United States as they had done in the early 1930s.[99] Furthermore, by 'October 1943 the Americans were also reading some traffic', although 'Irish codes never received more than intermittent attention' as the United States 'was pleased to leave this target to the British'. American code-breakers in fact experienced problems in obtaining copies of Irish traffic from Bletchley in 1943, but the cause was evidently a personality clash within the British organization rather than a policy decision to hold material back. It can safely be assumed that decrypted Irish material went as a matter of course to the Foreign Office and to the Dominions Office, the two departments with direct interest in Irish affairs. It is less clear whether the State Department regularly saw Irish decrypts, and it is not yet possible to see what impact, if any, such material had on British and American policy towards Ireland. It is also highly likely that Irish traffic was broken and read by other powers, including Germany and Italy, more or less whenever they wished.[100]

The British records indicate that almost all of the surprisingly large number of decoded Irish messages which were shown to Churchill, a confirmed signals intelligence addict, as part of his daily feast of intercepted communications between January 1941 and the spring of 1945 were ones dealing not with policy but with political gossip and general conditions in Axis and neutral countries.[101] Thus, Kerney's Madrid telegram of 7 October 1941 relaying rumours that the foreign minister 'Suner may be sent to the Vatican' and replaced by 'Franco's brother, who is . . . very pro-British', and that 'Hitler is very reliably stated to be acting to find some way to make peace with England' was seen by Churchill four days later.[102] It was Irish cables from Rome and later from Berlin, however, which seem to have contained the most meat. One of only two diplomatic decrypts shown to Churchill on 16 February 1943 was a report from MacWhite of a conversation with an Italian minister, who 'told me that if the Italians were to change sides, as many people advocated, they would never hold their heads up again. They must drain the bitter cup of defeat.' Further reports from MacWhite which Churchill saw described the collapse of Italian morale, bomb damage, shifts in German military policy in and around Rome, and German preparations for withdrawal from the city. MacWhite was concerned both about the value and the security of his cables which 'by the time they reach you . . . must be rather insipid'; he was never to know that the British thought many of them sufficiently

[99] The organization was moved out of London to Bletchley shortly before war broke out. 'Bletchley' has become shorthand for British military and diplomatic code-breaking, even though much of this was done elsewhere.

[100] D. Alvarez, 'No Immunity: Sigint and the European Neutrals, 1939–45', *Intelligence and National Security*, 12/2 (Apr. 1997), 31–2; Smith to Birch, 23 Dec. 1945, enclosing table showing 'the figures of distribution to our various customers' of intercepted diplomatic traffic, 1939–45, PRO, HW3/162.

[101] Andrew, *Secret Service*, 462.

[102] Irish minister, Madrid, to Dublin, 11 Oct. 1941, PRO, HW1/133. I am grateful to Dr Neville Wylie for introducing me to this source.

interesting to bring to the personal attention of their prime minister.[103] After the fall of Rome, most of the Irish telegrams seen by Churchill were from Con Cremin in Berlin. These chronicled the cumulative impact of relentless bombing, the growing public realization of impending defeat, brief upsurges of optimism after isolated military successes at Arnhem and in the Ardennes, rumours of splits in the German leadership, and Cremin's assessment that Hitler would fight to the end. Only one dealt with a significant policy matter: in December 1944 Cremin reported that Dublin's query about the fate of Jews deported from Kaunas had received a very dusty answer from an official 'with whom I have excellent relations... they would find it difficult to understand how the question of Lithuanian Jews could affect us particularly'. Cremin sought advice on 'whether... the matter is important to us because of possible hostile propaganda if we were to seem to be indifferent'. One other Irish telegram seen by Churchill stands out, a 1944 cable from Chicago disclosing an American approach to Irish delegates at a civil aviation convention to secure 'unlimited frequencies to Shannon... as a port of entry into Europe' for American airlines.[104]

It is highly likely that Irish military communications were also routinely intercepted and read. Allied and Axis signals detection and location organizations would automatically have attempted to cover all Irish civil and military radio communications, if only because the identification of all 'unknown traffic', however nondescript it might be, was a prerequisite to the proper mapping of all signals activity.[105] Material intercepted would then have been available for attempts at decoding, depending on the intercepting power's priorities and resources. As with Irish diplomatic traffic, military communications would have posed no serious challenge for sophisticated cryptanalytical organizations. In 1946 the army's main cipher was dismissed by the state's leading codebreaker Richard Hayes as 'very inferior' and far easier to break than some of the hand ciphers used by German agents sent to Ireland. Its 'security factor... is very low... It is to be hoped that no Irish army will ever again face an emergency so ill-provided in this essential security device.'[106] The main constraint on foreign reading of Irish military traffic would, it appears, simply have been pressure of more urgent business.

---

[103] Irish minister, Rome, to Dublin, 11 Sept. 1942, 10 Mar. and 21 Dec. 1943, and 13 Feb., 10, 23, and 28 Mar., and 1 Apr. 1944, PRO, HW1/896, 1370, 2314, 2456, 2617, 2660, 2676, and 2684 respectively; McWhite to Walshe, 30 Apr. 1943, quoted in Keogh, *Ireland and Europe*, 137.

[104] Cremin to External Affairs, 29 July 1943, 13 Mar., 22 July, 28 Aug., 18 Sept., 8 Oct., 11 and 28 Nov., and 25 Dec. 1944, and 30 Jan. 1945, PRO, HW1/1876, 1902, 2624, 3360, 3124, 3202, 3227, 3265, 3302, 3339, 3397, and 3506 respectively. The Irish decrypts are discussed in detail in E. O'Halpin, ' "According to the Irish Minister in Rome . . .": British Decrypts and Irish Diplomacy in the Second World War', *Irish Studies in International Affairs*, 6 (1995), 95–105.

[105] 'GCHQ diplomatic intercept history 1939–45' by C. Williams, pp. 3–4, with note by Williams, 30 July 1946, PRO, HW3/162, cited hereafter as 'GCHQ intercept history'.

[106] Valedictory report on code-breaking from 1940 to 1945 by Dr Richard Hayes, 2 Jan. 1946, National Library of Ireland, Richard Hayes MS 22984, cited hereafter as 'Hayes report'.

Communications to and from the Dublin missions of the belligerent powers presented a rather greater challenge to those interested in knowing their contents. In security terms, the advantages lay firmly with the Allies. Maffey's office had a range of means by which to communicate with London, including official and clandestine radio transmitters, telephone and teleprinter land lines to Northern Ireland, messages carried by courier by train or car to Belfast or by mail boat to Holyhead, officials carrying verbal instructions by scheduled civilian flights from Dublin airport or from Rineanna (Shannon) to Britain, and for a time even a clutch of carrier pigeons surreptitiously housed in the air attaché's attic. While routine telephone tapping and the interception of personal correspondence consigned to the ordinary post protected only by a stamp stating 'Exempt from censorship' yielded useful material for G2 from time to time, it appears that neither the Irish nor Axis signals intelligence organizations managed to read any confidential communications transmitted or cabled between Maffey's office and London in the course of the Emergency. Despite this, we may note Maffey's warning to his American counterpart in 1944 that the Irish had 'a very skilled cryptographer', Richard Hayes, with whose abilities the British were familiar from the close Anglo-Irish co-operation on German agent ciphers which developed after 1941, who 'had broken his code messages from London'. This led the secretary of state Cordell Hull to speculate after the 'American note' crisis of February 1944 that 'the Irish might be decoding some of our messages . . . The text of the proposed note' had been telegraphed to Gray 'in Brown code in which we no longer place great reliance', and 'we did not exclude the possibility that it might become known to the Irish authorities . . . it was believed that no great harm would come should they obtain a copy in advance'.[107] In fact Hayes in his valedictory report wrote that he had made no serious efforts to study, let alone to break, American traffic, and stated that 'we had experience of only one British cipher . . . picked up during March 1945 from a British transmission to a resistance group inside Germany'.[108] American concerns could more accurately have been directed at their closest ally, as the British were reading State Department traffic to Dublin in the months up to Pearl Harbor: one of the two decrypts supplied to Churchill on 23 November 1941 was a cable from Hull to Gray.[109] The Irish mounted their intelligence efforts against the American legation through the technically less demanding methods of postal interception, telephone tapping, and possibly the suborning of some legation employees. With so indiscreet a target, the pickings were usually good.

G2 adopted the same approach in respect of most of the other Dublin diplomatic missions. The exception was that of German cable and radio traffic.

---

[107] Gray to Washington, 22 Feb., and Hull to Gray, 21 Apr. 1944, USNA, State Department, 841.D01/240 and 342; 'Hayes report'.

[108] 'Hayes report'.

[109] Text of Hull to American Legation, Dublin, 18 Nov., decrypted 23 Nov. 1941, PRO, HW1/251.

When war broke out, all G2 had to guide it was its very limited pre-war studies on cryptanalytical problems, plus the advice of signals officers. The army did, however, have one crucial additional resource in Hayes, the director of the National Library and a War of Independence veteran who was both a self-taught codes and ciphers expert and an accomplished linguist. Hayes's cryptanalytical achievements during the Emergency have frequently been distorted, yet the documentary evidence indicates that in real terms they have not been exaggerated. Starting 'more or less from scratch' in August 1940, when a number of 'documents' were captured with the German agent Wilhelm Preetz which disclosed the cipher 'system used and [the] book containing the keywords . . . no work was necessary beyond writing a report on the system', Hayes almost singlehandedly provided G2 with the capability for the informed analysis of complex signals intelligence issues and, crucially, for breaking the only enciphered traffic which really mattered for the government during the war, that is the communications of individual German agents.[110]

The first serious cipher problem to be addressed, however, related not to agent but to German diplomatic traffic. It arose in February 1941, after the British said they had picked up transmissions in a German diplomatic cipher from a point north of Dublin. Dan Bryan and a signals officer went to the area on a 'preliminary speculative adventure which in hindsight was merely a waste of time'. A hastily established G2 signals section soon made the unwelcome discovery that the transmissions were coming from a clandestine radio transceiver housed in the German legation. Bryan later expressed some surprise that the British, whose Radio Security Service had been set up specifically to detect all clandestine and illegal traffic, were so wide of the mark in their initial fix: 'it raises . . . what they knew about the whole German diplomatic network of transmissions at this time . . . I would have expected the British people studying the diplomatic code should have tumbled to the fact that there was something in Dublin much sooner than they started corresponding with us'.[111] Bryan's suspicions are vindicated by the documents: Maffey raised 'the possibility of the German Legation having a secret wireless' with Walshe on 19 February 1941, and a recently released Bletchley document indicates that by the time the Irish were tipped off the British had already uncovered

a clandestine W[ireless] T[elegraphy] network (later to be known as 'Group 14'), connecting Berlin with most of the German embassies and a number of consulates. Traffic was . . . mainly . . . diplomatic, but a considerable proportion of Abwehr material was carried; one or two stations carried Abwehr traffic only. The nature of this group was brought to light by the capture of some German secret documents when the British occupied Reykjavik [on 10 May 1940]. The controlling transmitters were at Nauen . . . only two locations were known . . . [in February 1941]—Dublin and Madrid.

---

[110] 'Hayes report'; Bryan interview.
[111] Bryan transcripts, p. 19; on the RSS see Hinsley and Simkins, *British Intelligence*, 13, 72–3.

Detection of the radio presented the Irish with an appalling problem. On the one hand, it might be broadcasting intelligence or weather reports to Berlin; on the other, the legation could not be prevented from using it. Germany still appeared the most likely victor in the war, and undue pressure on Hempel might be impolitic. It was decided to conceal from the British the precise source of the transmissions until more was known about the traffic. For their part, the British decided to withhold technical data which they had obtained, together with the fact that they knew the traffic was German diplomatic.[112]

Once the source of the transmissions was established, a continuous radio watch was established in an adjacent army barracks. This enabled G2 to keep a record of all the enciphered radio traffic to and from the legation, a prerequisite to the proper management of the problem by External Affairs—without this, it would have been impossible to know whether or not the radio was in regular use, and so would have weakened the hands of Irish officials in their dealings with Hempel. At the behest of de Valera, a keen though indifferent mathematician, Hayes was asked to attempt to break the traffic. He sought 'the assistance of two or three men with high university qualifications in science or mathematics', but 'this help was not forthcoming and I was instead given three [army] lieutenants ... These men did useful work in tabulating material and compiling statistics, but had no special ability for cryptography.' The enterprise was set up amidst great secrecy: Kevin Boland, son of the minister for justice, was recruited only after he swore not to disclose anything of the work even to his father. After 'three or four months' spent 'in establishing that the German code was not of the simple dictionary code book type', the 'work was ... abandoned ... as there was not the slightest prospect of success with the staff available'. Three years later Hayes mounted 'a continuous investigation' of German cable traffic, as there was a 'high probability' that three cables to Berlin were relaying information smuggled out to the legation in enciphered messages by the imprisoned agent Herman Goertz, the contents of which G2 were already aware. Again he did not succeed:

The investigation was founded on the assumption that the code was based on a machine. An interesting mathematical system was worked out which made it possible to test the code for the more probable possibilities ... the theoretical value of the work done was of great interest, and may at some future date prove invaluable.[113]

Since the British already knew of the radio, and of the fact that it was part of a network of clandestine stations capable of communicating with each other as well as with Berlin, the Irish decision not to tell the British about its location

---

[112] Note by Walshe for de Valera, 19 Feb. 1941, DFA, A2; GCHQ intercept history, p. 3; Maltby to Kenworthy (Radio Security Service), 25 Oct. 1941, PRO, HW 14/21.

[113] Bryan transcripts, p. 21; remarks of Mr Kevin Boland at meeting of the 1916–1921 club, Dublin, 27 Apr. 1988; 'Hayes report'.

caused great strain in the spring of 1941. For a time all dealings between G2 and MI5 ceased. In November, however, when the Irish had good news to convey about the imminent arrest of Goertz, Bryan visited London for discussions. The importance attached to these talks is reflected in a minute from the deputy head of MI6 to his chief Sir Stewart Menzies:

Our plan is that Colonel Bryan should be asked to bring a technical advisor with him and that Maltby should have a preliminary talk with them to find out . . . (1) what has actually been done in the way of D[irection]/F[ind]-ing and picking up the German diplomatic wireless transmission from Dublin . . . and (2) whether the Eire authorities have been able to detect any other enemy wireless station transmitting from Eire . . . We propose to tell Colonel Bryan that in spite of [Joseph] Walshe's confidence, the German . . . station has been transmitting since the Eire authorities believed they had disposed of it and, under due safeguards, it will probably be necessary . . . to put certain technical data before Colonel Bryan in order to convince him of this point.

Menzies agreed, though 'the Eire delegate must not know too much of what we do over here'. Bryan, too, was under orders not to be completely frank. He told the British that the transmitter had been located (though not where it was housed), that it was being continuously monitored, and that it would soon cease broadcasting. In December the British proposed close co-operation on 'suspicious signals heard in either country', arguing that this would be mutually beneficial because 'radio signals in general can be heard only within a very few miles from their source . . . or at a considerable distance' and offering additional detection apparatus. The records suggest that some collaboration did take place thereafter on illicit signals problems. However, before this began to operate effectively the problem of the legation transmitter blew up again.[114]

Here there is a clash of evidence. Bryan recollected that External Affairs had not actually yet raised the matter with Hempel, and that the transmissions continued: 'I sent a copy of the transmissions each day to External Affairs and could do nothing more about the matter', whereas the British official history states that the transmitter went off air 'in the middle of 1941'. Furthermore, the External Affairs files carry reports and some enciphered text of traffic between August 1941 and February 1942: as an example, Bryan rang on 5 December 1941 to report 'very heavy traffic both ways'.[115] In February 1942 the German battle cruisers *Scharnhorst* and *Gneiseneau* slipped up through the narrow waters of the English Channel, taking advantage of dense fog caused by a sudden change in the weather. The British press carried claims that the Germans had acted on a meteorological report from the Dublin legation, which 'transmitted what were assumed to be weather reports during the passage' of the two ships. A memoir

---

[114] Minute to Menzies, and his reply, 22 and 23 Oct. 1941, PRO, HW 14/21; Bryan to Walshe, enclosing British proposals, 15 Dec. 1941, DFA, A25.

[115] Bryan transcripts, pp. 21–3; Hinsley and Simkins, *British Intelligence*, 205; note of telephone call, 5 Dec. 1941, DFA, A25.

by a British specialist in German diplomatic traffic also speaks of 'the accurate weather reports which had emanated from Ireland'.[116] In the immediate aftermath of the drama, Walshe told de Valera that the British 'would be justified in concluding that there was some connection between the sudden resumption after a long interval' of Hempel's 'wireless activities and the German coup in the Channel'. On the other hand, the meteorological service told Bryan that the 'weather which caused the snowstorm came from the east', a point made independently by a veteran meteorologist in 1994. Furthermore, in his unpublished memoirs, which in places evidently paraphrase intelligence reports, Admiral Godfrey wrote that 'the idea that meteorological reports were made and passed on by the German legation was discounted by the experts. Germany was receiving ample meteorological reports from their aircraft in the Atlantic.'[117] Whatever the facts of the matter, the public row led External Affairs to approach Hempel about the transmitter. He gave an undertaking that it would not be used again. When the British broke the German diplomatic code in January 1943, they discovered that, 'while refusing requests from Berlin to resume transmissions' in October 1942, Hempel had 'undertaken to do so should he receive any vital operational intelligence'. From Irish records, it is known that the British did intercept a number of attempts by Germany to call up the Dublin station '(which has not been heard for some months) and asked them to reply every hour' on 27 and 28 October 1942. The British asked the Irish to 'listen in'. That evening Walshe urged Hempel not to reply to the transmissions, and this appears to have worked. In December 1943 further British pressure, prompted by fears about security in the build-up to the invasion of Europe and by decrypts which 'revealed that Berlin was pressing the legation for information about Allied intentions', prompted External Affairs to ask Hempel to surrender the set. It was collected from the legation by Fred Boland of External Affairs and the G2 signals expert Commandant Neligan, who 'declared that every detail in the set was complete', and it was then placed in a Dublin bank vault. As neither the Allies nor Berlin learned of this arrangement, presumably on foot of a gentlemen's agreement between Hempel and External Affairs, the radio remained a cause of great concern. American code-breakers noted that in the spring of 1944,

despite assertions by the Eire Government that illicit communications no long exist between Berlin and Dublin, the Berlin control station . . . continued to transmit to secondary station BK (Dublin) throughout this period. However, there was no evidence of reply by radio from Dublin.[118]

---

[116] Hinsley and Simkins, *British Intelligence*, 205; P. Filby, 'Floradora and a Unique Break into One-Time Pad Ciphers', *Intelligence and National Security*, 10/3 (July 1995), 416.

[117] Walshe to de Valera, 17 Feb. 1942, DFA, A25; Bryan transcripts, p. 23; Bourke interview; xerox of pp. 182–205 of typescript initialled at end 'JH G[odfrey]', evidently an extract from a document in the Godfrey papers at Churchill College Cambridge, Bryan papers, P71/138, cited hereafter as 'Godfrey memoir'.

[118] Hinsley and Simkins, *British Intelligence*, 195 and 205; Bryan transcripts, p. 24; Hankinson (BRO)

The British also had to worry about Axis diplomatic traffic. All such cables were, like all other cables to and from Ireland, automatically routed through London. There they were delayed for security reasons for a few days, to lessen the value of any operational intelligence they might contain, before being passed on to Berne and thence to Berlin and Rome respectively.[119] The British evidently broke the Italian cables. So too did the Americans, who read Italian traffic between Dublin and Italian missions in neutral South American states. However, German diplomatic traffic remained impervious to Allied cryptanalysts until January 1943. The British were then able to read some earlier Dublin/Berlin exchanges of which they had records. This was for the most part innocuous in intelligence terms, and it confirmed that the legation was not an active centre of espionage although it did report any information which came its way in the ordinary course of affairs—while one British code-breaker recalled that 'we found Dublin passing all manner of possible dates and places of landings in France' in the run up to D-Day, Godfrey commented that Hempel's 'reports to Berlin were chiefly concerned with indiscreet conversations of Irish members of HM Forces on leave in Eire, or British technicians visiting the country'.[120]

The handful of decrypted German telegrams concerning Ireland passed to Churchill, while they bear out the impression that Hempel was not bent on espionage and do not include weather reports, are otherwise of little intrinsic interest. The only substantive German message was shown to the prime minister in 1943 not because of what it disclosed about Nazi intrigue, but rather because, as Sir Stewart Menzies put it in a rare explanatory note, 'although I do not usually send you German messages from Dublin . . . the attached . . . is worth your notice, as it gives a plain statement of Irish policy'. Walshe had thanked Hempel for Germany's 'sympathetic appreciation of the difficulties here', had reiterated Ireland's position that partition ruled out 'participation on the side of the Allies', and had complained of British 'insinuations' that Ireland might emulate the neutral Portuguese, who had allowed the Allies to use the Azores. In the last year of the war Churchill saw other unremarkable Irish cables from Berlin, perhaps provided to illustrate the erosion of German confidence in ultimate victory. By contrast, the available American records suggest that neither Roosevelt nor Truman took the slightest interest in signals intelligence concerning Ireland: only a handful of German and Japanese telegrams to and from Dublin were forwarded to the White House between 1943 and 1945, and none of these shed any light on Irish affairs (as it happened, the text of the Japanese

---

to Boland, and transcript of Walshe/Hempel telephone conversation, both 28 Oct. 1942, DFA, A25; 'History of Special German Diplomatic Network . . .', USNA, RG459, box 1282, file CBTH62 18743.

[119] Filby, 'Floradora', 416, says messages were delayed seven days as a matter of policy. An Irish study of inward German telegrams from Berne found that in October 1941 the delay in London had been '4–5 days'. Bryan to Walshe, 9 Jan. 1942, DFA, A8.

[120] Hinsley and Simkins, *British Intelligence*, 195; Filby, 'Floradora', 416; 'Godfrey memoir', p. 196.

foreign ministry message to missions abroad conveying news of Japan's capitulation came from a Tokyo/Dublin telegram).[121]

A final concern was that communications between Hempel and Berlin might be maintained by covert post or by courier. The German legation did not operate a diplomatic bag, but there were strong suspicions that messages were sent by hand via ships plying between Ireland and neutral Portugal.[122] This route was certainly used for espionage purposes but not, it appears, by the Dublin legation or by the German Foreign Office. Once the British broke the German diplomatic code used for radio and cable traffic, consequently, they had complete mastery of Dublin/Berlin exchanges.

The other obviously dangerous diplomatic missions in Dublin were those of the Spanish, the Japanese, the Vichy French, and the Italian governments. While not all British decrypts are available, it is very likely that the traffic of all these missions was eventually, with varying degrees of difficulty, broken and read. The British could break Italian diplomatic traffic to and from Dublin at least from early in 1941, and the Americans could also read some material; although the Italians introduced very complex ciphers in mid-1942, it is also known that these were eventually mastered. Amongst the collection of decrypts supplied to Churchill were three Italian messages concerning Ireland, two of which deal with matters of some substance. In the first, the Italian minister Berardis reported Walshe as downplaying the significance of the presence of American troops in Northern Ireland, and complaining that the bombing of Belfast had played into British hands and 'seemed to be an act scarcely worthwhile from the point of view of the results it was supposed to produce in the prosecution of the war'. Walshe added that de Valera 'hoped to avoid trouble for his country, apart from such as inevitably arose from the economic situation'. On this Churchill minuted: 'Keep handy. I may want it', the only occasion on which he was moved to comment on a decrypt relating to Ireland. The second Berardis telegram recounted de Valera's highly charged views, 'because of his attachment to Italy and to the capital of Christianity', on the bombing of Rome in July 1943. The Allies, he reportedly declared, 'will be responsible before humanity for the destruction of the [eternal?] city . . . the English will go down in history . . . for the barbarous way in which they have waged this war', a conclusion which Churchill marked in red ink. While Berardis may have felt it politic to exaggerate even the most anodyne diplomatic conversations to his beleaguered masters, it is unlikely that the British made allowances for possible reporting bias.[123]

---

[121] Menzies to Churchill, undated, with German legation, Dublin, to Berlin, 16 Oct. 1943, PRO, HW1/2138; text of Tokyo to Dublin [consulate], 14 Aug., decrypted 15 Aug. 1945, USNA, RG457, box 1033, CBOM78.

[122] Godfrey to Greig, 22 Nov. 1939, PRO, DO 130/3.

[123] Berardis to Rome, 28 Mar. and 16 June 1942, and 20 July 1943, PRO, HW1/1454, 654, and 1876 respectively.

Such decrypts can only have reinforced their view of de Valera as a dissimulating Catholic fanatic. The American archives also contain decrypts of Italian material emanating from Dublin, as well as some from the Japanese consulate which suggest that it was not providing Tokyo with any intelligence. Overall, the decrypts now available support the conclusion which G2, relying on simpler and more local techniques such as postal interception and telephone tapping, reached about foreign diplomatic activities in Ireland. This was that, with the limited and half-hearted exception of the German legation, no Axis or pro-Axis mission attempted to provide any intelligence of strategic or military value for their governments. That, however, was something which only mastery and a continuous watch of their enciphered communications could confirm. That the British and Americans remained nervous about the dangers posed by these diplomatic missions is, accordingly, entirely understandable.

While the state can be faulted for the low level of security of its own encoded diplomatic and military communications, in the event this did not much matter. G2 and External Affairs can, furthermore, generally be congratulated for the way in which they addressed the key signals intelligence problems which arose during the Emergency, those centred on unreadable German diplomatic traffic and on the clandestine legation radio, and those which arose from the operations within the state of German agents. The remarkable code-breaking work of Richard Hayes meant that G2 was able to deal with the British on a basis of equality in respect of such agent traffic, rather than depending on them for possibly misleading summaries of the contents of intercepted German communications. This in turn undoubtedly contributed to the high regard in which G2 came to be held by both British and American security organizations.

vii. Irish Exiles and Axis Covert Activities Relating to Ireland, 1939–1945

The final aspect of external security which requires consideration arose from the 'possibility of co-operation between the IRA and Germany' in the event of an invasion of the British Isles. This, along with the danger that Germany would use Ireland for espionage, was an acute concern.[124] Espionage is dealt with in the following chapter; here the threats posed by republican activities abroad are considered.

The pre-war exchanges between Jim O'Donovan and the Abwehr had gone undetected. Furthermore, while the government anticipated that the IRA would seek to help a German invasion on the assumption that British defeat would lead to the ending of partition, until the summer of 1940 there was very

---

[124] Draft report on year 1940, Bryan papers, P71/30.

little concrete evidence to go on in assessing the existence, extent, and results of a definite German/IRA understanding.[125] The answers to these riddles lay in Berlin and in the United States, not in Dublin, and it took years to acquire a reasonably complete picture of the nature, extent, and limits of German involvement with the Irish abroad. In February 1940, for example, External Affairs were told that the Garda could not furnish even basic information such as the names of potential Irish subversives based in the United States.[126]

The man identified as the likely linchpin of any possible Irish/German arrangements was Sean Russell, who had gone to the United States at the end of 1938, but his whereabouts remained a mystery until 1942. Russell, who had sought German support for IRA activities as early as 1936, had in fact travelled from the United States to Italy in 1940, and had sought weapons and military support for an IRA uprising timed to coincide with a German attack (a rumour along these lines was in fact reported to Dublin by the Irish consulate in Geneva in 1940, but was evidently discounted).[127]

In Germany Russell was brought into contact with his former comrade Frank Ryan, who had been captured and sentenced to death during the Spanish civil war while serving in the International Brigade. Until July 1940 he had languished in Burgos jail despite considerable diplomatic and public pressure to have him released—including an official request for British intercession in 1939 and, remarkably, a telegram to Franco from the former Blueshirt leader General O'Duffy.[128] The Irish minister in Madrid, Leopold Kerney, had then taken it upon himself to arrange and pay for Ryan's contrived escape from captivity into German hands. Kerney, who had been dismissed from the fledgling diplomatic service during the civil war because of his republican views, before being rehabilitated after Fianna Fáil took office in 1932, was always a man of hopeless judgement—in 1934 he had achieved the unhappy distinction of being personally 'admonished' by de Valera for making intemperate and unfounded complaints about another department. He displayed a naive faith in the integrity of the diplomatic bag, and he allowed his bag to be used by friends attempting to evade the normal postal censorship.[129] When he belatedly informed External Affairs of his role in Ryan's escape in August 1940, he claimed that he had acted on the understanding that Ryan would be smuggled to safety in the United States.[130] In reality Ryan, who despite his radical pedigree was evidently willing to co-operate with Germany, travelled to Paris. There he met with Helmut

---

[125] Note by O'Donoghue of his June 1940 talk with Tom Barry, 23 Nov. 1943, MA, G2/X/0093.

[126] Justice to External Affairs, 2 Apr. 1940, DFA, A12/1.

[127] Geneva to External Affairs, 4 Jan. 1940, DFA, A20/4.

[128] A. Ó'Canainn, 'Eilís Ryan in her Own Words', *Saothar*, 21 (1996), 137–40; Fianna Fáil national executive minutes, 28 Aug. 1939, FF/342; Kerney to Walshe, 5 July 1939, DFA, A20/1.

[129] Twomey (Agriculture) to External Affairs, 3 July, and Walshe to Twomey, 16 Nov. 1934, DFA, S. 31; Kerney to Walshe, 26 Aug. 1940, DFA, S. 31.

[130] Note of interview between Bryan and Kerney, 20 Oct. 1941, MA, G2/0257.

Clissman and Jupp Hoven, whom he knew from their pre-war sojourns in Ireland, who took him to Berlin to join Russell.

In August, in an echo of Roger Casement's ill-fated homecoming prior to the 1916 rebellion, the two men embarked for Ireland by U-boat. The intention was to galvanize the IRA as opportunity permitted, including action in support of a German attack or in resistance to a British seizure of the ports, although the claim that they were to organize an uprising on a signal from the German legation—the signal being a flowerpot placed on a legation window sill—seems implausible. During the voyage Russell fell ill and died, and the ship returned to Germany with Ryan still on board.[131] Early in 1942 he wrote that Russell 'died of an ulcerated stomach . . . I was with him, day and night, throughout his illness'.[132] In Berlin in 1944 Francis Stuart, whom G2 correctly viewed as a link between the IRA and the German authorities as well as an English-language broadcaster, reportedly told a fellow Irishman that he, Russell, and Ryan 'had undertaken to run guns . . . The other two were to go by submarine and make the arrangements for the reception of the cargo'. On their safe arrival they were to send for Stuart 'to follow with the cargo. After some time' Stuart 'received word from the German authorities telling him that Russell had died suddenly on the way and the other man was not in possession of the ability to carry out the proposed plans and so he had returned and the scheme fell through.'[133] Russell's whereabouts and fate remained a preoccupation of both the Irish and the British authorities because he was seen as the key to German/IRA co-operation: a rumour gained currency that he had been poisoned at Gibraltar by British agents, and in March 1941 G2 was still attempting to 'establish the truth or otherwise' of claims that Russell 'either went to Germany or contacted German agents'. In the absence of a German invasion or weapons, Russell would have been limited in the activities which he would have been able to organize had he reached Ireland. However, he might have injected more purpose, drive, and venom into the fitful operations which the IRA did attempt on both sides of the border than was evident under the bibulous Stephen Hayes and his jumpy successors. Ryan himself became an object of considerable interest because of indications that the German Foreign Office was toying with the idea of using him as an intermediary with de Valera. In fact, however, they found little further use for him after Russell's death, although he played some part in further efforts to exploit Irish grievances against Britain.[134] He died in Dresden in 1944.

[131] Bryan to minister for defence, 21 Dec. 1945, DFA, A12/1; Hinsley and Simkins, *British Intelligence*, 90; Duggan, *A History of the Irish Army*, 195. [132] Ryan to Kerney, 14 Jan. 1942, DFA, A52/1.

[133] Statement by W. J. Murphy, 6 Feb. 1945, PRO, HO 45/25839. See O'Donoghue, *Hitler's Irish Voices*, 163–4 n. 1, for Stuart's claim that Murphy 'was, or became, a minor British Intelligence agent', a far-fetched assumption.

[134] Archer to Walshe, 18 Mar. 1941, attaching memorandum on 'Irish-German-American Notes', DFA, A12/1; statement of John Codd, undated [May/June 1945], MA, G2/4174; Carter, *The Shamrock and the Swastika*, 125–35.

Somewhat incongruously given his Nazi links, he later became a patron saint of the Irish Republican Left.[135]

In Madrid Kerney not only facilitated correspondence between Ryan and his Irish friends via the diplomatic bag, but, as he belatedly informed External Affairs shortly after Ryan's death, for a time kept in touch with Ryan by post. Forwarding two letters which Ryan had written in 1940 and 1941, he commented that 'hitherto I have treated them as private communications having no particular importance and to which it might not have been prudent to refer in official despatches', an explanation which begged the question of why he had not said anything about his continuing contacts with Ryan during visits back to Dublin in 1941 and 1942. Then he had been quizzed both by External Affairs and by G2 about Ryan's escape and its ramifications, and was warned 'about the need for extreme care and prudence in security matters, particularly in view of the prospect of a second front being opened. The Taoiseach saw Kerney . . . and dealt with this matter himself.'[136]

That was not the limit of Kerney's indiscretions, as he was also in private touch with Helmut Clissman. Through Clissman, Kerney accepted an invitation to meet Veesenmayer, the German ambassador to Yugoslavia who had previously been the Foreign Office's main adviser on Irish affairs and who had specialized in the manipulation of nationalist movements for German policy ends. After the war a former Abwehr officer told an Irish diplomat that Veesenmayer had sought the meeting because the German Foreign Office could 'get nothing out of the then [Irish] Chargé d'Affaires in Berlin', but that sole reason was hardly sufficient to merit Veesenmayer's personal involvement. German documents indicated that there was some hope of encouraging a rapprochement between the IRA and de Valera, in anticipation of a German victory and the possible ending of partition, and in 1946 Dan Bryan reported evidence from a British source that Veesenmayer, who in 1942 was also 'connected in some way with a plan for the landing of parachutists and airborne troops' in Ireland, had argued along 'the lines "Russia will soon be finished. We are then going to tackle and finish off England. You have some interests in an area held by her, what are you going to do about it." '[137]

The Germans approached Kerney, rather than the more orthodox Warnock, because of his known republican views. Kerney belatedly reported on the Madrid meeting in guarded terms as 'Conversation with a German'. While he emphasized that he had offered no concessions and made no promises, the very fact of such unauthorized discussions with a senior German official in a neutral

[135] Ó'Canainn, 'Eilís Ryan', 141–2; papers on the 1966 row between his family and the Irish Left concerning the return of his remains are in DFA, A20.

[136] Bryan to Walshe, 7 Mar. 1941 and 29 Oct. 1942, DFA, A8 and A52/1; Kerney to Boland, 22 Jan. 1945, DFA, A52/1; Boland to Nunan, 3 Mar. 1954, DFA, A47.

[137] Report by C. C. O'Brien of conversation with Kurt Haller, 29 Sept. 1954, DFA, A34; Bryan to Boland, 18 June 1946, DFA, A47.

country potentially exposed the Irish government to the charge that it was secretly negotiating with Germany. It is not surprising that, reflecting on the debacle after the war, Joseph Walshe wrote of Kerney's 'Madrid betrayal'.[138] The evidence now available suggests that, in respect of Veesenmayer as of Ryan, Kerney was not a knave but rather a monumental fool whose unsuitability for diplomatic work had been obvious even before the war and who should never have been given a sensitive posting abroad. His antics contrast with the sheer common sense and professionalism displayed by other Irish officials in Rome, the Vatican, and Berlin.

Other Irish people on the continent also gave cause for concern through possible involvement in espionage. The Germans trained a handful of Irish civilians and prisoners of war for clandestine work in Ireland, Britain, and the United States, although only three of these—Joseph Lenihan, John Kenny, and John O'Reilly—were actually sent on missions. Another, John Codd, was recruited from a prisoner-of-war camp by Jupp Hoven, and at various times was apparently to be sent to Britain, to the United States, and to Northern Ireland. On his return from Germany in 1945, he gave a lengthy (though in G2's view somewhat dissembling) account of his training as an agent from 1942 to 1944.[139] The postal censorship seems to have been very effective in giving G2 early intimations that individuals living under German control might have been approached for special work.

Rogue diplomats, transient IRA men, and would-be spies apart, the set of Irish exiles who caused the state most anxiety were those involved in German propaganda. Between 1940 and 1945, a congeries of Irish men and women worked on and off for a number of German English-language stations, operated by the propaganda ministry's Buro Concordia, which were intended to serve a range of overt and clandestine propaganda purposes. The best known broadcaster was Francis Stuart.[140] None of these volunteers achieved the notoriety of Lord Haw Haw, the English renegade William Joyce (the son of Irish parents who belatedly rediscovered his Irish roots when it appeared that these might save him from the gallows in 1946), and they were a very motley crew. John Francis O'Reilly, a German agent dropped in Clare in 1943, gave G2 an unedifying description of life in the broadcasting service. In September 1941 he 'applied for a job writing articles for . . . broadcasts and was brought to Berlin', and found himself the only Irishman amongst a bizarre menagerie of people working on Irish matters. Amongst them was one hapless Englishwoman, 'unreliable and fond of drink', who lost her job after she 'used endearing terms' to a colleague

---

[138] Walshe to Nunan, 6 July 1953, ibid.

[139] Statement of John Codd, MA, G2/4174; 'Hayes report'.

[140] E. Howe, *The Black Game: British Subversive Operations against the Germans in the Second World War* (London, 1982), 62–9. The activities of Irish broadcasters are discussed extensively in O'Donoghue, *Hitler's Irish Voices*.

'while he was in the announcing box and still on the air'.[141] W. J. Murphy, a Tyrone Protestant whom the Germans had mistaken for a republican because of his name, had a similarly farcical tale to tell. Teaching English in Germany since the 1920s, he described to MI5 how in 1944 William Joyce had secured him a month's employment 'translating news . . . into English for the Irish Editing Dep[artmen]t at Luxembourg Rundfund . . . most of my work was thrown into the waste paper basket'. He claimed that Stuart later got him a broadcasting job while they both waited for shipment by submarine to Ireland 'in order to establish contact with the IRA'. He had to record news items, although

so far as I am aware none of my material was broadcast . . . This station . . . was broadcasting to the British people as a British station. The technique . . . was purposely to mislead the listeners both in regard to the items of news and talk. The latter were of an anti-Jewish or Fascist character . . . Adami [a German official] . . . from time to time made criticisms of my manner of speaking . . . he said that I would do better when I had some new teeth and he gave me a letter . . . [to a dentist] . . . stating that as I was to be employed as a broadcaster the loss of my front teeth was an impediment and requesting that the matter be remedied for me.[142]

The Irish authorities naturally did what they could to identify and keep track of Irish citizens involved in such broadcasts—participation bespoke a degree of sympathy with German war aims, and possible involvement in more sinister activities, as the cases of Stuart and O'Reilly demonstrated—but these people were breaking no Irish or international law. By the end of 1941 the view was taken that such broadcasting posed no direct serious threat to Irish interests, and any embarrassment caused could be offset by the fact that English and American renegades were similarly employed.

viii. Conclusion

Ireland was effectively defenceless when Germany and Britain went to war in September 1939. She was, furthermore, a strategic client of Britain's, entirely dependent on her neighbour for air and sea defence, and almost completely reliant on her for weapons, munitions, and other military equipment. To some extent this was the result of pre-war purchasing policy, which served the interests both of the Irish taxpayer and of British defence planners; in the main, however, it was an unavoidable consequence of geography and of economic and political relations between new state and former ruler. In these circumstances, Irish adherence to the long-declared policy of military neutrality while con-

---

[141] G2 note on O'Reilly, 31 Dec. 1943, DFA, A52/1. G2 placed O'Reilly on a watch list after he began broadcasting in 1942, once his identity had been established through postal censorship.

[142] Statement by W. J. Murphy, 6 Feb. 1945.

sistent was entirely predicated on British tolerance. That tolerance was initially forthcoming because the British government, while angered by Irish policy, broadly understood its political underpinnings. So long as Ireland made concessions on security, intelligence, and operational matters, Britain would put up with the refusal to allow use of the ports and associated facilities. This policy, already under attack from Churchill at the Admiralty, was drastically revised with the collapse of France, after which Churchill became prime minister of a coalition fighting for national survival. Britain and Ireland now found themselves confronted with circumstances which no responsible official in either country had envisaged when the Irish policy of military neutrality had been articulated in the 1920s. In contradiction of all planning assumptions, with the collapse of France the British Isles had become prime targets for German invasion.

This transformed the calcuations: Britain now saw the need for a foothold in Ireland not only to defend her Atlantic shipping, threatened as never before because of Germany's command of Europe's coastline from Norway to the south of France, but to thwart a German invasion. The Irish government drew precisely the opposite conclusion from the same set of facts: to extend help to Britain, apparently on the verge of defeat, would be to antagonize Germany, provoke widespread unrest, and expose an unprepared people to aerial attack and other horrors of war. In the event, despite her bitterness at Irish policy, Britain refrained from taking by force what she could not persuade de Valera to volunteer. This restraint was never unconditional: Britain, from 1941 joined by the United States, extracted a considerable price for tolerating Irish neutrality, one which was largely paid in secret. Those exchanges are dealt with in the following chapter.

6

Security Operations and Covert Activities, 1939–1945

i. Introduction

The state was relatively well prepared for the acute security problems which it faced in the autumn of 1939. Many essentially technical matters such as the control and censorship of communications, and supervision of the movements of people into and out of the state, had been under consideration for some time, while the continuing threat to Anglo-Irish relations posed by the IRA had been brought home by its English bombing campaign. Problems of espionage by both sets of belligerents, and of covert interference in Irish affairs, were also anticipated. The result was the rapid imposition of a highly intrusive domestic security regime. These drastic arrangements and practices won both public acceptance and the eventual grudging private commendation of the Allies. Irish security successes against Axis and republican activities undoubtedly contributed considerably to Allied acceptance of military neutrality; successes against Allied covert activities also made a useful contribution to the management of the state's external relations.

The state's main security worry in September 1939 was the republican movement. It was obviously intolerable that the IRA's bombing campaign in Britain should continue. Furthermore, it took no great leap of the imagination for the government to see that for militant republicans England's difficulty remained Ireland's opportunity, and that the IRA would seek to exploit the fact that Britain was at war as best it could both in Northern Ireland and on the British mainland. But the state also faced other pressing security problems. Amongst these were the need for effective communications censorship and movement controls between Ireland and the United Kingdom. More problematic because less evident and less easy to deal with was the issue of espionage or of sabotage mounted from the state against the United Kingdom by Germany or her friends. For as long as Ireland declined to join in the war on Britain's side, there was also the probability of covert activity in Ireland, in the realms both of espionage and of propaganda, by Britain and other powers sympathetic to her. There was also a possibility that the tiny communist movement, whose contacts with Moscow had apparently been revitalized through the participation of its leading lights in the Spanish civil war, might be covertly mobilized to serve the Soviet Union's foreign policy interests, perhaps in support of the CPGB. Finally, it had to be assumed that some of the remaining elements of the Blueshirts, not least O'Duffy, might be tempted to lend Germany some kind of hand, perhaps in association with the British fascist movement. Experience was to show that these were threats of unequal magnitude, and that it was the activities of the IRA, and the possibility of German espionage, which were to present the government with its greatest headaches.

ii. Emergency Legislation and Security Organization, 1939–1945

The most obvious register of a constitutional polity's willingness to act in any area of national life is the list and extent of laws under which government operates. Despite the liberal provisions successively of the 1922 and the 1937 constitutions, independent Ireland was well accustomed to the rapid passage and selective employment of emergency legislation. Furthermore, the existence and use of such measures evidently enjoyed a high degree of public tolerance.

The main internal threat was a familiar one, the republican movement. However, the extensive powers of inquiry, supervision, and detention which the state acquired were not predicated simply on the need to combat IRA subversion. They were also required to prevent Ireland being used as a base for espionage or sabotage against Britain, to prevent the leakage of war information of any kind, and to enable the state generally to deal with the covert activities of other countries within its frontiers. A number of new public order and security statutes had been passed as European war loomed: the Air Raid Precautions Act, the Treason Act, the Offences Against the State Act, and the catch-all Emergency Powers Act. Of these the OAS, which became law in June, proved the most important. It allowed for the establishment of special criminal courts, in which persons accused of certain categories of offences could be tried by a court of five military judges sitting alone. It also prohibited a range of seditious or potentially seditious activities, including membership of proscribed organizations, possession of treasonable documents, obstruction of the government or its servants, and the holding of certain meetings. In addition, it greatly increased the state's powers of search, arrest, and of detention, enabling recourse to the familiar device of internment without trial.[1] In its 'original conception' the EPA had been modelled on 'the lines of' a British draft bill circulated to all dominions, but its anti-subversive provisions were a replica of the Constitution (Amendment No. 17) Act of 1931 which had been so bitterly opposed by de Valera when

---

[1] Hogan and Walker, *Political Violence*, 177–8.

in opposition.[2] It became law on 3 September 1939, in tandem with a constitutional amendment to confer on the government the right to take emergency measures hitherto allowed only 'in time of war'. In addition to its public order provisions, clearly aimed primarily at the IRA, the EPA conveyed very wide powers on the government to act by emergency order in every aspect of national life. The real sting, however, came in an amending EPA in 1940. This provided for the summary trial of designated offences by a military tribunal, equipped with the sole sanction of execution upon conviction. In an amendment rushed through after the murder of two detectives, the right of appeal to another court was removed. The lives of those brought before this court were thus placed entirely in the hands of military men unfamiliar with the law and quite untrained in judicial processes. It was under this drastic legal regime that a number of IRA men were convicted and executed between 1940 and 1943. The six so dealt with included one hardened assassin, George Plant, whose prosecution before a civilian court for the murder of an informer had collapsed. He was promptly rearraigned before the military tribunal, effectively for the same offence, and was duly convicted. His fate provided an echo of the executions policy which the Cosgrave government had operated during the civil war.[3] As in the early 1930s, the government's recourse to the army for such grave judicial purposes reflected both the seriousness of the danger to the state and an unspoken belief that military men would present the IRA with more problematic targets for assassination than the civil judiciary.

The formidable array of powers approved by the Oireachtas in 1939 quickly proved insufficient. The family of a republican prisoner soon won a high court declaration that his internment under the OAS was unconstitutional, obliging the government to release all internees. The problem was overcome by the hasty passage of the Offences Against the State (Amendment) Act of 1940, which provided substantively the same powers of detention and internment. After referral by the president to the Supreme Court for a judgement as to its constitutionality, the bill was signed into law.[4] It enabled the use of internment as a selective tool, resulting in the prolonged detention in miserable conditions in makeshift army compounds of hundreds of republican suspects.[5] The legal difficulties which the government encountered in exercising its new powers illustrated an emerging characteristic of Irish jurisprudence: judicial acknowledgement of the legitimacy of emergency laws was balanced by a concern to protect individual rights.

One significant gap remained in the state's legal armoury. Neither the OSA nor the EPA directly addressed one of the central problems of any neutral country, that of the use of its territory for espionage against other countries. G2 had

[2] Justice memorandum on the emergency powers bill, 6 Oct. 1938, DT, S. 10834A.
[3] Bell, *The Secret Army*, 209.   [4] Ibid. 216–17. Cabinet papers on the bill are in DT, S. 11552A.
[5] Bell, *The Secret Army*, 179–81.

pointed this out in 1938, suggesting that it be addressed in the drafting of the OSA, and had later been supported by External Affairs, who asked that a provision against espionage should be included in the Emergency Powers bill, but they were thwarted by the attorney-general's argument that 'the Taoiseach's decision not to include special provisions in one bill must be taken as applying equally to the other'.[6] Consequently there was no law against spying in Ireland on Britain or any other foreign state, nor against possessing such information or transmitting it. Unlike other defects in security legislation, however, this was not remedied by an amending act during the Emergency.

There already existed a domestic legal basis for some of the policies adopted and the measures pursued. For example the interception and censorship of postal communications, cable traffic, and telephone conversations could be carried out under warrant under the 1908 Post Office Act. Similarly, state controls on private radio transmission were already in place under the 1926 Wireless Telegraphy Act. What distinguished the 1939–45 period from other times of crisis was not the nature of the laws in force but the breadth and duration of their application. Cumulatively this battery of repressive laws, some new and some dusted off, marked the revival, not the creation, of a draconian domestic legal regime. They were planned, drafted, and brought into operation by an administration accustomed to the rapid formulation and embodiment in law of extraordinary legal measures. The constitutional price of safeguarding neutrality was to be a considerable diminution of domestic liberty. Public acceptance of this can be explained by a number of factors. While the most obvious was popular support for the policy of military neutrality, other influences also played a part. Since 1922 the public had been accustomed to the operation of harsh though transient measures directed against the republican movement. Furthermore, the population had been subjected to broadly analogous restrictions and controls on their lives during the First World War under the umbrella Defence of the Realm Act, which embraced everything in a sliding scale of offences which ran all the way from treason and espionage to profiteering, to infecting the soldiery with venereal disease, and to the sale of seed potatoes for consumption. The practical experience of life under such legislation between 1914 and 1919 probably made the measures adopted in 1939 somewhat less of a novelty, if still an unwelcome shock, for the majority of Irish adults.

iii. Army–Garda Relations, 1939–1945

The 1939–45 era saw a dramatic shift in the balance of power between the army and the police. On the declaration of the Emergency de Valera agreed that 'a

---

[6] Attorney-general to Moynihan, 8 Apr. 1939, DT, S. 10834C.

number of questions affecting the security of the state, especially in its external aspect', should be the responsibility of G2.[7] This expansion of the counter-espionage brief it had been given in 1938 turned G2 into a ubiquitous security organization. While the Special Branch retained its primacy as the state's front line against the republican movement—it was Garda officers who made the arrests, and it was Garda officers who died at the hands of IRA gunmen—a combination of government decisions and incidental developments ensured that through G2 the army became the dominant influence on every aspect of security policy with any bearing on external relations. From the outset G2 gained effective control of communications censorship and of covert interception. Cumulatively these sources provided a mass of useful information, and it meant that G2 became exceptionally well informed on general conditions and opinion in Ireland and abroad. In the name of state security, G2 investigated the activities and loyalties of Irish citizens, including some politicians and public servants, as well as of aliens at home and abroad. It advised on the admission of aliens to the country, and on the issue of travel documents to people wishing to leave the state. It spied on foreign diplomats, and wherever possible intercepted their communications. G2 gradually developed close links with MI5, which enabled it to trade intelligence with the British; once the 1926 injunction against prying into domestic political intrigue was informally lifted following the IRA's Magazine Fort raid in December 1939, G2 quickly began to monitor internal subversion, drawing on long-dormant sources within the republican movement; perhaps most importantly for its overall standing, however, G2 reported directly on all political, subversive, or military matters having any international dimension to the two most senior officials in External Affairs, Joseph Walshe and Fred Boland, whose minister was also the taoiseach. The fact of this link undoubtedly explains the leeway increasingly accorded G2's officers in their activities.

The Department of Justice's tacit acceptance of G2 primacy in security matters until May 1945 merits consideration. G2 did encounter some difficulties about intercept warrants with Justice after 1941, when the combative Peter Berry became involved as head of a newly created intelligence division, but relations with that department and with some sections of the Garda remained reasonably good. There were a number of reasons for this. Most obviously, G2 had a strong mandate which came directly from the taoiseach, while the Garda had never taken any interest in espionage problems until prompted by G2 in 1938. Furthermore, most of the actual investigation of individuals and organizations throughout the state was done by the Garda, as G2 had neither the field organization nor the power to mount independent investigations. In addition, G2's

---

[7] Memorandum on 'Defence security intelligence', with Bryan to minister for defence, 21 June 1945, DFA, A8/1. Bryan was second in command of G2 until Colonel Archer was promoted out in May 1941, but he had handled all the security work from 1938 onwards.

effective monopoly on telephone tapping and postal interception appears only to have applied in the postal sorting offices and telephone exchanges in Dublin city: elsewhere, such interception appears to have been carried out under the direction of local Garda superintendents, who passed on the material to the Garda security section C3 from where it was forwarded to G2.

There were, however, important points of friction. In 1939 G2 was initially warned off inquiring into republican affairs, although Bryan and other officers had some old contacts from earlier days. Through such channels one G2 man, 'a kind of ignorant, uneducated queer bird . . . who could always pick up information', came across indications that the IRA were planning some sort of operation in west Dublin. The local Garda superintendent said that the rumours were unfounded, and the G2 man was 'told to lay off'. It later became clear that what he had uncovered were traces of the preparations for the Magazine Fort raid. G2 also received the unwelcome tip that there were no less than five 'wrong people' within the Special Branch, Garda officers originally recruited as Broy Harriers who had never lost their republican sympathies and were passing on information to their former comrades in the IRA. After some consideration Bryan decided not to raise this with Chief Superintendent Carroll of C3, because he had no hard evidence, feared it would poison relations, and might provoke a wider row about the proper boundaries of G2's activities. In the event, it was the IRA itself which provided incontrovertible evidence that there was something amiss by smuggling in a bomb to Special Branch headquarters in April 1940. The net results of that ludicrous gesture were increased Garda pressure on the IRA, and a belated emphasis on security within the Special Branch. It nevertheless took another year before Jim Crofton, the ex-Broy Harrier who was the IRA's most important Garda agent, was detained in Kerry while attempting to arrange the escape of the German agent Herman Goertz. This was a result of intelligence gathered by Florence O'Donoghue of G2 through his SIS. Even then O'Donoghue initially had difficulty in persuading the local police not to release Crofton, who purported to be on undercover duty. Bryan believed that other policemen compromised a number of security operations in 1939 and 1940, and claimed that Carroll of C3 later admitted that one important surveillance operation following the Magazine Fort raid had been betrayed to the IRA by a Garda who 'gave away some of the [stolen] amm[uniti]o[n] that was to be raided for'. G2 later came across evidence of British attempts to penetrate the Garda at a low level, resulting in nothing more than the perhaps innocent relaying of station gossip by a handful of policemen to drinking acquaintances. British agents also recruited some former members of the disbanded DMP, who had been assimilated into the Garda before retiring, as paid agents. [8]

---

[8] Bryan transcripts, pp. 49–50; Bryan's notebook of comments on the transcripts, Bryan papers, P71/89, p. 13; private information.

In retrospect Bryan was very critical of the Garda at headquarters level, maintaining that they were generally slow to share information and were frequently responsible for 'bad co-ordination [on] Intell[igence] matters'. He commented that 'I was annoyed with them often, but I had to . . . keep my tongue, play up to them'. The surviving files bear out the impression that C3, which collated police intelligence and directed the activities of the Special Branch, kept its distance from G2—correspondence between the two organizations was couched in tones far more formal than those evident in exchanges between G2 and External Affairs or even MI5. It is, however, worth noting that Bryan himself spoke highly of the work done by Wymes of the Aliens Office, which continued to investigate the activities of resident aliens until 1945. Furthermore, it is unarguable that, after early disasters, the Special Branch did secure spectacular results against the IRA. This was thanks largely to men such as Inspector Michael Gill, in Bryan's view 'a rough, crude uneducated man . . . with some kind of supreme talent for penetrating this kind of thing' and for handling information intelligently. Gill had had a chequered Special Branch career before the war, being demoted from sergeant to detective in 1934 apparently for political reasons before successfully contesting the commissioner's decision through legal action. He was soon promoted to inspector, and after the passage of the OAS in June 1939 he was given a very free hand by his superiors. Gill kept his cards very close to his chest because 'he knew what was wrong' within the Special Branch and appreciated the need for security. Despite the coolness at headquarters level between the Garda and G2, Gill won the 'complete confidence' of the two G2 officers dealing with republican activities in the eastern command area, and 'he told them everything [including things] that he wouldn't even tell his bosses for a while'.[9] Together with other vigorous officers such as Denis O'Brien, an ex-Broy Harrier, Gill took on the IRA and, aided by the state's enormous emergency legislative armoury, won the contest hands down: by the end of 1941 the RUC inspector-general had concluded that as a result of resolute Garda action 'the IRA was a spent force'. Despite the initial security lapses within the Special Branch, and the puzzling failure to track down Herman Goertz for a full eighteen months in 1940–1, in the main the Garda did the job demanded of them very efficiently, a point later made by Admiral Godfrey with the observation that 'having only recently emerged from a . . . civil war' they 'were particularly good at detecting underground conspiracies'.[10]

While documentary traces are uncommonly hard to find, good if highly discreet links between the RUC and the Garda on both ordinary crime and on some aspects of republican activities had evidently developed before the war. In August 1941 Godfrey advised the JIC that the 'best source of intelligence as

[9] Bryan transcripts, pp. 6 and 50; Bryan notebook, p. 13; Brady, *Guardians*, 181, 237–8.
[10] 'Godfrey report'; 'Godfrey memoir', p. 199; Bell, *The Secret Army*, 191.

regards both Ulster and Eire is Sir Charles Wickham', the RUC inspector-general, whose 'officers collaborate closely with the Civil Guard . . . he is thus able to keep close watch on German and IRA activities on both sides of the Border'. This view of RUC/Garda relations is borne out independently by the recollections both of Bryan, who emphasized Wickham's close Garda links, and of an MI5 officer who worked on Irish liaison and who found Wickham and one of his officers particularly familiar with Garda thinking. It is also plain from the available documents that the Security Executive placed considerable faith in Wickham's judgement.[11]

This north/south liaison appears to have been maintained at headquarters level, on the Garda side most probably through C3. Only a couple of instances have come to light: in November 1941, at G2's behest External Affairs interviewed a Garda officer experienced in RUC liaison to see whether he had told his Northern analogues anything about the Goertz case—he had not, and so Bryan did not discuss it during a subsequent meeting with MI5 in London—and in 1945 Justice approached External Affairs about rumours of the sale of weapons by American troops to the IRA in Tyrone, which Justice wanted to pass on to the RUC 'in the interests of good relations between the two police forces'. For some reason—perhaps the fact that the European war and its attendant security complications for Ireland were about to end—External Affairs decided that the Garda should not pass on this scrap of intelligence.[12]

One curious aspect of the surveillance regime operated by both the Garda and G2 illustrates the advantage which the combination of popular legitimacy, emergency powers, and abundant manpower confers on security organizations in the search for intelligence. The state had continued the British practice of having an annual appropriation for secret service which, because it did not have to be accounted for in the normal way, was potentially prone to abuse.[13] Despite the myriad of inquiries mounted, and all the pressure for quick results, spending from the secret service vote was surprisingly modest throughout the Emergency. At its height in 1944, the vote stood at £41,000. Most of that money was handled by the Garda—Bryan said G2 never spent more than a couple of thousand pounds a year between 1940 and 1945, mainly on liaison visits to and from Britain which for reasons of secrecy could not be accounted for through the normal channels. He believed that Defence sometimes treated the vote as a general contingency fund for expenses quite unconnected with security. External Affairs certainly did: in September 1942 Joseph Walshe, a man

---

[11] 'Godfrey report'; Bryan and Stephenson interviews.

[12] Bryan transcripts, p. 28; Berry to Walshe, 23 Apr., and attached Garda memorandum, 13 Apr. 1945, DFA, A12/1.

[13] E. O'Halpin, 'Financing British Intelligence: The Evidence up to 1945', in K. Robertson (ed.), *British and American Perspectives on Intelligence* (Basingstoke, 1987), 192–3.

whose probity was equalled only by his devout Catholicism, wrote to a Finance official:

Your minister and the Taoiseach have decided to make a present to the [Papal] Nunciature of five tons of coal and twelve tons of coke from state resources . . . I understand that, on a similar occasion, you fixed the price which the Board of Works should receive through the customary channels.[14]

The nature of the 'customary channels' is abundantly clear from the file, which is marked 'Secret Service Vote'. Presumably the public, reduced to burning sodden turf because of the severe shortage of imported fuel, never got to hear of the state's benefaction to a foreign diplomat. Untraceable funds have their uses.

The surviving evidence on army/police co-operation during the Emergency demonstrates that things did not always run smoothly. First, there was the security problem within the Special Branch, which remained suspect in G2's eyes up to the capture of Goertz. Secondly, C3 evidently resented army intrusions on what it regarded as its patch, whereas G2 felt that it should have been given a greater role in the penetration of the republican movement, and that intelligence which it did glean and pass on should have been given more heed. Thirdly, G2's effective control of telephone tapping and involvement in postal interception undoubtedly irritated some officials in Justice, particularly Peter Berry, and presumably Garda officers also. On the other hand, the fact that the Garda relinquished no police powers to the army, and that they handled liaison with the RUC, while G2 dealt directly with MI5 and from 1942 also with the American Office of Strategic Services (OSS) in Dublin and London, meant that an equilibrium of sorts was maintained between the two arms of the state's security forces: each needed the other, and neither was in sole possession of all the strands of security policy. This institutional balance, however irritating at times for those involved, was an appropriate check on each of them given the quite exceptional powers which both enjoyed.

iv. Press, Radio, and Cinema Censorship, 1939–1945

In order to demonstrate her credentials as a thoroughgoing neutral, to assuage British concerns about the management of information, and to thwart efforts by the belligerents to influence Irish opinion, in September 1939 the state set out to regulate what even its most loyal and law-abiding citizens could and could not hear and read. The result was a system of public and private censorship which attempted, if it did not entirely accomplish, the suppression of all public

---

[14] Walshe to Hanna, 22 Sept. 1942, DFA, P67.

controversy about the war. The result was an information policy which, by preventing the public dissemination and informed discussion of war news and commentary, in effect appeared to serve Axis rather than Allied interests.

The first point to note is the state's fear that the media would be used as a vehicle for covert propaganda by the belligerents. There was good reason to suppose that the warring countries would attempt to influence opinion in a neutral state through planting stories in newspapers and the like, just as they had done during the First World War, and so it proved. Both the Axis and the British and American diplomatic missions in Dublin naturally attempted to sway press opinion, while both sides also used less direct means to attempt to influence what was written about the conflict. The second point to note is the diplomatic sensitivity of whatever appeared, and whatever was suppressed, in newspapers. While constantly pressing the authorities to prevent the appearance of news or comment unduly favourable to Germany, for example, British officials were naturally concerned to insinuate as much pro-British material as possible into Irish papers. The German legation in turn set out to minimize British influence by continual complaint about an allegedly pro-Allied slant in the press and the cinemas, and by the assiduous courtship of Irish opinion. The press attaché Karl Petersen was a particular object of Allied suspicion, as much for his overt work as for his alleged espionage activities. He was infamous for his louche behaviour—the Canadian high commissioner noted that he 'mixes in disreputable Bohemian circles'—and he was said to be living with a mistress. His propensity to play the Nazi did not endear him to the authorities: after a drunken brush with some Gardai he allegedly remarked: 'If any one of them are alive at Christmas, congratulate them.' In December 1940 Walshe complained to Hempel that Petersen was 'addicted to drink, went with bad companions and was extremely imprudent'.[15] The real and suspected efforts of the belligerents to influence Irish opinion seem to have received far more intensive ministerial attention than their covert intelligence activities.

G2 had advanced tentative media and communications censorship plans in the mid-1920s. Planning was resumed under the broader aegis of an interdepartmental committee in 1935, and after the Munich crisis it was pursued with some vigour. This meant that once war broke out a censorship organization was rapidly put into place. As with postal and telephone controls, in planning the censorship the Irish drew largely on Britain's First World War experience. But British press censorship had in the course of that war become part of a wider approach to information and opinion management which included the suppression of domestic dissent, external propaganda, and the demoralization and strategic deception of the enemy amongst its aims. This philosophy naturally

[15] Hinsley and Simkins, *British Intelligence*, 17; 'Report on the German legation, Dublin', undated [1941], PAC, RG24, C1, C5258; Garda report, 29 Nov., and note by Walshe, 16 Dec. 1940, DFA, P41.

underpinned British inter-war discussion of censorship and propaganda machinery.[16] As a neutral Ireland had rather different information policy aims; the essentially British machinery adapted to achieve these, however, was more appropriate to a country at war.

The first controller of censorship was Joseph Connolly, a notoriously difficult ex-minister who had been made chairman of the Board of Works after his political demise in 1936, to whom the appointment 'came as an unpleasant shock'. A Belfast republican forced south by partition, Connolly had no doubts where the main difficulties would lie. On 19 September 1939 he wrote that

our lines have all been aimed at preventing publication of anything that would in the slightest degree impair our neutrality but it is already evident that it is going to be difficult to keep out of 'opinions', leaders and sub leaders the suggestions (a) that we are not really neutral, (b) that we cannot continue to be neutral, (c) that the big majority of the people are opposed to the enemies of Britain . . . it seems likely that we will have definite difficulty in the case of certain papers such as the 'Irish Times' in restraining them from tincturing all or most of their material with a definitely pro-British tinge and, particularly in their leading articles, getting them to follow a strictly neutral line of argument . . . a very considerable number of our own people (I would say the big majority including Government supporters and nationalists generally) are watching . . . to see what latitude will be permitted to what are looked upon as pro-British elements and will be quick to criticise anything that may seem to favour the British or pro-British tendencies and that will seem to 'cut across' our avowed neutrality.[17]

Press censorship would, in short, be aimed as much at the suppression of pro-British views as of military or security information. During the period of the invasion scare of 1940–1, the government became acutely sensitive about British attempts to influence opinion. Consequently a very strong protest was delivered in July 1940 about 'interference in the internal affairs of our country', warning 'how quickly the excellent work of the British Representative in Ireland could be brought to naught by well-meaning busybodies' sent over to spread British propaganda.[18] It was this aspect of Allied activities—the considerable efforts both open and covert which were made to change Irish attitudes towards the war— which caused the most suspicion. Any public expression of pro-Allied views, even if not aimed directly or indirectly at Irish policy, was thought likely to infect the body politic: thus the publicity activities of citizens of states such as Poland, Czechoslovakia, and Belgium, who could hardly do other than complain of their countries' fates, provoked both rigorous censorship and thorough

---

[16] On the inception of British strategic deception planning, see M. Howard, *British Intelligence in the Second World War*, v: *Strategic Deception* (London, 1989), 3–30.

[17] J. Gaughan (ed.), *Memoirs of Senator Joseph Connolly (1885–1961), a Founder of Modern Ireland* (Dublin, 1996), 396; memorandum by Connolly for discussion with taoiseach, 19 Sept. 1939, DT, S. 11306; Bryan interview.

[18] External Affairs to Dulanty (high commissioner in London), 17 July 1940, conveying representations to be made to the British government, DFA, A6.

G2 'supervision' for their authors, while those who sought to raise the issue of Germany's treatment of Jews were regarded as thoroughgoing Zionists bent on luring innocent Irishmen into Allied colours.

Connolly eventually stood down as controller in September 1941, and was succeeded by his rather more emollient deputy, T. J. Coyne of Justice. Policy, however, proceeded along the lines set down in 1939. The operation of the press censorship has been very effectively analysed by Donal O'Drisceoil, whose work demonstrates the extent to which decisions were taken at a political level, principally by the minister for the co-ordination of defensive measures Frank Aiken.[19] Aiken was generally believed to be strongly Anglophobe, and there was a good deal of speculation that he was also personally sympathetic to Germany. Whether or not this was so—and no one has produced evidence to suggest that he was anything other than a convinced nationalist with no ideological interest in either of the major European belligerents—the markedly pedantic approach to media censorship on which he insisted is completely explicable in terms of purely Irish political and security considerations.

The media censorship operated along straightforward lines. Under the controller were two discrete organizations. One of these dealt with control of the media; the other was responsible for communications censorship, and its operations are discussed separately below. As a state organization, Radio Éireann presented no great problems, though there was an armed police guard at the station and detectives also stood by during outside broadcasts lest anyone attempt to interfere.[20] The press, however, were less tractable. The government had hoped to put the media censorship organization in the hands of the trusted *Irish Press* journalist and one-time republican propagandist Frank Gallagher. In the event they appointed instead Michael Knightly. As editor of the official journals of the Dáil and Seanad, he was presumably no stranger to bombast and untruths; his credentials as a press censor were otherwise less clear. Knightly operated under unequivocal policy guidelines: nothing that could be of any possible military use to either set of belligerents should appear in newspapers, be broadcast, or shown in cinema newsreels; nothing should be published which seriously questioned neutrality; and even material on purely domestic economic and social issues should be subject to scrutiny lest, intentionally or not, it might undermine the national consensus on staying out of the war or harm public morale.[21] The net result was, as Admiral Godfrey later recalled, that despite the best efforts of the more independent minded journalists the newspapers became 'dull and insipid'—even sports events had to be reported without any reference to weather conditions, and the severe winter of 1943–4 'could

---

[19] D. O'Drisceoil, *Censorship in Ireland 1939–1945: Neutrality, Politics and Society* (Cork, 1996), and 'Moral Neutrality: Censorship in Emergency Ireland', *History Ireland*, 4/2 (Summer 1996), 46–50.

[20] Assistant commissioner to Garda commissioner, 11 July 1940, DT, S. 11982.

[21] O'Drisceoil, *Censorship in Ireland*, 104–5.

not be recorded in picture or word'. The government could not, of course, prevent people reading British newspapers, stop them tuning into either British or German English-language radio broadcasts, or prevent them from receiving newsletters disseminated by the various warring powers, while the constant movement of people between the state and the United Kingdom meant that plenty of war news circulated by word of mouth. This made the rigidity of the media censorship appear all the more absurd, and it became an increasing irritant in press/government relations. This was particularly so once the tide of war began to change. To many the retention of so rigid a censorship for so long was simply another manifestation of de Valera's pedantic insistence on retaining all the forms of absolute neutrality even when the outcome of the war was no longer in doubt and when overwhelming evidence of Germany's extermination policies was emerging. It also had the effect of suppressing public comment on and analysis of domestic issues. The *Irish Independent* spoke for all journalists when it commented in June 1944 that the press censorship had been 'grossly abused'. Even so staunch a de Valera loyalist as the journalist Liam Skinner, in his otherwise adulatory *Politicians by Accident*, described the censorship as 'both inelastic and unintelligent'; it 'overstepped the limits intended by the Oireachtas'.[22] The spirit of the censorship was concisely expressed by Coyne, who told Fred Boland in 1942 that

policy is to prevent the publication of matter which would endanger our security, directly or indirectly, including propaganda and matter which would be likely to give offence to other countries especially, of course, to either group of belligerents, as well as of matter which would be prejudicial to the maintenance of public order, or the provision of essential supplies and services . . .

The difference between the British censorship and ours is that ours doesn't even pretend to be voluntary . . . we do insist on seeing matter which comes under any of the fifty five categories which are set out in our printed directions and . . . we ruthlessly 'blue pencil' anything the publication of which we think would not be in the interests of the State.[23]

By restricting the publication of war news, and by curbing public debate on the rights and wrongs of neutrality and on the related issue of partition, the censorship undoubtedly facilitated the maintenance of a national consensus on neutrality. In addition, it probably operated to the government's political benefit: de Valera won the two general elections of 1943 and 1944. It also acted as a minor instrument of international news management, in that journalists attempting to send out critical reports were routinely subject to petty restrictions by the communications censors in consultation with External Affairs and G2.[24]

---

[22] 'Godfrey memoir', p. 193; O'Drisceoil, *Censorship in Ireland*, 102; extract from the *Irish Independent*, 28 June 1944, DT, S. 10834C; L. Skinner, *Politicians by Accident* (Dublin, 1946), 175.

[23] Coyne to Boland, 7 Aug. 1942, DFA, A/11.

[24] O'Drisceoil, *Censorship in Ireland*, 200–13.

The government remained unabashed about the rigidity and frequent absurdity of the censorship regime. After its termination on 11 May 1945 Aiken had the good grace to entertain newspaper editors to dinner and to listen to their recitations of their efforts to circumvent the state's blue pencil.[25]

v. Communications Censorship

Censorship on postal, cable, and telephone communications into and out of the state was introduced on similar lines to that exercised on the media, and was operated under the same controller. A key difference, however, was that collaboration with Britain was a prerequisite.[26] Over the six years of its operation there were considerable developments in censorship between the state and Britain, between the state and Northern Ireland, and between Northern Ireland and mainland Britain. The topic of interstate censorship awaits its historian: here, only a sketchy account is attempted.

Cable censorship between the state and the British mainland was more or less complete: British control of Irish cable communications had been built into the 1921 treaty precisely to protect her communications security in wartime, and to prevent likely enemies from running their own transatlantic cables through Ireland (the German government approached the Americans about such a development in the mid-1930s).[27] In September 1939 the Irish acquiesced in the routeing of all external cable traffic, other than telegrams to and from Northern Ireland, through London. With the exceptions of diplomatic traffic, of organizations such as oil and shipping companies whose communications the British agreed should be enciphered, and of meteorological reports sent in a British cipher, all such messages had to be in plain text. This arrangement was crucial to British security, and it also conferred other advantages. The enciphered messages to and from Axis and neutral diplomatic missions in Dublin could be accurately recorded for code-breaking purposes, and such cables were also deliberately delayed for a few days.[28] Until the autumn of 1940 there was, however, no censorship within Northern Ireland of telegrams passing between the two jurisdictions on the island, a gap in the United Kingdom's security fence which caused considerable alarm after the fall of France.[29]

Telephone calls between the state and both Northern Ireland and Britain required operators, and by the close of 1940 such calls were openly monitored

---

[25] Unsigned, undated note, DT, S. 11306; Andrews, *Man of no property*, 124.
[26] Maffey to Machtig (Dominions Office), 9 Oct. 1939, PRO, DO 130/3.
[27] Moffat (head of West European Division, State Department) to Livesey, 3 Dec. 1934, Houghton Library, Harvard, J. P. Moffat papers, bMS Am 1549, vol. 33.
[28] Filby, 'Floradora', 416.
[29] Report on visit by MI5 representatives to 'North Ireland', 28–30 Aug. 1940, with note by chairman, Security Executive, 4 Sept. 1940, PRO, HO 45/20570, cited hereafter as 'MI5 report'.

and were subject to sudden termination. Such power could be abused: the conversations of troublesome people such as hostile journalists were sometimes interrupted simply out of spite. In general, the telephone censorship adequately served both British and Irish needs. Once the build-up of forces for the invasion of Europe got seriously under way in Britain in 1943, the British tightened controls further on cross-channel calls. While this caused additional inconvenience, it shifted the onus for telephone security more clearly onto the British themselves. The various diplomatic missions in Dublin presumably took it for granted that their own telephone traffic was also subject to covert 'supervision', as was indeed the case from very early in the Emergency. Connolly had initially sought control of the covert interception of communications, and had wanted to begin with Maffey's office. Bryan, then responsible for security and counterespionage within G2, argued that interception was a security rather than a censorship function, and that the German legation should be the first priority. The difference of opinion was eventually settled in G2's favour.[30]

Postal censorship presented more problems. Internal post could only be checked systematically when routed through Dublin, where almost three hundred were employed in the censorship headquarters.[31] Thus, correspondence between, say, Sligo and Donegal could generally not be watched, although a local Garda superintendent could intercept mail under warrant. The same problem arose with mail to and from Northern Ireland, much of which did not pass through Dublin. Irish censorship of external mail soon came in for criticism: in July 1940 Maffey, who 'was somewhat shamefaced', complained that the censorship was causing undue delays, and relayed a British offer either to 'carry out our entire censorship' or to train Irish officials on censorship procedures. The prickly Connolly was convinced that these complaints were the work of pro-British elements alarmed that their post was being opened. So far from yielding to Maffey's blandishments, it 'is desirable not only to continue but to see if we can extend the censorship further'.[32] In fact, while the British may well have had the basest of motives, there was nothing new in the idea that they might train Irish officials: they had already done so in respect of covert interception, while the Irish censorship organization had been designed partly by reference to Britain's First World War experience. Furthermore, despite Connolly's bluster censorship of external mail was far from complete. In addition, the British faced a genuine and intractable censorship problem arising from partition. What was there to stop anyone in the south evading censorship by sending letters by hand into Northern Ireland for onward posting to Britain, and maintaining a censorship-free correspondence by using a Northern Ireland return address?

The MI5 group which visited Northern Ireland in August 1940 found that all censorship and security issues were complicated by politics: the telephone

---

[30] Bryan interview.　　[31] Connolly, *Memoirs*, 398.
[32] Connolly to Purcell, 11 July 1940, DFA, A9(1); Connolly, *Memoirs*, 400.

system was considered highly insecure because 'among the officials ... are some who are sympathisers with the IRA', who might either eavesdrop on official traffic or disrupt it. MI5 reported that 'criticism of the censorship is universal from all three [armed] services and from the police. The present position appears to be that there is no telegraph or postal censorship between North [*sic*] Ireland and Eire, although there is a scrutiny of telegrams, which undoubtedly is of value.' MI5 suggested that, while 'the frontier ... is admittedly completely open from a security intelligence point of view ... considerable value would be derived by imposing [cross-border] telegraph and postal censorship'. Telegraph and telephone censorship was eventually put on a satisfactory footing. Similarly, an effective mail and freight censorship between Northern Ireland and mainland Britain was set up despite the fears of Northern businessmen about commercial confidentiality: MI5 recommended abandoning 'local recruitment of censorship staff', a policy which also disposed of the problem of politically unreliable officials. The British authorities also posted a number of 'Travellers Censorship Officers' on the border. In April 1942, however, the Security Executive heard that, because the border 'is long and there is nothing to prevent anyone crossing on foot across the fields', the RUC thought this 'service ... of no practical use'. Any 'increase in the security measures ... which fell short of effective control might well be more prejudicial to real security than the present state of affairs ... any control which gave apparent but not real security would at once give rise to the suggestion that the censorship of communications between Northern Ireland and Great Britain could be relaxed'. The outcome could be that 'the intensification of ... [overt] control on the Border had resulted, on balance, in a decrease in security'.[33]

The Irish were just as anxious as the British that communications censorship should be effective. This was not only to counter British complaints about the leakage of secrets through Ireland, but because the postal censorship produced work 'of the highest quality' in terms both of security control and of intelligence on affairs both in Ireland and abroad. For example, G2 used the censorship to chart developments in Irish-American opinion on Irish neutrality, where a considerable change was reported after Pearl Harbor, and to monitor postal applications to join the British forces. It was crucial in the uncovering of the German agent Werner Unland, in Bryan's words 'an example of a suspect against whom by a process of continuous investigation an exceedingly strong case had been built up', through 'an immense amount of work' by G2, 'Postal Censorship, [the] Postal Investigation Branch and the Garda'.[34] The censorship threw

---

[33] 'MI5 report'; report by Herbert on postal and telegraphic censorship, undated, and Security Executive minutes, 29 Apr. 1942, PRO, HO 45/21985.

[34] Bryan transcripts, p. 4, and his lecture to the Military History Society of Ireland, 17 Feb. 1983; G2 report on Irish-American opinion, undated, with note to Bryan of 10 Apr. 1942, MA, G2/X/0825; Bryan to Boland, 13 June 1946, DFA, A71.

incidental light on the sometimes complex private lives of Irish residents: Connolly recalled that there were 'letters that emerged from time to time that one wanted to forget about . . . they were a revelation of the depths to which the human mind can sink'.[35] It also led to the uncovering of various incidents of smuggling and other misdemeanours without any political or subversive aspect. An indiscreet letter sent to Britain by a malingering corporal illustrates this nicely: 'I have reason to feel O.K. today, because I told the doctor a yarn and he sent me to hospital and that is where I am now, so I expect to work my ticket out of this army in about two weeks time and then I will be seeing you all again.' As this was, unkindly, relayed to Dublin by the British under the heading 'attempt to be made to evade further military service in the Irish Army', the planned reunion was probably delayed by many months.[36] The censors on both sides of the Irish Sea also came across compromising correspondence addressed to the German legation. Some of these letters were from obvious crackpots: Mrs Irma Corlette, a niece of General Sir Bindon Blood ('one of the Bloods of Clare'), wrote from England to Hempel asking him to 'please make some Jews give me what [money] I have lost through one of them here':

when Herr Hitler was beginning to do so much for Germany. I sent him a . . . book written by my uncle . . . to show him that we had some brilliant soldiers here too; I never heard from him, but he must have got it, as it never came back. Also when the Spanish [civil] war started, and General Franco was not doing well, I sent him a four-leafed shamrock, which is supposed to be the luckiest thing in the world, and the most rare.

Mrs Corlette was presumably left alone. Not so William Craven, a former member of the British Union of Fascists, whose offer of services to the German legation was picked up by the British censors (the British later apologized for a ministerial statement implying that the letter had got through). He received a life sentence, although the Garda afterwards heard that he was considered a 'mental case' who would be released once the war ended. His case illustrates the point that even the most overt forms of communications surveillance, intended almost entirely as a deterrent rather than as a snare for the unwary, could yield positive as well as preventive results.[37]

There was one important exception to the overt censorship of external mails: this was diplomatic correspondence sent under seal. Whether sent through the ordinary post marked 'Exempt from censorship', or consigned in diplomatic bags, this was liable to covert interception by any or all of the states through which it passed. G2 was well aware of how insecure such channels were. The constraints on Irish interception of diplomatic mail were technical rather than ethical: could unescorted bags and packets be quickly and discreetly opened and resealed? The

---

[35] Connolly, *Memoirs*, 401.   [36] Postal intercept, 14 July 1940, DFA, A8.
[37] Irma Corlette letter, 30 July 1940, ibid.; Carroll (C3) to Walshe, 22 June 1944, DFA, P93; Hinsley and Simkins, *British Intelligence*, 320.

External Affairs and G2 files contain numerous copies of the personal correspondence of diplomats sent in the ordinary post which had been carefully
opened and transcribed or photographed, although only one significant official
communication, a 1941 letter from the American legation to the United States
embassy in London, has come to light. As the British and Americans generally
used couriers to carry written communications between Dublin and London—
in February 1944 there was one 'secret bag . . . a week to Dublin'—that document
most likely came into G2's hands by means other than postal interception.[38]

The near certainty that various foreign powers were similarly reading Irish
diplomatic mail did not worry anyone unduly at first. However, in 1941 comments in a letter opened in the normal course of external postal censorship indicated that the Irish minister at Madrid, Leopold Kerney, was permitting
personal friends to use his bag for private correspondence. As well as passing on
family messages to the one-time Irish minister in Berlin and notorious pro-
German intriguer Charles Bewley, and facilitating correspondence between
members of an order of nuns with houses in Ireland and in Spain, Kerney was
acting as a conduit for letters to and from the exiled IRA man and potential
leader of a German-backed uprising in Ireland, Frank Ryan, and the Mulcahy
family, one of whom was married to Helmut Clissmann.[39] The Dublin/Madrid
bag was then placed under G2 surveillance. Quite apart from his naivety in
allowing friends to use his bag, Kerney was by turns hopelessly indiscreet and
deliberately dissimulating in his own written communications with Dublin. G2
later found their British counterparts deeply suspicious of and alarmingly well
informed about Kerney's activities, and at one point two British officials
'insisted on showing' Bryan and Joseph Walshe that the maverick diplomat's
name was in 'the British Black List'.[40] Together with other evidence, this strongly
suggests that Irish diplomatic post was routinely intercepted, both to read Irish
communications and to determine if the Irish bag was being used by other
powers. External Affairs prudently declined requests from the Germans in 1939
and from the Italians in 1941 to allow their correspondence to be carried in the
Irish bag, something which would certainly have come to British notice and which
would presumably have exacerbated Anglo-Irish relations even if the British
chose not to complain openly (when MI5 discovered that a Spanish diplomat in
London was using his country's bag for German espionage purposes, they used
the agent as an unwitting channel for disinformation).[41] That the British were

---

[38] H. M. Hyde, *Secret Intelligence Agent* (London, 1982), 35–6, 96, and 104–5, describes difficulties
involved in resealing diplomatic packets; the American document mentioned is in the Hayes papers,
MS 22981; Back (Foreign Office) to Roy (Home Office), 10 Feb. 1944, PRO, HO 213/2209.

[39] Archer to Walshe, 7 Mar. 1941, DFA, A8; copies of letters to Bewley from his father are in MA,
G2/3666; Bryan interview.

[40] Walshe to Nunan, 6 July 1953, DFA, A47.

[41] Warnock (Berlin) to Walshe, 25 Sept. 1939, and Brennan (Washington) to Walshe, 18 Apr. 1941,
DFA, P24; J. Masterman, *The Double-Cross System in the War of 1939 to 1945* (New Haven, 1972), 93.

alive to such possibilities is indicated by a warning in 1939 from the British ambassador in Rome that Leo Macauley, the Irish minister to the Vatican, was handling German postal and cable traffic to and from Berlin, although further inquiries suggested that he 'was only being used by the Eire Government as a channel for their [own] communications with the Eire Minister in Berlin'. The British also investigated a report that the Dutch minister in Dublin had secretly extended bag facilities to Hempel.[42] Despite its limitations, the external postal and telephone censorship appears to have served both its preventive purpose in respect of the innocent or malicious leakage of war information, and its exemplary aim of assuaging British fears about Irish security.[43]

vi. Domestic Surveillance, 1939–1945

Many aspects of the Emergency, such as rationing, the internment of republicans, the depredations of the 'glimmer man', and the operation of press censorship, are etched into the popular memory. Other aspects of the state's activities in its struggle to defend neutrality are, by contrast, little known. The period from 1939 to 1945 saw the operation of a remarkably intrusive security regime, as the authorities sought to detect and to thwart the variety of dangers they feared.

Inquiries were directed not only at obvious targets such as foreign diplomats, visiting journalists, and active republican and communist subversives, and at resident aliens who were more or less automatically placed under security 'supervision', however nondescript their lives and blameless their activities. Many people were also investigated because of their links, real or imagined, with one or other set of belligerent powers, with foreign or international organizations of every description, and with suspect political organizations, parties, and movements within the state. The rationale for the many covert inquiries mounted was the straightforward one of state security in a time of international crisis. While their purpose was clear enough, and while the evidence indicates that they were conducted in that spirit rather than for party political ends, such investigations often had unexpected results. One harrowing illustration is that of an unmarried woman on the fringes of IRA/German intrigue, whose intercepted correspondence revealed that an elderly couple were fostering her illegitimate child. Such discoveries seem to have been treated with appropriate discretion: there is nothing to suggest that anyone personally compromised through surveillance was subject to official coercion. External Affairs were, however,

---

[42] Hyde, *Secret Intelligence Agent*, 25, 33–4, 89, 96, and 105; Lorraine (Rome) to Cadogan (Foreign Office), 18 Sept., Jebb (Foreign Office) to Stephenson (Dominions Office), 30 Sept., and Maffey to Machtig, 16 Oct. 1939, PRO, DO 130/3.

[43] Memorandum by Hill (Home Office), 12 Jan. 1944, PRO, HO 213/2209.

sometimes briefed where diplomatic complications might arise. For the same reasons all aliens were watched quite carefully by the Garda and by G2, even when no positive suspicions arose: their correspondence was also routinely scanned for evidence of espionage or political intrigue, and files were kept on them. This applied both to Axis loyalists and to people who had come as refugees. An example was the distinguished theoretical physicist Erwin Schroedinger, in whose case 'the Taoiseach was interested', copies of whose intercepted correspondence can be seen in G2 records. Nothing untoward came to light.[44]

Surveillance had its lighter side. In 1944 Bryan wrote to External Affairs about one German resident, who tutored Hempel's children and whose considerable correspondence with women had initially aroused suspicions of espionage because some of the recipients made occasional visits to the United Kingdom. Interception of this correspondence had revealed that, while entirely innocent of spying or subversion, he was 'carrying on love affairs', 'some of which are conducted by correspondence with ladies he has never met', in various parts of Ireland and in Germany: 'He appears to have the faculty of playing on women's emotions through correspondence which in due course develops a lascivious tone'. External Affairs were told about this unlikely Casanova, somewhat grudgingly termed an 'expert in sexual psychology', because he was also giving lessons to the teenage daughter of a neutral diplomat, although 'there is no suggestion of anything other than an academic interest there'.[45]

The External Affairs and G2 records also show how some politicians, public figures, groups, and associations were watched because of their sympathies for one or other set of belligerents. Investigation of organizations which might well be used as rallying points for pro-British or pro-German opinion and covert activities, and which would certainly be publicly accused of doing so, presented no great dilemma; inquiries into the activities of politicians, however, raised altogether more delicate problems. In hindsight, it is the surveillance of those considered pro-Ally which is the more striking. Relations between the outspoken opposition TD James Dillon, who was alone in the Dáil in publicly urging active co-operation with Britain and the United States, and the American minister David Gray came under G2's disapproving scrutiny: for example, in August 1941 a G2 officer reported allegations 'that there is very close association between ... Gray and Mr Dillon TD and that in fact Mr Dillon's recent appeal in the Dáil ... was made on the instructions of Mr Gray'. The former Fine Gael senator and journalist Frank McDermott, who was avowedly pro-Ally, was also regarded with suspicion:

Senator McDermott has the advantage of his wealth in meeting journalists and can afford to entertain them generously and others who visit this country. He has the added

---

[44] Bryan to Commandant?, undated [Aug. 1940], MA, G2/0760; undated post-war G2 report, DFA, A55/1; note by Boland, 5 Jan. 1944, DFA, A63.
[45] Bryan to Boland, 12 Jan. 1944, DFA, A62; undated report [July 1944], MA, G2/2457.

status as a member of the Oireachtas which, coupled with his wider social contacts, including citizens with British titles, and others whose political leanings are strongly in favour of Great Britain, enables him to get willing ears for his own and his associates' views.[46]

The surviving evidence suggests, however, that the politician who came under the closest scrutiny was not a member of the opposition but a government back-bencher, the Jewish TD Bob Briscoe. This was less because of his political views than of his religion. His case throws some light on the sometimes intermingled questions of anti-Semitism and pro-German activities during the Emergency.

vii. Alien Influences, 1939–1945

The success of the highly restrictive immigration policy operated since independence was demonstrated by the remarkably small number of political refugees and of conventional immigrants who had obtained rights of residence. Between 1938 and 1946, only 558 aliens were granted residency rights, most of them Germans or Austrians. While all aliens were regarded with disfavour, there is no doubt that Jewish immigration had long been particularly discouraged on a variety of grounds, including the alleged reluctance of Jews to assimilate with Irish society, fears that anti-Semitism would be inflamed by any increase in the Jewish population, and anxiety not to give diplomatic offence to Germany by becoming a haven for those fleeing from her.[47] After the outbreak of war, these anxieties were compounded by the tide of events in Europe.

Bob Briscoe had come to Ireland in the early years of the century. He and his family had been involved in gun-running during the War of Independence and the civil war, and he was a long-time de Valera loyalist. He was undoubtedly the man best placed to defend the interests of Ireland's small and fearful Jewish community. Briscoe's relations with Jewish aid groups abroad were closely monitored lest these prove embarrassing to the state, and his links were much resented by security officials. Early in 1941 he was 'rather strongly suspected of conducting recruiting campaigns for the Allies abroad, using his official status in this country for that purpose', he was regularly accused of furthering Zionist interests at Ireland's expense, and he was believed to hold 'a high place in the councils of international Jewry'. Chief among G2's concerns were the possibility that his activities might expose the state to the charge that it was a centre of Zionist organization; that some of his contacts abroad might seek to use him to

[46] Keogh, *Ireland and Europe*, 129 and 156; O'Donoghue to Bryan, 12 Aug. 1941, MA, G2/X/1122; Archer to Walshe, 13 Jan. 1941, attaching memorandum on McDermott, DFA, A8; Bryan to Boland, 7 July 1941, DFA, P6.

[47] E. Ward, ' "A big show-off to show what we could do"—Ireland and the Hungarian Refugee Crisis of 1956', *Irish Studies in International Affairs*, 7 (1996), 133; D. Keogh, *Jews in Twentieth Century Ireland: Refugees, Anti-Semitism and the Holocaust* (Cork, 1998), 115–52.

influence Irish opinion in favour of the Allies; and that his support for Jewish enlistment in the LSF might be linked to plans for the eventual formation of an international Jewish army. In November 1942 a G2 report stated that he was

In constant contact with International Jewry . . . and is apparently an important figure in the New Zionist Organization . . . Mr Briscoe is a frequent visitor to London. He interests himself in visas for Jews on the Continent and is, as is to be expected of one of his race, an internationalist indulging in any and every line of business that will bring financial benefits.

While this report did note that Briscoe had defended Irish neutrality abroad, it and other documents unarguably illustrate the particular mistrust which the Irish Jewish community inspired in security circles. This was both because of the 'supra-national character of the Jewish race', and because it was thought that public opinion could easily be inflamed by too conspicuous a Jewish presence in the country. Zionism was seen as a pernicious doctrine which threatened to subvert the allegiance of Jews of all nationalities—we have already noted the army's apprehensions about Jews enlisting in the defence forces—and despite his loyalty to de Valera, as a Jew with international contacts Briscoe was evidently regarded as a troublemaker if not an outright intriguer acting in Allied interests.[48]

In reality, such fears were utterly unfounded. Briscoe had to strike an agonizing balance between the entreaties of his co-religionists seeking refuge and the likelihood of an anti-Semitic backlash. As a result he took great pains not to cause the government any public difficulties, and he defended de Valera and neutrality to a sceptical American press. The fact that he eschewed publicity was, nevertheless, grist to the mill of conspiracy theorists, who saw it as evidence that behind the scenes he was prising open the floodgates on behalf of rapacious international Jewry. In fact the immigration gates remained almost totally closed to foreigners, although at Roosevelt's prompting in 1943 de Valera did agree in principle to accept five hundred Jewish refugees—in reality, only about sixty continental Jews were admitted during the war years. In 1943 the government also began to make fruitless representations to the German Foreign Ministry about specific groups of Jews, although they kept such interventions quiet for fear of arousing domestic troubles. Even when clear evidence of German extermination policy had emerged, Irish policy remained 'reactive rather than proactive'.[49]

[48] Archer to Walshe, 13 Jan. 1941, DFA, A8; G2 report on Briscoe, undated [1943 or later?], MA, G2/X/40. The argument that Zionism was incompatible with patriotism was also used against American Jews. S. Cohen, *American Modernity & Modern Jewry* (New York, 1983), 154–5. European Jews who emigrated to Israel in the 1950s commented that they were regarded as 'tainted' and suspect because of their links with their former homelands. Elinor Lev, speaking on BBC Radio 4's *Exiles*, 14 May 1997.

[49] Keogh, *Jews in Twentieth Century Ireland*, 173–92; memorandum by Costigan, Justice, 24 Sept. 1945, DT, S. 11007A.

G2's watch on Briscoe produced far less disturbing material than did surveillance of his most vitriolic opponents, whether staunch republicans whose sympathies for the Axis cause derived primarily from atavistic anti-British feeling
such as the maverick Fianna Fáil TD Dan Breen, or those with more convoluted
anti-Semitic obsessions. Amongst the latter the most prominent was probably
the Holy Ghost priest Denis Fahey, who paraded his pseudo-scholarship in the
Catholic press and in a succession of publications. Fahey's world-view is encap-
sulated in a message which this 'rabid anti-Mason' sent to G2 indicating his willingness to 'give any assistance he can'. Fahey began by explaining that early in
1940 an unnamed friend had discovered that

Judaeo-Masonry [had decided] . . . to give Hitler a free hand at France and England . . .
At the same time, my friend learned that Ireland was to be centre of World Masonry
after the war, with Headquarters at Rushbrook [in County Cork] . . . In addition to making Ireland the headquarters . . . they will aim at uniting North and South on Masonic
terms . . . P. S. Stalin, that is the Jews who rule Russia, gave Hitler a guarantee of a safe
Eastern front at the beginning of the war.

By turning against Russia, Hitler seemingly wanted to make use of German power in
Europe. After having been nursed to power by the Jews and Masons, Russia wished to
break with them, in order to make the German race and German finance supreme in
Moscow.[50]

For all their fighting talk, Ireland's avowed anti-Semites did very little, confining themselves mainly to inconsequential meetings where Jewish moneylend-
ing was denounced and German victory predicted. Overt anti-Semitism drew
together an unholy alliance: at one extreme were unbalanced cranks such as
George Griffin and other long-time admirers of Nazism who had come to official attention before the Emergency. Amongst these were the egregious Liam D.
Walsh, formerly O'Duffy's right-hand man in the Blueshirts and subsequently
an enthusiastic fascist and erratic employee of the Italian legation, and Dr Francis O'Sullivan of the Department of Education, who supplied Walsh with
'names of officials' who might have similar sympathies. There were also a few
hard-nosed businessmen such as the one-time minister and ardent protectionist J. J. Walsh, 'regarded in British circles as one of four potential Quislings in
this country'.[51] These initially coalesced in the 'Irish Friends of Germany', a
group whose activities 'indicated that they hoped for a German victory and
were preparing the ground for their own selection as leaders in Irish politics'
when it came. The group disintegrated once a number of its leading lights were
interned, but others produced 'pro-German pamphlets and pamphlets ostensibly in favour of neutrality but really indicting the Government for anti-

---

[50] Breen to Briscoe, 18 Apr. 1941, DFA, P40; Capt. Daly to Commandant O'Connell, 28 Feb. 1942,
enclosing undated notes by D[enis] F[ahey], MA, G2/X/0040A.
[51] 'Notes on persons mentioned in attached memorandum', with Bryan to Walshe, 17 Sept. 1941,
DFA, A8.

German bias', some of the material in which, G2 later learned, 'was got indirectly from ... the German Legation'. They had some success with 'certain members of the Defence Forces' who, while 'loyally performing their duties ... under different circumstances and influences ... would require careful attention'. There is also fragmentary evidence that a handful of businessmen set out, in the name of thwarting Jewish moneylenders and capitalists, to strengthen the position of provident societies and of enterprises with which they were involved: one spoke in 1943 of the need for preventing the theft of 'Irish assets' by 'the gang of para-sites that had come in here in the last thirty years ... I doubt very much if they are human'. Because of his prominence in business and his standing as a former minister, it was J. J. Walsh whose activities caused most concern (although G2 was refused a warrant to tap his telephone). In 1941 his attempts 'surreptitiously to gain favour with certain Germans by passing on ... information of a military nature concerning Northern Ireland' became known to G2, and he also attempted to organize protests against the stationing of American troops in Northern Ireland. However, he appears to have abandoned hope of German victory after 1942, and to have concentrated thereafter on his various business interests. Apart from expressions of admiration for the German people and of loathing of Britain and of aliens, his dyspeptic *Recollections of a Rebel*, published in 1944, shed no light on his wider political sympathies. The Emergency also saw the brief emergence of a brace of what might be termed Catholic nativist polit-ical parties, Córas na Poblachta and Ailtirí na hAiseírghe, whose ideas appeared a mélange of extreme republican and German influences. They proved electoral non-starters, and absorbed the energies of some of the state's most quixotic political activists who might otherwise have caused more trouble.[52]

A strong undercurrent of public hostility towards Jews was perceptible throughout the Emergency, as G2 reports and other material indicate (interest-ingly, a confidential survey by the OSS in 1942 noted that Irish-Americans were strongly anti-Semitic). This was most publicly expressed from 1943 onwards by the newly elected independent TD Oliver J. Flanagan, an enthusiastic waver of the Axis flag in his Dáil contributions. Flanagan, whose ideas on Catholicism and on social credit largely echoed those of Father Fahey, praised Hitler for rid-ding Germany of Jews and repeatedly claimed that the government was unduly pro-Jewish, an accusation he continued to level after the war. What is more depressing, while few TDs rushed to support such declamations in the Dáil, none attempted to challenge them.[53]

The official attitude towards Jews reflected two realities. On the one hand, it

---

[52] Carroll to Archer, 26 May 1939; extract from *Irish Times* report banned by censors, 15 Mar. 1943; G2 report on 'Anti-Jewish Association', undated [1940?], all in MA, G2/X/40.

[53] Even after the war, Flanagan alleged favouritism towards non-Christian refugees, a bizarre charge to level against Justice. *Dáil Debates*, vol. 91, cols. 569–73, 9 July 1943, and vol. 92, col. 1911, 1 Mar. 1944; report by Friediger for Allen Dulles, 24 Aug. 1942, USNA, RG226, box 2, file 15.

is clear that the security authorities were both aware of and shared much of the general public prejudice. On the other hand, it was reasonable to look very carefully at any links which Jewish people had with organizations, movements, or governments abroad, just as it was necessary to probe similar connections which others, be they pro-Axis or pro-Ally, pro-communist, or irredentist republicans, had with the world outside. Furthermore, all aliens, be they of any religion or of none, were automatically suspect. The evidence suggests that in this sense the Jewish community, whether refugees or citizens, were treated no differently than were any other individuals or groups outside the mainstream of the Catholic Irish citizenry.[54] In retrospect, this does not look a proud record; in the circumstances of the time, for a combination of reasons from indigenous prejudice to realpolitik it was probably as much as could have been hoped for.

One externally inspired group of political activists proved surpassingly quiescent after 1939. Because 'Irish Communism and its individual members have a number of international affiliations which have to receive attention', G2 and the Garda kept an eye on left-wing organizations and individuals. Since most leftists were also convinced republicans with strong IRA links, and in the light of the IRA's enthusiasm for Germany, they found themselves in an awkward position as war loomed. These local ideological complications fortuitously evaporated after the Ribbentrop–Molotov pact enabled the Comintern in September 1939 to denounce the war as 'imperialist' and to enjoin all communist parties to 'act so as to shatter the capitalist system'. Until Hitler's invasion of Russia in June 1941, this was the fixed policy for loyal communists everywhere. Under this rubric, the CPI 'advocated the withdrawal of the Six Counties from the war', a formulation calculated to appeal to republican sentiment.[55] After June 1941, this doctrine was abruptly revised. G2, evidently drawing on Garda intelligence, reported that the general secretary had advised

a policy of continued opposition to Britain and Germany as imperialist, even though the British Government was now an ally of Russia . . . it could be shown in propaganda that while seeking the downfall of Germany the Irish people also sought the downfall of British imperialism . . . By opposing Britain . . . it was hoped to still hold the sympathy of those who had anti-British feelings and who hitherto had supported indirectly the Communist Party.

Although the authorities naturally viewed communists with some disfavour— one Englishwoman against whom 'there was a suspicion . . . of espionage activities, whether official or private', was arrested and immediately deported to England in April 1941—there is nothing to suggest that either the CPI or indi-

---

[54] For discussion of a comparable if more extreme and tragic exercise in ethnic paranoia see R. Daniels, *Prisoners without Trial: Japanese Americans in World War II* (New York, 1993), 27–47.

[55] G2 memorandum, 28 Jan., with Bryan to minister for defence, 2 Feb. 1944, DFA, A55/1; Hinsley and Simkins, *British Intelligence*, 36, 79–85, 305, and 320; Guy Liddell (MI5) to Holderness (Home Office), 26 Sept. 1939, PRO, HO 45/25521; Bryan to Duff (Justice), 5 Apr. 1945, MA, G2/X/0244.

vidual communists were pressed into covert service in the Soviet interest, unlike some of their British comrades, in either a political or an intelligence role. Nor does it appear that, as had been the case during the 1920s, Irish communists were under the thumb of the CPGB—the only external assistance to the CPI which came to light were modest monthly remittances send by Earl Browder and later by others in the American communist movement. In 1944 Bryan nevertheless expressed alarm about the development of a communist 'policy of infiltration into the Labour Party'. This he saw as a harbinger of trouble: 'Given the growth of Russian prestige and the impact of Russia on west European political problems, I anticipate that . . . Communism in the future will raise far more security problems for this country than Nazism or Fascism ever did'.[56] Post-war experience was to show that, the development of the Cold War notwithstanding, such fears were largely misplaced. The state's indigenous communist movement remained diminutive, while geography meant that Ireland's usefulness as a centre for Soviet covert activity was minimal. Precautions against such activity were, nevertheless, to become a submerged keystone of Anglo-Irish and Irish–American relations in the post-war era.

viii. The Irish–Allied Security Relationship, 1939–1945

Ireland presented obvious security problems for Britain. The United Kingdom and Ireland shared a highly permeable land border, and operated a common passport area. The unrestricted movement of people between the two jurisdictions, the presence in Britain of large Irish populations, the continuing tradition of large-scale Irish enlistment in the British armed services, and the bitterness of the nationalist minority within Northern Ireland, might facilitate an enemy in mounting espionage or sabotage operations from Ireland against the United Kingdom. The G2 'Fundamental Factors' document had warned in 1936 that 'there will always be an active if small minority that can be exploited' by a foreign power, and once war broke out it was correctly assumed both in Britain and in Ireland that Germany would step up her courtship of the IRA. There were also predictable problems arising from the presence of Axis diplomats, of citizens of Axis states, and of other aliens who might be mobilized to help Britain's enemies, as well as more prosaic matters requiring collaboration such as the control and censorship of communications out of Ireland to restrict the leakage of information to third countries and ultimately to the Axis powers. Finally, both Britain and France expressed concerns about Irish coastal security, although liaison with the French had not developed to any extent by the time France fell in June 1940.[57]

---

[56] Bryan to minister for defence, 2 Feb. 1944.
[57] 'Fundamental Factors', 79; private information.

Of the three British armed services, the Admiralty had the greatest interest in Ireland in 1939 because of questions of coastal defence and coastwatching. Churchill, brought into the war cabinet as First Lord of the Admiralty, shared the widespread suspicion that U-boats would be succoured in remote Irish bays: Gordon Campbell, hero of the First World War 'Q-ships', wrote in November, 'my appreciation of the submarine and radar situation leads me to think that the submarines are using inlets on the north western and south western coasts of Ireland as bases'.[58] With the agreement of the Irish authorities, Captain A. B. Greig was attached to Sir John Maffey's staff to cover naval affairs from 3 November. After undertaking a tour of the southern coast with G2 officers, he submitted a 'surprisingly favourable' report on the new coastwatching system, and he and his successors worked closely with G2 on submarine sightings, shipping issues, and other maritime matters: at Christmas 1939 an Irish diplomat told the Canadians that Greig 'has been most helpful in putting to an end unfounded rumours about the adventures of German submarines in Irish bays and harbours', and in 1941 the British chiefs of staff heard that 'there have been many rumours of submarines off the Irish coast but no authentic reports'.[59]

Shortly after his arrival, Greig warned London that efforts at espionage by patriotic amateurs 'tend to cloud the co-operation between us and [Irish] . . . officials'. G2 had 'evidently got a very good line on' one retired British officer, who claimed to be working under cover for naval intelligence and was attempting to recruit helpers. Although G2 pointed out to Greig that this man's 'services would no longer be of any value' since they knew all about him, a clandestine reporting network was established along the southern coastline to watch for suspicious marine activity, and possibly to act as the nucleus of an invasion warning and 'stay behind' organization should the Germans come—G2 got its hands on one British transceiver secretly supplied to someone wrongly thought loyal to Britain, and it was assumed that other sets had been distributed. Duly penetrated by G2, the network of agents 'really had nothing to report', and as it was merely confirming what the Irish were saying, it was simply kept under observation. G2 officers were similarly fatalistic about the flat-footed wanderings of the British air attaché appointed in 1940, complaining only about his lack of discretion. The pragmatism underpinning Irish attitudes was illustrated in

[58] Campbell to Commander Loly, 30 Nov. 1939, PRO, ADM 199/146. This file also contains instructions to various Q ships dispatched to hunt U-boats in Irish waters in 1939. For contrasting assessments of the First World War Irish U-boat scares, see P. Beesly, *Room 40: British Naval Intelligence 1914–1918* (London, 1982), 184–6 and 313, and O'Halpin, 'British Intelligence in Ireland, 1914–1921' in Andrew and Dilks (eds.), *The Missing Dimension*, 58.

[59] Greig to Godfrey, 9 Nov. 1939, PRO, DO 130/7; 'Godfrey memoir', pp. 66–7; aide-mémoire by Irish high commissioner in Ottawa, 22 Dec. 1939, PAC, RG25/31, vol. 781, file 398; there is a file on submarine sightings in MA, G2/X/0152.

The Irish U-boat legend became part of post-war British defence folklore, and it has been sustained in popular fiction. On this see K. Jeffery and E. O'Halpin, 'Ireland in Spy Fiction', in W. Wark (ed.), *Spy Fiction, Spy Films and Real Intelligence* (London, 1991), 97–8.

1941 with de Valera's instruction to act on an Admiralty request for detailed maps of various ports, as 'if they wanted to go to the trouble, the British could get all the information without having recourse to us'.[60] The Irish might have been rather more alarmed by amateur spies had they realized the 'seminal influence' on British policy of the alarmist report in June 1940 of Sir Charles Tegart, a retired Indian policeman who returned to Whitehall from Ireland with wild stories of U-boat incursions and IRA preparations for a German invasion. Tegart's tales evidently took precedence over Greig's more measured and better informed reports.[61]

A certain amount of improvised espionage was understandable in the first months of the war, when it appeared imperative to get information quickly and when nothing was known about Irish coastwatching and security arrangements. In the longer term, however, through Greig's dealings with G2 it became clear that, unless Britain intended to dispose of her Irish security problem by forcible reoccupation, effective security of all kinds, from counter-espionage to postal censorship, would best be obtained with Irish co-operation. It was this assumption which came to underpin MI5's approach to Irish affairs: from a slow and tentative start in 1938, when British warnings about German plans to use Irishmen to spy were received with 'extreme caution and reticence' by G2, in the course of the war liaison became very close. From the beginning of the war, the German and Italian legations, together with Irish organizations and individuals considered sympathetic to the Axis cause, were placed under very detailed G2 and police 'supervision' by a variety of means, from telephone and postal interception to infiltration.[62] Much, though not all, of the intelligence gained eventually found its way in modified forms to MI5. The Irish records contain a wealth of material illustrating the development of these links, which were somewhat cumbersomely maintained through External Affairs, the British Representative's Office, and the Irish High Commission in London. The liaison was facilitated by the personal connections of the MI5 officers directly responsible. Guy Liddell, who was head of the counter-espionage side of MI5 throughout the war, was a frequent visitor to his cousin Lord Revelstoke on Lambay Island. So too was his brother Cecil, whom he brought into MI5 in 1940 to establish and run an Irish section. Coincidentally, Cecil Liddell's assistant from 1940 to 1943, Joe Stephenson, also had Irish connections: his great-uncle Lord Frederick Cavendish had been murdered by the Invincibles in 1882—Dan Bryan took him to the spot in the Phoenix Park on one of his wartime visits—while his father had been involved in the prosecution of Roger Casement in 1916.[63] The liaison had its ups and downs

---

[60] Greig to Slade, 28 Nov., and reply, 1 Dec. 1939, PRO, DO 130/4; P. Beesly, *Very Special Admiral: The Life of Admiral John H. Godfrey CB* (London, 1980), 136–8; Bryan transcripts; Walshe to Archer, 14 May 1941, DFA, A3.

[61] Sloan, *Geopolitics*, 206.   [62] Bryan transcripts, p. 7.

[63] Stephenson interview.

but, fortified by the regular dispatch by Bryan of parcels of Irish meat, it became very close. This is reflected in a letter from the philosopher Gilbert Ryle, who visited Dublin early in 1944 for discussions with G2 on Abwehr ciphers:

I just write to tell you how grateful I am for all you did for me. My whole visit to Dublin was, thanks to you & [Dr Richard] Hayes, one of the pleasantest periods I have had since the war began . . . it was also profitable to my organisation & may, I hope, in the end be so to you . . . Please give my regards & thanks to . . . Neligan [a G2 signals officer], whom, with you, I want to meet again, whether on business or pleasure.[64]

A telegram from Cecil Liddell to G2 in January 1944 shortly after the capture of the German agent John O'Reilly also reflects how closely the two organizations had come to work:

Page and self delighted [to] come over when you think suitable stage of interrogation reached . . . Information about cyphers and device of great interest. Your preliminary report on radio indicates it may be of type not hitherto known here.[65]

In fact Hayes had found 'a hitherto unknown method of turning letters into figures on [a] keyword in such a way that some letters were represented by a single figure and others by . . . two digits'. This, 'discovered in the rough work in O'Reilly's cell when he was asked to prepare specimens of messages', appeared interesting but 'of quite minor insignificance at the time'. In the last year of the war, however, the Germans used the technique in 'an entirely new system of substitution and transposition ciphers'. Hayes was told 'that this whole set of ciphers would never have been solved without this vital piece of information culled from O'Reilly's work'.[66]

This, and other evidence, bear out the broad picture of the 1939–45 Anglo-Irish security relationship described elsewhere, though the Irish files show that the British official history is unduly conservative in stating that liaison was 'always strictly confined to counter-espionage'.[67] What is also clear is that each of the two security agencies principally involved were operating under broad guidelines, and that these were consistent with the declared policies of their respective governments. G2 and MI5 corresponded mainly through diplomatic channels—there are many MI5/G2 exchanges in the External Affairs files—and so those responsible (at least on the Irish side) for Anglo-Irish diplomatic relations had a fair idea of the nature of much of the material being shared or exchanged. This point while obvious is fundamental. So too is the rider that the close co-operation which slowly developed on security and on Axis counter-

[64]   Ryle to Bryan, 23 May 1945, Bryan papers, P71/454.
[65]   Archer (BRO) to Boland, conveying message from Liddell for Bryan, 3 Jan. 1944, DFA, A60. Denys Page, an expert on Abwehr ciphers, later became Master of Jesus College Cambridge. On 23 Apr. 1948 Cecil Liddell told Bryan that Page 'has just been made Regius Professor . . . He always remembers the days he spent in Dublin.' UCDA, Bryan papers, P71/455.
[66]   'Hayes report'.   [67]   Hinsley and Simkins, *British Intelligence*, 17.

espionage problems was never coterminous with complete frankness. On the other hand, from 1942 onwards there was close co-operation even on so sensitive a matter for the British as signals intelligence: in his valedictory report in 1946 Hayes showed himself remarkably well informed about many aspects of British and American code-breaking organizations and operations. There were also occasions when, in Bryan's laconic words, 'we knew things that the British were after that we didn't tell them. That . . . happens in all intelligence organisations.' The issue of the German legation radio was one such matter. There were also some recriminations about Irish failure to provide advance warning of the IRA's cross-border raids in 1942. G2 had a tip-off that such raids were being planned, a report which 'the police just pooh-poohed'. As a result, Bryan did not say anything to MI5: 'If I had told them this thing was pending, my credit was up. I didn't.' When next in London for consultations he was 'brought up formally to meet the boss of MI5', Sir David Petrie, who 'challenged me about these raids'. Bryan said nothing: 'You have to keep your own rows between yourselves at times'.[68]

The generally effective liaison which evolved between MI5 and G2 naturally remained highly secret. Consequently it could not be publicly adduced to counter the claims frequently aired in the British and American press that the IRA was running amok and that Dublin was a nest of Axis spies. OSS records indicate that, America's alliance with Britain notwithstanding, Washington had precious little intelligence on Ireland to hand other than scare stories from the press and from the American legation, which Bryan had criticized in 1940 as 'probably a greater centre of pro-British influence . . . than the office of the United Kingdom Representative'. The American minister David Gray combined his understandable dislike of Irish policy with both an appetite for private political intrigue and a chronic neglect of basic security—after the war a censorious G2 document described him as 'most unsympathetic to . . . neutrality and . . . most indiscreet in his conversations'—and he and his subordinates were closely watched. Surveillance disclosed that American diplomats were not only hostile to neutrality on political grounds but, in contrast to their British counterparts, also had spies on the brain. They were, furthermore, in G2's view markedly lazy, and never 'took any great pains to carry out their work efficiently'. In consequence, 'at no time was there any real liaison with the [American service] attachés', in contrast to the generally good relations with British service representatives.[69] The outlook of Gray and his staff was a serious problem because he enjoyed President Roosevelt's confidence, and it threatened a situation where all the efforts to demonstrate the effectiveness of Irish security

---

[68] Bryan transcripts, pp. 38, 48–9.
[69] Draft G2 annual report for 1940, Bryan papers, P71/33; Bryan to Walshe, 31 Jan. 1944, DFA, A8; O'Donoghue to Bryan, 12 Aug. 1941, MA, G2/X/1122; undated document, in file on 'Correspondence with the American army', MA, 18 MM. 24.

might be set at naught by alarmist reports from Dublin to Washington. These considerations determined the Irish attitude towards 'Spike' Marlin, the OSS official who was posted to Ireland in the autumn of 1942. He devoted most of his time to investigating the efficiency of Irish security, and to liaison with G2. He argued that American interests lay emphatically in prudent co-operation rather than in clandestine investigation. In March 1943 David Bruce, the head of OSS in Europe, visited Dublin and had very constructive talks with G2 and the Garda, and G2 supplied OSS with material on German agents and their ciphers. Gray, however, wished to be the sole conduit of information from Dublin to Washington, and he eventually forced Marlin out.[70] Marlin's good working relationship with G2 was reflected in the OSS's appraisal of Irish security arrangements in 1944. By then the main concern was that intelligence on the Normandy invasion build-up—and the massive deception operations which accompanied it—might reach Germany through Ireland. These fears led Washington to issue what became known as the 'American note' in February 1944. Such an approach had been canvassed by Gray from as early as January 1942, when he also said he was 'inclined to doubt efficacy of British secret service here'. Despite the 'entirely unfavourable' attitude of Sir John Maffey and of the British government towards the proposal, a note was eventually unilaterally issued which amounted to an ultimatum to close the Axis diplomatic missions in Dublin as a threat to Allied security. The note was also leaked to the press. The Irish were not the only ones taken aback: a Canadian official told his prime minister that the démarche was 'a mistake in judgement'. We are not concerned here with the wider impact of the crisis, which was to put Ireland on the spot about its pedantic adherence to neutrality and to lessen Irish-American sympathy about partition, nor to probe the British view.[71] The row did, however, alarm Allied security agencies because it threatened their generally constructive relationship with G2 and discounted their assessments of Irish security. In March Walshe visited London for discussions with OSS. Bruce was emollience personified:

He regretted very much that our relations should have been clouded by recent mishandling on the American side . . . the organisation of the State Department was most unfortunate. Nobody there seemed to have a complete knowledge of American relations with Ireland, and they certainly did not seem to know how close our relations with the American Intelligence people had been.[72]

This was not simply diplomatic soft soap: a month later Sir David Petrie and

[70] Hull (secretary of state) to Gray, 5 Dec. 1942; OSS 'Report on the present state of Eire', 27 Jan. 1943, USNA, State Department, 841D.00/1358A, and RG226, entry 106, box 0039, file 347; G2 documents on Abwehr ciphers passed to OSS are in RG457, CB2J73, 6285A, box 771.

[71] Gray to Washington, 18 Jan. 1942, USNA, State Department, 841D.00/1323; Kearney (Dublin) to Robertson (Ottawa), 15 Oct. 1943, and Robertson to MacKenzie King, 25 Feb. 1944, PAC, RG25 1989–90/029, box 45, file 126 (s), and RG25, D1, vol. 781; Bowman, *De Valera and the Ulster Question*, 251–2; T. Ryle Dwyer, *Irish Neutrality and the USA, 1939–1947* (Dublin, 1977), 192–3.

[72] Walshe to de Valera, 14 Mar. and 13 Apr. 1944, DFA, A2.

Bruce's OSS deputy asked the American ambassador in London to warn Washington not to press Ireland too hard, as the Irish were 'making every effort to co-operate on security measures' and too much criticism might provoke them to change this policy. In June two visiting OSS officials told Walshe they 'knew the excellence of Marlin's work . . . and how much he had contributed to better relations', and deplored Gray's attitude. In return Walshe delivered an extraordinary encomium on Marlin, but for whose 'patriotism in the interests of America and . . . complete understanding of this country, the liaison between our Security officials would never have been established'. The OSS Official History takes a similar line, describing Marlin's liaison work as his 'greatest achievement' and his 'main difficulties' as those which arose from his differences with Gray about the efficacy of Irish security against German espionage.[73]

ix. The Problem of Movement between the Two Jurisdictions

The initial Anglo-Irish exchanges on security matters focused mainly on the immediate danger of German espionage, and from May 1940 on the likelihood of a German strike against Ireland as part of an assault on the United Kingdom.[74] But other problems also loomed large. MI5 was relieved in August to find Sir Charles Wickham of the RUC, 'a most valuable friend and counsellor', dismissive of the likelihood of significant IRA activity in Northern Ireland unless an invasion were actually in train. Nevertheless, even a relatively quiescent IRA might achieve a good deal through discreet intelligence-gathering and sabotage in Northern Ireland and in Britain. In November 1940 the JIC concluded that 'there is not, and cannot be, any effective control over border traffic', and in April 1942 the Security Executive heard that about twenty thousand people crossed at recognized checkpoints each week. While there were some security procedures, 'there appears to be no practicable way of making this control effective'. Derry was in a particularly difficult situation, akin in some respects to that of Gibraltar in relation to pro-Axis Spain. Overlooked by independent Ireland across Lough Foyle, hundreds of people came from Donegal each day to work in the dockyards. It was regarded as particularly vulnerable both to espionage and to sabotage, and MI5 came to the conclusion that its security and that of the ships using it could only be maintained with active Irish co-operation.[75]

Even if it had been possible to fence off Northern Ireland from its southern neighbour, the option was deeply unattractive: besides being an important

---

[73] Winant (London) to Washington, 15 Apr. 1944, USNA, State Department, 841D01/333; Walshe to de Valera, 23 June 1944, DFA, A2. The quotation from the OSS Official History is as given in Marlin's obituary notice in *The Irish Times*, 2 Jan. 1995.

[74] Hinsley and Simkins, *British Intelligence*, 17, 90, and 280.

[75] 'MI5 report'; JIC (40) 355, 11 Nov. 1940, PRO, CAB 81/98; memorandum by Herbert, with minutes of 66th meeting of Security Executive, 29 Apr. 1942, PRO, HO 45/21985; Stephenson interview.

producer of food, Ireland was also a key manpower reservoir both for the British armed forces and for British industry. From the Orkneys to the south coast, and in Northern Ireland, southern Irish workers were a familiar and important element of the labour market.[76] Furthermore, most of the larger manufacturing centres in Scotland and in the English north-west and midlands had large Irish immigrant populations, as did western ports such as Liverpool. Such communities retained strong Irish links through visits, through correspondence, and through the assimilation of friends and relations travelling over in search of work. Even with strict postal censorship, unless all movement of people between Britain and the island of Ireland were stopped the passage of news of all sorts between the two countries was unavoidable. Prevention of such travel would, however, deprive Britain of much needed labour. It also risked alienating Irish people already resident in Britain and contributing to the war effort, whether as civilians or in the armed services.

The problem of travel to and from Ireland, and of travel by Irish citizens through neutral countries to the continent, greatly exercised MI5. In January 1940 its deputy director wrote that because 'of the anomalous position of citizenship of Eire in this country, an open channel exists for communications between enemy agents on the continent, in this country and in Eire'. In April another officer warned that once on the continent Irish travellers

can secure visas to enter Germany as neutrals. It is often impossible for us to prove that these people have acted as messengers or agents for the enemy . . . all that we can be sure of is that they may be acting as such agents or messengers and that . . . the means of communication exist. In other words, the problem primarily concerns the preventive rather than the detective side of the security service. What we want is the power to destroy the facilities to injure this country which Irish citizens at present enjoy.

The Home Office and the Dominions Office were against the proposed restrictions, on grounds both of policy and of practicality. After the invasion of the Netherlands, however, MI5 returned to the charge because 'Eire citizens', including some of German or Italian origin who had been naturalized after years of residence, could come and go from the United Kingdom 'as of right', thus extending 'the front which the security service has to guard'. This lessened MI5's ability to concentrate on 'potentially dangerous individuals'. As things stood, MI5 suspicions about Irish travellers were insufficient grounds for preventing them from travelling through the United Kingdom: 'As watch-dogs we bark when we see strangers—but we are told to prove that they are also dangerous strangers, which we can only do in few cases'.[77] MI5's fears were not entirely

---

[76] K. Jeffery, 'The British Army and Ireland since 1922', in T. Bartlett and K. Jeffery (eds.), *A Military History of Ireland* (Cambridge, 1996), 438.

[77] Holt-Wilson (MI5) to Maxwell (Home Office), 9 Nov. 1939 and 31 Jan. 1940; Turner (MI5) to Maxwell, 1 Apr., and MI5 notes for Maxwell, 10 May 1940, PRO, HO 213/1905.

fanciful: for example, Francis Stuart, who travelled through Britain on his way back to Germany in the autumn of 1939, later acted as a conduit between the IRA and the key republicans Sean Russell and Frank Ryan in Berlin, while his estranged wife Iseult was the first Irish contact for the German agent Herman Goertz.

The collapse of France finally provoked a change in policy, and in June travel permits were introduced for anyone wishing to move between Britain and either jurisdiction on the island of Ireland. Even in the midst of the invasion scare, however, it proved difficult to maintain tight controls. A Home Office official later told his minister that 'within a few weeks' the government 'were forced to make concessions to various categories of travellers . . . in the first week of June 1940 only 440 exit permits for travel to Ireland were granted, but by the middle of July that total had increased to 1600'.[78] The travel issue became very acute during the build-up to the invasion of Europe. In January 1944 MI5 warned the chiefs of staff of 'the danger of leakage of operational material via Ireland'. The 'greatest danger lay among the 150,000 Irish labourers', many 'working in the operational areas involved'. MI5 based its case on 'recent evidence . . . that the Germans were making increased efforts to obtain information from Ireland re Operation Overlord'; such evidence included the two parachutists captured in County Clare, as well as decrypts of messages to the German legation. The introduction of a blanket ban on the movement of people from Britain to Ireland nevertheless proved a vexed question. One official remarked that while 'at first sight the possibility of travel to Eire opens the door to the leakage of information . . . it is . . . by no means established that information has ever leaked through Eire; nothing so far as I know has ever been caught in the censorship'. It was argued that any restrictions should be temporary, should exclude the freight trade, and should not apply to Irish people seeking work in Britain. There was also a strong compassionate case for permitting restricted home leave for 'Irish merchant seamen whose ships dock in UK' after running the gauntlet of U-boat attacks. Although General Eisenhower insisted on a travel ban, the armed services were also mindful of the impact on morale and of recruitment of a lengthy prohibition of leave visits to Ireland. An indefinite ban was eventually imposed from 10 March, but it was attenuated with surprising speed once Overlord began: on 15 June the Home Office noted that 'it is now possible to relax the restrictions on certain classes of traveller . . . No public pronouncement will be or should be made at present.' A few years after the war, the British foreign secretary Ernest Bevin, 'in good spirits' at a function in Brussels, 'suddenly turned' to an Irish diplomat and loudly stated that he wanted

our Irish friends to know that, during all those months of preparation [for the invasion of Normandy], not a single leakage of information occurred through Ireland. In order

---

[78] Newsam to Morrison (home secretary), 2 Feb. 1944, PRO, HO 213/2209.

to enforce our restrictions on travel and communications, which were very severe, we had to take the top Irish officials into our confidence . . . they gave . . . co-operation unstintingly, and (he repeated this with emphasis) not one single leak occurred. This is a great tribute to the Irish government and the Irish officials concerned.[79]

The universal restrictions initially introduced in 1940 engendered much public criticism for the remainder of the war, in part because of the alleged administrative inefficiency of the British Permit Office (and MI6 cover organization) set up in Dublin in June 1940, but they were regarded by Irish security officials with a combination of equanimity and of relief. As well as lessening the administrative burden on the Irish authorities, the British permit system on occasion evidently enabled G2 to secure the temporary exclusion of troublesome foreigners and even Irish citizens, by having MI5 block their departures from the British mainland. The Irish may have learnt their lesson from Prince Milo of Montenegro, the somewhat implausible possessor of a Mexican passport and of a British travel permit, who made his way to Kildare before kicking up a fuss because he 'wants to be treated as a royal person'. The British authorities were subsequently asked 'not to issue exit permits to Ireland in future without first consulting [the] Irish government'.[80] The operation of the British system facilitated the timely exchange of information on suspects, and so made it much easier to keep track of suspects who were issued permits. Thus in 1942 Bryan was asked to keep a watch on an RAF sergeant who had escaped from a German prison camp and who wished to visit his Mayo home, 'in case he should attempt [to] contact Axis elements' to pass on information. Suspicions had arisen because he was a cousin of the renegade 'Lord Haw-Haw', who had visited him in captivity. Again, when the adventurer and would-be double-agent Joseph Lenihan told his MI5 controllers that he wished to take a short holiday in Ireland in 1943, the British were informed that while 'there is no objection to . . . a short visit', G2 'would not care to have Lenihan here indefinitely', and that 'owing to the man's habits and character' they could not 'guarantee a 100% fool-proof check on his doings'.[81]

The British were also concerned about the possibility of people travelling on the various 'cargo vessels . . . which ply between Eire and the continent'. While 'it is appreciated that . . . Eire discourages' such travel, early in 1940 MI5 argued that these shipping links presented a considerable danger to security. Experience was to bear out these fears. It was also to demonstrate that the only means of plugging

---

[79] Copy of COS (44) 63 (o), 22 Jan., signed by Beddle Smith, quoting MI5 document of 3 Jan.; memorandum by Hill (Home Office), 12 Jan.; draft report by Stewart (chairman, Security Executive), 31 Jan.; unsigned minute, 15 June 1944, all PRO, HO 213/2209; Fay (Washington) to McCann (External Affairs), 2 July 1965, DT, 96/6/412. Fay was almost certain that he had reported this conversation immediately it took place in 1948.

[80] Bryan minute, 20 Nov. 1940, MA, G2/X/0244.

[81] Hankinson (BRO) to Boland, relaying text of MI5 message for Bryan, 10 Nov. 1942; same to same, relaying message from Liddell for Bryan, and Bryan's reply, 30 Jan. and 4 Feb. 1943, DFA, A60.

these leaks was to work in co-operation with the Irish. The same applied though with less force, to Irish air links. The British raised no objections to the initiation of seaplane services by Pan American Airways from Foynes to the United States and to Lisbon in 1942. They found the Irish very anxious to help, agreeing to allow a British passport official to monitor seaplane passenger traffic, although the precaution seemed pointless as the traffic consisted almost exclusively of civilian officials and military personnel in mufti travelling on official business. The Irish also accepted uncomplainingly the very cumbersome arrangements put in place for incoming airmail (which was sent from Foynes to Liverpool for censorship before being passed on to Dublin). Shortly after the arrival of a Mr Carruthers as a passport control officer, a G2 report from Foynes predicted that 'he will content himself with the minimum amount of work . . . He is far more interested in getting his salary and allowances raised . . . than he is at getting on with his job.' Carruthers had reportedly admitted: 'Confidentially and off the record, the job is an absolute farce.'[82] However easy a billet Foynes proved, however, passport and movement controls remained a crucial element in the British security system. Here there was already a useful precedent in the manner in which the British and Irish governments had dealt with the movements of foreigners into and out of the British Isles since the early 1920s, and there were no serious security hiccups—MI5 found more to complain of in the increasingly lax attitude of Pan American after D-Day than in Irish movement controls.[83]

The problem of aliens, whether refugees from tyranny or adherents of it, by comparison with that of the cross-channel movements of British and Irish citizens proved easily managed. The few hundred resident aliens in September 1939, of whom only a minority were refugees, were already subject to registration and restrictions under the 1935 Aliens Act. The Axis émigré communities posed a threat, because of the Irish branches of the Nazi and Fascist parties. Here Ireland had a stroke of luck, because when war broke out some of the leading German émigrés, including their political leader Adolf Mahr of the National Museum, were on Nazi party business in Nuremberg, and so were unable to return. Furthermore, another fifty German citizens chose to return home: G2 and MI5 quickly made arrangements which allowed them to travel through Britain to Europe, an episode which served to improve relations between the two organizations. This left just over three hundred Germans within the state, of whom 141 were refugees (this did not exempt them from suspicion and surveillance). One further small category of Irish resident caused MI5 some worries: naturalized Irish citizens originally from Germany or Italy. However, Irish naturalization policy had always been far stricter even than Britain's—where as late as March 1939 the home secretary had ignored MI5 advice to refuse

---

[82] Turner to Maxwell, 1 Apr. 1940; G2 report by Hewett (Foynes), 27 July 1942, DFA, A60.
[83] Minutes of 63rd and 101st meetings of Security Executive, 1 Apr. 1942 and 20 Dec. 1944, PRO, CAB 93/2.

naturalization to any citizens of Axis countries—and as a result there were only a handful of Irish citizens of Axis origin. These were closely watched; with a few exceptions, they gave no cause for serious concern.[84]

After war broke out official opposition to the admission of and naturalization of aliens hardened. G2's line was particularly clear: the more aliens let in for any reason, the greater the security and political risks incurred. All foreigners, whether refugees from tyranny or supporters of it, were an embarrassment and a burden. Problems arose in relation to the meteorological service because only one of its professional staff was Irish. Others were from Northern Ireland and from Britain, and two were European refugees: Dr Deporto, a Basque inaccurately rumoured to have fought against Franco in the Spanish civil war, and Dr Pollak, a Czech Jew. This placed the state in a cleft stick, because the maintenance of an efficient meteorological service reporting hourly to its British analogue was a crucial element of the secret modus vivendi which underlay much of the public bluster of Anglo-Irish relations. Industry and Commerce supported naturalization, but G2 argued against this: 'we object to the naturalisation of any alien during this war and . . . Justice has accepted our general objection.' The two men were nevertheless retained on their particularly sensitive work, close co-operation with the British was maintained, and Deporto was ultimately granted citizenship and became director of the service.[85]

Requests for sanctuary were influenced both by realpolitik and by prejudice. While Archer of G2 opposed the admission of the family of a Greek shipping magnate 'on general grounds', Justice thought it might 'be very unwise for us to refuse' lest he 'take reprisals against us'—his ships carried most of Ireland's grain imports. The pre-war tendency to make exceptions for the Catholic Church remained: thus three Polish seminarians were allowed to come from Britain to study in the autumn of 1940. In general, Irish aliens policy created no problems for the British, because it continued to be operated with the stringency which had characterized immigration control since the foundation of the state. We may, however, note some nuances of which the British might not have approved: in the panic after the fall of France, the Defence Conference wanted 'all aliens (other than British subjects)' to be made to report to Garda stations daily. Walshe objected strongly to this: 'it would create new difficulties between us and the German Government . . . It appears to be entirely within the probabilities that we shall soon have to deal with the German Government, without any hope that we can look to another Government for support.'[86]

[84] Costigan (Justice) to Miss Murphy (External Affairs), 9 July 1940, DFA, P11; Bryan and Stephenson interviews.

[85] Fergusson (Industry and Commerce) to Walshe, 6 June 1940, DFA, A14; Archer (G2) to Walshe, 2 Dec. 1940, DFA, A17; Bourke interview; L. Shields (ed.), *The Irish Meteorology Service: The First 50 Years, 1936–1986* (Dublin, 1987), 8, 44–5.

[86] Duff (Justice) to Archer, and reply, 8 and 9 Nov. 1940, and External Affairs to Archer and reply, 9 Sept. and 17 Sept. 1940, MA, G2/X/0244; Walshe to Roche (Justice), 23 June 1940, DFA, A23.

Other and more colourful aspects of Anglo-Irish security relations are dealt with below, but we may note that the two countries' separate though inter-related security interests depended upon the effectiveness of the mundane pre-ventive measures outlined here.

x. Covert Activities in Ireland, 1939–1945

It is impossible to do justice in a few paragraphs to the Wodehousian galaxy of characters and devices involved in clandestine activities in Ireland between 1939 and 1945. Amongst these are Mr Austin, the counterfeit English butler; the 'decrepit' though still libidinous elderly ex-weightlifter turned spy Ernst Weber Drohl; the rakish 'Captain Higgins', who on arrest in Killarney bearing a gun and documents indicating that he 'is a British Secret Service agent, unless of course such papers are faked', admitted that the 'lady with whom he was living' as 'Captain and Mrs Price' was in fact 'a Mrs Walker from Jamaica'; the French-speaking maid whom MI6 planted in the home of a Vichy diplomat; the snob-bish naval reservist Lieutenant Mason, who came 'on behalf of the British Government to obtain certain information about German submarines', assum-ing 'the personality of an Irish tradesman on holiday with a bicycle and an Irish accent and a vile assortment of readymade clothes', a disguise which un-accountably failed to protect him from rapid detection and arrest; the MI6 agent suspected of misappropriating secret funds to buy himself a car; and a clutch of carrier pigeons concealed in the air attaché's Castleknock attic.[87] This discussion will, accordingly, focus on the general problems for the state thrown up by the espionage, counter-espionage, and other covert activities of the belligerent powers.

These activities can be broken down into three broad categories of unequal importance: (i) British attempts initially to acquire information of military value about Irish defensive preparations, and subsequently to uncover Axis activities; (ii) American efforts to uncover Axis activities and to assess Irish security; and (iii) Axis espionage and other clandestine activities directed against Allied interests. In a review of counter-espionage for the year 1940, Dan Bryan wrote that 'certain persons . . . in the panic following the collapse of France' had discussed

tentative measures for the establishment of intelligence centres in Ireland on behalf of Great Britain. It is not certain that these measures were in the fullest degree official.

---

[87] Austin to Whyte (BRO), 8 Oct. 1940, PRO, DO 130/4; report on Weber Drohl, 19 Apr., with de Buitléar (G2) to Walshe, 22 Apr., and Bryan to Walshe, 30 Oct. 1943, DFA, A71; undated [*c.*25 May 1940] note by G2 duty officer, DFA, A8; private information; Mason to Maffey, undated, with Antrobus (BRO) to Stephenson (Dominions Office), 3 Nov. 1939, and memorandum by Raynes (Air Ministry), 14 July 1940, both PRO, DO 130/4.

There is no recent evidence of such an organisation or activity and it is reasonably certain that a proposed organisation for certain radio work has been discontinued. The position of Germany and Britain for the collection of information in this country is . . . completely different. Germany is practically isolated and has no contacts here . . . British officers, officials and privileged members of the public generally can visit this country at will. They have friends in all parts and all classes and meet frequently people who are usually fully informed as to the general position . . . Further, in the ultimate there are no effective restrictions on the transmission of information from this country to Great Britain and, therefore, little need for the creation of a special organisation either for the collection of information or for its transmission.[88]

This assessment was broadly borne out by the pattern of British clandestine activity up to 1945. There was an initial flurry of intelligence-gathering by patriotic amateurs and by thinly disguised officers and ex-officers, directed first at coastal surveillance, secondly at checking the lie of the land for a possible military incursion from Northern Ireland, and (most likely) thirdly at surveying ports, airfields, power stations, and other facilities for sabotage purposes should a German invasion succeed. In 1941 the British escape service MI9 also organized one break out of nine airmen from internment, a stunt which caused embarrassment to the Irish authorities and probably delayed the eventual introduction of the covert release of Allied internees, and which—contrary to a rather sketchy British account—was successful only because G2 were directed by External Affairs not to pick up the escapers in their Dublin refuges. The irregular warfare agency Special Operations Executive (SOE) also took an interest at some point between 1940 and 1942, but received 'a bloody nose' from MI5 and withdrew.[89] British clandestine activity after the summer of 1940 was, however, primarily concerned with counter-intelligence, the uncovering of Axis covert activities through the investigation of aliens, Axis residents, and pro-Axis individuals and groups. As early as January 1940 the Garda reported that the British Trade Office had initiated an abnormally high number of inquiries through private detectives about 'certain aliens', and in June a passport control officer (PCO), Captain Collinson, was sent to open a Permit Office for people wishing to travel to Britain. A PCO in Paris before the war, he was automatically suspect to G2 because they were aware that passport control work had been the main peacetime cover for MI6 officers abroad. Collinson and his assistant PCO ran into the same difficulties which other PCOs had encountered in Europe in the 1930s, because the sheer volume of travel permit work got in the way of covert intelligence-gathering. Furthermore, the latter activity was hopelessly compromised: from January 1941 until its final dissolution amid much

---

[88]　Draft G2 annual report for 1940.

[89]　M. Foot and J. Langley, *MI9: Escape and Evasion, 1939–1945* (London, 1979), 116–17; Bryan and Stephenson interviews; conversation with Group Captain Hugh Verity, one of the escapers, 1986. On the experience of internees see T. R. Dwyer, *Guests of the Nation: The Story of Allied and Axis Servicemen Interned in Ireland during World War II* (Dingle, 1994). SOE briefly revived its interest in 1945.

backbiting and recrimination in April 1945, Collinson's Dublin counter-intelligence network, based in the credit investigation agency Stubbs Gazette, was comprehensively blown by one of its most trusted operatives. The result was that G2 had an excellent line not only on the extent of British clandestine inquiries but on their outcome, including much useful information on Axis activities and on political affairs, as well as on British attempts to penetrate the army and the Garda and tentative plans for a post-war intelligence network. It is of course possible that MI6 were aware of G2's success against Collinson's operations, but the sheer volume of good intelligence which the Irish obtained over such a long period suggests otherwise.[90]

American covert activities were mounted without consultation with their allies. Perhaps in unconscious imitation of the theatrical figures on whom the British appeared so frequently to rely, however, Bill Donovan, Roosevelt's 'Coordinator of Intelligence' and the founder of OSS in July 1942, initially planned to dispatch Errol Flynn 'to act as a public relations and intelligence agent'; instead he had to make do with an undistinguished stand-in, who on a trip in 1942 recruited a Kerry cattle dealer to develop a network of people around the south-west to collect information for transmission to the American legation. These arrangements were quickly uncovered by Florence O'Donoghue of G2, and with the aid of informants were kept under observation. In February 1944 O'Donoghue also confronted Smale, the American vice-consul in Cork, considered a particular 'busybody' responsible for various scare stories about German activities. Smale, who seemed 'in a nervous and excited condition', claimed to be 'horrified and indignant' at the suggestion that he was paying locals for information, but added that 'he knew Hathaway [the military attaché] was letting them down and may be paying money out of his own pocket'. This kind of amateurish spying caused particular difficulties because the wild stories it generated were fed back to Washington through diplomatic rather than security channels.[91]

Axis clandestine activities presented far larger problems. The Axis legations were natural objects of Allied suspicions. We have seen that the legations themselves did not act as controlling centres for espionage at any time, although German diplomats naturally passed on to Berlin any useful gossip or firmer military information which came their way and were involved in intrigues with some politicians and army officers which in different circumstances could have resulted in a coup. The Italians, similarly, stuck to overt and clandestine

---

[90] Garda report, 30 Jan. 1940, DFA, A8; Andrew, *Secret Service*, 379–80; Stubbs had been suggested as a possible cover operation for MI6 in discussions between Sir William Bull, Walter Long, and Basil Thomson, 14 and 18 Dec. 1918, Wiltshire Record Office, Long papers, 947/672; Bryan interview; private information.

[91] B. Smith, *The Shadow Warriors: OSS and the Origins of the CIA* (London, 1983), 101 and 141; undated G2 report with additions by de Buitléar, 9 Feb. 1942, MA, G2/X/0902; O'Donoghue to Bryan, 28 Feb. 1944, G2/X/1122.

propaganda and political work: in 1944 Walshe noted Hempel's comment that in 1939 the Italian minister Berardis 'had made "the most fantastic proposals" about the use which could be made of the Italians and the Germans residing in this country', and Hempel's claim that he had 'saved us a great deal of anxiety by his successful efforts' to discourage such 'anti-Irish activities'.[92] Although 'the personnel of the Legation and the higher-class Italians' adroitly shifted their allegiance with the formation of the pro-Allied Badoglio government, a congeries of lesser lights—ice cream parlour proprietors, chip shop owners, and the like—became 'a serious embarrassment' in 1944 through their secret endeavours to keep the fascist flame alight.[93] They did not, however, do any obvious harm. The two-man Japanese consulate also caused some alarm, as its secretary Ichihashi associated with 'Irish subversive elements' and with 'a group of Indians', presumably in furtherance of Japanese policy towards the Indian separatist movement. This intrigue ceased in the run-up to D-Day after two strong warnings from Walshe, who told de Valera that the consul 'got as pale as a Japanese can, and looked astonished and very guilty'. Walshe had then made the remarkable suggestion that 'security officials should interview Mr Ichihashi for the purpose of asking him questions and informing him more fully of the indiscretions of which they considered him guilty', and asked him point-blank whether his consulate possessed a radio transmitter. The Vichy French legation gave no such cause for complaint, while the Spanish also seem to have confined themselves to conventional diplomatic work (although some suspicions attached to one diplomat transferred from London in 1942).[94]

The main and the most dangerous sources of espionage were German agents sent to Ireland. In all, twelve arrived between August 1939 and December 1943 (see Table 6.1). The espionage, sabotage, and subversive operations which were attempted by these agents, while they caused intense difficulties for the state, were very small-scale efforts as compared with the efforts made in other neutral states in Europe and Latin America, which were of rather greater strategic interest once the possibility of an invasion of the British Isles had gone. Furthermore, German agent operations were generally characterized by the inadequacy of those involved, although precisely the same could be said of the ill-prepared spies whom the Abwehr hastily dispatched to Britain in 1940. On the other hand, at least six of those sent between 1939 and 1941—Unland, Goertz, Simon, Preetz, Obed, and Schutz—had had peacetime experience of espionage. Furthermore, a number of them were to contact other agents in Britain, an aspect of their missions which particularly alarmed MI5 because all such agents

[92] Memorandum by Walshe, 28 Feb. 1944, DFA, A52/1.
[93] Note by Boland, 5 Jan. 1944, DFA, A53. One of those named later taught this writer in prep school, in the 1960s.
[94] Walshe to taoiseach, 27 May and 1 June 1944, DFA, A2; Bryan to Walshe, 3 July 1942, DFA, A8/1. By contrast, note the covert activities of Japanese and Spanish diplomats in Britain up to 1941, in Masterman, *The Double-Cross System*, 57 and 93–4.

Table 6.1. **German agents dispatched to Ireland, August 1939–December 1943**

Agent	Date & means of arrival	Employer	Mission	Means of communication supplied	First detained
Werner Unland	August 1939, passenger ship, Dublin?	Abwehr	General intelligence on UK?	Coded letters in ordinary post	March 1941
Ernst Weber Drohl	February 1940, U-boat, Sligo	Abwehr	Courier with radio & money for IRA	None?	27 February 1940
Herman Goertz	12 May 1940, aircraft, Meath	Abwehr	IRA liaison re Northern Ireland	Radio (lost on landing)	12 November 1941
Walter Simon	12 June 1940, U-boat, Kerry	Abwehr	Shipping & weather	None found (may have buried radio)	13 June 1940
Wilhelm Preetz	25/26 June 1940, U-boat, Kerry	Abwehr	Weather, UK bomb damage	Radio (captured)	26 August 1940
Henry Obed	7 July 1940, small boat, Cork	Abwehr	Sabotage in UK	None	7 July 1940
Dieter Gaertner	7 July 1940, small boat, Cork	Abwehr	Sabotage in UK	None	7 July 1940
Herbert Tributh	7 July 1940, small boat, Cork	Abwehr	Sabotage in UK	None	7 July 1940
Guenther Schutz	12 March 1941, aircraft, Wexford	Abwehr	Weather; money for Unland; radio for agent in UK	Radio; coded letters in ordinary post	13 March 1941
Joseph Lenihan	18 July 1941, aircraft, Meath	Abwehr	Weather	Radio; secret inks for ordinary post	23 July 1941 (in Northern Ireland)
J. F. O'Reilly	16 December 1943, aircraft, Clare	SD (Nazi Party foreign intelligence)	Infiltration of Scottish radical groups	Two radios, secret inks for ordinary post	16 December 1943
John Kenny	19 December 1943, aircraft, Clare	Abwehr	Allied naval and military build-up	Radio (with O'Reilly)	19 December 1943

Note: This composite table is based mainly on material in DFA, A71 and A34. It excludes John Codd, who was trained as an agent but never sent (MA, G2/4174), and James O'Neill, who according to the Hayes report arrived with encoding materials at the end of 1942 although there is no reference to this in his file, G2/4174. Also excluded are Jan Van Loon, a Dutch sailor who was interned after he approached the German legation offering to spy, and the Belfast/Dublin and Dublin/Lisbon couriers Henry Lundborg (arrested in Belfast in 1942) and Christopher Eastwood (arrested in Dublin in 1943). DFA, A71. See also Carter, *The Shamrock and the Swastika, passim*.

had been captured and by late 1940 some were already being used as channels for disinformation in what became known as the double-cross system. Both

Goertz and Simon had been imprisoned for spying in Britain before the war, and Simon's Abwehr controller thought him 'the perfect classical secret agent', who 'had carried out all his assignments with discretion, élan, and pluck' although the farcical nature of his detection and arrest, after taking 'a good deal of drink' and 'talking indiscreetly to detectives whom he met on the train from Killarney', scarcely bespeaks great mastery of tradecraft.[95]

As Table 6.1 indicates, the majority of these agents were not at liberty for long (the key exception, Goertz, is discussed separately below). Preetz, who had lived in Ireland before the war, 'spent a good deal of . . . time in dissipation' at the Abwehr's expense in Dublin, and managed to transmit a few enciphered reports on weather conditions (which were intercepted by both the Irish and the British), before being tracked down and arrested by the Garda. His radio and enciphering materials were seized, together with the text of the messages he had transmitted. Henry Obed, 'a Mohomedan, born [in] Lucknow', and his German South African companions Gaertner and Tributh, stuck out a mile in Cork and, not surprisingly, were soon captured. Schutz similarly fell foul of watchful Gardai in Wexford, and was found to be carrying material implicating Unland, who was already under surveillance and who was then pulled in. Schutz later regained face by escaping from Mountjoy jail disguised as a woman with IRA help: he remained at large for six weeks in 1942 before being recaptured in the home of the strongly republican Brugha family while awaiting possible escape to the continent by boat. Ernst Weber Drohl reported to the Garda after carrying out his courier mission to the IRA. When charged with illegal entry he explained that while touring Ireland as 'Atlas the Strong' in 1907 he had fathered two sons whom he hoped to track down. This picaresque story, evidently the inspiration for the background of a SMERSH assassin in Ian Fleming's *From Russia with Love*, was true in so far as it went, and after a week's internment in June 1940 he was released. However unlikely an agent, Weber Drohl shared at least one attribute with Fleming's 007: despite the ravages wrought by age and ill-health, he quickly fixed himself up with a woman, 'the wife of a soldier absent on service', by whom he fathered yet another child. He was reinterned in 1942 after information on his initial mission came to light.[96]

The last three agents to arrive were all Irishmen who had fallen into German hands while in the Channel Islands in 1940. Joseph Lenihan, the black sheep of

---

[95] See the account of Germany's extensive Latin American espionage in S. Hilton, *Hitler's Secret War in South America, 1939–1945: German Military Espionage and Allied Counterespionage in Brazil* (1st edn., 1981; New York, 1982). Masterman, *The Double-Cross System, passim*; G2 reports on captured German agents, 17, 20, and 22 Apr. 1944, DFA, A71; Ritter of the Abwehr, quoted in David Kahn, *Hitler's spies* (1st edn., London, 1978; Arrow edn., 1982), 292.

[96] G2 report on captured German agents; decrypt of Schutz message of 22 July 1940, Hayes papers, MS 22983; G2 report on Weber Drohl, 19 Apr. 1944, DFA, A71; Jeffery and O'Halpin, 'Ireland in Spy Fiction', 101. DFA, A71 also contains a touching letter from one of the missing sons, an ARP warden in London. Ian Fleming served as Godfrey's personal assistant in naval intelligence.

a prominent Athlone family—his nephew Brian was to hold many ministerial posts including those of Justice and of Foreign Affairs between the 1960s and 1990—was briefed and equipped to transmit weather reports from Sligo. Instead, he went to Northern Ireland and surrendered. He gave useful information about the Abwehr in France and the Netherlands, and MI5 considered using him as part of the double-cross system, the intricate counter-intelligence and deception operation which had developed from the more straightforward practice of 'playing back' false reports by captured agents. However it was eventually concluded that he could not be so used, as his weather reporting mission was one in which any sustained deception would quickly become apparent. Furthermore, it was a cardinal rule of 'double-cross' that nobody could be used whose capture was known outside a very small circle of British security officials, lest the realization that one apparently active agent had been 'turned' lead the Germans to suspect that others had suffered the same fate. O'Reilly and Kenny, both dropped by parachute in Clare in 1943, had been recruited for espionage in much the same fashion as Lenihan. Kenny was injured on landing and gave no further trouble, but despite surrendering himself to the Garda O'Reilly proved a truculent and devious prisoner. He set out to mislead his inquisitors, and as an unusually skilled cryptographer he made elaborate 'false statements' about his ciphers which it took Hayes, despite British help, 'months to correct', although as already noted the investigations ultimately yielded very important results.[97]

None of the German agents in Ireland achieved anything substantial in intelligence terms. This was also true of the various Irish people who for a variety of motives tried to gather information of use to Germany. Of these the most significant were the maverick Charles McGuinness, a marine service NCO whose offers of information about shipping to the German legation were picked up in postal and telephone surveillance and led to his being jailed for seven years in 1942, and the adventurer Joseph Andrews, a one-time courier for the imprisoned Goertz. Early in 1943 the British discovered that Andrews had styled himself Goertz's chosen successor and was sending enciphered messages to Portugal via a cook on a ship plying between Dublin and Lisbon. After 'a great amount of work' the British and Irish broke the cipher—for a time, incredibly, an inept subordinate of Bryan's, a man 'of limited understanding', withheld news of Hayes's success because he thought Bryan would give it to the British—and in August 1943 Andrews and the courier were arrested and the text of all the traffic seized. Thus a potentially dangerous link between Ireland and the continent was severed in a timely fashion in a joint MI5/G2 operation just as preparations for D-Day intensified.[98]

---

[97] G2 report on Lenihan, 15 Apr. 1944, DFA, A71; Masterman, *The Double-Cross System*, 49, 99–100; Hinsley and Simkins, *British Intelligence*, 92; Sir Dick White, who worked on double-cross, to the author, 4 Apr. 1990; 'Hayes report'.

[98] 'Hayes report'; Bryan interview; Bryan transcripts, p. 52; Hankinson (BRO) to Boland, conveying messages for Bryan from Liddell, 16 Feb. and 13 Mar. 1943, DFA, A34.

The one agent who made a serious impact was Goertz. His mission was essentially to explore the possibility of effecting a reconciliation between the IRA and the Irish state with the object of supporting German operations in Northern Ireland. In addition, however, he nursed a personal ambition to inspire northern republicans into rebellion. He had been supplied with 'a first class cipher . . . the best in our experience used by the Germans during the war', which was 'evidently reserved for very special purposes' and which indicated an agent of high status. Having lost his radio during his parachute descent, however, he had no means of communicating regularly with Germany. A makeshift replacement transmitter was supplied by the IRA, but this was seized when the Garda raided the house where Goertz was staying, missing him but arresting its owner Stephen Held, an Irishman of German extraction who had earlier travelled to Berlin seeking arms for the IRA. Also seized were twenty thousand American dollars, eighteen enciphered messages which were eventually read after a combined Anglo-Irish effort resulted in the breaking of the Goertz cipher in April 1943, and papers disclosing *Plan Kathleen*, a scheme for German arms drops to the IRA and for a projected IRA/German campaign in Northern Ireland. Dublin was soon 'simply reverberating with rumours and talk'. Realization that a garbled version of events would soon reach British ears prompted Bryan to advise External Affairs to pass on copies of everything seized immediately. Fred Boland of External Affairs 'took the bull by the horns', and with de Valera's sanction the material was handed over to the British the next morning.[99]

The discoveries made in Held's house came as a bombshell. They indicated that the IRA had far more effective German links than had been suspected and had developed a plan for joint action in Northern Ireland, the scenario which de Valera most feared. While analysis of *Plan Kathleen* revealed its complete operational inadequacy—it was evidently an IRA document, not a military blueprint—its very existence raised grave questions about German intentions. It also added to the mystery surrounding Goertz, who during his eighteen months on the run acquired almost mythic status in Ireland, being rumoured to enjoy the protection of powerful government figures, and to be an unofficial ambassador. The failure for so long to catch him raised questions about both the efficiency of the security services and the instructions they were under, while the enthusiasm with which he pursued his aims marked him out as a serious figure. He quickly became disillusioned with the IRA and attempted to pursue his two main goals independently of them: the collection of military intelligence inside Northern Ireland, and the promotion of an understanding with people of influence in political and military circles. Fortunately for the state, his chosen instru-

---

[99] 'Hayes report', citing British experts on the Goertz cipher. Bryan's superior Archer, and Boland's superior Walshe, were both away when the crisis blew up. Bryan transcripts, pp. 9, 29–30, 37; Hinsley and Simkins, *British Intelligence*, 90.

ments for espionage in Northern Ireland 'had no idea of military organisation' and produced 'a lot of meaningless reports', most of which came into G2's hands. It was, nevertheless, deeply alarming to have such an operation running from within the state, particularly as Goertz also began 'feeding information' through an intermediary to army officers stationed along the border, with the aim of entangling them in various negotiations'. The most important was Major Niall MacNeill, Command IO in his cousin Hugo's Northern division and, according to Bryan, a self-proclaimed 'Nazi' who 'was inclined to act on his own and . . . to feel free of me', and who was also in touch with the German legation.[100] In pursuing army links Goertz may have been following advice given by the ailing General O'Duffy in November 1940. In the voluminous enciphered account of his mission which he 'thought was going by a secret channel to the German Legation, but which we [G2] intercepted' and decrypted, he wrote:

It had long been my wish to see this personality, who stood close to National Socialism. The contact was established via 44 [Jim O'Donovan] . . . We spoke for some two hours alone . . . He spoke with Irish power of expression. I could not do much, he said . . . with the IRA. I had probably seen this myself already. He had started his Blueshirt movement unfortunately too early. Ireland was not yet ripe. He could understand that Germany had interest only in a really independent Ireland. This goal could be reached only by means of a military dictatorship. De Valera could never get that done. They did not want it at all. It was with the army that Germany should get in touch—this was realised by leading heads within the army.[101]

The capture of Goertz was soon followed by the internment of his original IRA contact and the mainspring of the link with the Abwehr, Jim O'Donovan, who according to Bryan 'fancied himself as the future Irish Quisling or Fuhrer'.[102] With him gone, there was no one in what remained of the IRA leadership with either the knowledge or the inclination to promote further contacts with Germany.

xi. Republican Activities, 1939–1945

The IRA's reaction to the outbreak of war demonstrated a combination of naivety, incoherence, and unpreparedness. Plans for action to coincide with a German attack were sketchy, and they depended on people marooned abroad, while O'Donovan's Abwehr link had not been properly tested. The development of a workable strategy was hampered by uncertainty about what the IRA's aims should be, which in turn reflected the confusion which existed about the

[100] Bryan transcripts, pp. 34–7; Bryan interview; Duggan, *Neutral Ireland*, 181–90.
[101] Translation of Goertz's account of his mission, p. 37, undated [Dec. 1944], NLI, Hayes MS 22983.
[102] Bryan to minister for defence, 21 Dec. 1945, DFA, A12/1. Bob Bradshaw recalled how single-minded and solitary O'Donovan was in his management of the link with Germany. Bradshaw interview.

possibilities of German aid, about Germany's strategic intentions, and about Russell's activities abroad. The ineffectual chief of staff Stephen Hayes sent him an urgent note: 'The war has changed the whole position here . . . You will be needed here at once. Ask Clan [na Gael] to try and rush supplies.'[103] The timing of the S-plan ensured that the machinery of detection and suppression of republican activities in both Britain and Ireland was already in gear, minimizing the IRA's capacity to act as a sophisticated instrument of either sabotage or espionage against the United Kingdom in the changed circumstances of war, because many of its activists and organizers were either already in custody or on the run, and much of its support framework in Britain was compromised. While the IRA did remain fitfully active on the island of Ireland, one remarkable feature of its wartime history was to be its utter failure in Britain despite the opportunities for infiltration and action offered by Britain's acute need for Irish manpower. The mistiming of the S-plan did, however, have the accidental benefit for the IRA that the state's response, and in particular the passage of the OAS in June 1939, was viewed through the prism of peacetime conditions. It seemed simply another round in the government versus republican movement struggle which had been going on since 1922. It took time both for the public and for some members of the political elite to realize that the outbreak of war between Britain and Germany put the state/IRA conflict on an entirely different footing.

This largely explains the government's essentially peacetime approach to the management of its IRA problem. Widespread raids were mounted against the IRA in September, resulting in the capture in Dublin of most of its headquarters officers and a good deal of American money. In December, an IRA radio which had intermittently broadcast republican propaganda was finally pinpointed in Dublin by an army signals unit using an improvised direction finder—an order for modern equipment from the German firm Telefunken had lapsed on the outbreak of war—and the transmitter and its operators were captured by the Garda.[104] To the general public, much of this republican activity appeared relatively harmless. In consequence, there remained considerable sympathy for individual republicans, and the state began quickly to release some suspects unconditionally. Four others, however, remained in custody awaiting trial. When a number went on hunger strike in November, the government at first set its face against meeting their demands. This reflected experience of republican use of the hunger strike against both the British and the Irish states since 1917, which indicated that concessions served mainly to increase republican morale and public standing. There were, however, arguments on the other side: the September raids appeared to have nipped the IRA's plans for widespread action

---

[103] Undated letter quoted in FBI report on IRA, undated, with Hoover to Berle (State Department), 30 Sept. 1943, USNA, 841D.00/1421. This lengthy and detailed report is evidently a close paraphrase of an MI5 document, which in turn would have been drawn largely from material supplied by G2.

[104] Bryan transcripts, pp. 24–6.

in the bud, and some argued that by its firm action the state had made its point and that there was no virtue in remaining completely inflexible towards old comrades now on hunger strike. One of these, Patrick McGrath, still carried a British bullet in his body. There was unease within Fianna Fáil about his case, and the Labour party also argued for concessions. Liam Tobin, the leader of the 1924 army mutiny, wrote to de Valera about the 'great record which Paddy McGrath and his family have earned in the national struggle. It would be a tragedy if he lost his life, no matter what we may think of the aims and methods pursued by himself and those associated with him.' Public resentment at the death sentences passed on the Coventry bombers Barnes and McCormack added to the pressure to bring an end to the hunger strikes, and the government did not wish to appear to be marching too closely in step with the old enemy. In December, accordingly, a number of republicans were released early, and it was announced that the strikers would be freed unconditionally.[105]

Considerable efforts were also made to persuade Britain to display leniency towards the Coventry bombers. In the confused logic of republican martyrology, the fact that Barnes had smuggled the explosives used and that McCormack had assembled the device which had killed five people did not justify the sentence as they 'were as horrified as anyone that the bomb had gone off in the wrong place'—accidental detonation was not then such a threadbare excuse for IRA atrocities as it has since become. De Valera and his old antagonist Cosgrave each made private representations to Sir John Maffey arguing for clemency 'despite the gravity of the crimes'. Although the British cabinet took the matter very seriously, especially in terms of the effect on American opinion—Chamberlain's private secretary wrote that 'the IRA executions continue to exercise everybody's mind'—the hangings went ahead. Maffey, whom the IRA apparently planned to shoot in retaliation for the executions, was angered at de Valera's 'violent reaction ... He has moved sharply to the Left ... his administration is unpopular and incompetent, his eyesight is fading fast.' Nevertheless, 'it seems advisable to go to extreme limits of patience'.[106]

The Magazine Fort raid soon gave de Valera cause to regret his own leniency towards IRA hunger strikers. A humiliation for the army, and a tremendous shock to the government and the public, it underlined the real danger posed by domestic subversives, and it demonstrated that the IRA's ambitions had grown despite the fiasco of the S-plan and the delicacy of the national position. As well as dispelling any residual national complacency, the raid prompted a flood of

---

[105] Fianna Fáil national executive minutes, 6 Nov. 1939, Fianna Fáil archives, FF/342; Bell, *The Secret Army*, 170–1; parliamentary Labour party to de Valera and Tobin to de Valera, both 8 Nov. 1939, DT, S. 51515.

[106] Maffey to Eden (Dominions Secretary), 25 Jan.; noted to Maffey from James Dillon TD, 30 Jan.; Maffey to Machtig, 31 Jan. 1940, PRO, DO 130/9. U. MacEoin, *The IRA in the Twilight Years*, 890, reports the assassination plan.

information from the public to both the Garda and the army.[107] So far from taking careful stock of the changed political and military conditions created by the European war, the IRA intensified its activities in a way certain to increase the wrath of the authorities, yet without any clear plan in mind. On 2 January 1940 Thomas MacCurtain, son of the lord mayor of Cork murdered by British forces in 1920, killed a detective while attempting to resist arrest. He was duly sentenced to death. As the progeny of one of the martyrs of the Irish revolution, however, his punishment was commuted to life imprisonment shortly before the execution date in July 1940: Maffey wrote that de Valera has 'followed the weak course, as usual . . . Nevertheless he will not escape bitter criticism— Mr Cosgrave has already voiced it to me.' McCurtain was released in 1948, and later figured in the IRA's border campaign of 1956–62. Others with less exalted lineages were not so fortunate: in April 1940 two prisoners detained since September 1939, Tony D'Arcy and John McNeela, were allowed to starve themselves to death. A few days later the hunger strike of which they were part was abandoned without securing any significant concessions. With IRA/state conflict now taking place against the backdrop of European war and the real possibility of invasion, such strikes had ceased to be an effective means of extracting concessions.[108]

1940 saw a marked upsurge in violence, as IRA men showed increasing willingness to take on the Garda. The Dublin Castle bomb was clearly calculated to kill, and it indicated that the IRA now considered plain-clothes Gardai to be legitimate, indeed priority targets for assassination. That was followed by a bungled attempt to seize Maffey's mail, resulting in a gunfight in which two more detectives were seriously wounded. In August Patrick McGrath, the IRA veteran whom de Valera had released in December 1939, was involved in the killing of two detectives in Rathgar, an offence for which he and one of his companions were eventually convicted and executed. These shootings provoked a further amendment of the law: henceforth there could be no appeal from the verdict of the military tribunal. The state continued to bear down very hard on the IRA, and the combination of draconian legislation and incessant harassment proved very effective: an Admiralty intelligence summary of April 1941 stated that 'the general impression is that . . . the Government have the IRA well in hand', an observation supported by RUC reports.[109]

During 1941 the IRA was thrown into turmoil by the pressure exerted on it. One faction, composed mainly of northerners, sought an explanation for repeated failure in the charge that Stephen Hayes was an informer. Hayes was not a commanding figure: appointed to succeed the widely respected Russell, he had a weakness for drink, and he appears to have had few supporters. Between

---

[107] Bryan interview.   [108] Maffey to Machtig, 13 July 1940, DO 130/12; Coogan, *The IRA*, 189–90.
[109] Admiralty weekly intelligence report no. 59, 25 Apr. 1941, Churchill College Cambridge, Drax papers 5/6; 'Godfrey report', citing RUC assessments.

June and September 1941 his accusers imprisoned him, beat a lengthy confession out of him, and had him court-martialled and sentenced to death. This process was undertaken with an ineptitude which, had the principal actors reflected on the point, would itself have provided a sufficient explanation for the organization's litany of disasters since 1939. Hayes persuaded his captors to delay shooting him while he further gilded his already extraordinary confession. He then managed to escape, and found undignified sanctuary in a Garda station. A British official in Dublin wrote that the confession 'has somewhat fluttered the dovecots here', but its contents were so fantastic as to command disbelief. The confession, in which every calamity to befall the IRA since 1935 was explained by the machinations of Hayes and his Fianna Fáil mentors, would not have disgraced a Stalinist show trial: it stated that details of the S-plan had been betrayed to Scotland Yard, that the Magazine Fort raid was a government ploy to discredit the IRA and to enable the removal from the army of various 'men who would not do their bidding and replace them with men who were more pliable', that the Dublin Castle bomb had been the brainchild of the minister for agriculture Dr James Ryan, and so on. Although Hayes was subsequently jailed for IRA offences, many of his accusers felt that there was no smoke without fire and that, however far-fetched his confession, he must have been a traitor. So far as can be judged he was not. But in becoming the focal point of his comrades' paranoia, he unintentionally did the state an enormous favour. The Hayes affair diverted the IRA's energies for months, it further discredited the movement in the eyes of the public, and it left a legacy of confusion and bitterness in republican circles. As 'Spike' Marlin told Washington in January 1943, 'the IRA . . . in Eire completely lacks anything resembling cohesion, organisation or discipline'.[110]

The IRA was reduced to a minor irritant after 1941, the majority of its leading lights interned in harsh conditions in the Curragh, and most of its remaining activists concentrating on avoiding capture. The organization did, however, carry out one further very significant action in 1942. This was the shooting of Sergeant Denis O'Brien, the first calculated IRA killing of a Garda since the murder of Superintendent Curtin in 1931. It was one thing to kill a policeman in a gunfight, quite another to pick him off without warning (in fact, membership of the force was usually considered a form of life insurance, as demonstrated by government decisions to offer 'public interest' appointments to the force to two civilian witnesses to crimes whose lives had been threatened for giving evidence resulting in the jailing of two republicans). IRA folklore has it that O'Brien, an ex-Broy Harrier, was singled out for killing because he was an exceptionally greedy and brutal officer: 'of all the Special Branch men he had achieved by far

[110] Bryan interview; Archer (BRO) to Costar (Dominions Office), 4 Oct. 1941, and accompanying text of the Hayes confession, DO 130/23; Coogan, *The IRA*, 195–206; 'Report on the present state of Eire', unsigned, 27 Jan. 1943, USNA, RG226, entry 106, box 0039, file 347.

the greatest notoriety, not only for his successes but his brutality. He had entered into the great game of searching out and often shooting down the IRA men with far more dedication and satisfaction than any of his colleagues.'[111] This is, perhaps unintentionally, illustrative of the confusion in republican minds not only about the morality but the expediency of calculated murder: whatever the satisfaction to be had in assassinating a tough detective, experience since 1940 ought to have suggested that it was a very foolish action in terms both of its effect on public opinion and on the state's treatment of militant republicanism. The other detectives killed during the Emergency were, by contrast, in IRA eyes simply Free State stooges who happened to be hit during exchanges of fire. Those who died defending the state against subversion have been largely forgotten, apart from the tainted caricatures of republican folklore; the memory of those of their IRA killers who were executed, by contrast, has been kept alive by their admirers and exemplars.

Charlie Kerins, by then possessor of the largely empty title of chief of staff, was eventually executed for the O'Brien killing. A second IRA man suffered the same fate for killing Detective Officer Mordaunt during the intensive police searches which followed the O'Brien murder, although another gunman, Harry White, escaped. Some months later he survived a further clash during which another IRA man and another guard were killed, and he stayed out of the state's clutches until 1945. He was then arrested in Northern Ireland and handed over to the Garda. Initially charged with Mordaunt's murder—ironically for such a hardened republican, the British authorities asked the Irish authorities to delay executing him until his appeal against extradition from the United Kingdom had been ruled on by the House of Lords—by the time of his trial the sense of national crisis had eased and the judicial climate had changed. Ably represented by the one-time IRA chief of staff Sean MacBride, he was convicted only of manslaughter and was released after serving two years as an act of clemency when the Costello interparty government, fortuitously including his former lawyer MacBride, came to power in 1948 and let free the state's remaining political convicts.[112] White's experience provides an instructive contrast with that of George Plant, whose conviction and execution in 1942 has already been noted. As a number of ministers had personal reason to recall from the 1916–23 era, in deciding whether or not to exercise clemency where the death penalty had been imposed the government was choosing not between death and life imprisonment, but between the death of a convict and his almost certain release within a couple of years if political conditions calmed down.

Despite British fears of an IRA offensive within Northern Ireland in 1940, the organization was slow to act. This largely reflected its internal problems, both

---

[111] Brady, *Guardians*, 237–8; Justice memoranda, 31 Dec. 1942 and 29 Mar. 1943, DT, S. 10156A; Bell, *The Secret Army*, 227.

[112] Archer (BRO) to McCauley, 22 Jan. 1947, DFA, P115.

those posed by constant arrests and those caused by the leadership's indecision. Yet Northern Ireland appeared to offer considerable opportunities. The nationalist minority, still unreconciled to partition and resentful at political, social, and economic discrimination, together with the conspicuous British wartime military presence, provided both a promising environment for and plenty of targets for significant action. There were also opportunities for espionage, though this was never more than a minor consideration—there was no reliable means of getting intelligence to the Germans, and the IRA was committed to overt action and was not geared to the sustained and specialized tasks of military intelligence-gathering. IRA activity in Northern Ireland had the additional advantage of being likely to garner vague public support rather than criticism in the south, where resentment at partition still ran high: as late as August 1939, the Fianna Fáil national executive had agreed that the 'time is opportune' for members of the Oireachtas to take part in anti-partition meetings in Northern Ireland, 'all speakers to be prepared for arrest and imprisonment'.[113] Until the turn of the tide of war in 1942, many nationalists entertained hopes that a German invasion would end partition. In August 1940 northern members of the 'Irish National Unity Council' met with Hempel, who was critical of IRA inactivity in Northern Ireland, while in November Eamon Donnelly, the Armagh man who had long served as Fianna Fáil's conscience on partition, was reportedly planning 'a new organisation which would be more virile than the present Council of Unity', claiming that the German and Italian ministers had 'promised support and said they would have the case of partition broadcast in the German- and Italian-controlled radio stations'.[114] Republicans consequently had some grounds for thinking that action in Northern Ireland might have political benefits. It was partly for this reason that towards the end of 1941 the residual IRA leadership, themselves mostly northerners, decided to shift operations almost entirely onto Northern Ireland. The IRA thus stumbled into a variety of the strategy which had been pressed by Tom Barry in the late 1930s. This switch in priorities, two years late as it now appears, seemed to offer real possibilities for effective action.

The practical results of the IRA's reorientation were, however, derisory. This was partly because the movement had neither the means nor the purpose to mount a sustained offensive, but it was also due to the approach adopted. Had the IRA set out to damage the British war effort through a concerted programme of intelligence-gathering and sabotage within Northern Ireland, it might have achieved significant results and would certainly have caused the British much trouble. Instead, however, it contented itself with a series of uncoordinated operations directed primarily against the RUC and calculated mainly

[113] Fianna Fáil national executive minutes, 28 Aug. 1939.
[114] E. Phoenix, *Northern Nationalism: Nationalist Politics, Parties and the Catholic Minority in Northern Ireland 1890–1940* (Belfast, 1994), 207–15; Carroll (C3) to Justice, 9 and 18 Nov. 1940, DFA, A23.

to garner publicity and to maintain the semblance of an overt war against the northern state. These produced nothing except a few RUC and IRA deaths, and one martyr. That was Thomas Williams, one of six IRA men convicted of the murder of a policeman in Belfast at Easter 1942 during a minor diversionary operation which went wrong. Nationalist opinion in both parts of Ireland was inflamed by the passing of the six death sentences, and there were large public protests in Belfast and in Dublin, where de Valera and others sought to persuade the British government to exercise clemency. These pleas had some effect: in the end only Williams was executed. His comrades, amongst them Joe Cahill, later to become a chief of staff of the Provisional IRA, received life sentences and were eventually granted early release. Within hours of Williams's death, the first of a planned series of retaliatory cross-border IRA raids was mounted. The IRA party ran into, overwhelmed, and disarmed a small RUC patrol near the border, but then abandoned their operation. It was to be the last serious cross-border attack launched for fourteen years. Inside Northern Ireland, the IRA did manage to kill a few more policemen and to stage some minor operations in 1942 and 1943, but these were in the nature of isolated gestures of defiance and they served no wider purpose. The IRA's northern activities inspired one good British novel which became an outstanding film, F. L. Green's *Odd Man Out*. They were otherwise devoid of worthwhile achievements. By 1945, the organization appeared almost dead in Northern Ireland.[115]

xii. Conclusion

The security policies and practices adopted during the Emergency were justified not only by the potential but by the actual activities both of indigenous subversives and of foreign powers. Dan Bryan's courageous pre-war warnings in 'Fundamental Factors' were borne out by events, as the two sets of belligerents took a covert interest in Irish affairs and as the IRA/German alliance took shape. The preventive measures which the state took were crucial elements not simply in containing subversion and espionage, but in providing a private balance to what was in public a volatile and acrimonious Anglo-Irish relationship. The most serious failure for the discreet diplomacy of security understandings enthusiastically pursued from the autumn of 1939 occurred, contrary to expectations, not because of friction between Dublin and London or any hiccups in co-operation between Irish and Allied security agencies, but because of American bureaucratic politics which meant that alarmist and wildly inaccurate diplomatic reporting on Irish security took precedence in Washington over the more measured conclusions of Allied security agencies.

[115] Coogan, *The IRA*, 232–6.

One of the unrecognized costs of the state's maintenance of neutrality was an extraordinary level of domestic surveillance and control, together with robust measures against proven and suspected subversives, a remarkably intolerant approach to the public expression of views contrary to the official line on any aspect of the war, and a policy of the rigid exclusion of refugees. A person's post, his newspaper, his telephone, his travel arrangements, all were subject to draconian government interference. The individual views and private lives of ordinary people were systematically scrutinized, and the most harmless as well as the most sinister of groups and associations were investigated for traces of anti-national sentiment and intrigue. The few hundred resident aliens were automatically treated as suspect, however well connected socially or politically and whatever their backgrounds and politics.

Curiously enough, security policy was made and decisions were taken almost entirely at administrative levels within the Garda, the army, Justice, and External Affairs. There is nothing to indicate that ministers played a decisive part in the implementation of security policy, and the documents suggest that they averted their eyes from even the most intriguing or salacious results of police and army inquiries—unlike some of their successors, they did not read the transcripts. The Emergency also saw dramatic changes in the institutional balance of power. The army, kept in abject subjection since 1925, became the dominant influence in state security operations; through its liaison role with British and American agencies, it became a key instrument of Irish–Allied diplomacy; through the imposition of internment, it once again became jailer to the state's subversives; most strikingly of all, through the operation of the military tribunal, its officers became not only a supplementary judiciary to deal with political offences, but the sole arbiters of life and death for people accused of the most serious subversive crimes.

Ireland preserved its neutrality during the Second World War only by the partial abandonment of the key democratic presuppositions underlying its constitution. But, as events since 1922 had demonstrated, that was nothing new.

7

Ireland in the Post-War World, 1945–1969

i. The Post-War Consequences of Neutrality: Anglo-Irish Relations and the Irish World-View

In a controversial passage in his *Ireland since the Famine*, F. S. L. Lyons wrote that the consequence of neutrality for Ireland was

her almost total isolation from the rest of mankind . . . It was as if an entire people had been condemned to live in Plato's cave, with their backs to the fire of life and deriving their only knowledge of what went on outside from the flickering shadows thrown on the wall before their eyes by the men and women who passed to and fro behind them. When after six years they emerged, dazzled, from the cave into the light of day, it was to a new and vastly different world.[1]

This now seems at once an overstatement and an underestimate of the impact of neutrality on the state and its people. It is hard to see how participation in the war would have done much to broaden the horizons of the Irish psyche, even harder to believe that a sense of shared suffering would have bound Ireland more firmly into the international community. It was not the practice of neutrality, but the form which retrospective justification of that policy took, which fostered enduring illusions about the moral basis of staying out of other people's wars.

The physical benefits of successful neutrality were enormous. People had only to look to Belfast or to Britain to see the consequences of sustained bombing. For all her suffering from aerial bombardment, furthermore, the United Kingdom had got off lightly as compared with continental Europe, which in Donald Watt's powerful words 'in May 1945 . . . was near death'.[2] Apart from isolated German bombings, and an occasional explosion caused by drifting mines, independent Ireland suffered not at all. Furthermore, unlike continental neutrals the Irish were largely shielded from any sight or sound of the catastrophe which had befallen most of Europe: the intervening bulk of the United Kingdom ensured that there had been no streams of importunate refugees at border

---

[1] F. S. L. Lyons, *Ireland since the Famine* (London, 1971; revised edn., London, 1973), 557–8.
[2] Watt, *How War Came*, 3.

crossings or seaports pleading for their lives, while the extraordinarily strict press censorship helped to mask the horrors which unfolded as the Allies over-ran Hitler's concentration camps and extermination centres.

Despite minor privations which have passed into folklore, people in the state also had a far easier time in a material sense than did most other Europeans. Dublin 'and most of our border towns were invaded by hordes of visitors with plenty of money and insatiable appetites not only for food and drink but for every conceivable commodity that their home restrictions denied them'.[3] This is graphically illustrated in a young British servicewoman's breathless account of an 'utterly ecstatic' visit in April 1945. The Irish cave which she describes was less Plato's than Aladdin's:

Woolworth's—you just can't imagine! All the little things amaze you as much as the big things—paper hankies, lead soldiers, combs, zip fasteners, bath salts. We all wanted zips, but they were rather expensive . . . Then we started on cosmetics. Every imaginable make—Cyclax, Max Factor, Elizabeth Arden, Coty, Yardley, Gale. And everything was beautifully arranged in boxes with coloured shavings and ribbons and cellophane . . . Everything you buy is *wrapped up* in paper and tied with string, sometimes wrapped in layers of tissue paper first . . . We must have looked idiotic, just wandering about with our mouths open . . . And Dad should have seen Dunhill's—full of pipes and pouches and lighters and tobacco . . . [On lunch in Arnotts restaurant:] Just tea and—cakes!! And what cakes! Light and foamy as air. With layers and layers of coloured whipped cream in scrolls along the top. And chocolate cakes of every species. And cream buns, eclairs, meringues, all melting in the mouth. I will spare you further description . . . The Dolphin, which by repute is *the* place for steaks . . . [after lobster soup] the STEAK—we had thought by this time that we were immune to shock, but when they set it down before us we just gaped in astonishment. They were about two inches thick and about a foot across . . . [the next day] we rather hesitantly asked a policeman the way to the German Embassy, but our time was short and his instructions very difficult to follow.

Their contraband carefully hidden and their stomachs bloated with rich food, the girls reluctantly caught the Belfast train, and returned to the altogether more austere precincts of Larne.[4]

Neutrality undoubtedly soured Anglo-Irish relations, and widened the psychological gulf between de Valera's Ireland and unionist Ulster. These, however, had been largely anticipated in 1939 as consequences which would inevitably follow from staying out of the war. Neutrality as advanced in 1939 was a policy based firmly on realpolitik, defencelessness, the likelihood of republican insurrection if the state attempted to participate on Britain's side, and fear of the consequences of modern warfare. In setting out to stay neutral, Ireland did no more than what almost every other small state sought to do: twenty-seven European

---

[3] Connolly, *Memoirs*, 404.
[4] Two letters from S. M. Batstone to her parents, both 30 Apr. 1945, Imperial War Museum, 86/61/1 & Con Shelf.

countries elected to avoid war in September 1939, though only five maintained their neutrality unscathed, and the three Baltic states simply disappeared from the political map after invasion and absorption by the Soviet Union.[5] A combination of circumstances, including geography, diplomatic adroitness, the running sore of partition, covert security co-operation and British restraint, meant that Irish neutrality proved not only domestically popular but externally sustainable. Up to May 1940 strict adherence to neutrality was based partly on a naive assumption that Britain could survive comfortably and act as the state's strategic guarantor without the use of Irish facilities, and from the fall of France until the summer of 1941 on the belief that Germany was going to win and that Ireland must not antagonize her. Even the Churchillian carrot of the possible ending of partition in return for participation had been insufficient to lure de Valera into taking sides. Churchill's VE day attack on Irish policy, which argued that it was only thanks to Britain's unparalleled restraint that the Irish had been able to 'frolic with the German and . . . Japanese representatives to their hearts' content', could not have come at a better time for a state whose people were becoming uncomfortably aware that the emerging stories of the Nazis' systematic and unparalleled atrocities against whole peoples were not the figment of Allied propagandists' imaginations but the sober, indeed initially understated truth. Churchill's comments were eminently understandable, coming just a fortnight after de Valera had astounded the diplomatic world by formally conveying his condolences to Hempel on the demise of Hitler, a pedantic gesture of independence which even the Führer's erstwhile protégé Franco forbore to make. So far from presaging a permafrost in Anglo-Irish relations, however, Churchill's remarks were in the nature of a boxer's robust final swing as the bell rang to end the contest. The British neither contemplated nor pursued a punitive policy towards post-war Ireland: they still desperately needed Irish food and Irish manpower and, as Nicholas Mansergh has pointed out, 'they had a social revolution and an Indian de-colonisation on their hands' and they wanted only a prolonged period of calm in Anglo-Irish affairs: 'We should', the Dominions secretary advised the new Attlee government, 'endeavour, by steady but not dramatic moves, to rebuild and restore friendly relations.'[6] Churchill himself soon got over his apoplexy: in opposition in September 1945 he remarked that 'he thought that if he had gone on [as prime minister] he would have been able to bring her [Ireland] back into the fold. Anyway, as far as he was concerned, there would always be a candle burning in the window for the wandering daughter', and he afterwards spoke very warmly of de Valera.[7]

⁵ P. Keatinge, *A Singular Stance: Irish Neutrality in the 1980s* (Dublin, 1984), 26.

⁶ Mansergh, *The Unresolved Question*, 316; memorandum by secretary of state for dominion affairs, 7 Sept. 1945, PRO, CAB 129/2/8–10.

⁷ Lord Moran, *Winston Churchill: The Struggle for Survival 1940/1965* (1st edn., London, 1966; Sphere edn., 1968), 330, 497, and 499, entries for 10 Sept. 1945 and for 11 and 15 Sept. 1953.

The main result of Churchill's 'personal attack' was, as Maffey pointed out, that it afforded de Valera the opportunity to reclaim the moral highground after the embarrassment of his bizarre genuflection to the departed Führer.[8] His dignified speech, with its facile riposte that 'it is, indeed, hard for the strong to be just to the weak', received a rapturous domestic reception—'the greatness of the man, and the capacity of the statesman, were never so brilliantly displayed than when he went to the microphone to answer Mr Churchill'. It also established a holier than thou fashion in ministerial pronouncements on foreign policy issues which long outlasted its author.[9] The presumption that neutrality was a moral and sempiternal as distinct from a contingent and necessary measure gained further ground with America's recourse to nuclear weapons at Hiroshima and Nagasaki. These two acts of war were so devastating both in their immediate effects on the unfortunate people of Japan, and in their inauguration of a new dimension of warfare and of potential global destruction, as to give succour to moral absolutists. In a comparative context what was most singular about Irish neutrality was surely not the suppression of public debate and the curtailment of the circulation of war news during the Emergency— matters whose domestic rationale have already been discussed—but the illusions which afterwards grew up about the moral basis of Irish foreign and defence policy. By the end of the war, to quote Patrick Keatinge, 'the basis for a national tradition of neutrality, both as a value and a policy, had been laid; an orthodoxy, if not a dogma, had been established'.[10]

The retrospective couching of neutrality in high moral terms had the incidental benefit for the republican movement of limiting public discussion of the IRA's pursuit of an alliance with a regime so manifestly noxious as Hitler's Germany, of the peril in which this had placed neutrality, and of what would have been the likely and catastrophic outcome had the republican dream of an IRA-assisted German assault on Northern Ireland come to pass.

ii. New Lessons, Old Habits: External Defence Policy and Practice, 1945–1969

'We must start in the next war where we left off in this, not surely from scratch again.'[11] So wrote Richard Hayes in January 1946. Hayes's comments were made in support of the proposal that the state should in peacetime retain a small cryptographic bureau to advise the government on the security of its own external communications and to research the encrypted traffic of foreign governments

---

[8] Memorandum by Maffey, an annexe to secretary of state's memorandum of 7 Sept. 1945.

[9] Longford and O'Neill, *De Valera*, 413–14; P. Keatinge, *The Formulation of Irish Foreign Policy* (Dublin, 1973), 26; Skinner, *Politicians by Accident*, 37.

[10] Keatinge, *A Singular Stance*, 20.   [11] 'Hayes report'.

and agencies in so far as this affected Irish interests. They could have applied equally well to the wider question of post-war defence organization.

The Emergency had posed a number of stark questions about the nature of independence and the organization of national defence. It had laid bare the inadequacies of War of Independence tactics as a basis for the defence of the territory and people of a sovereign state, something to which senior politicians had remained emotionally attached; it had underlined the strategic paradox which defence procurement policy had created—that the state's main source of material was also the one with the strongest vested interest in keeping such supplies at starvation level; it had demonstrated the inadequacy of pre-Emergency policy as a basis for credible independent defence; and it had shown the need for the state to develop the capacity to police its own seas and skies. Once the success of D-Day made an eventual Allied victory a near certainty, the army advanced its views of what would be necessary in future to avoid the panics of the past. Its proposals echoed pre-war plans for a properly equipped and trained standing army which would act as the kernel for much larger first- and second-line reserves who could be called to full-time service as conditions dictated. What differentiated these arguments from previous efforts to persuade the government to act in accordance with the policy of independent defence in operation since 1925 was the authority and the vigour with which they were advanced by McKenna in his annual report for the year ending 31 March 1945:

On examining my previous reports, I find that every year I have had to draw particular attention to the deficiency of the necessary personnel to fill the relatively small establishments which were in being . . . I pointed out that the capacity of the army to implement our defence plans was gravely handicapped by the fact that we had not sufficient men to handle even the inadequate quantity of weapons which we possessed . . .

Almost every other civilised country has attempted to rely on voluntary recruitment to fill their armies and all have been forced to adopt some type of compulsory military service . . . [He wished to] again stress the absolute necessity for some kind of compulsory military service in this country, for I am confident that without it we can never achieve a proper state of preparedness for defence.[12]

The government, however, took a different view. So far from reviewing future defence policy in the light of the state's uncomfortable experience during the Emergency, of wider strategic considerations such as Atlantic security which had proved so crucial, of the unexpected armed threat which the IRA had presented, and of the likely shape of the post-war world, they simply reached for the financial axe. It was as though neither the Emergency nor the Second World War had happened, as though there was nothing useful which the state could learn one way or the other from six years of international catastrophe culminating in the advent of nuclear warfare. There was certainly a powerful case, in the

---

[12] Annual Report, 1944–5.

light of what had happened to other small European states, for the view that geography, not weapons, alliances with stronger powers, or international guarantees, had been the key determinant of national survival. But if this was the government view, it was not publicly put. Instead, the defence forces were honoured for their Emergency service with the staging of a military tattoo at the Royal Dublin Society's grounds. Once these ceremonial niceties had been observed, reduction of the defence forces to pre-war levels began in earnest.

While the pressure points in Ireland's external relations since 1939 had involved the management of defence and security issues—the likelihood of invasion after June 1940, the frantic British pressure for Atlantic ports and air bases in 1940 and 1941, the American note crisis of 1944—the government devoted no time to reflecting on the possible recrudescence of such difficulties if Britain and the United States again found themselves fighting a common enemy. Despite covert acceptance in 1940–1 of the reality that Ireland could only be militarily defended on land, at sea, and in the air on an all-island basis, the politics of partition ensured that there was no post-war Anglo-Irish dialogue on defence issues. Irish policy remained fixed on the doctrine of independent defence through the maintenance of armed forces sufficient to deter all but the most powerful invader; defence practice ensured nothing of the kind.[13] British and American planners undoubtedly made their own calcuations accordingly on how best to cope with a neutral Ireland should a new European war break out.

Within a year of the ending of the Emergency the number of men on full-time service in the first-line defence forces fell from thirty-eight thousand to nine thousand. As in pre-war days, these were distributed amongst a myriad of barracks, posts, and other installations throughout the state. Had the drastic reduction been accompanied by the creation of a proper system of first-line reserves, a will-o'-the-wisp pursued by successive chiefs of staff since 1923, it would have marked a turning point in the practice of national defence policy. Unsurprisingly, such a reserve system did not materialize. Furthermore, the government declined to grasp the nettle of compulsory national service which McKenna had proffered, opting instead for what was essentially a continuation of the pre-war Volunteer Force in the new guise of the *Fórsa Cosanta Áitiúil* (FCA). Intended as a territorial force capable of rapid absorption into the regular army in a time of crisis, this became the main component of the second-line reserve in army organization charts. From the first its training and other activities were bedevilled by familiar shortages of equipment and by the consequent difficulty of attracting and keeping sufficient volunteers with the meagre incentives on offer (although the greatcoat and footwear supplied to members were much prized during the hard winter of 1947).

[13] Report on Irish defence forces by W. A. Turgeon, high commissioner, Dublin, to secretary of state, Ottawa, 28 Apr. 1948, PAC, RG25-1983-1939-1110, part 7.

The departure of Fianna Fáil from office in February 1948 after sixteen years in government brought no improvement for the defence forces although the new Costello interparty government included Richard Mulcahy, the long-time champion of military professionalization. Costello's somewhat incoherent five-party coalition included at one extreme his Fine Gael party, which usually subjected army promotions to a political litmus test; and at the other Clann na Poblachta, a short-lived radical party headed by Sean MacBride, which had temporarily filched some of Fianna Fáil's constitutional republican clothes, and some of whose leading lights took a highly revanchist view of the partition issue. More alarmingly for the army, despite his metamorphosis into a constitutional politician MacBride retained strong links with extreme republicans.[14]

Despite the initial reversion to the pre-Emergency approach to defence policy, the government was forced to take one key decision. This arose out of approaches made by the United States following the formation of the NATO alliance as a bulwark against Soviet expansionism in 1949. The American initiative was, ironically in view of his later career as an outspoken scourge of American imperialism, rebuffed by MacBride on the sole grounds that the wrong of partition must first be undone: otherwise, Ireland would be prepared 'to participate in the [Atlantic] Pact'. The fact that this represented an important shift in policy, as the most de Valera had been prepared to offer in return for Irish unity in 1940–1 had been benevolent neutrality, was rather lost sight of in the fact of the refusal to join. The United States and Britain were less exercised by Irish particularism than Dublin assumed—the war had shown that effective eastern Atlantic defence cover could be provided from air and sea bases in Northern Ireland and Scotland, while the presence of British forces in Northern Ireland was regarded as sufficient protection against a Soviet attempt to occupy any part of the island—and they did not renew their overtures (the commonwealth secretary, the veteran pacifist and slightly muddle-headed Philip Noel-Baker, privately applauded Irish neutrality on moral grounds, although he gave no hint of this at the time).[15] Opinion in Ireland on the NATO issue differed: while de Valera, in unaccustomed exile as leader of the opposition, endorsed the government's position because of partition, the *Irish Times* inclined towards joining NATO.[16] The radical Catholic peace group Pax Christi inveighed against the proposition in a document which nicely illustrates the mélange of moralistic and political arguments which were later to become enduring features of the neutrality debate. Dismissing the *Irish Times* as 'the Royalist newspaper ... the

---

[14] Conversation with the late The (Mac) O'Rahilly, who was a senior figure in Clann na Poblachta and a friend of Sean MacBride, 1977.

[15] N. Browne, *Against the Tide* (Dublin, 1986), 134–7; Keatinge, *A Singular Stance*, 21; Bowman, *De Valera and the Ulster Question*, 293; External Affairs memorandum of 7 May 1949, quoted in Fanning, *Independent Ireland*, 177; Noel-Baker's MS notes on Pax Christi document on Ireland, n.d. [1949], Churchill College Cambridge, Noel-Baker papers, NBKR 4/219.

[16] *The Irish Times*, 24 Jan. 1949.

printed mouthpiece of the Protestant Ascendancy, and Imperialist "die-hards" trying to goad and taunt us into a war', the document continued:

Can we *afford* to join up with a dangerous gang who would think nothing of starting a war tomorrow, if they thought it would keep their airplane factories in employment?... America is the present day imperialist nation—she is doing what England used to do . . . This grandiose 'defence' scheme of Benelux and the rest is only a cover up scheme for an attack on Russia, because too many people are flocking to her banner for the liking of American refrigerator manufacturers . . . Ireland will be united and one country all in good time, but no Christian government will join up with a war-mongering 'Atlantic Pact', and still have a clear conscience . . . why doesn't someone hold out the hand and make *some* concession to Russia—she would appreciate friendship and not enmity and planning for war.[17]

The decision not to join NATO had grave implications for national defence. The army's view was, most unusually, put forward at some length for cabinet consideration. In many respects an echo of 'Fundamental Factors', a memorandum argued that in a future non-nuclear war involving NATO and the Soviet Union, the Atlantic sea and air lines of communication between Europe and the United States would be crucial. Geography would ensure that the state could not avoid being dragged into such a conflict unless it was capable of genuinely defending itself from a sustained attack. As it was, the NATO powers knew full well that the 'Irish defence forces are inadequate' to resist a Soviet assault on her ports, airfields, and communications facilities. By contrast, the army argued that 'no western nation is relatively better prepared for war' than Sweden, another state which had elected to remain outside the new alliance: 'Her defence effort is proportionately many times greater than the Irish . . . and is directed to protection against . . . Russia'. It followed that the NATO powers 'must also conclude that Irish defences are a danger to the Atlantic Pact defence system because of their inadequacy'. In consequence, NATO planners might well arrange for the 'establishment by their forces of defences in Ireland on the outbreak of war' whether the Irish liked it or not—the Americans, it was argued, had shown far less regard for the sovereignty of small states during the war than had Britain, and had if anything been more resentful and less understanding of Irish neutrality after Pearl Harbor, as the needless American note crisis had shown. In a mortal struggle with the Soviet Union they would have no qualms about using Ireland, whatever the views of the Irish on the matter. The document might have added that with Northern Ireland playing a key role in NATO air and sea defence, the idea that independent Ireland could avoid the horrors of war simply by remaining neutral was risible.[18]

---

[17] Pax Christi document, n.d.
[18] Undated memorandum [1949?], NA, DFA, A89. This bears such stylistic similarities to 'Fundamental Factors' that it is probably the work of Dan Bryan; Sloan, *Geopolitics*, 250–4.

The choice which the army was trying to get the government to make was, on the face of it, a rational one between two kinds of military credibility, that which came from being a member of a powerful alliance, and that which depended on independent national defensive strength as a meaningful deterrent against aggression. The problem which the army faced, however, was that no Irish government had any intention of accepting military credibility as the keystone of neutrality. There is, however, evidence that for a time the government did take the argument about the desirability of assuaging America's Atlantic defence concerns seriously: in March 1951 MacBride made tentative overtures about a bilateral defence pact. Although nothing came of this, within army circles there remained hope for some years that some Irish/American defence accord might be reached which would bring with it military largesse on the scale which the United States was already lavishing on other states with which it had understandings. In 1952 Aiken, now back in office as minister for external affairs, made sustained efforts to persuade the Americans to supply military and civil defence equipment, emphasizing that Ireland's refusal to join NATO was due solely to partition. Although there was some sympathy within the Dublin embassy, where memories of wartime co-operation remained fresh, Washington was unimpressed.[19] Successive governments were quite happy to agree to continue neighbourly co-operation in time of war in respect of the weather forecasting system, communications controls, and other matters which had been satisfactorily handled during the Emergency.[20] The Irish also recognized that the development of Shannon into a major transatlantic airport carried with it the need always to be conscious of American security concerns, and usually made the appropriate genuflections: in 1949 assurances were given that Ireland would not give Eastern Bloc aircraft easy access to the airport. Furthermore, in foreign policy terms Ireland was emphatically in the Western democratic camp, although after the state was belatedly admitted to the United Nations it adopted an independent-minded stance on issues such as decolonization and disarmament.[21] In official circles, arguments for reviewing the explicit linkage of partition with refusal to join NATO gathered weight in the late 1950s, as European Common Market membership gradually emerged as a real possibility. It was quite clear to anyone watching developments that the term 'Common Market' was a minimalist one, and that the explicit intention of its main promoters was to increase

---

[19] Keatinge, *A Singlular Stance*, 21; McIvor, *The Irish Naval Service*, 114; see the various reports in *Foreign Relations of the United States*, vi: *Western Europe and Canada*, part 2 (Washington, 1986), 1547–60; Chapin (Dublin) to Washington, 18 Jan. 1949, State Department, 841D20/1–1849.

[20] Moynihan to minister for industry and commerce, 28 Aug. 1953, DT, S. 15499; Bryan to Nunan, 7 Nov. 1951, DFA, A25/1.

[21] J. O'Grady, 'Ireland, the Cuban Missile Crisis, and Civil Aviation: A Study in Applied Neutrality', *Eire Ireland*, 30/3 (Fall, 1993), 70. J. M. Skelly, *Irish Diplomacy at the United Nations 1945–1965: National Interests and the International Order* (Dublin, 1997), *passim*.

the security as well as the economic prosperity of its members both by reducing economic and social friction between and within western Europe states and by strengthening western Europe's external defences. That in turn might ultimately involve some form of mutual defence pact—indeed, defence had been envisaged as one of the first pillars of the new European arrangements by its creators, until negotiations for a European Defence Union went awry in 1954.[22] Although as the custodians of the conscience of constitutional republicanism Fianna Fáil had to tread warily with the decoupling of neutrality and partition, it is clear that, under Sean Lemass as taoiseach, such a process was under way by 1960. This was done primarily to smooth the path towards eventual membership of the European Common Market, as distinct from signing up with NATO, an act which some argued would be tantamount to accepting partition in perpetuity—indeed, smooth words were required to dispel some disquiet within the Fianna Fáil parliamentary party in 1962 after a minister was reported as endorsing NATO membership as a logical consequence of joining the Common Market.[23] Nevertheless, the point is that the Lemass government was prepared, in order to take advantage of the economic and social benefits of EC membership, to find a way around the partititon/NATO conundrum which would allow Ireland eventually to make an appropriate contribution to strengthening the security of the bloc which it was attempting to join, even if the main means of providing such security was to be NATO. Furthermore, although Ireland had taken a prominent role at the United Nations in the formulation and eventual acceptance of the Nuclear Non-Proliferation Treaty, in their infrequent comments on defence and on neutrality in the 1950s and 1960s ministers steered clear of the potentially powerful argument that it would be morally wrong to participate in any multi-national defence arrangement or system which was underpinned by nuclear weapons. Neutrality, therefore, remained a contingent rather than an absolute value in foreign policy.[24]

The post-war years, then, saw a wholesale reversion to defence policy and practice as seen since 1925, combined with an increased emphasis on partition as the main basis for military neutrality. Underpinning this, however, was a feature which had only come to prominence with the Second World War, that is public fear of the consequences of war for the civilian population.[25] In external defence, the defence forces' role would continue to be largely symbolic, at most sacrificial lambs should the state be attacked. Even this was too much for some people: Patrick Kavanagh commented in 1952 that 'as a military force we would

---

[22] G. Murphy, 'The Politics of Economic Realignment, 1948–1964' (unpublished Ph.D. diss., Dublin City University, 1996) casts fresh light on the developing ideas on Europe of the Irish administrative elite; John Horgan, *Sean Lemass: The Enigmatic Patriot* (Dublin, 1997), 221–5.

[23] Horgan, *Lemass*, 223–4.

[24] Keatinge, *A Singular Stance*, 24–9; Skelly, *Irish Diplomacy*, 248–65; TS note, illegible initials, of talk with permanent representative of Luxembourg, 20 Jan. 1962, DT, S. 14291 B/62.

[25] See, for example, 'Soldiers are we', *Kavanagh's Weekly*, 1/9 (7 June 1952).

stand no chance and we should not be flaunting our red flag in the face of the bull of the world . . . we should have an army of about 500 for the purposes of giving us the thrill of the parade'. While the poet's exhortations found no apparent echo even within Finance, his observation about the significance of ceremonial for the army were prescient: military displays such as those mounted for the state visit of President Kennedy in 1963, and to mark the fiftieth anniversary of the Easter Rising in 1966, and even the prowess of army horsemen, were crucial to the maintenance of public confidence in the overall competence and strength of the defence forces. However poor an indicator of the overall effectiveness of a modern army, the uninitiated public are more likely to be impressed by a well-marshalled parade of a couple of thousand men marching in unison to the sound of a military band than by the sort of inchoate and muddied spectacle that serious training would be likely to throw up.[26]

There were some reports in the late 1940s that the army, faced with the inevitability of its permanent inadequacy for conventional defence, was actively developing a doctrine of resistance based on guerrilla warfare should the state be invaded and its main towns, ports, and facilities seized. It is, however, difficult to believe that the defence forces would have been allowed to promote the systematic study of, and training in, irregular warfare, with its necessarily decentralized system of command. Such an approach might weaken the state's iron grip on the army which had been the cardinal feature of military/civil relations since 1924. There was also the danger that the development of a force partly geared towards and trained in irregular warfare might fuel patriotic dreams of fostering insurrection within Northern Ireland. The emaciated defence forces instead remained organized for conventional warfare against a conventional external enemy. The imperatives of local politics meant that the wasteful pre-war pattern of garrisons was retained, with a predictable impact on effectiveness.[27] The launch of the IRA's 'border campaign' in 1956 did something to break the monotony of peacetime soldiering, with the deployment of troops along the border to aid the Garda in deterring republican operations. From December 1957 the army also had to operate the reopened internment camp at the Curragh. Border duty became an instrinsic part of military life until the final cessation of the IRA's half-hearted campaign in 1962. It placed considerable strain on the army without, unlike the other new demand of UN service, providing compensation through the variety and excitement involved. It was also a frequently thankless task: while opinion was clearly against the IRA campaign in principle, in practice there was considerable if myopic admiration for the courage and self-sacrifice of individual IRA volunteers killed in amateurish cross-border raids. Like the Garda, the army consequently endured a certain

[26] 'What is truth?', *Kavanagh's Weekly*, 1/3 (26 Apr. 1952).
[27] Report by W. A. Turgeon, 28 Apr. 1948; D. O'Carroll, 'Defence in the Context of Neutrality and the Single European Act', *Studies*, 77/305 (Spring 1988), 46.

amount of local opprobrium in border counties for its security efforts. As the units involved were drawn mainly from those counties, such pressures were all the more keenly felt. Whether or not they were sufficient to induce a degree of collusion between some soldiers and local IRA men—a suggestion still sometimes made *sotto voce* by British officials—cannot be judged.

As the defence forces shrank, so the paper and procedures needed to administer them expanded as Defence reasserted its administrative supremacy over the warriors. The council of defence, in principle still the supreme advisory body to the minister for defence and the management board for the defence forces, became an administrative fiction: although until 1954 it was statutorily required to meet every six months, it evidently ceased to play any meaningful role. Under the 1954 Defence Act the statutory requirement to meet disappeared altogether, and between 1958 and 1991 the council is said to have convened just seven times— useful discussion of 'matters arising' from the minutes of the previous meeting must have severely strained the skills of the chair.[28] Defence organization also suffered acutely from a chronic weakness which handicapped the effectiveness of many elements of central government in independent Ireland, the so-called 'dual structure' under which all actions or decisions recommended by the technical or professional experts were subject to further detailed scrutiny and review by the mainstream civil service. In addition to attenuating the decision-making process, the implicit subordination of their professional judgement to that of the civilian side of Defence undoubtedly had a debilitating effect on the officer corps, much of whose energies were perforce devoted to complying with largely pointless administrative fine print. The net result was, as the Devlin report pointed out in 1969, an enormously wasteful administrative system where everything was in effect done twice, once in the military and once in the civilian side of Defence, and which placed a pointless premium on checking and control at the expense of effectiveness. Ministerial efforts to increase the use of the Irish language in the defence forces, notably the decision in the late 1950s to make it the primary medium of instruction for cadets, acted as a further drag.[29]

It was predictable that, with the great crisis of 1939–45 successfully overcome, Defence should revert to its leisurely pre-war purchasing habits. Despite all the problems encountered in attempting to secure adequate and timely military supplies during the Emergency, for over a decade afterwards no serious efforts were made to improve the army's supply position with a view to strengthening the country's hand in future international crises, either by purchasing suitable modern weapons and equipment or by lessening reliance for supplies on Britain. As numbers fell, for a time those who continued to serve in the defence

---

[28] Gleeson report, 20; G. Doherty, 'The Ministers and Secretaries Act 1924 and the Council of Defence: A Neglected Controversy', *Administration*, 43/4 (Winter 1995–6), 76–88.

[29] *Report of the Public Services Organisation Review Group* (Dublin, 1969), 247. For illustration of how the system could frustrate executive-minded people, see Andrews, *Man of no property*, 127–30.

forces did have the luxury of training with relatively modern equipment and munitions in plentiful supply, including a handful of Churchill tanks acquired in 1948. That, however, proved a temporary aberration, because as stocks ran down and equipment wore out there was no replenishment. The decision to stay out of NATO made procurement even more problematic (tentative inquiries about the possibility of 'purchasing arms in Switzerland', like Ireland an ostentatious neutral, fell at the first fence in 1950 when the Swiss replied that Ireland would have to provide the requisite raw materials). The difficulty of obtaining armaments was compounded by British strategic calculations which regarded the state as an irrelevance in a likely future war against the Soviet Union, despite the importance of the Atlantic sea routes. A Whitehall committee in 1952 produced classifications on the desirability of exporting weapons to various states, on a scale which ran from A (crucial) to E (completely negligible).[30] Ireland's ratings were scarcely those of a strategic linchpin (see Table 7.1).

Table 7.1. **Ministry of Defence estimate of desirability of selling weapons to Ireland, 1952**

Politically	Economically	Strategically (Naval)	Strategically (Land)	Strategically (Air)
C	D	D	D	C

In the same year, and again in 1953, the British discreetly persuaded the United States to reject Irish overtures for defence supplies on the grounds that there was no likelihood of an invasion of Ireland, that a strengthened Irish army would unsettle Northern Ireland, and that the Irish continued to adopt an uncooperative attitude towards NATO. Britain had two further reasons which officials kept to themselves: they did not want the Irish spending money outside the sterling area, and they feared that what appeared a one-off purchase might develop into an ongoing American/Irish military supply relationship. While he appreciated the political problems, the British military attaché urged some concessions in the interests of long-term co-operation: 'everything possible [should] be done to ensure all possible similarity of equipment in the interests of easy logistical supply in war' as 'the small Irish army is so very largely based on the British model and would presumably fight alongside us (if they come to abandoning neutrality)'. In fact, however, the Irish could not afford the British weapons offered.[31]

While the army's supplies conundrum was never satisfactorily resolved— there was never enough money, and the procedures of Defence remained so

---

[30] Warnock (Berne) to Bryan, 18 Aug. 1950, DFA, P168/2; papers of arms export committee meeting, 2 Oct. 1952, PRO, DEFE 10/3.

[31] Pennells to Chadwick (Dublin embassy), 28 Feb., Fraser to Le Tocq (Dublin embassy), 20 July, and minute by Colonel Stewart (Dublin embassy), 27 July 1953, DO 130/122.

Byzantine as to turn even the most insignificant purchase into a bureaucratic marathon—efforts from the late 1950s to move away from excessive dependence on Britain gradually bore fruit. The Swedish Gustav sub-machine gun was purchased, and in 1961 the army, which had just embarked on its first large-scale commitment to UN service in the Congo, settled on the Belgian FN rifle as its standard infantry weapon. A number of French Panhard armoured vehicles were also acquired. When the crucial step of securing helicopters for the Air Corps was finally taken in 1963, these too were French.[32] This gradual shift in purchasing policy was of considerable significance not only in lessening dependence for equipment on Britain but in broadening the psychological horizons of the defence forces.

If the immediate aftermath of the Emergency generally saw an indiscriminate reversion to political neglect of defence issues, one small exception must be noted. That is the establishment in 1946 of a naval service as a permanent arm of the defence forces. The comic opera vicissitudes of the Marine Service between 1940 and 1945 had ensured its demise. Despite the recruitment of an ex-Royal Navy officer to head the new service, and the acquisition of three corvettes—the *Macha*, the *Maev*, and the *Cliona*, based on a whaleboat design and originally built in great haste for the British as rudimentary Atlantic convoy protection vessels—the new service was beset by much the same underlying problems as had bedevilled its Emergency predecessor. As an unloved adjunct to the army, it had little chance of developing into an effective organization. Its crews endured miserable conditions, its three main craft proved unsuitable for fisheries protection and the other essentially coastguard duties for which the service was intended, and it was not equipped for the coastal patrol work which would once again have become important had another Atlantic war broken out. As if that were not enough, the generally effective coastwatching service which had been organized with such difficulty in 1939 was quickly dismantled once peace came, thereby drastically lessening the state's knowledge of affairs in its own territorial waters and its ability to deploy its meagre forces effectively. Despite the best efforts of its members, the new service gradually became an object of ridicule as its corvettes and crews aged and ailed, and as financial stringency saw its operational capacity decline virtually to nil. By 1969 two of the corvettes had been consigned to the breakers' yard, leaving just the *Maev* to guard the state's territorial waters (until the 1970s there were apparently no votes to be garnered in effective fisheries protection).[33]

The post-Emergency Air Corps, which had inherited a bewildering miscellany of obsolescent aircraft and which acquired a few more in the immediate post-war years, also suffered from the state's continuing unwillingness to

---

[32] Duggan, *A History of the Irish Army*, 234–40. At the time of writing in 1998, some of these helicopters are still in service.

[33] McIvor, *The Irish Naval Service*, 97–132.

provide it with a realistic mandate and the aircraft and other equipment to discharge it. Baldonnel became less an operational installation than an air museum, its hangars clogged with antediluvian aircraft of value only to collectors. Even the one morale booster which the Air Corps received in the 1950s, the purchase of three brand new Vampire jet fighters in 1958, was tempered by the fact that these aircraft were already hopelessly obsolete for air defence. What saved the corps from terminal decline was the belated decision, already noted, to acquire helicopters. These rapidly proved so useful in all sorts of ways, few of them purely military in nature, that they quickly became the operational backbone of the corps. Their deployment in roles such as air ambulance duties and air-sea rescue also provided the corps with a modern image and a highly positive public profile.[34]

The fact that aerial defence was not a priority for post-war governments is hardly surprising. What is striking, however, is the almost complete neglect of the concomitant matter of civil defence. This was despite the widespread assumption, as one journal put it in 1959, that 'civilian defence on a properly organised and national scale is the only form of defence likely to contribute to our survival in the event of disaster'.[35] Despite the possibility of nuclear war, unlike almost every other northern European state Ireland never bothered to invest in shelters, food stores, protected communications, public education for the eventuality of a direct hit or of contamination from explosions elsewhere, air raid drills, or any of the other elements of a coherent civil defence programme in the nuclear age. Defence did establish a skeletal civil defence organization, its members decked out in lumpy black uniforms and equipped with elderly vehicles, painted an incongruously cheerful yellow, which the full-time defence and emergency services no longer wanted. This raggle-taggle body of retired army officers and callow youths was geared for little more than searching for missing hill walkers and occasional flood relief; it was certainly not equipped to cope with the aftermath of a nuclear explosion. In the wake of the Cuban missile crisis of October 1962, however, the government did, quite suddenly, issue a small illustrated booklet to every household containing advice on how best to cope in the event of a nuclear strike, and including the injunction that the pamphlet be kept in a safe place for handy reference in an emergency. This surreal document came like a bolt from the blue to the general public, hitherto schooled to believe that rhetorical neutrality was a shield sufficiently impermeable to protect the nation from the consequences of nuclear war, though anecdotal evidence suggests that once they had recovered their equanimity most people did not make even the preliminary dispositions advised.[36]

---

[34] J. P. Coyle, 'Transition to Peace', *Irish Sword*, 19/75–6 (1993–4), 72–4.

[35] Anon., 'Self-Defence: Deck-Chairs on the Abyss', *National Observer*, 2/3 (Sept. 1959), 12.

[36] In October 1961 fruitless overtures were made to Britain to allow Ireland to establish liaison with the British air raid warning organization. External Affairs to taoiseach, 2 Feb. 1962, DT, S. 14291.

It may be that to Irish minds, to prepare for possible catastrophe was to invite it to happen.

In concluding this discussion of the defence forces and of defence policy in the post-war world, it is worth recalling Dr Hayes's recommendation that the state should preserve the cryptanalytical capacity which it had built up during the Emergency, both for the purposes of reading other people's communications and of assessing the security of its own. Ireland had been naive before the war about communications security, and no one had studied the problem of how to monitor the coded communications of foreign representatives or of spies operating in Ireland:

> We must not enter the next emergency without a nucleus, however small, of experienced staff. If we do the danger will be over and the war lost or won before the necessary preliminary experience has been obtained . . . If the expenditure on this is not considered justifiable, on what grounds can the cost of a skeleton Corps of Engineers or Artillery or any other Army Service be justified?

Despite Hayes's prodigious achievements in cryptanalysis, his advice fell on deaf ears. No effort was made to preserve what he had created, although the state did continue to draw on his expertise and goodwill from time to time.[37] In 1948 he tested a Swedish cipher machine which had been offered to External Affairs. Dismissing the manufacturers' claims about their machine as 'very much exaggerated', he analysed a number of test messages and reported with his customary aplomb that 'to break the cipher in a few hours a staff of six persons to copy accurately and count frequencies is required . . . The machines are therefore unsafe . . . for messages over 2500 letters', as he had demonstrated by breaking one through 'a tedious but not very difficult method'.[38] No one in the state apparatus was briefed to succeed him or to cull his expertise for future study, in terms either of protecting Irish traffic or of reading anyone else's. It must be assumed, therefore, that Irish communications, civil and military, remained as vulnerable after the Emergency as they had been throughout it.

iii. Finding Salvation as Saviours: The Army and UN Service, 1958–1969

Soviet disapproval of Ireland's wartime neutrality, and perhaps more importantly their reluctance to add to the number of Western states in the organization until some of their own satellites were admitted, meant that Ireland's application to join the United Nations (UN), somewhat diffidently tabled in

---

[37] 'Hayes report'.
[38] Report by Hayes, n.d., in folder on 'Swedish cipher machines, 1948', Richard Hayes papers, MS 22984; Hayes to Boland, 28 Oct. 1948, DFA, P163.

1946, was not accepted until December 1955.[39] The delay was perceived in Dublin as at least a partial blessing, because it enabled the state to observe the somewhat depressing early development of the new organization into a Cold War cockpit without committing itself to it. Ireland had prided itself on its activism in the League of Nations, and the government was anxious that wartime neutrality should not lead to peacetime isolation in the new international system. Furthermore, de Valera's criticisms of the League had focused not on its aspirations but on its failure to protect small states from aggression, and on the selfish unwillingness of the great powers to pool their military resources to ensure the effectiveness of its resolutions. In so far as the UN aimed to protect the rights of all states, it too merited the support of those countries like Ireland which wished to steer clear of military alliances. On the other hand, there was some public and official apprehension lest UN membership might make the maintenance of military neutrality impossible; there was also a good deal of cynicism about the utility to a small country of an international organization where power was so unequally spread between the strong and the weak. The responsibilities and the potential military obligations of member states under the UN charter were, furthermore, formidable, so much so that close public perusal might well have drawn the conclusion that UN membership and continued neutrality were incompatible. The Soviet veto had the incidental benefit of sparing anti-partitionist Ireland from the embarrassment in 1950 of having to condemn a war of national unification, when South Korea was invaded by the Chinese-backed North Korean state.[40] By the time that Ireland was admitted, the balance of power between East and West ensured that UN activities had acquired a less confrontational and more pacific character. It was only when the collapse of the Soviet bloc in 1989 changed the rules of the UN game dramatically that awkward problems arising from the state's military obligations under the charter began to rear their heads again.

The opportunities for service which the League of Nations had offered to the defence forces had turned out to be purely theoretical. The UN, however, was a different proposition. Beginning in 1958, when some fifty officers volunteered for observer duty in the Lebanon, UN service provided the peacetime defence forces with a worthwhile external *raison d'être*. Their involvement also contributed handsomely to the state's wider foreign policy aims, by demonstrating Ireland's international good citizenship and its willingness as a small state to contribute to the management and resolution of armed conflict under UN auspices. The Irish had certain advantages as UN volunteers: first and obviously, they were professional soldiers; secondly, they came from a European state which had itself gained independence within living memory and which was

    [39] Skelly, *Irish Diplomacy*, 15.
    [40] J. M. Skelly, 'Ireland, the Department of External Affairs, and the United Nations, 1945–55: A New Look', *Irish Studies in International Affairs*, 7 (1996), 63–80.

untainted by colonialism. These assets were put to the test on a large scale in 1960, when the UN secretary-general asked the government to provide a composite battalion for peacekeeping service in the former Belgian Congo, where a secessionist war had broken out in the province of Katanga. The government agreed to this with alacrity—partition anywhere on the globe was an evil to be thwarted—and the army met this quite unexpected challenge with remarkable effect: within a fortnight the first battalion of 700 troops was on its way. Soon afterwards, a further battalion was dispatched, which meant that by the end of the year 20 per cent of the full-time defence forces were on operations in the middle of Africa. Over the next three years, eight such battalions were dispatched, involving a total of over three thousand members of the defence forces.[41] Equatorial Africa proved a far cry from Mullingar, but the units sent rose to the novel challenges posed by climate, disease, distance, and operating within a multinational force, as well as by the sheer complexity of the Congolese political and military situation. The mandate of the UN force was a peacekeeping one, to help to restore order so that the new Congolese government could operate effectively. Nevertheless, the Irish battalions became involved not only in patrolling and protective duties but in robust operations in conjunction with troops from other countries including Sweden, India, Ethiopia, and Malaysia. There were a number of sustained engagements to secure key installations involving the use of artillery and air support as well as infantry, the first offensive operations in which the army had been involved since April 1923. The appointment of the chief of staff General Sean McKeown as UN force commander from January 1961 to November 1962 was a further boost to morale. In all Ireland provided some four thousand five hundred troops over the duration of the UN's Congo mandate.[42]

The Irish units acquitted themselves well, particularly in the Elizabethville area, where there were fierce engagements in which a number of men were killed. There were also two serious reverses. One company cut off at Jadotville in September 1961 were allegedly tricked into laying down their arms after a four-day siege and were captured by a large force of Congolese secessionists.[43] Worse still, at Niemba nine soldiers died when attacked by tribesmen on 8 November 1960. The public response to this reverse was remarkable for the sense of national pride and of purpose which it reflected: the Niemba deaths were regarded not as a price too high but as an affirmation of Ireland's willingness as a neutral state to risk the lives of its soldiers in defence of peace rather than in prosecution of war. The tragedy underlined the particular dangers which a peacekeeping mandate and mentality placed on soldiers, as accounts

---

[41] Skelly, *Irish Diplomacy*, 268–70; Sean McKeown, 'The Congo (UNUC): The Military Perspective', *Irish Sword*, 20/79 (Summer 1996), 43–7.

[42] Gleeson report, 294.   [43] Duggan, *A History of the Irish Army*, 250–8.

suggest that the patrol might have been able to defend themselves more effectively had they been deployed for combat at the outset.[44] Irish troops on UN
service have had to become very adept at striking an appropriate balance, often
in the face of provocation and of acute danger, between a purely military
appraisal of a situation and an approach which takes account of local political
and cultural sensitivities.

Sixteen Irish soldiers were killed in action in the Congo. Despite this,
involvement there and in subsequent UN operations revitalized the army from
top to bottom. For individuals, peacetime service no longer revolved solely
around training, guard duty, border security, otiose administration, and ceremonial tasks within the state. In the course of their service soldiers could now
expect at least one extended period of UN service, with the attendant variety of
duty, extra money, and opportunities to see the world. For the army, UN service
brought enormous opportunities for improving the effectiveness of troops and
units in operational conditions and working in tandem with detachments from
foreign armies, as well as for the further education of officers detached for UN
service on observer and liaison duties. UN service was also of use in persuading
the government to provide some decent equipment. There were only two real
drawbacks. First, UN service contributed to the difficulties of units at home,
which routinely lost officers, men, and scarce equipment to high-profile operations abroad. Secondly, the commitment of Irish forces to UN service may
have muted robust discussion of national defence issues, and it undoubtedly
gave External Affairs a policy stranglehold in matters which were essentially
military in nature. It is striking how, despite the complexity of the military
issues involved in many of the international disputes and issues with which the
UN sought to deal between the 1950s and the 1970s, from peacekeeping missions
to the promotion of arms control, the army was evidently discouraged from
providing professional appraisals and advice.

The Congo was quickly followed by other missions. Of these the most significant up to 1969 was undoubtedly that in Cyprus, which involved a full battalion
(over six hundred troops). Initially the government baulked at contributing
troops, because of 'the sensitivities of the Irish people about the question of partition', but changed its line on receiving UN assurances that the aim of intervention was to prevent rather than to facilitate the break up of the existing pluralist
Cypriot constitution. Cyprus presented a somewhat different operational challenge than had the Congo: intervention was intended to re-establish calm after
serious inter-ethnic fighting by inserting a lightly armed buffer and mediating
force. UN troops themselves were not a direct target of attack for either side.
Cyprus remained a major commitment for the remainder of the decade,
absorbing between 5 and 7 per cent of the defence force's effective strength at any

---

[44] T. McCaughren, *The Peacemakers of Niemba* (Dublin, 1966), *passim*.

one time. By the time that the Irish contingent was withdrawn in 1974, over nine thousand men had served there.[45]

By the close of the 1960s, what had begun as a quiet experiment in 1958 had transformed the outlook of the defence forces. They had also become an important arm of foreign policy in a manner which no one had expected, and the public had grown used to the idea that through army involvement in UN service the state could make a meaningful contribution to the enhancement of security and the promotion of peace in different parts of the world. It was only in the early 1980s, with the army's hazardous involvement in the intractable mire of southern Lebanon, that the gloss began to fade from the public image of UN service as an unequivocally useful and efficacious way of contributing to world peace.

iv. The Civilianization of Responsibility for Internal Security, 1945–1946

By the spring of 1945 it was obvious that the Allies were on the point of victory in Europe. Once that came, the Emergency in Ireland would clearly be over. Dan Bryan anticipated a number of security problems which would continue, some arising out of the war, and others arising from the lessons which the war had taught the state about the necessity for careful monitoring of foreign activities.

One obvious area was the movement of people between Ireland and Britain; another, related, was the control of aliens wishing to visit Ireland and who might then avail themselves of the common travel area to slip into the United Kingdom unnoticed, as at least one German agent, Wilhelm Preetz, had done in 1938.[46] The big issue, however, was who would be responsible for detecting and monitoring the clandestine activities of foreign powers and their agents within the state. While the principle that G2 should do this work had been conceded in 1938, events were shortly to show that this was a matter not simply of nominal responsibility but of legal powers and operational capacity.

The blow fell in May with the ending of censorship. The Post Office, hitherto extremely co-operative, then told G2 that they could no longer either open letters or tap telephones 'in the absence of any apparent legal authority'.[47] During the Emergency such interception had been done on warrants supplied by Justice on G2's requests, but Justice was now willing to authorize only warrants specifically requested by the Garda commissioner for the prevention or detection of crime. This would cut G2 off from what was usually its main source of information.

---

[45] Gleeson report, 294; memorandum by ? [illegible], 25 Feb. 1964, DFA, P372; P. D. Hogan, 'UNI-CYP: Command and Staff Experiences', *Irish Sword*, 20/79 (Summer 1996), 48–52. Although the Irish battalion was withdrawn in 1974, from 1992 to 1994 the post of UN force commander was held by an Irish general.

[46] Bryan to Walshe, 6 Apr. 1945, DFA, A8/1.

[47] G2 memorandum, 16 May, with Bryan to minister for defence, 25 May 1945, DFA, A8/1.

Bryan made the best case possible for the restoration of the wider rubric applied during the Emergency, describing how G2 had acquired a counter-espionage role in 1938 and pointing out that this had been reaffirmed by the taoiseach personally in September 1939. He invoked the view of the attorney-general that there was no law prohibiting many of those clandestine activities which G2 had been dealing with since 1938. He also sought and received general support from External Affairs for the proposition that the state should know of matters in its own backyard which might affect its relations with other coun-tries. (Presumably in furtherance of this cause, he sent Joseph Walshe, who had a bee in his bonnet about freemasonry, a translated letter which 'is the first instance noticed of Masonry in this country being asked to take a hand in extra-national affairs . . . Owing to the removal of the censorship it will no longer be possible to keep a watch on this sort of activity.') Bryan complained that while Justice claimed they were merely reverting to the pre-Emergency status quo, in fact G2 had been organizing communications interception under warrant since May 1939 precisely because it was recognized that espionage directed against Britain, and externally aided subversive activities, were beyond the scope of the existing criminal law and the associated protocols under which warrants were usually granted to the Garda. In Bryan's despairing words, reversion to the pre-May 1939 rules would mean that the use of such warrants would be ruled out in regard to much of the more important work of his organization, on the basis that such activities were not criminal in themselves, and that

as shown by . . . experience . . . prior to and during the Emergency one of the problems confronting the state is the necessity of being in a position to prove that the activities in Ireland of certain foreign states, their nationals here, and their Irish friends, are not harmful to other states. The only way in which this can be satisfactorily achieved is for the Defence Security Intelligence Section . . . to keep itself fully informed of all such activities.

The experience of G2 Branch in the last seven years shows that many of the incidents and problems that worry foreign states . . . come to their notice through matter directed by post to and from Ireland. If the Defence Security Intelligence Section here is to con-tinue to keep itself informed of these matters, at least equally as well as the authorities of the foreign states concerned, postal supervision in selected cases is clearly essential.

Anticipating the question of what particular perils the state now faced, Bryan detailed a number of matters. These included residual links between Irish people and former German intelligence operatives which might under some circumstances be reactivated, and British activities such as the recruitment of Irishmen for the armed services, both of which required continued postal observation. The main new threat, however, was the 'Russian and communist problem'. He pointed to a long history of 'Russian propaganda and even of interference in subversive activities . . . and one known case of the attempted use of the IRA for espionage in Great Britain' (in 1925), and furnished evidence that Irish communists toed the Moscow line in everything which they did, as demonstrated by the propaganda gymnastics of the CPI between 1939 and 1941. The communist movement was, he argued, in effect

a unit of an international organisation; is subsidised and directed from outside the state and bases its general policy on that of a foreign state. This aspect of the Communist problem makes it fundamentally different from that of such organisations as the IRA which, even when they collaborated with the agents of a foreign state, did so as an indirect means to their particular ends.

The existence . . . of such an organisation, the first allegiance of which is to an international organisation or to a foreign state, provides an organised group, many members of which would undoubtedly, on request or direction, engage in espionage, propaganda or other activities.

For these reasons, he submitted, Justice must continue to provide interception warrants on G2's request subject to the provision of 'ample grounds' and the maintenance of 'great discretion' in their execution.[48]

Underlying the problem of postal and telephone warrants was a bigger question about the proper role of G2 in peacetime. The reality was that there were sound constitutional grounds for restricting military involvement in what amounted to political surveillance. In addition, interdepartmental rivalries played a part. Relations between G2 and Justice had been difficult ever since the pugnacious Peter Berry had become his minister's main adviser on security issues in 1941.[49] Berry was to prove himself an outstandingly courageous civil servant, but at times a difficult one. He was to dominate internal security policy as he rose through the department until his embittered retirement as its secretary in 1971. It is hardly surprising that, at his prompting, Justice reassumed primacy in internal security affairs at the ending of the Emergency.[50] While G2 did retain the counter-espionage remit acquired in 1938, it became in effect almost entirely dependent for information on Justice and C3. Its only other worthwhile source of information, apart from odd scraps which came from personal contacts, and material occasionally furnished by Irish diplomats abroad, was that gleaned from its dealings with foreign intelligence and security agencies, and in June 1945 it was not at all clear how extensive such contacts would be. While External Affairs did continue to consult it independently on matters which Justice probably felt lay within their purview, such as the granting of passports to people on watch lists because of alleged associations with communist

---

[48] Bryan to Walshe, 2 June (about the masons), and 25 June, enclosing copy of Bryan to minister for defence, 25 May and 25 June and attached memoranda, and Bryan to Philip O'Donoghue (Attorney-General's Office), 21 June 1945, DFA, A8/1.

[49] Bryan interview.

[50] Private information; interview with a former comptroller and auditor general, 1984; V. Browne, 'The Berry File', *Magill*, 3/9 (June 1980), 44.

organizations abroad, and general appraisals of the strength and intentions of the republican movement, the action taken in June 1945 effectively consigned it to a peripheral status in internal security affairs.[51]

The action taken at the conclusion of the Emergency also had the effect, presumably, of depriving External Affairs of the benefits of the interception of the telephone and postal communications of diplomatic missions in Dublin. On this, and on the wider issue of communications interception generally, the records are silent: in spectacular contrast to the profusion of materials for the 1939–45 period, there are almost no documents to show the nature and extent of state interception activities for internal security, counter-espionage, diplomatic intelligence, criminal investigation, or domestic political purposes. The decision in 1954 to make permanent three temporary positions held by Post Office officials responsible for telephone interception, on the advice of both Justice and Defence, does suggest that the practice had become firmly rooted.[52]

Reassertion of Garda primacy in intelligence on domestic subversion brought a shift in emphasis, just as it had done in 1925. From the relatively few appraisals of post-war subversive activity which are available, it appears that the Garda continued to be quite successful in securing good information from within republican circles. It is also clear that the Special Branch and C3 placed rather less emphasis on the analysis of material than had been G2's practice. The Garda role was, rather, to supply written information to Justice and to leave them to make the judgements and predictions and to issue directions for action. Within that department, the management of counter-subversive activities was dealt with by a handful of officials, and their deliberations and advice have remained largely secret. So far as can be judged, successive ministers played little part in the administration of internal security policy, although their consent was obviously needed for big decisions as well as for legal matters such as the issuing of interception warrants. There were rumours of widespread abuse of telephone tapping in the early 1960s for party political purposes, but in the absence of evidence these charges cannot be evaluated.[53]

From what emerged in the wake of the 1970 arms crisis, it appears that the quality of Garda intelligence on the republican movement within the state was quite good throughout the 1960s. While much of this came from overt and covert surveillance, it is plain that in this era the Special Branch had well-placed informants. It was these sources which led to the uncovering of the plan to import arms in 1970, a scheme the unmasking of which rocked the state to its foundations.

---

[51] See e.g. Bryan to Boland, 15 Nov. 1946, and External Affairs [unsigned] to Col. Callanan, G2, 9 Jan. 1958, DFA, A55/1.

[52] Papers on this are in NA, Department of Communications, H3013/35; for an unsatisfactory survey, see B. Munnelly, *Who's Bugging You? Inside Ireland's Secret World of Electronic Surveillance* (Cork, 1987).

[53] Munnelly, *Who's Bugging You?*, 17–18.

v. External Security Organization and Co-operation, 1945–1969

Garda/RUC and Garda/Scotland Yard liaison appears to run on largely un-changed after 1945. However, the very close security links built up between Britain and Ireland in the course of the Emergency gradually loosened in the post-war era. The main outstanding issues involved the debriefing of and treat-ment of the non-Irish German agents in Irish custody. The British relied on an understanding reached during the war that such agents would be handed over. The minister for justice Gerry Boland, however, was not party to that under-standing and he forthrightly repudiated it. He told Sir John Maffey that he had no time for spies in wartime and would have been glad to have had them shot. However, having secured so comprehensive a victory, the Allies should not be bothered pursuing small fry who had been locked up out of harm's way for years and who could do no damage. Once released from internment, therefore, such men should not be sought for possible arraignment or compulsory debriefing, and should be free to travel back to their homeland subject to normal civilian regulations.[54] The result was that, even after their release from custody, the ex-agents were kept for some time in a legal limbo as the British and Irish govern-ments sought a compromise. In the end it was agreed that former agents would not be prosecuted by the Allies for anything done during the war. In one case this understanding had a tragic outcome: in February 1947 the highly strung Herman Goertz, under a complete misapprehension about the Allied screening to which he would be subjected, and who had an exaggerated idea of his own importance, swallowed poison and died outside the Aliens Office after being informed by the Garda that the government had no choice but to send him home. Goertz was much liked by his former captors, and alone of the agents sent he was admired for his single-mindedness. His needless death created embar-rassment all round, and made further deportations of ex-agents impossible.[55]

Beyond clearing up the historical details of Axis activities, initially there was not all that much for MI5 and G2 to discuss. G2 was precluded from any exchanges regarding the IRA, except in respect of its possible dealings with for-eign powers or with extremist nationalist movements abroad—the Welsh, the Scots, the Bretons, and the Flemish—in what might be termed the 'Celtic Inter-national' (cordial relations between the handful of Scottish and Breton nation-alist extremists living in Ireland and mainstream republicans naturally gave some cause for concern).[56] However, the British were evidently quite keen to

---

[54] Walshe to Maffey, 4 July 1945, NA, DFA, A7/I.

[55] Note by Maffey of his talk with the minister for justice, 23 Dec. 1946; Maffey to Boland, 30 July 1947, DFA, A74.

[56] Bryan to chief of staff, 9 Mar. 1949, and Nunan to Coyne, 3 Feb. 1953, DFA, P/168 and A74. For an example of post-war pan-Celticism see the cover illustration of G. Evans, *Welsh Nationalism* (Denbigh, n.d. [1947?]), which picks out the island of Ireland as well as Scotland, Wales, Brittany, and Cornwall in

maintain established links, with the emphasis now on communist activities (it is clear from External Affairs records that G2 was the conduit for information from abroad on the activities of Irish communists, and this presumably came through foreign security sources). Cecil Liddell continued to do some work for MI5: he told Bryan in December 1945 that he was 'still . . . working on a note of the work of the past six years . . . I am always coming across instances of your kind help & co-operation', and a fortnight later wrote that 'I should like to come over, tho' I think Guy might make a trip to Lambay & combine it with a visit to you before I have a chance'.[57] In February 1947 he told Bryan that 'Guy's No. 1 Dick White has never been to Ireland, & is longing for an excuse to visit Dublin' together with Cecil's successor in MI5's Irish section, and later in the year proposed that Bryan visit London.[58] When Cecil died in 1952, Guy, who had become deputy director-general of MI5, wrote to thank Bryan for

your message of sympathy . . . Please convey, too, my thanks to Joe Guilfoyle for his message. I know how much importance Cecil attached to the friendships that he made in Ireland . . . I need not tell you how much we value the association, which Liam [Archer, director of G2 up to 1941] and you have done so much to promote, and how anxious we are that it should continue with your successor.

I cannot say how much I regret your departure [from G2 to become commandant of the military college] . . . I should like to wish you the very best of luck . . . and to thank you for your wholehearted co-operation and many kindnesses in the past. I hope you feel, as I do and as I know Cecil did, that Liam and you have laid the foundations of something really worthwhile.[59]

Cecil Liddell remained informally in touch with G2 until his death. Within MI5, the Irish brief was taken over by Dick White, who had been involved with the Lenihan case, and who later became the first man to head successively MI5 and then MI6, before becoming the first Cabinet Office adviser on intelligence in 1972. White, who visited Dublin for discussions with G2 once or twice in the late 1940s, became director-general of MI5 in 1956, and responsibility for the Irish link passed to Brigadier Bill Magan, a former Indian Army soldier originally from County Meath (in 1938 he had been master of the South Westmeath Hunt). Both were on very good terms with their G2 equivalents.[60]

While it is difficult without seeing the relevant British and Irish records to say much about the importance of the exchanges between G2 and MI5, for some years it is possible to count the number of packets of correspondence and

---

green on an otherwise black background. It must also be presumed that the French government took some interest in the doings of Breton exiles in Ireland, perhaps in collaboration with the Irish authorities.

57 Cecil Liddell to Bryan, 9 and 29 Dec. 1945, Bryan papers, P71/424 and 427.
58 13 Feb. 1947, P71/437.   59 Guy Liddell to Bryan, 18 and 26 Mar. 1952, P71/455.
60 Sir Dick White to the author, 4 Apr. 1990; Nunan to Boland, 5 June 1956, DFA, P168 1/C; private information.

documents consigned by G2 for the London embassy bag for onward transmission to MI5. The figures for the period from 1949 to 1960 are given in Table 7.2.

Table 7.2. G2 packets sent to MI5, 1949–1960

1949	1950	1951	1952	1953	1954	1955	1956	1957	1958	1959	1960
17	28	41	49	56	36	33	68	81	100	30	93

The reciprocal British figures for these years are harder to calculate. However, a London embassy log of packets received from MI5 suggests the figures given in Table 7.3 for the years 1950 to 1959.

Table 7.3. MI5 packets sent to G2, 1950–1959

1950	1951	1952	1953	1954	1955	1956	1957	1958	1959
8	72	83	61	61	50	9*	142	135	138

* 1956 figure is only ascertainable up to 14 February.

The stock-in-trade undoubtedly included problems of alleged war criminals, as well as suspect aliens (particularly communists) and, most importantly, communist activity: in February 1951 Bryan commented that 'the bulk' of one packet bound for London 'is due to copies of Communist propaganda'. The arrangement even survived the arrival of Sean MacBride as minister for external affairs in 1948, perhaps because his defence counterpart was evidently vague in his description of the material involved.[61] This is quite significant, as there is some evidence to suggest that MacBride, who could never have been accused of being pro-British and who in later life developed acute paranoia about the machinations of Western intelligence services, thought that G2 should be answerable to him: 'I did on one occasion ask the head of the army intelligence', Dan Bryan, 'for statistical information concerning British forces in Northern Ireland. It would be hard to describe the air of embarrassment which prevailed . . . and he told me that he did not know that his services kept this information up to date', a suitably elliptical reply to so recent and contingent a convert to strictly constitutional nationalism (Bryan evidently did have relevant information).[62] G2 did,

[61] Nunan to Walshe (the Vatican), 22 Jan. 1954, DFA, A55/1; Bryan to Nunan, 19 Feb. 1951, and to Boland, n.d. [?1949], Ms Foxe to Ms Mooney, 16 Jan. 1953, DFA, P168/1/A; the figures on packets sent to and from the British are taken from DFA, P168/1/A, B, C, D, and E. There may be some inaccuracies, as the records are not always clear.

[62] S. MacBride, 'Reflections on Intelligence', *Intelligence and National Security*, 2/1 (Jan. 1987), 92–3; Bryan to chief of staff, 9 Mar. 1949, DFA, P168. At p. 95 MacBride says that he was also warned that the police had received a tip-off from the 'British [Secret] Services' that he was to be assassinated. While ministerial colleagues assumed that this was an IRA plan—MacBride, after all, was regarded by his former IRA colleagues as something of an apostate at the time—he reasoned that it was probably a British secret service plot. I know of no corroborative source for any aspect of this story.

however, apparently make some (arguably improper) inquiries at MacBride's behest about the publishing activities of the demented Father Denis Fahey, which suggests a desire to please an important customer.[63]

Security relations with the United States in the post-war era presented greater difficulties than did the maintenance of the established British link. David Gray's persistent wrong-headedness on security matters was recalled with considerable resentment in both External Affairs and G2, and there was a corresponding reluctance to have any dealings on security questions with the American mission in Dublin. Against this, the good relations built up between OSS and G2 were remembered with satisfaction and were maintained until 1947 through London, and Bryan was evidently anxious to develop an appropriate link in peacetime.[64] But there appears to have been a long hiatus in seeking an arrangement, perhaps because Gray remained in Dublin until 1948. There is no trace of any American overtures until after the election of the Costello inter-party government in 1948, an event which alarmed the State Department because of the alleged Leftist and undoubted republican leanings of MacBride's Clann na Poblachta party. Bryan was then approached by the American military attaché, who in a roundabout way queried the efficacy of Irish scrutiny of communist activities and suggested a security understanding. Bryan observed that the 'Americans are, of course at present hypersensitive to any suggestion of Soviet or Communist activity or influence—they were to German and even to alleged Japanese activity here during the war'. He argued that it was better to keep the Americans accurately informed, as had been done through OSS from 1942 onwards, than to leave them in panicky ignorance of Irish affairs: 'If intelligence services are reasonably informed as to any situation . . . they are not as nervous as when they suspect activities of which they know nothing'. He argued that 'from the strictly intelligence viewpoint the advantages are in favour of liaison and an exchange of information, but difficult personal and political problems will have to be handled'.[65]

In the event, nothing was agreed. Overtures were renewed in 1950 and in 1951, when its director General Bedell Smith told Bryan that 'a CIA representative' would be 'posted in Dublin late this summer and I am . . . particularly anxious that he be in contact with you on a mutually profitable basis'. On the direction of External Affairs, Bryan replied that such an appointment would be inopportune. The man selected for the post was instead sent to London. In November 1954 the Americans returned to the matter: they 'were not interested in military intelligence as such', and stressed that 'any liaison . . . would confine activities to (1) counter-espionage and (2) communist subversive activities'. In deference to

---

[63] Bryan to Boland, 27 Apr. 1949, DFA, P168. It may be that it was felt that the world-wide if not cosmic scope of Fahey's conspiracy theories made him fair game for army investigation.

[64] Bryan to Boland, 8 Oct. 1945, DFA, A60; private information.

[65] Browne, *Against the Tide*, 100–5; memorandum by Bryan, Mar. 1948, DFA, A55/1.

Irish sensitivities, the link would be maintained through the American embassy in London. This proposal was put formally in a letter from CIA director Allen Dulles to the minister for external affairs Liam Cosgrave a month later and it was accepted.[66]

Once established, this link apparently operated quite smoothly. Two CIA officers already based in London to liaise with British intelligence organizations were initially nominated to liaise with G2. The senior man had no interest whatsoever in visiting Ireland; by contrast, his deputy and later successor in charge of liaison with the British had originally come to Ireland in 1947 to complete research for a Ph.D. on Ireland's position within the British commonwealth, and he was delighted to handle Irish affairs. In conversation he recalled his regular Irish visits between 1955 and 1967 with pleasure, and commented that while obviously a small organization the Irish 'knew what they were doing'. The main purpose of the liaison was to determine whether there was any Soviet or Soviet-inspired espionage or subversive activity going on within Ireland, to monitor the revolutionary Left, and to keep up contacts in case of a future East–West crisis.[67] As the relevant files are still unavailable, it is impossible to gauge the extent of the exchanges under this arrangement, or to determine if the CIA took any other interest in Irish affairs (although the United States did adduce the danger of espionage as one argument against the granting of landing rights at Shannon to Eastern Bloc airlines in the early 1960s). It seems unlikely that G2 had either the resources or the mandate to do much more than ask C3 to supply whatever current confidential information was available, and to produce commentaries on and copies of the output of the radical press. It appears that in return for this material the CIA acted as a conduit for some information on matters of possible interest to the defence forces such as Soviet air and sea activities in the eastern Atlantic (obtaining even published information on foreign armies was an acute problem for G2: Bryan told External Affairs in 1951 that 'in the absence of any military attachés or other similar sources I am most anxious to obtain certain elementary information from your missions abroad', though there is little sign that much was forthcoming). G2 also wanted whatever the CIA could give them on IRA contacts abroad, but the Americans had very little as this lay within the purview of the FBI, who maintained their own link with the Garda through their legal attaché at the London embassy. Given the rather limited significance in Cold War terms of the material which G2 had to trade, it seems unlikely that they either sought or received any material support of the kind sometimes offered to friendly intelligence and security services such as the

---

[66] Bedell Smith to Bryan, 7 Aug. 1951, DFA, A60; MacMahon (Defence) to Nunan, 25 Jan., Dulles to Cosgrave, 26 Feb., Nunan to Boland (London embassy), 29 Aug., and Boland to Nunan, 30 Sept. 1955, DFA, A60/1.

[67] Interviews with a former CIA officer who worked on liaison with G2 in the 1950s and 1960s, Boston and Washington, 1992 and 1998; P. Wright, *Spycatcher* (New York, 1987), 135, 274–5.

Dutch BVD (internal security service), which between 1948 and 1964 was partly subsidized by the CIA. It must be assumed that regular G2 liaison with both MI5 and the CIA continued up to 1969 through the same rather cumbersome channels, and also that intermittent G2 and Garda exchanges with other foreign security or intelligence services also took place from time to time. The records contain two interesting examples where co-operation was sought by foreign powers but refused: in 1960 the Malaysian high commission in London sought material on allegedly communist Malaysian students in Ireland, a request which External Affairs thought reasonable 'in principle'. Peter Berry, however, was dismissive: to share such information would be 'contrary to our settled policy'. A few months later he wrote somewhat apologetically to say that he now had information that some Malaysian students were, after all, receiving communist publications, 'but I am not at all clear that we can do anything about it'. As they 'do not associate even with others in the Afro-Asian group who have Communist sympathies', and use 'a language which is practically unknown outside their own group', it is 'extremely difficult for the police to get any reliable detailed information about their activities'. An offer by a South African diplomat, appropriately named White, to provide information about communists within the anti-apartheid movement 'mainly connected with a small group in Trinity College', and about visiting South Africans, in return for 'information about selected Irish immigrants to his country' was also declined, as External Affairs would not consider 'cooperation with the South Africans on the apartheid issue'.[68]

vi. Irish Communists and Internal Security, 1945–1969

Germany's haphazard dealings with the IRA during the Emergency had shown how a foreign power could seek to manipulate domestic political conditions for its own ends in much the way that had been predicted beforehand. Even before the war had finally ended, G2 had evinced concern that the state might face similar difficulties in the future, this time not due to German inspiration but to communist activities: in February 1944 Bryan advised his minister that the internecine warfare which had broken out within the Labour party was the

---

[68] Bryan to Nunan, 9 May 1951, DFA, P168/2. External Affairs did permit Fergus FitzGerald, a former G2 officer working in the Food and Agriculture Organisation in Rome, to forward material to Bryan via the Rome embassy. In the 1960s and early 1970s G2 also provided External Affairs with confidential newsletters on world affairs, topped and tailed so their origins could not be determined and which were probably American or NATO briefing documents. DFA, 313/14. B. de Graaff and C. Wiebes, 'Intelligence and the Cold War behind the Dikes: The Relationship between the American and Dutch Intelligence Communities, 1946–1994', *Intelligence and National Security*, 12/1 (Jan. 1997), 44–7; Cremin (External Affairs) to Coyne (Justice), 3 Sept., and Berry to Cremin, undated, Sept. 1960 and 24 Mar. 1961, DFA, A55 II; Keating (London embassy) to ambassador, 23 Sept., and McCann (External Affairs) to Berry, 29 Sept. 1964, DFA, A55/10.

product of 'gradual infiltration' by communists working to an agenda largely set by the CPGB—the CPI had been formally dissolved in July 1941, and its organizational functions transferred to Belfast—and that 'the growth of Communism requires attention from the intellectual or cultural and economic' as well as from the 'security or subversive' angles.[69] The issue of communist activity and influence became more pressing with the advent of the Cold War. It also became entangled with other matters such as immigration policy.

In discussing surveillance of communism, it is important to stress a number of points. First, the state had drawn a lesson from its experience with pro-German cultural and political organizations in the 1930s, which was that even the most apparently insignificant groups of eccentrics and nonentities could in certain circumstances be manipulated by external interests and cause trouble. Secondly, until 1943 Irish communists had been under orders to do the bidding of the Soviet Union, working through the Comintern, even if political conditions and a tendency to improvise in response to local circumstances made literal adherence to instructions a rare event. Even after Stalin dissolved the Comintern in 1943 as a gesture of anti-fascist unity towards his wartime allies, Irish communists were known to maintain links with foreign communist parties and to dance to Moscow's tune.[70] Thirdly, the interpenetration of the communist and republican movements had been a source of admittedly exaggerated state concern since the late 1920s. Fourthly, despite the enduring imagery of witch-hunts and injustice which now customarily attaches to discussion of Western anxieties about communist enemies within, the general fear both of overt communist organizations and of covert communist political and espionage activity was based not simply on the declamations of drunken American demagogues such as Senator McCarthy, but on knowledge of the reality of Soviet clandestine activities in the post-war West. In most Western countries communist parties and kindred bodies, while largely composed of idealistic, able, and patriotic people with a burning desire for social justice and faith in the eventual triumph of socialism, were also used to further Soviet aims, whether through the dissemination of propaganda, the penetration of trade unions and the communications media, the fomenting of industrial unrest, or, in a very few cases, assisting in espionage or other clandestine activities. Finally, it should be noted that surveillance did not automatically translate into oppression. In the words of a Justice document, 'our Communists' activities are not unlawful'. Just as Irish devotees of Hitler's Germany had been watched but not penalized for their views in the late 1930s, so the ideologues of the revolutionary Left were allowed to go about their business. It is a matter of opinion whether or not this was an index of state respect for individual rights, a reflection of the view that

---

[69] Bryan to minister for defence, 2 Feb. 1944, DFA, A55I; Justice memorandum, 31 Dec. 1947, MacEntee papers, P67/548.

[70] I. Deutscher, *Stalin* (Oxford, 1949; revised edn., London, 1966), 464.

communism was too sickly a plant to worry about, or the product of the sheer familiarity and enduring comradeship which existed between its leading proponents and the political elite whom in principle they sought to topple: the presence in the 1948–51 Costello government of MacBride meant that Irish radicals had a powerful friend at the cabinet table, while Peadar O'Donnell's comment in 1959 that the new taoiseach Sean Lemass 'is the complete realist. Didn't I sit for years with him on the [IRA] Army Council?' need only be inverted to explain why most Fianna Fáil ministers did not quake in their boots every time a Special Branch report on communist activity reached their desks.[71] Once the abstract threat was personalized, much of the sting went out of it. The surveillance to which left-wing organizations and individuals were subjected in the post-war years should be seen in that light.

The professional security case for keeping tabs on the revolutionary Left was clearly stated by Bryan in 1947:

I judge the Communists solely from the extent to which they might interfere with Irish defence efforts in a crisis or, still more important, by the extent to which they might use sections of the Irish population in England, America and other countries during a war in a way that would affect Irish interests . . . how could Russia in a future war, or even in peace time, use the Irish . . . for anti-British and anti-American propaganda or for sabotage or espionage against these countries . . . if, as I am convinced, this is the Russian and Communist purpose, they are meeting with a fair measure of success, and are improving their potential organisation, whilst at the same time working on the nationalist and anti-Partition spirit skilfully selling their propaganda. So far no information of attempts to use the Irish people for espionage has come to my knowledge. This would, however, only follow after skilful penetration by propaganda etc. The Russians have attempted to use Irish organisations for this purpose before [*for espionage in Britain in 1925*] and will certainly do so again. In Ireland, prior to and during the recent emergency there was not half a dozen doctrinaire Nazis. There were a number of IRA people and some other people who were anxious to use Germany to aid what they considered were Irish interests . . . at present there are at least 1,000 people who are so indoctrinated with and sympathetic to Communist ideas that on international isssues they automatically take the Russian and not an Irish view. They, for external purposes, form the nucleus of a fifth column and except that their numbers are not so large there is no difference between them and the fifth columns which have attracted attention in Canada and Australia recently. Like the fifth columns in those countries, they include intellectuals and persons of good positions.

Bryan emphasized that he did not 'think that the Communists here are . . . a serious or important factor' in domestic politics, despite their efforts to penetrate the Labour party and the unions.[72]

---

[71] Costigan (Justice) to O'Driscoll (External Affairs), 12 Oct. 1951, DFA, A55/6A; Padraic O'Halpin's journal, 27 Nov. 1959; Andrews, *Man of no property*, 286–7. Lemass secured O'Donnell a temporary civil service position when he was hard up during the Emergency. See Ó'Canainn, 'Eilís Ryan', 132–43, for illustrations of the enduring comradeship between leading figures in Fianna Fáil and republican Leftists.

[72] Memorandum by Bryan, 23 June, with Bryan to Boland, 23 June 1947, DFA, A55 I.

The plausibility of Bryan's analysis remains a matter of opinion, because it was never put to the test of an international crisis on the scale of war. There is no doubt that some on the Left did develop a world-view in which the interests of mankind and of the Soviet Union became coterminous. This in turn led them into a wilderness of mirrors, where political reality was whatever the Moscow line happened to be at that moment, as consistency of argument and aims was completely subordinated to the incoherent but emotionally fulfilling world of ultramontane Stalinism. Mainstream communism in post-war Ireland was, in short, a cult, its devotion to Moscow's every word in some respects analogous to the immutable wisdom which the vast majority of Irish people, frequently in defiance of the available evidence, accorded to the papacy. It is clear that the communist movement remained very small, and that its overt brand of unyielding millenarianism was unable to attract significant public interest and support in a resolutely Catholic and conservative society. Its attempts at penetration of trade unions, the press, and the Labour party yielded little, and seem to have been well known to the police. Special Branch surveillance of the Left revealed not growing strength but only chronic weakness. It uncovered no great conspiracies to subvert or to spy, and precious little evidence to indicate that Moscow took its Irish adherents seriously: the only external subsidy to communists which was traced between 1939 and 1948, the $100 a month remittted to the veteran publicist Sean Nolan by American comrades, was pathetically small.[73] The Soviet intelligence services, prodigiously active in most other states in western Europe, were conspicuous by their almost complete absence in the three decades following the war, while the most dramatic—and perhaps the only— significant Irish assistance given to the KGB in the period was provided not by any bearded ideologue, but by the emphatically non-socialist though deeply proletarian figure of Sean Burke, an habitual criminal who arranged the escape of the British traitor George Blake from Wormwood Scrubs prison in 1966. There was also an Irish angle in the case of another British traitor, Kim Philby, whose third wife, the American Eleanor Pope Brewer, tired of his infidelities and left Moscow for good in 1965: in July G2 told External Affairs that she had 'arrived in Britain on Wednesday evening', and it was feared that she intended 'settling down in Ireland. She is very anti-American, drinks too much and receives considerable money from Russia (from her husband or what?).'[74]

Attempts at reforging a synthesis between socialism and republicanism, begun in 1945 through organizations such as the Connolly clubs in Ireland and

---

[73] Browne, *Against the Tide*, 249–50; G2 memorandum, 12 Oct. 1948, DFA, A55I. The list of consignees included the leading American communists Earl Browder and Albert Benson (who in 1916 had been the Socialist candidate in the presidential election).

[74] N. West, *MI5 1945–72: A Matter of Trust* (1st edn., London, 1982; Cornet edn., 1983), 201–4; Hefferon (G2) to Gallagher (External Affairs), 17 July, and Gallagher's minute, 18 July 1965, DFA, A55 II; A. Boyle, *The Climate of Treason* (London, 1979; revised edn., 1980), 457–8, 470.

Britain, did yield some results. This was potentially far more dangerous to the state than communist attempts to penetrate the trade union movement, or the sisyphean efforts of communist publicists to spread the revolutionary word. The mainstream IRA had gratefully jettisoned most traces of socialist thought after the Republican Congress breakaway in 1934. In the changed circumstances of the post-war years, the old aspiration for a 'workers' republic' began to creep back into republican thinking despite the predominance within the organization of traditionalists who would have no truck with anything smacking of socialism. The gradual regeneration of a coherent doctrine of republican socialism was not the product of any externally inspired scheme to turn the IRA into an instrument of Soviet policy, but a natural development arising from the demonstrable failures of mainstream republicanism since the mid-1930s, the superior intellectual and literary abilities of the proponents of a new leftward shift, a general realization that social and economic conditions were issues upon which support might be garnered in both parts of the island, and the promise of a better world that revolutionary socialism appeared to offer. Although this alarmed a few people in national politics, most notably the veteran Fianna Fáil minister Sean MacEntee, official Ireland was not unduly perturbed. While the mainstream IRA continued to shy away from anything smacking of Marxism for over a decade after 1945, seeds had been planted in the minds of key activists which were to flower in the dismal course of the 1956–62 border campaign.[75] In the meantime, leftists continued to dream their dreams of pan-Irish, non-sectarian revolutionary unity: in 1957 the veteran proselytizer Peadar O'Donnell 'gave a talk . . . on the general situation in the Six Counties'. He was taxed about his endorsement of the IRA:

'Surely Peadar you don't trust those boys in the green berets . . .?' . . . He [O'Donnell] said with great venom: 'Those! Those are not the IRA, they are armed Catholics.'
   He seemed somewhat taken aback by his own vehemence. After a silence he said suddenly: 'When McCurtain gets out of jail I'll have plenty of influence over him.'[76]

O'Donnell, George Gilmore, and other stalwarts of the republican Left continued to their dying day to nurture hopes of a class-based non-sectarian revolutionary politics. The political class with whom they had broken continued not to worry overmuch about them.
   The Russophile Left were, of course, not the only group to proclaim varieties of the Marxist gospel. The 1960s saw the development both of small Trotskyite sects and of a coterie of Maoists. For some unfathomable reason the latter briefly aroused the particular wrath of conventional Ireland. In a celebrated

---

[75] Berry to Nolan (secretary to the government), 23 June 1947, DT, S. 5074B; G2 memorandum on the IRA, 19 Dec. 1951, with Callanan (G2) to Nunan, 19 June 1952, DFA, A12/1.
[76] O'Halpin journal, 8 July 1957. Thomas MacCurtain had been convicted of the murder of Detective Officer Roche in 1940, but was eventually released in 1948. He was interned in 1957.

demonstration of provincial intolerance, a Maoist bookshop in Limerick was burnt out and dark threats were uttered by local politicians against those spreading the pernicious teachings of the little red book. They would have done better to turn their attentions to purveyors of books and ideologies of the nationalist green variety, because it was the visceral tenets of Irish republicanism rather than Mao's eclectic Asiatic precepts which were about to threaten the fabric of Irish democracy.

vii. The Peril from Without: Foreign Involvement in Irish Affairs, 1945–1969

Indigenous communists formed only one part of the tapestry of potential externally inspired subversion. The other was provided by people coming to Ireland as refugees, as immigrants, or as visitors. Here antipathy to communism overlapped with other long-held policy assumptions within the bureaucracy, amongst them the imperative of maintaining the integrity of the Anglo-Irish common travel area, the general desirability of keeping foreigners out lest they pollute the body politic and take Irish jobs, and a sustained distrust of European Jews as social irritants and the devious authors of their own misfortunes first under Hitler and subsequently under Stalin.

It is not generally possible to separate fears of importing communism from the wider set of anti-immigration sentiments which the records reveal. Indeed, the files suggest that imputed communist leanings in immigration cases were simply another stick with which to beat back supplicant foreigners, rather than a major source of worry. As External Affairs explained to the Canadian embassy in 1951 in declining an approach to become involved in exchanges of information on the travel movements of communist suspects, 'the number of known Irish supporters of the Communist programme is extremely small', and the communist organization almost non-existent (although the Canadian security authorities later established good links with the Garda). Justice was, creditably, also concerned that it might be improper to disclose the names of law-abiding communists to foreign governments, a line to which it adhered for many years: in 1964 Berry loftily informed External Affairs that 'the activities of Communists, as such, are not contrary to law and it is the established practice . . . not to permit the police to disclose any police information in . . . matters of that kind'.[77] The post-war years did, however, see a few curious cases where foreigners were suspected of espionage or other clandestine activities. In 1948 two central Europeans were denounced to the Irish high commission in London as secret agents.

[77] Nunan to Priestman (Canadian embassy), n.d., Feb., and Costigan (Justice) to O'Driscoll (External Affairs), 12 Oct. 1951, DFA, A55/6A; Berry (Justice) to McCann (External Affairs), 2 Oct. 1964, DFA, A55/10.

Investigations were inconclusive, although a Justice official reported ominously that 'I have heard it said' of one of them 'that his [Irish] wife's family have formed a very poor opinion of him'. Doubts about the spying allegations were increased by the fact that their author had himself just been precipitately forced out of his employment in Ireland by Justice, not on security grounds but simply because, although 'a married man', he had been discovered to be 'keeping company with and proposing to marry' the niece of a prominent Catholic clergyman.[78]

In other cases, genuine possibilities of skulduggery arose. Thus in 1955 the London correspondent of *Izvestia*, whom G2 believed to be also 'an MVD officer operating under cover', made an unauthorized visit with a delegation of Soviet scientists attending a conference. It was surmised that his real mission was to keep an eye on the scientists and to glean whatever general information he could about Ireland. More dramatically, in December of that year one of two Russian residents 'about whom we had doubts . . . has been found dead hanging from a rope in a hotel bedroom in Malahide', a mystery on which the available records are sadly incomplete. It is hardly surprising that Russian visitors continued to excite security interest: in 1964 Justice warned External Affairs about one Zhiltsov, a third secretary in the Soviet embassy in London who 'ranks as Major in the Russian Intelligence Service and is an experienced Secret Service Agent. During his stay in Dublin from 23rd to 27th December', on the face of it a curious time to forsake the cosmopolitan pleasures of London, 'he was observed to act suspiciously'.[79]

Post-war concerns about possible covert activity were not confined to the machinations of international communism. There were also problems involving individuals who came to Ireland and who were alleged to, or were known to, have acted in the Axis interest during the war. There were persistent rumours that Ireland was being used as an 'escape route for wanted Nazis etc.', and in June 1948 Bryan, whose attention had been directed to one case 'by a special source' [MI5], sought Fred Boland's help in prising information out of the Garda as 'this matter is drifting so long it has now reached the stage in which neglect may reflect on my good-will and good credit'. While he was later to deprecate the suggestion that any war criminal of any importance escaped justice via Ireland, the surviving files indicate that at the time Bryan was not so sure. There are suggestions that some suspected of complicity in atrocities, for example the Croat Archbishop Artukovich, found succour in the state through the good offices of the Catholic Church.[80]

[78] Private information.
[79] Callanan to Murphy (External Affairs), 21 Oct.; Justice to Murphy, 21 Dec. 1955, DFA, A88. The MVD was one of the forerunners of the KGB; Berry (Justice) to McCann (External Affairs), 1 Jan. 1964, DFA, A55 II. On other problems with Russian visitors, see DFA, A55/9(B)1.
[80] Bryan to Boland, 24 June, attaching copy of Bryan to Carroll (Garda), 22 June 1948, DFA, P/168; Bryan interview; H. Butler, 'The Artukovich file', in *Escape from the Anthill* (Mullingar, 1985), 121–8.

Rumours also grew in the 1950s that Germans buying land in Ireland were acting in the interests of wanted ex-Nazis. The most celebrated such purchaser was the flamboyant Otto Skorzeny, famous for his rescue of Mussolini from captivity in 1943. Skorzeny had been acquitted of war crimes charges, ironically largely due to the evidence of a British agent who had suffered horribly at German hands, but he remained an object of interest to the British and American governments because of his alleged links with the ex-Nazi underground in Europe, the Middle East, and South America.[81] In 1957 he applied for a visa to visit Ireland, where he later bought a house and sought a right of permanent residence. Skorzeny, whose 'name appears in the British Home Office Suspect Index', was rumoured to be involved in arms smuggling to Algeria. As his interest in Ireland deepened, so official alarm grew at what he might be up to: in a rare demonstration that it retained some external sources of information, in this case probably MI5, G2 in February 1961 passed on to External Affairs and to the Garda 'information . . . from a delicate but very reliable source . . . that international arms dealers have been in touch with . . . Skorzeny with a view to setting up an arms dump in this country for later transhipment to Africa'. Shortly afterwards, he was reportedly in touch with assorted undesirables including the Belgian Quisling Leon Degrelle and Sir Oswald Mosley. While it was impossible 'to assess the reliability of this information, and although some of it sounds improbable', if any of it was accurate it could have 'international repercussions'. In fact Skorzeny seldom visited after 1960, and there is no evidence that he attempted anything untoward while in the state.[82]

Another embarrassing visitor was Sir Oswald Mosley, the erstwhile leader of British fascism. In 1946 he indicated that he would like to live in Ireland, but after consulting de Valera Justice advised him to wait for a more auspicious time. Mosley eventually took up residence in Eyrecourt in Galway in 1951, while also maintaining a home outside Paris. Dan Bryan wrote that 'there are two organisations . . . in which he might be interested, Aontas (semi-Fascist) and the German–Irish Society', the latter a body under the influence of former proponents of IRA/Nazi links, 'but there is no indication that he has been in touch with them'. In 1953 the British embassy asked External Affairs if they could observe meetings between Mosley and two of his former adherents who travelled over from Britain to see him. That Mosley might be using Ireland to plot the revival of his movement was obviously of some concern. G2 did its best to

---

[81] M. Seaman, *Bravest of the Brave: The True Story of Wing Commander 'Tommy' Yeo-Thomas—SOE Secret Agent—Codename 'The White Rabbit'* (London, 1997), 221–5.

[82] Whelan (Madrid) to External Affairs, Belton to External Affairs, 20 May and 28 June 1957; Cremin (External Affairs) to Berry (Justice), 10 Feb. 1960; Barry (G2) to Cremin, 21 Feb. and 27 July 1961, DFA, P316; Chief Superintendent Lincoln (Garda) to Hefferon (G2), 11 June 1968, MA, G2/C/1140. On another alleged international arms smuggler who wanted to set up a business in Ireland in 1950, and who may have been in touch with the IRA, see Whelan (G2) to Boland, 14 Aug. 1950, and subsequent correspondence, DFA, P168/3.

furnish External Affairs with useful material, although its capacity for inquiry was limited. The meagre information provided was evidently gleaned by quizzing employees of the Russell Hotel, and by having Mosley's visitors watched back on to the Holyhead boat. A report was duly passed on to the British embassy, as were those on further meetings. Demonstration of the embarrassment which Mosley's presence could cause was given in 1960, when the ambassador to France told External Affairs that his Japanese colleague had informed him that 'a number of his friends in Paris and elsewhere' had received a letter from Mosley, sent from Ireland, 'expressing strong criticism of both political parties in Britain'.[83]

While Irish unease at the presence of such prominent icons of the far Right was largely explained by the fact that it 'is . . . exploited to our disadvantage from time to time' in the British and American press, and by the fear that these men might be using Ireland as a base for covert activities in Europe, there was also some concern that they might inspire a fascist revival within Ireland. September 1951 saw a poster campaign in Dublin seeking recruits for a Black Legion, and funds for a 'United Christian Nationalist Party'. As the instigator was 'an adventurer with a criminal record', G2 did not at first think these enterprises would come to anything. However, in January 1953 an ex-serviceman's association received correspondence from the *Stahlhelm* ('Steel Helmet'), a sinister-sounding German veterans' organization, adverting to a forthcoming 'World Congress of ex-Soldiers' to be held in Dublin. It transpired that this was being organized by an Irishman 'of rather unbalanced mentality . . . at present in the RAF', and that it had the support of a network of extremist organizations in England and Germany. There was an obvious danger that this might attract Irish ex-servicemen and members of the defence forces into the fascist net—it was, after all, only twenty years since the Blueshirts—but the event never materialized, while the Black Legion and the United Christian Nationalist Party mercifully faded away. Other far right political and cultural organizations, for example the Irish National Socialist Workers Party which appeared in the late 1960s, came and went like the mayfly, and all belonged strictly to the lunatic fringe of Irish life. It should be noted, however, that anti-Semitic groups made some efforts to spread propaganda in the army once Ireland became involved in the UN mission in Lebanon in 1978.[84]

If neither Soviet-inspired communism nor residual international fascism proved serious external threats to Irish life, what of the covert interference of

---

[83] Costigan to Nunan, 27 Feb. 1951, Bryan to Nunan, 28 Feb., Chadwick (British embassy) to Nunan, 8 May and 18 Sept., Callanan (G2) to Nunan, 3 Oct. 1952 and 28 Feb. 1953, and MacDonald to External Affairs, 13 Oct. 1960, DFA, P211; on the German–Irish society see Bryan to Nunan, 19 Dec. 1951, DFA, P168.

[84] Cremin to Berry (Justice), 11 Oct. 1961, DFA, A74; Bryan to Nunan, 19 Dec. 1951, Callanan to Fay (External Affairs), and attached note, 26 Jan., and note of talk with Baron Von Richoften of the German embassy, 30 Jan. 1953, DFA, P168/5; H. MacDonald, *Irish Batt: The Story of Ireland's Blue Berets in the Lebanon* (Dublin, 1993), 93.

other powers in Irish affairs? As a result of its partial penetration of the Admiralty's and MI6's Irish networks during the Emergency, G2 was in possession of a good deal of information about British clandestine methods, including vague plans for a scaled-down peacetime intelligence organization in Ireland.[85] As most of the people likely to be involved had already been identified by G2, it is to be assumed that someone kept an eye on them in the post-war years. If so, surveillance appears not to have had positive results. The files and even the folklore are barren of worthwhile suspects, although they reveal the bizarre possibility that 'the British are using Castletownshend' in Cork 'as a hideout for their Cypriot spies': in 1958 a retired English officer who claimed he had been wounded in the EOKA insurgency in Cyprus arrived there to recuperate, and told a Garda that 'the appearance of a Cypriot national in this area would mean no good for him'. The Garda took 'precautions in case some subversive elements may decide to take a pot shot at him', as 'it was in Castletownshend the late Admiral Somerville was shot . . . and the reason . . . was trivial in the extreme'. A British embassy official dismissed the EOKA story as 'simply crazy', and asked that the local Garda scotch it quickly. (Curiously, however, there was a genuine Cyprus/Ireland link in being in 1958, in that representatives of EOKA and of the IRA reportedly met in London to discuss both a joint escape of prisoners from Wormwood Scrubs prison, and proposals that the IRA would train some EOKA men.)[86]

British concern about the IRA grew gradually in the mid-1960s, to the point where in 1966 a special unit was set up in the Ministry of Defence to analyse all relevant intelligence. At the time MI5 maintained that 'IRA activities constituted a "law and order" problem and were not a security one'. It must be remembered, however, that the pressures of the Cold War and of decolonization meant that the British intelligence and security services had a great deal more on their plate than Ireland. Furthermore, it is likely that MI5 would have been mindful of the difficulties for their existing liaison with G2 which could arise if other British agencies began to pry clandestinely into Irish affairs. It is consequently a fair guess that the organization which maintained the closest watch on Irish affairs from the 1940s to the 1960s, other perhaps than the ubiquitous codebreakers of GCHQ, was the RUC, because of Northern Ireland's particular concern about republican plans and activities. The RUC kept up its headquarters links with the Garda just as MI5 did with G2, individual officers maintained local understandings with their Garda counterparts in border counties, and the force undoubtedly continued to attempt to penetrate the IRA and other republican bodies on both sides of the border. There is one tantalizing scrap of evidence on such activity, a warning from Bryan to External Affairs about a 'new

---

[85] Bryan interview; private information.

[86] Report by Chief Superintendent Croke, 5 Dec., and Belton to Murphy, 16 Dec. 1958, DFA, P351A. A British counter-terrorism officer who served in Cyprus during the EOKA campaign was unable to shed light on this in 1997. Bell, *The Secret Army*, 320.

Anti-Partition League' launched at a meeting in Birmingham in 1946. He wrote that 'I am aware that one of the most active people on this committee was formerly an agent of the Special Branch of the RUC . . . in fact I am practically convinced . . . that he still is, and this really accounts for his interest in the League'.[87]

If traces of British intrigue remain elusive up to the late 1960s, so too does evidence of American covert involvement in Irish affairs. We have seen that the CIA's London station held a watching brief on Irish affairs, and it must be assumed that the FBI and other American law enforcement agencies at least maintained files on some Irish-American organizations. Broadly speaking, however, the same arguments apply as in the case of the British, though for different reasons: while Britain was relinquishing her empire, the United States was asserting itself as a world power and as the military leader of the Western world. Ireland was a stable democracy which, apart from its military neutrality and a tendency after joining the UN in 1955 to preach about the evils of nuclear weapons, was firmly in the Western camp. By 1950, furthermore, the tiny indigenous communist movement, which American diplomats had initially watched with some anxiety, was plainly going nowhere.[88]

viii. Refugees and Immigration

The final set of problems to be considered are those which arose in the sphere of immigration policy. In its declared aims and in its subtexts, this changed remarkably little in the post-war era. In contrast to the pre-war era, however, the known suffering and sheer scale of the European refugee crisis in 1945/6 makes Irish policy, both implicit and expressed in documents, appear shamefully mean-spirited. It is clear, furthermore, that what acknowledgement there was of Europe's human catastrophe was couched almost entirely in terms of the sufferings of Europe's displaced Christians.

There were two strands to post-war immigration policy. The first was the straightforward one advanced by Industry and Commerce. Ireland was simply too poor to throw open the gates to more than a handful of refugees, although judicious exceptions might be made on an individual basis for those with money or with particular skills. Irish war workers in Britain would soon flock home seeking employment, and domestic jobs had, after all, to be preserved for our own people. In fact, no such phenomenon occurred, because the British post-war reconstruction drive had an insatiable appetite for Irish labour (the opportunities in Britain were such as to create a minor crisis for the Irish middle classes, causing an acute shortage of Irish girls willing to work as domestic

---

[87] Extract from minutes of meeting, 17 Mar. 1966, COS (66) 15, in R. Aldrich (ed.), *Espionage, Security and Intelligence in Britain 1945–1970* (Manchester, 1988), 128–9; Bryan to Boland, 15 Nov. 1946, DFA, A8/1.
[88] See their reports in USNA, State Department, 841D.OOB/2-1048.

servants which the state addressed by temporarily lowering the immigration barrier to admit two hundred women, subject to medical checks for TB and VD and to their being of good character, from European countries 'where conditions do not preclude deportation in undesirable cases').[89] The quasi-economic argument against immigration could also be bolstered by pointing to factors such as the age and health of those wishing to come in—children, the sick, and the old would not be economically productive and would make disproportionate demands on the state's already stretched social services.

However small-minded such arguments may appear in the face of humanitarian catastrophe, they represented a continuation of the state's settled policy since 1922. The same cannot be said for the other grounds adduced for restricting immigration to a token number. In December 1945 Justice, apparently moved by 'the plight of millions of displaced persons in Europe', suggested that 'this country should make a contribution towards the relief of suffering by offering temporary refuge . . . to a limited number (say 250) of refugees within the next twelve months'. By Justice standards this was profligacy run riot, but it was hedged by noxious caveats. The department explained that

the immigration of Jews is generally discouraged. The wealth and influence of the Jewish community . . . appear to have increased considerably in recent years and there is some danger of exciting opposition and controversy if this tendency continues. As Jews do not become assimilated with the native population, like other immigrants, any big increase in their number might create a social problem.[90]

A similar argument—that more Jews would lead to more anti-Semitism—had been advanced by Bryan shortly before the end of the war. In future, he maintained, all aliens should only be granted rights of residence subject to strict conditions about their behaviour and activities. Furthermore,

writing with full recognition that the Jewish problem is a very thorny and contentious one and that accusations of anti-Semitism are easily aroused, I wish to state that the extent to which Dublin has become what may be described as Jew-conscious is frequently coming to the notice of this Branch. It is a problem which has only a limited security aspect but I am quite satisfied that any relaxation of the control on aliens entering this country will lead to an influx of continental Jews here, in addition to those Jews who enter here as British subjects.[91]

Despite such warnings, there were signs that the government wished to make a radical break with its previous highly restrictive immigration and refugee policies. At a meeting in December 1945 between de Valera, the minister for

---

[89] Industry and Commerce memoranda, 12 Dec. 1945, DT, S. 11007A, and 20 June 1947, and note of government decision, 27 June 1947, DT, S. 13931.

[90] Justice memorandum, 30 Nov. 1945, DT, S. 11007A.

[91] Bryan to Walshe, 6 Jan. 1945, DFA, P90.

justice, and officials of Justice, External Affairs, and Industry and Commerce, it was agreed that

our policy should be liberal and generous, due regard being had to our own interests in regard to certain matters, such as employment, foreign relations and the necessity for excluding undesirable persons . . . we should be as helpful as possible and we should try positively to give asylum to aliens seeking refuge . . . Mr Maguire [of Industry and Commerce] said that his minister had instructed him to adopt a more liberal attitude than had previously been authorised . . .

In summing up the Taoiseach again emphasised the necessity for a positive and liberal policy. Financial considerations should not be allowed to present an insuperable difficulty . . . He would be prepared to contemplate the admission, ultimately, of at least 10,000 aliens.[92]

In fact nothing of the sort happened. The government's paltry efforts, directed mainly at succouring German and Polish orphans, came in for some fierce political criticism, not on account of their lack of liberality but because they were held to be on too great a scale and to be unduly skewed towards Jews, whom Justice in 1946 termed 'a potential irritant in the body politic', at the expense of Christian children. This line of argument was vigorously advanced in the Dáil by Oliver J. Flanagan and others. In fact such guardians of Catholic ethnicity had little to fear. Immigration remained an area of post-war policy where the bureaucrats, particularly those in Justice, remained firmly in charge. Between 1945 and 1952 'about 1000 refugees', just 10 per cent of the target set by de Valera, were actually 'absorbed into the national economy'. This was largely because the process of securing even temporary admission remained so labyrinthine as to dissuade most agencies dealing with the European refugee crisis from turning to Ireland for significant help.[93] It was also the state's clear policy to demonstrate to any refugees who did get in that life for unwanted foreigners would not be a bed of roses. Official Ireland was thrown into paroxysms in 1948 by the unscheduled arrival in Cork of the *MV Victory*, a converted landing craft carrying almost four hundred Baltic refugees from Sweden to Canada, which the harbour authorities had inconveniently impounded as unseaworthy. The government's response reflected the underlying sentiment that indigent foreigners must be penalized for turning up unannounced, and deterred from thinking of Ireland as a possible home. The refugees were, accordingly, housed in miserable conditions in an army barracks outside Cork city. The Irish Red Cross, which struggled hard to alleviate their plight, was informed that the state would neither assist the refugees in moving on, nor support them if they chose to remain. The great majority of the refugees were eventually granted Canadian visas, although a handful obtained work locally and were allowed to stay.[94]

92 Note of meeting of 15 Dec. 1945, DT, S. 11007A.
93 Roche (Justice) to Moynihan, 25 Oct. 1946, DT, S. 11007.
94 Papers on this episode are in DT, S. 11107B/1.

In general, the state adhered to the view that refugees were an undesirable encumbrance. Paradoxically, efforts to address those concerns only gave further offence. In particular, the practice which Jewish refugee agencies and committees adopted of giving guarantees that groups applying for admission would move to a third country within a couple of years, and of agreeing to meet living expenses—'the bait thrown out that ample money will be forthcoming for . . . maintenance', as Peter Berry sourly put it in 1952—was then turned against its authors as evidence that Jews were engaged in organized queue-jumping at the expense of other refugees (described in uncharacteristically compassionate terms as 'thousands who have been waiting in fear and misery for an opportunity to start life anew in another country'). Berry remained fixed in his views: declaiming against Briscoe's request that ten Jewish families be admitted as refugees in 1952, he wrote that because 'Jews have remained a separate community within the community . . . and, for their numbers, appear to have disproportionate wealth and influence', to let more in would only cause social trouble. Furthermore, 'sympathy . . . has not been particularly excited by the recent news that . . . thousands are fleeing westwards because of the . . . round-up of a number of communist Jews who had been prominent in Governments . . . in East European countries'. Perhaps embarrassed by such vehemence, the government did rule that five Jewish families might be allowed in for up to two years. The offer was so slow in the making, however, that it was not taken up.[95]

The state's inability to think through its approach to immigration even after the immediate post-war refugee crisis had faded was graphically illustrated following the Hungarian rising in 1956. During Ireland's maiden speech to the UN general assembly, the minister for external affairs proudly announced that the government would accept over five hundred Hungarian refugees as permanent immigrants. While the intention was evidently to demonstrate Ireland's desire to be a good international citizen, the outcome was farcical. Still mindful of the desirability of keeping Jews out, the government was at pains to ensure that most of its guests would be Catholics. Although this seemed an obvious key to assimilation—it was, after all, the obverse of the standard line against admitting Jews—a shared devotion to the Pope proved a disappointing litmus test of the Hungarians' capacity to adapt happily to Irish life at its most dismal. Housed, again under the supervision of the Irish Red Cross, in a disused army camp in a remote quarter of County Limerick—'we are being kept in unheatable wooden huts, on unhealthy food without the possibility of schooling'—the refugees soon tired of the limited comforts available. In May 1957 the men in the party went on hunger strike to demand better conditions and the right to resettle in another country. This display of base ingratitude and the attendant

---

[95] Berry to secretary, Justice, 16 Feb. 1953, and attached undated memorandum, S. 11007B/2. Post-war immigration policy is discussed in depth in Ward, 'A big show-off', esp. 131–6.

international publicity outraged the Dáil and embarrassed the government, though the Red Cross had given ample warning that the refugees were close to mutiny, and it could only hope that some other country would offer to take them off Ireland's hands. As an interim palliative gesture, the refugees were offered the chance to relocate to an army barracks in Tipperary town, an offer which they unaccountably refused. By the autumn of 1958 most of the group had left Ireland for other countries—some even returned to Hungary—and the camp was closed down.[96] Whether or not the episode caused Justice to change its views about immigration criteria is not known. No further such expansive gestures towards refugees were made up to 1969, when emergency arrangements again fell well short of perfection.

There were significant developments in less public and less vexatious areas of immigration policy. First, the development of air travel brought with it the need for immigration officers at Irish airports to deal with an increasing number of unwanted visitors who arrived by plane. Such people never got the chance to seek legal advice: it is clear that for decades it was established policy to deal with them simply by pushing them back onto the aircraft, however eloquent their pleas or strident their demands. That policy only came under public scrutiny in the mid-1970s, after the granting of landing rights at Shannon Airport to the Soviet airline Aeroflot produced a steady stream of asylum seekers optimistically flinging themselves on the mercy of battle-hardened immigration officers. Secondly, rather to Irish surprise the British in 1952 scrapped their movement controls and proposed a reversion to the common travel area which had operated from 1922 to 1941. After some discussion this was agreed, though with de Valera's silent reservation that Ireland would 'withhold information . . . in any individual cases in which we may deem it proper to do so'. A case in point may have been that of Ralph Schoenman, an American who had been secretary to the British philosopher and veteran pacifist Bertrand Russell. In 1968 he was apparently 'on the British Visa Black List', but his Dublin lawyer was assured that he would be admitted to Ireland in the normal fashion. The system saw some readjustment in the early 1960s, as Britain's venerable preoccupation with security issues was superseded by concern at the level of coloured immigration from her former colonies: the ambassador in London wrote that 'officials will not deny privately that the coloured problem is at the root of the question'. Explaining new immigration rules, the Home Office emphasized that 'in actual practice white "non-belongers" from Commonwealth countries, not known to be criminals, will be admitted freely to Britain, and the British . . . would not expect Irish immigration officers to be too particular in regard to them': it was only coloured people whom the Home Office wished to exclude. As Britain continued to fulfil its side of the immigration bargain by turning away people

---

[96] This account relies on Ward, 'A big show-off', 137–41.

whom they knew the Irish would not want, the common travel arrangement continued to work to mutual satisfaction.[97]

ix. The State, the IRA, and Anglo-Irish Relations, 1945–1969

In 1945 the IRA was in a sorry condition. Within the state its indiscretions since launching the S-plan in 1939 had sundered the remaining bonds between it and Fianna Fáil, its rank and file had had the stuffing knocked out of them by arrest and internment, the public seemed completely indifferent to the armed republican cause, and the Garda and army had built up an intimate knowledge of the movement. In Northern Ireland, where republicans could at least count on widespread sympathy if not active support amongst the nationalist population, conditions for a revival were also inauspicious due to the vigilance of the Northern security forces and the weakness of the IRA's support structure.

In May 1945 the government agreed that the remaining seventy-two IRA internees should be 'released in small batches'. Within two months, however, Justice warned that since the first such releases 'attempts have been made to revive the IRA organisation which had more or less ceased its activities and it has already been found necessary . . . to reintern one man'. The government consequently agreed to bring into operation a tribunal to consider any further releases.[98] The IRA's early attempts to regain momentum were dealt a further blow early in 1946 with the rearrest of a number of key men from around the country. These included ex-internees who had been released towards the end of the Emergency, amongst them Michael Conway, whose death sentence for the 1936 murder of John Egan had ultimately mutated into less than two years of incarceration. The Garda success delayed IRA reorganization, although once those jailed had completed their short sentences they redoubled their efforts.[99] In the meantime, the cause was provided with another martyr in May 1946 through the death after a hunger and thirst strike of Sean McCaughey, a hardened republican who had demanded his unconditional release from internment. This embarrassed the government, though ministers must have been conscious of how quickly other IRA men released from detention had resumed their subversive activities. It may nevertheless have prompted a further review of detention policy: in December Thomas Doyle, the former Defence official jailed after the

---

[97] Bryan to Walshe, 6 Apr. 1945, DFA, A8; Justice memoranda, 3 July 1950 and 15 Feb. 1952, DT, S. 11512B and S. 15273A; note by O'Gallaghoir, 17 May 1968, DFA, A55 II; McCann to External Affairs, 3 Nov. 1962, and undated [1961] note of talk with a Home Office official by Andrew Ward (Justice), S. 15273 B/62; interview with Mr K. B. Paice, an assistant under secretary in the Home Office dealing with immigration matters in the early 1960s, 1981.

[98] Justice memoranda of 11 May and 20 July, and note of government decisions of 11 May and 24 July 1945, DT, S. 11552B.

[99] Bell, *The Secret Army*, 241–2; Bryan to minister for defence, 14 Mar. 1946, DFA, A12/1.

Magazine Fort raid, was released early and resumed his republican career. The energies of some activists were, however, temporarily siphoned off into politics, as Sean MacBride embarked on the creation of his Clann na Poblachta party. When in March 1948 MacBride found himself in an incongruous partnership in government with Fine Gael and three other parties, he promptly arranged for the unconditional release of the remaining republican prisoners.[100]

The IRA's activities in the decade after 1945 did not amount to much. There was a certain amount of drilling in some areas, an occasional anti-British gesture, a few arms were acquired by suborning soldiers or by theft, publicity material was produced from time to time, and the public flame of republicanism was kept alight through occasional street meetings and the annual Bodenstown pilgrimage. There were a couple of minor schisms—in 1950 disaffected IRA men formed an organization, named first Rosc Catha and then Arm na Saoirse (Army of Freedom), and others attempted to revive the IRB, in each case with the intention of adopting a more aggressive approach towards Northern Ireland—but these came to nothing, and their proponents were either warned off by or reassimilated into the IRA.[101] There were, however, signs of a gradual improvement in IRA organization and morale in the early 1950s, marked and sustained by a number of arms raids on military installations in Northern Ireland and Britain. Not all were successful—while those in Derry in 1951 and in Armagh in 1954 went well, the latter due to the IRA's success in infiltrating a volunteer into the British army, there was one heroic failure at Omagh and one fiasco at Felsted School in Essex which resulted in the jailing of three men including Cathal Goulding, later to become a left-leaning chief of staff—but they demonstrated that the movement's fighting spirit had been successfully rekindled and, because they took place outside the state and were directed against the British military, they 'aroused some measure of sympathy . . . in the public mind . . . mainly actuated by anti-partition sentiment and influences'.[102]

The gradual increase in IRA activity during the early 1950s brought some British pressure for more vigorous law enforcement by the Garda and the courts—an Irish diplomat reported from London in 1955 that 'the belief is widely held here that the IRA operates freely' within the state—but under both Fianna Fáil from 1951 to 1954, and the Costello coalition government, which relied for its majority on the support of the republican-minded Clann na Poblachta, not much could be done. There was, Fred Boland informed a British official, no question of agreeing to British suggestions that the state permit the extradition of IRA suspects, which 'would be entirely contrary to international

---

[100] Archer (BRO) to McCauley (External Affairs), 22 Jan. 1947, DFA, P115; memorandum by attorney-general, 14 Feb. 1947, and note of government decision of 5 Mar. 1948, DT, S. 13975.

[101] G2 memoranda, 11 Dec. 1951, June 1952, 11 Dec. 1953, and 27 Oct. 1954, DFA, A12/1; Bell, *The Secret Army*, 245–52.

[102] Ibid. 257–69; G2 report on IRA organization, with Callanan to Nunan, both 27 Oct. 1954, DFA, A12/1.

practice . . . something which no Irish government could contemplate in principle' and which 'Irish public opinion could never be brought to stand for',
while British complaints about inadequate Garda/RUC liaison were simply
noted. The Irish view was that republican violence inside the state was a grave
danger which had to be met with the full force of law; such activity outside the
state was a futile but understandable response to partition and to the repressive
and sectarian nature of Northern Ireland. The reality was that the IRA, while it
came under continuous pressure from the Special Branch, was no longer
regarded as a serious threat to state security. This was because of its continuing
military weakness, and because it had adopted a policy of avoiding confrontation with the security forces. This undoubtedly coloured the government's
approach to the problem of cross-border security. Even the hoary question of
sorting out the long-standing anomalies which existed in respect of extradition
for non-political offences, something which Justice, the Home Office, and the
Northern Ireland Ministry of Home Affairs had tossed about amongst themselves for decades, was deemed too sensitive for solution—the state was to sum-
mon up the courage to legislate on this only in 1965, the same year in which Sean
Lemass thumbed his nose at anti-partitionist sensibilities by paying an official
visit to Stormont to meet the prime minister of Northern Ireland, Captain
Terence O'Neill.[103]

There were considerable changes in security policy once the IRA, buoyed up
by the public impact of its cross-border activities, decided to embark on a more
sustained offensive against the Northern Ireland security forces in December
1956. This was the 'border campaign', which lasted on and off until 1962. It
brought the IRA two martyrs—Sean South and Fergal O'Hanlon—and a few
minor successes against customs posts and police barracks.[104] Inception of the
campaign, which cast embarrassing light on security on the southern side of the
border, led to considerable British pressure for a vigorous Irish response, and
repeated complaints that half-hearted law enforcement, and the weakness of
the existing Irish law, meant that the IRA could mount cross-border raids with
virtual impunity. There is little doubt that the state's initial reaction was complicated by the composition of the second Costello government, which relied
for its majority on the support of what remained of MacBride's Clann na
Poblachta. Once Fianna Fáil was returned to office in March 1957, however,
there was a marked shift in policy. While anti-partitionist rhetoric continued
unabated, practical steps were taken to deal with the IRA. Despite all the

---

[103] Boland (London) to Nunan, 2 Sept. 1954 and 12 Nov. 1955, and chargé d'affaires, London, to
External Affairs, 20 Aug. 1955, DFA, A12/1/A; Fay (External Affairs) to secretary and minister, 19 Oct.
1954, DFA, P263; Paice interview.
[104] M. L. R. Smith, *Fighting for Ireland? The Military Strategy of the Irish Republican Movement*
(London, 1995), 68–72. Smith provides a commanding analysis of post-1969 IRA strategy. The names of
O'Hanlon and of South quickly passed into popular memory through the medium of two striking songs,
'The patriot game' and 'Sean South of Garryowen'.

political sensitivities, Garda/RUC liaison apparently worked well. In addition, the deployment of extra police and soldiers in border areas was backed up by the reintroduction of internment for republican suspects in July. This was, crucially, mirrored by similar action in Northern Ireland. Brian Faulkner, a member of the Northern Ireland government during the period, was later to write that 'the vital factor in stamping out terrorism . . . was the introduction of internment' in both jurisdictions, combined with 'prompt co-operation between the Gardai and the RUC'.[105] Although sporadic attacks in Northern Ireland continued for a number of years, internment, ineffectiveness, and public indifference quickly broke the back of the IRA's campaign. In the autumn of 1958 the situation had so much improved that the Lemass government released its internees, much to British displeasure. The campaign was by then almost dead, but before it was formally ended the IRA managed to kill a couple more RUC men during a flurry of activity in 1961. There was one final and in retrospect particularly sinister twist, the assassination of an RUC constable in County Fermanagh, apparently sanctioned because the officer was believed to be collecting intelligence in the locality. The premeditated nature of the murder set it apart from the other five RUC and indeed the eight IRA deaths during the campaign. It was a harbinger of the tactics of the succeeding generation of IRA men. The government reacted to the border killings not by reintroducing internment but by reactivating the military tribunal. Whether or not this was necessary remains a matter of opinion: despite its killings the IRA appeared worn out. It was consequently no great surprise when in February 1962 its army council ordered a cessation 'in view of the general situation', a suitably vacuous phrase with which to end so inept a campaign.[106] In succeeding years a handful of stunts were mounted within the state by republicans—the felling of a few telegraph poles during a private visit by Princess Margaret in 1965, the firing of shots at a British naval vessel in Cork by the maverick Richard Behal, the blowing up of Nelson's Pillar in O'Connell Street in March 1966, and a series of bank robberies by the radical splinter group Saor Éire which began in 1967—but the republican leadership appeared bent on moving away from armed and towards political action.

The dismal failure of the 1956–62 campaign, coupled with the time for reflection and debate conferred by prolonged incarceration, saw a recrudescence of vaguely Marxist thought amongst some of the leading activists. This rekindled the old tensions between the pure physical force men and those who argued that partition could only be ended and a just Ireland created through a revolution which embraced radical economic and social change as well as the reclamation of Northern Ireland. Taking heart from the rhetoric of anti-colonialism, pro-

---

[105] B. Faulkner, *Memoirs of a Statesman* (London, 1978), 24.
[106] Coogan, *The IRA*, 386–418; Bell, *The Secret Army*, 310–34 (including the quotation from the army council announcement).

ponents of a decisive widening of the IRA's agenda argued that what was needed was a war of national liberation, and that this could only be won by a movement which mobilized the people for revolutionary change. By 1962, within the IRA leadership the initiative was held by men who drew their inspiration at least as much from James Connolly as from Patrick Pearse.

This development was significant for a number of reasons. First, it altered the preoccupations of the republican movement, both by promoting debate on the link between economic and political oppression and by highlighting the reactionary nature of independent Ireland. In this sense it must have appeared a modernizing force, enabling republicans to place their struggle in the wider context of the world-wide battle for national self-determination and for socialism. Secondly, by so doing it reintroduced complications into the republican movement's relationship with the state not seen since the failure of the Republican Congress in 1934, and it rekindled the old fear of communist influence on the IRA not only in official circles but amongst traditionalist republicans. That had some impact amongst Irish-Americans, whose sympathy for the IRA was at least equalled by their general loathing for socialism and their fear of international communism. Thirdly, the temporary predominance of the republican socialist paradigm within the IRA leadership not only sowed the seeds of future dissension, but lured some of the movement's brightest minds into the byways of doctrinal exegesis. It also sucked republican sympathizers into campaigns for social justice, for world peace, and, in Northern Ireland, for civil rights which, while not antithetical to the movement's traditional concerns, tended to blur the issues. Protesting against the Vietnam war or nuclear weapons outside the American embassy was all very well, but what had it got to do with the struggle against partition? However intellectually fulfilling for the participants, too much talk and too broad a set of political concerns held the danger of diverting energies from purposeful action on the fundamental problem of the British presence and unionist supremacy in Northern Ireland. Finally, the shift in thinking had the effect of widening the gulf between those within the republican movement, mainly southerners, who talked about Northern Ireland, and those who actually had to live there. This tension was to result in a spectacular parting of the ways in 1970, as the republican movement struggled to cope with the unfolding crisis inside Northern Ireland.

Despite the abandonment of the border campaign in 1962, the Northern authorities remained apprehensive about a renewal of IRA activities. At a meeting in October 1963, Peter Berry told the Northern Ireland Minister for Home Affairs William Craig and his permanent secretary that reports of an upsurge in training activities in border areas were without foundation. Furthermore, from Berry's account it seems clear that C3 was in closer communication with the RUC Special Branch and with Scotland Yard than Craig himself had been aware of: 'I formed the impression that the Minister (and the Secretary) knew very little about the IRA and the police machinery for dealing with the organisation'. In the event, Berry was vindicated. Three years later, when the fiftieth anniversary of the Easter Rising again set alarm bells ringing both north and south, Berry was surprised to discover that Garda headquarters had set up a radio network along the border in expectation of a renewed IRA campaign, despite authoritative Special Branch intelligence that no serious action was likely.[107] He directed that this be dismantled, a prudent measure as the Northern authorities subsequently approached him 'for a meeting between our respective Ministers for a joint plan against anticipated IRA violence'. It would have been difficult to refuse this request had the Garda preparations not been quietly rescinded.[108] In the event, republican commemorative violence was confined to the destruction of Nelson's Pillar, a petty act which deprived O'Connell Street of its main focal point.

x. Conclusion

The decades between 1945 and 1969 saw a transformation in the state's relations with the outside world. While military neutrality was elevated from being a doctrine of necessity to one apparently based on moral considerations, the practical steps which Ireland took to integrate into the post-war international community demonstrated a willingness to accept some of the responsibilities as well as the pleasures of independent statehood. Once acquired in 1955, UN membership was enthusiastically embraced as a means not only of securing protection from aggression but of making a positive contribution to the promotion of world peace and the betterment of mankind. In its campaign to join the Common Market in the early 1960s, itself a dramatic demonstration of Lemass's success in weaning the country away from the protectionist illusions which had crippled its post-war economic and social development, the government explicitly—albeit delicately—acknowledged that this would eventually entail participation in the maintenance of the security of the evolving European economic and political alliance. In the meantime, however, what remained of the army was left with the impossible charge of developing and maintaining a credible system of independent defence, a doctrine in which no one remotely believed. Once police primacy in internal security work had been re-established in 1945, what remained of the defence forces after retrenchment were confined to a largely ritualistic existence until 1956, when the IRA's new border campaign, and the almost simultaneous opening up of opportunities for UN service, breathed new life into the army.

While the problem of partition continued to overhang Anglo-Irish relations,

---

[107] Browne, 'The Berry File', 74–5.   [108] Ibid. 45

the period saw the continuation of the discreet security and immigration understandings which had been reached before or during the Emergency, and the restoration of security links with the United States government. Time and again ministers stressed that ideologically they stood with the Western democracies. This, the dictates of contiguity, and the hidden benefits which co-operation conferred on the state in matters such as immigration control, ensured that there continued to be considerable willingness to help out Britain wherever possible, provided only that such collaboration was decorously shrouded and that it did not conflict with Irish interests

The republican movement continued to pose the state intermittent though sometimes acute security problems. In its generally relaxed policy towards the IRA in the immediate post-war years the government undoubtedly underestimated the republican movement's remarkable capacity for survival in inauspicious times. It also let the IRA off the hook by not hammering home the extent of German/IRA collusion and the threat which that had posed to national survival. The internal politics of the first Costello government produced a further softening of the official line, with the precipitate release of two unrepentant killers of Gardai and a general easing of pressure on the republican movement. It was not until 1957, in the face of the IRA's border campaign, that a new Fianna Fáil government resorted to more robust tactics against republican activists through the reintroduction of internment. This was an explicitly temporary expedient, though a highly effective one.

The early 1960s saw a growth in intellectual cross-currents between republicanism and the wider world of revolutionary and anti-colonialist politics. While these theoretically added a new dimension to the threat which the IRA posed to the Irish state and society, in reality these external doctrinal influences had a generally positive diversionary effect on the republican movement, both in diluting the atavistic, sectarian venom of traditional republicanism and in distracting the IRA leadership from addressing purely Irish problems and imperatives. But developments across the border were about to throw Northern Ireland into turmoil, and also to precipitate the greatest domestic crisis which independent Ireland had faced since the definitive subordination of the military to civilian rule in 1924.

8

Unresolved Questions: Defence, Security, and Subversion since 1969

i. Introduction

The state's experience since the late 1960s in the realms of internal security and external defence, while linked so much to the old problems of partition and republicanism, must be seen against the broader backdrop of the modernization and internationalization of the Irish economy, and of the transformation of the country's relations both with the United Kingdom and with continental Europe.

ii. The Irish State and the Northern Ireland Crisis, 1969–1970

Despite the rash of civil rights marches, demonstrations, counter-demonstrations, and riots seen in Northern Ireland in 1968, the Irish government and the political system generally were quite unprepared for the serious and sustained street violence which broke out in 1969. Public opinion was unanimous in its support of nationalist demands for equal civil rights, but this was hardly evidence of a new radicalism on the partition issue: in fact it was paralleled in Britain, where '*bien pensant* opinion' accepted the claims of the civil rights movement uncritically, while 'dismissing Unionist opposition . . . as utterly prejudiced and benighted'.[1] For a combination of reasons, not least wishful thinking, the Irish state appears to have laid no plans to cope with the possible consequences of renewed political disturbances north of the border. Neither did the British government take any significant precautionary steps, leaving affairs entirely in the inadequate hands of the Stormont administration and its security forces.[2] The pot of sectarian passion bubbled fitfully throughout the autumn and winter of 1968/9. Political feeling ran high, and outbreaks of

---

[1] J. Grigg, *The History of the Times*, vi: *The Thomson years 1966–1981* (London, 1993), 109.
[2] J. B. Bell, *The Irish Troubles: A Generation of Violence 1967–1992* (London, 1993), 77–9. Like his *The Secret Army*, this work while useful has its weaknesses. For a critique see E. O'Halpin, 'Republican Standards', *TLS*, 1 Oct. 1993.

violence became commonplace between civil rights demonstrators and the RUC or Protestant counter-demonstrators. The pot dramatically boiled over following the annual Apprentice Boys march in Derry on 12 August 1969, when the 'Battle of the Bogside' broke out after nationalist demonstrators clashed with the RUC, a force then incapable of discharging its public order responsibilities either impartially or effectively and which relied extensively on the part-time USC (Ulster Special Constabulary, generally known as the 'B Specials'), a frankly partisan and ill-disciplined body.[3] The mayhem in Derry in turn inspired widespread attacks by Protestant mobs, sometimes including B Specials and with the apparent connivance of the full-time RUC, on Catholic districts elsewhere in Northern Ireland. The worst violence took place in Belfast, which saw the destruction of hundreds of houses in nationalist streets, the deaths of seven people over a three-day period, and the flight across the border of over three thousand people burnt out or intimidated out of their homes.

The government's political response to the unfolding events in Northern Ireland was confused. It supported the demands of Northern nationalists for equal political rights, and it condemned the failure of the Stormont government to administer the law even-handedly and to protect Catholic areas, particularly in Belfast. When Derry erupted, as the government had warned the British it would if the Apprentice Boys march was allowed to proceed as planned, the dilemma which faced the Irish cabinet was acute. At least one minister, Neil Blaney, argued that the army should be prepared to move into nationalist parts of Northern Ireland, such as Derry, Newry, Dungannon and South Armagh, not to reclaim them for the nation but rather to defend Catholic districts which they feared would otherwise be overrun by armed Protestant rioters acting in collusion with the Northern security forces. The government would then explain to the British that the troops were there only 'in a purely peace-keeping role', a formulation which they thought would assuage British concerns about the uninvited presence of a foreign army on United Kingdom soil. In fact the army was utterly unprepared for such a role, having neither the men, the equipment, the information, nor the plans necessary to mount such operations. In any case, even the most cursory glance at a map should have shown the utter implausibility of attempting to seize and to hold any ground within Northern Ireland. Furthermore, the scheme took no account of how unionists might react, both within the annexed areas and in other places such as Belfast where Catholic enclaves were and would remain defenceless, or of the possible British military response.[4] More cautious counsels prevailed in cabinet. The taoiseach Jack Lynch made a television broadcast in which, while he declared that the state could 'not stand by' while innocent people were being endangered in Northern Ireland, he prudently limited positive actions to the strengthening of border

---

[3] Hennessey, *A History of Northern Ireland*, 150–4.
[4] S. Brady, *Arms and the Men: Ireland in Turmoil* (Dublin, 1971), 35.

security, the establishment of field hospitals and refugee camps, and the dispatch of the Minister for External Affairs to the United Nations to request international intervention, the last a predictably barren gesture. An international publicity campaign was also launched, and temporary press attachés were dispatched to Irish diplomatic missions abroad to spread the official gospel that only the ending of partition could bring peace to Northern Ireland. Finally, the government agreed to provide an initial sum of one hundred thousand pounds for the relief of distress in Northern Ireland, to be controlled by the minister for finance Charles Haughey.

The deployment of British troops to protect nationalist areas after 15 August was successful in restoring public order. In addition, in the private words of the British home secretary to a *Times* journalist, it 'radically changed the situation' because the Stormont administration was 'no longer in full control of Ulster'.[5] The Irish government's public reaction to the northern crisis had the desired effect within the state of calming things down. However, other arrangements which were secretly made were to have precisely the opposite effect. On 13 August, at the height of the Derry violence and as the disturbances in Belfast began which were to cost seven lives over three days, a cabinet subcommittee on Northern Ireland was established. In apparent defiance of common sense, none of the ministers whose departments were most obviously involved in aspects of the Northern issue—Defence, Justice, External Affairs, taoiseach—nor the attorney-general, were involved. Of the four ministers on the committee, three came from border counties (Blaney and Joseph Brennan from Donegal, Paudraic Faulker from Louth). The fourth, Charles Haughey, was from Dublin. In practice Blaney and Haughey, widely regarded as particularly able and energetic ministers, were the only ones who counted.[6] The committee as such apparently never functioned or reported to the full cabinet. Blaney was no milk-and-water nationalist but a man of strong republican views, who believed that Northern nationalists could never be free until the link with Britain was broken and who had chafed at the restraining bit of his colleagues' fatalism about partition for years. By contrast Haughey had not been seen as a particularly prominent nationalist: it may be that it was thought that he would counteract the supposed border hotheads.[7] If that was the plan, it was a dismal failure.

For policy purposes Northern Ireland in 1969 might as well have been North Korea, so sparse was the reliable information available. In order to repair this deficit after the August disturbances, a number of army officers were dispatched north under cover to collect intelligence and to assess political feeling. In furtherance of the possibility of intervening, the army also embarked on a

---

[5] James Callaghan's off-the-record briefing, 15 August 1969, quoted in Grigg, *The Times*, 111.
[6] Blaney was described by one experienced official as much the best minister he had ever worked with. Interview, March 1996.
[7] B. Arnold, *Haughey: His Life and Unlucky Deeds* (London, 1993; paperback edn., 1994), 75.

series of 'purely military' studies of Northern Ireland, something which it had not done systematically since 1925—one former staff officer recalled the prodigious efforts which went into trying to assemble an accurate organization chart of the RUC on the basis mainly of gossip, before it was realized that the information was available in Northern Ireland official publications on sale in Dublin. Military involvement did not, however, stop at the planning stage.[8] Captain James Kelly of army intelligence had been in Derry during the August disturbances while officially on holiday, and had then had informal discussions with nationalists and republicans in various parts of Northern Ireland. On returning to duty he was detailed to develop these contacts further. Over the following months he became a crucial link between Northern republicans and a coterie of ministers and others in Dublin. Kelly reported mainly to Haughey and Blaney: the extent to which his superiors and the minister for defence were briefed on all his activities later became a matter of dispute, as the schemes in which he became embroiled threatened to bring down the government.

The clandestine arrangements made were apparently designed to succour northern nationalists in their hour of need by enabling them to defend their communities from further attacks. There were a number of strands to the action taken. First, a handful of men from Derry were given weapons training at an army camp in Donegal. Whether or not these men were being trained purely to contribute to the protection of their areas in the event of further assaults on the scale already seen in Belfast, or whether the intention was to build up a nationalist fifth column to aid an Irish army incursion, remains uncertain. In any event, they were hastily sent away once the press got hold of the story.[9] Secondly, some of the government money assigned for Northern relief was channelled to the families of people manning the barricades in nationalist areas. Public money was also used for an inept foray into the murky world of unattributable propaganda: this was *The Voice of the North*, a rabidly nationalist publication 'written by Northerners for Northern readership', although the taoiseach cut off the funding when he learnt of it. Plans were also made for an illicit mobile radio station, which would broadcast nationalist material at points along the border.[10] More importantly, however, in October 1969 a scheme was launched to import arms through the state for transfer to the 'citizens defence committees' which had sprung up in nationalist enclaves throughout Northern Ireland during the summer disturbances. This would be funded partly from the Northern relief grant. The plan undoubtedly had Blaney's blessing, although Haughey later denied all knowledge. It has also been claimed that it was known

---

[8] Conversation with a former staff officer, June 1992; *Committee of Public Accounts: Interim and Final Report (Order of the Dáil of 1 Dec. 1970)* (Dublin, 1972), 61–3.

[9] Evidence of Colonel Hefferon, director of intelligence from 1962 to 1969, *Final Report*, 647; P. Bishop and E. Mallie, *The Provisional IRA* (1st edn., London, 1987; Corgi edn., 1988), 129; J. Kelly, *Orders for the Captain?* (Dublin, 1971), 12–13.

[10] Brady, *Arms and the Men*, 90–7.

in outline to a third member of the cabinet, the minister for defence Jim Gibbons. A generally reliable history of the Provisional IRA goes further, saying that for a time in 1969/70 it was government policy to get arms covertly to northerners for defensive purposes. This remains the view of Captain James Kelly, whose successful defence against subsequent criminal charges was predicated on the argument that through Blaney, Haughey, and Gibbons the government as a whole had been well aware of what was going on.[11]

The Special Branch had for some months been reporting to Peter Berry in Justice on Captain Kelly's northern IRA contacts, most importantly in respect of a meeting with leading republicans in a County Cavan hotel in October 1969 in which he promised that the government would obtain weapons for use in Northern Ireland. It also reported that Kelly had met the IRA chief of staff Cathal Goulding. As evidence accumulated of clandestine arrangements in place or in prospect which went far beyond overt policy on succouring Northern nationalists, Berry endeavoured to obtain the political authority necessary to take decisive action. For months he was unsuccessful: what was apparently his own edited account, published after his death, suggests that the ministers whom he approached in essence did not want to know what was going on. There were also claims that Scotland Yard had photographed and passed on to the Garda warnings about two Irishmen who had been shadowed in London while discussing arms purchases with a supposed middle man. Dublin was awash with rumours, including the charge that Fianna Fáil was attempting to split the IRA, using money and guns to seduce Northern republicans from the Marxist faith, and the government remained immobilized by its own divisions.[12] The importation plan almost came to fruition in April 1970 when, having failed to get weapons in by sea, Captain Kelly, who has always maintained that he was acting quite properly under orders, arranged for a consignment to be flown into Dublin airport, from where they would be quietly transferred to a lorry for eventual movement to a monastery pending agreement on their distribution. (Apparently unknown to him, however, the IRA, who were to collect the weapons from the airport, intended to bring them north there and then.)[13] The scheme was thwarted by the vigorous actions of the Special Branch and of Peter Berry. Fearing that ministerial indecision might once again prevail, he directed the Special Branch to surround the airport's cargo terminal, and he then approached the octogenarian president Eamon de Valera, the founding father of Fianna Fáil. De Valera advised Berry to tell the taoiseach that action was imperative.[14]

Berry's actions were decisive. When it became clear that the weapons shipment would be impounded if it arrived, it was cancelled. Lynch then began a

---

[11] Arnold, *Haughey*, 87–100; FitzGerald, *All in a Life*, 92–7; Bishop and Maille, *The Provisional IRA*, 129.　　　　　　　　　[12] Brady, *Arms and the Men*, 85–9, 116.

[13] V. Browne, 'The Arms Crisis 1970: The Inside Story', *Magill*, 3/8 (May 1980), 51.

[14] Extracts from Berry's memoir are in Browne, 'The Berry File', 39–75.

series of interviews with the main protagonists, and initiated other inquiries. At the end of April he invited both Haughey and Blaney to resign from the government, which they declined to do. It may be that he was preparing the ground carefully for their dismissal, but his apparent prevarication in the face of compelling evidence caused alarm and apprehension in security circles. On 5 May Lynch was approached by the leader of the opposition Liam Cosgrave, who told him that he had information that ministers had been involved in an illegal conspiracy. This approach had historical resonances—Cosgrave's own father William T. had been faced with an analogous crisis in the early months of 1924 which had culminated in the army mutiny, and like Lynch he had been *hors de combat* for medical reasons as the drama unfolded—and it hastened Lynch's next steps if it did not force them. He eventually won through, despite some turmoil within his party. Lynch secured the resignation of Michael O'Morain, the ailing and ineffectual minister for justice, belatedly took the difficult decision to ask president de Valera to dismiss both Haughey and Blaney from the government, and accepted the resignation in protest of Kevin Boland, who saw the taoiseach's actions as a betrayal of northern nationalists and an abrogation of the state's constitutional claim to sovereignty over the whole island of Ireland. Haughey, Blaney, Captain Kelly, the northern republican John Kelly, and Albert Luykx, a friend and neighbour of Blaney's and a naturalized citizen who had come to Ireland after imprisonment in Belgium for Flemish nationalist activities and alleged collusion with the German occupation forces during the Second World War, were accused of conspiracy to import arms. All were eventually cleared of the charges laid against them, but the court proceedings and the subsequent Dáil inquiry left no room for doubt about the reality of clandestine encouragement for possible armed defensive action by nationalists within Northern Ireland. The key questions left hanging were the degree of contemporaneous knowledge of other ministers of these plans, and the extent to which those involved, other than the IRA, genuinely believed that the weapons promised would be used purely for defensive purposes if nationalist enclaves were again attacked.[15]

What of the consequences? The arms scheme was an indictment not only of the competence of its authors but of their political judgement. By the time that the scheme was hatched in October 1969, circumstances in Northern Ireland had changed dramatically. Public order had been restored through the deployment of British troops, an initiative generally welcomed in nationalist areas, the immediate crisis had passed, and many of the Northern refugees had gone back. There clearly remained a political vacuum, but placing more weapons in nationalist hands was hardly going to improve the situation. Furthermore, by the autumn of 1969 the Northern IRA had secured complete control of the

---

[15] Kelly, *Orders*, 22.

citizens defence committees and, as Garda intelligence indicated, were gearing up not to repel further pogroms but for offensive action against the Northern state. Whatever justification there might have been in the heat of the moment in mid-August 1969 for getting guns to people trying to keep armed mobs from burning them out of their homes had long gone with the restoration of public order, the announcement of the phasing out of the B Specials, and the move towards reforming and disarming the RUC. The British government was also clearly committed to the introduction of measures to address specific nationalist grievances in other matters such as housing and local government elections. In such circumstances, it was monumental folly to seek to put guns in the hands of Northern republicans, whose aim was the destruction of the Northern state rather than the acquisition of equal rights and security within it.

The eventual inquiry by the Dáil committee of public accounts (PAC) into the misappropriation of the money, while unable to provide a definitive account of what had happened to every penny, produced a great deal of evidence from witnesses about the diversion of funds for arms purchases and other clandestine activities, about Garda intelligence on the republican movement and its links with some ministers, and about the army's involvement in the covert schemes. Chief Superintendent Fleming of the Special Branch made very strong claims of apparent collusion over a period of months between Haughey and the IRA, and in so doing disclosed the extent of police penetration of parts of the republican movement.[16] The army was embarrassed by disclosure of Captain Kelly's involvement in the importation scheme, and by his strong argument that he had simply been following orders—while he had been dealing mainly with Haughey and Blaney, he maintained that the director of intelligence and the minister for defence had been kept in the picture, and that he was sacrificed to protect the government. (One member of the PAC later commented that until he took part in its inquiry into the missing funds, he had thought having both military and police intelligence organizations was unnecessary. After it, he thought it essential because they could keep an eye on each other's activities.)[17] The plot also raised grave doubts in Britain about Irish bona fides, weakening the state's ability to influence British policymaking on Northern Ireland.[18] The cabinet uncertainty which had allowed the clandestine initiatives to mature, and which undoubtedly had an impact on the enforcement of the law in respect of republican activities seen as relating primarily to Northern Ireland, meant that for nine months before and after the definitive split within the republican movement the IRA had a good deal of room for manoeuvre south of the border.[19] Finally, the fact that the lengthy

---

[16] Evidence of Chief Superintendent Fleming, 9 Feb. and 3 Mar. 1971, *Final Report*, 417–28, 745–53.
[17] Comment of Dr Garret FitzGerald at a meeting of the Irish Historical Society, 11 Oct. 1996.
[18] M. Rees, *Northern Ireland: A Personal Perspective* (London, 1983), 15–16.
[19] Brady, *Arms and the Men*, 114–16.

hiatus after Lynch received definite information about the plot was only ended by the leak of Special Branch information to the opposition appears to have tainted some senior police officers in Fianna Fáil eyes. The problem of the real or imagined politicization of the senior ranks of the Garda was to continue to dog the force at least until the end of the Haughey era in 1992.

Peter Berry, who with Chief Superintendent Fleming emerged with considerable credit from the debacle, did not gain much from the risks which he took. The unaccustomed glare of publicity took its toll—he unsuccessfully sued *The Irish Times* for publishing a photograph of republican demonstrators outside his home holding up placards denouncing him, and he was reported to be one of the intended victims of a kidnap plot hatched by Saor Éire, which had carried out a number of bank robberies, in one of which an unarmed Garda had been killed—and when he retired early in January 1971, he claimed that pledges about his pension rights were not fully honoured.[20]

If the arms crisis had a positive aspect, it was that it forced the government and the political system to begin to face up to the Northern Ireland problem as something which had to be addressed by patient diplomacy and by cautious statecraft rather than by impetuous speeches and nod and wink encouragement of irredentist militancy, and as a matter which required the constant attention of the serving taoiseach and of a standing cabinet committee of appropriate ministers. But both the state and Northern Ireland were to pay dearly over many years for the mistakes made between August 1969 and May 1970.

iii. The Evolution of Mainstream Republican Subversion within the State since 1969

The outbreak and extent of political violence in Northern Ireland took the IRA largely unawares. While there was undoubtedly considerable republican sympathy for and some influence on the Northern Ireland civil rights campaign, it was a broadly based movement which drew its inspiration less from revolutionary struggles elsewhere than from the overwhelmingly peaceful American civil rights campaigns, where the focus had been on equality within rather than on separation from the existing state: the Derry marchers of 5 October 1968 were somewhat dismissively described by one Derry journalist as 'a collection of left wing entities from all parts of Ireland, and even from Britain'.[21] So far as the Northern Ireland administration and most unionist politicians were concerned, however, the civil rights movement was simply a republican front.

In December 1969 the leadership of the republican movement, both political and military, split definitively on ideological and on broadly geographic lines.

---

[20] Browne, 'The Berry File', 73.   [21] Brady, *Arms and the Men*, 10.

The bulk of the southerners endorsed the then intellectually fashionable argument that what was now needed was a pan-island national liberation front, which would combine non-sectarian and essentially defensive violence with a political strategy embracing the abandonment of the policy of abstention from the Irish, the British, and the Stormont parliaments. At the Sinn Féin ard fheis, held in the incongruously bourgeois setting of Dublin's Intercontinental Hotel on 11 January 1970, this approach secured the backing of a clear majority of the delegates present. As in 1925, however, when de Valera and a group of TDs left Sinn Féin after another acrimonious ard fheis, it was the minority on the day who emerged the long-term victors. Led by Sean MacStiofain, but dominated by Northern republicans, the dissident group sought and received the benediction of the veteran republican and survivor of the legitimist Second Dáil Tom Maguire, established a Provisional army council and a supporting Sinn Féin party, and set about making war in Northern Ireland.[22]

At the time of the split it was by no means clear that the Provisionals would be the long-term victors in the struggle for custody of the republican flame. Their opponents retained many of the assets of the republican movement—weapons, facilities, premises, money—as well as its lines of contact with Eastern Bloc countries which might be expected to lend a hand. But the Provisionals had the priceless asset of credibility and legitimacy on the nationalist streets of Northern Ireland. In Ireland and in America, that translated into growing command of republican opinion, which in turn ensured that the organization's initial weaknesses of finance, propaganda, and weaponry were gradually overcome. While they retained some interest in wider issues of social justice at home and abroad and of international revolution—in 1984 a leading republican political strategist publicly remarked that he was a 'socialist first and a republican [only] second'—the IRA never let this get in the way of their core activities in Ireland, the United Kingdom, and further afield.[23] The patina of Marxist internationalism which was to be found in the speeches and statements of Provisionals at conferences in Europe and elsewhere, while it put the wind up some intelligence and counter-terrorism analysts, was conspicuous by its absence in republican appeals to their key Irish-American audience. There, the Provisionals happily purveyed an unreconstructed, visceral anti-British rhetoric calculated to warm the heart of even the most fervent anti-communist.

The Provisional IRA suffered many setbacks, both military and political, in its first years. Its leadership had agreed to use the traditional weapon of the hunger strike as a means of applying pressure when arrested by the Garda. Irish sensitivities were such that this initially worked well—Joe Cahill and other prominent figures were released for lack of evidence after refusing food.

---

[22] Bishop and Mallie, *The Provisional IRA*, 132–8.
[23] In a discussion with a group of American students accompanied by this writer, Derry, Oct. 1984.

However, Sean MacStiofain, who had initially appeared set fair to become another Terence MacSwiney, eventually abandoned first his thirst and then his hunger strike when it became clear that the government would not let him go. This humiliation, an unexpected victory for the state, finished him in the republican movement. It also temporarily removed such strikes from the republican armoury of weapons to be used against the state.[24] Despite such setbacks, however, the harsh reality is that in the post-1969 phase of the troubles the mainstream republican movement became very much more efficient than it had been since 1922 in mounting a sustained terrorist campaign, whilst gradually building a considerable political presence in precisely those areas in Northern Ireland which have suffered most from the perpetuation of violence and of the concomitant state security presence. This was not simply a function of modernity. After all, the Irish and British security forces engaged in combating the IRA had rather greater access to sophisticated equipment and the like—as one RUC Special Branch officer, admittedly speaking somewhat in his cups, put it in 1992, not one terrorist 'boy' in his area could so much as leave a house without the police knowing, an omniscience which begs the question of why so many terrorist operations continued to be mounted.[25] Unlike both their predecessors and their fringe competitors in both parts of Ireland, the Provisionals have shown the capacity to develop, to sustain, and to adapt a military strategy which, however incoherent, counter-productive, inconsistent, and immoral it may be, and however doomed to ultimate failure it may appear to be in terms of its teleological objectives, has not hampered the development of a deep-rooted political base within the nationalist population in Northern Ireland, and has succeeded in drawing initially the British and subsequently the Irish and even the American administrations into secret and more recently into semi-public negotiations with Sinn Féin.[26] The Provisionals also proved able to respond to shifts in tactics by the British and Irish security forces, and they succeeded in compartmentalizing the IRA's operational and support structures for damage limitation purposes as never before, so that even significant breaches of security or high-level betrayals did not cripple the organization. (In this they were probably helped by the 1970 split, as it appears that the Garda Special Branch's main informants were in what became Official Sinn Féin and the Official IRA.)[27]

The Provisionals took a crucial decision soon after their foundation: while they did not recognize the southern state, they would not confront it directly. It was instead to be a base for operations, support, fund-raising, and refuge, and in border areas for the mounting of attacks from inside Irish territory. The

---

[24] Bishop and Mallie, *The Provisional IRA*, 243–5, 358.

[25] Conversation with an RUC officer, 1992.

[26] Smith, *Fighting for Ireland?*, 91–227; B. O'Brien, *The Long War: IRA and Sinn Féin, 1985 to Today* (Dublin, 1993), 281–95.

[27] This was certainly the educated guess of Dan Bryan in 1983.

doctrine had the advantage that, while it did not prevent some conflict with the army and Garda, it initially allowed the IRA to pass themselves off as the defenders of Northern Catholics rather than as a cancer in the body politic of independent Ireland, and that in turn strengthened the political argument in the south against undue repression. Despite the Provisionals' self-denying ordinance eschewing offensive action against the security forces, however, the Northern crisis soon brought a marked increase in political violence within the state. This was partly the inevitable consequence of the reliance of the IRA and of splinter groups on bank robberies and kidnappings, activities which naturally attracted Garda interdiction and which saw the murder of a number of members of the force, most of them unarmed (or if armed, caught totally unawares, as was the case with detectives Hand in 1984 and McCabe in 1996, each killed while escorting money shipments). It also resulted from the IRA's wish to terrorize or kill individuals for their real or suspected anti-republican sympathies: thus Senator Billy Fox of Fine Gael, a Protestant from County Monaghan, was pursued and shot dead by an IRA gang raiding a Protestant home near the border town of Clones in 1974 (at the time IRA apologists first denied responsibility, then dismissed this murder as being accidental and complained that the jailing for life of some of the perpetrators was unduly harsh). There were also cases where the IRA plainly calculated that the publicity benefits of individual atrocities would outweigh the opprobrium which they would earn. In this category can be placed the murders of the British ambassador Christopher Ewart Biggs and his secretary in Dublin in 1976, and of Earl Mountbatten and British and Irish members of his fishing party in Sligo in 1979 (at the time some sympathizers justified the killing on the characteristically specious grounds that as an admiral of the fleet the 79-year-old Mountbatten remained technically a serving officer). Those assassinations were perhaps the greatest of many humiliations inflicted on the state by the republican movement after 1969.[28] They raised grave questions about the efficiency of the Irish security apparatus which have never been publicly addressed.

Provisional IRA spectaculars within the state, or those mounted from it—for example, the 1987 Enniskillen bombing—carried with them the danger of provoking a strong response not only in terms of an upsurge in searches and arrests, but of changes in the framework of anti-terrorist laws. In recent years, and in particular since the initial IRA ceasefire of August 1994, it appears that such atrocities were more carefully controlled so as not to damage Sinn Féin's evolving political strategy. It is also obvious that the latter party was remarkably successful in representing even acts which caused enormous public revulsion and anger—for example the murders of Detective McCabe in Adare in 1996, and of two RUC officers in Lurgan in 1997—as proof not of the need for a renewed

---

[28] FitzGerald, *All in a Life*, 126, 311; conversation with an IRA apologist, 1975.

security clampdown, but of the urgency of accommodating Sinn Féin in all-party talks without requiring the IRA to pass under the yoke of a permanent and credible cessation of violence. Atrocities which in the 1970s and 1980s might have prompted a legislative response inspired only temporary condemnation followed by renewed *pourparlers* with Sinn Féin. The extent to which this represented consummate damage limitation by the Sinn Féin leadership, as opposed to the deliberate use of IRA violence to remind the British and Irish governments of the alternatives to constructive engagement with the republican movement, remains a matter of opinion.

The Provisional movement's gradual engagement with politics from the mid-1980s caused a significant and telling rift within the republican family when a coterie of traditionalists, outraged at the 1986 decision to end abstentionism as a policy for elections to the Dáil, split away to form Republican Sinn Féin and claimed to be the true and only heirs of republican legitimacy. For some years this development appeared inconsequential—indeed, the departure of some of the movement's traditionalist dinosaurs was probably something of a blessing to those modernizers bent on turning Provisonal Sinn Féin into an electorally vibrant political party. With the IRA ceasefires of 1994 and 1997, however, traditionalist sentiment has seen the emergence of the Continuity Army Council and of other groupings committed to continuing the armed struggle and with the capacity to mount serious terrorist attacks. Whether or not these succeed in derailing the Provisional movement's journey towards broadly peaceful politics remains to be seen; what is clear is that their appearance bears out the thesis that splits and reformations are, paradoxically for a legitimist movement claiming to possess an unbroken chain of argument from 1916 onwards, integral to republican politics.

iv. The Erosion of the Republican Left since 1969

The splintering of the republican movement saw the Provisionals' rapid acquisition of military predominance. However, the biggest headache for the state in the first year after the split was posed by neither of the main IRA factions, but by a small left-leaning republican group, Saor Éire, which carried out a number of armed robberies, one of which resulted in the murder of the unarmed Garda Fallon. But Saor Éire soon faded from the picture, leaving the field clear for the Provisionals and the remnants of the 1960s leadership to contest the leadership of republicanism. After the January 1970 Sinn Féin ard fheis, opponents of the Provisionals regrouped under the banner of 'Official Sinn Féin', and retained as their armed wing the Official IRA. Both the Officials, or 'Stickies' as they became known, and their more extreme and ideologically eclectic offshoot which became the Irish Republican Socialist Party (IRSP) and for terrorist purposes the Irish National Liberation Army (INLA), remained broadly Marx-ist and espoused what might loosely be described as a communist world-view. Although the Officials carried out a number of significant terrorist acts in the early 1970s, including the inept and bloody Aldershot bombing and the notori-ous killing of Ranger Best in Derry in 1972, the organization was soon over-shadowed by the far better organized Provisionals. In any case, the sheer logic of non-sectarian socialism drove the Officials inexorably away from political vio-lence. At the same time, the organization's revolutionary credentials were placed under intermittent threat by the IRSP and INLA, whose ideologically more eclectic approach allowed for overtly sectarian slaughter. These factors ensured that it was seldom a significant element in terrorist activities on either side of the border after 1972, when it declared a military ceasefire, being reduced effectively to a protection force and, through activities ranging from racketeer-ing to forgery, a fund-raising arm for Official Sinn Féin and elements of that party's successors.[29]

The Officials' political leadership underwent a remarkable metamorphosis in the course of the late 1970s and early 1980s, as their party developed from Official Sinn Féin into Sinn Féin the Workers Party and on into the Workers Party, by which time it had become a Moscow-orientated communist party in all but name. In parallel with this came a shift in its core concerns, as espousal of political violence was supplanted by arguments about the need to tackle the economic and social oppression which, in its analysis, had created the condi-tions in which sectarianism and atavistic nationalism flourished: an Irish republic could only be achieved by peaceful means, through the gradual build-ing of socialism in both parts of the island. The party also put much energy into commentary on international affairs, warning against incorporation into the Western military alliance, declaiming against American imperialism and the modernization of NATO's nuclear arsenal, deploring Western interference in the Third World and the toleration of apartheid, and preaching the glories of socialist achievement in the Soviet Union, Cuba, North Korea, and other show-pieces of Marxian state-building.

As the Workers Party, what had been Official Sinn Féin received a major boost when it won three Dáil seats in the February 1982 general election. The party continued to pursue a broadly Moscow line in ideological matters: as the rhetorical climate in Europe about nuclear force modernization heated up in the mid-1980s its TDs were vociferous on Western and particularly on Ameri-can iniquity in international affairs, assiduous in their pursuit of issues such as American military overflights, and persistent in their demands that Ireland join the effectively anti-Western non-aligned movement. When the party won its

[29] Bell, *The Irish Troubles*, 320–2, 438–40; P. K. Clare, 'Subcultural Obstacles to the Control of Racketeering in Northern Ireland', *Conflict Quarterly*, 10/4 (Fall 1990), 26, 31–3.

first European Parliament seat in 1989, furthermore, its MEP joined not the fashionable Eurocommunist group but the rusting 'tankies' of the European hard Left. In this period, it is clear that the party still looked to Moscow, that the Soviets regarded it as the operational successor of earlier Irish communist parties, and that the international song which it sang suited the Soviet tune.[30] There are also contested indications of some fitful financial assistance from the Communist Party of the Soviet Union—it would be surprising if there was none—as was certainly given to pro-Moscow groups in many other countries for decades.[31] The party was also dogged by persistent allegations that the Official IRA remained in being as an illegal fund-raising arm. Tensions within the Workers Party grew in the late 1980s, however, as the contradictions evident in Stalinism and the incongruity of lauding such reprehensible totalitarian states as North Korea began to grate on the nerves of most of the party's TDs, who, paradoxically for a group theoretically opposed to liberal democracy, had shown themselves to be by Irish standards unusually assiduous, parliamentarians. The party underwent a Pauline conversion to the mixed economy, and this precipitated a crisis which resulted in six of its seven TDs leaving to form Democratic Left in 1992. The residual Workers Party was left alone to continue valiantly if ineffectually to raise the Stalinist banner, its veterans undaunted by the demise of state socialism around the world and by the disappearance of the Soviet Union, and its activities tainted by charges that its paramilitary arm remained in being for protective and other purposes.[32]

It would be tempting to argue that the Workers Party had a disproportionate anti-Western influence on public debate in international affairs in the 1980s and 1990s. The reality, however, is that public sentiment on matters such as NATO membership, military neutrality, and the evils of nuclear proliferation long predate the emergence of a coherent and respected voice on the Left. Furthermore, while the promotion of a neutralist agenda in foreign affairs may well have tied in with what the Soviet Union wished for, the last two decades have seen the Irish public embrace the European integration project more consistently and with greater fervour than any other member state, and this public approval has transformed the historic opposition of the Irish Left into wholehearted endorsement of the European project. This is precisely the opposite of the line

[30] As an illustration of Soviet propaganda priorities, see the agenda for 1978 set by the KGB for its Copenhagen station as reproduced in C. Andrew and O. Gordievsky, 'Residency Priorities: The Case of Denmark', *Intelligence and National Security*, 7/1 (Jan. 1992), 28–31.

[31] Translation of CPSU document of 14 Apr. 1988 in J. F. Burke, 'Recently Released Material on Soviet Intelligence Operations', *Intelligence and National Security*, 8/2 (Apr. 1993), 248; see also reports from the second de Rossa libel trial in *The Irish Times*, 1, 5, and 8 Mar. 1997.

[32] J. Coakley, 'The Foundations of Statehood', in J. Coakley and M. Gallagher (eds.), *Politics in the Republic of Ireland* (2nd edn., Dublin, 1993; repr. 1996), 20; *The Irish Times*, 1 Mar. 1997; R. Dunphy, 'The Workers Party and Europe: Trajectory of an Idea', *Irish Political Studies*, 7 (1992), 20–39; high court testimony of Chief Superintendent Egan, as reported in the *Sunday Tribune*, 24 Aug. 1997.

preached by Moscow once it began to take the European Community (EC) seriously in the mid-1970s.[33]

The IRSP and the INLA have neither courted nor achieved the same respectability. The IRSP was briefly supported by the fiery nationalist Bernadette McAliskey, the diminutive icon of the Battle of the Bogside, but it has remained on the fringes of republican political life. Unlike the Provisionals, it has produced an explicitly revolutionary analysis of the Northern crisis, drawing its inspiration from Trotsky rather than from Moscow. The actions of its military wing, however, have served to expose a gaping hole between its pretensions to cerebral revolutionary exegesis and its bloody and sectarian instincts. The latter have prevailed within the INLA, which in its various mutations has included some of the Troubles' most notorious—or celebrated—gunmen, amongst them the 'Border Fox' Dessie O'Hare and the late Dominic 'Mad Dog' McGlinchey. With the exception of the murder of the Conservative MP Airey Neave in 1979, it has never been able to match the IRA's capacity for mounting sophisticated terrorist operations in Britain or elsewhere despite its superficially impeccable international revolutionary credentials. It has, however, exhibited a lack of discipline and strategic coherence which sets it apart from the mainstream IRA, from whom it has attracted some disaffected recruits. Paradoxically for an organization which denounces sectarianism, it was associated with particularly egregious sectarian murders such as the notorious machine-gunning of worshippers in a Pentecostal hall at Darkley in 1983. Its commitment to the wider struggle against imperialism internationally found expression only with the bizarre bombing of an air traffic control radar installation in County Cork in 1982 on the grounds that it could be used for NATO purposes.[34] Despite the organization's small size, the INLA and people associated with it and its transient and bickering offshoots have habitually adopted a more aggressive approach towards the southern state than has the IRA: during the 1980s three Gardai were shot dead after first being disarmed or disabled, and two others were also killed, while a senior prison officer was assassinated. In the last decade, however, the INLA has expended much of its energies on both sides of the border on violent feuds incomprehensible to all outside the fractious and self-destructive world of militant republican socialism. In one two-year period from 1987 to 1989, internal dissension within the small IRSP/INLA family saw a dozen deaths, including those of most of its leading killers, initiated by the machine-gunning of three activists in broad daylight in the lobby of a Drogheda hotel. 1995 and 1996 saw a recrudescence of that feud, with murders on both sides of the border, most notably those of McGlinchey and of Gino Gallagher, leader of one of the INLA factions in

[33] C. Andrew and O. Gordievsky, *KGB: The Inside Story of its Foreign Operations from Lenin to Gorbachev* (London, 1990), 471–3.

[34] Bell, *The Irish Troubles*, 658.

Belfast. Further deaths, including the Garda killing of an armed INLA activist during an abortive robbery in Dublin in 1997, and persistent reports that the residue of the organization's Dublin group had become heavily involved both in armed robberies and in the illegal drugs trade, reinforce the view that it has been less a disciplined, coherent revolutionary force than a nihilistic, self-indulgent movement, the spoilt child of the republican terrorist family. There appears little doubt that it subsists only on sufferance of the mainstream IRA—in 1994 an Irish diplomat commented that the government had been assured by Provisional sources that the INLA and other republican splinter groups would simply not be allowed to jeopardize any republican ceasefire. The activities both of the INLA and of other factions which emerged following the ceasefires of 1994 and of 1997 indicate that this was wishful thinking.[35]

Finally, it should be noted that political violence within the state since 1969 has included a few actions by what might be termed genuinely revolutionary Left groups. Of these the most serious was the murder in 1975 of an off-duty Garda after an abortive bank robbery by a married couple, the Murrays, who belonged to an arcane political sect. Convicted of capital murder, their case aroused some sympathy in progressive circles—after all, a woman was involved, the couple appeared genuine Leftist ideologues rather than republican misfits, they had no way of knowing that the man they gunned down was a policeman, and in any case as tools of the state policemen were perhaps expendable. As in all such cases since the 1940s, their sentences were commuted to life imprisonment. The forces of proletarian internationalism were less fatally deployed in 1981, when an executive of a strike-riven British car company giving a talk in Trinity College was wounded by an Italian gunman, one of a curious coterie of student radicals and hangers-on of a broadly Trotskyite persuasion. The episode stands out not only for its brutality and for its incongruity, but also because it demonstrates how thin the line can be between an essentially juvenile interest in revolutionary politics in the abstract and the harsh reality of using a gun. While the hapless Italian was jailed, his Trinity associates escaped prosecution, perhaps on the grounds that the whole affair was little more than an ill-judged jape by people who would eventually be reabsorbed by the bourgeoisie to which they properly belonged.[36]

v. Republicanism's External Links since 1969

What has distinguished the contemporary IRA's external links from its previous dealings with sympathetic foreigners has been both their extent and the fact that

[35] *The Irish Times*, 13 June 1997; conversation with an Irish official, 1994.
[36] There are some parallels with European terrorist movements which sprang from student politics. For a somewhat dated but still gripping discussion of the Red Army Faction see J. Becker, *Hitler's Children: The Story of the Baader-Meinhof Gang* (London, 1977; revised edn., 1978).

significant covert help has come from time to time not only from states such as Libya hostile to Britain, but also from terrorist groups such as the Basque ETA and the Palestine Liberation Organization waging their own freedom wars. The republican movement has reportedly reciprocated when it could. Nearer home it has also lent a fraternal hand to would-be Welsh and Scottish terrorists.[37] Amongst the benefits of such external links are their apparent value in delivering a degree of foreign support, access to cash, weapons, equipment, and explosives from a variety of sources, and contacts with groups and regimes in various parts of the world willing to exchange expertise or to assist IRA personnel on operations abroad. While the IRA has continued to make common cause with anyone whom they calculate will help them in their fight against Britain, mainstream republican terrorism obviously has far more in common with nationalist groups elsewhere than with organizations such as the German Red Army Faction, the French Action Directe, or the Italian Red Brigades which were driven primarily by a desire for left-wing revolution. It is instructive to compare the relative transience of the latter category, particularly since the collapse of Soviet power, with the vitality and resilience of the former. Ethnocentric nationalism has far outstripped essentially neurotic revolutionary socialism as an organizing force for terrorism in Western Europe.[38]

Quite apart from their continued willingness to befriend analogous movements abroad, the modern IRA and its offshoots have also been quicker to seize the opportunities presented by European integration than individual countries have been to grasp the nettle of interstate collaboration, as the IRA's many operations against British targets in Belgium, the Netherlands, and Germany, and the INLA's rather less successful European adventures over the last two decades, have demonstrated. It is evident that to a degree republican activities in Europe were facilitated by underground contact with other terrorist groups and their support networks. This has led to claims that there exists what might be termed a 'terrorist international', and that until the 1990s this operated largely under Soviet manipulation, stemming from a Politburo decision in 1964 to invest heavily in the encouragement of Western terrorist groups.[39] The main peacetime advantage to be had for the Soviet Union in indirectly assisting terrorist organizations was neither in intelligence gathering nor 'fifth column' work—the rationale behind Nazi Germany's courtship of the IRA and of analogous separatist movements—but rather in the subversion of the Western political order, in forcing Western governments to devote vast security resources to coping with internal and transnational terrorist activity, and in offering the spectre

[37] Institute for the Study of Terrorism, *IRA, INLA: Foreign Support and International Connections* (London, 1988), 41–2, 65–70.

[38] W. Laqueur, *The Age of Terrorism* (London, 1987), 206.

[39] R. Goren, *The Soviet Union and Terrorism* (London, 1984), 95–106 and 169–72; J. M. Poland, *Understanding Contemporary Terrorism: Groups, Strategies, and Responses* (Englewood Cliffs, 1988), 227–9.

of orchestrated terrorist action in support of Soviet strategic aims at times of international crisis or during an actual East–West war.

The reality of Soviet interest in terrorism internationally was cogently argued by various writers in the 1960s and 1970s, frequently in the face of official reticence and general media disbelief. Compelling evidence has accumulated since the collapse of Soviet power to show that the Soviet Union did indeed attempt to manipulate some foreign guerrilla/terrorist groups, just as did the United States in various parts of the world, but that their influence was far more limited than analysts allowed. Some fell into a logical trap: because the Soviet Union and its proxies encouraged and sometimes covertly supported international terrorism as well as 'wars of national liberation', they reasoned that the Russians were amongst the main progenitors and the ultimate controllers of such activity. Cold War warriors have, consequently, argued with varying degrees of authority that external support for Irish republicans was all part of a seamless web of Moscow-inspired subversion.[40] To quote one work particularly highly regarded by intelligence professionals,

the Irish Republican Army is linked to the . . . PLO, the PLFP, Algeria and Libya . . . Each [terrorist] group is linked with the others . . . on and on the connections grow. It is a worldwide web of terror, and each strand can be traced back to the Soviet Union.[41]

The subtlety and contingency of the ideological, strategic, and logistical relationships between terrorist groups and the Soviet Union, be they in the Bogside or in Bogota, remained something which many analysts seemed unable to grasp.[42] While some terrorist groups undoubtedly served as conduits through which the Soviet Union could indirectly provide assistance to other international mischief-makers, often through its client states such as East Germany and Cuba, it does not follow that these were simply Russian pawns in the Cold War game. Rather, they had their own agendas to pursue, arising out of ethnic, social, or political grievances in their own areas of operations. In short, they were to varying extents opportunists, who in return for political and sometimes material support would graze selectively on the dismal steppes of Soviet orthodoxy, rather than committed revolutionary socialists whose only aim was to do Moscow's bidding. The emergence as recognized sponsors of terrorism of 'rogue states' such as Iraq and Libya, the latter with disastrous consequences for Ireland, also undermined the argument that Russian intrigue lay at the heart of the phenomenon of international terrorism—in fact there is evidence that by the mid-1980s the Soviets were almost as alarmed by Qadhafi as was the

---

[40] Institute for the Study of Terrorism, *IRA, INLA*, 7; Goren, *Soviet Union and Terrorism*, 95–106.

[41] Comment of a discussant to S. Gazit and M. Handel, 'Insurgency, Terrorism and Intelligence', in R. Godson (ed.), *Intelligence Requirements for the 1980s. Number Three: Counterintelligence* (Washington, 1980), 150. This series was described by the late John Bruce Lockhart, a former deputy head of MI6, as the best available on modern intelligence problems. Interview, 1985.

[42] Goren, *Soviet Union and Terrorism*, 194–9; K. Campbell, *ANC: A Soviet Task Force?* (London, 1986), 5–8.

West.[43] The sudden demise of Soviet power has left many terrorism experts with egg on their faces, as they search for an alternative explanatory device for its continuance in the Western and developing worlds.[44]

The state has faced considerable difficulties in coping with the problem of foreign support for the republican movement. The intermittent interest of the Soviet Union and its satellites during the first decade of the Northern Ireland crisis was not confined to rhetoric but included the clandestine provision of some weapons and other material and support, and an adjustment of the Soviet attitude towards the republican movement was undoubtedly one of the desiderata which the Irish sought through the establishment of diplomatic relations in 1974.[45] That may have played its part in changing Soviet policy on Ireland—by the early 1980s Soviet officials in Ireland were apparently under orders not to respond to any overtures from the IRA—although the Soviets evidently did abuse Irish hospitality to some extent, because in 1983 three people attached to the Dublin embassy were dramatically expelled. Despite speculation that these had had IRA contacts, the then taoiseach has written that they were 'engaged in improper activities that had involved the use of our territory for the secret transfer of information concerning the military affairs of another power', a formulation of which Dan Bryan would have been proud.[46] It is also said that the KGB's main interest in Ireland in the 1980s was in using it as a training ground for English-speaking 'illegals', that is agents equipped with false identities and Western nationality who would eventually be placed in a target country (the powerful East German foreign intelligence agency HVA reportedly listed one agent of its own, a 'lecturer . . . codenamed "Klavier"', in the country in the late 1980s).[47] The KGB may also have sought intelligence in Ireland on the EC, as from the late 1970s its officers in Western countries were under instructions both to gather information on and to develop lines of propaganda against further economic and political integration—it is said that a senior KGB official visited Dublin in 1985 to reprimand KGB staff because of dissatisfaction with the intelligence being produced (by contrast, a British Kremlinologist was at pains to stress the high quality of Irish diplomatic reporting on the internal politics of Soviet bureaucracy in the early 1980s, which was shared with Britain under the umbrella of the European political co-operation process).[48]

---

[43] Andrew and Gordievsky, *KGB*, 531–2; B. Woodward, *Veil: The Secret Wars of the CIA 1981–87* (1st edn., London, 1987; paperback edn., 1988), 506.

[44] M. Tugwell, 'Politics and Propaganda of the Provisional IRA', in P. Wilkinson (ed.), *British Perspectives on Terrorism* (London, 1981), 23–4, 36–7. At p. 24 Tugwell ludicrously argues that 'it may have been more than coincidental that the visit' of a London-based *Pravda* correspondent, allegedly a KGB officer, to an internment camp in Northern Ireland 'was followed within the month by . . . "Bloody Sunday"'.

[45] FitzGerald, *All in a Life*, 124–6; Burke, 'Recently Released Material', 243.

[46] FitzGerald, *All in a Life*, 603; Andrew and Gordievsky, *KGB*, 372.

[47] Andrew and Gordievsky, *KGB*, 532. *Sunday Tribune*, 12 Oct. 1997.

[48] C. Andrew and O. Gordievsky, *Instructions from the Centre: Top Secret Files on KGB Foreign Operations 1975–1985* (London, 1991), 140–69. Included are the translated texts of KGB instructions to its

The state has greeted evidence of foreign involvement with the IRA and republican splinter groups with extraordinary reticence. Its most public efforts to dissuade outsiders from assisting republican terrorism have been directed at the Irish-American community which, as in earlier phases of republican violence, has been a crucial source of financial and logistical support for the IRA. As with the Soviet Union, Ireland has favoured a path of quiet persuasion in dealings with Libya, which was an early and active supporter of the republican movement both in words and in deeds. In March 1973 the Naval Service, tipped off by Britain, intercepted the small *MV Claudia*. On board were five tons of arms which had been loaded in Tripoli, accompanied by the IRA's Joe Cahill.[49] The government's public response to this blatant interference in Irish affairs was undermined by the inappropriately jovial remark of the minister for defence that the *Claudia* would receive 'a boot up the transom' if she returned to Irish waters. Efforts were made softly to disabuse Colonel Qadhafi of his misconceptions about the Irish situation through the good offices of other Arab leaders, and by 1976 this approach appeared to have borne fruit.[50] Experience was to show, however, that Libya continued to provide the IRA with both money and weapons, which were used to kill people both in the United Kingdom and in Ireland. Against this, Libya simultaneously represented itself as well disposed towards Ireland, and it became a very important customer of the Irish beef industry. The government remained privately uneasy about Libya's attitude: during the decisive meeting in 1984 which ultimately led to the 1985 Anglo-Irish agreement, the taoiseach Garret FitzGerald pointed out to Margaret Thatcher that Qadhafi was 'deeply involved' in supporting the IRA.[51] In public, however, successive governments of varying political hues remained reticent. In 1986 when the Garda seized boxes of ammunition with Libyan markings, the government kept its diplomatic representations private. A year later press allegations that Libya was supplying the highly effective explosive Semtex, a point the truth of which was soon to be graphically demonstrated, produced a remarkably low-key Dáil statement by the minister for foreign affairs, who argued for the need to 'retain a sense of perspective', said that the allegations were unproven, and in general sought to suggest that there was nothing to worry about.[52] The fatuity of this response was demonstrated that autumn, when the French authorities intercepted the freighter *Eksund* with 150 tons of Libyan arms, including ground to air missiles, on what was apparently her fifth such trip to Ireland. All this produced in diplomatic terms was a mild, almost apologetic squeak of protest, after which Irish/Libyan relations were allowed to

residencies in member states between 1976 and 1984; Andrews and Gordievsky, *KGB*, 532. Conversation with a former British official, London, 1995.

[49] Andrews and Gordievsky, *KGB*, 72–6; Cahill is quoted in Bishop and Malley, *The Provisional IRA*, 246.   [50] FitzGerald, *All in a Life*, 284 and 311.
[51] Ibid. 548.   [52] *Dáil Debates*, vol. 372, cols. 2097–2105, 14 May 1987.

return to normal. Crucially, the lucrative cattle trade continued undisturbed.[53] There was a slight public contretemps in the early 1990s, but not on the issue of help for the IRA—it was said that the largesse had ceased to flow—but of Libya's awkward questions about Irish cattle disease, which threatened beef exports. Libya has since provided details of covert assistance to the IRA. Ironically in view both of her declared sympathy for nationalist Ireland and of her hatred of imperialism, these details were given not to the Irish government but to a British diplomat in Geneva.[54] It may be that the progressive development of a co-ordinated European Union response in matters of foreign policy and security, which in June 1997 resulted in unprecedented collective diplomatic action by all member states in response to the involvement of Iranian agents in assassinations in Germany, will see a more overt reaction should foreign powers again become involved in covert support of republican terrorism— unless, that is, the interests of Irish beef processors are again put into the scales.

The mainstream republican movement's external links since 1969 are entirely consonant with its previous history. They demonstrate two enduring elements: the movement's willingness to co-operate with even the most ideologically incongruous bedfellows, and its capacity to retain control of its own agenda. The IRA will accept help from anyone, but will be bought by no one.

vi. The State and the Northern Ireland Crisis since 1970

The state's response to the Northern crisis and to the overspill of political vio-lence into the state—both republican and, intermittently since 1970, loyalist— has been conditioned both by national political circumstances and by what might be termed its institutional memory of previous upsurges in political crime. Until the arms crisis, public attention focused overwhelmingly on what was seen as the manifest injustices and bigotry of the Northern state, and the imperative to secure the protection of Catholic life and property and full civil rights. While the nostrum of a united Ireland as the solution to all such woes was generally endorsed, there was some recognition that this could not happen overnight. The arms crisis forced a reconsideration of attitudes at least within the political elite, most importantly inside Fianna Fáil. Without abandoning its fundamental aspiration for a united Ireland, the party unequivocally reverted to the broad policy towards IRA activities within or launched from the state which de Valera had adopted from 1936 onwards. It and the other parties which have been in government since have all kept Northern Ireland high on their list of priorities, and have ensured that, in contrast to the murky events of 1969–70,

---

[53] O'Brien, *The Long War*, 142.   [54] Private information, 1997.

Northern Ireland policy and the related security issues have been dealt with within the framework of cabinet government.

On the face of it, the government had formidable legal instruments already to hand in 1969: the Offences against the State Act (OSA) of 1939 remained in operation, and the state of emergency declared in September 1939 had never been rescinded. However, the government initially held back from bringing key provisions of these measures into operation despite the ascending violence in Northern Ireland and a concomitant rise in subversive crime within the state, although it is said that ministers toyed with the idea of introducing internment in the autumn of 1970 to deal with an alleged kidnap plot by Saor Éire.[55] It was not until May 1972, after a particularly galling failure to secure a conviction in the Garda Fallon murder case, that the non-jury Special Criminal Court was reactivated under the OSA. Even then, there was a marked departure from previous practice in that membership was confined to judges or retired judges: army officers were no longer required to discharge the state's most perilous judicial functions.[56] Furthermore the government, perhaps conscious of the disastrous failure of internment as so incompetently and brutally introduced in Northern Ireland in August 1971, held back from imposing a similar measure within the state although it had proved highly effective when last used in 1957. The abjuring of internment in the early 1970s appeared a moderate and sensible approach at the time; in retrospect, historians may fairly speculate on whether an intelligently applied system of internment in both parts of Ireland, and embracing both republican and loyalist paramilitaries, might not have yielded beneficial long-term results just as it had done before. The persistence of republican crime, and a sudden shift in IRA policy whereby those arraigned were permitted to contest charges against them in the courts, forced the government to propose a key amendment to the OSA in November 1972 under which the offence of IRA membership could be taken as proved on the word of a Garda chief superintendent. Ironically, this provoked a leadership crisis not within Fianna Fáil but in the far less republican-minded opposition Fine Gael party, whose leader Liam Cosgrave was entirely sympathetic to the measure as proposed despite the reservations of the majority in his party who were concerned about the inherent erosion of civil liberties. At the eleventh hour, news that a bomb in the city centre had killed two people filtered through to the Dáil, and Fine Gael TDs followed their leader and did not contest the government's proposal.[57] The atrocity was subsequently attributed not to the IRA but to loyalists on a mercifully rare foray south of the border—on the basis of a *cui bono?* analysis, republicans and some others argued that the bomb was, directly or indirectly, the work of Britain. In practice, the robust independence of the courts in

---

[55] For a concise though vivid account of the growth of republican violence, see Bishop and Mallie, *The Provisional IRA*, 139–245; Browne, 'The Berry File', 72–3.

[56] Hogan and Walker, *Political Violence*, 179.   [57] FitzGerald, *All in a Life*, 106–8.

applying stern laws meant that the measure introduced was neither as draconian nor as effective as either its proponents or its critics predicted.

The OSA of 1939 remains the state's basic legal weapon against political crime, although a number of ancillary measures were introduced in the 1970s and 1980s. The three most striking were the ban on the broadcasting of interviews with members of republican and loyalist paramilitary organizations and their political arms, a measure introduced by the Cosgrave government in 1973 (the previous Fianna Fáil government had ducked the issue of overt censorship by attempting to pressure RTE, the national broadcasting service, voluntarily not to broadcast inconvenient material), the Emergency Powers Act of 1976 which allowed detention of suspects arrested for certain offences for up to seven days before arraignment or release, and a bill which went through every stage of the legislative process in a single day in 1985 in order to permit the government to seize over two million pounds held in bank accounts believed to be under IRA control.[58]

The prelude to the 1994 IRA ceasefire saw a number of significant changes in the legal provisions covering political crime. The ban on broadcast interviews with republicans and loyalists was lifted with great fanfare, and the state of emergency in being from 1939 to 1978, and which had subsequently been renewed every year by resolution of the Oireachtas, was allowed to lapse. These steps were taken as confidence-building measures on the road to persuading the IRA to put down the gun forever, and the IRA's subsequent though temporary abrogation of its ceasefire was not sufficient to provoke a reappraisal of the changes.

The state's legal difficulties in adjusting to the Northern Ireland crisis extended beyond striking the appropriate balance between police powers and individual rights in emergency legislation. The big problem has been the difficulties surrounding extradition for alleged terrorist offences, which has at times been an acute irritant in Anglo-Irish relations. Until 1982 a person wanted by another country with whom Ireland had extradition arrangements could avoid extradition if he or she could show that the alleged crime was political in nature or was committed for political ends. In this Irish courts were simply upholding an accepted principle of international law, as required by article 29.3 of the constitution, ironically one based on British jurisprudence. The result was that the state was a legal safe haven for terrorist suspects. British politicians and commentators saw what one minister described as the 'black comedy' of the extradition problem as essentially political rather than judicial, and were dismissive of the 1976 Criminal Law (Jurisdiction) Act and of measures such as all-Ireland courts proposed to overcome the problem.[59] It was obvious that extradition was

[58] FitzGerald, *All in a Life*, 608.
[59] N. Lawson, *The View from No. 11: Memoirs of a Tory Radical* (1st edn., London, 1992; Corgi edn., 1993), 670; FitzGerald, *All in a Life*, 213–14, 534.

a very sensitive domestic political issue, particularly for Fianna Fáil: republican sympathizers argued that no one should be extradited simply for fighting for Ireland, while civil libertarians pointed to the arguably unsatisfactory nature of the Northern Ireland Diplock courts and to apparent miscarriages of justice involving Irish people in Britain.[60] Governments were consequently only too glad to leave the problem with the courts despite British criticisms. In 1982 there was considerable surprise when the Supreme Court abruptly reversed its view of what constituted a political offence in the case of Dominic McGlinchey, essentially restricting the term to non-violent action. This was reinforced in further cases, through Irish accession to the European Convention on the Suppression of Terrorism, and through the eventual passage of a new Extradition Act in 1987, albeit one with procedural features which outraged British ministers. While the McGlinchey and subsequent decisions got the government off the hook to some extent, extradition proceedings never became the production line process which the British appeared to expect. There is a tradition in Irish law of close scrutiny of arrest and detention procedures, and of any warrants or other documents involved, and extradition procedures even in ordinary criminal cases are characterized by highly technical legal argument.[61] On a number of occasions the British authorities, evidently unused to the pedantic traditions of the Irish bar, made mistakes in preparing extradition papers, on others it appeared that errors were made in Dublin. The result was a series of courtroom fiascos, where wanted republicans had to be released. In November 1988 there was particular controversy when the attorney-general declined to seek the extradition to Britain of the alleged IRA quartermaster, Father Patrick Ryan, because of publicity given to prejudicial comments made by apoplectic MPs. This enraged the British government, who saw it as further proof of Irish duplicity (Belgium, which had chosen not to extradite Ryan to Britain, instead deporting him to Ireland, mysteriously escaped criticism). However, the later release on appeal in Britain of the 'Winchester Three', on the grounds that ill-considered public remarks by one of their alleged targets during their trial might have influenced their jury, suggests that the attorney-general's finding in the Ryan case might have been justified.

At times during the 1970s and 1980s the British government gave the impression that they believed that the IRA could easily be beaten if only Ireland would stop playing semantic games and make extradition work. But the removal of the political exception, and the success of the majority of extradition applications after 1987, while it may have put some dangerous people behind bars did not bring republican violence to a grinding halt. The British attitude to the extradition issue appeared 'irrational' to the Irish, given the unavoidable legal

---

[60] For an impassioned criticism of extradition see Farrell, *Sheltering the Fugitive?*
[61] A. E. Owen, *The Anglo-Irish Agreement: The First Three Years* (Cardiff, 1994), 219; Hogan and Walker, *Political Violence*, 279–307.

complexity and delicacy of the process for any country, the availability of an alternative in Ireland in the form of the 1976 Criminal Law Jurisdiction Act and Irish willingness to consider other ideas such as all-Ireland courts, and the severity with which Irish courts treat terrorist crimes.[62] There is also an element of selective amnesia in the British position, as extradition from the United Kingdom can be a lengthy and uncertain affair: in the non-political Heysel Stadium case it took almost three years for Belgium to get hold of twenty-six suspects through the British courts, while in 1989 a London court refused to extradite a man wanted for gun-running to Fiji on the grounds that the alleged offence was 'of a political character'.[63] Mrs Thatcher's reaction to that judgement is not recorded.

The growth in political violence and in armed crime since 1969 placed great strain on the Garda, a force already under pressure because of the increasing urbanization of Irish society. While unrest within the rank and file of the force was contained in the 1970s and 1980s largely through a transformation in pay and conditions, underlying problems of organization and direction persisted. There has been frequent friction between those who favoured the development of specialist investigative and rapid response units to deal with particular problems and those who argued for the concentration of resources in the standard geographic Garda divisions, arguments which show no signs of ending. In the mid-1970s the force's public stock fell because of widespread allegations of the existence of a 'heavy gang' of officers who used third-degree methods in the interrogation of suspects.[64] These issues were complicated by the curse of politicization within the higher ranks of the force: as in earlier decades, each senior officer had attached to him, whether fairly or not, an imputed political allegiance, and in the wake of the arms crisis, the question of who was for whom became even more sensitive. This made effective management of the force very difficult. Matters became very fraught in 1978, when the new Fianna Fáil government precipitately dismissed the Garda commissioner Edmund Garvey, believed by some to be the man who had leaked news of the arms importation scheme to Liam Cosgrave in 1970.[65] Simply by being the government's choice to replace Garvey, his successor was placed in an invidious position. After Charles Haughey became taoiseach in 1979, matters became more complicated still within the higher echelons of the force. While considerable resources were invested in modern equipment for detective and security work, the belief grew that the Garda was experiencing considerable political interference in its operations. The apogee of such interference came during the short-lived Haughey minority government of 1982, when the Justice portfolio was given to Sean Doherty, a colourful former Garda who was a Haughey loyalist. Rumours soon

---

[62] Interview with a former minister, 1989.　　　[63] *Independent*, 21 Mar. 1989.

[64] FitzGerald, *All in a Life*, 313–15.

[65] J. Joyce and P. Murtagh, *The Boss: Charles J. Haughey in Government* (Dublin, 1983), 133–5, 141–2.

spread of the tapping of the telephones of a number of journalists, ostensibly in the name of national security but in fact to determine who in Haughey's cabinet was feeding the press with details of internecine disputes. This was an abuse both of the process of seeking a tap—the initiative was supposed to come from the Garda, whereas it had in fact come from Doherty—and the purpose. A Garda tape recorder was also provided to allow one minister to record a telephone conversation with another. Hard evidence on this emerged after the November 1982 election, when the new FitzGerald coalition government made it public after securing the resignations both of the Garda commissioner, Patrick McLoughlin, and of the head of the ISB (Intelligence and Security Branch, the former C3). The two officers had reluctantly yielded to political pressure to initiate the taps, although it was evident that their recommendations had been strongly resisted by officials in Justice.[66] In the aftermath of the affair, in which Haughey said he had had no hand, act, or part, the Fianna Fáil parliamentary party temporarily expelled Doherty. Two journalists won substantial damages from the state, and a third later received an out-of-court settlement. Doherty, who resented being Fianna Fáil's sacrificial lamb, had belated but spectacular revenge a decade later, when Haughey was in the third year of his time as taoiseach of an unlikely coalition with his one-time sworn enemies in the small Progressive Democrats party. Doherty stated that Haughey had indeed known of the taps and had been provided with transcripts from them. This produced a dignified denial from the taoiseach, but his coalition partners believed Doherty rather than him and he was obliged to resign.[67]

vii. The Complexities of Interstate Security Co-operation since 1969

Since 1970 the state has attempted to cope with the problem of political violence arising from the Northern Ireland crisis (including the occasional though vicious loyalist terrorist acts which republican activities have provoked) in co-operation with the British government and its security forces. While fraught with difficulties, this approach quickly became a fact of life, and since 1973 it has been accorded public acknowledgement through intergovernmental agreements. The discussion below falls into two parts: security relations up to 1979, when aspects of security co-operation became the ostensible reason for the ousting of Jack Lynch from the leadership of Fianna Fáil and from the office of taoiseach, to be succeeded by the Lazarus-like Charles Haughey; and security relations since that political watershed.

The 1970s saw considerable developments in Anglo-Irish security relations.

---

[66] Ibid. 194–200, 385–96; Arnold, *Haughey*, 208–12.
[67] Arnold, *Haughey*, 275–9.

It is said that despite the debacle of the arms crisis, 'the Irish government was more than willing to co-operate with British security forces provided they showed some understanding of the need for intelligence, in both senses of the word', and that 'G2, the Irish Intelligence Service . . . co-operated' in the introduction of internment in 1971 and retained good links with British security agencies in subsequent years. The same reportedly held good for co-operation between the Garda and the RUC under both the Lynch government of 1969–73 and the Cosgrave government of 1973–7, although mutual suspicion, 'together with political restraints and reservations', prevented liaison 'from becoming really effective'.[68] The ex-Fianna Fáil minister Kevin Boland, ironically the son of the man who had crushed the IRA during the Emergency, claimed in 1984 that security co-operation had been marginally more effective under the Cosgrave and FitzGerald Fine Gael-led governments because 'they have not got the same sense of guilt in the role of Britain's partners' as did Fianna Fáil in office, but the evidence does not support this.[69] Despite disagreement on the political future of Northern Ireland, despite Southern anger at aspects of British security policy and operations—the state successfully prosecuted Britain under the European Convention on Human Rights over the treatment of people detained in Northern Ireland following the introduction of internment in 1971—and despite British despair at the workings of the Irish court system in relation to extradition, the two states shared much common ground. It was in both their interests to try to end political violence, and to stop weapons reaching the IRA and other terrorist groups. The RUC and British police forces needed access to Garda intelligence, and the Irish government was plainly dependent on Britain and other friendly countries for information about arms smuggling and other republican activities outside Ireland, because it had no significant capacity itself to gather intelligence abroad. Similarly, the Irish authorities had little information on loyalist paramilitaries, who from time to time carried out cross-border bombings, and had no choice but to rely on the RUC for information. Political developments in Northern Ireland, particularly the prorogation of the Stormont parliament in March 1972 and the Sunningdale agreement of December 1973, were also important in improving the climate for co-operation. Under that agreement, in the words of the Unionist Party leader Brian Faulkner, 'formal co-operation against terrorism' was 'agreed for the first time'. This unionists saw 'as the major step forward, and we had a firm commitment that there would be operational and intelligence co-operation from the Gardai', although problems persisted: the British complained continually about Irish reticence, while the Irish suspected that the British sometimes chose to use intelligence for

---

[68] A. Verrier, *Through the Looking Glass: British Foreign Policy in an Age of Illusions* (London, 1983), 301–2, 304; E. O'Ballance, *Terror in Ireland* (Novato, 1983), 216.

[69] K. Boland, *Fine Gael: British or Irish?* (Dublin, 1984), 74. See also Boland's *The Rise and Decline of Fianna Fáil* (Dublin, 1982).

black propaganda purposes instead of sharing it, most notoriously in respect of information on thefts of explosives from a County Meath factory.[70]

An Anglo-Irish legal commission was established to explore the treatment of fugitive offenders wanted for terrorist crimes, who were protected by Irish legal precedent from extradition. While this group could not agree on extradition, its work bore some fruit in the 1976 Criminal Law (Jurisdiction) Act, which allowed for trial in Ireland in respect of specified offences committed in the United Kingdom. A reciprocal law was passed in Britain. This legislation has seldom been used—there were considerable practical problems concerning witnesses, custody of evidence, and other matters, and in any case the British government has always regarded it as a very poor substitute for extradition—but it was, nevertheless, a very significant departure for Ireland, which for the first time claimed competence in the prosecution of people for certain crimes committed outside the state. It was to be followed in the succeeding decade by further efforts to create not merely a bilateral but a pan-European legal framework for dealing with political crime.

Despite Irish acknowledgement after Sunningdale of the need for security co-operation, its continuing sensitivity was dramatically underlined in the autumn of 1979. Jack Lynch, who had led Fianna Fáil back to power in 1977 with an unprecedented Dáil majority, came under public attack from backbenchers worried at what they claimed was the dilution of the party's constitutional republican ethos. The pressure on Lynch increased with press reports that the government, as part of a package of security measures agreed after the Mountbatten and Warrenpoint murders in August, had secretly sanctioned limited British overflights of Irish territory—overflights, like rights of 'hot pursuit', were issues about which the British government had an obsession at the time. Speaking at a press function in New York, Lynch took the opportunity to say that there was 'no truth' in such stories. Unfortunately for him, he then departed from his script by adding the qualification 'or almost none'. This indiscretion prompted an official next to him to mutter 'Oh, Jesus', a comment picked up by the microphone. Lynch's remark had major consequences: the overflights issue became the subject of the party debate which preceded his resignation weeks later. He was succeeded by Charles Haughey, who thus triumphantly completed his recovery from the debacle of the 1970 arms crisis. Irish sanction for British overflights effectively lapsed, although it was eventually revived on a reciprocal basis for bomb detection and disposal work in January 1987.[71]

Charles Haughey ousted Lynch as Fianna Fáil leader and taoiseach on a republican ticket. Ironically, it was probably these credentials which enabled

---

[70] Faulkner, *Memoirs*, 237; FitzGerald, *All in a Life*, 256.
[71] Private information; *The Irish Times*, 28 Sept. 1988; Arnold, *Haughey*, 149–54.

him quickly to embark on a major initiative in Anglo-Irish relations, one which confounded predictions that he would take a tougher line with the British. In May 1980 he and Margaret Thatcher agreed at the 'teapot summit' to closer political co-operation on a continuing basis, and they 'noted with satisfaction the efforts being made by the two Governments, both separately and in co-operation, in the field of security'. They announced a meeting between the chief constable of the RUC and the Garda commissioner, an important breakthrough because it was a public acknowledgement by the Haughey government that security co-operation was essential if political progress was to be made on Northern Ireland. At an operational level, furthermore, the British found the Garda under Haughey particularly helpful. The importance of sustained co-operation against terrorism was again stressed in the 1985 Anglo-Irish agreement, and it was undoubtedly a major element of the deal for the British.[72]

Exchanges of intelligence and joint assessments of terrorist capabilities and intentions appear to have become the stock-in-trade of cross-border co-operation, together with the provision of cover from the Irish side for British security forces investigating incidents near the border. Some major search operations have also been mounted in concert on each side of the border, for example during the massive Operation Mallard search for IRA arms dumps following the seizure of the *Eksund* in November 1987, and there have been reports that in recent years Garda/RUC intelligence co-operation has been particularly fruitful in the north-west. Although many in the Garda developed considerable admiration for the RUC, co-operation has not always run smoothly.[73] Quite apart from political issues, sources within each force have at times been critical of the other's performance. In 1974 the Irish government expressed its 'concern at the lack of co-ordination between the British army and the RUC, which contrasted with the effective liaison . . . between the RUC' and the Garda. The same point was made five years later, at a time of acute friction between the RUC and the British army over security policy, when a Garda officer told the newly appointed Security Co-ordinator Sir Maurice Oldfield that 'we find it hard to believe any police force can get along so badly with its own army. We are baffled by the lack of co-ordination between them. How can you hope for help from us in this situation?' Garda sources were forthright in their comments on the RUC's inability to operate at all in many border areas, and could also point to the findings of the Stalker 'Shoot to kill' inquiry which revealed at best a high degree of incompetence within specialist RUC anti-terrorist units.[74] From United Kingdom

---

[72] Quoted in P. Arthur and K. Jeffery, *Northern Ireland since 1968* (Oxford, 1988), 15; British official source, 1989; Lord Armstrong interview, 1992; Lawson, *The View from No. 11*, 670; FitzGerald, *All in a Life*, 570.

[73] *The Irish Times*, 27 Sept. 1997; Joyce and Murtagh, *The Boss*, 133.

[74] FitzGerald, *All in a Life*, 232; R. Deacon, *'C': A Biography of Sir Maurice Oldfield, Head of MI6* (London, 1985), 229; *The Irish Times*, 23 Aug. 1988.

sources there came suggestions that a separate Garda intelligence gathering and security unit be established in border counties, although the Irish concluded that this was a recipe for confusion and decided to leave overall responsibility with a Garda superintendent in each geographic area—it is at this level that most operational Garda/RUC liaison takes place.[75] Complaints have also been aired about weaknesses in the training, organization, motivation, and deployment of the Garda: the then RUC chief constable Sir John Hermon was quoted in 1986 as saying that 'it was evident their capacity and contribution was small', while in 1992 an experienced detective remarked that, while Gardai were good fellows to drink with, his force was far ahead in the collection and management of intelligence.[76] The available evidence suggests that cross-border police co-operation has been affected less by political considerations than by other factors. It was said that Lawrence Wren, the Garda commissioner from 1983 to 1987, refused to meet his Northern counterpart Jack Hermon for some years because of Hermon's refusal to investigate the farcical 'Dowra affair' of 1982, an improper use of RUC/Garda liaison to prevent a witness giving evidence in a case against the brother-in-law of the minister for justice Sean Doherty.[77] Inevitably over the course of almost three decades, there have also been security disasters. In 1991 it emerged that a Limerick-based detective arrested for passing information was a long-term IRA agent rather than a casual informant, an alarming indication of the sophistication of republican intelligence work. There were suggestions, indignantly denied, that the murders near the border of Lord Justice Gibson and his wife in 1987 and of two senior RUC officers returning from a meeting in Dundalk Garda Station in 1989 were the results of leaks from the Garda, while the acquisition by loyalist paramilitaries of material originally supplied to the RUC by the Garda about IRA suspects in Donegal obliged the Garda to warn and to take steps to protect people some of whom were themselves suspected of atrocious crimes.[78]

While operational co-operation is run principally through the two police forces, British and Irish military units are also deployed in border areas. The roles of the two armies are, however, very different. Since 1969 the Irish army has always acted strictly in aid of the Garda along the border, providing cover so that the police can do their work. This is because the conventions of life south of the border mean that republican paramilitaries seldom engage troops directly. For the most part, consequently, the army's border operations have been essentially preventive in nature and effect. This undoubtedly irked the British government, who consistently pressed in the 1970s and 1980s for a more aggressive approach

[75] K. Jeffery, 'Security Policy in Northern Ireland: Some Reflections on the Management of Violent Conflict', *Terrorism and Political Violence*, 2/1 (Spring 1990), 29.
[76] *The Times*, 10 Oct. 1986; conversation with an RUC officer, 1992.
[77] Joyce and Murtagh, *The Boss*, 239–50.
[78] *The Irish Times*, 30 Sept. 1991; *Independent*, 21 and 23 Sept. 1989.

to border security, and who argued that the Irish should establish a separate border command instead of continuing to rely on locally recruited, trained, and garrisoned units which, by implication, might sometimes be inclined to look the other way. The British also repeatedly sought direct army to army communications in those areas where the British army operates in tandem with or in lieu of the RUC, in order to facilitate the interception of terrorists crossing the border, but the government and its military advisers always refused to allow this. Army to army communications consequently are mediated through the respective police forces, an arrangement which undoubtedly lessens operational effectiveness. British criticism of the army's border performance has usually met with three related responses: first, the evidence is that the vast majority of republican terrorist incidents in Northern Ireland—over 96 per cent—were planned and carried out within the United Kingdom and did not involve any crossing of the border; secondly, the army's duty along the border is not to ambush and destroy, but rather to deter and, in support of the Garda, to secure the arrest of suspected terrorists; and thirdly, an argument which British officials naturally find particularly hard to take, that the border areas most notorious for terrorism were those in places within Northern Ireland such as South Armagh where the RUC and the British army themselves have been unable to patrol effectively.[79]

In the absence of evidence it is difficult to say anything useful about contemporary Dublin/London security links and how and by whom they are managed at either end. The only recent indication involving counter-terrorism concerns Sean O'Callaghan, who after leaving the IRA was persuaded by the Garda to rejoin it in 1979 and in six years rose to become a senior commander, a remarkably successful penetration by any standards. After he quit the IRA in 1985, he was passed from the Garda to MI5 for a thorough debriefing, a transfer that suggests close co-operation.[80] It is also impossible to say what more can be done by either state, or to determine what more either demands of the other, to make security co-operation against terrorism more effective. The British have continuously pressed for a greater flow of intelligence and for more vigorous patrolling in border areas. They have also been critical of the secondary role allotted to the Irish army, and of perpetual Irish obfuscation on the issue of extradition. For their part, successive Irish governments have complained that improvements in cross-border security co-operation, and the eventual circumvention of the major obstacle of extradition, were not paralleled by imaginative reforms of policing and security within Northern Ireland. They have also pointed to continuing friction within the British security forces about who should have primacy in the struggle against republican terrorism, disputes

---

[79] Information from a former minister, and from British officials; O'Ballance, *Terror in Ireland*, 217; FitzGerald, *All in a Life*, 232.

[80] See O'Callaghan's article in *The Irish Times*, 7 Jan. 1997.

which continued into the 1990s with the increased role now accorded to MI5. For years the British authorities countered Irish criticism on such matters with the argument that the Garda Special Branch were slack and inefficient, and met accusations of security force collusion with loyalist paramilitaries with blanket denials, until the Stevens inquiry—established only after loyalist paramilitaries had publicly boasted that their selection of victims for assassination was based on official intelligence—confirmed in 1990 that the leakage of low-grade information was widespread. This strengthened Irish arguments that security co-operation would only become truly decisive in the struggle against terrorism when the security forces in Northern Ireland can command the confidence of the majority of the nationalist community.[81]

The Anglo-Irish security relationship has developed in tandem with another set of considerations which arise from the reality that each partner had good grounds for not fully trusting the other. For the British there were initially the legacy of the arms crisis, suspicions about Irish tolerance of republican cross-border activities, a sense that the Irish lacked the will to overcome the legal obstacles to extradition for political offences, and intense resentment at the partially successful Irish action taken against Britain under the European Convention on Human Rights in respect of the treatment of prisoners taken following the introduction of internment in Northern Ireland in 1971. On the Irish side there was at first considerable local sympathy for republican activists who had come south and who were sometimes regarded as the victims rather than as the perpetrators of political violence, although this wore off with the growth in republican violence on both sides of the border; in the early 1970s there was also considerable and as it transpired justified fear that the British government was pursuing an understanding with the IRA behind the back of the Irish authorities; there was concern at what was sometimes seen as Britain's reluctance to support constructive political developments in Northern Ireland; and there was resentment of British covert activities within the state. While primarily directed against the republican movement, these created acute domestic difficulties for successive governments and they were grist to the mill of conspiracy theorists. Concrete evidence of British espionage emerged in 1972 when a sergeant working in C3, the security section at Garda headquarters, was convicted of passing official documents to a British intelligence officer. Both men were treated with extraordinary clemency, being given suspended sentences and allowed to leave the country. It is still not known how this penetration was detected. The subsequent episode of the bank-robbing Littlejohn brothers, two Englishmen who after capture claimed to be operating with the knowledge of British intelligence—ironically enough, they were eventually extradited from Britain to face charges in the Irish courts—also lent colour to suspicions that Britain

[81] *Independent,* 18 May 1990.

continued to play a covert hand within the state. These cases were, naturally, repeatedly adduced in support of the argument that Britain maintained agents throughout the state apparatus and the media; more fantastically, the episodes were also resurrected to support the argument that the devious hand of British intelligence lay behind the misfortunes of the short-lived Haughey government of 1982, an ill-starred regime whose greatest mishaps were fuelled by ministerial infighting and indiscipline and by paranoia about leaks of information from the cabinet, and which needed no external stimulus in its drive to self-destruction. (This is not to argue that British agencies might not have worked to undermine Haughey, the financing of whose opulent lifestyle was the subject of a whispering campaign. But an eventual judicial inquiry showed the rumours to be well founded.)[82]

In the 1970s and early 1980s there were also alarming indications of covert cross-border counter-terrorist operations by British forces, including the shadowing of suspects within the state and possible involvement in the kidnapping and even the murder of republicans. In 1976 two groups of soldiers of the elite Special Air Service (SAS) regiment, arrested by a Garda patrol, proffered the implausible excuse that they had misread their maps and had crossed the border by mistake. Despite intense British political pressure to have the incursion forgotten, their weapons were checked to make sure that none had been used in unsolved murders which had taken place along the border—itself an indication that the Garda suspected that British forces might have already brought their undercover campaign against the IRA onto state territory—and the soldiers were charged with firearms offences for which they were subsequently convicted and fined. Other *causes célèbres*, including the RUC killings in Armagh in 1982 which gave rise to the Stalker inquiry, and the allegations made by a handful of former British officers of cross-border incursions and assassinations in the mid-1970s, added weight to the view that British forces engaged in counter-terrorist operations were not overawed by lines on the map and were quite capable of operating within the state if they could do so undetected. In the 1980s this writer encountered alarmingly naive attitudes amongst some British specialists, who viewed Irish terrorism almost exclusively as a cross-border problem and who yearned for what was familiarly termed a 'gloves off' approach under which the supposed twenty or so kingpins of the IRA campaign

---

[82] FitzGerald, *All in a Life*, 259–61; J. M. Feehan, *The Statesman: A Study of the Role of Charles J. Haughey in the Ireland of Tomorrow* (Dublin, 1985), 56–7, and *Operation Brogue: A Study of the Vilification of Charles Haughey Codenamed 'Operation Brogue' by the British Secret Service* (Dublin, 1984), *passim*; the best account of Mr Haughey's 1982 government remains Joyce and Murtagh, *The Boss*. David Spedding, who became head of MI6 in 1994, had reportedly been in charge of its Irish desk between 1981 and 1983, at the height of Mr Haughey's travails. *Lobster*, 27 (Apr. 1994), 12; *Report of the Tribunal of Inquiry (Dunnes Payments)* (Dublin, 1997), 70–3. Wright, *Spycatcher*, 352–3, says that in the early 1970s he proposed installing 'a device no larger than a packing case' in the attic of the British embassy to enable the monitoring of Irish telephone traffic.

would be hunted down and killed wherever they were. Similar sentiments were publicly aired in 1997 by the maverick Conservative MP and one-time defence minister Alan Clarke.[83]

Other long-standing aspects of the Anglo-Irish security understanding also underwent change. The state continued its venerable passport control arrangements with Britain, which have survived even the European Union's insistence on the free movement of people within its frontiers.[84] There are, however, indications that this understanding is no longer the shield against unwanted immigration that it was in earlier days. Citizens of other member states can now live and work freely within Ireland, a development which has caused little friction because such rights are reciprocal. More alarming for public opinion, however, people from outside the European Union can now arrive at Irish ports direct from continental Europe, or by aircraft from almost anywhere in the world. While the immigration authorities for years dealt expeditiously with supplicant refugees slipping off Aeroflot flights at Shannon simply by shoving them back on the aircraft—a practice which presumably formed part of the deal made with the Soviet airline in the first place—in recent years a combination of factors, including the passage of a liberal Refugees Act in 1996, has transformed the way that issues of immigration and of the granting of refugee status are managed. In 1996/7 there was a hiatus in administrative arrangements to cope with refugees, resulting in an upsurge in illegal immigrants seeking asylum amid strong suspicion that the word had got out that Ireland, from being virtually impregnable, had become a soft touch. It remains to be seen whether this new-found liberalism will continue or whether government will pander to public unease by shutting the gates once more.

The 1980s also saw a number of embarrassing revelations about Irish passport security. Two of those captured on the *Eksund* had false passports which were from a bundle of blanks stolen from the Passport Office. More exotically, during the Irangate inquiry it transpired that President Reagan's National Security Adviser Robert Macfarlane and other American officials used false Irish passports while visiting Tehran for secret meetings in 1986. Further embarrassment was to follow in 1987 when a London embassy official was arrested by British police for selling Irish passports, an offence for which he was later jailed in Ireland.[85] Other evidence has since emerged to show how liberally the state

---

[83] FitzGerald, *All in a Life*, 281; J. Stalker, *Stalker* (London, revised edn., 1988), 52–3. For broadly republican analyses of such episodes see J. Bloch and P. Fitzgerald, *British Intelligence and Covert Action: Africa, Middle East and Europe since 1945* (London, 1983), 210–36, P. McArdle, *The Secret War: An Account of the Sinister Activities along the Border involving Gardai, RUC, British Army and the SAS* (Dublin, 1984), and F. Doherty, *The Stalker Affair* (Dublin, 1986). Conversations with British former counter-insurgency specialists; *The Irish Times*, 7 Oct. 1997.

[84] The Amsterdam treaty signed in May 1997 allowed both Britain and Ireland to keep their border controls with the rest of the European Union and thus to preserve the common British Isles travel area.

[85] *Dáil Debates*, vol. 371, cols. 155–7, 24 Mar. and vol. 372, cols. 1320–9, 7 May 1987; Woodward, *Veil*, 510–12.

had bestowed its passport favours in the past, including the provision of blanks to an Irish missionary order during the Nigerian civil war. This succession of fiascos, and other irregularities discovered in the course of the consequent investigations, led to considerable reforms in passport procedures. However, a murky 'passports for investments' scheme aimed at wealthy foreigners of unimpeachable backgrounds, which in 1990 netted two financiers implicated in 'the biggest banking scandal in history', the collapse of the Bank of Credit and Commerce International, suggests that passport procedures may still be open to abuse.[86]

A final set of security relationships deserves mention. The European integration process has been characterized not only by successive treaties, but by parallel intergovernmental collaborative arrangements in areas outside the treaties proper. Since 1973 Ireland has been involved through these evolving frameworks, at first hesitantly but in the last decade with considerable enthusiasm, in exchanges with her European partners on crime, security, and immigration matters. While much secrecy still surrounds Irish involvement in the European Union-wide mafia of interior ministries known as the 'Trevi group'—because these arrangements remained outside the ambit of the treaties until 1992, it was virtually impossible to obtain any information about them in Ireland—it is clear that Justice has been a fully fledged member for years. Such arrangements now operate within the framework of the 'third pillar' laid down in the treaty of Maastricht, and the state moved to put them on a statutory footing in the autumn of 1997 with the introduction of a bill to allow ratification of the European convention on Europol. While ministers have placed most public emphasis on co-operation 'in such areas as the fight against drugs, immigration, customs, police cooperation and judicial matters', it is clear that counter-terrorism has been on the collaborative agenda since the early 1980s and will also come within the remit of the Europol arrangements (the army came close to securing direct involvement in the Trevi network in the 1980s because of its explosives and ordnance responsibilities arising from terrorist activity, only to be blocked by the Garda).[87] These European developments in turn presumably mean that intelligence on republican activities abroad is no longer simply a matter of Anglo-Irish co-operation, and that the Irish security authorities have developed their own bilateral links with their European analogues in addition to their long-established exchanges with United Kingdom police and security

[86] *The Irish Times*, 3 Jan. 1997; coincidentally, the British embassy in Dublin recently found itself at the centre of a fraudulent passport scheme. See *The Irish Times*, 4 July 1997. Jim Higgins TD, quoted in V. Browne, 'The Politics of a Cover Up', *Magill* (Oct. 1997), 42; *The Irish Times*, 4 Oct. 1997.

[87] Department of Foreign Affairs, *Challenges and Opportunities Abroad: White Paper on Foreign Policy* (Dublin, 1996), 80–2; M. Anderson, *Policing the World: Interpol and the Politics of International Police Co-operation* (Oxford, 1989), 3 and 28; J. Lodge, 'The European Community and Terrorism', in J. Lodge (ed.), *The Challenge of Terrorism* (Brighton, 1988), 22–5, 247–9; private information; *The Irish Times*, 1 Oct. 1997.

agencies. It must also be assumed that the liaison arrangements established in the early 1950s with the CIA and FBI still obtain (it is said that a CIA presence in Ireland was established in the 1970s—probably when the Soviet Union opened its Dublin embassy in 1974—but that it has since been withdrawn).

viii. The Army, External Defence Policy, and the Making of a New Europe

The development of the defence forces since 1969 has taken place largely in the shadow of the Northern crisis. The army appears quickly to have overcome the early disaster of the involvement of army intelligence in the arms crisis, just as it had the 1924 mutiny (again, centred on intelligence), although it had to endure inadvertent involvement in a major constitutional clash in 1976. This arose from extraordinary post-prandial remarks made by the minister for defence Patrick Donegan, a celebrated bon viveur, while opening new catering facilities in a barracks in Mullingar. Donegan attacked President Ó'Dálaigh for exercising his power to refer legislation to the Supreme Court for a binding verdict on its constitutionality—in this case, two bills granting additional powers to deal with political crime in the wake of the murder of the British ambassador. The minister reminded the officers present that the army must 'stand behind the state', in apparent contrast to the president, the titular commander-in-chief of the defence forces, whom he reportedly called 'a thundering disgrace' (he apparently used a rather more familiar expletive). President Ó'Dálaigh was a distinguished constitutional lawyer and jurist and a man of considerable courage—in 1975, after the Dutch industrialist Tiede Herrema was kidnapped by maverick republicans, he had contemplated offering 'myself as a substitute . . . in the fair knowledge that there can be no Government compromise with blackmail. I believe I could bring the kidnappers to reason; if I fail, I do not mind dying—it will vindicate Ireland's honour before the world.' So far from disowning Donegan's gaffe for what it was, the taoiseach Liam Cosgrave initially refused to accept his now remorseful old friend's offer of resignation. Instead he issued what a cabinet colleague fairly described as a 'somewhat half-hearted' statement of apology, which provoked the resignation of President O'Dálaigh.[88] Donegan was, however, translated to another cabinet post, so saving the army from further embarrassment.

Once it became obvious in 1970 that political violence was likely to persist, and that this would inevitably spill over into the state both through republican activities and through loyalist attacks, a gradual expansion in permanent

---

[88] Information from a person present, 1995; Ó'Dálaigh to the taoiseach, 22 Oct. 1975, UCDA, Ó'Dálaigh papers, P51/163; FitzGerald, *All in a Life*, 316–18. It is not known whether President Ó'Dálaigh's letter was actually sent to Mr Cosgrave.

defence force numbers began (actual strength rose by over 30 per cent in the succeeding decade, and in the 1980s the army began a cautious experiment in the recruitment of women, initially as officer cadets and more recently also as enlisted soldiers in both the permanent defence forces and the FCA). As had happened in 1956, border duties became an integral part of military life. This again demonstrated the core importance of the army's internal security role, a point reinforced in May 1974 with the withdrawal of a battalion of Irish troops from UN service in the Middle East after the Dublin and Monaghan car bombings. The state also made extensive use of the army for essentially non-military duties arising from the Northern crisis, such as the escorting of cash shipments and the guarding of prisons. While professional soldiers complain that such work is irksome, boring, and an impediment to training activities, pride is taken in the claim that, in contrast to the Garda, the army has never 'lost a penny or a prisoner' in its care. Occasionally subversives have engaged troops on security duty: a soldier was killed during the rescue of the IRA kidnap victim Don Tidey in 1983—a botched affair which some army sources blamed on Garda failings— and the maverick gunman and kidnapper Dessie O'Hare was wounded and captured and his companion killed at an army/Garda roadblock in 1987. Both the Air Corps and the Naval Service have also frequently been deployed to counter republican activities: the seizures of the gun-runners *Claudia* and *Marita Ann* demonstrated the security value of having a naval arm, however small.[89] The problems posed by indigenous and cross-border terrorism have also seen developments which tie in with rather than cut across the wider military interests of the defence forces: the army handles bomb disposal work, for example, which is also important on some of its UN missions, and it has a special forces unit which is frequently deployed on a range of security and protective duties.

Since the late 1980s there has been a sustained effort to reappraise the purpose, structure, and operations of the defence forces. The initial impetus evidently came from a desire to save money: the government announced a major defence review 'with the particular objective of developing the most realistic and cost-effective defence arrangements'. The outcome of that exercise remains secret, but the thinking behind it led to significant changes. A programme of disposal of some of the decaying barracks and other legacies of British rule was embarked on. To date this has seen the closure of two large barracks in Dublin, and the announcement of six phased closures elsewhere. In 1989 growing unrest about pay and conditions led first to the fielding of a number of 'soldiers' wives' candidates in some constituencies during the general election, and subsequently to the creation and official recognition of representative bodies for

---

[89] I am grateful to Dr Margaret O'hÓgartaigh for pointing out that the first woman to join the army was Dr Bridget Lyons Thornton, who was commissioned as a medical officer in 1922; conversations with various officers. A trainee Garda also died during the Tidey rescue.

officers, for enlisted men, and for members of the reserve. While some observed this development with trepidation, it has had no obvious impact on discipline or effectiveness. Furthermore, the representative bodies have proved their value not only in the specifics of protecting the interests of their members, but in promoting informed discussion on wider issues of defence policy and practice which hitherto could not be publicly aired by serving soldiers, those best qualified to comment on them.

In reaction to the 1989 unrest, the government also established a major inquiry into pay and career structures within the defence forces. The outcome—the 1990 Gleeson report—is perhaps the most lucid and revealing analysis of the defence forces ever published, depicting an army militarily ineffective in proportion to its size, strangled by red tape, mainly engaged on essentially non-military duties, and with remarkably elderly soldiers who had come to see the army as a job for life.[90] In addition to some improvements in pay, the report led to the introduction of a new merit-based selection process for senior officers to supplant the twin evils of seniority and political or personal favouritism which had previously often been what mattered. A second study was also initiated by an 'Effectiveness Audit Group', the findings of which caused acute alarm because of their core proposal that the permanent defence forces should be reduced to about three thousand men. In 1994 a third study commissioned from Price Waterhouse produced recommendations for a radical reduction in the size of the permanent defence forces—by about 40 per cent of establishment, and about 25 per cent of actual strength—and a much greater investment in weapons and equipment: in the pointed words of one of its authors, the Canadian general Lewis MacKenzie, 'you want an army that can fight'.[91] In 1996 the chief of staff announced a radical restructuring which, together with an early retirement scheme, more spending on equipment, modernized administrative procedures, and the systematic recruitment of young blood on short service contracts, is intended to make the defence forces slimmer but more operationally effective both in Ireland and on UN service. There are limits to what rationalization processes can achieve, however: despite compelling cost and effectiveness arguments, it has proved enormously difficult for political reasons to shut any barracks outside Dublin, and there is no guarantee that any real manpower and other savings achieved through reorganization will in fact be devoted to improving equipment and training (the assumption underlying the army's approach to reorganization). The avalanche of over nine thousand compensation claims for hearing damage caused by firearms practice, in 1998 estimated likely to cost the state perhaps two billion pounds when all are settled, will undoubtedly drastically reduce the funds available for equipment purchases. While the representative associations recognize the need for

---

[90] Gleeson report.　　[91] Speaking on RTE's *Prime Time*, 8 Nov. 1994.

greater investment in military hardware, furthermore, in public they advance arguments, designed to protect the jobs of their ageing members, which fly in the face of military effectiveness. The point that the aim of rationalization should be to increase effectiveness rather than to save money was, unprecedentedly, publicly and forthrightly made by the chief of staff General McMahon in 1996. He also dwelt on the need for reorganization, modernization, and investment in weapons, and he announced important changes of policy in relation both to the permanent defence force and to the FCA, which he described as 'underutilised, poorly trained and ill equipped to carry out an effective role' after decades of neglect. Remarking that it was 'ludicrous' that the army possessed just two modern armoured personnel carriers, he also warned that the army may find itself increasingly excluded from even the most pacific UN roles for want of proper training and of appropriate equipment.[92]

The recent experience and likely fate of the two subordinate arms of the defence forces require mention. The Naval Service, which in 1970 reached the extraordinary low point of having no seagoing craft at all, has seen significant developments in its capacity and duties. In 1972 the state inaugurated a period of relatively sustained modernization with the commissioning of two new purpose-built patrol vessels from an Irish dockyard. These were augmented by the purchase of further modern vessels from abroad. The main reason for the expansion was not maritime defence, or the interdiction of gun-runners, but fisheries protection: Ireland has responsibility for enforcing fisheries regulations in the second largest sea area of any EU state, and for this purpose the EU has met much of the considerable cost of re-equipping the naval service (Europe also helped to foot the bill for the Air Corps's maritime surveillance aircraft, which carry out fisheries protection work in tandem with the Naval Service). The realization in recent years that Ireland has become an important entrepôt for illegal drugs on passage to Britain or to mainland Europe has led to further requests to Brussels for money to buy more ships for essentially customs duties. While it is likely that it will undergo a radical reorganization before the millennium—the service is currently under review by a firm of management consultants—its long-term prospects in fisheries protection, coastguard work, and drug interdiction are very good.[93] The future of the Air Corps looks less promising: while it has acquired one new role in maritime surveillance, in recent years it has encountered considerable difficulties in retaining trained pilots disenchanted by the limited opportunities which it can offer and tempted by the higher salaries available in commercial aviation. It has also lost its

---

[92] *The Irish Times*, 20 Apr. 1998; comments by John Lucey, president of the enlisted men's association, Radio Ireland, 15 May 1997; speeches by Lt.-Gen. G. J. McMahon, 9 Oct. and [undated] Apr. 1996, as supplied by the Defence Forces Public Relations Branch.

[93] McIvor, *Irish Naval Service*, 135, 220–1; *Fianna Fáil manifesto—1997: People before Politics* (Dublin, 1997), 139.

monopoly on the provision of helicopter services to the state: a private contractor now provides search and rescue cover along the West coast, and in 1997 the Garda took delivery of their first helicopter. As air defence is now accepted as being outside its remit, it may be due for a reorganization to make it a more focused army support arm rather than the jack of all trades which it has attempted to be since the early 1960s.

Border duties and internal security tasks apart, most of the work of the defence forces is now 'concerned with matters other than the stated primary role of defence of the State against external aggression'. Of the variety of non-security activities in which it is engaged, the most challenging ones have been those connected with UN service. That remains a professional lifeline, providing variety, travel, extra money, familiarity with other armies, and some danger: the period from the ending of its major Cyprus involvement in 1974 until a battalion was provided for the UN force in southern Lebanon in 1978, was described in 1996 by the chief of staff as 'a low point which we can never allow to happen again'. The Lebanon has proved a particularly challenging and hazardous mission, as neither the Israeli Defence Forces and their south Lebanese proxies, nor the guerrilla groups operating in the area, are much impressed by blue helmets. What was supposed to be a UN-maintained cordon sanitaire in southern Lebanon instead became a guerrilla war zone, with UN forces confined to a fraction of the territory they were supposed to control, and even there under constant challenge by well-armed local groups. Since 1980 the army has lost a number of men on active service, including three kidnapped and later murdered. On occasion the Irish battalion has had to defend itself robustly against attack by different groups (including elements of the IDF). It is arguable that the army's difficult experience with Israeli forces and their proxies has had the general effect of increasing Irish sympathy for the Palestinian people: during his visit to Dublin to unveil a plaque outside his boyhood home in 1985, the Israeli president Chaim Hertzog complained bitterly of the attitude of Irish troops in Lebanon.[94]

The growing complexity and variety of the army's UN involvement brought significant change in the early 1990s: first, a separate UN training school was established within the military college; secondly, in 1993 legislation was passed to allow Irish military participation in UN peace enforcement as well as in peacekeeping operations, recognition that in the post-Cold War era the UN was facing new tests of its will in many parts of the world; thirdly, in 1996 the Bruton government committed itself to the appointment of a military adviser to the Irish mission to UN headquarters, reversing the long-held Foreign Affairs line that the army only wanted the post 'for the [subsistence] allowances . . . We've

---

[94] McMahon speech, 9 Oct. 1996; Robert Fisk, *Pity the Nation: Lebanon at War* (1st edn., London, 1990; Oxford, 1991), 151–4.

been blocking it for years!' and that career diplomats were well able to deal with even the most specialized military issues.[95]

The other area in which the horizons of the defence forces have changed is in respect of European security. Since 1983 the army has provided an officer as part of the Irish team at the Conference on Security and Co-operation in Europe (now the OSCE), a belated acknowledgement by Foreign Affairs that military expertise could sometimes be a necessary element in the foreign policy process. It is also likely that, as European integration proceeds, the state will increasingly look to the defence forces for specialist advice on the myriad of quite technical security issues which arise in the governance of the Union and in its dealings with the rest of Europe. This brings the discussion to formal defence policy. The policy-making process has arguably evolved scarcely at all since the 1960s. While the presence in cabinet of the minister for defence suggested a key input at the appropriate policy level to ensure proper representation of the professional military view, it appears that few ministers for defence have had any substantive role in policy discussions relating to defence. Instead, they have been the political heads of an essentially executive agency required only to do the government's bidding, not to advise the government on what to do. Given the lack of a supporting policy focus within the department, that is perhaps not surprising. The consequences for the defence forces have been severe: the first generation of ministers were men whose understanding of defence affairs was framed by their experience of the War of Independence and of the civil war, rather than by any broader exposure to modern warfare or to the promptings of a professional military establishment. One striking feature of affairs after 1969 is the perpetuation of these arrangements: when asked in 1994 about the role of his department in the formulation of contemporary defence policy, a senior Defence official responded in a tone of combined shock and indignation that policy questions were of course matters exclusively for Foreign Affairs and for the government.[96]

Formally, defence policy remains unchanged. The state still steers clear of other peoples' wars, and the defence forces are still expected to protect the state from external aggression without any outside help. Circumstances have, however, changed considerably. Most importantly, in 1973 Ireland joined the European Economic Community (now the EU). While this was done emphatically on economic rather than on political or foreign policy grounds, proponents of the move and the government clearly stated that they realized that Ireland was embarking in a direction which would take the state towards convergence with the other members, and that no state could expect to reap the economic benefits of membership without accepting some of the political obligations, including that of contributing to the security of the new Europe and its constituent states. The 1970s and 1980s, however, also saw the elevation of neutrality to the status of

---

[95] *White Paper on Foreign Policy*, 194–5; conversation with an Irish official, 1992.
[96] Exchange with a Defence official, 1994.

holy writ. Furthermore, environmental fears about nuclear pollution added to public unease about the morality of nuclear warfare, and consequently strengthened arguments against any military links with states having nuclear weapons. At the same time, all Irish governments since 1973 have supported the progressive integration of EC/EU foreign and security policy. The one significant departure from this came in 1982 in the wake of the Argentine invasion of the Falkland Islands, then as now British sovereign territory. Ireland initially joined with the rest of the EC in supporting the British position that Argentina should withdraw unconditionally, a principle also endorsed by the UN Security Council, of which the state was then a member, in resolution 502. This was, however, done only with obvious reluctance—there were clear parallels between Argentina's aspirations and the Irish claim to Northern Ireland. There may also have been resonances, for some connected with the minority Haughey government, of the 1969 dreams of a military *coup de main* to repossess parts of the fourth green field. Matters were further complicated by the precarious circumstances of the government, by the emotional legacy of the 1980–1 Northern Ireland hunger strikes and the parlous state of Anglo-Irish relations, and by an evident gap between the approach suggested by Foreign Affairs and the more abrasive noises emanating from other government quarters. Matters came to a head after the British sinking of the Argentine cruiser the *General Belgrano*. This produced an impromptu statement from, of all unlikely people, the minister for defence that Britain was now the aggressor. The official Irish line changed to demand the withdrawal of EC sanctions against Argentina, together with an immediate cessation of hostilities. While this policy switch may have reflected popular sentiment, public anger might more rationally have been directed against the Argentine junta who had dispatched the elderly *Belgrano* on her ill-conceived mission. The change made diplomatic sense only if framed as one element in a broader, bifocal policy aimed first at persuading the Security Council to rescind resolution 502, and secondly at ensuring that all European states should relinquish their remaining colonial holdings (whatever the wishes of their inhabitants). This reorientation at UN and EC levels brought Ireland onto a collision course with Britain, made more obvious by the fact that the government did not press the wider case for complete decolonization upon which its amended policy logically depended. Ireland continued to call for a ceasefire even after British forces had landed on the Falklands. While the government denied that its bizarre policy contortions were animated by anything other than the purest internationalism and a desire for the pacific settlement of disputes, their origins lay firmly in domestic political circumstances, together with antagonism towards the British government and its formidable prime minister.[97]

---

[97] Joyce and Murtagh, *The Boss*, 155–68; Keatinge, *A Singular Stance*, 105–8; on the hunger strikes see D. Beresford, *Ten Men Dead: The Story of the 1981 Irish Hunger Strike* (London, 1987).

Domestic political attitudes towards the UN have changed considerably in the post-Cold War era, due largely to a perception of increased American domination of its agenda. This was reflected in reactions to the Iraqi invasion of Kuwait and the subsequent UN-endorsed multinational military response which succeeded in evicting Iraq from the state which it had overrun. While the government fully supported the UN and EU positions that the Iraqi invasion was a flagrant piece of aggression against a sovereign state, many others argued that the West was only fighting to secure its oil supplies. Iraq's argument that it was merely reclaiming its historic nineteenth province may also have had a subconscious resonance for a public emotionally predisposed towards anti-partitionist imagery. None of those who raised their voices against a UN military response had any realistic alternative method of restoring Kuwait to statehood beyond the empty nostrum of indefinite negotiation: the core of their argument appeared to be that the use of force to succour a violated state, even if mandated by the United Nations, is somehow immoral simply because the states involved in such action are also protecting their own national security interests.

Public discussion about Ireland's position in the UN has been further complicated by the changes in NATO's role since the end of the Cold War which have seen it become an operational sub-contractor in UN peacekeeping and peace enforcement, most conspicuously in the former Yugoslavia. NATO has clearly become a key element in the network of institutions which Europe has created to promote the security of emerging as well as of long-established states, and even the Russians have been willing to place troops under NATO operational control. Such developments have proved something of an embarrassment to Irish politicians, who generally prefer to avert their eyes from questions of European security and defence. There appears to be a consensus that Ireland will not join a military alliance such as NATO, yet there is broad acceptance that the growing foreign policy co-ordination process which Ireland has heartily endorsed inevitably binds the state to stick by its European partners in security as in economic and political matters. Since 1983 the state has maintained military as well as civilian representation at the pan-European Organization for Security and Co-operation in Europe, and in 1992 assumed observer status at the Western European Union. In 1996 the Bruton coalition signalled its willingness to participate in Partnership for Peace (PfP), the European security confidence-building organization which all the former Cold War contestants and even Switzerland, hitherto the purest of pure neutrals, have joined. The Bruton government also allowed the posting of an Irish officer to Ifor, the NATO-led but UN-mandated international force in former Yugoslavia. A military police company was subsequently attached to its successor force, and a liaison officer assigned to NATO headquarters.[98] In opposition Fianna Fáil portrayed PfP as a

---

[98] *The Irish Times*, 3 Oct. 1996 and 15 May 1997.

NATO honeytrap, and speculated that the United States was attempting to seduce the country from military neutrality; in government, the party appeared reluctant publicly to move from that position, although its position may become clearer with the promised defence white paper in 1999.[99] The military view is that the state will only be able to continue to make a meaningful contribution to peacekeeping if it participates in the PfP framework, which has become the main vehicle for the development of the doctrines and practices necessary for effective multinational military co-operation in peace as well as in war, and that the army's high reputation and practical capacity in peacekeeping will be jeopardized if Ireland remains outside. It is, however, likely that the state's political and military contribution to the maintenance and enhancement of EU and of wider European security, as well as to future UN operations, will be hedged in with ingenious semantic caveats to avoid the charge that Ireland has sacrificed neutrality as well as sovereignty on the altar of economic and social development. Whether these will be sufficient indefinitely on the one hand to assuage neutralist sentiment, and on the other to placate Ireland's current and prospective EU partners, a number of which face very real regional security threats, remains to be seen. It may be that the small states which now constitute a majority in the EU will prove less tolerant of Irish exceptionalism than have the traditional NATO guarantors of Western European security since 1949 who, conspiracy theorists notwithstanding, were never greatly exercised by Irish refusal to join the alliance.

Predictions that the establishment of a foreign affairs committee as a parliamentary forum for the analysis of foreign policy issues would inevitably lead to more informed public debate about defence and security issues proved over-optimistic: since its inception in 1993 the committee, so far from becoming a focus of sustained inquiry and analysis, has hopped about like a performing flea from one headline-catching issue to another.[100] It has, however, at least taken evidence and had briefings both from Foreign Affairs and from defence forces personnel, in itself a notable innovation in Irish parliamentary history. Another important innovation was the publication in April 1996 of the first ever government white paper on foreign policy. This was intended as a comprehensive document not only setting out Ireland's specific policy positions in international relations but also spelling out 'the principles that underpin Ireland's commitment to peace, security and co-operation', increasing transparency in the formulation and conduct of foreign policy, and raising the public's awareness of and sense of ownership of the state's actions in the external

[99] *White Paper on Foreign Policy*, 128–32; *The Irish Times*, 12 Oct. 1996; R. McGinty, 'Almost like Talking Dirty: Irish Security Policy in Post-Cold War Europe', *Irish Studies in International Affairs*, 6 (1995), 127–43; press release by David Andrews TD, minister for defence, 30 June 1997.

[100] E. O'Halpin, 'Irish Parliamentary Culture and the European Union: Formalities to be Observed', in P. Norton (ed.), *National Parliaments and the European Union* (London, 1996), 131–3.

environment.[101] While an acknowledged novelty in Irish public affairs—in its own words, 'never before have the Irish Government sought to explain the full range of their foreign policy to the people through the medium of a White Paper'—the document fell at the first hurdle which it set itself. So far from being comprehensive, the intertwined issues of Northern Ireland and of Anglo-Irish relations, the 'fundamental priority of Irish foreign policy . . . since the foundation of the State', were left out—a chapter was excised at a late stage because of the sensitivity of the issues.[102] That had two effects. First, it meant that other matters assumed a false centrality in the public articulation of Irish foreign policy preoccupations. Secondly, while its chapters on the EU and European integration were very useful, by sidestepping the always complicated and sometimes seedy reality of the state's relations with its closest neighbour the white paper contributed to rather than dispelled illusions about the nature of interstate relations and the necessary primacy of national interest in the formulation and conduct of Irish foreign policy, and instead assigned itself a licence to moralize. Thus, gender inequity, military power, economic injustice in underdeveloped countries, 'drugs and international crime', and anti-personnel landmines all felt the lash of Mother Ireland's tongue.[103] On practical matters reflecting less glorious light on Ireland's external policies, such as the peculiar balance apparently struck between the imperatives of the beef export trade and wider national interests, it had nothing at all to say. Anyone perusing this 340-page document will see for themselves that the *Skibbereen Eagle* still flies.

ix. Conclusion

In the past thirty years the state has had to make a series of contingent adjustments in its approach to its external relations and its dealings with the international community, and these have had implications for defence and security policy. Some of these such as European integration have been eagerly embraced, without much prior thought for or informed discussion of the logical long-term consequences; others have been adopted more or less reluctantly in response to renewed threats from within and to a lesser extent from without. The main dangers which the state has had to cope with have come not from the activities or designs of foreign powers, but from the resurgence in militant republicanism on both sides of the border and, for the first time, from a concomitant though sporadic threat from loyalist paramilitaries. The state's response to these threats has embraced both a recourse to tried and tested

---

[101] Extract from the Bruton/Spring/de Rossa policy agreement *A Government of Renewal*, quoted in *White Paper on Foreign Policy*, 1.

[102] Ibid. 3 and 37; private information.   [103] *White Paper on Foreign Policy*, 9.

methods such as special courts, and new departures including the construction of a bilateral Anglo-Irish legal domain in respect of some terrorist offences and increasing recognition of the validity of the legal framework provided by a number of European conventions on extradition, on the suppression of terrorism, and on human rights.

The last thirty years have also seen a redefinition of the state's international relationships, particularly in respect of its enthusiasm for European integration, which are beginning to have a major impact not only in the spheres of economic and social policy but in even more sensitive areas such as immigration control, crime prevention, and defence. They have, however, also arguably seen a growing disjuncture between, on the one hand, Irish state interests and long-accepted national policy including support for European political integration, the need to ensure the rule of international law, and the primacy of the UN in international affairs, and, on the other, a public mythology which now portrays Ireland as the moral conscience of an otherwise depraved, cynical, and egotistical developed world.

Conclusion

The twenty-six-county Irish state was established as a parliamentary democracy, and it has remained one. Since independence, furthermore, it has avoided war and it has not been invaded or attacked by any other state—the fitful though unwelcome interference of Germany between 1939 and 1944, of the Soviet Union and its satellites up to 1990, and of Libya since the 1970s, have been construed as being aimed entirely against Britain rather than as interventions directed against Ireland. This history of unbroken democracy, and the dearth of external enemies, sets Ireland apart from the other European states which emerged after the First World War. It is all the more striking given the unresolved question of partition.

The consolidation of democratic government in a new state which owed its emergence largely to the use of force was neither automatic nor easy: it involved acceptance of something less than an all-island Ireland, a bitter (though not all that bloody) civil war which in the ultimate hinged on the issue of whether the clear wishes of the electorate or those of a self-referential militant elite ought to predominate, the difficult subordination of military to civilian authority in 1924, and an enduring struggle with armed republicanism. It also involved recognition of the imperative of protecting Britain's strategic interests, ironically a principle on which both those who supported the 1921 Treaty settlement, and Eamon de Valera, who denounced it, were implicitly agreed. This was complicated by the republican movement's penchant for making deals with Britain's enemies. These factors in combination contributed to the adoption by the state of a formal doctrine of external defence the primary subtext of which was not to enable Ireland to stand up for itself against military aggression from all comers and to police its own skies and waters, but rather to suppress militarism within the state. The imagery of an external threat was used to legitimize the use of the army to defend the state from its bitterest foes. These were not foreign powers but domestic enemies who believed that the project of a united, independent Ireland had been needlessly abandoned. The paradox of Irish defence policy up to the 1990s has, consequently, been that the state has used the army overwhelmingly as a guarantor of internal rather than of external security. Defending Ireland from without was, and remains, almost entirely the unavowed role of other powers and since 1949 of NATO.

Since its establishment the state has exhibited a combination of pragmatism and resolution in defining and in protecting its domestic security interests: hard laws have been passed and then permitted gradually to lapse, and harsh measures applied and then relaxed, in a calibrated response to the ebb and flow of republican violence. The underlying aim of internal security policy, as much under W. T. Cosgrave until 1932 as under de Valera and his Fianna Fáil successors, has consistently been not to extirpate republicanism as an ideology but to corral it within the framework of constitutional politics. At different times the Garda and the army predominated in internal security operations up to 1945, since when the police have had the lead role. The emphasis in this book has been on the army and on the Department of External (now Foreign) Affairs, simply because the files are largely available; those elements of the Garda and of the Department of Justice which handle problems of subversion, terrorism, and counter-espionage await their historians once their records are opened.

In the first decades of the state's existence external defence policy was, pieties uttered at the League of Nations notwithstanding, framed entirely by reference to the United Kingdom, which was at once independent Ireland's strategic guarantor, her unwelcome guest under the Treaty, and her only likely military enemy. There was clarity on only two key principles: Ireland would not be dragged into Britain's wars, and Ireland would not allow her territory to be used to harm Britain's strategic interests. Having embraced those ideas, however, both the Cosgrave and the de Valera governments shied away from the logical corollary, that of providing the state with forces which could act as a serious deterrent to aggression from any quarter on land, by sea, or in the air. This is not to say that the defence forces served no useful purposes up to 1939: on the contrary, the state needed the army as a badge of statehood, as a focus for national loyalty, as an armed bulwark against the republican movement, and as visible proof that the post-Treaty IRA were not the sole heirs to the Irish physical force tradition. But the first generation of Irish leaders was acutely aware of the perils of militarism, and of the need to keep soldiers firmly under the thumb of civil government. Furthermore, their perceptions of defence questions were bounded by their War of Independence experience: physical force was essentially a political device to be used against an occupying power, not an instrument of deterrence of external aggression or a means of enhancing Irish influence in the outside world.

The state's apprehensions about the role of the military has had unhappy consequences for the defence forces. These have been denied a clear long-term role beyond the vaguest and most implausible of injunctions to secure the independent defence of the national territory. In the years between 1939 and 1945 the government did make a half-hearted effort to provide the resources necessary for the task of independent defence. Even then, however, the reality was that Ireland could defend herself effectively only to the extent that Britain would allow her the necessary weapons, munitions, and equipment and would provide the air and naval power that the state utterly lacked. Independent defence in effect meant nothing more than the potential very briefly to contest the inevitable should either set of belligerents have decided to appropriate all or part of the state for their own purposes.

While maintaining the fiction of a policy of independent defence, contiguity and common interests ensured that, the problem of Northern Ireland notwithstanding, the state adopted and maintained close security relations with the United Kingdom in respect of the outside world. With the specific though significant exception of the problem of republican activities after 1923, Ireland has always been a co-operative peacetime neighbour, solicitous of British security interests and quietly aware of submerged reciprocal benefits in matters such as immigration control. The state has, similarly, been conscious of the security concerns of other friendly countries, in particular the United States of America, even at times when it has pursued independent lines of policy at the United Nations and elsewhere. Discreet security collaboration was used as a substitute for overt military co-operation with the Western powers both during and after the Second World War, an arrangement which suited the states involved, which met the domestic imperative of not openly supporting the old enemy England, which left intact the policy of formal neutrality, and which in the ultimate proved remarkably cost-effective.

The state has remained fearful of siren calls for military action, overt or covert, to complete the traditional nationalist agenda of uniting North with South. Canada's Lewis MacKenzie, consequently, is surely wrong in his remark that 'you want an army that can fight': for over seventy years the state has sought nothing of the kind, partly through negligence but also out of fear that such a force would inevitably turn its guns northwards. There have been moments—in 1922, in the mid-1930s, in the early years of the Emergency, and most dramatically in 1969–70—when cliques within army or political circles broke the taboo against even contemplating the use of military force to gain control of all or part of Northern Ireland. Such episodes strengthen, and for some may justify, the control by starvation philosophy implicit in the state's handling of its defence forces.

The contemporary Irish state is plainly happy to engage with its EU partners and with other friendly states in any security matters which do not involve the use of military force. Both the Garda and army intelligence have had long experience of selective liaison with analogous organizations abroad, and such collaboration has been codified and deepened through the Amsterdam treaty and the Europol Act. Where the state continues to have acute problems is in the public definition of what its external security interests, and its responsibilities both to its European partners and to the wider world, actually are. After forty years of successful though sometimes costly military involvement in well-intentioned but underpowered UN peacekeeping operations in far-flung corners of the world, the development in the post-Cold War era of modes of international intervention predicated on the use of serious force under UN mandate and, worse still, drawing on NATO's unrivalled organizational resources, has caused embarrassment to a state which prefers to regard itself as the Mother Teresa of the international community. Having long agonized about the inadequacy, tardiness, and selfishness of the West's response to atrocity and genocide, whether in Rwanda or in Bosnia, it now havers about involvement in the planning and training processes necessary to make UN and European military interventions to protect or to restore peace effective lest Irish neutrality somehow—and uniquely—be compromised. Nothing better highlights the inconsistencies and evasions which underscore that most convenient, malleable, and inexpensive of doctrines.

Addendum to Paperback Edition

Four significant developments since this book was completed must be mentioned.

First, in October 1999 a detachment from the army Ranger Wing was assigned to long-range reconnaissance duties on the East Timor/West Timor border, the first occasion on which such troops have been deployed operationally on UN service. Furthermore, in the same month a transport company was sent to provide logistical support for the UN-mandated and NATO-led 'Security Presence' in Kosovo. Thirdly, on 1 December 1999 Ireland finally bit the bullet of Partnership for Peace, joining without either fanfare or commotion after a Dáil resolution. This occasioned the appointment of officials from Foreign Affairs, Defence, and the army to deal with PfP and the Euro-Atlantic Partnership Council in Brussels. As a result of the December 1999 Helsinki summit decisions on Petersberg tasks, finally, Ireland now has a full-time representative at ambassadorial level on the EU's interim Political and Security Committee.

Against these broadly encouraging developments, however, must be put the black farce of the long-promised defence white paper. This was eventually laid before the Dáil in February 2000 amidst considerable controversy, not least because it had been prepared almost entirely without consultation with the general staff. Clothed in the language of modern public service management, it was in practice a straightforward essay in military emasculation. Amongst other contentious points, it sought to transfer ultimate responsibility for advice on defence policy from the chief of staff to the civilian head of the department, a proposal made doubly bizarre by that department's historic aversion to the very idea that policy formed any part of its brief. After much argument and the public intervention of the taoiseach, a codicil was produced which met some of the army's basic objections. A leaked Defence memorandum has since shown that, despite this temporary reverse, the civilian side still plan to tighten their stranglehold on military affairs. Plus ça change . . .

BIBLIOGRAPHY

(a) Official Records

National Archives, Dublin

Department of Communications
Department of Defence
Department of Finance
Department of Foreign Affairs
Department of Justice
Department of the Taoiseach

Military Archives, Dublin

Chief of Staff
Council of Defence
Intelligence/G2

Public Record Office of Northern Ireland, Belfast

Cabinet minutes and papers
Ministry of Home Affairs

Public Record Office, London

Admiralty
Cabinet committee papers and War Cabinet committee papers
Cabinet memoranda
Dominions Office
Foreign Office
Government Code and Cipher School
Government Communications Headquarters
Home Office
Ministry of Defence
Treasury

United States National Archives, Washington

National Security Agency
Office of Strategic Services
State Department

Public Archives of Canada, Ottawa

Department of External Affairs
Department of National Defence

(*b*) **Private Papers**

Abbreviations: CCC: Churchill College Cambridge; UCDA: University College Dublin Department of Archives.

Sheila Batstone	Imperial War Museum
Ernest Blythe	UCDA
Dan Bryan	UCDA
Dan Bryan transcripts	in my possession
Lionel Curtis	Bodleian Library, Oxford
F. N. Davidson	Liddell Hart Centre for Military Archives, King's College London
Geoffrey Dawson	Bodleian Library, Oxford
Reginald Drax	CCC
Fianna Fáil	Fianna Fáil headquarters, Dublin
Desmond FitzGerald	UCDA
Maurice Hankey	CCC
Michael Hayes	UCDA
Richard Hayes	National Library of Ireland
Hugh Kennedy	UCDA
Walter Long	Wiltshire Record Office, Trowbridge
Sean MacEntee	UCDA
Sean MacEoin	UCDA
Patrick McGilligan	UCDA
J. Pierpoint Moffat	Houghton Library, Harvard
Richard Mulcahy	UCDA
Philip Noel-Baker	CCC
Cearbhaill Ó'Dálaigh	UCDA
Padraig O'Halpin	in my possession
Diarmuid O'Hegarty	UCDA
Ernie O'Malley	UCDA

(*c*) **Parliamentary and Official Publications**

Challenges and opportunities abroad: White Paper on Foreign Policy (Dublin, 1996)
Committee of Public Accounts reports
Dáil Debates
Report of the Commission on Remuneration and Conditions of Service in the Defence Forces [Gleeson report] (Dublin, 1990)
Report of the Public Services Organisation Review Group [Devlin report] (Dublin, 1969)
Report of the Tribunal of Inquiry (*Dunnes Payments*) (Dublin, 1997)

(*d*) **Newspapers and Magazines**

Catholic Bulletin
An Cosantoir

Independent
Irish Times
Kavanagh's Weekly
Lobster
Magill
National Observer
Sunday Tribune

(e) Books, Articles, and Theses

ALDRICH, R., *Espionage, Security and Intelligence in Britain, 1945–1970* (Manchester, 1998).

ALVAREZ, D., 'No Immunity: Sigint and the European Neutrals, 1939–45', *Intelligence and National Security,* 12/2 (Apr. 1997).

ANDERSON, M., *Policing the World: Interpol and the Politics of International Police Co-operation* (Oxford, 1989).

ANDERSON, W. K., *James Connolly and the Irish Left* (Dublin, 1994).

ANDREW, C., *Secret Service: The Making of the British Intelligence Community* (London, 1985).

—— and GORDIEVSKY, O., *Instructions from the Centre: Top Secret Files on KGB Foreign Operations 1975–1985* (London, 1991).

—— —— *KGB: The Inside Story of its Foreign Operations from Lenin to Gorbachev* (London, 1990).

—— —— 'Residency Priorities: The Case of Denmark', in *Intelligence and National Security,* 7/1 (Jan. 1992).

ANDREWS, C. S., *Dublin made me: An Autobiography* (Dublin, 1979).

—— *Man of no property: An Autobiography Volume Two* (Dublin, 1982).

ARNOLD, B., *Haughey: His Life and Unlucky Deeds* (London, 1993; paperback edn., 1994).

ARTHUR, P., and JEFFERY, K., *Northern Ireland since 1968* (Oxford, 1988).

BECKER, J., *Hitler's Children: The Story of the Baader-Meinhof Gang* (London, 1977; revised edn., 1978).

BEESLY, P., *Room 40: British Naval Intelligence 1914–1918* (London, 1982).

—— *Very Special Admiral: The Life of Admiral John H. Godfrey CB* (London, 1980).

BELL, J. B., *The Irish Troubles: A Generation of Violence 1967–1992* (London, 1993).

—— *The Secret Army: A History of the IRA 1916–1970* (London, 1970).

BERESFORD, D., *Ten Men Dead: The Story of the 1981 Irish Hunger Strike* (London, 1987).

BISHOP, P., and MALLIE, E., *The Provisional IRA* (London, 1987; Corgi edn., 1988).

BLOCH, J., and FITZGERALD, P., *British Intelligence and Covert Action: Africa, Middle East and Europe since 1945* (London, 1983).

BOLAND, K., *Fine Gael: British or Irish?* (Dublin, 1984).

—— *The Rise and Decline of Fianna Fáil* (Dublin, 1982).

BOWMAN, J., *De Valera and the Ulster Question* (Oxford, 1982).

BOYLE, A., *The Climate of Treason* (London, 1979; revised edn., 1980).

BRADY, C., *Guardians of the Peace* (Dublin, 1974).

BRADY, S., *Arms and the Men: Ireland in Turmoil* (Dublin, 1971).

Broderick, E., 'The Corporate Labour Policy of Fine Gael, 1934', *Irish Historical Studies*, 29/113 (May 1994).

Browne, N., *Against the Tide* (Dublin, 1986).

Browne, V., 'The Arms Crisis 1970: The Inside Story', *Magill*, 3/8 (May 1980).

—— 'The Berry File', *Magill*, 3/9 (June 1980).

—— 'The Politics of a Cover Up', *Magill* (Oct. 1997).

Brunicardi, D., 'The Marine Service', *Irish Sword*, 19/75–6 (1993–4).

Burke, J. F., 'Recently Released Material on Soviet Intelligence Operations', *Intelligence and National Security*, 8/2 (Apr. 1993).

Butler, H., 'The Artukovich File', in *Escape from the Anthill* (Mullingar, 1985).

Campbell, K., *ANC: A Soviet Task Force?* (London, 1986).

Campbell, P., 'By the right—Go Mear Mearseail', in *The P-P-Penguin Patrick Campbell* (London, 1965).

—— 'Cuckoo in the nest', in *The P-P-Penguin Patrick Campbell* (London, 1965).

—— 'Sean Tar joins up', in *Come here till I tell you* (London, 1960).

Canning, P., *British Policy towards Ireland, 1921–1941* (Oxford, 1985).

Carroll, J., *Ireland in the War Years* (Newton Abbot, 1975).

—— 'US–Irish Relations, 1939–45', *Irish Sword*, 19/75–6 (1993–4).

Carter, C., *The Shamrock and the Swastika: German Espionage in Ireland in World War II* (Palo Alto, 1977).

Churchill, W., *The Second World War*, i: *The Gathering Storm* (London, new edn., 1949).

City and County Management: A Retrospective (Institute of Public Administration, Dublin, 1991).

Clare, P. K., 'Subcultural Obstacles to the Control of Racketeering in Northern Ireland', *Conflict Quarterly*, 10/4 (Fall 1990).

Coakley, J., 'The Foundations of Statehood', in J. Coakley and M. Gallagher (eds.), *Politics in the Republic of Ireland* (2nd edn., Dublin, 1993; repr. 1996).

Cohen, S. M., *American Modernity & Modern Jewry* (New York, 1983).

Colville, J., *The Fringes of Power: Downing Street Diaries*, i: *1939–1941* (London, 1985).

Constitution of the Irish Free State (Dublin, 1922).

Coogan, T. P., *The IRA* (London, 1970).

—— *Michael Collins* (London, 1990).

Coyle, J. P., 'Transition to Peace', *Irish Sword*, 19/75–6 (1993–4).

Cronin, M., 'Blueshirts, Sports and Socials', *History Ireland* (Autumn 1994).

—— 'The Socio-Economic Background and Membership of the Blueshirt Movement, 1932–5', *Irish Historical Studies*, 29/114 (Nov. 1994).

Cronin, S., *Frank Ryan: The Search for the Republic* (Dublin, 1980).

—— *The McGarrity Papers: Revelations of the Irish Revolutionary Movement in Ireland and America 1900–1940* (Tralee, 1972).

Cullen, J., 'Patrick J. Hogan TD, Minister for Agriculture, 1922–1932' (unpublished Ph.D. diss., Dublin City University, 1993).

Curran, J. M., *The Birth of the Irish Free State, 1921–3* (Alabama, 1980).

Daniels, R., *Prisoners without Trial: Japanese Americans in World War II* (New York, 1993).

Deacon, R., *'C': A Biography of Sir Maurice Oldfield, Head of MI6* (London, 1985).

DEUTSCHER, I., *Stalin* (Oxford, 1949; revised edn., London, 1966).

DOHERTY, F., *The Stalker Affair* (Dublin, 1986).

DOHERTY, G., 'The Ministers and Secretaries Act 1924 and the Council of Defence: A Neglected Controversy', *Administration*, 43/4 (Winter 1995–6).

DUGGAN, J. P., *A History of the Irish Army* (Dublin, 1991).

—— *Neutral Ireland and the Third Reich* (Dublin, 1985).

DUKES, J., 'The Emergency Services', *Irish Sword*, 19/75–6 (1993–4).

DUNPHY, R., 'The Workers Party and Europe: Trajectory of an Idea', *Irish Political Studies*, 7 (1992).

DWYER, T. RYLE, *Guests of the Nation: The Story of Allied and Axis Servicemen Interned in Ireland during World War II* (Dingle, 1994).

—— *Irish Neutrality and the USA, 1939–1947* (Dublin, 1977).

ENGLISH, R., '"Paying no heed to public clamour": Irish Republican Solipsism in the 1930s', *Irish Historical Studies*, 28/112 (Nov. 1993).

—— *Radicals and the Republic: Socialist Republicans in the Irish Free State, 1925–1937* (Oxford, 1994).

—— 'Socialism and Republican Schism in Ireland; The Emergence of the Republican Congress in 1934', *Irish Historical Studies*, 27/105 (May 1990).

—— and O'MALLEY, C. (eds.), *Prisoners: The Civil War Letters of Ernie O'Malley* (Dublin, 1991).

EVANS, G., *Welsh Nationalism* (Denbigh, undated but probably 1947).

FANNING, R., *Independent Ireland* (Dublin, 1983).

FARRELL, B. (ed.), *De Valera's Constitution and Ours* (Dublin, 1988).

FARRELL, M., *Sheltering the Fugitive? The Extradition of Irish Political Defenders* (Dublin, 1985).

FARRELL, T., 'The "Model Army": Military Imitation and the Enfeeblement of the Army in Post-Revolutionary Ireland, 1922–42', *Irish Studies in International Affairs*, 8 (1997).

FAULKNER, B., *Memoirs of a Statesman* (London, 1978).

FEEHAN, J. M., *Operation Brogue: A Study of the Vilification of Charles Haughey Code-named 'Operation Brogue' by the British Secret Service* (Dublin, 1984).

—— *The Statesman: A Study of the Role of Charles J. Haughey in the Ireland of Tomorrow* (Dublin, 1985).

Fifteen Years of Dublin Opinion (Dublin, n.d.).

FILBY, P. W., 'Floradora and a Unique Break into One-Time Pad Ciphers', *Intelligence and National Security*, 10/3 (July 1995).

FISK, R., *In Time of War: Ireland, Ulster and the Price of Neutrality 1939–45* (London, 1983).

—— *Pity the Nation: Lebanon at War* (1st edn., London, 1990; Oxford, 1991).

FITZGERALD, G., *All in a Life: An Autobiography* (Dublin, 1991).

FITZPATRICK, D., '"Unofficial emissaries": British Army Boxers in the Irish Free State, 1919–31', *Irish Historical Studies*, 30/118 (Nov. 1996).

FOOT, M. R. D., and LANGLEY, J., *MI9: Escape and Evasion, 1939–1945* (London, 1979).

Foreign Relations of the United States, vi: *Western Europe and Canada*, part 2 (Washington, 1986).

GALLAGHER, M. (ed.), *Irish Elections 1922–44: Results and Analysis* (Dublin, 1993).

GARVIN, T., *1922: The Birth of Irish Democracy* (Dublin, 1996).

GAUGHAN, J. A. (ed.), *Memoirs of Senator Joseph Connolly (1885–1961), a Founder of Modern Ireland* (Dublin, 1996).

GILBERT, M., *Churchill: A Life* (London, 1991).

GILLMAN, L. and P., *Collar the Lot! How Britain Interned and Expelled its Wartime Refugees* (London, 1980).

GILMORE, G., *The Republican Congress 1934* (Dublin, undated).

GOREN, R., *The Soviet Union and Terrorism* (London, 1984).

GRAAFF, B. de, and WIEBES, C., 'Intelligence and the Cold War behind the Dikes: The Relationship between the American and Dutch Intelligence Communities, 1946–1994', *Intelligence and National Security*, 12/1 (Jan. 1997).

GRIGG, J., *The History of the Times*, vi: *The Thomson Years 1966–1981* (London, 1993).

HARRINGTON, N., *Kerry Landing August 1922: An Episode of the Civil War* (Dublin, 1992).

HART, P., 'The Protestant Experience of Revolution in Southern Ireland', in R. English and G. Walker (eds.), *Unionism in Modern Ireland: New Perspectives on Politics and Culture* (Basingstoke, 1996).

HAWKINS, R., '"Bending the beam": Myth and Reality in the Bombing of Coventry, Belfast and Dublin', *Irish Sword*, 19/75–6 (1993–4).

HENNESSEY, T., *A History of Northern Ireland, 1920–1996* (Basingstoke, 1997).

HERLIHY, J., *The Royal Irish Constabulary: A Short History and Genealogical Guide* (Dublin, 1997).

HILTON, S. E., *Hitler's Secret War in South America, 1939–1945: German Military Espionage and Allied Counterespionage in Brazil* (1st edn., 1981; Ballantine edn., New York, 1982).

HINSLEY, F. H., and SIMKINS, C. A. G., *British Intelligence in the Second World War*, iv: *Security and Counter-Intelligence* (London, 1990).

HOGAN, G., and WALKER, C., *Political Violence and the Law in Ireland* (Manchester, 1989).

HOGAN, J., *Could Ireland become Communist?* (Dublin, 1933).

HOGAN, M., 'International Military Show-Jumping', *An t-Óglách*, 2/2 (Aug. 1929).

—— 'Irish Army International Show-Jumping', *An t-Óglách*, 3/1 (Jan. 1930).

HOGAN, P. D., 'UNICYP: Command and Staff Experiences', *Irish Sword*, 20/79 (Summer 1996).

HOPKINSON, M., *Green against Green: The Irish Civil War* (Dublin, 1988).

HORGAN, J., *Sean Lemass: The Enigmatic Patriot* (Dublin, 1997).

HOWARD, M., *British Intelligence in the Second World War*, v: *Strategic Deception* (London, 1989).

HOWE, E., *The Black Game: British Subversive Operations against the Germans in the Second World War* (London, 1982).

HUDSON, W. J., and STOKES, H. J. W. (eds.), *Documents on Australian Foreign Policy 1937–49*, iv: *July 1940–June 1941* (Canberra, 1980).

HYDE, H. M., *Secret Intelligence Agent* (London, 1982).

Institute for the Study of Terrorism, *IRA, INLA: Foreign Support and International Connections* (London, 1988).

JEFFERY, K., 'The British Army and Ireland since 1922', in T. Bartlett and K. Jeffery (eds.), *A Military History of Ireland* (Cambridge, 1996).

—— 'Security Policy in Northern Ireland: Some Reflections on the Management of Violent Conflict', *Terrorism and Political Violence*, 2/1 (Spring 1990).

—— and O'HALPIN, E., 'Ireland in Spy Fiction', in W. Wark (ed.), *Spy Fiction, Spy Films and Real Intelligence* (London, 1991).

JOYCE, J., and MURTAGH, P., *The Boss: Charles J. Haughey in Government* (Dublin, 1983).

KAHN, D., *Hitler's Spies* (1st edn., London, 1978; Arrow edn., 1982).

KEATINGE, P., *The Formulation of Irish Foreign Policy* (Dublin, 1973).

—— *A Singular Stance: Irish Neutrality in the 1980s* (Dublin, 1984).

KELLY, J., *Orders for the Captain?* (Dublin, 1971).

KENNEDY, M., *Ireland and the League of Nations, 1923–1946* (Dublin, 1996).

—— 'Prologue to Peacekeeping: Ireland and the Saar, 1934–5', *Irish Historical Studies*, 30/119 (May 1997).

KEOGH, D., 'De Valera, the Catholic Church, and the "Red Scare", 1931–1932', in J. A. Murphy and J. P. O'Carroll (eds.), *De Valera and his Times* (Cork, 1983).

—— *Ireland and Europe, 1919–1948* (Dublin, 1988).

—— *Jews in Twentieth Century Ireland: Refugees, Anti-Semitism and the Holocaust* (Cork, 1998).

KOHN, L., *The Constitution of the Irish Free State* (London, 1932).

LAQUEUR, W., *The Age of Terrorism* (London, 1987).

LAWSON, N., *The View from No. 11: Memoirs of a Tory Radical* (London, 1992; Corgi edn., 1993).

LEE, J., *Ireland 1912–1985: Politics and Society* (Cambridge, 1989).

LLOYD, M., *The Guiness Book of Espionage* (Enfield, 1994).

LODGE, J., 'The European Community and Terrorism', in J. Lodge (ed.), *The Challenge of Terrorism* (Brighton, 1988).

LONGFORD, the Earl of, and O'NEILL, T. P., *Eamon de Valera* (London, 1970).

LYONS, F. S. L., *Ireland since the Famine* (London, 1971).

MACARDLE, D., *The Irish Republic* (1st edn., London 1937; Corgi edn., London, 1968).

McARDLE, P., *The Secret War: An Account of the Sinister Activities along the Border involving Gardai, RUC, British Army and the SAS* (Dublin, 1984).

MACBRIDE, S., *A Message to the Irish People* (Dublin, 1988).

—— 'Reflections on Intelligence', *Intelligence and National Security*, 2/1 (Jan. 1987).

McCAUGHREN, T., *The Peacemakers of Niemba* (Dublin, 1966).

MACDONALD, H., *Irish Batt: The Story of Ireland's Blue Berets in the Lebanon* (Dublin, 1993).

MAC EOIN, U., *The IRA in the Twilight Years, 1923–1948* (Dublin, 1997).

McGINTY, R., 'Almost like Talking Dirty: Irish Security Policy in Post-Cold War Europe', *Irish Studies in International Affairs*, 6 (1995).

McIVOR, A., *A History of the Irish Naval Service* (Dublin, 1994).

McKEOWN, S., 'The Congo (UNUC): The Military Perspective', *Irish Sword*, 20/79 (Summer 1996), 43–7.

McLOUGHLIN, B., and O'CONNOR, E., 'Sources on Ireland and the Communist International, 1920–1943', *Saothar*, 21 (1996).

McMahon, D., '"A transient apparition": British Policy towards the de Valera Government, 1932–5', *Irish Historical Studies*, 22/88 (Sept. 1981).

—— *Republicans and Imperialists: Anglo-Irish Relations in the 1930s* (London, 1984).

McNiffe, L., *A History of the Garda Síochána: A Social History of the Force, 1922–52, with an Overview of the Years 1952–97* (Dublin, 1997).

Mac Ruairi, M., *In the Heat of the Hurry: A History of Republicanism in County Down*, (Castlewellan, 1997).

Mangan, C., 'Plans and Operations', *Irish Sword*, 19/75–6 (1993–4).

Manning, M., *The Blueshirts* (Dublin, 1974).

—— *Irish Political Parties: An Introduction* (Dublin, 1972).

Mansergh, N., *The Unresolved Question: The Anglo-Irish Settlement and its Undoing, 1912–1972* (London, 1991).

Masterman, J. C., *The Double-Cross System in the War of 1939 to 1945* (New Haven, 1972).

Milotte, M., *Communism in Modern Ireland* (Dublin, 1984).

Moran, Lord, *Winston Churchill: The Struggle for Survival 1940/1965* (1st edn., London, 1966; Sphere edn., 1968).

Munnelly, B., *Who's Bugging You? Inside Ireland's Secret World of Electronic Surveillance* (Cork, 1987).

Murphy, B., *Patrick Pearse and the Lost Republican Ideal* (Dublin, 1990).

Murphy, G, 'The Politics of Economic Realignment, 1948–1964' (unpublished Ph.D. diss., Dublin City University, 1996).

Neary, J. P., and O'Grada, C., 'Protection, Economic War and Structural Change: The 1930s in Ireland', *Irish Historical Studies*, 27/107 (May 1991).

Nicolson, N. (ed.), *Harold Nicolson: Diaries & Letters 1939–45* (1st edn., London, 1967; Fontana, 1970).

O'Ballance, E., *Terror in Ireland* (Novato, 1983).

O'Brien, B., *The Long War: IRA and Sinn Féin, 1985 to Today* (Dublin, 1993).

O'Brien, T. H., *Civil Defence: History of the Second World War* (London, 1955).

O'Broin, L., *Just like Yesterday . . . an Autobiography* (Dublin, undated).

—— *No Man's Man: A Biographical Memoir of Joseph Brennan—Civil Servant & First Governor of the Central Bank* (Dublin, 1982).

Ó'Canainn, A., 'Eilís Ryan in her Own Words', *Saothar*, 21 (1996).

O'Carroll, D., 'Defence in the Context of Neutrality and the Single European Act', *Studies*, 77/305 (Spring 1988).

—— 'The Emergency Army', *Irish Sword*, 19/75–6 (1993–4).

O'Connor, E., *Syndicalism in Ireland, 1917–1923* (Cork, 1988).

O'Donnell, P., *The Gates Flew Open* (Dublin, 1932).

O'Donoghue, D., *Hitler's Irish Voices: The Story of German Radio's Wartime Irish Service* (Belfast, 1998).

O'Donoghue, F., *No Other Law: The Story of Liam Lynch and the Irish Republican Army, 1916–1923* (Dublin, 1954).

O'Donovan, D., *Kevin Barry and his Time* (Dublin, 1989).

O'Drisceoil, D., *Censorship in Ireland 1939–1945: Neutrality, Politics and Society* (Cork, 1996).

O'DRISCEOIL, D., 'Moral Neutrality: Censorship in Emergency Ireland', *History Ireland*, 4/2 (Summer 1996).

O'DUFFY, E., *Crusade in Spain* (Dublin, 1938).

O'GRADY, J., 'Ireland, the Cuban Missile Crisis, and Civil Aviation: A Study in Applied Neutrality', *Eire Ireland*, 30/3 (Fall, 1993).

—— 'The Irish Free State Passport and the Question of Citizenship, 1921–4', *Irish Historical Studies*, 26/104 (Nov. 1989).

O'HALPIN, E., '"According to the Irish minister in Rome . . .": British Decrypts and Irish Diplomacy in the Second World War', *Irish Studies in International Affairs*, 6 (1995).

—— 'Army, Politics and Society in Independent Ireland, 1923–1945', in T. G. Fraser and Keith Jeffery (eds.), *Men, Women and War: Historical Studies*, xvii (Dublin, 1993).

—— 'British Intelligence in Ireland, 1914–1921' in Christopher Andrew and David Dilks (eds.), *The Missing Dimension: Governments and Intelligence Communities in the Twentieth Century* (Basingstoke, 1984).

—— *The Decline of the Union: British Government in Ireland, 1892–1920* (Dublin, 1987).

—— 'Financing British Intelligence: The Evidence up to 1945', in K. G. Robertson (ed.), *British and American Perspectives on Intelligence* (Basingstoke, 1987).

—— *Head of the Civil Service: A Study of Sir Warren Fisher* (London, 1989).

—— 'Intelligence during the Emergency', *Irish Sword*, 19/75–6 (1993–4).

—— 'Intelligence and Security in Ireland', *Intelligence and National Security*, 5/1 (Jan. 1990).

—— 'Irish Parliamentary Culture and the European Union: Formalities to be Observed', in Philip Norton (ed.), *National Parliaments and the European Union* (London, 1996).

—— 'The Origins of City and County Management', in *City and County Management: A Retrospective* (Institute of Public Administration, Dublin, 1991).

—— 'Republican Standards', *TLS*, 1 Oct. 1993.

OWEN, A. E., *The Anglo-Irish Agreement: The First Three Years* (Cardiff, 1994).

PARSONS, D., 'Mobilisation and Expansion, 1939–40', *Irish Sword*, 19/75–6 (1993–4).

PEDEN, G. C., *British Rearmament and the Treasury, 1932–1939* (Edinburgh, 1979).

PHOENIX, E., *Northern Nationalism: Nationalist Politics, Parties and the Catholic Minority in Northern Ireland 1890–1940* (Belfast, 1994).

POLAND, J. M., *Understanding Contemporary Terrorism: Groups, Strategies, and Responses* (Englewood Cliffs, 1988).

QUIGLEY, A., 'Air Aspects of the Emergency', *Irish Sword*, 19/75–6 (1993–4).

QUINN, O., 'The Coastwatching Service', *Irish Sword*, 19/75–6 (1993–4).

REES, M., *Northern Ireland: A Personal Perspective* (London, 1983).

ROSENBERG, J. L., 'The 1941 Mission of Frank Aiken to the United States: An American Perspective', *Irish Historical Studies*, 22/86 (Sept. 1980).

RYAN, D., *Sean Treacey and the Third Tipperary Brigade IRA* (Tralee, 1945).

SALMON, T., *Unneutral Ireland: An Ambivalent and Unique Security Policy* (Oxford, 1989).

SEAMAN, M., *Bravest of the Brave: The True Story of Wing Commander 'Tommy' Yeo-Thomas—SOE Secret Agent—Codename 'The White Rabbit'* (London, 1997).

SHIELDS, L. (ed.), *The Irish Meteorology Service: The First 50 Years, 1936–1986* (Stationery Office, Dublin, 1987).

SINNOTT, R., *Irish Voters Decide: Voting Behaviour in Elections and Referendums since 1918* (Manchester, 1995).

SKELLY, J. M., 'Ireland, the Department of External Affairs, and the United Nations 1945–55: A New Look', *Irish Studies in International Affairs*, 7 (1996).

—— *Irish Diplomacy at the United Nations 1945–1965: National Interests and the International Order* (Dublin, 1997).

SKINNER, L. C., *Politicians by Accident* (Dublin, 1946).

SLOAN, G. R., *The Geopolitics of Anglo-Irish Relations in the Twentieth Century* (London, 1997).

SMITH, B. F., *The Shadow Warriors: OSS and the Origins of the CIA* (London, 1983).

SMITH, M. L. R., *Fighting for Ireland? The Military Strategy of the Irish Republican Movement* (London, 1995).

STALKER, J., *Stalker* (London, revised edn., 1988).

STUART, C., *Secrets of Crewe House: The Story of a Famous Campaign* (London, 1920).

SWEENEY, O., 'The Coast Watching Service', *Irish Sword*, 19/73–4 (1993–4).

TAYLOR, P. M., and SANDERS, M., *British Propaganda during the First World War, 1914–18* (London, 1982).

TUGWELL, M., 'Politics and Propaganda of the Provisional IRA', in Paul Wilkinson (ed.), *British Perspectives on Terrorism* (London, 1981).

VALIULIS, M., *Portrait of a Revolutionary: General Richard Mulcahy and the Founding of the Irish Free State* (Dublin, 1992).

VERRIER, A., *Through the Looking Glass: British Foreign Policy in an Age of Illusions* (London, 1983).

WALSH, J. J., *Recollections of a Rebel* (Tralee, 1944).

WARD, E., '"A big show-off to show what we could do"—Ireland and the Hungarian Refugee Crisis of 1956', *Irish Studies in International Affairs*, 7 (1996).

WATT, D. C., *How War Came: The Immediate Origins of the Second World War, 1938–1939* (1st edn., London, 1989; Mandarin, 1990).

WEST, N., *MI5: British Security Service Operations, 1905–1945* (London, 1983).

—— *MI5 1945–72: A Matter of Trust* (1st edn., London, 1982; Cornet edn., 1983).

WHITE, S., 'Ireland, Russia, Communism, Post-Communism', *Irish Studies in International Affairs*, 8 (1997), 156–8.

WHITE, T. DE V., *Kevin O'Higgins* (1st edn., London, 1948; Tralee, 1996).

WINANT, J. G., *A Letter from Grosvenor Square: An Account of a Stewardship* (London, 1947).

WOODWARD, B., *Veil: The Secret Wars of the CIA 1981–87* (1st edn., London, 1987; paperback edn., 1988).

WRIGHT, P., *Spycatcher* (New York, 1987).

'XYZ', 'Why should we Apologize?', *An t-Óglách*, 3/1 (Jan. 1930).

—— 'NCOs and Men', *An t-Óglách*, 3/1 (Jan. 1930).

YOUNG, P., 'Defence and the New Irish State, 1919–39', *Irish Sword*, 19/75–6 (1993–4).

—— 'Pageantry and the Defence Forces', *An Cosantoir*, 45/9 (Sept. 1985).

INDEX